HANDBOOK OF

Volatility Models and Their Applications

Wiley Handbooks in
FINANCIAL ENGINEERING AND ECONOMETRICS

Advisory Editor

Ruey S. Tsay

The University of Chicago Booth School of Business, USA

The dynamic and interaction between financial markets around the world have changed dramatically under economic globalization. In addition, advances in communication and data collection have changed the way information is processed and used. In this new era, financial instruments have become increasingly sophisticated and their impacts are far-reaching. The recent financial (credit) crisis is a vivid example of the new challenges we face and continue to face in this information age. Analytical skills and ability to extract useful information from mass data, to comprehend the complexity of financial instruments, and to assess the financial risk involved become a necessity for economists, financial managers, and risk management professionals. To master such skills and ability, knowledge from computer science, economics, finance, mathematics and statistics is essential. As such, financial engineering is cross-disciplinary, and its theory and applications advance rapidly.

The goal of this Handbook Series is to provide a one-stop source for students, researchers, and practitioners to learn the knowledge and analytical skills they need to face today's challenges in financial markets. The Series intends to introduce systematically recent developments in different areas of financial engineering and econometrics. The coverage will be broad and thorough with balance in theory and applications. Each volume will be edited by leading researchers and practitioners in the area and covers state-of-the-art methods and theory of the selected topic.

Published Wiley Handbooks in Financial Engineering and Econometrics

Bauwens, Hafner, and Laurent · *Handbook of Volatility Models and Their Applications*
Viens, Mariani, and Florescu · *Handbook of Modeling High-Frequency Data in Finance*

Forthcoming Wiley Handbooks in Financial Engineering and Econometrics

Bali and Engle · *Handbook of Asset Pricing*
Brandimarte · *Handbook of Monte Carlo Simulation*
Chan and Wong · *Handbook of Financial Risk Management*
Cruz, Peters, and Shevchenko · *Handbook of Operational Risk*
Sarno, James, and Marsh ·*Handbook of Exchange Rates*
Szylar · *Handbook of Market Risk*

HANDBOOK OF
Volatility Models and Their Applications

Edited by

LUC BAUWENS
CHRISTIAN HAFNER
SEBASTIEN LAURENT

WILEY

A John Wiley & Sons, Inc., Publication

Published by John Wiley & Sons, Inc., Hoboken, New Jersey
Published simultaneously in Canada

Library of Congress Cataloging-in-Publication Data:

Bauwens, Luc, 1952–
Handbook of volatility models and their applications / Luc Bauwens, Christian Hafner, Sebastien Laurent.
p. cm. – (Wiley handbooks in financial engineering and econometrics; 3)
Includes bibliographical references and index.
ISBN 978-0-470-87251-2 (hardback)
1. Banks and banking–Econometric models. 2. Finance–Econometric models. 3. GARCH model. I. Hafner, Christian. II. Laurent, Sebastien, 1974– III. Title.
HG1601.B38 2012
332.01′5195--dc23

2011044256

10 9 8 7 6 5 4 3 2 1

MIX
Paper from responsible sources
FSC® C013604
FSC www.fsc.org

Contents

PART THREE

Realized Volatility

Preface

This book is a collection of 19 chapters that present a broad overview of the current state of knowledge, developed in the academic literature, about volatility models and their applications.

Volatility modeling was born 30 years ago, if we date it to the publication (in 1982) of the paper where Rob Engle introduced the autoregressive conditional heteroskedasticity (ARCH) modeling idea (even if, for sure, there have been earlier signs of interest in the topic). Volatility modeling is still, and will remain for long, one of the most active research topics of financial econometrics. Despite the enormous advances we have seen during the last 30 years, we conjecture that 30 years from now, the models available today, most of which are described in this book, will be considered as classical, with some respect, but many advances and new approaches will have been achieved in between.

The development of econometric models of volatility has gone along with their application in academia and progressive use in the financial industry. The very difficult situation of the financial sector of the global economy since the financial crisis of 2008, and its dramatic economic consequences, have made it clear that academics, regulators, and financiers have still a lot of progress to make in their understanding of financial risks. These risks are compounded by the development of sophisticated financial products and the strong linkages between financial institutions because of the globalization. We hope that the chapters of this book will be useful as a basis on which to extend a scientific approach to study and to ultimately manage financial risks and related issues.

The volume is split into three distinct parts, preceded by a survey that serves to introduce the models and methods covered in the book. The first part, consisting of seven chapters, presents ARCH and stochastic volatility models. Given the enormous literature that already exists on these models, we have mainly focused our choice of topics on recent contributions. The second part, with four chapters, presents alternative approaches, such as multiplicative error models, nonparametric and semi parametric models, and copula-based models of (co)volatilities. The third part consists of seven chapters dealing with the issues of the measurement of volatility by realized variances and covariances, as well as of modeling and forecasting these realized measures.

We express our deepest gratitude to all the authors for their willingness to contribute to this book, and their efficient and quick cooperation that has resulted in a manuscript written within two years. We also warmly thank all the persons at Wiley who were helpful in the editing process of this handbook.

Luc Bauwens
Christian Hafner
Sébastien Laurent

Louvain-La-Neuve (Beligum) and
Maastricht (The Netherlands)
January 18, 2012

Contributors

Yacine Aït-Sahalia, Princeton University and NBER, USA

Francesco Audrino, University of St. Gallen, Switzerland

Luc Bauwens, Université catholique de Louvain, CORE, Belgium

Charles S. Bos, VU University Amsterdam, The Netherlands

Kris Boudt, K.U.Leuven, Lessius, Belgium

Christian T. Brownlees, New York University, USA

Francesco Calvori, Florence University, Italy

Massimiliano Caporin, University of Padova, Italy

Fabrizio Cipollini, Università di Firenze, Italy

Jonathan Cornelissen, K.U.Leuven, Belgium

Fulvio Corsi, University of St. Gallen, Switzerland

Christophe Croux, K.U.Leuven, Belgium

Giampiero M. Gallo, Università di Firenze, Italy

Eric Ghysels, University of North Carolina, USA

Markus Haas, University of Kiel, Germany

Christian Hafner, Université catholique de Louvain, Belgium

Aamir R. Hashmi, National University of Singapore, Singapore

Andréas Heinen, Université de Cergy-Pontoise, France

Tsunehiro Ishihara, University of Tokyo, Japan

Sébastien Laurent, Maastricht University, The Netherlands; and Université catholique de Louvain, Belgium

Oliver Linton, London School of Economics, UK

Cecilia Mancini, Florence University, Italy

Michael McAleer, Erasmus University Rotterdam, The Netherlands

Santosh Mishra, West Virginia University, USA

Yasuhiro Omori, University of Tokyo, Japan

Marc S. Paolella, University of Zurich, Switzerland
Sujin Park, London School of Economics, UK
Roberto Renò, University of Siena, Italy
Kevin Sheppard, University of Oxford, UK
Liangjun Su, Singapore Management University, Singapore
Anthony S. Tay, Singapore Management University, Singapore
Timo Teräsvirta, Aarhus University, Denmark
Aman Ullah, University of California, Riverside, USA
Alfonso Valdesogo, Universidad Carlos III de Madrid, Spain
Rossen Valkanov, University of California San Diego, USA
Sébastien Van Bellegem, Université catholique de Louvain, Belgium and Toulouse School of Economics, France
Francesco Violante, Maastricht University, The Netherlands, and Université catholique de Louvain, Belgium
Yun Wang, University of California, Riverside, USA
Dacheng Xiu, Princeton University, USA

CHAPTER ONE

Volatility Models

LUC BAUWENS, CHRISTIAN HAFNER, and SÉBASTIEN LAURENT

1.1 Introduction

This chapter presents an introductory review of volatility models and some applications. We link our review with other chapters that contain more detailed presentations. Section 1.2 deals with generalized autoregressive conditionally heteroskedastic models, Section 1.3 with stochastic volatility (SV) models, and Section 1.4 with realized volatility.

1.2 GARCH

1.2.1 UNIVARIATE GARCH

Univariate ARCH models appeared in the literature with the paper of Engle (1982a), soon followed by the generalization to GARCH of Bollerslev (1986). Although applied, in these pathbreaking papers, to account for the changing volatility of inflation series, the models and their later extensions were quickly found to be relevant for the conditional volatility of financial returns observed at a monthly and higher frequency (Bollerslev, 1987), and thus to the study of the intertemporal relation between risk and expected return (French et al., 1987; Engle et al., 1987). The reason is that time series of returns (even if

Handbook of Volatility Models and Their Applications, First Edition.
Edited by Luc Bauwens, Christian Hafner, and Sebastien Laurent.

adjusted for autocorrelation, typically through an ARMA model) have several features that are well fitted by GARCH models. The main stylized feature is volatility clustering: "large changes tend to be followed by large changes, of either sign, and small changes tend to be followed by small changes" (Mandelbrot, 1963). This results in positive autocorrelation coefficients of squared returns, typically with a relatively slowly decreasing pattern starting from a first small value (say, <0.2). Said differently, volatility, measured by squared returns, is persistent, hence to some extent predictable even if it is noisy. Another stylized property of financial returns that was known long before ARCH models appeared is that their unconditional probability distributions are leptokurtic, that is, they have fatter tails and more mass around their center than the Gaussian distribution (Mandelbrot 1963). In this and later papers (e.g., Fama, 1963, 1965; Mandelbrot and Taylor, 1967), the returns are modeled as independently and identically distributed (i.i.d.) according to a stable Paretian distribution. But clearly, if squared returns are autocorrelated, they are not independent. A great advantage of GARCH models is that the returns are not assumed independent, and even if they are assumed Gaussian conditional to past returns, unconditionally they are not Gaussian, because volatility clustering generates leptokurtosis.

We illustrate the stylized facts with the percentage daily returns of the S&P 500 index, that is, the returns (y_t) are computed as $100(p_t - p_{t-1})$, where $p_t = \log P_t$ and P_t is the closing price index value adjusted for dividends and splits (available at http://finance.yahoo.com) and t is the time index referring to trading day t. The sample period starts on January 3, 1950 and ends on July 14, 2011 for a total of 15,482 returns. Table 1.1 contains descriptive statistics of the original and demeaned returns, the latter being the residuals of an AR(2) model fitted to the original returns. The descriptive statistics of the two series hardly differ and the large excess kurtosis coefficients confirm their leptokurtosis.

TABLE 1.1 Descriptive Statistics for S&P 500 Returns

	Returns	Demeaned Returns
Observations	15,482	15,480
Mean	0.02818	0
Standard deviation	0.97078	0.96897
Skewness	−1.0567	−1.0738
Kurtosis	32.035	31.623
Minimum	−22.900	−22.856
Maximum	10.957	10.571

Returns definition and source: (see text). Demeaned returns are residuals of an AR(2) model fitted to the returns by ordinary least squares (OLS). Skewness is the ratio of the third centered moment to the third power of the standard deviation. Kurtosis is the ratio of the fourth centered moment to the square of the variance.

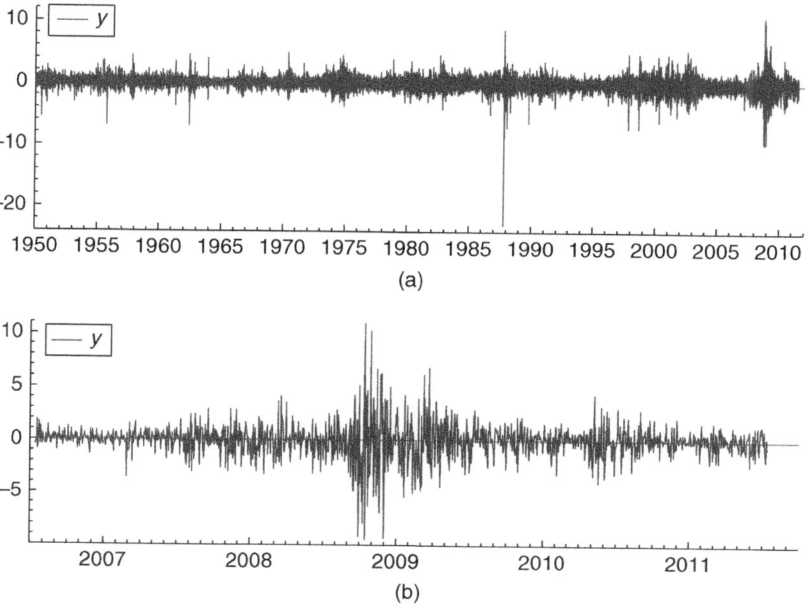

FIGURE 1.1 S&P 500 index returns (y).

Figure 1.1 displays the full sample series of returns (a) and the series for the last five years (2006/07/14–2011/07/14) (b). Figure 1.2 shows the full series of absolute demeaned returns (a), the sample ACF of the corresponding squared series until lag 100 (b), and the absolute demeaned returns or the last five years (c). The squared demeaned returns are positively autocorrelated: their ACF starts at 0.15, has a peak of 0.20 at lag 5, and decreases rather slowly. Volatility clustering is clearly visible on the top and bottom graphs of both figures. The leptokutrosis of the estimated density of the demeaned returns, shown over a truncated support—see maximum and minimum values in Table 1.1—is visible on Figure 1.3, where a Gaussian density with the same mean (0) and standard deviation (0.969) is drawn for comparison. The negative skewness coefficients reported in Table 1.1 illustrate that large negative returns are more probable than large positive ones. This is also a widespread feature, by no means universal, of financial return series, which we discuss below.

1.2.1.1 Structure of GARCH Models. We define a GARCH model for y_t (an asset return as defined above) by

$$y_t - \mu_t = \varepsilon_t = \sigma_t z_t, \tag{1.1}$$

where z_t is an unobservable random variable belonging to an i.i.d. process, with mean equal to 0 and variance equal to 1, $E(z_t) = 0$ and $\mathrm{Var}(z_t) = 1$. The symbols μ_t and σ_t denote measurable functions with respect to a σ-field $\mathcal{F}_{t-1}$ generated

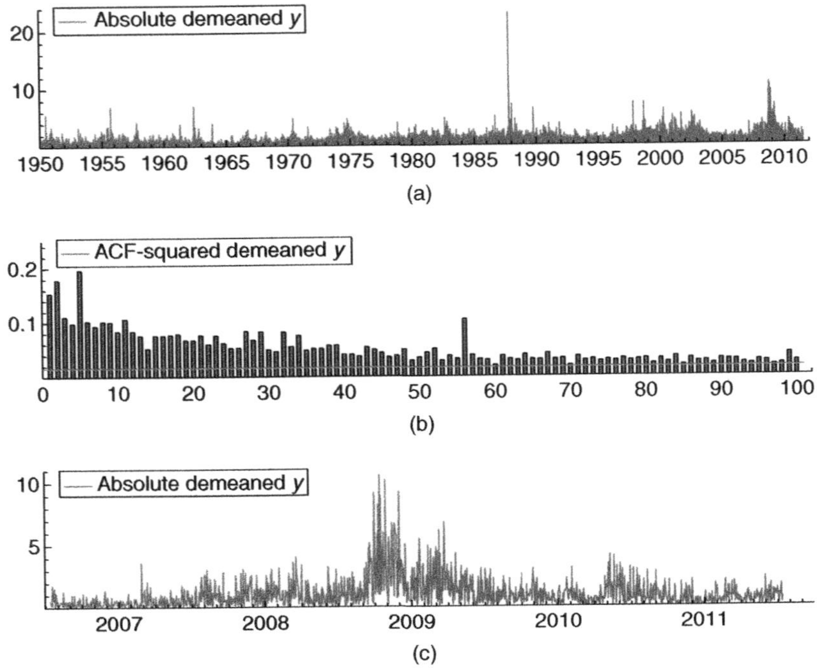

FIGURE 1.2 S&P 500 index demeaned absolute returns and ACF of their square.

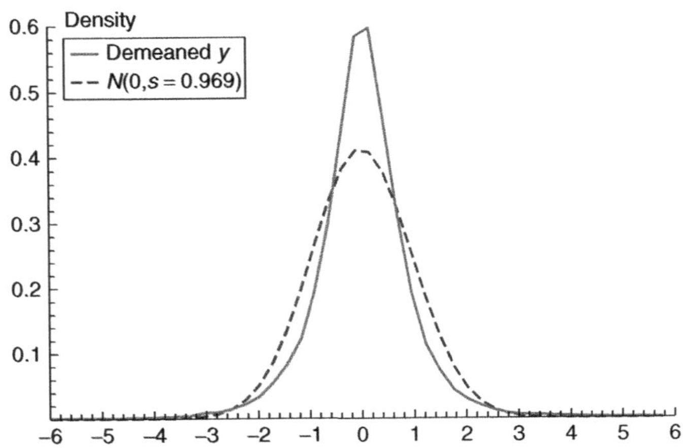

FIGURE 1.3 Density estimate of S&P 500 index demeaned returns and Gaussian density.

by y_{t-j} for $j \geq 1$ and possibly by other variables available at time $t-1$. It follows that μ_t and σ_t^2 are the conditional mean and variance of y_t, respectively, that is, $\mu_t = E(y_t|\mathcal{F}_{t-1}) = E_{t-1}(y_t)$ and $\sigma_t^2 = \mathrm{Var}(y_t|\mathcal{F}_{t-1}) = \mathrm{Var}_{t-1}(y_t)$, so that $E_{t-1}(\varepsilon_t) = 0$ and $\mathrm{Var}_{t-1}(\varepsilon_t) = \sigma_t^2$. The i.i.d. hypothesis for the z_t process can be replaced by the assumption that the process is an m.d.s. (martingale difference sequence), such that $E_{t-1}(z_t) = 0$ and $\mathrm{Var}_{t-1}(z_t) = 1$.

The model is fully parametric if μ_t, σ_t^2, and $f(z_t)$, the probability density function (pdf) of z_t (assumed to be time invariant), are indexed by a finite dimensional parameter vector denoted by $\theta \in \Theta$ (the parameter space). Otherwise, the model is nonparametric or semiparametric, see Su et al. (2012) in this Handbook for a review of this approach. In the parametric version, the conditional mean function is typically specified as an ARMA model, augmented by additional regressors according to the modeling objectives. We discuss briefly below the specification of the conditional variance as a function of the variables generating $\mathcal{F}_{t-1}$ and of the probability distribution of z_t.

1.2.1.2 Early GARCH Models. The GARCH(1,1) equation,

$$\sigma_t^2 = \omega + \beta\sigma_{t-1}^2 + \alpha\varepsilon_{t-1}^2, \tag{1.2}$$

where ω, β, and α are parameters, is the most widely used formulation. The positivity of σ_t^2 is ensured by the following sufficient restrictions: $\omega > 0$, $\alpha \geq 0$, and $\beta \geq 0$, but if $\alpha = 0$, β must be set to 0 as well, otherwise the sequence σ_t^2 tends to a constant and β is not identifiable. If q lags of ε_t^2 and p lags of σ_t^2 are included (instead of setting $p = q = 1$ as above), the model is named GARCH(p,q), as put forward by Bollerslev (1986). Tests of zero restrictions for the lag coefficients and model choice criteria result in choices of p and q equal to 1 in a vast diversity of data series and sample sizes, with p or q equal to two rarely selected and higher values almost never.

To understand why the GARCH(1,1) equation together with (Eq. 1.1) and the assumptions stated above is able to account for volatility clustering and leptokurtosis, let us note that the autocorrelation coefficients of ε_t^2, denoted by ρ_j, are equal to $\rho_1 = \alpha(1-\beta^2-\alpha\beta)/(1-\beta^2-2\alpha\beta)$, which is larger than α, and $\rho_j = (\alpha+\beta)\rho_{j-1}$ for $j \geq 2$, if $\alpha+\beta < 1$. The last inequality ensures that $\mathrm{Var}(\varepsilon_t) = \omega/(1-\alpha-\beta)$ (denoted by σ^2) exists and that ε_t is covariance stationary. Moreover, the autocorrelations of ε_t^2 are positive and decaying at the rate $\alpha+\beta$. The sum $\alpha+\beta$ is referred to as the persistence of the conditional variance process. For financial return series, estimates of α and β are often in the ranges [0.02, 0.25] and [0.75, 0.98], respectively, with α often in the lower part of the interval and β in the upper part for daily series, such that the persistence is close to but rarely exceeding 1. Hence, ρ_1 is typically small, and the autocorrelations decay slowly, though still geometrically. Table 1.2 reports quasi-maximum likelihood (QML) estimates (see Section 1.2.1.3) for the demeaned S&P 500 returns over the full sample and 12 subsamples of 5 years of data (except for the first and last subsamples, which are a bit longer). The

TABLE 1.2 GARCH(1,1) QML Estimates for S&P 500 Demeaned Returns

Period	T	α	β	$\alpha+\beta$	σ^2	KC	ρ_1
1950-01-06	15,480	0.079	0.915	0.994	1.301	∞	0.405
2011-07-14					0.939	31.62	0.154
2006-01-03	1393	0.092	0.898	0.990	1.762	16.08	0.351
2011-07-14					2.306	11.53	0.209
2001-01-02	1256	0.073	0.920	0.993	1.178	18.34	0.344
2005-12-30					1.320	5.34	0.186
1996-01-02	1263	0.094	0.882	0.977	1.638	4.91	0.238
2000-12-29					1.348	6.71	0.209
1991-01-02	1264	0.026	0.963	0.989	0.389	3.20	0.056
1995-12-29					0.423	5.62	0.027
1986-01-02	1264	0.156	0.755	0.911	1.397	4.20	0.250
1990-12-31					1.632	87.53	0.118
1981-01-02	1264	0.033	0.956	0.989	0.720	3.31	0.076
1985-12-31					0.756	4.77	0.050
1976-01-02	1263	0.044	0.943	0.987	0.602	3.54	0.111
1980-12-31					0.595	4.34	0.128
1971-01-04	1262	0.072	0.923	0.995	1.006	35.83	0.362
1975-12-31					0.885	4.84	0.165
1966-01-03	1233	0.138	0.817	0.955	0.499	5.33	0.285
1970-12-31					0.493	5.99	0.233
1961-01-03	1258	0.237	0.733	0.970	0.550	∞	0.599
1965-12-31					0.417	20.40	0.427
1956-01-03	1260	0.088	0.868	0.956	0.472	3.64	0.158
1960-12-30					0.471	5.29	0.124
1950-01-03	1500	0.020	0.975	0.995	0.651	3.29	0.062
1955-12-30					0.537	12.81	0.104

T, number of observations; σ^2 is estimated as $\omega/(1-\alpha-\beta)$ using the (unreported) estimate of ω, KC using Equation 1.3 with $\lambda = 3$ (∞ means that the existence condition in Equation 1.3 is not satisfied), and ρ_1 as $\alpha(1-\beta^2-\alpha\beta)/(1-\beta^2-2\alpha\beta)$. The data in the second row (for each period) are the sample variance (σ^2 column), kurtosis coefficient (KC column), and first-order autocorrelation of squared returns. Results obtained with GARCH module of OxMetrics 6.20. demeaned returns are defined in Table 1.1.

kurtosis coefficient, defined as $E(\varepsilon_t^4)/\text{Var}(\varepsilon_t)^2$ and denoted by KC, is equal to

$$\text{KC} = \lambda \frac{(1-\alpha^2-\beta^2-\alpha\beta)}{(1-\lambda\alpha^2-\beta^2-2\alpha\beta)}, \quad \text{if } \lambda\alpha^2-\beta^2-2\alpha\beta < 1, \tag{1.3}$$

where $\lambda = E(z_t^4)$ is the kurtosis coefficient of z_t, so that KC is larger than λ. In particular, if z_t is Gaussian, $\lambda = 3$ and ε_t is leptokurtic. However, it is not easy to obtain jointly a small value of ρ_1 and a high kurtosis with a small value of

α, a large value of β and a Gaussian distribution for z_t: for example, $\alpha = 0.05$, $\beta = 0.93$, yield $\rho_1 = 0.11$, while KC $= 3.43$ if $\lambda = 3$. If λ is set to 5, KC increases to 6.69. In Table 1.2, it can be seen that estimates of the parameters fit the unconditional variance much better than the first autocorrelation and especially the kurtosis coefficients. The extreme value of the kurtosis in the period 1986–1990 is due to the extreme negative return of 19 October, 1987.

The GARCH(1,1) equation (Eq. 1.2) is the universal reference with respect to which all its extensions and variants are compared. An (almost) exhaustive list of GARCH equations in 2008 is provided in the ARCH glossary of Bollerslev (2008). Several of them are presented by Teräsvirta (2009). The formulation in Equation 1.2 is linear in the parameters but others are not, and most of these are presented in Chapter 2 by Teräsvirta (2012) in this Handbook. A widely used extension introduces an additional term in Equation 1.2, as given in Glosten et al. (1993):

$$\sigma_t^2 = \omega + \beta\sigma_{t-1}^2 + \alpha\varepsilon_{t-1}^2 + \gamma\varepsilon_{t-1}^2 I(\varepsilon_{t-1} < 0). \tag{1.4}$$

With $\gamma = 0$, the conditional variance response to a past shock (ε_{t-1}) of given absolute value is the same whether the shock is positive or negative. The news impact curve, which traces σ_t^2 as a function of ε_{t-1} for given values of $\omega + \beta\sigma_{t-1}^2$ and α, is a parabola having its minimum at $\varepsilon_{t-1} = 0$. If γ is positive, the response is stronger for a past negative shock than for a positive one of the same absolute value and the news impact curve is asymmetric (steeper to the left of 0). This positive effect is found empirically for many (individual and index) stock return series and may be interpreted as the leverage effect uncovered by Black (1976). This effect for a particular firm says that a negative shock—a return below its expected value—implies that the firm is more leveraged, that is, has a higher ratio of debt to stock value, and is therefore more risky, so that the volatility should increase. The extended GARCH model (Eq. 1.4) is named *GJR-GARCH* or just GJR and referred to as an *asymmetric GARCH equation*. There exist several other GARCH equations that allow for an asymmetric news impact effect, in particular, the EGARCH model of Nelson (1991b) and the TGARCH model of Zakoian (1994). The positive asymmetric response of stock return volatility to past shocks is considered as a stylized fact, but there is no consensus that the finding of positive γ estimates corresponds actually to the financial leverage effect. Negative estimates of γ are found for commodity return series as documented in Carpantier (2010), who names it the *inverse leverage effect*. Engle (2011) also provides evidence of this effect for returns of a gold price series, volatility indexes, some exchange rates, and other series and interprets this as a hedge effect (the mentioned type of series are from typical hedge assets).

1.2.1.3 Probability Distributions for z_t. The Gaussian distribution was the first to be used for estimation by the method of maximum likelihood (ML). The likelihood function based on the Gaussian distribution has a QML interpretation, that is, it provides consistent and asymptotically Gaussian estimators of the conditional mean and GARCH equation parameters provided that the conditional mean and variance are correctly specified. See Bollerslev et al. (1994, Section 2.3) for a short presentation of QML for GARCH and Francq and Zakoian (2010, Chapter 7) for more details and references. The (quasi-)log-likelihood function is based on the assumption of independence of the z_t innovations (even if the latter are only an m.d.s.). For a sample of T observations collected in the vector y, it is written

$$\ell_T(\theta; y) = \sum_{t=1}^{T} \ell(y_t; \theta), \tag{1.5}$$

where $\ell(y_t; \theta) = \log f(y_t|\theta)$, with $f(y_t|\theta)$ the density function of y_t obtained by the change of variable from z_t to y_t implied by Equation 1.1. Actually, $f(y_t|\theta)$ is conditional on $\mathcal{F}_{t-1}$ through μ_t and σ_t^2. For example, if $z_t \sim N(0, 1)$ and $y_t \sim N(\mu_t, \sigma_t^2)$, and apart from a constant $\log f(y_t|\theta) = -0.5[\log \sigma_t^2 + (y_t - \mu_t)^2/\sigma_t^2]$. As mentioned above, the Gaussian assumption implies conditional mesokurtosis for y_t (i.e., a kurtosis coefficient equal to 3 for z_t) and unconditional leptokurtosis if a GARCH effect exists, but the degree of leptokurtosis may be too small to fit the kurtosis of the data. For this reason, Bollerslev (1987) proposed to use the t-distribution for z_t, since it implies conditional leptokurtosis and, therefore, stronger unconditional leptokurtosis. The functional expression of $\ell(y_t; \theta)$, if $f(z_t)$ is a t-density with ν degrees of freedom, is given by (apart from a constant) $\log[\Gamma(\nu + 1/2)/\Gamma(\nu/2)] - 0.5\{(\nu - 2)\sigma_t^2 + (\nu + 1)(y_t - \mu_t)^2/[(\nu - 2)\sigma_t^2]\}$. Notice that θ includes ν in addition to the parameters indexing μ_t and σ_t^2, and the restriction that ν be larger than 2 is imposed to ensure the existence of the variance of y_t. When $\nu > 4$, the fourth moment exists and the conditional kurtosis coefficient, that is, the λ to be used in Equation 1.3, is equal to $3 + 6(\nu - 4)^{-1}$. Another family of distributions for z_t, which is sometimes used in GARCH estimation is the generalized error (GE) distribution indexed by the positive parameter ν. It was proposed by Nelson (1991b). It implies conditional leptokurtosis, if $\nu > 2$; platykurtosis, if $\nu < 2$; and corresponds to the Gaussian distribution, if $\nu = 2$.

The Gaussian, t, and GE distributions are symmetric around 0. The symmetry of the conditional distribution does not necessarily imply the same property for the unconditional one. He et al. (2008) show that conditional symmetry combined with a constant conditional mean implies unconditional symmetry, whatever the GARCH equation is (thus, even if the news impact curve is itself asymmetric). They also show that a time-varying conditional mean is sufficient for creating unconditional asymmetry (even if the conditional density is symmetric), but the conditional mean dynamics has to be very strong to induce nonnegligible unconditional asymmetry. Empirically, the conditional mean dynamics is weak for return series as their autocorrelations are small. Since it is obvious that conditional asymmetry implies the same unconditionally, an easy way to account for the latter, which is not rare in financial return series as illustrated above, is to employ a conditionally asymmetric distribution. Probably the most used asymmetric (or skewed) distributions in GARCH modeling is the skewed-t of Hansen (1994). Bond (2001) surveys asymmetric conditional

TABLE 1.3 GJR-GARCH(1,1) ML Estimates for S&P 500 Demeaned Returns for the Period 2006-07-14 Until 2011-07-14 (1260 Observations)

Density	BIC	α	γ	β	ω	ν	ξ
Gaussian	3.132	−0.0225	0.181	0.915	0.0212	—	—
		(7.3)	(0.9)	(0.0)	(0.0)		
GE	3.082	−0.0209	0.182	0.914	0.0137	1.24	—
		(11)	(0.9)	(0.0)	(2.9)	(0.0)	
t	3.087	−0.0255	0.196	0.920	0.0106	5.05	—
		(6.7)	(0.0)	(0.0)	(7.5)	(0.0)	
Skewed-t	3.074	−0.0289	0.206	0.919	0.0140	5.90	−0.18
		(1.4)	(0.0)	(0.0)	(2.9)	(0.0)	(0.0)

Results obtained with G@RCH module of OxMetrics 6.20. Demeaned returns are defined as in Table 1.1. In parentheses: p-values in percentage.

densities for ARCH modeling. Another way to account for asymmetry and excess kurtosis is to estimate the conditional distribution nonparametrically, as given by Engle and Gonzalez-Rivera (1991)—see also Teräsvirta (2012) in this Handbook.

The use of an asymmetric conditional density often improves the fit of a model as illustrated in Table 1.3—the Bayesian information criterion (BIC) is minimized for the skewed-t choice—and may be useful in Value-at-Risk (VaR) forecasting (see below). The skewed-t-density is indexed by an asymmetry parameter ξ in addition to the degrees of freedom parameter ν also indexing the symmetric t-density used by Bollerslev (1987). A negative ξ corresponds to a left-skewed density, a positive ξ to right skewness, and for $\xi = 0$ the skewed-t reduces to the symmetric t. The estimation results in Table 1.3 show that the conditional skewed-t is skewed to the left, which generates unconditional left skewness, in agreement with the negative skewness coefficient of the data, equal to -0.23. Notice that ξ is not the skewness coefficient, that is, the values -0.18 and -0.23 are not directly comparable in magnitude. The data kurtosis coefficient is equal to 10.9, hence it is not surprising that the estimated degrees of freedom parameter is of the order of 6 for the skewed-t, 5 for the symmetric t, and that the estimated GE parameter value of 1.24 is well below 2. Notice that, perhaps with the exception of ω, the estimates of the GJR-GARCH equation parameters are not sensitive to the choice of the density used for the estimation. An unusual feature of the results are the negative estimates of α, but except in the skewed-t case, α is not significantly different from 0 at the level of 5%.

1.2.1.4 New GARCH Models. Although early GARCH models have been and are still widely used, a viewpoint slowly emerged, according to which these models may be too rigid for fitting return series, especially over a long span. This is related to the rather frequent empirical finding that the estimated persistence of conditional variances is high (i.e., close to 1), as illustrated by the results in Table 1.2. In the GARCH infancy epoch, Engle and Bollerslev (1986) suggested that it might be relevant to impose the restriction that $\alpha + \beta$ be equal to 1 in the GARCH equation (Eq. 1.2), then named integrated GARCH (IGARCH) by analogy with the unit root literature. However, the IGARCH equation

$$\sigma_t^2 = \omega + \sigma_{t-1}^2 + \alpha(\varepsilon_{t-1}^2 - \sigma_{t-1}^2) \tag{1.6}$$

implies that the unconditional variance does not exist (since $\alpha + \beta < 1$ is necessary for this), and that the conditional expectation of the conditional variance at horizon s is equal to $\omega s + \sigma_{t+1}^2$.[1] Unless $\omega = 0$, there is a trend in $E_t(\sigma_{t+s}^2)$, which is not sensible for long-run forecasting.[2]

Diebold (1986), in his discussion of Engle and Bollerslev (1986), briefly mentions that the high persistence of conditional variances may be provoked by overlooking changes in the conditional variance intercept ω. The intuition for this is that changes in ω (or σ^2) induce nonstationarity, which is captured by high persistence. Lamoureux and Lastrapes (1990) document empirically this idea and show it to be plausible by Monte Carlo (MC) simulation, while Hillebrand (2005) provides a theoretical proof. Another possible type of change is in the persistence itself, as suggested by the results in Table 1.2 for some periods.

The GJR-GARCH equation (Eq. 1.4) has an undesirable drawback linked to the way it models the leverage effect for stocks ($\gamma > 0$). It implies that conditional variances persist more strongly after a large negative shock than after a large positive shock of the same magnitude ($\beta + \alpha + 0.5\gamma > \beta + \alpha$). This is somehow in disagreement with the view that after the October 87 crash, the volatility in US stock markets reverted swiftly to its precrash normal level. Evidence of this based on implied volatilities from option prices is provided by Schwert (1990) and Engle and Mustafa (1992).

All this has promoted the development of more flexible GARCH models, in particular, models allowing for changing parameters. There are many ways to do this, and somewhat arbitrarily, we present a selection of existing models into three classes.

1-Component and smooth transition models. Component models are based on the idea that there is a long-run component in volatilities, which changes smoothly, and a short-run one, changing more quickly and fluctuating around the long-run component. The components may be combined in an additive way or in a multiplicative way. The component model of Engle and Lee (1999) is additive and consists of the equations

$$\sigma_t^2 = q_t + \beta(\sigma_{t-1}^2 - q_{t-1}) + \alpha(\varepsilon_{t-1}^2 - q_{t-1}), \tag{1.7}$$

$$q_t = \sigma^2 + \rho q_{t-1} + \phi(\varepsilon_{t-1}^2 - \sigma_{t-1}^2), \tag{1.8}$$

[1]From the GARCH(1,1) equation, one gets that $E_t(\sigma_{t+s}^2) = \omega + (\alpha + \beta)E_t(\sigma_{t+s-1}^2)$, hence $E_t(\sigma_{t+s}^2) = \omega \sum_{i=1}^{s} (\alpha + \beta)^{i-1} + (\alpha + \beta)^s \sigma_{t+1}^2$. If $\alpha + \beta < 1$, this tends to σ^2 as s tends to ∞, but if $\alpha + \beta = 1$, this diverges because of the linear trend.

[2]The RiskMetrics model (J.P. Morgan, 1996) sets $\omega = 0$ in addition to $\alpha + \beta = 1$ and $\alpha = 0.94$ for daily returns. Thus, it avoids the trend but implies forecasts that stay at the level of date t.

where β, α, σ^2, ρ, and ϕ are parameters. If $\phi = \rho = 0$ and $\alpha + \beta < 1$, the equations above are equivalent to the GARCH(1,1) equation (Eq. 1.2), where $\omega = \sigma^2(1 - \alpha - \beta)$. If ϕ and ρ differ from 0, q_t is an AR(1) process with 0 mean error $\varepsilon_{t-1}^2 - \sigma_{t-1}^2$ (an m.d.s.). If $\rho = 1$, Equation 1.8 has the IGARCH format of Equation 1.6. The equation for σ_t^2 is a GARCH(1,1) allowing for volatility clustering around the component q_t that evolves more smoothly than the σ_t^2 component if $\rho > \alpha + \beta$, which justifies the interpretation of q_t as long-run component. If moreover $\rho < 1$, the forecasts of both q_t and σ_t^2 converge to $\sigma^2/(1 - \rho)$ as the forecast horizon tends to infinity. By combining the Equations 1.7 and 1.8, the model is found to be equivalent to a GARCH(2,2). In an application to the daily S&P 500 returns over the period 1971–1991, Engle and Lee (1999) do not reject the hypothesis that the q_t component is integrated ($\hat{\rho} = 0.9982$), and that shock effects are stronger on σ_t^2 than on q_t ($\hat{\alpha} = 0.089 > \hat{\phi} = 0.032$), while $\hat{\beta} = 0.80$, such that the persistence of the short-run component ($\hat{\alpha} + \hat{\beta} = 0.89$) is much lower than for the long-run one. However, the slowly moving component q_t reverts to a constant level (assuming $\rho < 1$), a feature that does not fit to the viewpoint that the level of unconditional volatility can itself evolve through time, as suggested by the different subsample estimates of σ^2 in Table 1.2. A related additive component model is put forward by Ding and Granger (1996), where the conditional variance is a convex linear combination of two components: $\sigma_t^2 = w\sigma_{1,t}^2 + (1 - w)\sigma_{2,t}^2$. One component is a GARCH(1,1)—$\sigma_{1,t}^2 = \omega_1 + \beta_1\sigma_{1,t-1}^2 + \alpha_1\varepsilon_{t-1}^2$—and the other is an IGARCH equation—$\sigma_{2,t}^2 = (1 - \alpha_2)\sigma_{2,t-1}^2 + \alpha_2\varepsilon_{t-1}^2$. The restriction to IGARCH form with 0 intercept is necessary for identifiability. Bauwens and Storti (2009) extend this model by letting the fixed weight w become time-varying and specifying w_t as a logistic transformation of σ_{t-1}^2. This allows to relax the restriction that one of the components must be integrated. That model is close to a smooth transition GARCH (STGARCH) model. In a STGARCH model, the parameters of the GARCH equation change more or less quickly through time. For example, to allow for a change of the intercept, ω in the GARCH(1,1) equation is replaced by $\omega_1 + \omega_2 G(\varepsilon_{t-1})$, where $G()$ is a "transition" function taking values in $[0, 1]$. For example, if $G(\varepsilon_{t-1}) = \{1 + \exp[-\gamma(\varepsilon_{t-1} - \kappa)]\}^{-1}$, the intercept is close to ω_1 if ε_{t-1} is very negative and to ω_2 if it is very positive. The parameter γ is restricted to be positive and represents the speed of the transition; if it is large, the transition function is close to a step function jumping at the value of κ. The parameter κ represents the location of the transition. Smooth transition models are presented in detail in Chapter 2 by Teräsvirta (2012) in this Handbook. Multiplicative component models are briefly discussed below and in more detail in Chapter 9 by Brownlees et al. (2012b) in this Handbook.

2-Mixture and Markov-switching models. The log-likelihood function of the component model of Ding and Granger (1996) is of the type of Equation 1.5, so that estimation is not complicated. A mixture model is also based on two (or more) variance components $\sigma_{i,t}^2 = \omega_i + \beta_i\sigma_{i,t-1}^2 + \alpha_i\varepsilon_{t-1}^2$ (for $i = 1, 2$) that appear in a mixture of two Gaussian distributions. It is assumed that $\varepsilon_t|\mathcal{F}_{t-1} \sim wN(\mu_1, \sigma_{1,t}^2) + (1 - w)N(\mu_2, \sigma_{2,t}^2)$. The means of the Gaussian distributions are related by $w\mu_1 + (1 - w)\mu_2 = 0$ to ensure that the mixture has a null expectation. This model is a particular "mixed normal GARCH" (MN-GARCH) model, see Haas et al. (2004a) for several extensions. One interpretation of it is that there are two possible regimes: for each t, a binary variable takes one of the values 1 and 2 with respective probabilities of w and $1 - w$. Once the regime label is known, the model is a GARCH(1,1) with given mean. One regime could feature a low mean with high variance (bear market) and the other a high mean with low variance (bull), for example, if $\mu_1 < \mu_2$ and $\omega_1/(1 - \beta_1 - \alpha_1) > \omega_2/(1 - \beta_2 - \alpha_2)$. Haas et al. (2004a) derive the existence conditions for the fourth-order moments of MN-GARCH models. In the model described above, the unconditional variance exists if $w(1 - \alpha_1 - \beta_1)/(1 - \beta_1) + (1 - w)(1 - \alpha_2 - \beta_2)/(1 - \beta_2) > 0$, so that it is not necessary that $\alpha_i + \beta_i < 1$ holds for $i = 1$ and $i = 2$. If $w = 1$, the model reduces to the GARCH(1,1) case and the previous condition to $\alpha_1 + \beta_1 < 1$. The model is useful to capture not only different levels of variance (according to the regimes) but also unconditional skewness and kurtosis, since a mixture of Gaussian densities can have such features. In an application to a series of NASDAQ daily returns over the period 1971–2001, for two components, the ML estimates are $\hat{w} = 0.82$, $\hat{\mu}_1 = 0.09$, $\hat{\alpha}_1 = 0.05$, $\hat{\beta}_1 = 0.92$, $\hat{\mu}_2 = -0.42$, $\hat{\alpha}_2 = 0.51$, and $\hat{\beta}_2 = 0.73$. These values are in agreement with the interpretation suggested above of bull and bear regimes. The second regime thus has $\hat{\alpha}_2 + \hat{\beta}_2 > 1$, yet the variance existence condition holds. The estimates imply a variance level equal to 0.53 in the first variance process and 1.74 in the second, thus on average 1.06. The single regime GARCH(1,1) Gaussian ML estimates are $\hat{\alpha} = 0.12$, $\hat{\beta} = 0.87$, and $\hat{\sigma}^2 = 0.99$. The likelihood ratio statistic is about 140, indicating a much better fit of the MN-GARCH model with two components.

The idea that the regime indicator variables that are implicit in the MN-GARCH model are independent through time does not seem realistic. Intuitively, if the market is bullish, it stays in that state for a large number of periods and likewise if it is bearish. Thus, some persistence is likely in each regime. Following the idea of Hamilton (1989), this is modeled by assuming that the regime indicator variables are dependent, in the form of a Markov process of order 1. Thus, once in a given regime, there is a high probability to stay in the same regime and a low to move to the other regime. This idea can be combined with the existence of two different means and conditional variance processes within each regime, as in the MN-GARCH model (the extension to more than two regimes is obvious). Haas et al. (2004b) develop this type of Markov-switching GARCH model. This model is much easier to estimate than a Markov-switching model featuring path dependence. Such a model is defined by assuming that the parameters of the GARCH equation change according to a Markov process. Let s_t denote a random variable taking the values 1 or 2 in the case of two regimes. Then, if $\varepsilon_t(s_t) = \sigma_t(s_t)z_t$ and $\sigma_t(s_t)^2 = \omega_{s_t} + \alpha_{s_t}\varepsilon_{t-1}(s_{t-1})^2 + \beta_{s_t}\sigma_{t-1}(s_{t-1})^2$, the model features path dependence. This means that to compute the value of the conditional variance at date t, one must know the realized values of all s_τ for $\tau \leq t$. Since the s_t process is latent, the realized values are not known and thus for estimation by ML, these variables must be integrated out by summation over 2^t possible paths (K^t for K regimes). This renders ML estimation infeasible for the sample sizes typically used in volatility estimation. Notice that path dependence does not occur if $\beta_{s_t} = 0$ for all possible values of s_t, that is, in the ARCH case, see Cai (1994) and Hamilton and Susmel (1994). However, Bayesian estimation of a Markov-switching GARCH model using a MCMC algorithm is feasible, as shown by Bauwens et al. (2010). Chapter 3 by Haas and Paolella (2012) in this Handbook presents in detail the mixture and Markov-switching GARCH models and contains empirical illustrations.

3-Models with a changing level of the unconditional variance. The models in the previous classes (when stationary) have a constant level of unconditional variance even if they let the conditional variances fluctuate around a changing level. This moving level changes smoothly in the model of Engle and Lee (1999), and it changes abruptly in a Markov-switching GARCH model whenever there is a switch. In the third class discussed hereafter, the models are nonstationary since the unconditional variance is time-varying. The level of the unconditional variance is captured either by a smooth function or by a step function, independently of the short-run GARCH dynamics.

The models of Engle and Rangel (2008) and Amado and Teräsvirta (2012) let the unconditional variance change smoothly as a function of time.[3] In their models, Equation 1.1 is extended by including a factor τ_t multiplicatively, as follows:

$$\varepsilon_t = \tau_t \sigma_t z_t. \tag{1.9}$$

In the spline-GARCH model of Engle and Rangel (2008), the factor τ_t is an exponential quadratic spline function with k knots and is multiplied by a GARCH component:

$$\sigma_t^2 = (1 - \alpha - \beta) + \beta\sigma_{t-1}^2 + \alpha(\varepsilon_{t-1}/\tau_{t-1})^2, \tag{1.10}$$

$$\tau_t^2 = \omega \exp\left(\delta_0 t + \sum_{i=1}^{k} \delta_i[(t - t_{i-1})_+]^2\right), \tag{1.11}$$

where β, α, ω, and δ_i are parameters for $i = 0, 1, \ldots, k$, $x_+ = x$ if $x > 0$ and 0 otherwise, and $\{t_0 = 0, t_1, \ldots, t_{k-1}\}$ are time indices partitioning the time span into k equally spaced intervals. The specification of σ_t^2 may be chosen among other available GARCH equations[4] with an adapted identification constraint for the intercept (e.g., $1 - \alpha - \beta - \gamma/2$ for the GJR-GARCH(1,1) equation and a symmetric distribution for z_t). Given this type of constraint on the constant of the GARCH equation, it is obvious that $\text{Var}(\varepsilon_t) = \tau_t^2$, so that the τ_t^2 component is interpretable as the smoothly changing unconditional variance, while σ_t^2 is the component of the conditional variance capturing the

[3]Another model with this feature is the STGARCH model where the variable triggering the transitions is the index of time, see Section 2.4.7 in Chapter 2 Teräsvirta (2012) in this Handbook.

[4]Notice that ε_{t-1} is divided by τ_{t-1} in Equation 1.10.

clustering effect. The model of Amado and Teräsvirta (2012) uses a transition function type of functional form for τ_t, see Section 8 of Teräsvirta (2012) in this Handbook for more details. Baillie and Morana (2009) put forward an additive model where the unconditional variance component τ_t^2 evolves smoothly via another type of function known as the *Fourier flexible form*, given by $\omega + \sum_{i=1}^{k}[\gamma_i \sin(2\pi it/T) + \delta_i \cos(2\pi it/T)]$. The GARCH component of their model is a fractionally integrated one (FIGARCH) that is useful to capture a long-memory aspect in squared returns, see Baillie et al., (1996). Table 1.4 shows the ML estimates of the spline-GARCH model with three knots for the period January 2006 to mid-July 2011, and Figure 1.4 displays the estimated spline component, which clearly reflects the volatility bump due to the financial

TABLE 1.4 Three Knot Spline-GARCH(1,1) ML Estimates for S&P 500 Demeaned Returns for the Period 2006-01-03 Until 2011-07-14 (1393 Observations)

Parameter	Estimate	p-Value, %
ω	0.727	0.04
δ_0	−4.432	39.7
δ_1	21.48	8.50
δ_2	−49.71	1.40
δ_3	49.56	0.62
α	0.077	0.00
β	0.892	0.00

Results obtained with OxMetrics 6.20. Demeaned returns are defined as in Table 1.1.

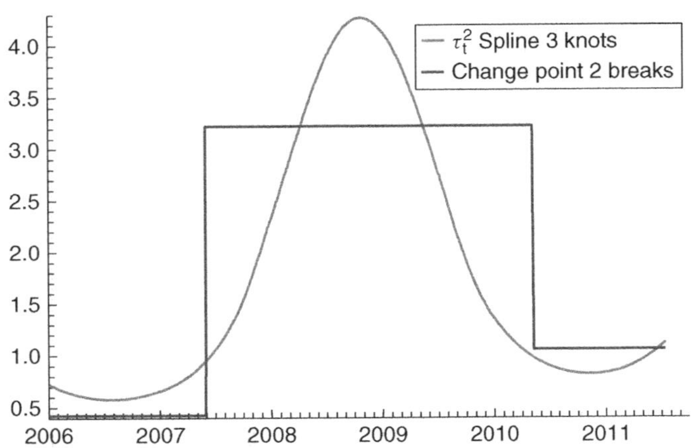

FIGURE 1.4 Three knot spline-GARCH component and variance of change-point model with two breaks of S&P 500 index demeaned returns, 2006-01-03/2011-07-14 (1393 observations).

crisis of 2008 and anticipates the increase of the summer of 2011. The persistence of the conditional variance component σ_t^2 is estimated to be 0.97 versus 0.99 in the simple GARCH(1,1) model (Table 1.2).

In Chapter 10 by Van Bellegem (2012) in this Handbook, more general multiplicative models that feature nonstationarity are reviewed. The spline-GARCH model is also briefly presented with an empirical illustration.

Models allowing sudden changes in the level of the unconditional variance are scarce. The model of Amado and Teräsvirta (2012) has this feature if the transition function becomes a step function (or a superposition of such functions). He and Maheu (2010) propose a change-point GARCH model based on the change-point modeling framework of Chib (1998). It is a Markov switching model that excludes recurrent states: once in a given state, the time series can only stay in it (with some probability) or move to the next state (with the complementary probability). He and Maheu (2010) use this approach for the univariate GARCH(1,1) model (with 0 mean and student errors), using a particle filter for implementing Bayesian estimation. Applying such a model (with Gaussian innovations) to the same data as for the spline-GARCH model above and assuming two breaks, the estimated unconditional variance increases from 0.43 to 3.22 on 2007-05-31 and decreases to 1.05 on 2010-12-10. This is shown graphically by the piecewise constant line in Figure 1.4. The estimates of α and β for the three successive regimes are $(0.034, 0.900)$, $(0.099, 0.890)$, and $(0.002, 0.753)$. For details on algorithms and model choice in this type of models, see Bauwens et al. (2011).

1.2.1.5 Explanation of Volatility Clustering. According to financial theory, the price of an asset should equal the expected present value of its future income flows. An asset price then changes because the expectations of investors about these future incomes change over time: as time passes, new information (news) about these is released, which modifies the expectations. This explains why prices and, hence, returns are random and therefore volatile. Volatility fluctuates over time because the contents and the arrival rate of news fluctuate. For example, crisis periods correspond to more news releases: in particular, bad news tend to happen in clusters. Volatility clustering is thus due to clusters of arrivals of different types of news. For a more extensive discussion, see Engle (2004). This fundamental explanation is difficult to test empirically. For the example of the S&P 500 index returns, there are many types of news that might be relevant in different importance: news affecting the constituent stocks (earnings announcements, profit warnings, etc.) and the industries to which they belong, news affecting the real activity of the US economy, news about the monetary policy... The contents of these news must be measured. The way they affect volatility is through expectations of many investors, raising an issue of aggregation. It is not known how these expectations are formed, and it is likely that there is a degree of heterogeneity in this process. Parke and Waters (2007) provide an evolutionary game theory model based on heterogeneous agents, who form different types of expectations and adjust these over time. The model is able to generate volatility clustering.

Thus, at best, a reduced form, partial, approach is feasible, that is, relating volatility to some macroeconomic variables and news measures. Relevant papers about the relation between macroeconomic variables and stock volatility include Schwert (1989a, b) and Engle and Rangel (2008). In the latter, the authors use the estimated unconditional variances (the τ^2 of Equation 1.11) of their spline-GARCH model to compute time series of annualized estimates of volatilities for different countries and relate them to macroeconomic variables through a panel data model. Other authors study the impact of news announcements on the intraday volatility of exchange rate returns using a GARCH model, by including variables representing news occurrences and measurements (Degennaro and Shrieves, 1997; Melvin and Yin, 2000; Bauwens et al., 2005).

1.2.1.6 Literature and Software. Extensive surveys of GARCH include Bollerslev et al. (1992), Bera and Higgins (1993), Bollerslev et al. (1994), Diebold and Lopez (1996), Pagan (1996), Palm (1996), Shephard (1996), Li et al. (2002), Giraitis et al. (2006), Teräsvirta (2009), and Hafner (2008). Introductory surveys include Engle and Patton (2001), Engle (2001, 2004), and Diebold (2004). Introductory econometric textbooks briefly mention or explain ARCH (see Stock and Watson (2007) and Wooldridge (2009)) intermediate and advanced books provide more details (Hamilton, 1994; Greene, 2011; Tsay, 2002; Verbeek, 2008). Specialized books are Gouriéroux (1997), Francq and Zakoian (2010), and Xekalaki and Degiannakis (2010). Andersen et al. (2009) contains nine chapters on GARCH modeling.

Several well-known software for econometrics and statistics (EVIEWS, OxMetrics, SAS, SPSS, STATA) contain menu-driven modules for GARCH modeling, avoiding the need to program inference tools for applying GARCH models. See Laurent (2009) for the OxMetrics documentation.

1.2.1.7 Applications of Univariate GARCH. Univariate GARCH models are useful for financial applications such as option pricing and risk measurement.

Option pricing. We take the example of a European call option. Such an option is an acquired right to buy a security (called the *underlying*) at a price (the *premium*) set in advance (the *exercise price*) and at a fixed date (the *maturity*). It is well known that the value of an option is a function of several parameters, among which is the volatility of the return on the underlying security until the maturity. According to the financial theory, see Cox and Ross (1976), "options are priced *as if* investors were risk-neutral and the underlying asset expected return were equal to the risk-free interest rate" (denoted by r below). This is called *"risk-neutral" pricing*. Let C_t^T denote the premium at t for maturity T, $T - t$ thus being the time to maturity. Let P_T be the random value of the underlying security at T and K the exercise price. Then,

$$C_t^T = \mathrm{e}^{-r(T-t)} E_Q[\max(P_T - K, 0)] \tag{1.12}$$

is the discounted expected cash flow of the option, where the expected value is computed using Q, the "risk-neutral" probability distribution. So, C_t^T is a function of r, $T-t$, K, and the parameters of Q, which determine the variance of the return on the underlying. The risk-neutral density function must have as expected return (until maturity) the risk-free interest rate, and its variance must be the same as in the process generating the observed returns. Duan (1995) showed that risk-neutralization cannot be used with a GARCH model both for the unconditional variance and the conditional variance at all horizons. He uses a "locally" risk-neutral probability for GARCH processes, that is, for the one-step-ahead conditional variance. For the GARCH process defined by Equations 1.1 and 1.2, where $z_t \sim N(0,1)$, the locally risk-neutralized process is given by $y_t = r + v_t$, where $v_t = \mu_t - r + \varepsilon_t$ is $N(0, \sigma_t^2)$ and $\sigma_t^2 = \omega + \alpha(v_{t-1} - \mu_{t-1} + r)^2 + \beta\sigma_{t-1}^2$. The parameters of Q are denoted by θ and consist of the parameters indexing μ_t in addition to (ω, α, β). Thus, denoting $C_t^T = C_t^T(r, K, \theta)$, the premium can be computed by numerical simulation if θ is known or, in practice, replaced by an estimate. Given N simulated realizations $\{P_{T,i}\}_{i=1}^N$ of P_T using the risk-neutralized process,[5] $C_t^T(r, K, \theta)$ is estimated by $\hat{C}_t^T(\theta) = \mathrm{e}^{-r(T-t)} \frac{1}{N} \sum_{i=1}^N \max(P_{T,i} - K, 0)$. Bauwens and Lubrano (2002) apply this procedure in a Bayesian setup, which makes it possible to compute a predictive distribution of the premium and not only a point estimate as is the case when θ is simply replaced by a point estimate. Such predictive distributions have a positive probability mass at 0, corresponding to the probability that the option will not be exercised, while the remaining probability is spread over the positive values through a continuous density function. Among many others, some references about option pricing in relation with GARCH models are Noh et al. (1994), Kallsen and Taqqu (1998), Hafner and Herwartz (2001), and Rombouts and Stentoft (2009).

Value-at-risk. The VaR of a financial position provides a quantitative measure of the risk of holding the position. It is an estimate of the loss that may be incurred over a given horizon, under normal market conditions, corresponding to a given statistical confidence level. For example, an investor holding a portfolio of stocks might say that the daily VaR of his trading portfolio is €5 million at the 99% confidence level. That means there is 1 chance in 100 that a loss >€5 million will occur the next day under normal market conditions. Indeed, the VaR is a quantile (the 1% quantile in the example above) of the probability distribution of the position. The distribution can be, for example, the conditional distribution implied by a GARCH model estimated at the date when the VaR must be computed. The model is estimated using historical data of past returns on the portfolio and provides a value of the 1% quantile of the next day return distribution. Multiplying this quantile by the portfolio value gives the VaR estimate.

Formally, assume that $y_t = \mu_t + \sigma_t z_t$, where σ_t is defined by a GARCH equation and $z_t \sim N(0,1)$. Let n_α be the left quantile at α% of the $N(0,1)$ distribution, and $n_{1-\alpha}$ be the right quantile at α% (e.g., $n_1 = -n_{99} = -2.326$). The one-step-ahead VaR (computed at date $t-1$) for a long position of

[5]Since $P_T = P_t \prod_{s=t+1}^T (1 + y_s)$, one must simulate sequentially the returns $y_{t+1}, y_{t+2}, \ldots, y_T$ from the risk-neutral GARCH process.

€1 is given by $\text{VaR}_t(\alpha) = \mu_t + n_\alpha \sigma_t$. For a short position, $\text{VaR}_t(1-\alpha) = \mu_t + n_{1-\alpha}\sigma_t$. In practice, the GARCH model is estimated with data until date $t-1$, and μ_t and σ_t are replaced by their one-step-ahead forecast in the VaR formula. If we assume another distribution for z_t, we use its quantiles. For example, for a t-density with ν degrees of freedom, we replace ν by its ML estimate and find the corresponding quantiles. Angelidis et al. (2004) evaluate GARCH models for VaR and illustrate that the use of a t-density instead of a Gaussian one improves VaR forecasts. Giot and Laurent (2003) show that the use of a skewed-t instead of a symmetric distribution may be beneficial. VaR forecasts are evaluated using statistical tests (Kupiec, 1995; Christoffersen 1998; Engle and Manganelli, 2004).

1.2.2 MULTIVARIATE GARCH

Multivariate ARCH models appeared almost at the same time as univariate models. Kraft and Engle (1982) was a first attempt, and Engle et al. (1984) put forward a bivariate ARCH model, applied to the forecast errors of two competing models of US inflation, so that their conditional covariance matrix adapts over time. The move to financial applications was done by Bollerslev et al. (1988) who also extended multivariate ARCH to GARCH. They used the capital asset pricing model (CAPM) in the framework of conditional moments rather than unconditional moments. The multivariate GARCH (MGARCH) model of that paper, known as the *VEC model*, has too many parameters to be useful for modeling more than two asset returns jointly. A natural research question was then to design models that can be estimated for larger dimensions. Important milestones are the BEKK model of Engle and Kroner (1995), the factor model of Engle et al. (1990), and the constant conditional correlation (CCC) model of Bollerslev (1990). The latter was followed 12 years later by the time-varying correlation (TVC) model of Tse and Tsui (2002) and the dynamic correlation model (DCC) of Engle (2002a).

In this section, we review briefly the conditional correlation models and factor models. Chapter 4 by Sheppard (2012) in this Handbook is partly complementary to what follows, since it contains more models and is oriented by their use in forecasting. Some surveys and books cited in Section 1.2.1.6 cover the topic of MGARCH models (Bollerslev et al., 1994; Hafner 2008; Francq and Zakoian, 2010). More detailed and extensive surveys of MGARCH models are those of Silvennoinen and Teräsvirta (2009) and Bauwens et al. (2006). The discussion paper version of the latter (Bauwens et al. (2003)) includes a review of applications of MGARCH models to asset pricing, volatility transmission, futures hedging, Value-at-Risk, and the impact of financial volatility on the level and volatility of macroeconomic variables. In Chapter 5 of this Handbook, Hashmi and Tay (2012) apply factor models that not only allow for volatility spillovers between different stock markets but also for time-varying skewness and spillovers in skewness effects. Multivariate models can be used also for pricing options that are written on more than a single underlying asset, so that their price depends on the correlations between the assets (Rombouts and Stentoft, 2011).

1.2.2.1 Structure of MGARCH Models. We denote by y_t a column vector of N asset returns, by μ_t the vector of conditional expectations of y_t, and by $\Sigma_t = (\sigma_{tij})$ the conditional variance–covariance matrix of y_t. The elements of μ_t and Σ_t must be measurable with respect to the σ-field $\mathcal{F}_{t-1}$ generated by y_{t-j} for $j \geq 1$ and possibly by other variables available at time $t-1$. An MGARCH model for y_t is then defined by

$$y_t - \mu_t = \varepsilon_t = \Sigma_t^{1/2} z_t, \tag{1.13}$$

where $\Sigma_t^{1/2}$ is any square matrix such that $\Sigma_t = \Sigma_t^{1/2}(\Sigma_t^{1/2})'$ and z_t is an unobservable random vector belonging to an i.i.d. process, with mean equal to 0 and variance–covariance equal to an identity matrix, $E(z_t) = 0$ and $\mathrm{Var}(z_t) = I_N$. It follows that $\Sigma_t = \mathrm{Var}(y_t|\mathcal{F}_{t-1}) = \mathrm{Var}_{t-1}(y_t)$, so that $\mathrm{Var}_{t-1}(\varepsilon_t) = \Sigma_t$ (note that $E_{t-1}(\varepsilon_t) = 0$). The model is parametric and the definition is complete when the pdf of z_t is defined and the functional form of μ_t and Σ_t is specified. These functions are altogether indexed by a parameter vector of finite dimension. In what follows, we assume that $\mu_t = 0$ and concentrate on the specification of the other elements.

Concerning the pdf of z_t, the reference is the multivariate Gaussian, that is, $z_t \sim N(0, I_N)$, since it provides the basis of QML estimation as in the univariate case. The quasi-log-likelihood function of a sample of T observed vectors y_t (altogether denoted by Y) for a model defined by Equation 1.13 and for known initial observation is

$$\ell_T(\theta; Y) = -\frac{1}{2}\sum_{t=1}^{T}(\log|\Sigma_t| + \varepsilon_t'\Sigma_t^{-1}\varepsilon_t), \tag{1.14}$$

where θ denotes the vector of parameters appearing in μ_t, Σ_t, and in the pdf of z_t (if any). Another choice of density for ε_t is the multivariate t. Multivariate skewed distribution, such as the skewed-t of Bauwens and Laurent (2005), can also be used. As in the univariate case, distributions with fat-tails and skewness are usually better fitting data than the Gaussian, see Giot and Laurent (2003) for an example in the context of Value-at-Risk evaluation.

1.2.2.2 Conditional Correlations. In conditional correlation models, what is specified is the conditional variances σ_{tii} (equivalently denoted by σ_{ti}^2) for $i = 1, 2, \ldots, N$, and the conditional correlations ρ_{tij} for $i < j$ and $j = 2, 3, \ldots, N$. The conditional covariance σ_{tij} is equal to $\rho_{tij}\sigma_{ti}\sigma_{tj}$. In matrix notations,

$$\Sigma_t = D_t R_t D_t, \tag{1.15}$$

where $D_t = \mathrm{diag}(\sigma_{t1}, \sigma_{t2}, \ldots, \sigma_{tN})$ is a diagonal matrix with σ_{ti} as ith diagonal element, and $R_t = (\rho_{tij})$ is the correlation matrix of order N (implying $\rho_{tii} = 1$ $\forall i$ and $\forall t$). The matrix Σ_t is positive-definite if σ_{ti}^2 is positive for all i and R_t is positive-definite.

With this approach, the specification of Σ_t is divided into two independent parts: a model choice for each conditional variance and a choice for the conditional correlation matrix.[6] Concerning the first part, an important simplification is obtained in QML estimation if each conditional variance is specified as a function of its own lags and the ith element of ε_t (denoted by ε_{ti}), for example, by a GARCH(1,1) equation written as

$$\sigma_{ti}^2 = \omega_i + \beta_i \sigma_{t-1,i}^2 + \alpha_i \varepsilon_{t-1,i}^2 \tag{1.16}$$

or any other univariate GARCH equation (Section 1.2.1). This type of model excludes transmission (or spillover) effects between different assets, that is, the presence of terms involving $\varepsilon_{t-1,j}$ or $\sigma_{t-1,j}^2$ for $j \neq i$ in the previous equation. To explain why the assumption of no spillovers simplifies the estimation of conditional correlation models, we substitute $D_t R_t D_t$ for Σ_t in Equation 1.14 to define "degarched" returns

$$\tilde{\varepsilon}_t = D_t^{-1} \varepsilon_t \tag{1.17}$$

and split the likelihood function into two parts:

$$\ell_T(\theta; Y) = -\frac{1}{2} \sum_{t=1}^{T} \left(2 \log |D_t| + \log |R_t| + \tilde{\varepsilon}_t' R_t^{-1} \tilde{\varepsilon}_t\right) \tag{1.18}$$

$$= -\frac{1}{2} \sum_{t=1}^{T} \left(2 \log |D_t| + \tilde{\varepsilon}_t' \tilde{\varepsilon}_t\right) \tag{1.19}$$

$$-\frac{1}{2} \sum_{t=1}^{T} \left(\log |R_t| + \tilde{\varepsilon}_t' R_t^{-1} \tilde{\varepsilon}_t - \tilde{\varepsilon}_t' \tilde{\varepsilon}_t\right). \tag{1.20}$$

It is clear that Equation 1.19 depends only on the parameters (denoted by θ_V) of the conditional variances that appear in D_t, while Equation 1.20 depends on the whole θ that includes, in addition to θ_V, the parameters (denoted by θ_C) of the conditional correlation matrix R_t. If there are no spillover terms in the conditional variance equations, maximizing Equation 1.19 with respect to θ_V provides a consistent and asymptotically normal estimator under usual regularity conditions. Moreover, it is easy to see that Equation 1.19 itself can be split into N functions that correspond to the quasi-log-likelihood functions of univariate

[6] A generalization of this model is the class of copula-MGARCH models. Such models are specified by univariate marginal GARCH models for each asset, and a copula function capturing the dependence between the different assets. If the margins are Gaussian and the copula is multivariate Gaussian, the dependence is captured by the correlation matrix. Other copula function can be used to model dependence in a more refined way, see Jondeau and Rockinger (2006) and Patton (2006a) for examples. Chapter 12 by Heinen and Valdesogo (2012) in this Handbook reviews copula-based volatility models.

GARCH models.[7] Once θ_V is estimated, its value can be injected in Equation 1.20 and the latter maximized with respect to θ_C. To do this, the term $\tilde{\varepsilon}_t'\tilde{\varepsilon}_t$ can be neglected in Equation 1.20, since it does not depend on θ_C.

The separate estimation of each conditional variance model and of the correlation model is the key to enable estimation of MGARCH models of conditional correlations when N is large, where large means more than, say, 5. The price to pay for this is the impossibility of including spillover terms in the conditional variance equations. If spillover effects are included, one can, in principle, maximize Equation 1.19 with respect to θ_V, and then Equation 1.20, where θ_V is replaced by the previous estimate, with respect to θ_C. The first step of maximization will be limited by the dimension of θ_V, which is of order N^2 if all spillover terms are included in each conditional variance equation.

Models for R_t. Several specifications are available from the literature. The challenge is to ensure that R_t be positive-definite and not depending on so many parameters by which the model is not estimable. Bollerslev (1990) solves the issue by setting $R_t = R\ \forall t$, that is, by assuming CCCs, where R is a correlation matrix. Notice that R has $N(N-1)/2$ parameters, but they can be estimated easily even if N is large. It follows from Equation 1.18 that if $R_t = R\ \forall t$, and if D_t is known, the ML estimator of R, given by

$$\widehat{R} = \frac{1}{T}\sum_{t=1}^{T} \tilde{\varepsilon}_t\tilde{\varepsilon}_t', \tag{1.21}$$

is consistent (under usual regularity conditions and if $T > N$) and remains so if D_t is replaced by a consistent estimator for all t (obtained by computing D_t using the consistent estimator of θ_V resulting from the maximization of Equation1.19 as explained above). In finite samples, the diagonal elements of $\widehat{R}$ are not exactly equal to 1, so that $\widehat{R}$ should be transformed to a correlation matrix. This is done by replacing the elements of $\widehat{R}_t$ by $\widehat{\rho}_{tij}/\sqrt{\widehat{\rho_{tii}\rho_{tjj}}}$. In matrix notation, the transformed matrix is

$$\widetilde{R} = (I_N \odot \widehat{R})^{-1/2}\widehat{R}(I_N \odot \widehat{R})^{-1/2}, \tag{1.22}$$

where the symbol $\odot$ is the element by element multiplication operator (Hadamard product).

The hypothesis of CCCs is not tenable except for specific cases and short periods. Several tests of the null hypothesis of constant correlations exist: see Longin and Solnik (1995), Tse (2000), Engle and Sheppard (2001), Bera and Kim (2002a), and Silvennoinen and Teräsvirta (2005). The tests differ because of the specification of the alternative hypothesis. Smooth transition-type CCC models are proposed by Silvennoinen and Teräsvirta (2005) and Silvennoinen and Teräsvirta (2007).

[7] If the GARCH equations are as in Equation 1.6, θ_V consists of the vectors $(\omega_i\, \beta_i\, \alpha_i)$, $i = 1, 2, \ldots, N$.

The CCC model has been generalized in different ways, so that the conditional correlations change over time. One dynamic model of conditional correlations is the TVC model of Tse and Tsui (2002). The dynamic process generating R_t is specified as

$$R_t = (1 - \alpha - \beta)R + \beta R_{t-1} + \alpha S_{t-1}, \tag{1.23}$$

where β and α are scalar parameters, R is a constant correlation matrix parameter, and $S_t = (s_{tij})$ is the correlation matrix computed from the past degarched returns $\tilde{\varepsilon}_{t-1}, \tilde{\varepsilon}_{t-2}, \ldots, \tilde{\varepsilon}_{t-M}$, with $M > N$ to ensure that S_t be positive-definite. Thus, if R_0 is a positive-definite correlation matrix, α and β are positive and satisfy $\alpha + \beta < 1$, R_t is a positive-definite correlation matrix for all t. By writing the above constant part of R_t as $(1 - \alpha - \beta)R$, R is interpretable as the expected value of R_t. Hence R is estimated consistently by $\tilde{R}$ defined in Equation 1.22. This can be used to ease estimation of the model when N is large: instead of maximizing Equation 1.20 with respect to R, α, and β, we can replace R by $\tilde{R}$ in Equation 1.20 and maximize it with respect to α and β, that is, only two parameters instead of $2 + N(N-1)/2$. This procedure is called *correlation targeting* (or *tracking*) and is unavoidable if N is large.

Another generalization of the CCC model is the DCC model of Engle (2002a), who specifies the dynamic process on the variance–covariance matrix of $\tilde{\varepsilon}_t$, denoted by Q_t, and transforms it to the correlation matrix R_t:

$$Q_t = (1 - \alpha - \beta)Q + \beta Q_{t-1} + \alpha \tilde{\varepsilon}_{t-1}\tilde{\varepsilon}'_{t-1}, \tag{1.24}$$

$$R_t = (I_N \odot Q_t)^{-1/2} Q_t (I_N \odot Q_t)^{-1/2}. \tag{1.25}$$

where β and α are scalar parameters and Q is a $N \times N$ symmetric and positive-definite matrix parameter. If Q_0 is symmetric and positive-definite and β and α satisfy the same restrictions as in the TVC model above, Q_t is symmetric and positive-definite and R_t is a correlation matrix for all t. The parameter matrix Q can be estimated by $\widehat{R}$ as defined in Equation 1.21 and inserted in Equation 1.20 to ease estimation as explained for the TVC model.[8] However, Aielli (2009) showed that the estimation of Q by $\widehat{R}$ is inconsistent since $E(\tilde{\varepsilon}_t\tilde{\varepsilon}'_t) = E\left(E\left(\tilde{\varepsilon}_t\tilde{\varepsilon}'_t|\mathcal{F}_{t-1}\right)\right) = E\left(R_t\right) \neq E\left(Q_t\right)$. He proposes a consistent specification of Q_t (cDCC, consistent DCC),

$$Q_t = (1 - \alpha - \beta)Q + \beta Q_{t-1} + \alpha P_t \tilde{\varepsilon}_{t-1}\tilde{\varepsilon}'_{t-1} P_t, \tag{1.26}$$

where $P_t = \mathrm{diag}\left(q_{t11}^{1/2}, q_{t22}^{1/2}, \ldots, q_{tNN}^{1/2}\right) = (I_N \odot Q_t)^{1/2}$, so that, by construction, Q is the unconditional variance–covariance matrix of $P_t\tilde{\varepsilon}_t$. The available empirical evidence suggests that the cDCC and DCC estimates are close to each other.

[8] Sheppard (2012) in this Handbook (Section 4.4.6) reviews alternative estimation methods to the maximization of Equation 1.20, which are especially useful when N is large.

Although estimation for a large dimension is in principle feasible, it raises problems. First, as one sees in Equation 1.18 directly, a large matrix (R_t) has to be inverted for each observation in the sample, which is time consuming for the sample sizes typically used in applications, and may raise numerical difficulties for large N. Even if estimation is done in two steps, based on Equation 1.20, with or without correlation targeting, the same issue arises. A model that circumvents this problem is the dynamic equicorrelation (DECO) model of Engle and Kelly (2008). Secondly, Engle et al. (2008) show by simulation that the QML estimates of α and β in the DCC model (estimated with correlation targeting) are subject to a bias problem (toward 0) that is more and more acute as the dimension N increases relative to the sample size T. The source of the problem seems to be that when N approaches T, the estimator (Eq. 1.21) is ill-conditioned, as it approaches a singularity. Better conditioned estimators can be built and are useful to reduce the bias problem, see Hafner and Reznikova (2010b).

Both the TVC and DCC models extend the CCC model by making the conditional correlations time-varying. Notice that a test of $\alpha = \beta = 0$ can be based on the Wald statistic to test the null hypothesis of CCCs. The fact that only two additional parameters suffice to render the correlations time-varying is very useful to deal with large dimensions, but of course, the price to pay is the constraint that all the correlations have the same dynamic pattern. This may be viewed as unrealistic. Several extensions of the DCC model have been proposed to relax this constraint, at the price of introducing more parameters in the process of Q_t and thus being applicable only for moderate values of N (say up to 5 or 10 depending on the number of additional parameters): see Engle (2002a), Billio and Caporin (2006), and Hafner and Franses (2009). Cappiello et al. (2006) introduce asymmetric ("leverage") effects in a DCC model. More extensions are on the agenda of several researchers.

The conditional correlation models described above share the same feature: that the conditional correlations revert to a constant level. Like for univariate GARCH models, this is considered too restrictive for long data series. In particular, the correlation level usually increases in periods of financial turbulence. Thus, models that allow for a smoothly changing level of the correlations are in development. The DCC-MIDAS model of Colacito et al. (2011) and the factor spline-GARCH model for high and low frequency correlations of Rangel and Engle (2009) are of this type. The latter is reviewed in Section 4.4.3 of this Handbook.

1.2.2.3 Factor Models. Factor MGARCH models rest on the idea that the volatilities of assets might be driven by a few common forces. This is related to factor models in finance where excess returns of financial assets are related to factors such as the market excess return in the CAPM or macroeconomic and financial factors, though it should be noted that these models were developed to explain the cross-section of returns rather than their time-series evolution. In the MGARCH literature, the factor structure is a convenient way to reduce the number of parameters with respect to the VEC and BEKK models. Basically, the factor structure says that the unexpected excess return vector $\varepsilon_t = y_t - \mu_t$

(of N elements) is a linear function of p factors (with $p < N$) collected in the vector f_t:

$$\varepsilon_t = Bf_t + \nu_t, \tag{1.27}$$

where B is a matrix of factor loadings, of dimension $N \times p$ and rank equal to p, and ν_t is a white noise vector, called the *indiosyncratic noise*. Assuming that $\mathrm{Var}_{t-1}(\nu_t) = \mathrm{Var}(\nu_t) = \Psi$ with Ψ of full rank, that $\mathrm{Var}_{t-1}(f_t) = \Phi_t$, and that $\mathrm{Cov}(f_t, \nu_t) = 0$, the conditional variance–covariance matrix of ε_t is given by

$$\Sigma_t = B\Phi_t B' + \Psi, \tag{1.28}$$

which is positive-definite.

The specification is completed by a choice of an MGARCH process for Φ_t. The most simple choice is to constrain Φ_t to be a diagonal matrix of univariate GARCH processes, $\Phi_t = \mathrm{diag}(\phi_{t1}^2, \phi_{t2}^2, \ldots, \phi_{tp}^2)$, as in Engle et al. (1990).[9] Thus if $p = 1$, this yields $\Sigma_t = BB'(\omega_1 + \beta_1\phi_{t-1,1}^2 + \alpha_1 f_{t-1,1}^2) + \Psi$. If y_t is a vector of stock returns, the factor can be chosen as the market return. Another choice is to take the factor as a linear combination of ε_t, denoted by $\lambda_1'\varepsilon_t$, where λ_1 is a vector of weights that can be estimated (after normalizing their sum to unity). This model implies that the conditional variances of the unexpected returns have the same dynamics. If λ_1 is known, the number of parameters to estimate is $N + 3 + N(N+1)/2$. The $N(N+1)/2$ elements of Ψ can be estimated by covariance targeting and injected in the (Gaussian) log-likelihood to estimate the remaining parameters. If the factor is observed directly (such as the market return), the parameters of its conditional variance can be estimated in a preliminary step, as an univariate GARCH model.

One can add more factors provided some identification restrictions are imposed, see Bauwens et al. (2006) for details. For two factors $f_{ti} = \lambda_i'\varepsilon_t$ $(i = 1, 2)$, these restrictions are that $B_1'\lambda_2 = B_2'\lambda_1 = 0$, where B_i is the ith column of B. It follows that the two factors have a constant conditional covariance. The fact that factors are conditionally correlated can be viewed as a drawback since they may catch similar features of the data. Several factor models avoid this feature; the orthogonal GARCH (O-GARCH) model of Alexander and Chibumba (1997), the generalized orthogonal GARCH model of van der Weide (2002), the full factor GARCH model of Vrontos et al. (2003), and the generalized orthogonal factor GARCH model of Lanne and Saikkonen (2007). See the surveys of Bauwens et al. (2006) and Silvennoinen and Teräsvirta (2009) for more information.

If the viewpoint is taken that the factors can be correlated, then a DCC model can be chosen for the factor vector f_t, for the idiosyncratic noise vector ν_t, or for the correlations between f_t and ν_t. Engle (2009b) and Rangel and Engle (2009) contain such extensions (in a single factor model) that enrich considerably the conditional correlation structure of the factor model.

[9]If Φ_t is not diagonal and the off-diagonal elements are constant, they can be absorbed in Ψ.

1.3 Stochastic Volatility

An alternative to GARCH-type models is the class of SV models, which postulate that volatility is driven by its own stochastic process. For example, the standard Gaussian autoregressive SV model in discrete time, as first introduced in this form by Taylor (1982), is given by

$$y_t - \mu_t = \varepsilon_t = \sigma_t z_t \quad z_t \sim N(0,1), \tag{1.29}$$

$$\log \sigma_{t+1}^2 = \omega + \beta \log \sigma_t^2 + \sigma_u u_t, \quad u_t \sim N(0,1), \tag{1.30}$$

and, in the standard case, the innovations z_t and u_t are independent. This discrete time model can be thought of as the Euler approximation of an underlying diffusion model,

$$\mathrm{d}p(t) = \sigma(t)\mathrm{d}W_1(t), \tag{1.31}$$

$$\mathrm{d}\log\sigma(t)^2 = \omega + \phi \log\sigma(t)^2 + \sigma_u \mathrm{d}W_2(t), \tag{1.32}$$

where $\mathrm{d}p(t)$ denotes the logarithmic price increment (i.e., $\mathrm{d}p(t) = \mathrm{d}\log P(t)$), and $W_1(t)$ and $W_2(t)$ are two independent Wiener processes.

The major difference to GARCH models is that, conditional on the information set $\mathcal{F}_{t-1}$, volatility σ_t^2 is not known but rather an unobserved random variable. As we will see, this renders estimation and inference of SV models more complicated than for GARCH models. On the other hand, SV models have some advantages compared with GARCH models. For example, SV models offer a natural economic interpretation of volatility, are easier to connect with continuous-time diffusion models with SV, and are often found to be more flexible in the modeling of financial returns.

The economic motivation is based on the so-called mixture-of-distributions hypothesis, which states that financial returns are driven by a convolution of two random variables as in Equation 1.29, one being an independent noise term, the other a stochastic process representing an information arrival process. For example, Clark (1973) uses trading volume as a proxy for the information arrival process, while Tauchen and Pitts (1983) study the joint distribution of returns and volume, which are driven by the latent information flow. A common feature of models motivated by the mixture-of-distributions hypothesis is that, conditional on the latent variable σ_t, returns follow a normal distribution: $\varepsilon_t|\sigma_t \sim N(0, \sigma_t^2)$. However, as σ_t is assumed to be a random variable, the unconditional distribution of ε_t is no longer Gaussian but, in particular, has fatter tails than the normal distribution, which corresponds to the empirical evidence for financial returns.

While Clark (1973) and Tauchen and Pitts (1983) did not specify any dynamics for the information flow process, Taylor (1982) was the first to propose the popular model in Equation 1.30, where the logarithm of volatility follows a first-order Gaussian autoregressive process. This allows, through a positive parameter β, to model volatility clustering as in GARCH models, that is, alternating periods of high and low volatility. Moreover, because of the simplicity of the model, stochastic properties such as stationarity, distributions, or moments are straightforward to derive. For example, by Theorem 2.1 of Andersen (1994), the stochastic process $\{\varepsilon_t\}$ is strictly stationary (which in the SV case is equivalent to covariance stationary) and ergodic if $|\beta| < 1$. This contrasts with GARCH models, for which conditions for strict and covariance stationarity do not coincide, although they do coincide for the EGARCH model. Moreover, we know the unconditional distribution of log-volatility, given by $\log \sigma_t^2 \sim N(\omega/(1-\beta), \sigma_u^2/(1-\beta^2))$, which can, for example, be used to draw initial values for σ_1^2 when simulating the model. It also implies that volatility itself follows a log-normal distribution.

For the model in Equations 1.29 and 1.30, we can calculate the autocorrelation function of squared demeaned returns, ε_t^2, and the kurtosis of ε_t (Ghysels et al., 1996). They are given by, respectively,

$$\rho(\tau) = \frac{\exp(\sigma_u^2/(1-\beta^2)\beta^\tau) - 1}{\kappa - 1}, \tag{1.33}$$

$$\kappa = 3\exp(\sigma_u^2/(1-\beta^2)), \tag{1.34}$$

which shows that, unless the error term of volatility is degenerate (i.e., $\sigma_u = 0$), the kurtosis κ is strictly larger than 3, and returns have a leptokurtic or fat-tailed distribution. Furthermore, the ACF $\rho(\tau)$ decays exponentially with β. Both properties are shared with GARCH-type models. However, Carnero et al. (2004) show that the SV model in Equations 1.29 and 1.30 is more flexible than the standard GARCH(1,1) model with Gaussian innovations in fitting kurtosis and persistence of empirical autocorrelations of squared returns, although both models have the same number of parameters. They attribute the often used fat-tailed distributions for the innovations of a GARCH model to this lack-of-fit of standard GARCH models, which requires adding additional parameters such as the degrees of freedom parameter of a t distribution to better explain kurtosis and persistence of empirical data. In the SV model, however, it is typically not necessary to relax the normality assumption of innovations.

1.3.1 LEVERAGE EFFECT

The classical SV model in Equations 1.29 and 1.30 with independent error terms z_t and u_t cannot take into account the leverage effect mentioned above, that is, the effect that negative news tend to increase volatility stronger than positive news. It is, however, possible to incorporate this effect in the standard model by introducing a dependence between the two error terms. It turns out that there are basically two ways of doing this, which is discussed in the following sections, and the conclusion is that the second one should be preferred.

Jacquier et al. (2004) propose to let (z_t, u_{t-1}) follow a bivariate normal distribution with correlation ρ. They propose estimation and inference methods for this model in a Bayesian framework. A critique of this model, however, is the fact that returns are no longer martingale difference sequences in the sense that

$E[\varepsilon_t|\varepsilon_{t-1},\sigma_{t-1}] \neq 0$, violating the efficient market hypothesis, see (Harvey and Shephard, 1996).

As an alternative to introduce the leverage effect, Harvey and Shephard (1996) propose to let (z_t, u_t) follow a bivariate normal distribution with correlation ρ. This makes a small but important difference: The two components of ε_t, that is, σ_t and z_t, remain independent and, hence, ε_t has the martingale difference property. Moreover, this model is the discrete time Euler approximation of the diffusion model in Equations 1.31 and 1.32, where $\mathrm{d}W_1(t)\mathrm{d}W_2(t) = \rho \mathrm{d}t$. Yu (2005) provides a comprehensive comparison of these two specifications of the leverage effect in the SV model and concludes that, both from a theoretical and empirical perspective, the model of Harvey and Shephard (1996) should be preferred to that of Jacquier et al. (2004).

1.3.2 ESTIMATION

The estimation problem is certainly the main reason why GARCH models have been more often used in empirical applications than SV models, although much progress has been made over the last 15 years. While in GARCH models the predictive density of returns depends on volatility, which is measurable with respect to the information set, estimation by ML is straightforward. Unfortunately, this is not the case for SV models, since the likelihood function for a sample of T observations can be written as

$$L(\theta; Y_T) \propto \int f(Y_T|H_T;\theta)f(H_T|\theta)\mathrm{d}H_T, \tag{1.35}$$

where Y_T is a vector containing all observed returns, $H_T = (\sigma_1^2, \ldots, \sigma_T^2)'$ is the vector containing all latent volatilities, and θ is the parameter vector, which in the classical model without leverage effect is $\theta = (\omega, \beta, \sigma_u)'$. The problem is the integral appearing in Equation 1.35, which is a multiple integral of dimension T. It cannot be solved analytically, and direct numerical methods are infeasible even for moderately large samples. Other techniques have to be employed, and this is what we discuss in the following paragraphs.

Chapter 6 by Bos (2012) in this handbook gives a broad overview of existing estimation methods of the standard univariate SV model, emphasizing the relationship between them and providing an empirical comparison. Estimation methods of SV models can be roughly categorized into moment methods and simulation methods, where the former are often simpler but inefficient, while the latter attempt to achieve a close approximation of the likelihood function through computationally expensive simulation methods.

Let us first discuss some estimators based on moment expressions. If only the estimation of the model parameter θ is of interest but not the filtration of the underlying volatility process, then simple moment-based estimators can be used based, for example, on the moments given in Equations 1.33 and 1.34. Even closed-form estimators for θ are available, see (Taylor, 1982; Dufour and Valéry, 2006; Hafner and Preminger, 2010), which however are quite inefficient.

Generalized method of moment (GMM) estimators have been proposed, for example, by Melino and Turnbull (1990) and Andersen and Sorensen (1996).

Harvey et al. (1994a) propose a QML estimator based on the linear state space representation of model (Eqs. 1.29 and 1.30), whose measurement equation is given by $\log \varepsilon_t^2 = \log \sigma_t^2 + \xi_t$ and transition equation for the volatility state variable given by Equation 1.30. If $u_t \sim N(0, \sigma_u^2)$, then the noise term $\xi_t = \log u_t^2$ has a highly skewed log chi-square distribution, which Harvey et al. (1994a) approximate by a Gaussian distribution with the same mean and variance. On the basis of this Gaussian linear state space model, they obtain a QML estimator for θ and filtered and smoothed estimates of volatility by using the Kalman filter. While this approach is simple and straightforward to implement, it is not fully efficient because of the skewness of ξ_t.

The influential paper by Kim et al. (1998) extends the approximation of the log chi-squared error term ξ_t to a Gaussian mixture with unobserved mixture weights. Since volatility depends on these latent state variables, the resulting state space model is no longer linear and the Kalman filter cannot be used directly as in Harvey et al. (1994a). Kim et al. (1998) propose to use a Bayesian Markov Chain MC algorithm with data augmentation. For given sampled mixture weights, the state space model is again linear and Kalman filtering can be employed in the estimation and inference procedure. Omori et al. (2007) extend the approach of Kim et al. (1998) to allow for the leverage effect.

Turning to the second category of estimation methods, those based on simulation to approximate as close as possible the likelihood function of the model, Bos (2012) emphasizes importance sampling methods in which much progress has been made recently. Early examples of estimation by simulated ML are Danielsson (1994), Durbin and Koopman (1997), and Sandmann and Koopman (1998). The basic idea of importance sampling, as first used in the SV context by Durbin and Koopman (1997), is to approximate the likelihood function given in Equation 1.35 by the simulation mean of $f(Y_T, H_T^{(i)}; \theta)/g(H_T^{(i)})$, where the ith sequence of volatilities, $H_T^{(i)}$, is drawn from the approximating importance density $g(H_T)$. Extensions of the basic importance sampling estimator of Durbin and Koopman (1997) have been proposed, for example, the efficient importance sampler (EIS) of Liesenfeld and Richard (2003) and Richard and Zhang (2007). The alternative methods differ in the way they construct the importance density $g(H_T)$, which depends on auxiliary parameters.

Bos (2012) discusses other estimation techniques such as simulated method of moments as in Gallant and Tauchen (1996) or the multimove sampler of Shephard and Pitt (1997). Methods based on MCMC and particle filtering are more extensively reviewed in Broto and Ruiz (2004) and Andersen (2009). In this case, estimation and inference is typically investigated in a Bayesian context, the earliest example being Jacquier et al. (1994).

1.3.3 MULTIVARIATE SV MODELS

As for multivariate GARCH models, the variety of multivariate stochastic volatility (MSV) models is remarkable, ranging from a rigid model with independent volatilities and constant correlations to highly complex models incorporating dynamic correlations and leverage effects. A review of proposed MSV models is given by Asai et al. (2006), see also Yu and Meyer (2006).

The basic model due to Harvey et al. (1994a) can be written as

$$\varepsilon_t = H_t^{1/2} z_t, \quad z_t \sim N(0, \Sigma_z), \tag{1.36}$$

$$H_t = \mathrm{diag}(\exp(h_{1t}), \ldots, \exp(h_{Nt})), \tag{1.37}$$

$$h_{t+1} = \omega + \beta \odot h_t + u_t, \quad u_t \sim N(0, \Sigma_u), \tag{1.38}$$

where $h_t = (h_{1t}, \ldots, h_{Nt})'$ is the vector of volatilities, ω and β are $(N \times 1)$ parameter vectors, Σ_z is a correlation matrix, and $\odot$ designates the Hadamard (elementwise) product operator. Note that, since Σ_z is constant, the model is similar to the CCC model of Bollerslev (1990) discussed above. As a straightforward extension of univariate SV models, Harvey et al. (1994a) propose to use QML with the Kalman filter to estimate this model, while Danielsson (1998) uses simulated ML methods. Obviously, the model may be too restrictive since correlations are restricted to constants, there is no Granger causality in volatilities and leverage effects are not present. However, it is a reasonable starting point and extensions are usually encompassing this basic model.

According to the empirical analysis of Yu and Meyer (2006), the two most successful models to explain volatilities and correlations of a bivariate exchange rate series were explicitly taking into account temporal variation of correlations. The first of these two is a model similar in spirit to the DCC-GARCH model of Engle (2002a) discussed above and can be written as

$$\varepsilon_t = H_t^{1/2} z_t, \quad z_t \sim N(0, \Sigma_{z,t}), \tag{1.39}$$

$$\Sigma_{z,t} = \mathrm{diag}(Q_t^{-1/2}) Q_t \mathrm{diag}(Q_t^{-1/2}), \tag{1.40}$$

$$Q_{t+1} = S \odot (\iota\iota' - A - B) + B \odot Q_t + A \odot v_t v_t', \tag{1.41}$$

$$v_t \sim N(0, I_N),$$

where $\iota = (1, \ldots, 1)'$. Restricting A, B, and $(\iota\iota' - A - B)$ to be positive-definite will ensure that Q_t is positive-definite and, hence, $\Sigma_{z,t}$ is a valid correlation matrix. The volatilities are given as in Equations 1.37 and 1.38.

The second possibility to allow for TVCs is a factor-type SV model of the form

$$\varepsilon_t = Df_t + z_t, \quad z_t \sim N(0, \Sigma_{z,t}), \tag{1.42}$$

$$f_t = \exp(h_t/2)\eta_t, \quad \eta_t \sim N(0, 1), \tag{1.43}$$

$$h_{t+1} = \omega + \beta h_t + u_t, \quad u_t \sim N(0, \sigma_u^2), \tag{1.44}$$

where $D = (\delta_1, \delta_2, \ldots, \delta_N)$ and z_t, η_t, u_t are mutually independent. For identification, one usually imposes $\delta_1 = 1$. The common factor f_t captures comovements in volatilities. In a bivariate framework, Yu and Meyer (2006) estimate this factor model using Bayesian MCMC, while Liesenfeld and Richard (2003) use the EIS in a frequentist approach. Note that the model

(Eqs. 1.42–1.44) has much less parameters than the DCC-SV model in Equations 1.39–1.41. However, it may again be quite restrictive. For example, in the bivariate case, it is straightforward to show that conditional on the factor volatility, the correlation coefficient is given by

$$\mathrm{Corr}(\varepsilon_{1t}, \varepsilon_{2t}|h_t) = \frac{\delta}{\sqrt{(1+\sigma_{z1}^2\exp(-h_t))(\delta^2+\sigma_{z2}^2\exp(-h_t))}},$$

which depends on δ and h_t. Clearly, as h_t increases, correlations increase as well, which corresponds to empirical findings, but the functional form of the dependence between volatilities and correlations might be too rigid in many cases.

Omori and Ishihara (2013), in this handbook, propose very general forms of MSV models that allow, for example, for leverage effects, cross-leverage effects, and heavy-tailed innovation distributions. Their factor MSV model extends the model in Equations 1.42–1.44 to multiple factors, while estimation is performed using Bayesian MCMC based on the multimove sampler of Kim et al. (1998), see also Omori et al. (2007) and Omori and Watanabe (2008).

1.3.4 MODEL SELECTION

Caporin and McAleer (2012), in this handbook, give a survey of recent advances in model selection in the context of volatility models. GARCH and SV models are not nested, which renders the choice based on statistical criteria nontrivial. If the problem is to choose between the exponential GARCH model of Nelson (1991b) and the standard SV model, then an encompassing model could be specified such as

$$\log\sigma_{t+1}^2 = \omega + \alpha_1 z_t + \alpha_2|z_t| + \beta\log\sigma_t^2 + \sigma_u u_t,$$

see Danielsson (1994) and Fridmann and Harris (1998). The SV model results if $\alpha_1 = \alpha_2 = 0$ and the EGARCH model if $\sigma_u = 0$. For the latter case, Kobayashi and Shi (2005) propose a Lagrange Multiplier test. Furthermore, one can test for the leverage effect by testing the hypothesis $\alpha_1 = 0$.

Choosing between GARCH and SV models can be more complicated since standard model selection criteria such as BIC or Bayesian posterior odds are inconsistent (Hong and Preston, 2005). Several approaches have been proposed to address this problem. Franses et al. (2008) suggest to augment the GARCH model by a contemporaneous stochastic error term, whose variance collapses to 0 if the true model is standard GARCH. Under the alternative of nonzero variance, the resulting model is a variant of an SV model but not equivalent to the standard SV model. Hafner and Preminger (2010) propose a set of simple, strongly consistent decision rules to choose GARCH or SV. Their selection procedure is based on a number of moment conditions that is allowed to increase with the sample size. This method leads to choosing the best and simplest model with probability 1 as the sample size increases.

Furthermore, statistics of standard tests such as likelihood ratio have non-standard distributions (Vuong, 1989). Kim et al. (1998) propose an algorithm based on simulations to obtain empirical p-values of testing one model against the other, which might be inconclusive when hypotheses are reversed. Caporin and McAleer (2012) then continue by giving an extensive review of out-of-sample comparisons, an area with a lot of new results.

1.3.5 EMPIRICAL EXAMPLE: S&P 500

We give a small illustration of estimation results for the daily returns of the S&P 500 index over the period 2006-07-14 until 2011-07-14 (1260 observations). This series was analyzed above using an asymmetric GARCH model, and the leverage effect was found to be highly significant. We therefore would like to allow for leverage effects, also in the SV model. To estimate the SV model, we choose a Bayesian framework and use the MCMC algorithm of Omori et al. (2007).[10] First, the algorithm also relaxes the assumption of normality of the innovation term z_t, which however in our case did not turn out to be necessary: The estimated posterior mean of the degrees of freedom parameter of a t-density is 22.8 with a large 95% confidence interval given by [15.71, 31.89], so that we decided to use the normal distribution for simplicity. We estimate a reparametrized version of model (Eqs. 1.29 and 1.30),

$$\varepsilon_t = \sigma_t z_t, \tag{1.45}$$

$$\log \sigma_{t+1}^2 = \mu + \beta(\log \sigma_t^2 - \mu) + \sigma_u u_t, \tag{1.46}$$

$$\begin{pmatrix} z_t \\ u_t \end{pmatrix} \sim N\begin{pmatrix} 1 & \rho \\ \rho & 1 \end{pmatrix}, \tag{1.47}$$

where $\mu = \omega/(1-\beta)$. Prior distributions are chosen similar to Omori et al. (2007) as $(\beta+1)/2 \sim \beta(20, 1.5)$, $\sigma_u^{-2} \sim \Gamma(5/2, 0.025)$, $(\rho+1)/2 \sim \beta(1, 1)$ and $\mu \sim N(-10, 1)$. For the MC sampler, 5500 draws of the posterior distribution are obtained, and the first 500 are discarded as in Omori et al. (2007).

Table 1.5 shows the estimation results for the posterior distributions of the parameters. It is quite common to find that the persistence parameter β is close to 1, which is again the case here. Remarkably, however, the correlation parameter ρ is strongly negative with a posterior mean of -0.7263, which is probably due to the financial crisis present in the sample. Previous precrisis studies such as Yu (2005) find that correlation is significantly negative but much smaller in absolute value, of the order -0.3 to -0.5. This may indicate that the leverage effect depends on time and, in particular, the state of the economy. The last column of Table 1.5 reports the inefficiency factor defined as $1 + 2\sum_{i=1}^{\infty} \rho_i$, where ρ_i is the sample autocorrelation of order i of the sampled parameter. The small values compared with Kim et al. (1998) indicate the efficiency of the employed sampler

[10]An OxMetrics program is available at http://jnakajima.web.googlepages.com.

TABLE 1.5 Posterior Statistics of SV Parameters Estimated for S&P500 Returns

Parameter	Mean	Standard Deviation	95%L	95%U	Inef.
β	0.9777	0.0050	0.9670	0.9868	4.23
σ_u	0.2030	0.0244	0.1593	0.2560	7.14
$\exp(\mu/2)$	0.0117	0.0011	0.0097	0.0140	1.15
ρ	−0.7263	0.0694	−0.8435	−0.5789	7.07

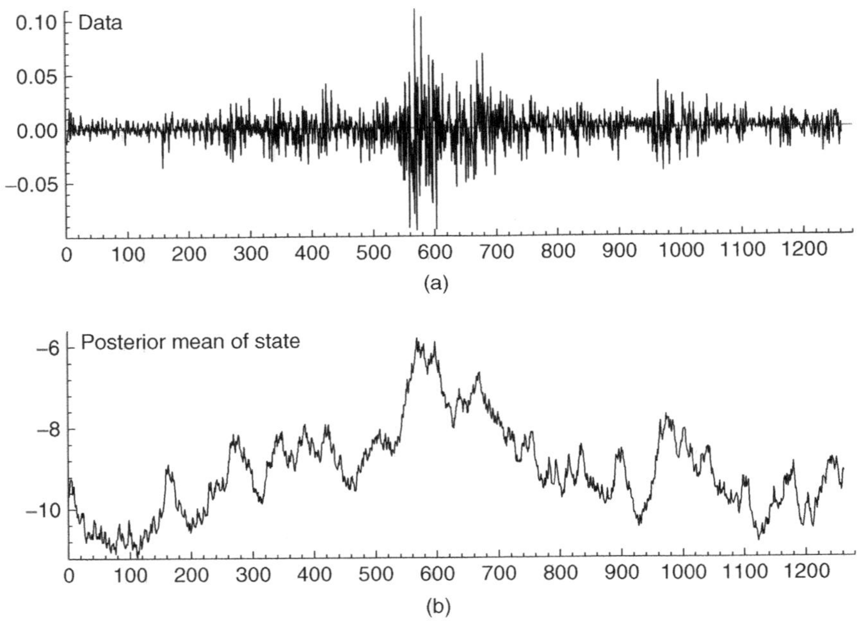

FIGURE 1.5 (a) S&P 500 index returns, July 14, 2006 to July 14, 2011. (b) Posterior mean of log-volatilities.

(Omori et al., 2007). Figure 1.5 shows the index returns and the posterior means of log-volatilities.

1.3.6 LITERATURE

As the research on the modeling, estimation, and inference of SV models, especially in the multivariate case, is huge and still growing, our account can only be partial. We refer to more extensive reviews of the subject: An early monograph that discusses in detail the SV model is given by Taylor (1986). Andersen (1994) is an early review of discrete and continuous time SV models and their applications in finance. Some computational aspects of estimation and inference in SV models are discussed in Bauwens and Rombouts (2004). Shephard (2005) is a collection of important papers on SV, Broto and Ruiz (2004) provides a review of estimation methods in SV models, whereas Andersen (2009) gives a general review with particular focus on continuous-time SV models and their link with realized volatility measures, to be discussed in the next section.

1.4 Realized Volatility

The models described in the previous sections are essentially parametric and usually designed to estimate the daily, weekly, or monthly volatility using data sampled at the same frequency. Since French et al. (1987) and thanks to the widespread availability of databases providing the intradaily prices of financial assets (stocks, stock indices, bonds, currencies, etc.) econometricians have considered using data sampled at a very high frequency to compute ex-post measures of volatility at a lower frequency.

1.4.1 REALIZED VARIANCE

This method has been popularized by several authors, including Andersen, Barndorff-Nielsen, Bollerslev, Diebold, and Shephard, and is known as *realized volatility approach*.

It is clear that the trading and pricing of securities in many of today's liquid financial asset markets is evolving in a near continuous fashion throughout the trading day. It is thus natural to think of the price and return series of financial assets as arising through discrete observations from an underlying continuous-time process.

The intuition behind realized volatility is most readily conveyed within the popular continuous-time diffusion:

$$dp(t) = \mu(t)dt + \sigma(t)dW(t), t \geq 0, \tag{1.48}$$

where $dp(t)$ denotes the logarithmic price increment, where $\mu(t)$ is a continuous locally bounded variation process, $\sigma(t)$ is a strictly positive and càdlàg (right-continuous with left limits) SV process and $W(t)$ is a standard Brownian motion.

Assuming that the time length of 1 day is 1, what does model (Eq. 1.48) implies for the one-period daily return? It follows immediately that

$$r_t \equiv p(t) - p(t-1) = \int_{t-1}^{t} \mu(s)ds + \int_{t-1}^{t} \sigma(s)dW(s). \tag{1.49}$$

From Equation 1.49, we see that the volatility for the continuous-time process over $[t-1, t]$ is linked to the evolution of the spot volatility $\sigma(t)$. Furthermore, conditional on the sample path of the drift and the spot volatility processes,

$$r_t \sim N\left(\int_{t-1}^{t} \mu(s)ds, \text{IV}_t\right), \tag{1.50}$$

where IV_t denotes the so-called integrated variance (volatility), and is defined as follows:

$$\mathrm{IV}_t \equiv \int_{t-1}^{t} \sigma^2(s)ds. \tag{1.51}$$

It is clear from the above equation that IV_t is latent because $\sigma^2(s)$ is not observable. GARCH and SV models typically infer IV_t from a model that links the daily volatility of day t to past realizations of the one-period daily returns, that is, $r_{t-1}, r_{t-2}, \ldots$ This approach raises some natural questions:

- Which model to choose?
- How good is our GARCH/SV estimate of IV_t?
- By conditioning on past daily returns, do we not lose a significant part of the available information by throwing away all the intraday returns (if intraday data are available of course)?

One of the most popular measures to check the forecasting performance of the volatility models is the Mincer-Zarnowitz regression, that is, ex-post volatility regression:

$$\breve{\sigma}_t^2 = a_0 + a_1\hat{\sigma}_t^2 + u_t, \tag{1.52}$$

where $\breve{\sigma}_t^2$ is the ex-post volatility, $\hat{\sigma}_t^2$ is the forecasted volatility, and a_0 and a_1 are parameters to be estimated. Recall that if the model for the conditional variance is correctly specified (and the parameters are known) and if $E(\breve{\sigma}_t^2) = \hat{\sigma}_t^2$, we have $a_0 = 0$ and $a_1 = 1$.

To judge the quality of the GARCH forecasts, econometricians first used daily squared returns to approximate the ex-post volatility, that is, $\breve{\sigma}_t^2 = r_t^2$. The R^2 of this regression is used to measure the degree of predictability of the volatility models. However, the R^2 of the above regression is typically lower than 5% for GARCH models and this could lead to the conclusion that GARCH models produce poor forecasts of the volatility (see, among others, Schwert (1990) or Jorion (1996)).

In their seminal paper, Andersen and Bollerslev (1998) have shown that if r_t follows a GARCH(1,1), for example, $r_t = \sigma_t z_t$ with $\sigma_t^2 = \omega + \alpha_1 r_{t-1}^2 + \beta_1\sigma_{t-1}^2$, the R^2 of this regression is nothing but $\frac{\mathrm{var}(\breve{\sigma}_t^2)}{\mathrm{var}(r_t^2)} = \frac{\alpha_1^2}{(1-\beta_1^2-2\alpha_1\beta_1)}$. If κ is the kurtosis of the innovations z_t, we have that $\kappa\alpha_1^2 + \beta_1^2 + 2\alpha_1\beta_1 < 1$ to ensure the existence of the unconditional kurtosis of r_t. It follows then that $\kappa\alpha_1^2 < 1 - \beta_1^2 - 2\alpha_1\beta_1$ and

$$R^2 \equiv \frac{\alpha_1^2}{(1-\beta_1^2-2\alpha_1\beta_1)} < \frac{1}{\kappa}.$$

If z_t is i.i.d $N(0,1)$, the R^2 is thus necessarily lower than 1/3 (and even smaller if z_t has fat-tails).

Let us now illustrate this result by means of a simple MC simulation. In model (Eq. 1.48), $\sigma(t)$ was deliberately let unspecified. The simulated model is designed to induce temporal dependencies consistent with the GARCH(1,1) model. We first consider the continuous-time GARCH diffusion of Nelson (1991a). It is formally defined by

$$dp(t) = \sigma(t)dW_p(t), \tag{1.53}$$

$$d\sigma^2(t) = \theta[\omega - \sigma^2(t)]dt + (2\lambda\theta)^{1/2}\sigma^2(t)dW_d(t), \tag{1.54}$$

where $W_p(t)$ and $W_d(t)$ denote two independent Brownian motions.

We used a standard Euler discretization scheme to generate the continuous-time GARCH diffusion process, that is, $p(t+\Delta) = p(t) + \sigma(t)\sqrt{\Delta}Z_p(t)$ and $\sigma^2(t+\Delta) = \theta\omega\Delta + \sigma^2(t)\left[1 - \theta\Delta + \sqrt{2\lambda\theta\Delta}Z_d(t)\right]$, where $Z_p(t)$ and $Z_d(t)$ denote two independent standard normal variables.

We set $\theta = 0.054$, $\omega = 0.478$, and $\lambda = 0.480$ to replicate the behavior of the YEN-USD exchange rate during October 1987 to September 1992 like in Andersen and Bollerslev (1998). To simulate exchange rates, we choose $\Delta = 1/2880$, corresponding to 10 observations per 5-min interval. The number of simulated days is 510, but the first 10 days have been discarded, giving a total of 500 simulated days. Furthermore, we use the following initial values for the log-price and spot volatility: $p(0) = 1$ and $\sigma^2(0) = 0.1$. From the simulated log-prices, we computed 5-min log-prices (denoted $p_{t,i}$ for $i = 1, \ldots, M = 288$, and $t = 1, \ldots, T$) by selecting 1 price for every 10 observations. Five-minute returns $r_{t,i}$ are computed as the first difference of $p_{t,i}$. Finally, daily returns r_t are defined as $\sum_{i=1}^{M} r_{t,i}$.

Figure 1.6 graphs the simulated 5-min and daily returns for the above DGP.

Figure 1.7 plots four volatility measures computed on the simulated data. Let us concentrate on three of these for the moment.

1. Panel (a) displays the daily integrated volatility, that is, IV_t. Given the fact that $\text{IV}_t \equiv \int_{t-1}^{t} \sigma^2(s)ds$, the "daily" IV_t is computed as $\sum_{i=1}^{1/\Delta} \sigma^2(t - j/\Delta)\Delta$, where $1/\Delta = 2880$. Recall that in empirical applications this quantity is unknown.
2. Panel (c) displays the conditional variance obtained by estimating a GARCH(1,1) model by Gaussian QML on the daily returns r_t.
3. Finally, panel (d) plots the daily squared returns r_t^2.

Two comments are in order.

- Even though the daily squared return is known to be an unbiased measure of the daily volatility, this estimator is extremely noisy.
- Unlike the daily squared returns, the conditional variance of the GARCH(1,1) is much less noisy. Indeed, it generally tracks the level of the integrated volatility very well.

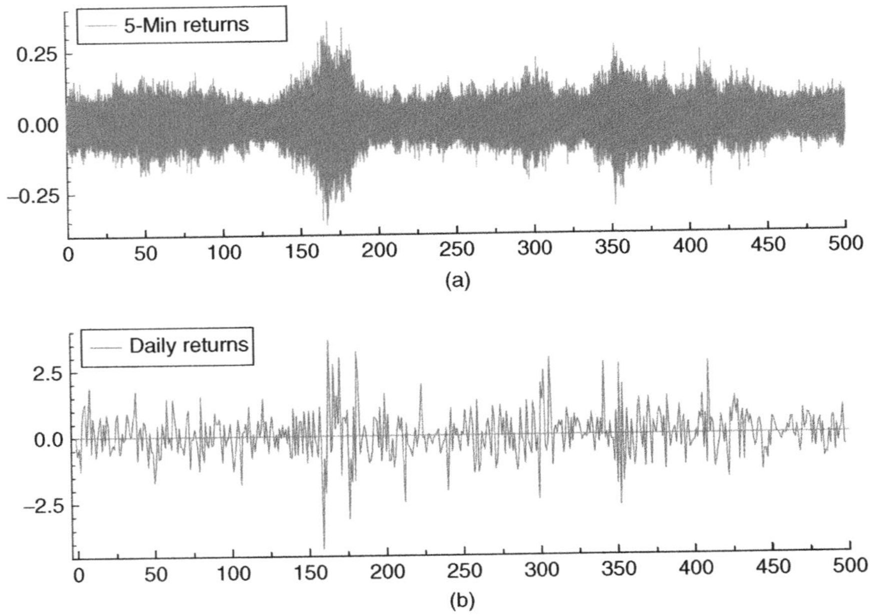

FIGURE 1.6 Simulated 5-min and daily returns from a continuous-time GARCH(1,1).

We also run the above Mincer-Zarnowitz regression to illustrate the findings of Andersen and Bollerslev (1998). When using the daily squared returns to measure the observed daily volatility, the R^2 of the regression is found to be extremely low, that is, 7% even though a_0 and a_1 are not significantly different from 0 and 1, respectively.

Naturally, this finding raises another question. Can we use the R^2 of this regression to discriminate between volatility models? Said differently, "is model 1 preferable to model 2 if the R^2 of this regression is higher for model 1?". It is not always true that using a conditionally unbiased proxy, such as r_t^2, will lead asymptotically to the same outcome that would be obtained if the true volatility was observed. When the evaluation is based on a target observed with error, such as r_t^2, the choice of the evaluation criterion becomes critical in order to avoid a distorted outcome. The problem of consistency, sometimes referred to as *robustness*, of the ordering between two or more volatility forecasts is discussed in Chapter 19 by Violante and Laurent (2012).

Note that if we consider the integrated volatility instead of the squared daily returns as an ex-post volatility measure, the R^2 now equals 53.3%, suggesting that the GARCH model explains more than 50% of the variability of the true volatility despite the fact that a large proportion of the data has been ignored. However, this regression in unfeasible because IV_t is not computable in practical applications.

Andersen and Bollerslev (1998) are the first to point out that a much more precise ex-post estimator than the daily squared return can be obtained by simply summing up intraday squared returns. They called this *estimator-realized*

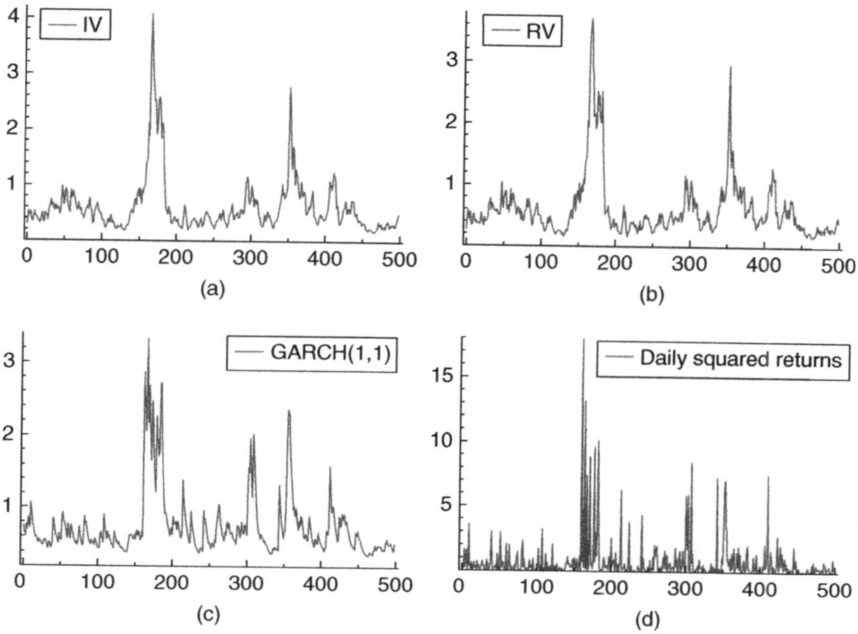

FIGURE 1.7 **Four volatility measures: (a) integrated volatility; (b) realized volatility; (c) GARCH(1,1) on daily returns; and (d) daily squared returns.**

volatility.[11] More formally, this estimator is defined as follows:

$$\mathrm{RV}_t = \sum_{i=1}^{M} r_{t,i}^2. \tag{1.55}$$

By summing high frequency squared returns, we may obtain an "error free" or "model free" measure of the daily volatility. This is illustrated in Figure 1.7. Panel (a) displays the daily realized volatility computed from the simulated 5-min returns, that is, $\mathrm{RV}_t = \sum_{i=1}^{288} r_{t,i}^2$. It is clear from this graph that realized volatility is indeed a very precise estimator of IV_t. The correlation between IV_t and RV_t equals 0.989.

We also computed the R^2 of the Mincer-Zarnowitz regression using the realized volatility as endogenous variable. Not surprisingly, the R^2 is very close to the value previously obtained for IV_t, that is, 52.7% versus 53.3%.

The properties of this estimator are presented in detail in Chapter 13 by Park and Linton (2012). The main findings of the literature are that under suitable conditions (such as the absence of serial correlation in the intraday returns) the

[11]The origin of realized volatility is not as recent as it would seem at first sight. Merton (1980) already mentioned that, provided data sampled at a high frequency are available, the sum of squared realizations can be used to estimate the variance of an i.i.d. random variable.

realized volatility is consistent for the integrated volatility in the sense that when $\Delta \to 0, \mathrm{RV}_t$ measures the latent integrated volatility IV_t perfectly. However, in practice, at very high frequencies, returns are polluted by microstructure noise (bid-ask bounce, unevenly spaced observations, discreteness, etc.). This "errors-in-variables" problem causes the high frequency returns to be autocorrelated. Recall that bid-ask bounce occurs in all high frequency transaction data as successive quotes tend to bounce between buys and sells, and sampling these as proxies for the mid-price gives an impression that markets are moving more than they actually are, adding an upward bias to the measured volatility. Note that Chapter 14 by Ait-Sahalia and Xiu (2012) show how maximum-likelihood estimators can be used to deal with the microstructure noise issue.

Empirical studies have shown that a continuous diffusion model as in Equation 1.48 fails to explain some characteristics of asset returns. Furthermore, standard GARCH models are not able to fully explain the excess kurtosis found in most financial time series. In a continuous-time framework, the inadequacy of the standard stochastic diffusion model has led to developments of alternative models. Jump diffusion and SV models have been proposed in the literature to overcome this inadequacy.

Suppose now that the log-price process belongs to the Brownian Semi-Martingale with Jumps (BSMJ) family of models. Under the BSMJ model, the diffusion component captures the smooth variation of the price process, while the jump component accounts for the rare, large discontinuities in the observed prices. Andersen et al. (2007) cite the work of several authors who found that this is a realistic model for the price series of many financial assets.

A BSMJ log-price diffusion admits the representation

$$\mathrm{d}p(t) = \mu(t)\mathrm{d}t + \sigma(t)\mathrm{d}W(t) + \kappa(t)\mathrm{d}q(t), t \geq 0, \tag{1.56}$$

where $\mathrm{d}q(t)$ is a counting process with $\mathrm{d}q(t) = 1$ corresponding to a jump at time t and $\mathrm{d}q(t) = 0$ otherwise. The (possibly time-varying) jump intensity is $l(t)$ and $\kappa(t)$ is the size of the corresponding jump.

Jumps in stock prices are often assumed to follow a probability law. For instance, the jumps may follow a Poisson process, which is a continuous-time discrete process.

Let us consider the following continuous-time GARCH diffusion process with jumps,

$$\mathrm{d}p(t) = \sigma(t)\mathrm{d}W_p(t) + \kappa(t)\mathrm{d}q(t), \tag{1.57}$$

$$\mathrm{d}\sigma^2(t) = \theta[\omega - \sigma^2(t)]\mathrm{d}t + (2\lambda\theta)^{1/2}\sigma^2(t)\mathrm{d}W_d(t), \tag{1.58}$$

$$\kappa(t) \sim \sigma(t)\sqrt{m}([-2,-1] \cup [1,2]) \tag{1.59}$$

$$\mathrm{d}q(t) \sim \mathrm{Poisson}(l). \tag{1.60}$$

The jump size $\kappa(t)$ is modeled as the product between $\sigma(t)$ and a uniformly distributed random variable on $\sqrt{m}([-2,-1] \cup [1,2])$. Note that in this DGP,

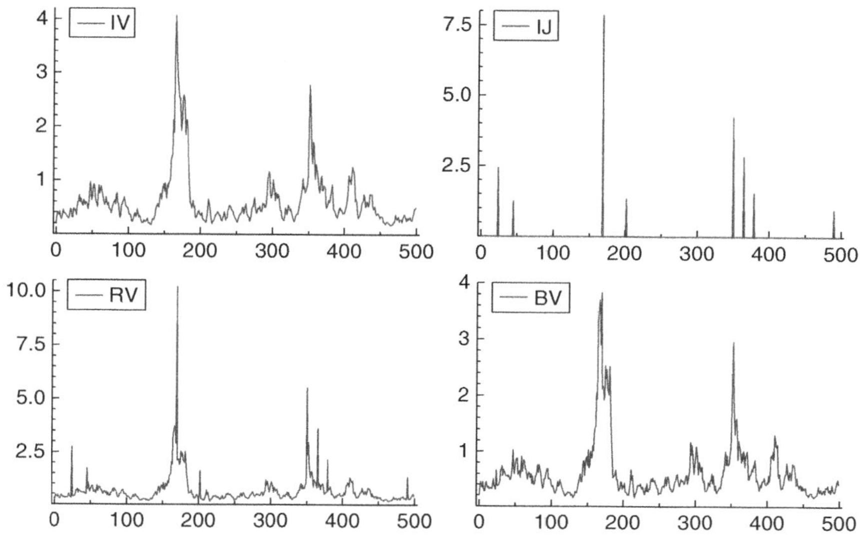

FIGURE 1.8 Four volatility measures in presence of jumps: (a) integrated volatility; (b) integrated jumps; (c) realized volatility, GARCH(1,1) on daily returns; and (d) bipower variation.

the intensity of the jumps (l) is assumed to be constant over time for simplicity. The parameter m determines the magnitude of the jumps.

Figure 1.8 plots four volatility estimates for 500 days of simulated intraday returns. The parameters of the continuous-time GARCH(1,1) are the same as for the previous simulation. For the jump component, l is chosen such that first jump is expected every 100 days (in this replication there are 8 days with at least one jump). About the magnitude of the jumps, we chose $m = 2$, which corresponds to a case of rare but very big jumps.

1. Panel (a) displays the daily integrated volatility, that is, IV_t;
2. Panel (b) displays the integrated jumps, defined as $IJ_t = \sum_{t-1<s\leq t} \kappa^2(s)$. Like IV_t, this quantity is latent and cannot be computed on real data;
3. Panel (c) displays the realized volatility computed from 5-min returns;
4. Finally, panel (d) plots the so-called bipower variation estimator BV_t (see below).

It is clearly visible that the realized volatility does not match the integrated volatility in presence of jumps. This result is not surprising since we know by the theory of quadratic variation that for $\Delta \to 0$, we have the following convergence in probability:

$$\mathrm{RV}_t \to \int_{t-1}^{t} \sigma^2(s)\mathrm{d}s + \sum_{t-1<s\leq t} \kappa^2(s). \tag{1.61}$$

In other words, in the absence of jumps, the realized volatility is a consistent estimator of the integrated volatility but not in the presence of jumps.

Several robust to jumps estimators of IV_t are discussed in Chapters 17 and 18 by Mancini and Calvori (2012) and Boudt et al. (2012), respectively. The pioneers are Barndorff-Nielsen and Shephard (Barndorff-Nielsen and Shephard (2004b)), who showed that for a subclass of BSMJ price diffusions (i.e., BSM with Finite Activity Jumps), the normalized sum of products of the absolute value of contiguous returns (i.e., bipower variation) is a consistent estimator for IV_t. Mancini and Calvori (2012) also discuss the case of infinite activity jump processes (Levy jumps).

The bipower variation is defined as

$$\text{BV}_t \equiv \mu_1^{-2} \frac{M}{M-1} \sum_{i=2}^{M} |r_{t,i}||r_{t,i-1}|, \tag{1.62}$$

where $\mu_1 \equiv \sqrt{2/\pi} \simeq 0.79788$.

Unlike the RV_t, BV_t is designed to be robust to jumps because its building block is the product between two consecutive returns instead of the squared return. If one of the returns corresponds to a jump and the next one follows the BSM diffusion process, then the product has a small impact on BV_t, being the sum of many of these building blocks. If the jump process has finite activity[12] then a.s. jumps cannot affect two contiguous returns for $\Delta \to 0$ (or equivalently $M \to \infty$) and the jump process has a negligible impact on the probability limit of BV_t, which coincides with the IVar. Under the BSM with finite activity jumps (BSMFAJ), one has

$$\text{plim}_{\Delta \to 0} \text{BV}_t = \int_{t-1}^{t} \sigma^2(s) ds. \tag{1.63}$$

Looking at Figure 1.8d, we see that unlike RV_t, BV_t is indeed a robust estimate of the integrated volatility in presence of jumps.

1.4.1.1 Empirical Application. The series we consider is the Dow Jones index. We use a 5-min sampling frequency corresponding to seventy-eight 5-min intraday price observations for each trading day (from 9:30 EST until the market closes, i.e., at 16:00 EST). The data set covers the periods from 1995-01-03 to 2009-12-31. The Dow Jones index data is provided by the Tickdata.

Figure 1.9 plots the daily returns, realized volatility and bipower variation for the Dow Jones index series computed from 5-min returns.

Figure 1.10 plots the autocorrelation function (50 lags) of these three series. The displayed 95% confidence bands (doted lines) are computed with the generalized Bartlett's formula of Francq and Zakoian (2009). This figure clearly suggests the presence of long memory in the realized volatility and bipower

[12]A jump process is defined to be of finite activity if the number of jumps in *any* interval of time is finite.

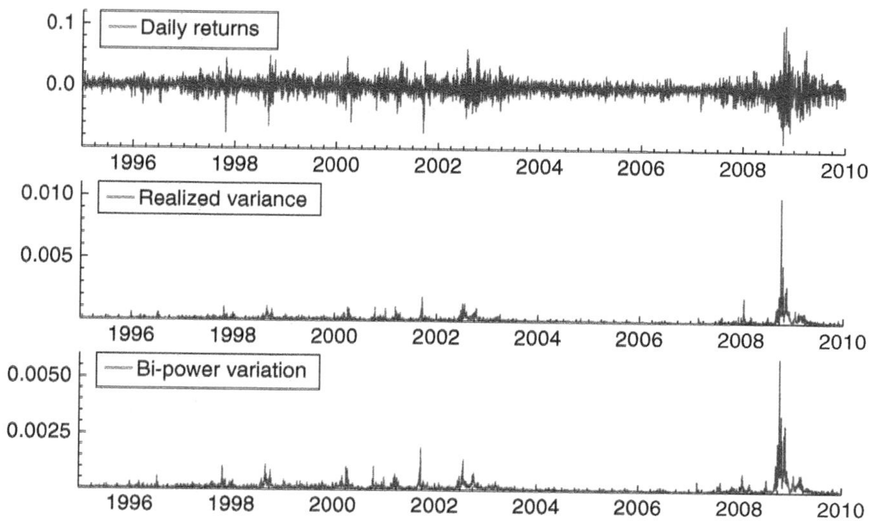

FIGURE 1.9 (a) Daily returns; (b) realized volatility; and (c) bipower variation for the Dow Jones index computed from 5-min returns.

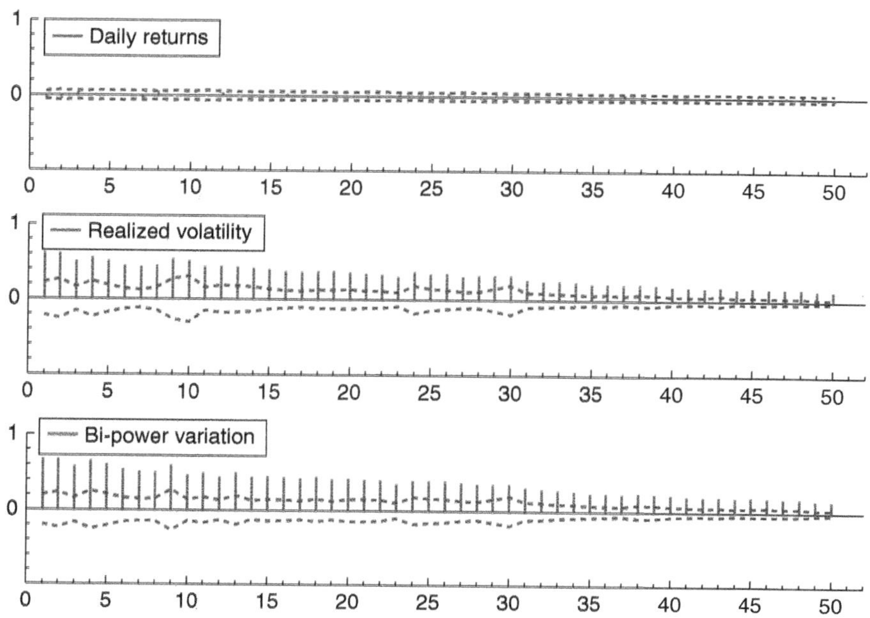

FIGURE 1.10 Autocorrelation function and robust 95% confidence interval on daily returns, realized volatility, and bipower variation for the Dow Jones index computed from 5-min returns.

variation but no serial correlation in the daily returns. The estimated long-memory parameters given by the log-periodogram regression method of Geweke and Porter-Hudak (1983) are equal to 0.28 and 0.33 for the realized volatility and bipower variation, respectively, suggesting that BV_t is slightly more persistent than RV_t (because of the presence of jumps in RV_t, see Andersen et al. (2007)).

The next step is naturally to formulate a model to forecast RV_t, and/or BV_t that takes into account their most important characteristics. ARFIMA models are usually estimated on these two series (or their log-transformation to ensure the positivity of the forecasts). Figure 1.11 plots $\log(BV_t)$ as well as the conditional mean and conditional variance of an ARFIMA$(1, d, 0)$-GARCH$(1, 1)$ estimated by ML with a skewed-t distribution (see Giot and Laurent (2003) and Bauwens and Laurent (2005) for more details on this distribution).

This figure suggests that this conditional mean captures the main features of the series. Furthermore, the conditional variance is not constant over time, suggesting that the variance of the variance is time-varying as well. Figure 1.11d plots a histogram of the standardized residuals of the estimated model, together with a kernel estimate (solid line) and the estimated (dotted line) of the unconditional density of the standardized residuals. This graph also suggest that the skewed-t density provides a good approximation of the true density (the estimated asymmetry coefficient is positive and highly significant and the degree of freedom is about 15).

In Chapter 15, Corsi et al. (2012) follow an alternative direction that generates very similar stylized facts for volatility series using a cascade of heterogeneous volatility components. This model leads to a simple AR-type

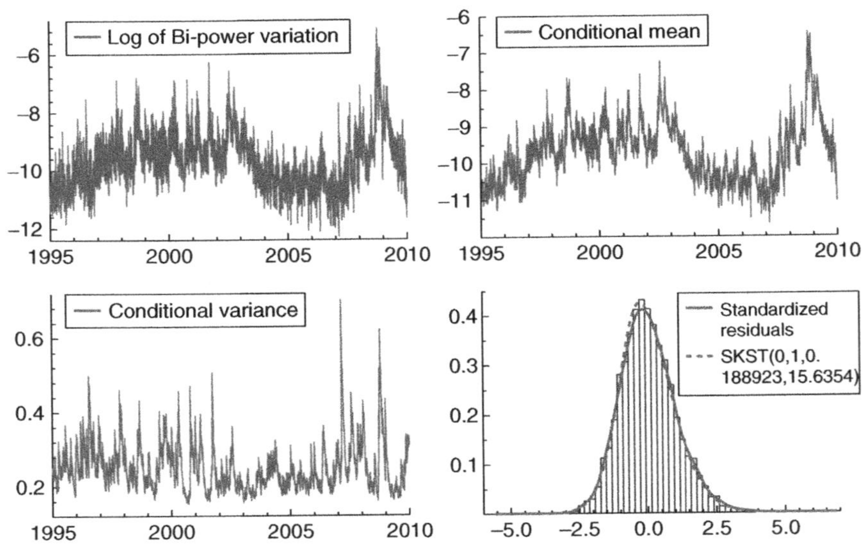

FIGURE 1.11 Log of bipower variation, conditional mean, and conditional variance of an ARFIMA$(1, d, 0)$-GARCH$(1, 1)$ on $\log(BV_t)$ and density estimate of the innovations for the Dow Jones index.

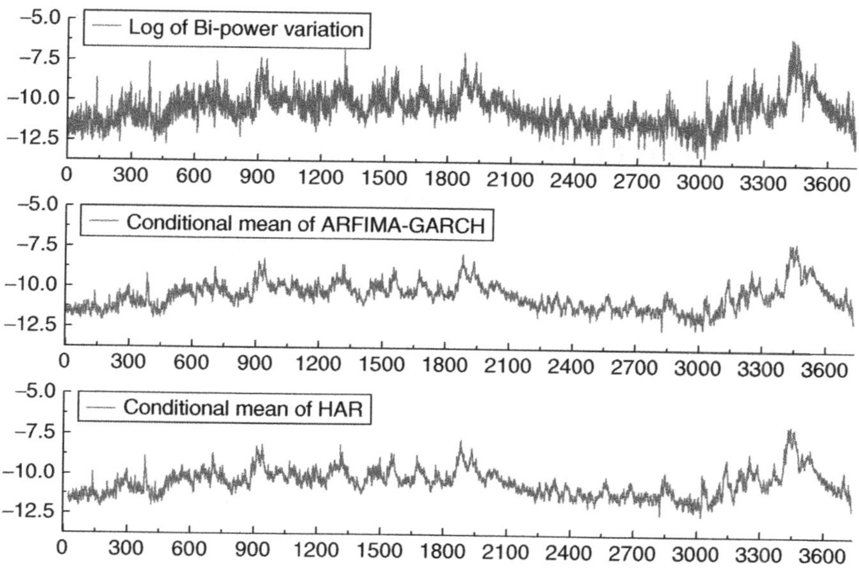

FIGURE 1.12 **Log of bipower variation, conditional mean of the ARFIMA($1, d, 0$)-GARCH($1, 1$), and HAR models on log(BV_t) for the Dow Jones index.**

model that considers volatilities realized over different time horizons and is thus called heterogeneous autoregressive (HAR). This framework turns out to be easier to handle than the above ARFIMA model, with a straightforward economic interpretation and an excellent fit to the data.

Figure 1.12 plots log(BV_t) as well as the conditional mean of the above ARFIMA($1, d, 0$)-GARCH($1, 1$) and the HAR model with a cascade of three volatility measures, that is, the log of the average of BV_t over the previous 1, 5, and 21 days. The difference between the fitted values of the ARFIMA and HAR models is hardly visible. Indeed, both models seem to track the dynamics of log(BV_t) rather well. The in-sample average of the errors equal 0.018871 and $1.2188e^{-14}$, respectively, for the ARFIMA and HAR models. The corresponding standard deviations are 0.56977 and 0.57120. Both models explain respectively 68.8879% and 68.5991% of the variability of log(BV_t), while the correlation between the fitted values (conditional mean) of the two models is 98.358%. The two models are thus hardly distinguishable.

The HAR model and the ARFIMA model described above have something in common. Both the endogenous and explanatory variables are aggregated measures of volatility (e.g., realized volatility) or some transformation of these measures (e.g., square root, log). Chapter 16 by Ghysels and Valkanov (2012) reviews an alternative strategy called MIDAS (*mi*xed *da*ta *s*ampling). For example, when we forecast daily volatility, we want to preserve the information in the intradaily data without computing daily aggregates such as realized volatility. Likewise, when we focus on, say, weekly or monthly volatility forecasts, we want to use daily returns or daily realized volatility measures. They focus on the issues pertaining to mixed frequencies—that arise typically because we would like to consider multistep volatility forecasts while maintaining information in high frequency data.

1.4.2 REALIZED COVARIANCE

In the case, where $y_{t,i}$ is an N-dimensional return vector generated by the multivariate counterpart of the BSMJ price diffusion model in Equation 1.56, the processes $p(s)$, $\mu(t)$, and $q(t)$ are all N-dimensional vector processes and $W(t)$ is a vector of N independent Brownian motions. Denoted by $\Omega(t)$, the $N \times N$ càdlàg process such that $\Sigma(t) = \Omega(t)\Omega'(t)$ is the spot covariance matrix process of the continuous component of the price diffusion. Let $K(t)$ be the $N \times N$ process controlling the magnitude and transmission of jumps such that $K(t)\mathrm{d}q(t)$ is the contribution of the jump process to the price diffusion. We then have that a N-dimensional log-price diffusion can be decomposed as follows:

$$\mathrm{d}p(t) = \mu(t)\mathrm{d}t + \Omega(t)\mathrm{d}w(t) + K(t)\mathrm{d}q(t). \tag{1.64}$$

The integrated covariance matrix (ICov) over $[t-1, t]$ is the matrix

$$\mathrm{ICov}_t = \int_{t-1}^{t} \Sigma(s)\mathrm{d}s. \tag{1.65}$$

Denoted by κ_j, the contribution of the jth jump in $[t-1, t]$ to the price diffusion.

1.4.2.1 Realized Quadratic Covariation. Andersen et al. (2003) have shown that the realized quadratic covariation (RCov)

$$\mathrm{RCov}_t \equiv \sum_{i=1}^{M} y_{t,i} y'_{t,i} \tag{1.66}$$

is a consistent estimator for the sum of the ICov and the realized jump variability

$$\mathrm{plim}_{\Delta \to 0} \mathrm{RCov}_t = \mathrm{ICov}_t + \sum_{j=1}^{j_t} \kappa_j \kappa'_j, \tag{1.67}$$

where $j_t = \int_{t-1}^{t} \mathrm{d}q^*(s)$, with $q^*(s)$ the univariate counting process derived from $q(s)$ such that $q^*(s)$ increases by 1 whenever $q(s)$ changes.

Compared to the univariate case, the additional issue of synchronicity arises, whereby trading for different assets occurs at different times. Park and Linton (2012) discuss two methods typically used to solve this problem, namely, the *fixed clock time* and the *refresh time*.

1.4.2.2 Realized Bipower Covariation. For disentangling the continuous and jump components in the RCov, we need an additional estimator for the

ICov that is robust to jumps. To this purpose, Barndorff-Nielsen and Shephard (2004b) introduce the Realized BiPower Covariation process (RBPCov) as the process whose value at time t is the N-dimensional square matrix with k-, lth element equal to

$$\frac{\pi}{8}\left(\sum_{i=2}^{M}\left|y_{(k)t,i}+y_{(l)t,i}\right|\left|y_{(k)t,i-1}+y_{(l)t,i-1}\right|\right.$$
$$\left.-\left|y_{(k)t,i}-y_{(l)t,i}\right|\left|y_{(k)t,i-1}-y_{(l)t,i-1}\right|\right), \tag{1.68}$$

where $y_{(k)t,i}$ is the kth component of the return vector $y_{t,i}$. The factor $\pi/8$ ensures that the RBPCov converges to the ICov under model (Eq. 1.64):

$$\text{plim}_{\Delta\to 0}\text{RBPCov}_t = \int_{t-1}^{t} \Sigma(s)\text{d}s. \tag{1.69}$$

Other estimators of the integrated covariance that are robust to the presence of jumps in assets returns are reviewed in the Chapters 17 and 13 by Mancini and Calvori (2012) and Park and Linton (2012), respectively, for example, the threshold realized covariation of Mancini and Gobbi (2012), and the outlyingness weighted quadratic covariation of Boudt et al. (2010).

A natural question is how these nonparametric covariance estimates can be used to model and forecast future values of the covariance, ensuring its symmetry and its positive semidefiniteness. Answers to this question are provided in this Handbook in the Chapters 4, 9, 13, and 15 by Sheppard (2012), Brownlees et al. (2012b), Park and Linton (2012), and Corsi et al. (2012), respectively. The existing models are the Wishart autoregressive (WAR) model of Gouriéroux et al. (2009), and standard univariate and multivariate models estimated on the elements of the Cholesky factorization (Chiriac and Voev, 2010) or the matrix log-transformation (Bauer and Vorkink, 2011) of the covariance estimates. New models based on the Wishart distribution are in development (Jin and Maheu, 2010; Golosnoy et al., 2010; Bauwens et al., 2012).

Acknowledgments

Research supported by the contract "Projet d'Actions de Recherche Concertées" 07/12-002 of the "Communauté francaise de Belgique," granted by the "Académie universitaire Louvain."

PART ONE

Autoregressive Conditional Heteroskedasticity and Stochastic Volatility

CHAPTER TWO

Nonlinear Models for Autoregressive Conditional Heteroskedasticity

TIMO TERÄSVIRTA

2.1 Introduction

One of the first occasions for at least European econometricians to hear about autoregressive conditional heteroskedasticity (ARCH) was at the 1979 Econometric Society European Meeting in Athens, where Robert Engle presented a paper with that title in a session named *Time Series II: Specification*, chaired by David Hendry. The published version of the paper appeared 3 years later, Engle (1982a). The number of models for describing and forecasting autoregressive conditional heteroskedasticity has increased dramatically from those early days, as has the number of applications. Recent overviews include Bauwens et al. (2011), in this handbook, and Teräsvirta (2009). Several chapters of Andersen et al. (2009) are devoted to various theoretical and computational aspects of these models.

The focus of this chapter is on univariate nonlinear generalized autoregressive conditional heteroskedasticity (GARCH) models. There are examples of nonlinear multivariate GARCH models, but they are not discussed here; for recent surveys, see Bauwens et al. (2006) and Silvennoinen and Teräsvirta (2009). The definition of a nonlinear GARCH model adopted in this overview

Handbook of Volatility Models and Their Applications, First Edition.
Edited by Luc Bauwens, Christian Hafner, and Sebastien Laurent.

is quite narrow and only covers parametric nonlinear models. The exponential GARCH model of Nelson (1991b) is excluded from the consideration, however, because the logarithm of the conditional variance is linear in parameters. The hidden Markov or Markov-switching models, such as the variance-switching model of Rydén et al. (1998) or its more complicated ARCH and GARCH variants, that can be viewed as nonlinear, are discussed in Chapter 3 of Haas and Paolella (2011) in this handbook and are not taken up here. The models to be considered include the smooth transition GARCH, the double threshold GARCH, the asymmetric power GARCH, and a particular class of time-varying GARCH models. The artificial neural network GARCH model is mentioned as well, although the number of applications of the model appears to be very small.

A general treatment of volatility models based on multiplicative decomposition of the variance can be found in Van Bellegem (2012), see also Brownlees et al. (2012), both in this handbook. That chapter contains a brief discussion of fully parametric variants of such models. A majority of them are semiparametric and are therefore not covered by this account.

The plan of this chapter is as follows. Sections 2.2 and 2.3 contain short presentations of the standard GARCH model and linear predecessors to nonlinear GARCH models. Smooth transition GARCH and related models are considered in Section 2.4. Testing linearity against various nonlinear GARCH models is discussed in Section 2.5 and parameter estimation in Section 2.6. Forecasting with nonlinear GARCH models is the topic of Section 2.7. Parametric special cases of models based on multiplicative decomposition of the variance are considered in Section 2.8 and Section 2.9 contains final remarks.

2.2 The Standard GARCH Model

Assume a random variable y_t can be modeled as follows: $y_t = \mu_t + \varepsilon_t$, where $\mu_t = \mathsf{E}\{y_t|\mathcal{F}_{t-1}\}$ and $\mathcal{F}_{t-1} = \{y_{t-j}, j \geq 1\}$ being the information set available at $t-1$, and ε_t is a random error with mean zero and variance σ^2. In the standard GARCH(p, q) model as defined by Bollerslev (1986), the error term is parameterized as follows:

$$\varepsilon_t = z_t h_t^{1/2} \tag{2.1}$$

with $z_t \sim$ i.i.d. (0, 1), and the positive-valued conditional variance function is

$$h_t = \alpha_0 + \sum_{j=1}^{q} \alpha_j \varepsilon_{t-j}^2 + \sum_{j=1}^{p} \beta_j h_{t-j}, \tag{2.2}$$

where $\alpha_0 > 0$. It is seen from Equation 2.1 that $\mathsf{E}\varepsilon_t\varepsilon_{t-j} = 0$ for $j \neq 0$. In what follows, we assume that the conditional mean $\mu_t \equiv 0$. Sufficient conditions for h_t being positive almost surely include $\alpha_j \geq 0, j = 1, \ldots, q$, and $\beta_j \geq 0$, $j = 1, \ldots, p$. Identification requires that at least one $\alpha_j > 0$ for $j > 0$. These conditions are not necessary, however, unless $p = q = 1$ (Nelson and Cao, 1992). The unconditional variance

$$\mathsf{E}\varepsilon_t^2 = \alpha_0 \left(1 - \sum_{j=1}^{q} \alpha_j - \sum_{j=1}^{p} \beta_j\right)^{-1}$$

provided the weak stationarity condition $\sum_{j=1}^{q} \alpha_j + \sum_{j=1}^{p} \beta_j < 1$ holds.

The GARCH model, defined by Equations 2.1 and 2.2, is linear in parameters. It has been generalized in many ways to accommodate things such as regime switches, asymmetries, and so on. A number of these extensions to the standard GARCH model are described in Bauwens et al. (2011) and Teräsvirta (2009). The next section looks at ones that may be regarded as predecessors to parametric nonlinear GARCH models.

2.3 Predecessors to Nonlinear GARCH Models

Predecessors to nonlinear GARCH models, as the concept is defined here, have the property that they are linear in parameters but could be made nonlinear by assuming a certain known quantity in them to be an unknown parameter. The most frequently applied models of this kind are the GJR-GARCH model by Glosten et al. (1993) and the threshold generalized autoregressive conditional heteroskedasticity (TGARCH) model by Rabemananjara and Zakoïan (1993) and Zakoian (1994). In applications, the GJR-GARCH model is typically assumed to be a first-order GARCH model. It can be generalized to have higher-order lags, although in practice, this almost never seems to happen. The conditional variance of this model has the following representation:

$$h_t = \alpha_0 + \sum_{j=1}^{q} \{\alpha_j + \kappa_j I(\varepsilon_{t-j} < 0)\}\varepsilon_{t-j}^2 + \sum_{j=1}^{p} \beta_j h_{t-j}, \tag{2.3}$$

where $I(A)$ is an indicator variable: $I(A) = 1$ when A holds, and zero otherwise. The idea of this model is to capture the leverage effect present in stock return series. This effect manifests itself as an asymmetry: a negative shock has a greater impact on the conditional variance than the positive one with the same absolute value. This implies a positive value for κ_j. As already mentioned, in applications $p = q = 1$, so one would expect that the estimate $\widehat{\kappa}_1 > 0$.

The GJR-GARCH model can be generalized by extending the asymmetry in Equation 2.3 to the other components of the model. The volatility-switching generalized autoregressive conditional heteroskedasticity (VS-GARCH) model of Fornari and Mele (1997) is such an extension. The first-order VS-GARCH model is defined as follows:

$$\begin{aligned} h_t = {} & \alpha_0 + \psi_0 \operatorname{sgn}(\varepsilon_{t-1}) + \{\alpha_1 + \psi_1 \operatorname{sgn}(\varepsilon_{t-1})\}\varepsilon_{t-1}^2 \\ & + \{\beta_1 + \psi_2 \operatorname{sgn}(\varepsilon_{t-1})\}h_{t-1}, \end{aligned} \tag{2.4}$$

where sgn is the sign operator: $\text{sgn}(x) = 1$ for $x > 0$, $\text{sgn}(x) = 0$ for $x = 0$, and $\text{sgn}(x) = 0$ for $x < 0$. It is seen that by setting $\psi_0 = \psi_2 = 0$ in Equation 2.4, one obtains a model that is equivalent to the first-order GJR-GARCH model.

The TGARCH model is similar to Equation 2.3 with one important difference: what is being modeled is the conditional standard deviation and not the conditional variance. The model is defined by replacing h_t in Equation 2.3 by its square root and each ε_{t-j}^2 by the corresponding absolute value $|\varepsilon_{t-j}|$. Some authors muddle the distinction between these two models by applying the term TGARCH model to the GJR-GARCH model.

Engle and Ng (1993) suggested the following (first-order) generalization of the (first-order) GJR-GARCH model (Eq. 2.3):

$$h_t = \alpha_0 + \sum_{i=0}^{m^+} \kappa_j^+ I(\varepsilon_{t-1} > \tau_i)(\varepsilon_{t-1} - \tau_i)$$

$$+ \sum_{i=0}^{m^-} \kappa_j^- I(\varepsilon_{t-1} < \tau_{-i})(\varepsilon_{t-1} - \tau_{-i}) + \beta_1 h_{t-1}, \tag{2.5}$$

where $\tau_i = i\sigma$, and σ is the unconditional standard deviation of ε_t. This is essentially a spline model, where $\tau_i, i = m^-, m^- + 1, \ldots, m^+$ are the knots. There is another difference: ε_{t-1} does not appear squared in Equation 2.5. As a consequence, even when the simplest case $m^+ = m^- = 0$ is considered, it seems that one cannot derive a closed form for the unconditional variance of ε_t^2, if it exists. This is because of the fact that an analytical expression for $\mathsf{E}h_t^{1/2}$ is not available. The necessary and sufficient positivity conditions for h_t in this case are $\alpha_0 > 0$, $\kappa_0^- < 0, \kappa_0^+ > 0$, and $\beta_1 \geq 0$. For the general model (Eq. 2.5), the corresponding conditions are $\alpha_0 > 0, \sum_{i=0}^{n^-} \kappa_j^- < 0, n^- = 0, \ldots, m^-, \sum_{i=0}^{n^+} \kappa_j^+ > 0, n^+ = 0, \ldots, m^+$, and $\beta_1 \geq 0$. They are not satisfied by the estimated model of Engle and Ng (1993, Table VII), where $m^- = m^+ = 4$ due to the estimates of parameters κ_3^+ and κ_3^-. The splines make the parameterization more flexible than that of Equation 2.3, but the latter does not have the discontinuities present in the former.

Finally, it may be mentioned that there exists a threshold autoregressive stochastic volatility model in which the threshold parameter, analogously to Equation 2.3, equals zero. It has been defined and applied in So et al. (2002). For overviews of stochastic volatility models, see Shephard and Andersen (2009) and Bos (2011) in this handbook.

2.4 Nonlinear ARCH and GARCH Models

2.4.1 ENGLE'S NONLINEAR GARCH MODEL

Let $g(\varepsilon_{t-1}; \theta)$ be a generic function representing the function of ε_{t-1} in Equations 2.3, 2.5, 2.8, and in the TGARCH model. For all these models, $g(\varepsilon_0; \theta) = 0$, that is, $\varepsilon_t = 0$ does not contribute to the conditional variance at $t+1$. This is no longer true for the nonlinear GARCH model of Engle (1990). The conditional variance of this model has the following (first-order) form:

$$h_t = \alpha_0 + \alpha_1(\varepsilon_{t-1} - \lambda)^2 + \beta_1 h_{t-1}, \tag{2.6}$$

where $\alpha_0, \alpha_1 > 0$, and $\beta_1 \geq 0$. Thus, $g(0; \theta) = \alpha_1\lambda^2$. When $\lambda = 0$, Equation 2.6 collapses into the standard GARCH(1,1) model (Eq. 2.2). These models share the same weak stationarity condition $\alpha_1 + \beta_1 < 1$, and for Equation 2.6, $\mathsf{E}\varepsilon_t^2 = (\alpha_1 + \lambda^2)/(1 - \alpha_1 - \beta_1)$. Although Equation 2.6 defines a rather simple nonlinear GARCH model, it has been less popular among users than, say, the GJR-GARCH model.

2.4.2 NONLINEAR ARCH MODEL

Higgins and Bera (1992) introduced a nonlinear autoregressive conditional heteroskedasticity (NLARCH) model that nests both the standard ARCH model and the logarithmic GARCH model of Pantula (1986) and Geweke (1986). It is an ARCH model with Box-Cox transformed variables:

$$\frac{h_t^\delta - 1}{\delta} = \alpha_0 \frac{\omega^\delta - 1}{\delta} + \alpha_1 \frac{\varepsilon_{t-1}^{2\delta} - 1}{\delta} + \cdots + \alpha_q \frac{\varepsilon_{t-q}^{2\delta} - 1}{\delta}, \tag{2.7}$$

where $0 \leq \delta \leq 1, \omega > 0, \alpha_0 > 0, \alpha_j \geq 0, j = 1, \ldots, q$, and $\sum_{j=0}^{q} \alpha_j = 1$. It can also be written as follows:

$$h_t = \{\alpha_0\omega^\delta + \alpha_1\varepsilon_{t-1}^{2\delta} + \cdots + \alpha_q\varepsilon_{t-q}^{2\delta}\}^{1/\delta}.$$

When $\delta \to 1$, Equation 2.7 approaches Engle's ARCH(q) model. The purpose of the restriction $\sum_{j=0}^{q} \alpha_j = 1$, which also helps identify ω becomes obvious from this special case. When $\delta \to 0$, the result is the qth order logarithmic ARCH model. As the GARCH family of models have become a normal specification in applications to financial time series, the NLARCH model has been rarely used in practice.

2.4.3 ASYMMETRIC POWER GARCH MODEL

Ding et al. (1993) introduced the asymmetric power generalized autoregressive conditional heteroskedasticity (APGARCH) model. The first-order APGARCH model has the following definition:

$$h_t^\delta = \alpha_0 + \alpha_1(|\varepsilon_{t-1}| - \lambda\varepsilon_{t-1})^{2\delta} + \beta_1 h_{t-1}^\delta, \tag{2.8}$$

where $\alpha_0 > 0, \alpha_1 > 0, \beta_1 \geq 0, \delta > 0$, and $|\lambda| \leq 1$, so it is nonlinear in parameters. Meitz and Saikkonen (2011) considered the special case $\delta = 1$ and called the model the *asymmetric GARCH (AGARCH) model*. Using the indicator variable, they showed that for $\delta = 1$ (Eq. 2.8) can be written as a GJR-GARCH(1,1) model with $p = q = 1$:

$$h_t = \alpha_0 + \alpha_1(1-\lambda)^2\varepsilon_{t-1}^2 + 4\lambda\alpha_1 I(\varepsilon_{t-1} < 0)\varepsilon_{t-1}^2 + \beta_1 h_{t-1}. \tag{2.9}$$

This implies that the conditions for the existence of unconditional moments of the AGARCH model can be obtained from the corresponding conditions for the first-order GJR-GARCH model. For the general APGARCH model, the only analytic "fourth-moment" condition available is for the fractional moment $\mathsf{E}|\varepsilon_t|^{4\delta}$ (He and Teräsvirta, 1999b). Ding et al. (1993) also discussed some stylized facts of return series. Considering a number of long daily return series, they found that the autocorrelations $\rho(|\varepsilon_t|^{2\delta}, |\varepsilon_{t-j}|^{2\delta})$ were maximized for $\delta = 1/2$. Fitting the APGARCH model to a long daily S&P 500 return series yielded (in our notation) $\widehat{\delta} = 0.72$. He et al. (2008) fitted the model to daily return series of the 30 most actively traded stocks in the Stockholm Stock Exchange and in all cases obtained an estimate of δ that was remarkably close to the value reported by Ding, Granger, and Engle. For similar results, see Brooks et al. (2000).

2.4.4 SMOOTH TRANSITION GARCH MODEL

As mentioned in Section 2.3, the GJR-GARCH model may be generalized by making it nonlinear in parameters. This is done, for example, by substituting an unknown parameter for the zero in the argument of the indicator function of Equation 2.3. The same substitution may be made for the TGARCH model. This generalization can be further extended by replacing the indicator function by a continuous function of its argument and extending the transition to also include the intercept. In the (p, q) case, this yields the following conditional variance

$$h_t = \alpha_{10} + \sum_{j=1}^{q} \alpha_{1j}\varepsilon_{t-j}^2 + \left(\alpha_{20} + \sum_{j=1}^{q} \alpha_{2j}\varepsilon_{t-j}^2\right) G_K(\gamma, \mathbf{c}; \varepsilon_{t-j}) + \sum_{j=1}^{p} \beta_j h_{t-j}, \tag{2.10}$$

where the transition function

$$G_K(\gamma, \mathbf{c}; \varepsilon_{t-j}) = \left(1 + \exp\left\{-\gamma \prod_{k=1}^{K} (\varepsilon_{t-j} - c_k)\right\}\right)^{-1}, \gamma > 0 \tag{2.11}$$

and $\mathbf{c} = (c_1, \ldots, c_K)'$. For $K = 1$, this model corresponds to the one that Hagerud (1997) introduced. The restriction $\gamma > 0$ is an identification restriction. Furthermore, global identification requires another restriction such as $c_1 \leq \cdots \leq c_K$, but this restriction does not have any practical significance in the estimation of parameters. The transition function is bounded between 0 and 1. The parameter γ represents the slope and $\mathbf{c}$ the location of the transition(s). When $K = 1$, the "ARCH parameters" and the intercept of the model change from α_{1j} to $\alpha_{1j} + \alpha_{2j}$ as a function of $\varepsilon_{t-j}, j = 0, 1, \ldots, q$. This means that the impact of each shock on the conditional variance is nonlinear. When $K = 1, \gamma \to \infty$ and $c_1 = 0$, Equation 2.10 becomes the GJR-GARCH model (Eq. 2.3). When $K = 2$, the transition function (Eq. 2.11) is nonmonotonic and symmetric around $(c_1 + c_2)/2$. The model (Eq. 2.10) could be called an additive smooth transition generalized autoregressive conditional heteroskedasticity (STGARCH) model. Hagerud (1997) also proposed the exponential transition function

$$G^E(\gamma; \varepsilon_{t-j}) = 1 - \exp\{-\gamma \varepsilon_{t-j}^2\}. \tag{2.12}$$

The limiting behavior of Equation 2.12 when $\gamma \to \infty$ is different from that of Equation 2.11. When $\gamma \to \infty$ in Equation 2.12, $G^E(\gamma, \mathbf{c}; \varepsilon_{t-j}) = 1$ except for $\varepsilon_{t-j} = 0$, where the function equals zero. As to Equation 2.11, the function equals 0 for $c_1 \leq \varepsilon_{t-j} < c_2$ and is 1 otherwise. At least for $q = 1$, Equation 2.11 may be preferred to Equation 2.12, because applying Equation 2.12, the STGARCH model (for all practical purposes) collapses into the standard GARCH(1,1) model when $\gamma \to \infty$. The transition function (Eq. 2.11) is symmetric around zero if $c_1 = -c_2$. Function G^E is symmetric around zero, but the center of symmetry can easily be moved away from zero by adding a location parameter to the exponent as in Teräsvirta (1994). Lubrano (2001) considered this extension in the STGARCH context.

In the model by Gonzalez-Rivera (1998), the intercept does not switch, and the same lag of ε_t controls the transition:

$$h_t = \alpha_{10} + \sum_{j=1}^{q} \alpha_{1j}\varepsilon_{t-j}^2 + \left(\sum_{j=1}^{q} \alpha_{2j}\varepsilon_{t-j}^2\right) G(\gamma, c_1; \varepsilon_{t-d}) + \sum_{j=1}^{p} \beta_j h_{t-j}, \tag{2.13}$$

where $d > 0$. It is also assumed that $c_1 = 0$, but that is not crucial. Anderson et al. (1999) extended Equation 2.13 by also allowing the conditional variance to switch according to the same transition function as in Equation 2.13.

Smooth transition GARCH models are useful in situations where the assumption of two distinct regimes is too rough an approximation to the asymmetric behavior of the conditional variance. Among other things, Hagerud (1997) discussed a specification strategy that allows the investigator to choose between $K = 1$ and $K = 2$ in Equation 2.11. Larger values of K may also be considered, but they are likely to be less common in applications than the two simplest choices.

The standard GARCH model has the undesirable property that the estimated model often exaggerates the persistence in volatility. This means that the estimated sum of the α- and β-coefficients in Equation 2.2 is close to 1. Overestimated persistence results in poor volatility forecasts in the sense that following a large shock, the forecasts indicate "too slow" a decrease of the conditional variance to more normal levels. In order to find a remedy for this problem, Lanne and Saikkonen (2005) proposed a smooth transition GARCH model, whose first-order version has the form

$$h_t = \alpha_0 + \alpha_1\varepsilon_{t-1}^2 + \delta_1 G_1(\theta; h_{t-1}) + \beta_1 h_{t-1}. \tag{2.14}$$

In Equation 2.14, $G_1(\theta; h_{t-1})$ is a continuous, monotonically increasing bounded function of h_{t-1}. Since $h_{t-1} > 0$ almost surely, Lanne and Saikkonen used the cumulative distribution function of the Gamma distribution as the transition function. A major difference between Equations 2.13 and 2.14 is that in the latter model the transition variable is a lagged conditional variance. In empirical examples given in the paper, this parameterization clearly alleviates the problem of exaggerated persistence.

Lanne and Saikkonen (2005) also considered a general family of models of the conditional variance of order $(p, 1)$:

$$h_t = g(h_{t-1}, \ldots, h_{t-p}) + f(\varepsilon_{t-1}), \tag{2.15}$$

where the functions g and f are defined in such a way that Equation 2.15 contains, as special cases, all the GARCH$(p, 1)$ models discussed in this chapter, including the smooth transition GARCH model (Eqs. 2.6 and 2.13). They find conditions for geometric ergodicity of h_t defined by Equation 2.15 and for the existence of moments of ε_t. These conditions are quite general in the sense that unlike the other conditions available in the literature, they cover the smooth transition GARCH models as well. For even more general results on first-order models, see Meitz and Saikkonen (2008).

2.4.5 DOUBLE THRESHOLD ARCH MODEL

The TGARCH model is linear in parameters, because the threshold parameter appearing in nonlinear threshold models is assumed to equal zero. A genuine nonlinear threshold model does exist, namely, the double threshold autoregressive conditional heteroskedasticity (DTARCH) model of Li and Li (1996). It is called a double threshold model, because both the autoregressive conditional mean and the conditional variance have a threshold-type structure. The conditional mean model is defined as follows:

$$y_t = \sum_{k=1}^{K} \left(\phi_{0k} + \sum_{j=1}^{p_k} \phi_{jk} y_{t-j} \right) I(c_{k-1}^{(\mathrm{m})} < y_{t-b} \leq c_k^{(\mathrm{m})}) + \varepsilon_t \tag{2.16}$$

and the conditional variance has the form

$$h_t = \sum_{\ell=1}^{L} \left(\alpha_{0\ell} + \sum_{j=1}^{p_\ell} \alpha_{j\ell} \varepsilon_{t-j}^2 \right) I(c_{\ell-1}^{(\mathrm{v})} < y_{t-d} \leq c_\ell^{(\mathrm{v})}), \tag{2.17}$$

where $c_0^{(\mathrm{m})} = c_0^{(\mathrm{v})} = -\infty$ and $c_K^{(\mathrm{m})} = c_L^{(\mathrm{v})} = \infty$. Furthermore, b and d are delay parameters, $b, d \geq 1$. The number of regimes in Equations 2.16 and 2.17 , K and L, respectively, need not be the same, and the two delay parameters need not be equal either. Other threshold variables than lags of y_t are possible. The conditional variance model (Eq. 2.17) differs from a typical GARCH model in the sense that the transition variable in Equation 2.17 is y_{t-d} and not a function of ε_{t-d}. This feature is somewhat analogous to the threshold moving average (TMA) model (Ling and Tong 2005; Ling et al., 2007). The TMA model is a generalization of the standard moving average model for the conditional mean, but the threshold variable is a lag of y_t and not ε_t.

2.4.6 NEURAL NETWORK ARCH AND GARCH MODELS

The literature on nonlinear GARCH models also comprises models based on artificial neural network (ANN) type of specifications. As an example, consider the following model by Donaldson and Kamstra (1997). It is an extension of the GJR-GARCH model; but for simplicity, it is here given without the asymmetric component as an extension to the standard GARCH model. The ANN-GARCH model of the authors has the following form:

$$h_t = \alpha_0 + \sum_{j=1}^{q} \alpha_j \varepsilon_{t-j}^2 + \sum_{j=1}^{p} \beta_j h_{t-j} + \sum_{j=1}^{s} \phi_j G(\mathbf{w}_{t-j}, \Gamma_j),$$

where the "hidden units" are defined as follows:

$$G(\mathbf{w}_{t-j}, \Gamma_j) = \left(1 + \exp\left\{\gamma_{0j} + \sum_{i=1}^{u} (\mathbf{w}_{t-j}' \gamma_{ji})\right\}\right)^{-1}, \tag{2.18}$$

where $j = 1, \ldots, s$. In Equation 2.18, γ_{0j} and $\Gamma_j = (\gamma_{j1} : \cdots : \gamma_{ju})$ are parameters such that each $m \times 1$ vector $\gamma_{ji} = (\gamma_{j1}, \ldots, \gamma_{ji}, 0, \ldots, 0)'$, $i = 1, \ldots, m$, and $\mathbf{w}_t = (w_t, w_t^2, \ldots, w_t^m)'$ with $w_t = \varepsilon_t / \sqrt{\mathsf{E}\varepsilon_t^2}$. Note that $G(\mathbf{w}_t, \Gamma_j)$ as a logistic function is bounded between zero and one. Each standardized and lagged ε_t appears in powers up to m. For a user of this model, specification of p, q, s, and u is an important issue, and the authors suggest the use of BIC of Rissanen (1978) and Schwarz (1978) for this purpose. More details about this can be found in Section 2.6.

A simpler ANN-GARCH model can be obtained by defining the hidden unit as in Caulet and Péguin-Feissolle (2000). This results in the following ANN-GARCH model:

$$h_t = \alpha_0 + \sum_{j=1}^{q} \alpha_j \varepsilon_{t-j}^2 + \sum_{j=1}^{p} \beta_j h_{t-j} + \sum_{j=1}^{s} \phi_j G(\gamma_{0j} + \varepsilon_t' \gamma_j), \tag{2.19}$$

where

$$G(\gamma_{0j} + \varepsilon_t' \gamma_j) = (1 + \exp\{\gamma_{0j} + \varepsilon_t' \gamma_j)\})^{-1}, \tag{2.20}$$

where $j = 1, \ldots, s$, with the $k \times 1$ parameter vector γ_j and $\varepsilon_t = (\varepsilon_{t-1}, \ldots, \varepsilon_{t-k})'$. In fact, Caulet and Péguin-Feissolle (2000) assumed $\alpha_j = 0, j = 1, \ldots, q$, and $\beta_j = 0, j = 1, \ldots, p$, in Equation 2.19, because their purpose was to set up a test of no conditional heteroskedasticity against conditional heteroskedasticity of rather general form. Nevertheless, their specification can be generalized to an ANN-GARCH model (Eq. 2.19) with (Eq. 2.20). Since Equation 2.20 is a positive-valued function, assuming $\phi_j \geq 0, j = 1, \ldots, s$, would, jointly with the restrictions $\alpha_0 > 0, \alpha_i, \beta_j \geq 0, \forall i, j$, guarantee positivity of the conditional variance. Because of the positivity of Equation 2.20, one could even think of deleting the linear combination $\sum_{j=1}^{q} \alpha_j \varepsilon_{t-j}^2$ from the model altogether.

2.4.7 TIME-VARYING GARCH

It has been argued (Mikosch and Stărică 2004) that the assumption of the standard GARCH model having constant parameters may not hold in practice unless the series to be modeled are sufficiently short. The standard model may be generalized by assuming that the parameters change at specific points of time, divide the series into subseries according to the location of the break points, and fit separate GARCH models to the subseries. The main statistical problem is then finding the number of the unknown break points and their location. It is also possible to model the switching standard deviation regimes using the threshold generalized autoregressive conditional heteroskedasticity (TGARCH) model discussed in Section 2.3. This is done by assuming that the threshold variable is the time. A recent survey by Andreou and Ghysels (2009) expertly covers this area of research.

Another possibility is to consider the smooth transition GARCH model (Eq. 2.13) to fit this situation. It is done by assuming the transition function in Equation 2.13 to be a function of time:

$$G(\gamma, \mathbf{c}; t^*) = \left(1 + \exp\left\{-\gamma \prod_{k=1}^{K} (t^* - c_k)\right\}\right)^{-1}, \gamma > 0,$$

where $t^* = t/T$ is rescaled time (T is the number of observations). The resulting time-varying parameter generalized autoregressive conditional heteroskedasticity (TV-GARCH) model has the form

$$h_t = \alpha_0(t) + \sum_{j=1}^{q} \alpha_j(t) \varepsilon_{t-j}^2 + \sum_{j=1}^{p} \beta_j(t) h_{t-j}, \tag{2.21}$$

where $\alpha_0(t) = \alpha_{01} + \alpha_{02} G(\gamma, c; t^*), \alpha_j(t) = \alpha_{j1} + \alpha_{j2} G(\gamma, c; t^*), j = 1, \ldots, q$, and $\beta_j(t) = \beta_{j1} + \beta_{j2} G(\gamma, c; t^*), j = 1, \ldots, p$. This is quite a flexible parameterization. The TV-GARCH model is nonstationary as the unconditional variance of ε_t varies deterministically over time.

Some of the time-varying parameters in Equation 2.21 may be restricted to constants *a priori*. For example, it may be assumed that only the intercept $\alpha_0(t)$ is time-varying. This implies that while the unconditional variance is changing over time, the dynamic behavior of volatility remains unchanged. If change is allowed in the other GARCH parameters as well, the model is capable of describing systematic changes in the amplitude of the volatility clusters. The standard weakly stationary constant-parameter GARCH model cannot accommodate such changes. For a general survey of time-varying ARCH and GARCH models, see Cizek and Spokoiny (2009).

2.4.8 FAMILIES OF GARCH MODELS AND THEIR PROBABILISTIC PROPERTIES

Some authors have defined families of GARCH models, often with the purpose of proving results on probabilistic properties of GARCH models for the whole family. The corresponding results for individual GARCH models in the family then follow as special cases. A rather general family of first-order GARCH models is defined by Duan (1997). The general process is called the *augmented GARCH(1,1) process*, and it is partly based on the Box-Cox transformation of the variables of the GARCH model. It accommodates several models presented in Sections 2.3 and 2.4. These include the TGARCH, the GJR-GARCH, and the nonlinear GARCH model by Engle (1990). Duan (1997) derived conditions for strict stationarity for the augmented GARCH model, and so they apply to these three special cases.

Hentschel (1995) has introduced another family of first-order GARCH models that is less general than that of Duan (1997). Nevertheless, it also nests the three aforementioned models and the NLARCH(1) model or its GARCH generalization. The idea is to define a general model, estimate its parameters and consider the adequacy of nested special cases by the likelihood ratio test. It appears, however, that this specification strategy has not been often used in practice.

He and Teräsvirta (1999a) define their family of first-order GARCH processes in order to obtain general results of weak stationarity, existence of the fourth moment, and the autocorrelation function of $\{\varepsilon_t^2\}$ of the processes belonging to this family. Since in that work the integer moments of GARCH processes are the object of interest, the family is restricted to models of $h_t^{1/2}$ and h_t. The more general case h_t^δ is excluded because there do not exist analytic expressions for the integer moments of ε_t except for the two special cases $\delta = 1/2$ and $\delta = 1$. This family contains as special cases, among others, the TGARCH, the GJR-GARCH, and the VS-GARCH models.

Meitz and Saikkonen (2008) consider a very general Markov chain with one observable and another unobservable process that contains a rather general family of first-order GARCH model as a special case. For example, in the standard GARCH(1,1) process (Eqs. 2.1 and 2.2), $\{\varepsilon_t\}$ is the observable process and $\{h_t\}$ is the unobservable one. The joint sequence $\{(\varepsilon_t, h_t)\}$ is also a Markov chain. Using the theory of Markov chains, the authors derive conditions for geometric ergodicity and β-mixing for a large number of GARCH(1,1) models. These include not only the Hentschel (1995) family of GARCH models but also a STGARCH model that nests both the model of Hagerud (1997) and the one considered by Lanne and Saikkonen (2005). The first-order GARCH version of the TARCH (threshold autoregressive conditional heteroskedasticity) model of Li and Li (1996), $p_\ell = 1$ for $\ell = 1, \ldots, L$ in Equation 2.17, is another special case.

2.5 Testing Standard GARCH Against Nonlinear GARCH

2.5.1 SIZE AND SIGN BIAS TESTS

After a GARCH model, for example, the standard GARCH model, has been estimated, it would be wise to subject it to misspecification tests to see whether the model adequately describes the data. In this section, we consider tests that are designed for alternatives that incorporate asymmetry or, more generally, missing exogenous variables or nonlinearity. The leading testing principle is the score or Lagrange multiplier principle, because then only the null model has to be estimated. As explained for example in Engle (1982b), these tests can be carried out in the so-called TR^2 form, and under the null hypothesis the test statistic has an asymptotic χ^2-distribution. When the null hypothesis is the standard GARCH model (Eq. 2.2), the test can be carried out in stages as follows:

1. Estimate the parameters of the GARCH model (Eq. 2.2) and compute "the residual sum of squares" $\mathrm{SSR}_0 = \sum_{j=1}^{T}(\varepsilon_t^2/\widetilde{h}_t - 1)^2$, where $\widetilde{h}_t$ is the estimated conditional variance at t.
2. Regress $\widetilde{z}_t^2 = \varepsilon_t^2/\widetilde{h}_t$ on the gradient of the log-likelihood function and the new variables (assuming the component excluded under the null hypothesis is linear in parameters), and compute the residual sum of squares SSR_1 from this auxiliary regression.
3. Form the test statistic

$$T\frac{\mathrm{SSR}_0 - \mathrm{SSR}_1}{\mathrm{SSR}_0} \xrightarrow{d} \chi^2(m)$$

under the null hypothesis of dimension m. When the null model is Equation 2.2, the gradient equals $\widetilde{\mathbf{g}}_t = \widetilde{h}_t^{-1}(\partial h_t/\partial\omega)_0$, where $\omega = (\alpha_0, \alpha_1, \ldots, \alpha_q, \beta_1, \ldots, \beta_p)'$, and

$$(\partial h_t/\partial\omega)_0 = \widetilde{\mathbf{u}}_t + \sum_{i=1}^{p} \widetilde{\beta}_i(\partial h_{t-i}/\partial\omega)_0$$

with $\widetilde{\mathbf{u}}_t = (1, \varepsilon_{t-1}^2, \ldots, \varepsilon_{t-q}^2, \widetilde{h}_{t-1}, \ldots, \widetilde{h}_{t-p})'$. The subscript 0 indicates that the partial derivatives are evaluated under H_0. They are available from the estimation of the null model and need not be computed separately.

The auxiliary regression is thus

$$\widetilde{z}_t^2 = a + \widetilde{\mathbf{g}}_t'\delta_0 + \mathbf{v}_t'\delta_1 + \eta_t, \tag{2.22}$$

where $\widetilde{z}_t^2 = \varepsilon_t^2/\widetilde{h}_t$ and $\mathbf{v}_t$ is the $m \times 1$ vector of the variables under test, so H_0: $\delta_1 = \mathbf{0}$. Many of the tests discussed in this section fit into this framework. Engle and Ng (1993) propose asymmetry tests such that $\mathbf{v}_t = I(\varepsilon_{t-1} < 0)$ (the sign bias test), $\mathbf{v}_t = I(\varepsilon_{t-1} < 0)\varepsilon_{t-1}$ (negative size bias test), and $\mathbf{v}_t = \{1 - I(\varepsilon_{t-1} < 0)\}\varepsilon_{t-1}$ (positive size bias test). They also suggest a joint test in which

$$\mathbf{v}_t = (I(\varepsilon_{t-1} < 0), I(\varepsilon_{t-1} < 0)\varepsilon_{t-1}, \{1 - I(\varepsilon_{t-1} < 0)\}\varepsilon_{t-1})'$$

and note that the tests can be generalized to involve more lags than the first one. These three tests are the most often used tests for asymmetry in empirical work.

2.5.2 TESTING GARCH AGAINST SMOOTH TRANSITION GARCH

An STGARCH model must not be fitted to a return series without first testing the standard GARCH model against it. The reason is that the STGARCH model is not identified if the data are generated from the standard GARCH model. As an example, consider the model (Eq. 2.10). If $\alpha_{2j} = 0, j = 0, 1, \ldots, q$, the model collapses into the GARCH model. In this case, the parameters γ and $c_1, \ldots, c_K$ in Equation 2.11 are nuisance parameters that cannot be estimated consistently. Setting $\gamma = 0$ also makes the model into a standard GARCH model, and in this case, $\alpha_{2j} = 0, j = 0, 1, \ldots, q$, and $c_1, \ldots, c_K$ are unidentified. The problem is that the lack of identification under the null hypothesis, which is the standard GARCH model, invalidates standard asymptotic inference. Consequently, the asymptotic null distribution of the customary χ^2-statistic is unknown. This is a common problem in testing linearity against many nonlinear conditional mean models such as the threshold autoregressive, the smooth transition autoregressive, or the hidden Markov model. It was first considered by Davies (1977); see Teräsvirta, Tjøstheim, and Granger (2010, Chapter 5) for further discussion.

A straightforward solution to the problem of testing a standard GARCH model against an STGARCH alternative would be to construct an empirical distribution of the test statistic by simulation (Hansen, 1996). Gonzalez-Rivera (1998) already mentioned this possibility in her discussion of testing for smooth transition GARCH. Since the time series in applications are often quite long, this approach, however, could be computationally demanding. Following Luukkonen et al. (1988), Hagerud (1997) and later Lundbergh and Teräsvirta (2012) suggested circumventing the identification problem by approximating the transition function (Eq. 2.11) by a Taylor expansion around the null hypothesis $\gamma = 0$. As a simple example, let $q = 1$ in Equation 2.10 and $K = 1$ in Equation 2.11. A first-order Taylor expansion of the transition function becomes

$$T_1(\varepsilon_{t-1}; \gamma) = 1/2 + (1/4)(\varepsilon_{t-1} - c_1)\gamma + R_1(\varepsilon_{t-1}; \gamma), \tag{2.23}$$

where $R_1(\varepsilon_{t-1}; \gamma)$ is the remainder. Substituting Equation 2.23 for the transition function in Equation 2.10 and reparameterizing yields

$$h_t = \alpha_{10}^* + \alpha_1\varepsilon_{t-1} + \alpha_{11}^*\varepsilon_{t-j}^2 + \alpha_{111}^*\varepsilon_{t-1}^3 + R_1^*(\varepsilon_{t-1}; \gamma) + \sum_{j=1}^{p} \beta_j h_{t-j},$$

where $R_1^*(\varepsilon_{t-1};\gamma)=(\alpha_{20}+\alpha_{21}\varepsilon_{t-j}^2)R_1(\varepsilon_{t-1};\gamma), \alpha_1=\gamma/4,$ and $\alpha_{11}^*=\gamma\alpha_{21}/4.$ Since the resulting test is a Lagrange multiplier test and $R_1(\varepsilon_{t-1};\gamma)\equiv 0$ under the null hypothesis, the remainder can be ignored in the test. The null hypothesis equals $\alpha_1=\alpha_{111}^*=0$. In the TR^2 version of the test, $\mathbf{v}_t=\widetilde{h}_t^{-1}(\partial h_t/\partial\omega)_0$, where

$$\left(\frac{\partial h_t}{\partial\omega}\right)_0=(\varepsilon_{t-1},\varepsilon_{t-1}^3)'+\sum_{j=1}^{p}\widetilde{\beta}_j\left(\frac{\partial h_{t-j}}{\partial\omega}\right)_0$$

and $\omega=(\alpha_1,\alpha_{111}^*)'$. The asymptotically (under H_0) χ^2-distributed test statistic has two degrees of freedom. The test requires $\mathsf{E}\varepsilon_t^6<\infty$. Generalizations to $q>1$ are obvious. When $p=q=1$ and $\alpha_{21}=0$, one obtains $\mathbf{v}_t=\widetilde{h}_t^{-1}\{\varepsilon_{t-1}+\beta_1(\partial h_{t-1}/\partial\alpha_1)_0\}$ and the test can be viewed as the test of the GARCH(1,1) model against the Quadratic GARCH(1,1) model of Sentana (1995).

2.5.3 TESTING GARCH AGAINST ARTIFICIAL NEURAL NETWORK GARCH

Caulet and Péguin-Feissolle (2000) developed a test of the hypothesis of independent, identically distributed observations against autoregressive conditional heteroskedasticity. The model was thus Equation 2.19 with $\alpha_i,\beta_j=0, i,j\geq 1$, and the null hypothesis was $\phi_j=0$ and $j=1,\ldots,s$. The model can be generalized for testing GARCH against Equation 2.19 with Equation 2.20. To solve the identification problem, the authors adopted the method introduced by Lee et al. (1993). The idea was to choose a large s and draw the nuisance parameters for each hidden unit from a uniform distribution after appropriate rescaling of $\varepsilon_t, t=1,\ldots,T$. It follows that

$$\mathbf{v}_t=\widetilde{h}_t^{-1}(G(\widehat{\gamma}_{01}+\varepsilon_t'\widehat{\gamma}_1),\ldots,G(\widehat{\gamma}_{0s}+\varepsilon_t'\widehat{\gamma}_s))',\tag{2.24}$$

where $\widehat{\gamma}_{0j}$ and $\widehat{\gamma}_j$ are the parameters from the jth random draw. The power of the test is dependent on s. The dimension of the null hypothesis and $\mathbf{v}_t$ may be reduced by considering the principal components of the hidden units corresponding to the largest eigenvalues. The test of Caulet and Péguin-Feissolle (2000) is a special case of the test mentioned here. Note that in that case, $\widetilde{h}_t$ in Equation 2.24 is a positive constant and can be ignored. Another possibility, discussed in Péguin-Feissolle (1999), is to develop each hidden unit into a Taylor series around the null hypothesis H_0: $\gamma_j=\mathbf{0}$ as in Teräsvirta et al. (1993). After merging terms and reparameterizing, a third-order Taylor expansion has the form

$$\begin{aligned}T_3(\varepsilon_t;\gamma_1,\ldots,\gamma_s)&=\phi_0^*+\sum_{j=1}^{k}\phi_j^*\varepsilon_{t-j}+\sum_{i=1}^{k}\sum_{j=i}^{k}\phi_{ij}^*\varepsilon_{t-i}\varepsilon_{t-j}\\&\quad+\sum_{i=1}^{k}\sum_{j=i}^{k}\sum_{j=\ell}^{k}\phi_{ij\ell}^*\varepsilon_{t-i}\varepsilon_{t-j}\varepsilon_{t-\ell}+R_3(\varepsilon_t;\Gamma),\end{aligned}$$

where $R_3(\varepsilon_t; \Gamma)$ is the combined remainder. Similarly, to the remainder in Equation 2.23, $R_3(\varepsilon_t; \Gamma) = 0$ under the null hypothesis H_0 and does not affect the asymptotic null distribution of the test statistic. The new null hypothesis is H_0': $\phi_j^* = 0, j = 1, \ldots, s, \phi_{ij}^* = 0, i \neq j$, and $\phi_{ij\ell}^* = 0, i = 1, \ldots, s; j = i, \ldots, s$; and $\ell = j, \ldots, s$. The moment condition is $\mathsf{E}\varepsilon_t^6 < \infty$. When $k = 1$, $H_0' : \phi_1^* = 0, \phi_{111}^* = 0$, and the test is the same as the test of GARCH against STGARCH when $q = 1$ in Equation 2.10. Since the power comparisons of Péguin-Feissolle (1999) only concerned the null hypothesis of no conditional heteroskedasticity, little is known about the power properties of these tests in the GARCH context. They may be regarded as rather general misspecification tests of the standard GARCH model.

2.6 Estimation of Parameters in Nonlinear GARCH Models

2.6.1 SMOOTH TRANSITION GARCH

Parameters of the smooth transition GARCH models can be estimated by the quasi-maximum likelihood (QML) method. The use of QML requires, among other things, that the slope parameter γ be bounded away from both 0 and ∞. General conditions for asymptotic normality of the QML estimators of nonlinear first-order GARCH models are discussed in Meitz and Saikkonen (2011). The moment conditions required for asymptotic normality include the existence of the fourth moment of ε_t. It is seen from Equation 2.1 that a necessary condition for this is $\mathsf{E}z_t^4 < \infty$, but it is not sufficient. One of the examples in Meitz and Saikkonen (2011) is the STGARCH model (Eq. 2.10) with $p = q = 1$, and it is shown how the model satisfies the general conditions given in the paper.

In practice, estimation of the parameters of the STGARCH model is quite straightforward. Numerical problems in the form of slow convergence may be expected, however, when the slope parameter γ is large, that is, much larger in magnitude than the other parameters. The reasons for this have been discussed in the context of smooth transition autoregressive model; see Teräsvirta, Tjøstheim, and Granger (2010, Chapter 16). A major reason is that even a substantial change in the value of γ only leads to a very small change in the shape of the transition function when the transition is very steep or, in other words, when γ is large.

Computing the partial derivatives is another numerical issue. Brooks et al. (2001) already emphasized the importance of using analytical derivatives in the estimation of parameters of standard GARCH models. It is even more important to apply them when the GARCH model to be estimated is nonlinear. The reason is increased precision of the estimates. If the user chooses to use the Berndt-Hall-Hall-Hausman (BHHH) algorithm discussed in many textbooks, then only the first derivatives are needed. This algorithm has been quite popular in the estimation of GARCH models, where computing the analytical second derivatives is most often avoided despite the work of Fiorentini et al. (1996).

The choice of initial values is important in the estimation of nonlinear models. The initial values of the conditional variance may be chosen in the same way as in linear GARCH models by setting them equal to the sample unconditional variance. The initial values $\varepsilon_0, \ldots, \varepsilon_{q-1}$ are set to zero as are the partial derivatives of the conditional variance. It may be harder to find appropriate initial values for the parameters of the STGARCH model. Obtaining them by applying a heuristic method such as simulated annealing or a genetic algorithm would be a possibility. That would help avoiding inferior local optima. For applications of these to standard GARCH models, see Amilon (2003) or Adanu (2006). The latter article considers and compares several heuristic methods with each other. Finally, it can be mentioned that smooth transition GARCH models can also be estimated using Bayesian techniques; see Lubrano (2001) for discussion. Wago (2004) later showed how estimation can be carried out using the Gibbs sampler.

2.6.2 NEURAL NETWORK GARCH

Estimation of ANN-GARCH models using analytical derivatives may be difficult because of many nonlinear parameters, unless the number of hidden units is very small. For this reason, Donaldson and Kamstra (1997) proposed to draw five sets of parameters $\Gamma_j, j = 1, \ldots, s$, randomly and then estimate the remaining parameters for each of these five sets with a grid on the dimensions p, q, s, u, and m, defined as $(p, q, s, u, m) \in [0, 5]$. Once this is done, a model selection criterion such as BIC is employed to choose the best model from the set of estimated models. The statistical properties of this *ad hoc* method are not known.

It seems that the parameters of the ANN-GARCH model (Eq. 2.19) could be estimated by simulated annealing, although empirical evidence of this is scarce. Goffe et al. (1994) considered applying simulated annealing in the situation where an autoregressive single-hidden-layer neural network model was fitted to a time series generated from a chaotic model. The results showed a number of local maxima. Furthermore, in repeated experiments with different starting values and temperatures, they were not able to find the same local maximum twice. The optima found were, nevertheless, better than the ones obtained using derivative-based estimation methods. The estimation of GARCH models offers an extra complication since the conditional variance h_t is not observed but has to be reestimated for each iteration. Estimation of a pure ANN-ARCH model would in this respect be a computationally easier problem. Simulations and applications would be needed to assess the usefulness of simulated annealing in the estimation of models such as Equation 2.19.

2.7 Forecasting with Nonlinear GARCH Models

2.7.1 SMOOTH TRANSITION GARCH

It may be useful to begin this section by considering the first-order GJR-GARCH model, one of the predecessors of the smooth transition GARCH model. What is being forecast is the conditional variance h_t. The forecasts are conditional means, so the forecast of h_{t+1} given the information $\mathcal{F}_t$ up to t equals (Zivot 2009)

$$h_{t+1|t} = \mathsf{E}(h_{t+1}|\mathcal{F}_t) = \alpha_0 + \alpha(z_t)h_t, \tag{2.25}$$

where $\alpha(z_t) = \alpha_1 z_t^2 + \kappa_1 I(z_t < 0)\}z_t^2 + \beta_1$. Accordingly, assuming that z_t has a symmetric distribution,

$$\begin{aligned} h_{t+2|t} &= \alpha_0 + \{\alpha_1 \mathsf{E}z_{t+1}^2 + \kappa_1 \mathsf{E}I(z_{t+1} < 0)\}z_{t+1}^2 + \beta_1\}h_{t+1|t} \\ &= \alpha_0 + \{\alpha_1 + (\kappa_1/2) + \beta_1\}h_{t+1|t} \\ &= \alpha_0(1 + \{\alpha_1 + (\kappa_1/2) + \beta_1\}) + \{\alpha_1 + (\kappa_1/2) + \beta_1\}\alpha(z_t)h_t. \end{aligned}$$

Generally, for $k \geq 1$,

$$h_{t+k|t} = \alpha_0 \sum_{j=0}^{k-1} \{\alpha_1 + (\kappa_1/2) + \beta_1\}^j + \{\alpha_1 + (\kappa_1/2) + \beta_1\}^{k-1}\alpha(z_t)h_t.$$

When $\alpha_1 + (\kappa_1/2) + \beta_1 < 1$, that is, when the unconditional variance of ε_t is finite,

$$h_{t+k|t} \to \alpha_0(1 - \{\alpha_1 + (\kappa_1/2) + \beta_1\})^{-1}$$

as $k \to \infty$.

Next, consider the first-order smooth transition GARCH model assuming $K = 1$ and $z_t \sim$ i.i.d. $(0, 1)$ with a continuous density $f_z(z)$. The forecast corresponding to Equation 2.25 equals

$$h_{t+1|t} = \alpha_{10} + \alpha_1 z_t^2 + \beta_1 h_t + \alpha(z_t, h_t)h_t,$$

where

$$\alpha(z_t, h_t) = (\alpha_{20} + \alpha_{21}z_t^2)(1 + \exp\{-\gamma(z_t h_t^{1/2} - c)\})^{-1}$$

is a nonlinear function of h_t. This makes a difference. Consider

$$h_{t+2|t} = \alpha_{10} + (\alpha_1 + \beta_1)h_{t+1|t} + \mathsf{E}\{\alpha(z_{t+1}, h_{t+1|t})|\mathcal{F}_t\}h_{t+1|t},$$

where

$$\mathsf{E}\{\alpha(z_{t+1}, h_{t+1|t})|\mathcal{F}_t\} = \int_{-\infty}^{\infty} \frac{\alpha_{20} + \alpha_{21}z^2}{1 + \exp\{-\gamma(z h_{t+1|t}^{1/2} - c)\}} f_z(z)\mathrm{d}z. \tag{2.26}$$

The expectation (Eq. 2.26) can be computed by numerical integration, but the integration becomes a multiple integral when the forecast horizon $k > 2$. A similar situation has been discussed in the context of forecasting with nonlinear conditional mean models, see Teräsvirta (2006), Kock and Teräsvirta (2012), or Teräsvirta, Tjøstheim, and Granger (2010, Chapter 14). The suggestion has been to compute an approximation to the integral by simulation or bootstrap, for details see the aforementioned references. As a by-product, this method generates a density forecast based on the simulated or bootstrapped values of the argument of Equation 2.26.

The same procedure applies to a few other nonlinear models including the ANN-GARCH model of Caulet and Péguin-Feissolle (2000) but is not necessary for Engle's nonlinear GARCH model (Eq. 2.6). For that model,

$$h_{t+1|t} = \alpha_0 + \alpha_1(z_t h_t^{1/2} - \lambda)^2 + \beta_1 h_t$$

is a nonlinear function of h_t. Nevertheless,

$$\begin{aligned} h_{t+2|t} &= \alpha_0 + \alpha_1 \mathsf{E}(z_{t+1} h_{t+1|t}^{1/2} - \lambda)^2 + \beta_1 h_{t+1|t} \\ &= \alpha_0 + \alpha_1 \lambda^2 + (\alpha_1 + \beta_1) h_{t+1|t}, \end{aligned}$$

which implies that forecasts for $k > 2$ can be obtained by a simple recursion.

2.7.2 ASYMMETRIC POWER GARCH

Consider first the special case of Equation 2.8 with $\delta = 1$, discussed by Meitz and Saikkonen (2011). Since this model can be written as a GJR-GARCH model, forecasting several periods ahead is straightforward. The one-period-ahead forecast equals

$$h_{t+1|t} = \alpha_0 + \{\alpha_1(1-\lambda)^2 + 4\lambda\alpha_1 \mathsf{E}I(z_t < 0)z_t^2 + \beta_1\}h_t. \tag{2.27}$$

where retaining the assumption that $z_t \sim \mathcal{N}(0,1)$, $\mathsf{E}I(z_t < 0)z_t^2 = \{(\pi/2) - 1\}/4$. Forecasts for longer horizons are obtained by recursion. In general,

$$h_{t+h|t} = \alpha_0 \sum_{j=0}^{h-1} \alpha(z,\lambda)^j + \alpha(z,\lambda)^{h-1} h_t,$$

where $\alpha(z,\lambda) = \alpha_1(1-\lambda)^2 + 4\lambda\alpha_1 \mathsf{E}I(z<0)z^2 + \beta_1$ and $z \sim \mathcal{N}(0,1)$. When $\delta \neq 1$, the forecast $h_{t+1|t}$ already has to be computed numerically. From Equation 2.8, one obtains

$$h_t = \{\alpha_0 + \alpha_1(|\varepsilon_{t-1}| - \lambda\varepsilon_{t-1})^{2\delta} + \beta_1 h_{t-1}^{\delta}\}^{1/\delta},$$

so

$$\begin{aligned} h_{t+1|t} &= \mathsf{E}[\alpha_0 + \{\alpha_1(|z_t| - \lambda z_t)^{2\delta} + \beta_1\}h_t^{\delta}]^{1/\delta} \\ &= \int_{-\infty}^{\infty} [\alpha_0 + \{\alpha_1(|z| - \lambda z)^{2\delta} + \beta_1\}h_t^{\delta}]^{1/\delta}\phi(z)\mathrm{d}z, \end{aligned}$$

where $\phi(z)$ is the density function of the standard normal random variable. The integral can be computed by simulation or by a bootstrap as in the case of the smooth transition GARCH model.

There is another special case that is of interest: $\delta = 1/2$. What is being modeled is the conditional standard deviation. In that case, it is natural to also forecast the conditional standard deviation and not the conditional variance. Thus,

$$h_{t+1|t}^{1/2} = \mathsf{E}[\alpha_0 + \{\alpha_1(|z_t| - \lambda z_t) + \beta_1\}h_t^{1/2}] = \alpha_0 + \{\alpha_1(2/\pi)^{1/2} + \beta_1\}h_t^{1/2} \tag{2.28}$$

and the forecasts for longer horizons follow by simple recursion from Equation 2.28.

2.8 Models Based on Multiplicative Decomposition of the Variance

So far the nonlinear extensions of the standard GARCH model considered in this chapter have concerned the parameterization of the conditional variance. There is another strand of literature aiming at extending the GARCH model by decomposing the variance into two components, one which is stationary and the other that can be nonstationary. Many of the models belonging to this category are semiparametric and discussed in Van Bellegem (2012). In this section, we shall look at two parametric models: one by Amado and Teräsvirta (2012) and the other by Osiewalski (2009) and Osiewalski and Pajor (2009).

The multiplicative variance decomposition is as follows: write

$$\varepsilon_t = z_t\sigma_t = z_t(h_t g_t)^{1/2}, \tag{2.29}$$

where the variance $\sigma_t^2 = h_t g_t$. The first component h_t is defined in Equation 2.2 or Equation 2.3, and the positive-valued function

$$g_t = 1 + \sum_{l=1}^{r} \delta_l G_l(t^*; \gamma_l, \mathbf{c}_l) \tag{2.30}$$

with

$$G_l(t^*; \gamma_l, \mathbf{c}_l) = \left(1 + \exp\left\{-\gamma_l \prod_{k=1}^{K}(t^* - c_{lk})\right\}\right)^{-1},$$
$$\gamma_l > 0,\ c_{l1} \le c_{l2} \le \cdots \le c_{lK} \tag{2.31}$$

is a flexible deterministic function of time describing shifts in the unconditional variance. This makes $\{\varepsilon_t\}$ a (globally) nonstationary sequence in variance. Analogously to Equation 2.11, the function (Eq. 2.31) is a generalized logistic function. In practice, typically $K=1$ or $K=2$. The function h_t characterizes volatility clustering as in the standard GARCH model. Rewriting Equation 2.29 as

$$\phi_t = \varepsilon_t / g_t^{1/2} = z_t h_t^{1/2}, \tag{2.32}$$

it is seen that after adjusting for shifts in the unconditional variance, the first-order conditional variance process h_t has the form:

$$h_t = \alpha_0 + \alpha_1 \phi_{t-1}^2 + \beta_1 h_{t-1}. \qquad (2.33)$$

The number of shifts in Equation 2.30 is determined by sequential testing after fitting a GARCH or GJR-GARCH model to the time series under consideration. Maximum likelihood estimation of the parameters in Equation 2.29 is carried out by maximizing the log-likelihood in parts as discussed in Song et al. (2005); see Amado and Teräsvirta (2012) for details. Evaluation of the estimated model is carried out by misspecification tests in Lundbergh and Teräsvirta (2012) that are generalized to this situation. Examples can be found in Amado and Teräsvirta (2012). Semi- and nonparametric alternatives to Equation 2.30 are considered in Van Bellegem (2012).

The hybrid volatility model of Osiewalski (2009) and Osiewalski and Pajor (2009) makes use of the decomposition (Eq. 2.29), but g_t is stochastic and defined as a first-order autoregressive stochastic volatility process:

$$\ln g_t = \psi \ln g_{t-1} + \eta_t, \qquad (2.34)$$

where $|\psi| < 1$, and $\{\eta_t\} \sim$ i.i.d. $\mathcal{N}(0, \sigma_\eta^2)$ and independent of $\{z_t\}$. The original version of the model is multivariate, and the conditional covariance matrix follows a BEKK-GARCH process. In this chapter, the focus is on the univariate special case. The authors distinguish between two different specifications. In the first one,

$$h_t = \alpha_0 + \alpha_1 \varepsilon_{t-1}^2 + \beta_1 h_{t-1},$$

so the conditional variance evolves independently of Equation 2.34. The second version bears resemblance to the model of Amado and Teräsvirta (2012) in that h_t is modeled as in Equation 2.33 using Equation 2.32. In that case, h_t is dependent on two independent sources of noise, z_t and η_t. Stationarity conditions for this model are probably not well known, and analytic expressions for unconditional moments of ε_t do not as yet seem to be available.

The treatment of these two models in Osiewalski (2009) and Osiewalski and Pajor (2009) is completely Bayesian, and the authors discuss appropriate algorithms for estimation. Multivariate applications to financial time series can be found in these two papers.

2.9 Conclusion

This chapter covers the most common nonlinear models of conditional heteroskedasticity. Parametric models in which the variance is decomposed into an unconditional component and a conditional component are also briefly considered. Many of these models can characterize various types of nonlinearity, such as asymmetric, or symmetric but nonlinear responses to shocks. Nevertheless, it seems that none of these models is widely used in practice. The practitioners often favor simpler models, of which, the GJR-GARCH model designed for describing asymmetric response to shocks constitutes an example. Increased computational power and improved numerical methods of optimization may be expected to change the situation in the future.

Acknowledgments

This research was supported by the Danish National Research Foundation. A part of the work was carried out when the author was visiting the Department of Economics of the European University Institute, Florence, whose kind hospitality is gratefully acknowledged. The author wishes to thank Christian Hafner for useful comments and Yukai Yang for technical assistance but retains responsibility for any errors or shortcomings in this work.

CHAPTER THREE

Mixture and Regime-Switching GARCH Models

MARKUS HAAS and MARC S. PAOLELLA

3.1 Introduction

The success of even the plain, standard GARCH model with a normally distributed innovations sequence for capturing the volatility of asset returns measured at weekly or daily (or higher) frequencies needs little introduction, along with the numerous subsequent generalizations that improved on the original simple recursion for the variance of the univariate equally spaced return series $\{r_t\}$. Most of these generalizations can be divided into two categories, the first being the parametric recursion, which dictates the variance of r_t as a function of lagged shocks, and the second being the distribution of the innovations $\{\eta_t\}$ in Equation 3.1 (which are assumed i.i.d.), this being without exception a distribution with thicker tails than the normal, or a distribution that can exhibit asymmetry.

In particular, and serving as a reference point for the regime-switching (RS) GARCH models discussed below, fully parametric models in this class assume that financial returns belong to a location-scale family of probability distributions

Handbook of Volatility Models and Their Applications, First Edition.
Edited by Luc Bauwens, Christian Hafner, and Sebastien Laurent.

of the form

$$r_t = \mu_t + \sigma_t \eta_t, \tag{3.1}$$

where η_t is i.i.d. with zero location and unit scale and may be characterized by additional shape parameters (such as the degrees of freedom parameter in the Student-t distribution). The classic GARCH(p, q) model allows the sequence of scale parameters $\{\sigma_t\}$ to be a function of past information as

$$\sigma_t^2 = \omega + \sum_{i=1}^{q} \alpha_i \varepsilon_{t-i}^2 + \sum_{j=1}^{p} \beta_j \sigma_{t-j}^2, \tag{3.2}$$

where $\varepsilon_t = r_t - \mu_t = \sigma_t \eta_t$, and the GARCH(1,1) with $p = q = 1$ is the most common formulation and will also set the stage for our discussion. A natural starting point, and indeed the assumption in the original ARCH and GARCH models, is to take η_t to be Gaussian, although this was soon realized to be inadequate and, in fact, of even more importance (with respect to Value-at-Risk, (VaR), and density prediction) than the functional form of the GARCH recursion (Mittnik and Paolella, 2000).

There are several other types of conditional heteroskedasticity models that do not yield Equation 3.2 as a special case, such as EVT-GARCH, filtered historical simulation, and CAViaR; see Kuester et al. (2006) for a review, original references, extensions, and comparisons of such models. While these models, particularly the first two, have been demonstrated to yield competitive VaR forecasts, they do not deliver an entire parametric density forecast for the future return. Having this density is of value for at least two reasons. First, interest might center not just on prediction of a particular tail quantile or tail moment (VaR and expected shortfall) but rather on the *entire* distribution. Indeed, density forecasting has grown enormously in importance in finance because of its added value in option pricing (Badescu et al., 2008) or when working with asymmetric loss functions and non-Gaussian data; see Tay and Wallis (2000) for a survey, Amisano and Giacomini (2007) for associated tests, and Paolella (2010) for a detailed illustration of its use in multivariate prediction of asset returns. The second reason for preferring models that deliver an entire (parametric) density forecast is that densities of individual assets can be analytically combined to yield the density of a *portfolio* of such assets, thus allowing portfolio construction using, for example, the mean and any desired risk measure that can be elicited from a parametric density, such as expected shortfall. This methodology is developed and demonstrated in Broda and Paolella (2009) and Broda et al. (2011).

A class of models that yields Equation (3.2) as a special case and delivers an entire parametric density forecast is that of RS-GARCH models, the subject of this chapter. As detailed in Section 3.2, these processes give rise to a conditional mixture distribution, where each of the mixture components is endowed with its own GARCH structure. One motivation for mixture GARCH models is that mixture distributions are rather flexible and have been found to fit the distribution of asset returns well; moreover, economic intuition can often be mapped to the model. To quote from Alexander's (2008, p. 163) recent book, "[t]he normal mixture GARCH model is like a powerful magnifying glass through which we can view the behavior of equity markets. It tells us a lot about the volatility characteristics of equity markets and allows one to characterize its behavior in two different market regimes." Another feature of these models not possible with the formulation in Equation 3.2 is *time-varying* skewness. A growing amount of literature indicates that not only are there asymmetries in the conditional return distribution but also that this asymmetry is time-varying; see, for example, Rockinger and Jondeau (2002) and Jondeau and Rockinger (2003) for empirical evidence, and Jondeau and Rockinger (2009) for an illustration of its importance for asset allocation. With more than one component, time-varying skewness is automatically accommodated in mixture GARCH models, that is, it is inherent in the model without requiring an explicit, ad hoc specification of a conditional skewness process appended to Equation 3.2. Relevant equations and graphical illustrations are given in Haas et al. (2004a).

This chapter is outlined as follows. In Section 3.2, various specifications of RS-GARCH models are discussed. Theoretical properties are considered in Section 3.3, and Section 3.4 discusses issues of estimation, regime inference, and volatility forecasting. An application to stock markets is provided in Section 3.5, and Section 3.6 concludes.

3.2 Regime-Switching GARCH Models for Asset Returns

The idea of the RS approach to modeling asset returns is that the distribution of returns depends on a (typically unobserved) state (or *regime*) of the market. For example, both the level and the time series properties of expected returns and variances may be different in bull and bear markets. The current section discusses various popular specifications of such models.

3.2.1 THE REGIME-SWITCHING FRAMEWORK

Assume that there are k different market regimes and that if the market is in regime j at time t, the conditional mean and variance of the return, r_t, are given by μ_{jt} and σ_{jt}^2, respectively, where $j = 1, \dots, k$. Generalizing Equation 3.1, an RS-GARCH model can be written as

$$r_t = \mu_{\Delta_t,t} + \sigma_{\Delta_t,t}\eta_t, \tag{3.3}$$

where $\Delta_t \in \{1, \dots, k\}$ is a variable indicating the market regime at time t, and $\{\eta_t\}$ is an i.i.d. sequence with zero mean and unit variance. In many applications, the distribution of η_t is taken to be Gaussian, so that the conditional distribution of r_t, based on the information that we are in regime j at time t, is likewise normal with mean μ_{jt} and variance σ_{jt}^2, that is,

$$f_{t-1}(r_t|\Delta_t = j) = \phi(r_t; \mu_j, \sigma_j^2) := \frac{1}{\sqrt{2\pi}\sigma_{jt}} \exp\left\{-\frac{(r_t - \mu_{jt})^2}{2\sigma_{jt}^2}\right\}, \tag{3.4}$$

where f_t denotes a conditional density based on the return history up to time t, that is, $\{r_s : s \leq t\}$.

Suppose that the conditional probability for the market being in regime j at time t is π_{jt}, that is,

$$p_{t-1}(\Delta_t = j) = \pi_{jt}, \quad j = 1, \ldots, k. \tag{3.5}$$

Then, if Equation 3.4 is adopted, the conditional distribution of r_t is a k-component *finite normal mixture distribution*, with density

$$f_{t-1}(r_t) = \sum_{j=1}^{k} \pi_{jt}\phi(r_t; \mu_{jt}, \sigma_{jt}^2), \tag{3.6}$$

where π_{jt} are the (conditional) *mixing weights*, and $\phi(r_t; \mu_{jt}, \sigma_{jt}^2)$ are the *component densities*, with *component means* μ_{jt} and *component variances* σ_{jt}^2, $j = 1, \ldots, k$; see Frühwirth-Schnatter (2006) for a monograph on mixture models. The conditional moments of Equation 3.6 can be derived from those of the component densities; for example, we have

$$\mathbb{E}_{t-1}(r_t) = \sum_{j=1}^{k} \pi_{jt}\mu_{jt}, \quad \text{and} \quad \mathbb{V}_{t-1}(r_t) = \sum_{j=1}^{k} \pi_{jt}(\sigma_{jt}^2 + \mu_{jt}^2) - \left(\sum_{j=1}^{k} \pi_{jt}\mu_{jt}\right)^2 \tag{3.7}$$

for the conditional mean and variance, respectively.

The class of finite normal mixture distributions (Eq. 3.6) is known to exhibit considerable flexibility with respect to skewness and excess kurtosis, which are important features of financial return data (cf. Rydén et al. 1998; Timmermann 2000; Haas and Mittnik 2009). Moreover, and in contrast to many other flexible distributions used for that purpose, normal mixtures often provide an economically plausible disaggregation of the stochastic mechanism generating returns, such as the distinction between bull and bear market dynamics referred to at the beginning of this section. See, for example, Haas et al. (2004a), Alexander and Lazar (2006), and Dean and Faff (2008) for further discussion and references relating to these issues.

We review several approaches to modeling the dynamics of the conditional component variances as well as the mixing weights in Equation 3.6, whereas conditional mean dynamics will not be treated in detail since the structure in the conditional mean of asset returns tends to be weak; see Francq and Zakoïan (2001) and Lange and Rahbek (2009) for a discussion of RS ARMA models. However, as long as the innovation η_t in Equation 3.3 has a symmetric distribution, allowing for different regime means is necessary to produce a skewed conditional density.

3.2.2 MODELING THE MIXING WEIGHTS

A particularly popular approach to modeling the dynamics of market regimes is the Markov-switching (MS) technique, which has become very popular in empirical finance since Hamilton (1989) and Turner et al. (1989). It formalizes the intuition that market regimes may be persistent; for example, if we are in a bull market currently, then the probability of being in a bull market in the next period will be larger than that if the current regime were a bear market.

It is assumed that the regime process $\{\Delta_t\}$ follows a Markov chain with finite state space $S = \{1, \ldots, k\}$ and $k \times k$ transition matrix $\boldsymbol{P}$,

$$\boldsymbol{P} = \begin{pmatrix} p_{11} & \cdots & p_{k1} \\ \vdots & \cdots & \vdots \\ p_{1k} & \cdots & p_{kk} \end{pmatrix}, \tag{3.8}$$

where the transition probabilities $p_{ij} = p(\Delta_t = j | \Delta_{t-1} = i)$, $i, j = 1, \ldots, k$. Let $\boldsymbol{\pi}_t = (\pi_{1t}, \ldots, \pi_{kt})'$ denote the distribution of the Markov chain at time t. It follows from the laws of probability that for $j = 1, \ldots, k$,

$$\pi_{j,t+1} = p(\Delta_{t+1} = j) = \sum_{i=1}^{k} p(\Delta_t = i) p(\Delta_{t+1} = j | \Delta_t = i) = \sum_{i=1}^{k} \pi_{it} p_{ij}, \tag{3.9}$$

or in matrix form, and then by iteration,

$$\boldsymbol{\pi}_{t+1} = \boldsymbol{P}\boldsymbol{\pi}_t, \quad \boldsymbol{\pi}_{t+\tau} = \boldsymbol{P}^{\tau}\boldsymbol{\pi}_t, \quad \tau \geq 1, \tag{3.10}$$

so that the elements of $\boldsymbol{P}^{\tau}$ are the $\tau-$step transition probabilities $p(\Delta_{t+\tau} = j | \Delta_t = i)$, $i, j = 1, \ldots, k$. Moreover, under general conditions (namely, assuming that $\boldsymbol{P}$ is irreducible and aperiodic; see, for example, Ch. 22 in Hamilton (1994) for a more detailed discussion), there exists a *stationary* or *long-run* distribution $\boldsymbol{\pi} = (\pi_1, \ldots, \pi_k)'$ with the property that, independently of $\boldsymbol{\pi}_t$,

$$\boldsymbol{\pi} = P\boldsymbol{\pi} = \lim_{\tau \to \infty} \boldsymbol{P}^{\tau}\boldsymbol{\pi}_t. \tag{3.11}$$

If regimes are persistent, this will be reflected in rather large diagonal elements of $\boldsymbol{P}$, the "staying probabilities", relative to the nondiagonal elements. The degree of regime persistence can be measured by the magnitude of the second largest eigenvalue of the transition matrix $\boldsymbol{P}$ (the largest eigenvalue is always equal to one). This can be seen by writing $\boldsymbol{P}^{\tau} = \boldsymbol{P}_{\infty} + \boldsymbol{R}^{\tau}$, $\tau \geq 1$, where $\boldsymbol{P}_{\infty} = \lim_{\tau \to \infty} \boldsymbol{P}^{\tau} = \boldsymbol{\pi} \boldsymbol{1}_k' = (\boldsymbol{\pi}, \ldots, \boldsymbol{\pi})$, and $\boldsymbol{R} = \boldsymbol{P} - \boldsymbol{P}_{\infty}$, so that $\boldsymbol{\pi}_{t+\tau} =$

$\boldsymbol{\pi} + \boldsymbol{R}^{\tau}(\boldsymbol{\pi}_t - \boldsymbol{\pi})$.[1] Matrix $\boldsymbol{R}$ has the same eigenvalues as $\boldsymbol{P}$ except the eigenvalue 1, which becomes zero, and so the rate of convergence to the unconditional distribution is governed by the largest (second largest) eigenvalue of $\boldsymbol{Q}(\boldsymbol{P})$ (cf. Poskitt and Chung, 1996). For some concreteness, in the practically important case of two regimes, Equation 3.9 becomes, on repeated substitution,

$$\begin{aligned}
\pi_{1,t+\tau} &= p_{11}\pi_{1,t+\tau-1} + p_{21}\pi_{2,t+\tau-1} = p_{11}\pi_{1,t+\tau-1} + (1-p_{22})(1-\pi_{1,t+\tau-1}) \\
&= (p_{11}+p_{22}-1)\pi_{1,t+\tau-1} + (1-p_{22}) \\
&= (p_{11}+p_{22}-1)^{\tau}\pi_{1t} + (1-p_{22})\sum_{i=0}^{\tau-1}(p_{11}+p_{22}-1)^{i} \\
&= \pi_1 + \delta^{\tau}(\pi_{1t}-\pi_1),
\end{aligned}$$

where $\delta := p_{11} + p_{22} - 1$ measures the persistence of the regimes, and $\pi_1 = (1 - p_{22})/(2 - p_{11} - p_{22})$. Another quantity that is frequently reported is the expected regime duration; it follows from the properties of the geometric distribution that, once we are in regime j, we expect it to last for $\sum_{d=1}^{\infty} dp_{jj}^{d-1}(1-p_{jj}) = (1-p_{jj})^{-1}$ periods.

When $\boldsymbol{P} = \boldsymbol{P}_{\infty} = (\boldsymbol{\pi}, \ldots, \boldsymbol{\pi})$, there is no persistence in $\{\Delta_t\}$ and we have an i.i.d. mixture model with constant weights, i.e., $\pi_{jt} = \pi_j$ for all $t, j = 1, \ldots, k$. When coupled with GARCH structure (Eq. 3.21) for the component-specific volatility dynamics (to be discussed in Section 3.2.3) and Gaussian innovations, this gives rise to the mixed normal (MN) GARCH process proposed by Alexander and Lazar (2006) and Haas et al. (2004a). In this specification, the conditional mean is typically decomposed into an overall mean component c_t (which may be driven by a standard ARMA model) and regime-specific (time-invariant) components $\mu_j, j = 1, \ldots, k$, that is,

$$r_t = c_t + \varepsilon_t, \tag{3.12}$$

where the error term ε_t is conditionally mixed normal as in Equation 3.6 with

$$\mu_k = -\sum_{j=1}^{k}(\pi_j/\pi_k)\mu_j \tag{3.13}$$

to ensure a zero mean of ε_t. Such a convenient decomposition is not feasible if the (conditional) mixing weights are time-varying. It is apparent from Equation 3.7 that in this case ε_t in Equation 3.12 would display conditional mean dynamics, which would hinder its interpretation as an unexpected shock. Moreover, this autocorrelation would be impossible to disentangle from the asymmetries that are likewise induced by the regime-specific means, which may be undesirable

[1] This follows since $\boldsymbol{P}_{\infty}$ is idempotent, $\boldsymbol{P}_{\infty}\boldsymbol{P} = \boldsymbol{P}\boldsymbol{P}_{\infty} = \boldsymbol{P}_{\infty}$, and it can checked by induction that $\boldsymbol{R}^{\tau} = (\boldsymbol{P} - \boldsymbol{P}_{\infty})^{\tau} = \boldsymbol{P}^{\tau} - \boldsymbol{P}_{\infty}$ (cf. Poskitt and Chung, 1996).

in certain applications. An alternative to generate skewness in case of persistent regimes is to set all the regime-specific means to zero and use skewed regime densities, as in Geweke and Amisano (2011) and Haas (2010b); see also the discussion in Haas et al. (2004b).

A further possibility to model the dynamics of the mixing weights is to make them depend on a set of predetermined variables, which Lange and Rahbek (2009) term "observation switching." For example, in the two-component logistic mixture model suggested by Wong and Li (2001a) and extended to mixture GARCH processes by Cheng et al. (2009), the weight of the first component is determined according to

$$\pi_t = \frac{\exp\{\boldsymbol{\gamma}'\boldsymbol{x}_t\}}{1+\exp\{\boldsymbol{\gamma}'\boldsymbol{x}_t\}}, \tag{3.14}$$

where $\boldsymbol{\gamma} = (\gamma_0, \gamma_1, \ldots, \gamma_{p-1})'$ is a vector of parameters and $\boldsymbol{x}_t$ is a vector of p predetermined variables, including perhaps a constant. For example, Bauwens et al. (2006) use $\boldsymbol{x}_t = (1, \varepsilon_{t-1}^2)'$, so that, with $\gamma_1 > 0$, $\pi_t \to 1$ as ε_{t-1}^2 tends to infinity. If the first component has lower volatility, this means that "large shocks have the effect of 'relieving pressure' by reducing the probability of a large shock in the next period." Other examples include the modeling of exchange rate behavior in target zones, where a jump component reflects the possibility of realignments and the probability of a jump depends on interest differentials and, possibly, further explanatory variables incorporating market expectations (Bekaert and Gray, 1998; Neely, 1999; Haas et al., 2006), or of a nonlinear relation between hedge fund returns and market risk factors (Tashman and Frey, 2009; Tashman, 2010). These models also bear some similarities to the class of smooth transition GARCH (STGARCH) models (cf. Teräsvirta, 2009; Medeiros and Veiga, 2009) and the component GARCH specification of Bauwens and Storti (2009). The difference is that, in the latter models, the weighting applies to the volatility parameters directly (as compared to the densities as in Equation 3.6), so that the conditional distribution is not a mixture.

Clearly, Equation 3.14 can be generalized to more than two components. For example, Haas et al. (2006) consider a specification of the form

$$\pi_{jt} = \frac{\theta_{jt}}{1+\sum_{i=1}^{k-1}\theta_{it}}, \quad j = 1, \ldots, k-1, \quad \pi_{kt} = 1 - \sum_{j=1}^{k-1}\pi_{jt}, \tag{3.15}$$

where, mimicking the structure of an asymmetric GARCH-type model,

$$\theta_{jt} = \exp\left(\gamma_{0j} + \sum_{i=1}^{u}\gamma_{ij}\varepsilon_{t-i} + \sum_{i=1}^{v}\kappa_{ij}\pi_{j,t-i} + \sum_{i=1}^{w}\delta_{ij}\left|\varepsilon_{t-i}\right|^{d}\right), \tag{3.16}$$

for $j = 1, \ldots, k-1$. In their particular application, Haas et al. (2006) set $v = w = 0$ and $u = 1$, so that, with $k = 2$ components, with the first component exhibiting lower volatility, $\gamma_{11} > 0$ implies a negative relation between the lagged shock and current volatility, that is, the "leverage effect." The sigmoidal weight function in this context is motivated by the shape received from fitting the model with a nonparametric weight function as follows. Let $m > 0$ be the number of intervals, and let $\boldsymbol{\theta} = (\theta_1, \ldots, \theta_{m-1})$ denote the sorted vector of interval bounds, where $\theta_i < \theta_{i+1}$. Then, the weight function is given by

$$\pi_{1t}(\varepsilon_{t-1}) = \begin{cases} b_1, & \text{if } \varepsilon_{t-1} < \theta_1, \\ b_2, & \text{if } \theta_1 \leq \varepsilon_{t-1} < \theta_2, \\ b_3, & \text{if } \theta_2 \leq \varepsilon_{t-1} < \theta_3, \\ & \vdots \\ b_{m-1}, & \text{if } \theta_{m-2} \leq \varepsilon_{t-1} < \theta_{m-1}, \\ b_m, & \text{if } \varepsilon_{t-1} \geq \theta_{m-1}, \end{cases} \tag{3.17}$$

where $\pi_{2t}(\varepsilon_{t-1}) = 1 - \pi_{1t}$ and $b_i \in (0, 1)$, $i = 1, \ldots, m$. For choosing the intervals in Equation 3.17, an equally spaced grid with $m = 10$ was used.

Figure 3.1a shows the estimated nonparametric weight function (Eq. 3.17) when applied to the daily NASDAQ returns from 2001 to 2011 and coupled with a mixture GARCH structure of the form (Eq. 3.21). Panel b shows the estimated weight function based on Equations 3.15 and 3.16 with $v = w = 0$, $u = 1$, and $k = 2$, that is, $\pi_{1t} = (1 + \exp\{-\gamma_0 - \gamma_1\varepsilon_{t-1}\})^{-1}$. Since the first mixture component represents the low-volatility regime, Figure 3.1 reveals that negative and positive shocks have an asymmetric impact on future volatility in the sense that negative news surprises increase volatility more than positive news surprises.

3.2.3 REGIME-SWITCHING GARCH SPECIFICATIONS

There exist different specifications of RS-GARCH models. These have in common that the coefficients of the GARCH equation and thus the conditional variance at time t depend on the current regime Δ_t, and they differ in the way the lagged variance term in the regime-specific GARCH recursions is specified. In our discussion, we concentrate on the volatility specification and ignore regime-specific mean terms.

In the first version, as considered by Cai (1994) and Hamilton and Susmel (1994), this term is taken to be the lagged variance conditional on the previous regime, that is, the time series of shocks, $\{\varepsilon_t\}$, is modeled as

$$\varepsilon_t = \sigma_{\Delta_t,t}\eta_t, \tag{3.18}$$

where the regime-specific conditional variances are

$$\sigma_{jt}^2 = \omega_j + \alpha_j\varepsilon_{t-1}^2 + \beta_j\sigma_{\Delta_{t-1},t-1}^2, \quad \omega_j > 0, \quad \alpha_j, \beta_j \geq 0 \quad j = 1, \ldots, k. \tag{3.19}$$

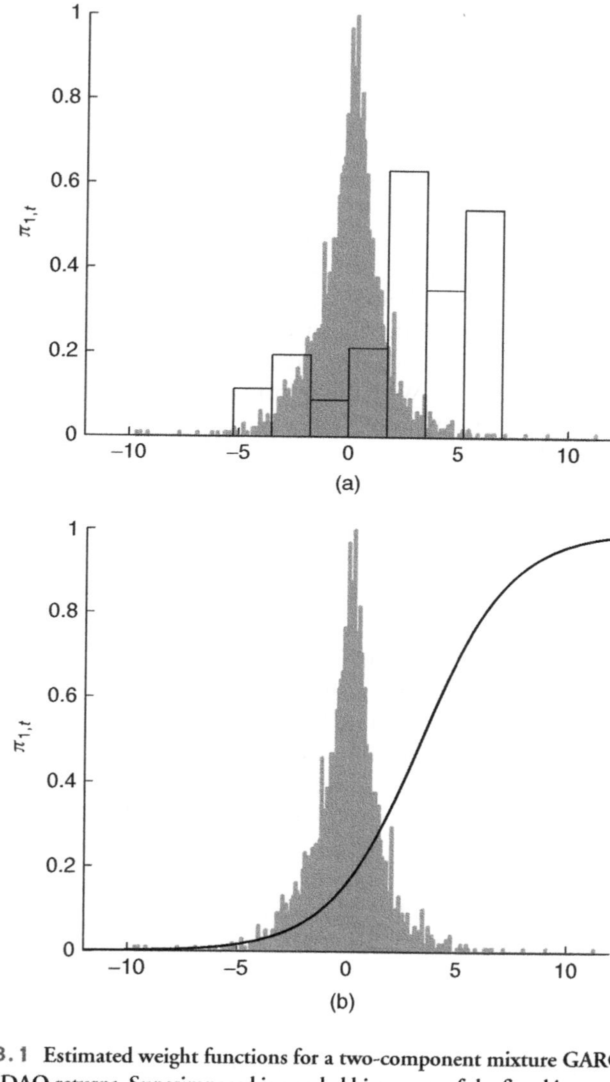

FIGURE 3.1 Estimated weight functions for a two-component mixture GARCH model for the daily NASDAQ returns. Superimposed is a scaled histogram of the fitted innovations. (a) The nonparametric mixing weights based on Equation 3.17 with $m = 10$ (some of estimated weights are essentially zero). (b) The sigmoidal mixing weights based on Equations 3.15 and 3.16 with $v = w = 0$, $u = 1$, and $k = 2$, that is, $\pi_{1t} = (1 + \exp\{-\gamma_0 - \gamma_1 \varepsilon_{t-1}\})^{-1}$.

However, Cai (1994) and Hamilton and Susmel (1994) observed that maximum likelihood (ML) estimation of this specification is not feasible because of the path dependence in Equation 3.19, and thus they employed MS-ARCH rather than MS-GARCH. To see the problem, suppose we want to calculate the likelihood function for model Equation 3.19. We face the problem that Δ_{t-1} and therefore $\sigma^2_{\Delta_{t-1},t-1}$ in Equation 3.19 is not observable, and so we have to integrate it out. However, $\sigma^2_{\Delta_{t-1},t-1}$ likewise depends on the previous regime, Δ_{t-2}, so that in the end, the conditional variance at time t depends on the entire regime history up to time t. Thus, the evaluation of the likelihood for a sample of T observations requires the integration over all k^T possible regime paths, rendering its calculation infeasible. More recently, Francq and Zakoïan (2008) considered GMM estimation, and Bauwens et al. (2010) and Henneke et al. (2011) showed how an MS-GARCH model built on (3.19) can be estimated via Bayesian Markov chain Monte Carlo (MCMC) methods. Pure MS-ARCH processes are also considered in Wong and Li (2001b), Kaufmann and Frühwirth-Schnatter (2002), and Kaufmann and Scheicher (2006).

To circumvent the path dependence, Gray (1996) replaces $\sigma^2_{\Delta_{t-1},t-1}$ in Equation 3.19 with the conditional variance of ε_{t-1}, given only the observable information up to time $t-2$. With this information, the conditional distribution of ε_{t-1} is a k-component mixture with variance (cf. Equation 3.7; abstaining from regime-specific means)

$$h_{t-1} := \mathbb{V}_{t-2}(\varepsilon_{t-1}) = \sum_{j=1}^{k} p_{t-2}(\Delta_{t-1} = j)\sigma^2_{j,t-1}, \tag{3.20}$$

where $p_{t-2}(\Delta_{t-1} = j)$, $j = 1, \ldots, k$, are the conditional regime probabilities (Eq. 3.5) implied by the model for the regime process; see Section 3.4 for their computation under MS dynamics. Quantity (Eq. 3.20) is then used instead of $\sigma^2_{\Delta_{t-1},t-1}$ in the regime-specific GARCH equations (3.19), which makes the calculation of the likelihood function straightforward by means of the methods described in Section 3.4. Similar solutions have also been proposed by Dueker (1997) and Klaassen (2002). Ane and Ureche-Rangau (2006) extend the model to allow for asymmetric volatility dynamics, and Chen and Hung (2010) consider its use in option pricing.

A third approach to RS-GARCH models, proposed by Haas et al. (2004a,b), can be viewed as a direct generalization of the single-regime GARCH model (Eq. 3.2). In this specification, each regime-specific conditional variance depends only on its own lag, that is,

$$\sigma^2_{jt} = \omega_j + \alpha_j\varepsilon^2_{t-1} + \beta_j\sigma^2_{j,t-1}, \quad \omega_j > 0, \quad \alpha_j, \beta_j \geq 0 \quad j = 1, \ldots, k. \tag{3.21}$$

To see the analogy between Equations 3.2 and 3.21, recall that a GARCH(1,1) process $\sigma^2_t = \omega + \alpha\varepsilon^2_{t-1} + \beta\sigma^2_{t-1}$ with $\beta < 1$ can be written as ARCH(∞),

$$\sigma^2_t = \frac{\omega}{1-\beta} + \alpha\sum_{i=1}^{\infty}\beta^{i-1}\varepsilon^2_{t-i}, \tag{3.22}$$

which shows that α is the reaction parameter reflecting the magnitude of a unit shock's immediate impact on the next period's variance, whereas β measures the memory in the volatility process, and the total impact of a unit shock on future variances is $\alpha/(1-\beta)$. Adopting Equation 3.21 implies a representation (3.22) for each regime, so that this specification allows a clear-cut interpretation of the regime-specific volatility processes; namely, the parameters α_j and β_j measure the immediate responsiveness to a shock and the memory of the volatility process in regime j, respectively. To rule out explosive volatility processes, an obvious requirement is therefore

$$\beta_j < 1, \quad j = 1, \ldots, k, \tag{3.23}$$

which is not required in Equations 3.19 and 3.20. The likelihood function of Equation 3.21 can likewise be evaluated by the methods in Section 3.4. Bayesian estimation of specification (Eq. 3.21) has been developed by Bauwens and Rombouts (2007b) and Ardia (2009), with the latter extending the model to allow for asymmetric volatility dynamics as well as Student-t innovations; see also Ausin and Galeano (2007), Giannikis et al. (2008), and Wu and Lee (2007). Option pricing with i.i.d. normal mixture GARCH processes of the form (Eq. 3.21) is considered in Badescu et al. (2008) and Rombouts and Stentoft (2009, 2010).

We may note that Haas et al. (2004a) also considered a slightly more general version of Equation 3.21 where the components are allowed to communicate directly. To illustrate, with two components, the general GARCH(1,1) specification would read

$$\begin{pmatrix} \sigma_{1t}^2 \\ \sigma_{2t}^2 \end{pmatrix} = \begin{pmatrix} \omega_1 \\ \omega_2 \end{pmatrix} + \begin{pmatrix} \alpha_1 \\ \alpha_2 \end{pmatrix} \varepsilon_{t-1}^2 + \begin{pmatrix} \beta_{11} & \beta_{12} \\ \beta_{21} & \beta_{22} \end{pmatrix} \begin{pmatrix} \sigma_{1,t-1}^2 \\ \sigma_{2,t-1}^2 \end{pmatrix}. \tag{3.24}$$

Process (Eq. 3.21) is nested in Equation 3.24 when the coefficient matrix of the lagged variances in Equation 3.24 is diagonal. The more general nondiagonal structure has been found by Haas et al. (2004a) not to improve the fit, and it also requires some restrictions for identification. For example, the early MN-GARCH model of Vlaar and Palm (1993), where $\sigma_{1t}^2 = \omega_1 + \alpha_1\varepsilon_{t-1}^2 + \beta_{11}\sigma_{1,t-1}^2$, and $\sigma_{2t}^2 = \sigma_{1t}^2 + \delta^2$, can be represented by Equation 3.24 *either* by setting $\omega_2 = \omega_1 + \delta^2$, $\alpha_2 = \alpha_1$, $\beta_{21} = \beta_{11}$, and $\beta_{12} = \beta_{22} = 0$, *or* by setting $\omega_2 = \omega_1 + \delta^2(1 - \beta_{11})$, $\alpha_2 = \alpha_1$, $\beta_{22} = \beta_{11}$, and $\beta_{12} = \beta_{21} = 0$, where the latter is a diagonal specification.

3.3 Stationarity and Moment Structure

To better understand the nature of multi-regime GARCH models as compared to their single-regime counterparts, we discuss some of their dynamic properties, focussing on specification (Eq. 3.21), which is relatively well understood, along with MS dynamics for the regime process. To do so, we write Equation 3.21 in vector form, that is,

$$X_t = \omega + C_{\Delta_{t-1},t-1}X_{t-1}, \tag{3.25}$$

where $X_t = (\sigma_{1t}^2, \ldots, \sigma_{kt}^2, \varepsilon_{t-1}^2)'$, $C_{\Delta_t,t} = \alpha e'_{\Delta_t}\eta_t^2 + \beta$, e_j is the jth unit vector in $\mathbb{R}^{k+1}, j = 1, \ldots, k+1$, and

$$\omega = \begin{pmatrix} \omega_1 \\ \vdots \\ \omega_k \\ 0 \end{pmatrix}, \quad \alpha = \begin{pmatrix} \alpha_1 \\ \vdots \\ \alpha_k \\ 1 \end{pmatrix}, \quad \beta = \begin{pmatrix} \beta_1 & \cdots & 0 & 0 \\ \vdots & \ddots & \vdots & \vdots \\ 0 & \cdots & \beta_k & 0 \\ 0 & \cdots & 0 & 0 \end{pmatrix}. \tag{3.26}$$

For any function $f : S \mapsto M_{n\times n'}(\mathbb{R})$, where $M_{n\times n'}(\mathbb{R})$ is the space of real $n \times n'$ matrices, and S is the state space of $\{\Delta_t\}$, define the matrix

$$\mathbb{P}_f^{(\tau)} = \begin{pmatrix} p_{11}^{(\tau)} f(1) & \cdots & p_{k1}^{(\tau)} f(1) \\ \vdots & \cdots & \vdots \\ p_{1k}^{(\tau)} f(k) & \cdots & p_{kk}^{(\tau)} f(k) \end{pmatrix}. \tag{3.27}$$

When $\tau = 1$, we drop the superscript and define $\mathbb{P}_f = \mathbb{P}_f^{(1)}$.

The following two basic results from Francq and Zakoïan (2005) will be useful in discussing the properties of MS-GARCH processes.

LEMMA 3.1 (Francq and Zakoïan, 2005, Lemma 1)

Let $f : S \mapsto M_{n\times n}(\mathbb{R})$, and $g : S \mapsto M_{n\times n'}(\mathbb{R})$. Suppose that π_{t-h} is given, that is, the regime probabilities at time $t-h$. Then, for $h > \tau > 0$,

$$\begin{aligned} &\mathbb{E}[f(\Delta_t)f(\Delta_{t-1})\cdots f(\Delta_{t-\tau+1})g(\Delta_{t-\tau})|\pi_{t-h}] \\ &\qquad = (\mathbf{1}'_k \otimes I_n)\mathbb{P}_f^\tau \mathbb{P}_g^{(h-\tau)}(\pi_{t-h} \otimes I_{n'}), \end{aligned} \tag{3.28}$$

where $\mathbf{1}_k$ is a k-dimensional column of ones.

If g does not depend on the prevailing regime, that is, $g := g(1) = \cdots = g(k)$, $\mathbb{P}_g^{(h-\tau)} = P^{h-\tau} \otimes g$, and the right-hand side of Equation 3.28 becomes

$$(\mathbf{1}'_k \otimes I_n)\mathbb{P}_f^\tau (P^{h-\tau} \otimes g)(\pi_{t-h} \otimes I_{n'}) = (\mathbf{1}'_k \otimes I_n)\mathbb{P}_f^\tau (\pi_{t-\tau} \otimes g). \tag{3.29}$$

LEMMA 3.2 (Francq and Zakoïan, 2005, Lemma 3)

For $\ell \geq 1$, if the variable $Y_{t-\ell}$ belongs to the information set generated by $\Psi_{t-\ell} := \{\varepsilon_s : s \leq t-\ell\}$, then

$$\pi_j \mathbb{E}(Y_{t-\ell}|\Delta_t = j) = \sum_{i=1}^{k} \pi_i p_{ij}^{(\ell)} \mathbb{E}(Y_{t-\ell}|\Delta_{t-\ell} = i),$$

where the $p_{ij}^{(\ell)} := p(\Delta_t = j|\Delta_{t-\ell} = i)$, $i, j = 1, \ldots, k$, *denote the* ℓ*−step transition probabilities, as given by the elements of* P^ℓ.

To see the logic behind Lemma 3.2, note that

$$\mathbb{E}(Y_{t-\ell}|\Delta_t = j) = \sum_{i=1}^{k} p(\Delta_{t-\ell} = i|\Delta_t = j)\mathbb{E}(Y_{t-\ell}|\Delta_{t-\ell} = i \cap \Delta_t = j).$$

Then, since $\pi_j p(\Delta_{t-\ell} = i|\Delta_t = j) = \pi_i p(\Delta_t = j|\Delta_{t-\ell} = i) = \pi_i p_{ij}^{(\ell)}$, Lemma 3.2 essentially states the intuitive result that "given the regime at time t, the expectation of any variable determined by the information up to time t does not depend on the future regime history," that is, $\mathbb{E}(Y_{t-\ell}|\Delta_{t-\ell} = i \cap \Delta_t = j) = \mathbb{E}(Y_{t-\ell}|\Delta_{t-\ell} = i)$.

3.3.1 STATIONARITY

To discuss the stationarity properties of the MS-GARCH process, let

$$C_{mm}(j) = \mathbb{E}(C_{jt}^{\otimes m}), \quad j = 1, \ldots, k, \quad m \in \mathbb{N}, \tag{3.30}$$

where $A^{\otimes m}$ denotes the mth Kronecker power of A,[2] and let $\rho(A)$ denote the spectral radius of a square matrix A, that is,

$$\rho(A) = \max\{|z| : \text{z is an eigenvalue of A}\}.$$

The conditions for the existence of a stationary solution of Equation 3.25 and the existence of moments are given by the following result (see also Haas et al., 2004b, for the second and fourth moment conditions).

THEOREM 3.1 (Liu, 2006, Corollary 1 and Theorem 2)

If $\rho(\mathbb{P}_{C_{mm}}) < 1$, *where* $\mathbb{P}_{C_{mm}}$ *is defined via Equations 3.27 and 3.30, then the MS-GARCH(*k*) process defined by Equations 3.18 and 3.21 has a unique strictly stationary solution with finite* $(2m)$*th moment.*

To develop some intuition for the result, assume that second moments are finite, so that we can write, by Lemma 3.2 and representation (Eq. 3.25),

$$\pi_j\mathbb{E}(X_t|\Delta_{t-1} = j) = \pi_j\omega + \sum_{i=1}^{k} p_{ij}C_{11}(j)\pi_i\mathbb{E}(X_{t-1}|\Delta_{t-2} = i), \quad j = 1, \ldots, k. \tag{3.31}$$

[2]For example, we have $C_{11}(j) = \alpha e_j' + \beta$, and $C_{22}(j) = \kappa_4(\alpha \otimes \alpha)(e_j' \otimes e_j') + (\alpha e_j') \otimes \beta + \beta \otimes (\alpha e_j') + \beta \otimes \beta$.

Now define the $k(k+1) \times 1$ vector Q as

$$Q = (\pi_1 \mathbb{E}(X_t|\Delta_{t-1} = 1)', \ldots, \pi_k \mathbb{E}(X_t|\Delta_{t-1} = k)')',$$

so that

$$Q = \pi \otimes \omega + \mathbb{P}_{C_{11}} Q. \tag{3.32}$$

Since all the parameters involved in Equation 3.32 are nonnegative, it follows that there is a nonnegative solution Q if and only if $\rho(\mathbb{P}_{C_{11}}) < 1$, so that the condition is clearly necessary (cf. Murata, 1977, pp. 53, 109). In this case, we can calculate the unconditional variance as

$$\begin{aligned}\mathbb{E}(\varepsilon_t^2) &= \sum_{j=1}^{k} \pi_j \mathbb{E}(\varepsilon_t^2|\Delta_t = j) = (\mathbf{1}_k \otimes e_{k+1})' Q \\ &= (\mathbf{1}_k \otimes e_{k+1})'(I_{k(k+1)} - \mathbb{P}_{C_{11}})^{-1}(\pi \otimes \omega).\end{aligned} \tag{3.33}$$

Matrices with the structure such as those in Theorem 3.1 appear rather naturally in time series models with MS dynamics, see, for example, Yao and Attali (2000) and Francq and Zakoïan (2001) for switching autoregressions. For MS-GARCH models, Liu (2007) generalizes Theorem 3.1 to asymmetric power GARCH processes à la Ding et al. (1993). Francq et al. (2001), Francq and Zakoïan (2005), and Bauwens et al. (2010) obtain results for processes of the form (Eq. 3.19), whereas Abramson and Cohen (2007) also consider Klaassen's (2002) specification similar to Equation 3.20. Note that Theorem 3.1 provides a *sufficient* condition for strict stationarity. Liu (2006, Theorem 3) also provides a weaker necessary and sufficient condition for strict stationarity which is, however, less practical. An implication of his result is that the MS-IGARCH process with $\rho(\mathbb{P}_{C_{11}}) = 1$ is strictly stationary with infinite variance (Liu, 2006, Theorem 4), which parallels Nelson's (1990) result for the IGARCH(1,1), see also Liu (2009a).

Theorem 3.1 implies that within-regime stationarity is not necessary for global stationarity, that is, "the process can occasionally behave in a nonstationary manner although being stationary in the long run" (Yang, 2000), provided that the nonstationary regimes do not occur too often in a row, a condition that depends both on the long-run probabilities as well as the "staying probabilities" of the regimes. This may be interpreted in the sense that markets are stable most of the time, but, occasionally, subject to severe, short-lived fluctuations that drive the system beyond the stability threshold.

For example, in the i.i.d. mixture GARCH model, the covariance stationarity condition $\rho(\mathbb{P}_{C_{11}}) < 1$ turns out to be equivalent to $\sum_j \pi_j \alpha_j/(1 - \beta_j) < 1$ (Haas et al., 2004a; Alexander and Lazar, 2006), which in view of Equation 3.22 can be interpreted straightforwardly in the sense that the *average* total impact of a unit shock on all the component variances is below unity. The unconditional variance of ε_t is then (with component-specific means satisfying Equation 3.13)

$$\mathbb{E}(\varepsilon_t^2) = \frac{\sum_j \pi_j(\omega_j/(1-\beta_j)+\mu_j^2)}{1-\sum_j \pi_j\alpha_j/(1-\beta_j)} = \frac{\sum_j \pi_j(\omega_j/(1-\beta_j)+\mu_j^2)}{\sum_j \pi_j(1-\alpha_j-\beta_j)/(1-\beta_j)}. \quad (3.34)$$

To illustrate the role of the regimes' persistence, we consider a restricted two-regime model, allowing for explicit treatment of the stationarity conditions and characterization of the moments. This model imposes the restriction $\beta_1 = \beta_2 \stackrel{\text{def}}{=} \beta$, which amounts to specifying the second regime's variance as a linear function of the first regime, that is, $\sigma_{2t}^2 = a + b\sigma_{1t}^2$, thus nesting the MN-GARCH specifications of Vlaar and Palm (1993) and Bai et al. (2003) for $b = 1$ and $a = 0$, respectively. To see this, consider the ARCH(∞) representation of $\sigma_{2t}^2 = \omega_2 + \alpha_2\varepsilon_{t-1}^2 + \beta\sigma_{2,t-1}^2$,

$$\begin{aligned}\sigma_{2t}^2 &= \frac{\omega_2}{1-\beta} + \alpha_2\sum_{i=1}^{\infty}\beta^{i-1}\varepsilon_{t-i}^2 = a + b\left\{\frac{\omega_1}{1-\beta} + \alpha_1\sum_{i=1}^{\infty}\beta^{i-1}\varepsilon_{t-i}^2\right\} \\ &= a + b\sigma_{1t}^2, \end{aligned} \quad (3.35)$$

where $a = (\omega_2 - \omega_1\alpha_2/\alpha_1)/(1-\beta)$, and $b = \alpha_2/\alpha_1$. As Equation 3.35 implies that "the same GARCH effect is present in [both] variances" (Vlaar and Palm, 1993), we can describe the dynamics of the process by the evolution of σ_{1t}^2 alone. To do so, we introduce an indicator variable S_t, which is unity if $\Delta_t = 2$ and zero otherwise. Then we can write

$$\begin{aligned}\sigma_{1t}^2 &= \omega_1 + \alpha_1\varepsilon_{t-1}^2 + \beta\sigma_{1,t-1}^2 = \omega_1 + \alpha_1\eta_{t-1}^2\sigma_{\Delta_{t-1},t-1}^2 + \beta\sigma_{1-t-1}^2 \\ &= \omega_1 + \alpha_1 a\eta_{t-1}^2 S_{t-1} + \{(\alpha_1 + \alpha_1(b-1)S_{t-1})\eta_{t-1}^2 + \beta\}\sigma_{1,t-1}^2 \\ &= \omega_1 + \alpha_1 a\eta_{t-1}^2 S_{t-1} + c_{\Delta_{t-1},t-1}\sigma_{1,t-1}^2, \end{aligned} \quad (3.36)$$

where $c_{\Delta_t,t} = (\alpha_1 + \alpha_1(b-1)S_t)\eta_t^2 + \beta = \alpha_1\eta_t^2(1-S_t) + \alpha_2\eta_t^2 S_t + \beta$, and the condition for covariance stationarity boils down to checking the larger eigenvalue of the matrix

$$\mathbb{P}_c = \begin{pmatrix} p_{11}c_1 & p_{21}c_1 \\ p_{12}c_2 & p_{22}c_2 \end{pmatrix}, \quad (3.37)$$

where $c_j = \alpha_j + \beta, j = 1, 2$. A necessary and sufficient condition for $\rho(\mathbb{P}_c) < 1$ is positivity of the leading principal minors of $I_2 - \mathbb{P}_c$ (cf. Murata, 1977, p. 109), that is, $p_{11}c_1 < 1$ and

$$\pi_1c_1 + \pi_2c_2 + \delta(\pi_2c_1 + \pi_1c_2 - c_1c_2) = p_{11}c_1 + p_{22}c_2 - \delta c_1c_2 < 1, \quad (3.38)$$

so that, for a given transition matrix, the covariance stationarity region in (c_1, c_2) space is described by the boundary curve

$$c_2^\star = \frac{1 - p_{11}c_1}{p_{22} - \delta c_1} = \frac{1 - (\pi_1 + \delta\pi_2)c_1}{\pi_2 + \delta(\pi_1 - c_1)}$$
$$= 1 + \frac{\pi_1(1 - c_1)(1 - \delta)}{\pi_2 + \delta(\pi_1 - c_1)}, \quad 0 \le c_1 < 1/p_{11}. \tag{3.39}$$

Regarding condition (Eq. 3.38), we note that its left-hand side consists of two parts. Its first two terms are just the sum of the regime-specific persistence parameters $c_j, j = 1, 2$, weighted by their *unconditional* state probabilities. Thus, this part of the condition says that nonstationary regimes must not occur too often *on average*. It is also easily confirmed from Equation 3.39 that for fixed long-run probabilities, the larger the δ, the stronger is the restriction on the regime-specific GARCH parameters. This is a plausible result, since a high δ leads to long regime durations during which regime-specific (nonstationary) volatility dynamics can unfold. Examples are presented in Figure 3.2, which shows Equation 3.39 for four different processes, where $p_{11} = p_{22} = 0.25, 0.5, 0.75$, and 0.95, and hence $\delta = 2p_{11} - 1 = -0.5, 0, 0.5$, and 0.9, respectively.[3] In all processes, $\pi_1 = \pi_2 = 0.5$, but whereas the restrictions on the GARCH parameters are very weak for the process with $\delta < 0$, the sum of the GARCH parameters in the

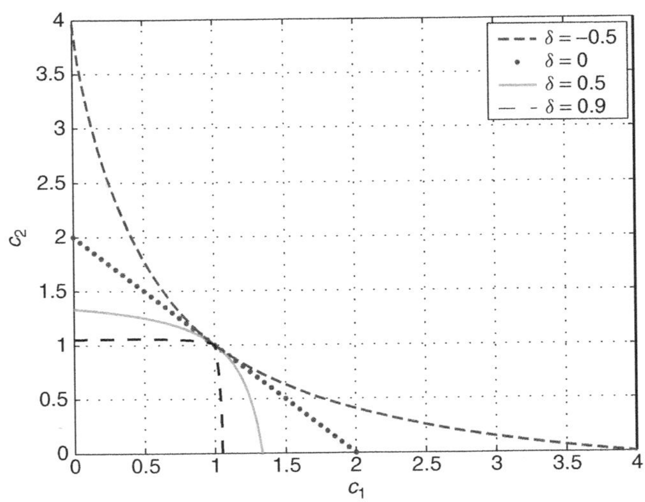

FIGURE 3.2 Stationarity regions (Eq. 3.39) for MS-GARCH processes of the form (Eq. 3.36) with common memory parameter β, where $c_j = \alpha_j + \beta$, $j = 1, 2$, is the regime-specific measure of volatility persistence. All processes have $\pi_1 = \pi_2 = 0.5$ but differ with respect to the persistence of the regimes.

[3] For a similar graph for MS-AR(1) models, see Figure 1 in Yao and Attali (2000).

high-persistence regime is only allowed to mildly exceed unity in the model with strong regime dependence ($\delta = 0.9$).

The evaluation of Liu's (2006) condition for *strict* stationarity of process (Eq. 3.21) requires simulation, whereas Francq et al. (2001) and Bauwens et al. (2010) show that for process (Eq. 3.19), strict stationarity requires

$$\sum_{j=1}^{k} \pi_j \mathbb{E}\{\log(\alpha_j \eta_t^2 + \beta_j)\} < 1, \tag{3.40}$$

that is, Nelson's (1990) stationarity condition for the GARCH(1,1) has to hold on average with respect to the long-run probabilities; see also Zhang et al. (2006) for the i.i.d. mixture case. Interestingly, in contrast to the moment conditions, the regimes' persistence does not appear in condition (Eq. 3.40). A consequence of Equation 3.40 is that if one of the regimes has constant variance ($\alpha_j = \beta_j = 0$), then, since this resets the process "to the start" from time to time, the parameters of the other regimes may become arbitrarily large (Francq and Zakoïan, 2001).

3.3.2 MOMENT STRUCTURE

Moment calculations for mixture and MS-GARCH models can be found, for example, in Abramson and Cohen (2007), Alexander and Lazar (2006, 2009), Francq and Zakoïan (2005, 2008), Haas et al. (2004a,b), Haas (2008), and Rombouts and Bouaddi (2010). We have already shown how to compute the variance for specification (Eq. 3.21), and calculations of higher moments and autocorrelations are similar. In this section, we shall thus concentrate on a particular two-regime case that allows for rather simple explicit expressions with clear-cut interpretation. In particular, as in Vlaar and Palm (1993), we further impose $\alpha_1 = \alpha_2 \stackrel{\text{def}}{=} \alpha$ (i.e., $b = 1$) in Equation 3.21 so that Equation 3.36 becomes

$$\sigma_{1t}^2 = \omega_1 + \alpha_1 a \eta_{t-1}^2 S_{t-1} + c_{t-1} \sigma_{1,t-1}^2, \tag{3.41}$$

where now $a = (\omega_2 - \omega_1)/(1 - \beta)$, and $c_t = \alpha \eta_t^2 + \beta$. Using Equation 3.41 along with Lemma 3.2, we calculate

$$\begin{aligned}\mathbb{E}(\varepsilon_t^2) &= \sum_{j=1}^{2} \pi_j \mathbb{E}(\sigma_{1t}^2 | \Delta_t = j) + \pi_2 a = \frac{\pi_1 \omega_1 + \pi_2 \omega_2}{1 - c_{11}} \\ &= \sum_{j=1}^{2} \pi_j \frac{\omega_j}{1 - \alpha - \beta}, \quad c_{11} = \alpha + \beta,\end{aligned} \tag{3.42}$$

which was also calculated by Cai (1994) for the MS-ARCH process. Thus, the unconditional variance is given by the weighted average of those of the single-regime GARCH processes that drive the individual components.[4] Rather lengthy and tedious calculations also show that provided $c_{22} = \kappa_4\alpha^2 + 2\alpha\beta + \beta^2 < 1$,

$$\mathbb{E}(\varepsilon_t^4) = \frac{\kappa_4(\pi_1\omega_1 + \pi_2\omega_2)^2(1 + c_{11})}{(1 - c_{11})(1 - c_{22})} + \frac{\kappa_4\pi_1\pi_2 a^2(\kappa(\tilde{\varepsilon}) - 1)}{\kappa_4 - 1}\left[1 + \frac{2\delta\rho_1(\tilde{\varepsilon}_t^2)}{1 - \delta c_{11}}\right], \tag{3.43}$$

where

$$\kappa(\tilde{\varepsilon}) = \frac{\kappa_4(1 - c_{11}^2)}{1 - c_{22}}, \quad \text{and} \quad \rho_1(\tilde{\varepsilon}_t^2) = \frac{\alpha(1 - \alpha\beta - \beta^2)}{1 - 2\alpha\beta - \beta^2} \tag{3.44}$$

are the unconditional kurtosis and the first-order autocorrelation of the squares of the single-regime GARCH(1,1) process with the same unconditional variance (Eq. 3.42) and the same volatility dynamics parameters α and β, respectively. The first expression on the right-hand side of Equation 3.43 is just equal to the unconditional fourth moment of this single-regime process, and the second term therefore determines the excess kurtosis over and above the single-regime process with the same volatility dynamics. Note that Equation 3.43 in general also depends on the persistence of the regimes, δ, which is in contrast to the basic MS model with homoskedastic regimes (cf. Timmermann, 2000).

The autocovariance function of the squared process turns out to be

$$\mathrm{Cov}(\varepsilon_t^2, \varepsilon_{t-\tau}^2) = \gamma(\tau) = \begin{cases} \phi_1 c_{11}^{\tau-1} + \phi_2 \frac{\delta^{\tau-1} - c_{11}^{\tau-1}}{\delta - c_{11}} & \delta \neq c_{11} \\ [\phi_1 + (\tau - 1)\phi_2/\delta]\,\delta^{\tau-1} & \delta = c_{11}, \end{cases} \tag{3.45}$$

where the constant ϕ_1 is a rather complicated function of all the model's parameters,[5], whereas $\phi_2 = \pi_1\pi_2 a^2\delta(\delta - \beta)(1 - \delta\beta)(1 - \delta c_{11})^{-1}$. For $\delta = 0$, we have $\phi_2 = 0$ in Equation 3.45 and hence, $\gamma(\tau) = c_{11}\gamma(\tau - 1)$ as in the single-regime process. Note that $\phi_2 = 0$ is also true, for $\delta = \beta$; so in this case, likewise, the autocorrelation function (ACF) resembles that of a standard GARCH(1,1). On the other hand, if $\alpha = \beta = 0$, that is, the basic MS model, we have $\gamma(\tau) = \pi_1\pi_2(\omega_1 - \omega_2)^2\delta^\tau$ (Timmermann, 2000). In the general case, Equation 3.45 shows that the decay of the ACF is a mixture of two exponentials with rates c_{11} and δ. Thus, if the persistence of the regimes dominates that of shocks to volatility, we expect that the persistence of shocks will be overestimated in case the shifts in the level parameter are ignored, since in that case all the persistence is "thrown into the persistence of an individual shock" (Gray, 1996). Initially, this has been one of the reasons to consider RS-GARCH models, see, for example, Lamoureux and Lastrapes (1990), Hamilton and Susmel (1994),

[4]We stress that there is no such simple relationship in the general case with regime-specific volatility dynamics.

[5]Details of the calculations are available from the authors on request.

Mikosch and Stărică (2004), Krämer and Tameze-Azamo (2007), and Krämer (2008) for discussion.

Moreover, if regimes are very persistent ($\delta \approx 1$), then the ACF may mimic that of a long memory process in the sense that Equation 3.45 exhibits a fast decay at the beginning (represented by the "shock component" c_{11}^{τ}) and a very slow decay afterward (via the RS component δ^{τ}). Since Ding et al. (1993) and Ding and Granger (1996), this behavior of the sample ACF has often been observed in financial data recorded over very long time spans. We also mention that, even without persistent regimes, the mixture GARCH process can display a similar shape of the ACF when the GARCH dynamics of the components are unrestricted. To illustrate, consider the two-component model with zero component means. Then by Equations 3.7 and 3.22, the conditional variance of ε_t^2, σ_t^2, is

$$\mathbb{E}_{t-1}(\varepsilon_t^2) = \sigma_t^2 = \pi_1\sigma_{1t}^2 + \pi_2\sigma_{2t}^2$$

$$= \frac{\pi_1\omega_1}{1-\beta_1} + \frac{\pi_2\omega_2}{1-\beta_2} + \left(\frac{\pi_1\alpha_1}{1-\beta_1 L} + \frac{\pi_2\alpha_2}{1-\beta_2 L}\right)\varepsilon_{t-1}^2,$$

where L is the lag operator, that is, $L^{\tau}x_t = x_{t-\tau}$, so that we get a GARCH(2,2) representation of σ_t^2,

$$\sigma_t^2 = \overline{\omega} + (\beta_1+\beta_2)\sigma_{t-1}^2 - \beta_1\beta_2\sigma_{t-2}^2$$
$$+(\pi_1\alpha_1+\pi_2\alpha_2)\varepsilon_{t-1}^2 - (\pi_1\alpha_1\beta_2+\pi_2\alpha_2\beta_1)\varepsilon_{t-2}^2, \qquad (3.46)$$

where $\overline{\omega} = \pi_1\omega_1(1-\beta_2) + \pi_2\omega_2(1-\beta_1)$. Note that, similar to the GARCH(2,2) representation of Ding and Granger's (1996) component GARCH process, the lag-two coefficients in Equation 3.46 are negative, but positivity of σ_t^2 is guaranteed. However, owing to the negativity, both roots of the characteristic equation associated with Equation 3.46 are positive, so the ACF of ε_t^2 is a mixture of two positive exponentials, which may capture both a rapidly and a slowly decaying component; see Haas et al. (2004a) for a more detailed discussion.

3.4 Regime Inference, Likelihood Function, and Volatility Forecasting

Since the regimes are not observable, we cannot use the transition probabilities p_{ij} in Equation 3.8 to directly forecast future regimes. However, we can use the return history to compute regime inferences once we have estimated the parameters of an MS GARCH process. These probabilities are also required for the likelihood function. To this end, we define, for each point of time, t, a k-dimensional random vector $\boldsymbol{z}_t = (z_{1t}, \ldots, z_{kt})'$, with elements z_{jt} such that

$$z_{jt} = \begin{cases} 1 & \text{if} \quad \Delta_t = j, \\ 0 & \text{if} \quad \Delta_t \neq j, \end{cases} \qquad j = 1, \ldots, k. \qquad (3.47)$$

Moreover, let $\boldsymbol{\varepsilon}_\tau = \{\varepsilon_\tau, \varepsilon_{\tau-1}, \ldots\}$ denote the process up to time τ, and let $z_{jt|\tau} = p(z_{jt} = 1|\boldsymbol{\varepsilon}_\tau), j = 1, \ldots, k$, be our probability inference of being in state j at time t, based on the process up to time τ, and let $\boldsymbol{z}_{t|\tau} = (z_{1t|\tau}, \ldots, z_{kt|\tau})'$. Then, assuming conditional normality, we have (Hamilton, 1989, 1994, 2008)

$$\boldsymbol{z}_{t|t} = \frac{\boldsymbol{z}_{t|t-1} \odot \boldsymbol{f}_t}{\mathbf{1}'_k(\boldsymbol{z}_{t|t-1} \odot \boldsymbol{f}_t)} \tag{3.48}$$

$$\boldsymbol{z}_{t+1|t} = \boldsymbol{P}\boldsymbol{z}_{t|t}, \tag{3.49}$$

where $\odot$ denotes the Hadamard product, that is, elementwise multiplication of conformable matrices, and

$$\boldsymbol{f}_t = \begin{pmatrix} \phi(\varepsilon_t; \mu_1, \sigma_{1t}^2) \\ \vdots \\ \phi(\varepsilon_t; \mu_k, \sigma_{kt}^2) \end{pmatrix} = (2\pi)^{-1/2} \begin{pmatrix} \sigma_{1t}^{-1} \exp\{-(\varepsilon_t - \mu_1)^2/(2\sigma_{1t}^2)\} \\ \vdots \\ \sigma_{kt}^{-1} \exp\{-(\varepsilon_t - \mu_k)^2/(2\sigma_{kt}^2)\} \end{pmatrix}.$$

Equations 3.48–3.49 can be used to calculate regime inferences recursively, and τ-step ahead regime probabilities are obtained as $\boldsymbol{z}_{t+\tau|t} = \boldsymbol{P}^\tau \boldsymbol{z}_{t|t}$.

To initialize the recursion, the stationary distribution of the chain may be used. However, for reasonably long time series, as usually available in financial applications, the choice of the initial distribution will have a negligible impact on actual out-of-sample regime forecasts. The same applies to the initial values of the regime-specific variances, which may be treated either as a parameter to estimate or else all set equal to the sample variance. The latter approach may be preferable to setting the initial variances equal to their unconditional values, which causes numerical instabilities if the spectral radius of $\mathbb{P}_{C_{11}}$ in Equation 3.33 is close to unity.

The conditional (predictive) density of ε_{t+1}, given the process up to time t, is

$$f(\varepsilon_{t+1}|\boldsymbol{\varepsilon}_t) = \sum_{j=1}^{k} z_{j,t+1|t}\phi(\varepsilon_{t+1}; \mu_j, \sigma_{j,t+1}^2) = \mathbf{1}'_k(\boldsymbol{z}_{t+1|t} \odot \boldsymbol{f}_{t+1}), \tag{3.50}$$

and the likelihood function for a sample of length T is

$$\log L = \sum_{t=1}^{T} \log f(\varepsilon_t|\boldsymbol{\varepsilon}_{t-1}) = \sum_{t=1}^{T} \log[\mathbf{1}'_k(\boldsymbol{z}_{t|t-1} \odot \boldsymbol{f}_t)]. \tag{3.51}$$

Note that the entire procedure simplifies considerably for the i.i.d. normal mixture GARCH model and for time-varying specifications à la

Equation 3.14, since the conditional regime probabilities are observable (or even constant) then.

In many applications, we are also interested in calculating the regime probabilities based on the entire sample information, that is, $z_{t|T}$, or, more generally, $z_{t|t'}$ for $t' > t$, which are referred to as the *smoothed* regime probabilities; a convenient algorithm for this purpose was derived by Kim (1994), which works backward through

$$z_{t|T} = z_{t|t} \odot [P'(z_{t+1|T} \oslash z_{t+1|t})], \tag{3.52}$$

where $\oslash$ denotes element-by-element division.

In practice, estimation of mixture GARCH models is most often done via ML, although alternative methods have been developed, as reviewed in Section 3.2.3. Hessian-based optimization routines with numerically determined derivatives are typically used to locate the maxima of the likelihood function, but we note that analytic first- and second-order derivatives of the log-likelihood of the normal mixture GARCH model are provided in Alexander and Lazar (2006, 2009). There can be several *plausible* local maxima of the likelihood function, and only via use of various starting values can one obtain what is likely to be the global maximum. A second issue in this regard involves maxima that are not plausible but, because of the nature of the mixture likelihood, can arise and plague estimation; see Day (1969), Hamilton (1991), and McLachlan and Peel (2000) for a discussion in the context of unconditional mixtures. A possible remedy for mixture GARCH models is proposed in Broda et al. (2011) and Krause and Paolella (2011), which works by appending to the log-likelihood, two judiciously chosen penalty and shrinkage terms and thus does not entail any more numeric work than is involved in directly maximizing the likelihood. While significantly more complicated and numerically more challenging, the Bayesian approaches mentioned in Section 3.2.3 provide another solution.

Francq et al. (2001) have shown that the ML estimator (MLE) is consistent for MS-ARCH models, whereas results for MS-GARCH models appear not to be available to date, and the same is true for results about the asymptotic distribution of the MLE. Alexander and Lazar (2006) conducted a simulation study with MN-GARCH models, suggesting asymptotic normality, with standard errors provided by the inverse Fisher information.

Most of the applications of MS-GARCH appear to be based on Gaussian regimes. However, as noted by Klaassen (2002), Ardia (2009), and Haas (2009), if regimes are not normal but leptokurtic, the use of within-regime normality can seriously affect the identification of the regime process and hence also of the within-regime GARCH processes. The reason is that, in this case, a Gaussian RS model will detect regime switches too frequently due to an untypical observation in an otherwise low- or high-volatility period, whereas leptokurtic components, such as Student-t, because of their higher peaks and fatter tails, can better accommodate such realizations within a given regime, leading to regimes that are more persistent. This implies, for example, that quasi-ML estimation based on

Gaussian components does not provide a consistent estimator. The importance of the conditional distribution for identifying the regime process is illustrated in Section 3.4.3.

3.4.1 DETERMINING THE NUMBER OF REGIMES

An issue that has not been completely resolved is the determination of the number of regimes (or mixture components), that is, the choice of k in Equation 3.6. Standard test theory breaks down, and straightforward likelihood ratio tests, for example, cannot be used to decide on k; Hansen (1992) is a standard econometrics reference on these issues. There is some evidence that, at least for unconditional mixtures, the Bayesian information criterion (BIC) provides a reasonably good indication for the number of components, and thus it is often used as a guideline in the literature; see McLachlan and Peel (2000) for some discussion. However, in applications to financial data, for reasons of parsimony and interpretability, it is often reasonable to *a priori* restrict the number of components to be small, for example, $k = 2$. In particular, in models with $k > 2$, at least one of the components tends to have a very small mixing weight and, consequently, its parameters are subject to a rather large estimation error (cf. Alexander and Lazar, 2006). Also, Rydén et al. (1998) observed that estimates of three-regime MS models are much less stable over time than those of two-component processes, with one component usually just capturing a few outliers.

3.4.2 VOLATILITY FORECASTS

In contrast to multistep densities, multistep conditional volatilities can be calculated straightforwardly for most GARCH specifications, and MS-GARCH models are no exception. As noted by various authors, for example, Davidson (2004) and Pelletier (2006), an attractive feature of MS models is that conditional expectations can be calculated analytically, which is in contrast to many other nonlinear time series models. We illustrate this for the MS-GARCH process described by Equations 3.18 and 3.21, where forecasts can be calculated by means of a simple recursive scheme (see Haas 2010a for development in a multivariate framework). Repeated substitution in Equation 3.25 yields

$$\begin{aligned}
X_{t+d+1} &= \omega + C_{\Delta_{t+d},t+d} X_{t+d} \\
&= \omega + C_{\Delta_{t+d},t+d}\,\omega + C_{\Delta_{t+d},t+d} C_{\Delta_{t+d-1},t+d-1} X_{t+d-1} \\
&\ \ \vdots \\
&= \sum_{i=1}^{d} \left\{ \prod_{\ell=1}^{i-1} C_{\Delta_{t+d+1-\ell},t+d+1-\ell} \right\} \omega \\
&\quad + \left\{ \prod_{\ell=1}^{d} C_{\Delta_{t+d+1-\ell},t+d+1-\ell} \right\} X_{t+1},
\end{aligned}$$

where we define $\prod_{\ell=1}^{0} C_{\Delta_{t+d+1-\ell},t+d+1-\ell} \stackrel{\text{def}}{=} I_{k+1}$. Let $\Delta_t = \{\Delta_s : s \leq t\}$. Then

$$\mathbb{E}_t(X_{t+d+1}|\Delta_{t+d}) = \sum_{i=1}^{d} \left\{ \prod_{\ell=1}^{i-1} C_{11}(\Delta_{t+d+1-\ell}) \right\} \omega + \left\{ \prod_{\ell=1}^{d} C_{11}(\Delta_{t+d+1-\ell}) \right\} X_{t+1}. \tag{3.53}$$

Applying Lemma 3.2 and Equation 3.29 to the product terms in Equation 3.53 gives

$$\mathbb{E}_t(X_{t+d+1}) = (\mathbf{1}_k' \otimes I_{k+1})M(d), \quad d \geq 0,$$

where $M(0) = \pi_t \otimes X_{t+1}$, and

$$\begin{aligned} M(d) &= \sum_{i=1}^{d} \mathbb{P}_{C_{11}}^{i-1}(\pi_{t+d+1-i} \otimes \omega) + \mathbb{P}_{C_{11}}^{d}(\pi_t \otimes X_{t+1}) \\ &= \pi_{t+d} \otimes \omega + \mathbb{P}_{C_{11}} \left\{ \sum_{i=1}^{d-1} \mathbb{P}_{C_{11}}^{i-1}(\pi_{t+(d-1)+1-i} \otimes \omega) + \mathbb{P}_{C_{11}}^{d-1}(\pi_t \otimes X_{t+1}) \right\} \\ &= \pi_{t+d} \otimes \omega + \mathbb{P}_{C_{11}} M(d-1), \quad d \geq 1. \end{aligned}$$

Hence volatility forecasts can be calculated as

$$\mathbb{E}_t(\varepsilon_{t+d}^2) = (\mathbf{1}_k \otimes e_{k+1})' M(d), \tag{3.54}$$

where

$$M(d) = \begin{cases} \pi_t \otimes X_{t+1} & d = 0 \\ \pi_{t+d} \otimes \omega + \mathbb{P}_{C_{11}} M(d-1) & d \geq 1. \end{cases} \tag{3.55}$$

In practice, we estimate π_t in Equation 3.55 via $\boldsymbol{z}_{t|t}$ in Equation 3.48, and then $\widehat{\pi}_{t+d} = \widehat{\boldsymbol{P}}^d \boldsymbol{z}_{t|t}$, $d \geq 1$.

3.4.3 APPLICATION OF MS-GARCH MODELS TO STOCK RETURN INDICES

We consider daily percentage log-returns, r_t, of the MSCI stock market indices for France, Germany, and the United Kingdom from January 1990 to August 2010 ($T = 5203$ observations). A few basic statistical properties of these are summarized in Table 3.1. We estimate a two-regime process of the form (Eq. 3.21) with both normal and unit variance Student-t components with common

TABLE 3.1 Statistical Properties of MSCI Stock Market Returns, 1990–2010

	Mean	Variance	Skewness	Kurtosis	JB
France	0.015	1.864	−0.053	7.997	5416.1 (0.000)
Germany	0.015	2.078	−0.150	8.156	5782.5 (0.000)
UK	0.015	1.292	−0.120	9.564	9353.5 (0.000)

Returns are defined as $r = 100 \times \log(I_t/I_{t-1})$, where I_t is the index level at time t. "Skewness" and "Kurtosis" denote the moments-based coefficients of skewness and kurtosis, respectively, that is, the third and fourth standardized moments of the returns, and JB is the Jarque–Bera test for normality, with p-values given in parentheses. The means of all three series have the same first four digits.

degrees of freedom parameter ν, where in the latter case, the density of η_t in Equation 3.18 is

$$f(\eta_t;\nu) = \frac{\Gamma\left(\frac{\nu+1}{2}\right)}{\Gamma(\nu/2)\sqrt{(\nu-2)\pi}}\left(1+\frac{\eta_t^2}{\nu-2}\right)^{-(\nu+1)/2}, \quad \nu > 2. \qquad (3.56)$$

Estimation results are reported in Table 3.2, where the regimes have been ordered with respect to a declining long-run probability, that is, $\pi_1 > \pi_2$. The results show some common characteristics that are typical of those reported in the literature. In all cases, the first component is the low-volatility regime since it has a smaller unconditional variance, that is, $\mathbb{E}(\varepsilon_t^2|\Delta_t = 2) > \mathbb{E}(\varepsilon_t^2|\Delta_t = 1)$. In the high-volatility states, the immediate effect of a shock on the conditional volatility tends to be higher than in the low-volatility states (i.e., $\alpha_2 > \alpha_1$), but the impact of shocks dies out soon in these regimes since they display a shorter memory ($\beta_2 < \beta_1$). Moreover, in the Gaussian models, the high-volatility regimes are driven by nonstationary GARCH dynamics in the sense that $\alpha_2 + \beta_2 \geq 1$. For the Student-$t$ models, this is the case only for the German index, where Regime 2 is IGARCH-like. However, all the switching GARCH processes are stationary by Theorem 3.1, since $\rho(\mathbb{P}_{C_{11}}) < 1$ in all cases. A comparison of the model-implied unconditional overall variances $\mathrm{E}(\varepsilon_t^2)$ with their sample analoges in Table 3.1 shows a relatively close agreement in most cases. The exceptions are the cases where $\rho(\mathbb{P}_{C_{22}}) > 1$, so that the fourth moment does not exist and the unconditional distribution is very fat-tailed.

As indicated at the end of Section 3.4, there are important differences between the models based on Gaussian and those based on Student-t innovations. Namely, with the exception of France, the regimes exhibit much more persistence in the Student-t models, and so in particular, for the German index, where the estimated Gaussian MS-GARCH model is basically an i.i.d. mixture GARCH process. The expected duration of regime 2 in this process, $(1 - p_{22})^{-1}$, is just 1, which means that this regime essentially only captures some isolated outliers. Consequently, when compared to the t-model, the unconditional probability of this regime (3%) is much lower, and the ratio between the expected volatility in the high-volatility regime and that in the low-volatility state is more extreme than

TABLE 3.2 **Parameter Estimates for Markov-Switching GARCH Processes**

	France		Germany		United Kingdom	
	Normal	t	Normal	t	Normal	t
ω_1	0.008 (0.002)	0.009 (0.002)	0.008 (0.003)	0.002 (0.001)	0.005 (0.001)	0.003 (0.001)
α_1	0.028 (0.006)	0.028 (0.006)	0.071 (0.008)	0.015 (0.004)	0.029 (0.006)	0.011 (0.004)
β_1	0.959 (0.007)	0.960 (0.008)	0.917 (0.008)	0.977 (0.005)	0.958 (0.007)	0.978 (0.006)
$\alpha_1 + \beta_1$	0.987 (0.002)	0.987 (0.002)	0.989 (0.003)	0.992 (0.002)	0.987 (0.002)	0.989 (0.002)
p_{11}	0.991 (0.003)	0.993 (0.003)	0.970 (0.011)	0.982 (0.009)	0.987 (0.006)	0.990 (0.007)
π_1	0.913	0.908	0.970	0.527	0.903	0.521
$(1 - p_{11})^{-1}$	114.2	135.9	33.8	55.0	79.6	98.8
$\mathbb{E}(\varepsilon_t^2 \mid \Delta_t = 1)$	1.394	1.402	1.919	1.604	1.181	0.637
ω_2	0.204 (0.191)	0.235 (0.163)	1.676 (1.125)	0.039 (0.020)	0.019 (0.029)	0.037 (0.015)
α_2	0.066 (0.033)	0.078 (0.037)	0.645 (0.483)	0.122 (0.022)	0.076 (0.031)	0.110 (0.018)
β_2	0.934 (0.056)	0.915 (0.055)	0.629 (0.205)	0.878 (0.022)	0.965 (0.027)	0.878 (0.022)
$\alpha_2 + \beta_2$	1.000 (0.032)	0.992 (0.031)	1.274 (0.340)	1.000 (0.010)	1.041 (0.014)	0.987 (0.012)
p_{22}	0.909 (0.024)	0.928 (0.022)	0.044 (0.082)	0.980 (0.014)	0.882 (0.029)	0.989 (0.011)
π_2	0.087	0.092	0.030	0.473	0.097	0.479
$(1 - p_{22})^{-1}$	10.9	13.8	1.0	49.4	8.5	90.7
$\mathbb{E}(\varepsilon_t^2 \mid \Delta_t = 2)$	6.764	6.582	8.236	3.995	5.915	2.017
ν	∞	23.43 (8.173)	∞	10.25 (1.378)	∞	15.29 (3.375)
δ	0.900 (0.025)	0.920 (0.023)	0.015 (0.083)	0.962 (0.022)	0.870 (0.032)	0.979 (0.018)
$\rho(\mathbb{P}_{C_{11}})$	0.988	0.987	0.991	0.994	0.996	0.989
$\mathbb{E}(\varepsilon_t^2)$	1.863	1.880	2.108	2.735	1.638	1.297
$\rho(\mathbb{P}_{C_{22}})$	0.978	0.978	0.994	1.024	1.008	0.996
$-\log L$	8158.4	8153.9	8237.2	8224.4	7007.3	7003.7

Shown are parameter estimates for two-regime MS-GARCH models of the form (Eq. 3.21) fitted to the MSCI return series, with approximate standard errors given in parentheses. $(1 - p_{jj})^{-1}$ is the expected duration of regime $j, j = 1, 2$; see Section 3.2.2. Calculation of the regime-specific unconditional variances $\mathbb{E}(\varepsilon_t^2 \mid \Delta_t = j), j = 1, 2$, is based on Equation 3.32, ν is the degrees of freedom parameter of the t density (Eq. 3.56), $\delta = p_{11} + p_{22} - 1$ is the degree of persistence in the regime process (cf. Section 3.2.2), and $\rho(\mathbb{P}_{C_{jj}}), j = 1, 2$, is the largest eigenvalue of the matrix $\mathbb{P}_{C_{jj}}$ defined via Equations 3.27 and 3.30. The unconditional process variance $\mathbb{E}(\varepsilon_t^2)$ is given by Equation 3.33 and $-\log L$ is -1 times the value of the maximized log-likelihood function.

in the model with Student-t regimes. Germany also has the lowest ν estimate, indicating that regimes are considerably fat-tailed, and the largest improvement in log-likelihood when allowing for t-innovations. The results for the UK market are similar, although less extreme, whereas the differences between the two models for France appears negligible. Figure 3.3 shows the index and return series along

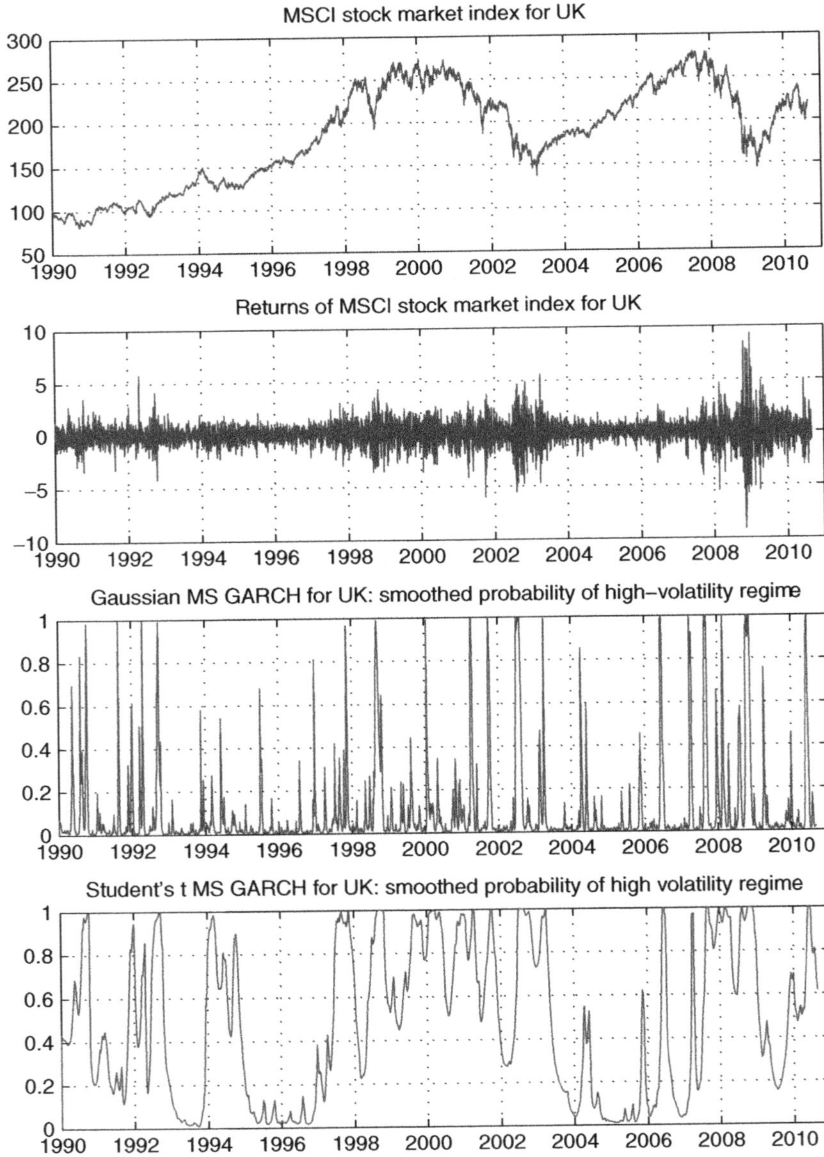

FIGURE 3.3 Index level, returns, and *smoothed* high-volatility regime probabilities (Eq. 3.52) of the UK MSCI stock market index.

with the *smoothed* probabilities (Eq. 3.52) of the high-volatility regime for the United Kingdom, highlighting the greater persistence in the Student-t model. Marcucci (2005) and Sajjad et al. (2008) report similar results for various stock market indices.

3.5 Application of Mixture GARCH Models to Density Prediction and Value-at-Risk Estimation

In this section, we evaluate the forecasting performance of various mixture GARCH models on an economic basis by employing the VaR concept, which is a widely used measure to describe the downside risk of a financial position.

3.5.1 VALUE-AT-RISK

Consider a time series of portfolio returns, r_t, and an associated series of ex-ante VaR measures with target probability ξ, $\text{VaR}_t(\xi)$. The $\text{VaR}_t(\xi)$ implied by a model $\mathcal{M}$ is defined by

$$\Pr_{t-1}^{\mathcal{M}}(r_t < -\text{VaR}_t(\xi)) = \xi, \tag{3.57}$$

where $\Pr_{t-1}^{\mathcal{M}}(\cdot)$ denotes a probability derived from model $\mathcal{M}$ using the information up to time $t-1$, and the negative sign in Equation 3.57 is because of the convention of reporting VaR as a positive number. For an appropriately specified model, we expect $100 \times \xi\%$ of the observed return values to not exceed the (negative of the) respective VaR forecast. Thus, to assess the performance of the different models, we examine the percentage shortfall frequencies,

$$U_\xi = 100 \times \frac{x}{T} = 100 \times \hat{\xi}, \tag{3.58}$$

where T denotes the number of forecasts evaluated, x is the observed shortfall frequency, that is, the number of days for which $r_t < -\text{VaR}_t(\xi)$, and $\hat{\xi} = x/T$ is the empirical shortfall probability. If $\hat{\xi}$ is significantly less (higher) than ξ, then model $\mathcal{M}$ tends to overestimate (underestimate) the risk of the position. In the present application, we focus on the target probabilities $\xi = 0.005, 0.01, 0.025$, and 0.05 for both long and short positions.

To formally test whether a model correctly estimates the risk (according to VaR), that is, whether the empirical shortfall probability, $\hat{\xi}$, is statistically indistinguishable from the nominal shortfall probability, ξ, we use the likelihood ratio test

$$\text{LRT}_{\text{VaR}} = -2\{x \log(\xi/\hat{\xi}) + (T-x)\log[(1-\xi)/(1-\hat{\xi})]\} \overset{\text{asy}}{\sim} \chi^2(1). \tag{3.59}$$

As a performance summary, we also calculate the mean absolute percentage error (MAPE) of a model, given by

$$\text{MAPE} = \frac{1}{8}\left\{\sum_{i=1}^{4}\left|\frac{\widehat{\xi_i}-\xi_i}{\xi_i}\right|_{\text{long}} + \sum_{i=1}^{4}\left|\frac{\widehat{\xi_i}-\xi_i}{\xi_i}\right|_{\text{short}}\right\}, \tag{3.60}$$

where $\{\xi_1, \xi_2, \xi_3, \xi_4\} = \{0.005, 0.01, 0.025, 0.05\}$.

3.5.2 DATA AND MODELS

We base our comparison on the European stock market indices described in Section 3.4.3. The index levels and returns of the UK index are shown in Figure 3.3, and they are representative for the other series as well. It is apparent that the sharp decline during the late-2000's financial crisis was accompanied by a burst of (at least in the sample) unprecedented volatility, which poses a serious challenge for all volatility models.

Based on the first 2500 return observations, we calculate one-day-ahead VaR measures based on parameter estimates obtained from a rolling data window, where the parameters are updated every month. Thus we get, for each model, 2703 one-day-ahead, out-of-sample VaR measures.

Although economic intuition suggests that market regimes are persistent, many applications have shown that i.i.d. mixture GARCH models tend to provide rather accurate predictive densities (Alexander and Lazar, 2006; Haas et al., 2004a; Kuester et al., 2006; Paolella and Steude, 2008; Paolella and Taschini, 2008). In fact, when directly compared with the less-restrictive MS-GARCH process, they even appear to be somewhat superior *out-of-sample* (Haas, 2010b). A possible explanation may be that regime changes are difficult to time *ex-ante*, or, as put by Greenspan (2009), "[w]e can model the euphoria and the fear stage [...] Their parameters are quite different. We have never successfully modeled the transition from euphoria to fear." This may explain why an agnostic view concerning the regime process may often be a reasonable choice when it comes to out-of-sample forecasting. In view of these remarks and those made at the end of Section 3.4.1, we focus on i.i.d. mixture GARCH processes with two regimes.

We consider the two-component MN-GARCH model both with and without regime-specific means, and the latter (symmetric) specification will be denoted by MN_s. Furthermore, the results in Haas (2010b) suggest that it may be more advantageous to model skewness by means of an asymmetric conditional density rather than by component-specific means, for example, by replacing the normal with the skew-normal (SN) distribution of Azzalini (1985), with density

$$f(z; \lambda) = 2\phi(z)\Phi(\gamma z), \quad \gamma \in \mathbb{R}, \tag{3.61}$$

where ϕ and Φ are the standard normal pdf and cdf, respectively, and γ controls the degree of asymmetry, with $\gamma < 0$ implying negative skewness; see Haas (2010b) for further details of the motivation and specification of mixed skew-normal (MSN) GARCH models. Furthermore, to put the mixture GARCH models into perspective, we include into the comparison the single-regime GARCH(1,1) process with Gaussian, Student-t, and Mittnik and Paolella's (2000) skew-t innovations.

To account for the fact that stock market volatility reacts asymmetrically to positive and negative shocks (leverage effect), we also follow Alexander and Lazar (2009) and Rombouts and Bouaddi (2009) and extend Equation 3.21 à la Ding et al. (1993), that is,

$$\sigma_{jt}^2 = \omega_j + \alpha_j(|\varepsilon_{t-1}| - \gamma\varepsilon_{t-1})^2 + \beta_j\sigma_{j,t-1}^2, \quad \gamma \in (-1,1), \quad j = 1,\ldots,k, \tag{3.62}$$

where the asymmetry parameter γ is common to both regimes, and $\gamma > 0$ implies that negative shocks have a deeper impact on future volatility.

3.5.3 EMPIRICAL RESULTS

Before we turn to the out-of-sample VaR forecasts, we first measure the models' in-sample fit by means of their likelihood values. Table 3.3 reports log-likelihood values as well as the Akaike information criteria (AIC) and BIC for the entire sample period. We note that the SN mixture GARCH process achieves the highest likelihood and lowest AIC for all three indices, and the lowest BIC for the German index. For the other two series, the skew$-t$ GARCH model is preferred according to the BIC. Moreover, models allowing for asymmetries are always preferred over their symmetric counterparts, that is, skew-t is preferred to t-GARCH and MN and MSN are preferred to MN_s GARCH, with the latter being nested in both. Note that the likelihood values in Table 3.3 cannot be directly compared with those in Table 3.2, since the models in the former incorporate volatility asymmetries via Equation 3.62.

Table 3.3 also reports the results of simple tests for correct specification of conditional mean, variance, skewness, and kurtosis, based on the one-step-ahead, out-of-sample Rosenblatt (1952) residuals, which should be i.i.d. standard normal (see, e.g., Haas et al., 2004a for details). The tests use the likelihood ratio framework of Berkowitz (2001b) along with the skewed exponential distribution of Fernandez et al. (1995), given by the density

$$f(z;\mu,\sigma,p,\theta) = \frac{\theta}{1+\theta^2}\frac{p}{\sigma 2^{1/p}\Gamma(1/p)}\begin{cases}\exp\left\{-\frac{1}{2}\left(\frac{|z-\mu|\theta}{\sigma}\right)^p\right\} & \text{if} \quad z < \mu \\ \exp\left\{-\frac{1}{2}\left(\frac{z-\mu}{\sigma\theta}\right)^p\right\} & \text{if} \quad z \geq \mu,\end{cases} \tag{3.63}$$

where $\sigma,\theta,p > 0$. This distribution nests the normal for $\theta = 1$ and $p = 2$. For $\theta < 1 (\theta > 1)$, the density is skewed to the left (right), and it is fat-tailed for $p < 2$. The results show that all the models pass the test for the specification of the conditional variance (σ^2) and, with the obvious exception of the Gaussian GARCH, of the kurtosis, whereas MSN is the only model that appears to predict the conditional skewness accurately for all series.

The results concerning VaR are reported in Table 3.4. It is apparent that models based on symmetric densities, that is, the single-regime Gaussian and Student-t GARCH and the symmetric MN_s, are inferior to those allowing for

TABLE 3.3 In-and Out-of-Sample Goodness-of-Fit

			AIC		BIC					
	K	$\log L$	Value	R	Value	R	$\mu \times 100$	σ^2	Skew (θ)	Kurt (p)
					France					
Single–component models										
nor.	5	−8186	16382	6	16414	6	-3.7^a	1.018	0.87^c	1.71^c
t	6	−8123	16257	5	16296	2	-4.3^b	1.004	0.87^c	2.04
sk−t	8	−8113	16243	2	16295	1	−2.6	1.005	0.94^b	1.97
Two–component mixture models										
MN_s	9	−8118	16254	4	16313	5	-4.3^b	1.005	0.87^c	1.93
MN	10	−8112	16243	3	16309	4	-3.7^a	0.998	0.93^b	1.94
MSN	10	−8107	16235	1	16300	3	-3.8^b	0.999	0.96	1.90
					Germany					
Single–component models										
nor.	5	−8331	16672	6	16705	6	-3.2^a	1.025	0.88^c	1.67^c
t	6	−8209	16430	5	16469	3	-4.2^b	1.014	0.88^c	2.03
sk−t	8	−8191	16397	2	16450	2	−0.8	1.017	0.97	1.94
Two–component mixture models										
MN_s	9	−8203	16423	4	16482	5	-4.2^b	1.019	0.88^c	1.87
MN	10	−8196	16411	3	16477	4	-3.2^a	1.011	0.95^b	1.94
MSN	10	−8179	16378	1	16443	1	-3.4^a	1.012	1.01	1.94
					United Kingdom					
Single–component models										
nor.	5	−7008	14027	6	14059	6	−2.2	1.009	0.85^c	1.77^c
t	6	−6975	13961	5	14000	2	−2.7	1.005	0.84^c	2.08
sk−t	8	−6965	13946	2	13998	1	−0.3	1.011	0.92^c	1.99
Two–component mixture models										
MN_s	9	−6969	13956	4	14015	5	−2.6	1.009	0.85^c	2.02
MN	10	−6964	13949	3	14014	4	−1.9	1.006	0.91^c	2.01
MSN	10	−6961	13943	1	14008	3	−2.0	1.009	0.96	1.99

The model type is in the leftmost column; see Section 3.5.2 for the acronyms. K is the number of model parameters, including the constant mean of the return equation, and $\log L$ is the maximized log-likelihood value. AIC $= -2\log L + 2K$ and BIC $= -2\log L + K\log T$ are the Akaike and Bayesian information criterion, respectively (for T observations); R columns give ranks. AIC and BIC are calculated for the entire sample from 1990 to 2010. The right part of the table is based on the one-step-ahead, out-of-sample standardized residuals from 2000 to 2010 (2703 observations), which are standard normal for a correctly specified model. The test is based on the skewed exponential power (SEP) distribution (3.63). To test for correct specification of mean and variance, we fix θ and p at their Gaussian values (i.e., as in Berkowitz (2001b), we use the normal likelihood), and then test for $\mu = 0$ and $\sigma^2 = 1$, respectively. Both likelihood ratio tests (LRTs) are approximately $\chi^2(1)$ distributed. To test for asymmetries and excess kurtosis, we use the full model (Eq. 3.63) and test the restrictions $\theta = 1$ and $p = 2$, respectively, with the corresponding LRTs again having an approximate $\chi^2(1)$ distribution. For all these tests, we report the estimate of the parameter of interest.

[a]Significance at 10% level.
[b]Significance at 5% level.
[c]Significance at 1% level.

TABLE 3.4 Evaluation of Value-at-Risk (VaR) Measures

	Long positions				Short positions				
Model	0.005	0.01	0.025	0.05	0.005	0.01	0.025	0.05	MAPE
				France					
Single-component models									
nor.	0.85[b]	1.52[b]	3.88[c]	6.33[c]	0.30	0.78	1.78[b]	3.59[c]	0.41
t	0.67	1.15	3.66[c]	6.40[c]	0.15[c]	0.52[c]	1.63[c]	3.51[c]	0.38
sk-*t*	0.48	0.96	3.22[b]	5.99[b]	0.30	0.74	2.15	4.37	0.19
Two-component mixture models									
MN_s	0.74[a]	1.37[a]	3.92[c]	6.36[c]	0.18[c]	0.59[b]	1.78[b]	3.59[c]	0.41
MN	0.52	1.11	2.96	6.07[b]	0.33	0.96	1.89[b]	3.88[c]	0.17
MSN	0.55	1.15	3.11[a]	5.73[a]	0.37	0.92	2.33	4.22[a]	0.15
				Germany					
Single-component models									
nor.	0.92[c]	1.44[b]	3.48[c]	6.55[c]	0.22[b]	0.63[b]	1.96[a]	4.25[a]	0.41
t	0.63	1.22	3.07[a]	6.84[c]	0.18[c]	0.41[c]	1.48[c]	4.22[a]	0.36
sk-*t*	0.48	0.96	2.59	5.99[b]	0.30	0.81	2.59	5.36	0.13
Two-component mixture models									
MN_s	0.63	1.41[b]	3.37[c]	6.84[c]	0.15[c]	0.48[c]	1.81[b]	4.29[a]	0.38
MN	0.55	1.04	3.03[a]	6.44[c]	0.30	0.67[a]	2.48	4.59	0.18
MSN	0.48	0.89	2.52	5.85[b]	0.41	1.00	2.70	5.22	0.08
				United Kingdom					
Single-component models									
nor.	1.11[c]	1.89[c]	3.63[c]	5.81[a]	0.22[b]	0.41[c]	1.59[c]	3.70[c]	0.56
t	0.78[a]	1.55[c]	3.48[c]	5.96[b]	0.07[c]	0.30[c]	1.41[c]	3.70[c]	0.49
sk-*t*	0.70	1.29	3.14[b]	5.70	0.22[b]	0.52[c]	2.11	4.99	0.29
Two-component mixture models									
MN_s	0.85[b]	1.70[c]	3.88[c]	6.18[c]	0.07[c]	0.37[c]	1.52[c]	3.92[c]	0.54
MN	0.59	1.18	3.44[c]	5.88[b]	0.18[c]	0.48[c]	2.00[a]	4.44	0.30
MSN	0.67	1.26	2.96	5.48	0.30	0.67[a]	2.18	4.85	0.22

Shown are the results of the tests for correct coverage of out-of-sample Value-at-Risk measures for the three European stock market indices. For the abbreviations of the models, see Section 3.5.2. Reported are the realized one-day-ahead percentage shortfall ratios, U_ξ, for given target probabilities, as defined in Equation 3.58. MAPE is the mean absolute percentage error (3.60).

[a] Significance at 10% level as obtained from the likelihood ratio test.

[b] Significance at 5% level as obtained from the likelihood ratio test.

[c] Significance at 1% level as obtained from the likelihood ratio test.

skewness. Just like the results in Table 3.3, this shows that skewness, an important property of mixture models, is an important feature of the data when it comes to calculating predictive densities.

The asymmetric models all do reasonably well in measuring the risk of the stock market indices. However, the mixture GARCH model based on the SN distribution appears to exhibit the best fit overall both in terms of the number and strength of rejections as well as the MAPE, for which it has the lowest value for all three series. The VaR results are therefore consistent with the predictive density results in Table 3.3 in that they favor the SN mixture GARCH specification.

3.6 Conclusion

In this chapter, we have reviewed the extensive literature on mixture GARCH models. Although we concentrated on univariate specifications, it is clear that many applications in finance require a multivariate framework in order to model the dependencies between assets. In this respect, multivariate RS models may be particularly useful since they can handle asymmetric dependence structures, that is, the observation that the dependencies between assets tend to be stronger in bear markets than in bull markets, which has important consequences for portfolio construction; see Pelletier (2006), Bauwens et al. (2007), Haas et al. (2009), Lee (2009), and Haas (2010a) for some multivariate models and applications. While these models are rich in their ability to model multivariate asset returns, their obvious drawback is, similar to many multivariate GARCH models, the curse of dimensionality. There are (at least) two ways of dealing with the general multivariate case but still having the benefit of mixture structures. The first is to use independent component analysis (ICA) with each univariate component modeled by a mixture GARCH model; see Broda et al. (2011). The second way is to forgo GARCH structures and instead use short windows of estimation and parameter shrinkage; see Paolella (2011) and the references therein.

Acknowledgments

The research of Haas was supported by the German Research Foundation (DFG). Part of the research of Paolella has been carried out within the National Centre of Competence in Research "Financial Valuation and Risk Management" (NCCR FINRISK), which is a research program supported by the Swiss National Science Foundation. The authors wish to thank Jochen Krause for computational assistance, proofreading, and other input, which led to an improved presentation. We also thank Luc Bauwens for many helpful comments and suggestions.

CHAPTER FOUR

Forecasting High Dimensional Covariance Matrices

KEVIN SHEPPARD

4.1 Introduction

Multivariate volatility models were introduced in Kraft and Engle (1982) and Engle et al. (1984); subsequently, a large literature has developed on measuring, modeling, and predicting conditional covariances, correlations, and betas. This chapter provides an overview of the multivariate models that are capable of forecasting covariance when the number of assets in large, which I define as staring at 50. These models range from simple moving average estimators to relatively rich dynamic models. All high dimensional forecasting models share the common feature that a closed form or other simple, analytically tractable estimator is used to avoid direct estimation of parameters in large parameter spaces.

Forecasting large dimensional covariances is challenging since the cross-sectional dimension is often similar to the number of observations available. Simple estimators are often poorly conditioned with some small eigenvalues and so are unsuitable for many real world applications including portfolio optimization and tracking error minimization. Many covariance forecasting methods directly address the conditioning of the forecast covariance to improve performance in these problems.

Handbook of Volatility Models and Their Applications, First Edition.
Edited by Luc Bauwens, Christian Hafner, and Sebastien Laurent.

This chapter is complementary to recent surveys or multivariate ARCH models (Bauwens et al., 2006; Silvennoinen and Teräsvirta, 2009), multivariate stochastic volatility models (Chib et al., 2009) and realized covariance (RC) (Andersen and Benzoni, 2009; Andersen et al., 2010).

This chapter is organized as follows. Section 4.2 defines the notation used throughout. Section 4.3 describes some common, simple to estimate moving average estimators. Section 4.4 covers the limited selection of dynamic models that are capable of forecasting high dimensional dynamic covariances. Section 4.5 explores some recent developments in the use of ultrahigh frequency (tick-by-tick) data in the estimation of high dimensional covariances. Section 4.6 discusses the evaluation of these models, and section 4.7 concludes and discusses directions for future research.

4.2 Notation

Let $\boldsymbol{\varepsilon}_t = [\varepsilon_{1,t}, \varepsilon_{2,t}, \ldots, \varepsilon_{k,t}]'$ denote a k by 1, a vector-valued variable. The information set used in defining the conditional variance is $\mathcal{F}_{t-1}$ and is assumed to include the history of past returns but may include other variables. Denote the conditional covariance $\mathrm{V}[\boldsymbol{\varepsilon}_t|\mathcal{F}_{t-1}] \equiv \mathrm{V}_{t-1}[\boldsymbol{\varepsilon}_t] = \boldsymbol{\Sigma}_t$, a k by k symmetric, positive-definite matrix composed of elements $\sigma_{ij,t}$ where $\sigma_{ii,t} \equiv \sigma^2_{i,t}$ denotes the conditional variance of the ith variable and $\sigma_{ij,t}$ denotes the conditional covariance between variables i and j. Throughout I will assume $\mathrm{E}_{t-1}[\boldsymbol{\varepsilon}_t] = \mathbf{0}$ and so $\boldsymbol{\varepsilon}_t$ can either be residuals constructed by subtracting the conditional mean or data where the conditional mean is sufficiently close to 0 so as to be unimportant in covariance forecasting.[1] "Devolatilized" returns are defined as $\mathbf{u}_t = \boldsymbol{\varepsilon}_t \oslash \boldsymbol{\sigma}_t$ where $\boldsymbol{\sigma}_t$ is a k by 1 vector of conditional standard deviations, $u_{i,t} = \varepsilon_{i,t}/\sigma_{i,t}$, and $\oslash$ is Hadamard (element-by-element) division. Standardized returns are defined $\mathbf{e}_t = \boldsymbol{\Sigma}_t^{-1/2}\boldsymbol{\varepsilon}_t$ and satisfy $\mathbf{E}_{t-1}[\mathbf{e}_t\mathbf{e}_t'] = \mathbf{I}_k$. T data points are assumed to be available, although some estimators will be based on $m < T$ observations. I assume the interest is in forecasting the one-step ahead conditional covariance, $\mathrm{E}_t[\boldsymbol{\varepsilon}_{t+1}\boldsymbol{\varepsilon}_{t+1}'] = \boldsymbol{\Sigma}_{t+1}$, although multistep forecasting, using either iterative or direct methods, is possible in all models described.

4.3 Rolling Window Forecasts

Rolling window forecasts based on simple estimators and a window length $m < T$ have been widely used in the academic finance literature both for the ease of implementation and their connection of factor models such as the Capital Asset Pricing Model (CAP-M) (Markowitz, 1959; Sharpe, 1964; Lintner, 1965), arbitrage pricing theory (Ross, 1976) or the intertemporal capital asset pricing

[1]When using high frequency financial data, such as daily returns of liquid equities, the variation due to the squared mean represents less than 1% of the total variation in squared returns and so it is often assumed that the conditional mean is 0 (Andersen and Bollerslev, 1998).

model (Merton, 1973). The choice of window length has been explored in a limited manner in Foster and Nelson (1996), Andreou and Ghysels (2002), and Liu (2009b). An alternative is to treat the window length as a parameter that can be estimated or calibrated to database under study.

4.3.1 SAMPLE COVARIANCE

The simplest estimator is the sample covariance, defined

$$\Sigma_{t+1} = m^{-1} \sum_{i=0}^{m-1} \boldsymbol{\varepsilon}_{t-i} \boldsymbol{\varepsilon}'_{t-i}, \tag{4.1}$$

where m is the sample size used in the rolling window. The sample covariance estimator will be positive-definite as long as $m \geq k$ although the estimation error when $m \approx k$ makes computing its inverse problematic. This requirement limits its use in forecasting high dimensional covariance since the choice of window length is substantially impacted by the cross-sectional dimension, at least when invertibility is a concern. The sample covariance is used in a number of more sophisticated estimators, and so it is included for completeness.

4.3.2 OBSERVABLE FACTOR COVARIANCE

Many panels used in finance and macroeconomics are thought to be well approximated by a factor structure. In most cases, the factor structure is assumed to be weak in the sense that the residuals from the factor model are not necessarily uncorrelated. Weak factor structures ultimately require using sample covariance estimators to consistently estimate the complete covariance matrix. If the assumption of a weak factor model is replaced by an assumption of a strong factor model, then the estimation of the covariance can be simplified. Define $\mathbf{f}_t = [f_{1,t}, f_{2,t}, \ldots, f_{p,t}]'$ to be returns from a set of p observable factors, assumed to have conditional expectation 0. The observable factor covariance forecast is constructed using estimates of the factor covariance, the factor loadings, and the idiosyncratic covariance as

$$\boldsymbol{\Sigma}_{t+1} = \boldsymbol{\beta}'_{t+1} \boldsymbol{\Sigma}^f_{t+1} \boldsymbol{\beta}_{t+1} + \boldsymbol{\Omega}_{t+1}, \tag{4.2}$$

where

$$\boldsymbol{\beta}_{t+1} = \left(\sum_{i=0}^{m-1} \mathbf{f}_{t-i} \mathbf{f}'_{t-i} \right)^{-1} \left(\sum_{i=0}^{m-1} \mathbf{f}_{t-i} \boldsymbol{\varepsilon}'_{t-i} \right), \tag{4.3}$$

$$\boldsymbol{\Sigma}^f_{t+1} = m^{-1} \sum_{i=0}^{m-1} \mathbf{f}_{t-i} \mathbf{f}'_{t-i}, \tag{4.4}$$

$$\omega_{jj,t+1} = m^{-1} \sum_{i=0}^{m-1} \xi_{j,t-i}^2, \quad \omega_{jk,t+1} = 0 \;\; j \neq k, \tag{4.5}$$

$$\boldsymbol{\xi}_{j,t} = \boldsymbol{\varepsilon}_{j,t} - \boldsymbol{\beta}'_{j,t+1}\mathbf{f}_t,$$

where $\boldsymbol{\beta}_{j,t+1}$ is the jth column of $\boldsymbol{\beta}_{t+1}$. $\boldsymbol{\Omega}_{t+1}$ is a diagonal matrix with idiosyncratic variance of each series along its diagonal, and so covariance forecasts based on a factor structure are positive semidefinite as long as $p < m$ so that the idiosyncratic error variance of each series is positive. In practice, p is typically between 1 and 5 and so this is not an issue. Observable factor models can also be trivially extended to allow for structure among the factors and variables where subsets of returns are restricted to have exposure to only a subset of factors by imposing 0 restrictions in the factor loading matrix. Fan et al. (2008) show that when a set of assets follow a factor structure the gains to exploiting it, relative to the sample covariance, are small. However, the gains to exploiting the factor structure in terms of the *inverse* of the covariance matrix and for the construction of optimal portfolio weights are substantial. The CAPM inspired single-index covariance, where the only included factor is the return on the market portfolio, is an important input in more complicated models.

4.3.3 STATISTICAL FACTOR COVARIANCE

Statistical factor covariance, such as observable factor covariance estimators, exploits a strict factor structure to estimate a covariance matrix that is positive semidefinite after a small number of observations. The difference between the observable and the statistical factor covariance estimators is the specification of the factors. Statistical factor covariance estimators extract the factors directly from returns using principle components. Using the rolling window covariance estimator, the original data can be transformed into a k by k matrix of factor loadings $\mathbf{V}$ and the m by k matrix of factors, $\mathbf{F}$, so that $\boldsymbol{\varepsilon} = \mathbf{FV}$. The factor loadings are estimated using the eigenvectors of the sample covariance. Statistical factor estimators make use of $p \ll k$ factors to capture the covariance between assets. Define $\tilde{\mathbf{V}}$ to be the first p rows of $\mathbf{V}$ with $\tilde{\mathbf{f}}_t$ the associated p factors. The statistical factor covariance estimator is defined

$$\boldsymbol{\Sigma}_{t+1} = \tilde{\mathbf{V}}'_{t+1}\boldsymbol{\Sigma}^f_{t+1}\tilde{\mathbf{V}}_{t+1} + \hat{\boldsymbol{\Omega}}_{t+1}, \tag{4.6}$$

where

$$\boldsymbol{\Sigma}^f_{t+1} = m^{-1} \sum_{i=0}^{m-1} \tilde{\mathbf{f}}_{t-i}\tilde{\mathbf{f}}'_{t-i}, \tag{4.7}$$

$$\boldsymbol{\xi}_{j,t} = \boldsymbol{\varepsilon}_{j,t} - \tilde{\mathbf{V}}'_{j,t+1}\tilde{\mathbf{f}}_t,$$

$$\omega_{jj,t+1} = m^{-1} \sum_{i=0}^{m-1} \xi_{j,t-i}^2, \quad \omega_{jk,t+1} = 0 \;\; j \neq k,$$

where $\tilde{\mathbf{V}}_{j,t+1}$ is the jth column of $\tilde{\mathbf{V}}_{t+1}$. The factor model residuals, ξ_i, are reestimated in each window. This estimator only differs from the observable factor covariance through the definition of the factors and the estimation of the factor loadings. Abadir et al. (2010) investigate a modified version of this estimator that uses a subsampling scheme to produce a positive-definite estimator even when all factors are used ($p = k$). In their estimator, the eigenvectors are estimated using a subsample of the data and then covariance estimator is computed using the remaining data.

4.3.4 EQUICORRELATION

The equicorrelation covariance estimator is a parsimonious model where volatilities are allowed to differ across assets, but correlation is assumed to be common in all pairs. The equicorrelation estimator may be appropriate when the assets are homogeneous and has been widely applied in credit modeling (Embrechts et al., 1999). This estimator requires the correlation among the set of assets to lie in the range $\left(-\frac{1}{k+1}, 1\right)$ and so it would not be appropriate for assets with substantial heterogeneity in correlation or with some negative correlations.

The equicorrelation estimator is defined as

$$\boldsymbol{\Sigma}_{t+1} = \boldsymbol{\sigma}_{t+1}\boldsymbol{\sigma}'_{t+1} \odot \left((1 - \rho_{t+1})\mathbf{I}_k + \rho_{t+1}\iota\iota'\right),$$

where the standard deviations are estimated

$$\sigma_{i,t+1} = \sqrt{m^{-1}\sum_{i=0}^{m-1}\varepsilon_{i,t}^2}, \tag{4.8}$$

ι is a k by 1 vector of 1s, and $\odot$ is Hadamard (element-by-element) product. The equicorrelation, ρ_{t+1}, is usually estimated using a moment estimator. Define $\varepsilon_{p,t} = k^{-1}\sum_{i=1}^{k}\varepsilon_{k,t-i}$ as the return to an equally weighted portfolio and $\sigma_{p,t+1}^2 = m^{-1}\sum_{i=0}^{m-1}\varepsilon_{p,t}^2$ as the variance of this portfolio. The moment-condition-based estimator of the equicorrelation is then

$$\rho_{t+1} = \frac{\sigma_{p,t+1}^2 - k^{-2}\sum_{i=1}^{k}\sigma_{i,t}^2}{k^{-2}\sum_{i=1}^{k}\sum_{j=i+1}^{k}\sigma_{i,t+1}\sigma_{j,t+1}}. \tag{4.9}$$

While the moment-based estimator is consistent, it may not always fall within $\left(-\frac{1}{k+1}, 1\right)$. Assuming normality, the maximum likelihood estimator is an alternative estimator of the equicorrelation and is defined as the *maximizer* of

$$L(\rho_{t+1}; \mathbf{u}) = -\frac{m}{2}\ln|\mathbf{R}_{t+1}| - \frac{1}{2}\sum_{i=0}^{m-1}\mathbf{u}'_{t-i}\mathbf{R}_{t+1}^{-1}\mathbf{u}_{t-i} \tag{4.10}$$

$$= -\frac{m}{2}\ln\left((1-\rho)^{k-1}(1+(k-1)\rho)\right)$$

$$-\frac{1}{2(1-\rho)}\sum_{i=0}^{m-1}\left[\sum_{j=1}^{k}u_{j,t-i}^{2}-\frac{\rho}{1+(k-1)\rho}\left(\sum_{q=1}^{k}u_{q,t-i}\right)^{2}\right],$$

where $\mathbf{u}_t$ is a k by 1 vector of devolatilized residuals and $\mathbf{R}_{t+1}$ is the k by k equicorrelation matrix. This likelihood is computationally simple and so maximization is very fast even if k is large by precomputing $\sum_{j=1}^{k} u_{j,t-i}^{2}$ and $\sum_{q=1}^{k} u_{q,t-i}$.

4.3.5 SHRINKAGE ESTIMATORS

Shrinkage estimators combine two or more rolling window estimators based on a bias-variance trade-off. The study of shrinkage estimators of the covariance is typically based around two assumptions. First, the data are i.i.d., which while not realistic, does allow for analytical tractability that is needed to provide usable results in high dimensions. The second assumption is that the cross-sectional dimension, k, is growing with the sample size, T. This assumption validates the use of shrinkage estimators since the sample covariance is no longer consistent. Shrinkage forecasts combine two common estimators, and so

$$\mathbf{\Sigma}_{t+1} = w\mathbf{\Sigma}_{t+1}^{\mathrm{R}} + (1-w)\,\mathbf{\Sigma}_{t+1}^{\mathrm{S}},$$

where $\mathbf{\Sigma}_{t+1}^{\mathrm{S}}$ and $\mathbf{\Sigma}_{t+1}^{\mathrm{R}}$ are two forecasts. In most applications, $\mathbf{\Sigma}_{t+1}^{\mathrm{S}}$ is the sample covariance and $\mathbf{\Sigma}_{t+1}^{\mathrm{R}}$ is a restricted, estimator such as a one-factor covariance or the equicorrelation forecast. Ledoit and Wolf (2003) studied these estimators in the context of shrinking the sample covariance ($\mathbf{\Sigma}_{t+1}^{\mathrm{S}}$) toward a one-factor model ($\mathbf{\Sigma}_{t+1}^{\mathrm{R}}$) and derived the optimal shrinkage weight

$$w^{\star} = \frac{1}{T}\frac{A-B}{C},$$

where

$$\mathrm{A} = \sum_{i=1}^{k}\sum_{j=1}^{k}\mathrm{avar}\left(\sqrt{T}\sigma_{ij,t+1}^{\mathrm{S}}\right),$$

$$\mathrm{B} = \sum_{i=1}^{k}\sum_{j=1}^{k}\mathrm{acov}\left(\sqrt{T}\sigma_{ij,t+1}^{\mathrm{S}},\sqrt{T}\sigma_{ij,t+1}^{R}\right),$$

$$\mathrm{C} = \sum_{i=1}^{k}\sum_{j=1}^{k}\left(E[\sigma_{ij,t+1}^{\mathrm{S}}] - E[\sigma_{ij,t+1}^{\mathrm{R}}]\right)^{2}.$$

This shrinkage estimator takes the familiar form of many James-Stein-type shrinkage estimators (James and Stein, 1956). The amount of shrinkage is increasing in the variance of the sample covariance (A) and is decreasing in the amount of covariance between the sample covariance estimator and the one-factor covariance estimator (B) and the squared bias between the two estimators and the sample size (C). The construction of this shrinkage estimator assumes that the one-factor model is not consistent, which is necessary to ensure that $C > 0$. These quantities are population values and so, in practice, they must be estimated using sample analogs. If C is small then the estimate of $w^\star$ may be unreliable, and it is common to restrict the weight to lie between 0 and 1 using $\tilde{w}^\star = \min(1, \max(0, \hat{w}^\star))$. This shrinkage estimator was derived under and assumption of i.i.d. data, which is empirically rejectable, and so optimal shrinkage derived in Ledoit and Wolf (2003) would be expected to underestimate the true optimal shrinkage since the sample covariance estimators would be more volatile (A would be larger). Other shrinkage targets have been studied, including the identity matrix (Ledoit and Wolf, 2004a) and the equicorrelation matrix (Ledoit and Wolf, 2004b).

4.4 Dynamic Models

4.4.1 COVARIANCE TARGETING SCALAR VEC

Bollerslev et al., (1988) introduced the vector generalized autoregressive conditional heteroskedasticity (GARCH) specification for modeling the conditional covariance which is a flexible specification that nests many other multivariate GARCH specifications. The scalar version of the VEC has covariance dynamics that evolve according to

$$\boldsymbol{\Sigma}_{t+1} = \mathbf{C} + \alpha \boldsymbol{\varepsilon}_t \boldsymbol{\varepsilon}_t' + \beta \boldsymbol{\Sigma}_t,$$

where $\mathbf{C}$ is a positive-definite intercept and both α and β are positive scalars. The model has $k(k+1)/2 + 2$ parameters and so estimation is not feasible when k is large. Engle and Mezrich (1996) show that the scalar VEC can be "targeted," which allows that intercept to be concentrated out using a simple moment-based estimator. Assuming the $\alpha + \beta < 1$,

$$\mathrm{E}[\boldsymbol{\Sigma}_{t+1}] = \mathbf{C} + \alpha \mathrm{E}[\boldsymbol{\varepsilon}_t \boldsymbol{\varepsilon}_t'] + \beta \mathrm{E}[\boldsymbol{\Sigma}_t], \tag{4.11}$$

$$\bar{\boldsymbol{\Sigma}} = \mathbf{C} + \alpha \bar{\boldsymbol{\Sigma}} + \beta \bar{\boldsymbol{\Sigma}}, \tag{4.12}$$

$$\mathbf{C} = \bar{\boldsymbol{\Sigma}}\,(1 - \alpha - \beta)\,, \tag{4.13}$$

where $\bar{\boldsymbol{\Sigma}}$ is the unconditional covariance of $\boldsymbol{\varepsilon}_t$. $\bar{\boldsymbol{\Sigma}}$ can be estimated using the usual moment estimator

$$\hat{\bar{\boldsymbol{\Sigma}}} = T^{-1} \sum_{t=1}^{T} \boldsymbol{\varepsilon}_t \boldsymbol{\varepsilon}_t',$$

and the parameters which determine the dynamics can be estimated by maximizing the likelihood over only α and β using the targeted likelihood,

$$\boldsymbol{\Sigma}_{t+1} = \hat{\hat{\boldsymbol{\Sigma}}}(1-\alpha-\beta) + \alpha\boldsymbol{\varepsilon}_t\boldsymbol{\varepsilon}_t' + \beta\boldsymbol{\Sigma}_t.$$

Other methods that can be used to estimate α and β are discussed in Section 4.4.6.

4.4.2 FLEXIBLE MULTIVARIATE GARCH

The flexible multivariate GARCH (FLEX-M) is an algorithm to estimate high dimensional diagonal VEC specification (Ledoit et al., 2003). Covariances in a diagonal VEC evolve according to

$$\boldsymbol{\Sigma}_{t+1} = \mathbf{C} + \mathbf{A} \odot \boldsymbol{\varepsilon}_t\boldsymbol{\varepsilon}_t' + \mathbf{B} \odot \boldsymbol{\Sigma}_t,$$

where **C**, **A**, and **B** are symmetric parameter matrices. Ledoit et al., (2003) show that $\boldsymbol{\Sigma}_{t+1}$ will be positive-definite as long as **A** and **B** and $\mathbf{D} = \mathbf{C} \oslash (1-\mathbf{B})$ are all positive-definite since

$$\boldsymbol{\Sigma}_{t+1} = \mathbf{C} \oslash (1-\mathbf{B}) + \sum_{i=0}^{\infty} \mathbf{B}^{\odot i} \odot \mathbf{A} \odot \boldsymbol{\varepsilon}_t\boldsymbol{\varepsilon}_t',$$

where $^{\odot i}$ is used to denote element-by-element exponentiation. This insight suggests that the diagonal model could be estimated using a multistep procedure:

1. For $i = 1, \ldots, k$ estimate univariate GARCH(1,1) models for $\varepsilon_{i,t}$,

$$\sigma_{i,t+1}^2 = \omega_{ii} + \alpha_{ii}\varepsilon_{i,t}^2 + \beta_{ii}\sigma_{i,t}^2,$$

   by maximizing univariate normal likelihoods and retain the estimates $\hat{\boldsymbol{\theta}}_i = [\hat{\omega}_{ii}, \hat{\alpha}_{ii}, \hat{\beta}_{ii}]$.
2. For $i = 2, \ldots, k, j = i+1, \ldots, k$ estimate $\theta_{ij} = [\omega_{ij}, \alpha_{ij}, \beta_{ij}]$ using a bivariate GARCH(1,1) conditioning on the previously estimates of θ_{ii} and θ_{jj} parameters where the conditional covariance is

$$\boldsymbol{\Sigma}_{ij,t+1} = \begin{bmatrix} \hat{\omega}_{ii} & \omega_{ij} \\ \omega_{ij} & \hat{\omega}_{jj} \end{bmatrix} + \begin{bmatrix} \hat{\alpha}_{ii} & \alpha_{ij} \\ \alpha_{ij} & \hat{\alpha}_{jj} \end{bmatrix} \odot \begin{bmatrix} \varepsilon_{i,t}^2 & \varepsilon_{i,t}\varepsilon_{j,t} \\ \varepsilon_{i,t}\varepsilon_{j,t} & \varepsilon_{j,t}^2 \end{bmatrix}$$
$$+ \begin{bmatrix} \hat{\beta}_{ii} & \beta_{ij} \\ \beta_{ij} & \hat{\beta}_{jj} \end{bmatrix} \odot \boldsymbol{\Sigma}_{ij,t},$$

   by maximizing the bivariate normal likelihood. The constraints $|\omega_{ij}| < \sqrt{\hat{\omega}_{ii}\hat{\omega}_{jj}}$, $|\alpha_{ij}| \le \sqrt{\hat{\alpha}_{ii}\hat{\alpha}_{jj}}$, and $|\beta_{ij}| \le \sqrt{\hat{\beta}_{ii}\hat{\beta}_{jj}}$, are sufficient to ensure that the bivariate covariance is positive-definite.

3. Assemble $\hat{\mathbf{C}}$, $\hat{\mathbf{A}}$, and $\hat{\mathbf{B}}$ from the estimates computed in the previous two steps.

This algorithm requires $k(k+1)/2$ optimizations that can be slow if k is very large, although each optimization is no more difficult than estimating a univariate GARCH model. The computational speed can be improved by saving the fit conditional variances in the first step and so only the conditional covariance between assets i and j needs to be recursively computed in the second step.

In large samples, these parameters should satisfy the constraints necessary for the conditional covariance to be positive-definite. In finite samples, the restriction may be violated, and if so, an additional step is needed to enforce the constraint. This is accomplished using an algorithm from Sharapov (1997). Suppose $\mathbf{Z}$ is a symmetric matrix with strictly positive diagonal elements. A positive-definite matrix $\ddot{\mathbf{Z}}$ can be constructed to be as close as possible in the Frobenius norm sense as

$$\min_{\ddot{\mathbf{Z}}} \|\mathbf{Z} - \ddot{\mathbf{Z}}\| \text{ subject to } \ddot{\mathbf{Z}} \text{ is positive semidefinite and } z_{ii} = \ddot{z}_{ii}, \quad i = 1, 2, \ldots, k.$$

This additional step is applied to $\hat{\mathbf{A}}$ and $\hat{\mathbf{B}}$ to produce $\ddot{\mathbf{A}}$ and $\ddot{\mathbf{B}}$ and then to $\hat{\mathbf{D}} = \hat{\mathbf{C}} \oslash \left(1 - \ddot{\mathbf{B}}\right)$ to produce $\ddot{\mathbf{C}} = \ddot{\mathbf{D}} \oslash \left(1 - \ddot{\mathbf{B}}\right)$. The conditional covariance is then forecast using

$$\boldsymbol{\Sigma}_{t+1} = \ddot{\mathbf{C}} + \ddot{\mathbf{A}} \odot \boldsymbol{\varepsilon}_t \boldsymbol{\varepsilon}_t' + \ddot{\mathbf{B}} \odot \boldsymbol{\Sigma}_t.$$

4.4.3 CONDITIONAL CORRELATION GARCH MODELS

Conditional correlation GARCH models all make use of the decomposition of the covariance into standard deviations and correlation,

$$\boldsymbol{\Sigma}_{t+1} = \mathbf{D}_{t+1} \mathbf{R}_{t+1} \mathbf{D}_{t+1},$$

where $\mathbf{D}_{t+1}$ is a diagonal matrix with the conditional standard deviation of the ith asset in its ith diagonal position and the evolution of $\mathbf{R}_{t+1}$ depends on the choice of the model. The conditional variances are typically modeled using univariate GARCH models, and so

$$\sigma_{i,t+1}^2 = \omega_i + \alpha_i \varepsilon_{i,t}^2 + \beta_i \sigma_{i,t}^2 \quad i = 1, 2, \ldots, k,$$

although other models, for example, EGARCH (Nelson, 1991b), GJR-GARCH (Glosten et al., 1993), or TARCH/ZARCH (Zakoian, 1994), could be used instead. The conditional correlations are modeled sequentially using the standardized residuals $\mathbf{u}_t$.

The constant conditional correlation (CCC-) GARCH assumes that $\mathbf{R}_{t+1} = \mathbf{R}$ for $t = 1, 2, \ldots, T$ (Bollerslev, 1990). This assumption allows for closed-form estimation of the conditional correlation using the usual correlation estimator,

$$\mathbf{R} = \mathbf{Q}^{*}\mathbf{Q}\mathbf{Q}^{*}, \tag{4.14}$$

$$\mathbf{Q} = T^{-1}\sum_{t=1}^{T}\mathbf{e}_t\mathbf{e}_t',$$

$$\mathbf{Q}^{*} = (\mathbf{Q} \odot \mathbf{I}_k)^{-\frac{1}{2}},$$

where $\mathbf{Q}^{*}$ is a diagonal matrix needed to ensure that $\mathbf{R}$ is a correlation matrix. Another possibility for estimating $\mathbf{R}$ would be to use a statistical factor model to limit the estimation uncertainty. The estimator would be Equation 4.7 applied to the devolatilized residuals. In this case, the conditional correlation would be defined as

$$\mathbf{R} = \mathbf{Q}^{*}\tilde{\mathbf{Q}}\mathbf{Q}^{*}, \tag{4.15}$$

where $\tilde{\mathbf{Q}}$ would be the p-factor statistical covariance of the devolatilized residuals. While I am not aware of any applications of this type of regularization, it may provide an improvement when the cross-sectional dimension is large and can be used to produce a positive-definite conditional correlation forecast when $T < k$. It is related to the modified dynamic conditional correlation (DCC) estimator studied in Hafner and Reznikova (2010b).

Engle (2002a) introduces the DCC-GARCH model that extends the CCC-GARCH to allow for simple scalar-*vec*-like dynamics for the conditional correlations. Like the CCC-GARCH model, conditional correlations are modeled using the devolatilized returns. The DCC-GARCH model is specified

$$\mathbf{Q}_{t+1} = (1-\delta-\gamma)\bar{\mathbf{Q}} + \delta\mathbf{u}_t\mathbf{u}_t' + \gamma\mathbf{Q}_{t-1}, \tag{4.16}$$

$$\mathbf{R}_{t+1} = \mathbf{Q}_{t+1}^{*}\mathbf{Q}_{t+1}\mathbf{Q}_{t+1}^{*},$$

$$\mathbf{Q}_{t+1}^{*} = \left(\mathbf{Q}_{t+1} \odot \mathbf{I}_k\right)^{-\frac{1}{2}}.$$

DCC models are typically estimated using a three-step strategy. The first step is identical to the first step in the CCC-GARCH model and requires the estimation of k scalar volatility models that are typically standard GARCH(1,1) specification but can also take other forms. The second step is to estimate the covariance of returns for use in "correlation targeting" and is identical to the estimator of $\mathbf{Q}$ in the CCC-GARCH model. The final step estimates the parameters that determine the dynamics of the DCC, δ, and γ using m-profile maximum likelihood estimation. Hafner and Reznikova (2010b) consider an alternative estimator for DCC models where shrinkage is used on the correlation intercept using the identity matrix, a one-factor model, or the equicorrelation model as restricted estimators. They find that shrinking the correlation target leads to substantial decreases in the bias when the number of assets is large relative to the number of time periods ($1 \leq k/T \leq 5$).

The factor DCC model of Rangel and Engle (2009) combines the standard DCC with a p-(weak) observable factor model where the errors are assumed to be unconditionally uncorrelated with the factors but may be conditionally correlated with the factors. Only the one-factor version of the model is presented and the p-factor extension is simple. The model begins with a standard factor model where

$$r_{i,t} = \alpha_i + \beta_i r_{m,t} + \nu_{i,t}, \tag{4.17}$$

and it is assumed that the factor and the residuals are unconditionally uncorrelated, $\mathrm{E}[r_{m,t}\nu_{i,t}] = 0$ for $i = 1, 2, \ldots, k$, although the conditional correlation may be nonzero. It is further assumed that the $k+1$ by 1 vector $\boldsymbol{\varepsilon}_t = [r_{m,t}\ \nu_{1,t}\ \nu_{2,t}\ \ldots\ \nu_{k,t}]'$ has conditional covariance given by

$$\mathrm{E}_{t-1}[\boldsymbol{\varepsilon}_t \boldsymbol{\varepsilon}_t'] = \mathbf{H}_t = \mathbf{D}_t \mathbf{R}_t \mathbf{D}_t,$$

where $\mathbf{D}_t$ is a diagonal matrix containing conditional standard deviations and $\mathbf{R}_t$ is the conditional correlation. The conditional standard deviations can follow any ARCH-family process (Rangel and Engle 2009) use a spline-GARCH, see Engle and Rangel, 2008), and $\mathbf{R}_t$ evolves according to a standard DCC. The factor structure underlying returns means that the conditional covariance forecast is

$$\boldsymbol{\Sigma}_{t+1} = \mathbf{B}\mathbf{H}_{t+1}\mathbf{B}' = \mathbf{B}\mathbf{D}_{t+1}\mathbf{R}_{t+1}\mathbf{D}_{t+1}\mathbf{B}', \tag{4.18}$$

where

$$\mathbf{B} = \begin{bmatrix} 1 & \mathbf{0}' \\ \boldsymbol{\beta} & \mathbf{I}_k \end{bmatrix},$$

where $\mathbf{0}$ is a k by 1 vector of 0s and $\boldsymbol{\beta}$ is the k by 1 vector of cross-sectional regression coefficients. Estimation of the factor DCC model only differs from the standard DCC with respect to the estimation of $\boldsymbol{\beta}$ that can be consistently estimated using a standard cross-sectional regression. DCC-class models, such as the scalar VEC, can be estimated using techniques other than maximum likelihood as discussed in Section 4.4.6.

4.4.4 ORTHOGONAL GARCH

Orthogonal GARCH assumes that the data are generated by an unconditional factor model where the factors are unconditionally uncorrelated and is related to the rolling window statistical factor model (Alexander, 2001; Alexander and Chibumba, 1997). O-GARCH forecasts begin with a principal components decomposition of the original data,

$$\boldsymbol{\varepsilon} = \mathbf{F}\mathbf{V},$$

where $\mathbf{F}$ is a T by k matrix of uncorrelated factors and $\mathbf{V}$ is a k by k matrix of factor loadings where $\mathbf{V}'\mathbf{V} = \mathbf{I}_k$. The simplest implementation of O-GARCH utilizes all k factors to forecast the covariance. The conditional covariance of the factors, $\mathbf{\Sigma}^f_t$, is defined

$$\mathbf{\Sigma}^f_{t+1,ii} = \omega_i + \alpha_i f^2_{i,t} + \beta_i \mathbf{\Sigma}^t_{t,ii}, \quad i = 1, \ldots, k, \tag{4.19}$$
$$\mathbf{\Sigma}^f_{t+1,ij} = 0, \quad i \neq j,$$

and so the forecast is

$$\mathbf{\Sigma}_{t+1} = \mathbf{V}'\mathbf{\Sigma}^f_{t+1}\mathbf{V}. \tag{4.20}$$

In most applications, using all the factors is undesirable and a modified version that uses $p \ll k$ factors can be constructed as

$$\mathbf{\Sigma}_{t+1} = \tilde{\mathbf{V}}'\tilde{\mathbf{\Sigma}}^f_{t+1}\tilde{\mathbf{V}} + \mathbf{\Omega}, \tag{4.21}$$

where $\tilde{\mathbf{V}}$ contains the first p rows of $\mathbf{V}$, $\tilde{\mathbf{\Sigma}}^f_{t+1}$ is the upper p by p block of $\mathbf{\Sigma}^f_{t+1}$, and $\mathbf{\Omega}$ is defined in Equation 4.7. The number of factors to use, p, can be selected using one of the information criteria in Bai and Ng (2002). A less restrictive estimator that does not require that the factors are conditionally uncorrelated has been considered in van der Weide (2002). Chib et al. (2006) propose a factor model in a stochastic volatility framework that is suitable for large panels.

4.4.5 RISKMETRICS

The RiskMetrics model is one of the best known forecasting covariance models and is popular for its transparency and ease of implementation. The usual RiskMetrics model is formally known as *RM1994* and covariance evolve according to an exponentially weighted moving average (EWMA) of the outer product of returns.

The RiskMetrics covariance is defined recursively as

$$\mathbf{\Sigma}_{t+1} = (1 - \lambda)\boldsymbol{\varepsilon}_t\boldsymbol{\varepsilon}'_t + \lambda\mathbf{\Sigma}_t, \tag{4.22}$$

for $\lambda \in (0, 1)$. It is equivalently defined through the infinite moving average

$$\mathbf{\Sigma}_{t+1} = (1 - \lambda)\sum_{i=0}^{\infty} \lambda^i \boldsymbol{\varepsilon}_t\boldsymbol{\varepsilon}'_t. \tag{4.23}$$

Implementation of the RiskMetrics covariance forecast requires an initial value for $\mathbf{\Sigma}_1$, which can be set to the average covariance over the first m days for some $m > k$ or could be set to the sample covariance. The single parameter, λ, is usually set to 0.94 for daily data and 0.97 for monthly data based on recommendations from RiskMetrics (J.P. Morgan, 1996).

The 1994 RiskMetrics Covariance has been surpassed by RM2006 that uses a *(pseudo) long memory* model for volatility , which requires that the weights on past returns decay hyperbolically rather than exponentially. The current methodology uses a three-parameter model that includes a logarithmic decay factor, τ_0 (1560), a lower cutoff, τ_1 (4), and an upper cutoff $\tau_{\max}$ (512), where suggested values are in parentheses (Zumbach, 2007). One additional parameter, ρ, is required to operationalize the model and RiskMetrics suggests $\sqrt{2}$.[2] The new methodology extends the 1994 methodology by computing the volatility as a weighted sum of EWMAs rather than a single EWMA.

The RM2006 covariance estimator is computed as the average of m-EWMA covariances according to

$$\begin{aligned}
\hat{\boldsymbol{\Sigma}}_{t+1} &= \sum_{i=1}^{m} w_i \tilde{\boldsymbol{\Sigma}}_{i,t+1}, \qquad (4.24)\\
\tilde{\boldsymbol{\Sigma}}_{i,t+1} &= (1-\lambda_i)\,\boldsymbol{\varepsilon}_t\boldsymbol{\varepsilon}_t' + \lambda_i \boldsymbol{\Sigma}_{k,t},\\
w_i &= \frac{1}{C}\left(1 - \frac{\ln(\tau_k)}{\ln(\tau_0)}\right),\\
\lambda_i &= \exp\left(-\frac{1}{t_i}\right),\\
\tau_i &= \tau_1 \rho^{i-1}, \quad i = 1, 2, \ldots, m,
\end{aligned}$$

where C is the normalization constant that ensures that $\sum_{i=1}^{m} w_i = 1$.

Both RiskMetrics estimators can be expressed as $\hat{\boldsymbol{\Sigma}}_{t+1} = \sum_{i=1}^{\infty} \gamma_i \boldsymbol{\varepsilon}_t \boldsymbol{\varepsilon}_t'$ for a set of weights $\{\gamma_i\}$. The 2006 methodology has both higher weight on recent data and higher weight on data in the distant past. One method to compare the two models is considering how many periods it takes for 99% of the weight to have been accumulated, or $\min_n \sum_{i=0}^{n} \gamma_i \geq 0.99$. For the RM1994 methodology, this happens in 75 days when $\lambda = 0.94$–the RM2006 methodology requires 619 days to achieve the same target (using the suggested parameter values). The first 75 weights in the RM2006 estimator contain 83% of the weight, and so 1/6 of the total weight depends on returns more than six months in the past.

One important limitation of either RiskMetrics covariance forecast is that the conditioning, as defined as the ratio of the largest to the smallest eigenvalue, of the covariance matrix deteriorates as k grows. This does not occur in a covariance targeting scalar VEC as long as the sum of the dynamics parameters is less than 1 and the target (or intercept) is positive-definite. This difference arises since the RiskMetrics forecast does not have a lower bound, unlike the scalar BEKK.

All the rolling window forecasts in Section 4.3 can be implemented as EWMA estimators by replacing the sum and average by the EWMA. The RM1994 forecast is the sample covariance where this has been done. An EWMA

[2] $\tau_{\max}$ does not directly appear in the equations for the RM2006 framework, but is implicitly included since $m = \ln\left(\frac{\tau_{\max}}{\tau_1}\right) / \ln \rho$.

observable factor model can be constructed by replacing the rolling window estimators' averages in Equations 4.3–4.5 with EWMA. Additionally, the EWMA decay parameter can be allowed to vary in the different equations, which allows the creation of a model with, for example, slowly moving factor loadings and a rapidly varying factor covariance. For example, an EWMA observable factor model is defined

$$\boldsymbol{\beta}_{t+1} = \left(\sum_{i=0}^{\infty}(1-\lambda_\beta)\lambda_\beta^i \mathbf{f}_{t-i}\mathbf{f}_{t-i}'\right)^{-1}\left(\sum_{i=0}^{\infty}(1-\lambda_\beta)\lambda_\beta^i \mathbf{f}_{t-i}\boldsymbol{\varepsilon}_{t-i}'\right),$$

$$\boldsymbol{\Sigma}_{t+1}^{f} = \sum_{i=0}^{\infty}(1-\lambda_f)\lambda_f^i \mathbf{f}_{t-i}\mathbf{f}_{t-i}',$$

$$\omega_{jj,t+1} = \sum_{i=0}^{\infty}(1-\lambda_\xi)\lambda_\xi^i \xi_{j,t-i}^2, \quad \omega_{jk,t+1} = 0 \;\; j \neq k,$$

where λ_β, λ_f, and λ_ξ control the decay in the factor loadings, factor covariance and idiosyncratic variance equations, respectively.

4.4.6 ALTERNATIVE ESTIMATORS FOR MULTIVARIATE GARCH MODELS

Two alternative but related methods for estimating the parameters that govern the dynamics of the DCC have been proposed in Engle (2009a), Engle (2009b), and Engle et al. (2008). Engle (2009a) proposed the "MacGyver" estimator for δ and γ. The MacGyver estimator is constructed by estimating all bivariate DCC-GARCH models that are nested within a complete k asset model—there are $k(k-1)/2$ unique pairings—and then taking the median value of each parameter. Let $\{\hat{\delta}_i\}$ and $\{\hat{\gamma}_i\}$, $i = 1, 2, \ldots, k(k-1)/2$ be the set of parameter estimates from the bivariate models, the estimator is $\hat{\delta}_{\mathrm{M}} = \operatorname{median}(\hat{\delta}_i)$ and $\hat{\gamma}_{\mathrm{M}} = \operatorname{median}(\hat{\gamma}_i)$. Engle (2009b) considered other functions to aggregate the parameter estimates in the models including the mean and the trimmed mean. The performance of the mean was notably worse than either the median or the trimmed mean because of the occurrence of some pairs where $\hat{\delta}_i \approx 0$ and so $\hat{\gamma}_i$ is not identified.

Engle et al. (2008) (hereafter ESS) also use pairs of assets to estimate parameters of targeted DCC and scalar BEKK models. Rather than using the full k-dimensional Gaussian likelihood, ESS use all pairwise likelihoods to construct a composite likelihood,

$$\mathrm{CL}(\boldsymbol{\varepsilon}_t; \boldsymbol{\lambda}, \boldsymbol{\theta}) = \frac{2}{(k-1)k}\sum_{i=1}^{k}\sum_{j=i+1}^{k}\ln f\left(\varepsilon_{i,t}, \varepsilon_{j,t}; \boldsymbol{\lambda}_{ij}, \boldsymbol{\theta}\right),$$

where $f\left(\varepsilon_{i,t}, \varepsilon_{j,t}; \boldsymbol{\lambda}_{ij}, \boldsymbol{\theta}\right)$ is a bivariate Gaussian density and the parameters of the model have been partitioned so $\boldsymbol{\theta} \in \boldsymbol{\Theta}$ contains all parameters that are common to all pairwise likelihoods while $\boldsymbol{\lambda}_{ij} \in \boldsymbol{\Lambda}_{ij}$ contains any parameters that are specific to the ijth pair. The parameters that are specific to the pair are considered to be "nuisance" parameters and are further assumed to be variation free in the sense $\boldsymbol{\Lambda} = \boldsymbol{\Lambda}_{11} \times \boldsymbol{\Lambda}_{12} \times \ldots \times \boldsymbol{\Lambda}_{k-1,k}$. Composite likelihood estimation has a number of advantages over the usual practice of using the k-dimensional Gaussian likelihood. First, the composite likelihood estimator only requires invertibility of the 2-by-2 covariance for each pair and so is applicable when $k > T$. Second, the assumption of variation free nuisance parameters allows for simple inference that does not require inversion of a high dimensional Hessian. Finally, the estimator is fast and computationally simpler than the usual ML in the sense that the number of calculations required to compute the composite likelihood is lower order in k than the full likelihood. Moreover, ESS show that a subset of the pairs can be used and propose choosing adjacent pairs (e.g., 1-2, 2-3, ...), which further reduces the order of the problem and allows models with hundreds of assets to be estimated in a few seconds.

4.5 High Frequency Based Forecasts

The most recent developments in covariance measurement and forecasting have focused on using ultrahigh frequency (UHF) financial data, either transaction prices or quotes, to provide estimates of the integrated covariance. In many ways, these estimators are the high frequency analogs of rolling window estimators and share many common features. Estimation of covariances using UHF data requires addressing some new problems which were not present when using lower frequency data: market microstructure noise and the effects of nonsynchronous trading.

Realized variance and covariance were introduced to econometrics by Andersen et al. (2001) (see also Andersen et al. (2001b) and Barndorff-Nielsen and Shephard (2002a)). Prices are assumed to be a semimartingale,

$$d\mathbf{p}_t = \boldsymbol{\mu}_t dt + \boldsymbol{\Omega}_t d\mathbf{W}_t,$$

where $\mathbf{p}_t$ is the log price at time t, $\boldsymbol{\mu}_t$ is the instantaneous drift, $\boldsymbol{\Sigma}_t = \boldsymbol{\Omega}_t \boldsymbol{\Omega}_t'$ is the instantaneous covariance of returns, and $\mathbf{W}_t$ is a standard k-variate Wiener process.[3] In this framework, it is tempting to estimate $\boldsymbol{\Sigma}_t$ as a basis for forecasting future returns. Estimation of the *spot covariance* is difficult since the estimator is slow to converge (Foster and Nelson, 1996). In practice, the *integrated covariance* is usually estimated,

$$\text{ICov} = \int_0^1 \boldsymbol{\Sigma}_s \, ds,$$

[3]Prices may also contain jumps. Most forecasting methods using UHF data are developed in a stochastic environment where jumps are excluded, and so this chapter also excludes jumps from the price process.

where 0 and 1 represent an arbitrary interval, usually one day. All the UHF-based forecasting methods assume that covariance follows a random walk, and so $\boldsymbol{\Sigma}_{t+1}$ is set to the last estimate of the integrated covariance.

4.5.1 REALIZED COVARIANCE

RC uses UHF data to estimate the integrated covariance. The RC on day t is computed as the outer product of high frequency returns. Define $\boldsymbol{r}_{i,t} = \mathbf{p}_{i,t} - \mathbf{p}_{i-1,t}$, $i = 1, 2, \ldots, m$ as a set of m high frequency returns constructed from transaction prices or mid-quotes. RC is defined

$$\mathrm{RC}_t = \sum_{i=1}^{m} \mathbf{r}_{i,t}\mathbf{r}_{i,t}'. \tag{4.25}$$

Under an assumption that prices follow an arbitrage-free semimartingale, Barndorff-Nielsen and Shephard (2004a) show that RC_t is a consistent estimator of the integrated covariance. In principle, RC can be trivially extended to high dimensional problems as long as prices can be sampled frequently (e.g., m is large). However, nonsynchronous trading and market microstructure noise both limit the highest sampling frequency. de Pooter et al. (2008) studies the optimal sampling frequency using a subset of the assets in the S&P 100 and find that the sampling between 30 and 65 min—between 6 and 13 samples per day—performs best using a set of economically motivated tests. In practice, it is often useful to improve the estimator by *subsampling* (Zhang et al., 2005). Subsampled RC improves on RC estimators whenever prices are not sampled at the highest frequency. Suppose m returns are available but due to market microstructure concerns—nonsynchronous trading and/or bid-ask bounce—blocks n returns are used to compute RC_t, so that

$$\mathrm{RC}_t = \sum_{i=1}^{m/n} \tilde{\mathbf{r}}_{(i-1)n+1,t}\tilde{\mathbf{r}}_{(i-1)n+1,t}', \tag{4.26}$$

where $\tilde{\mathbf{r}}_{k,t} = \sum_{j=1}^{n} r_{k+j-1,t}$ are the cumulative returns over the block of n returns beginning at index k. This estimator is inefficient since it does not make use of all data, and the subsampled RC is defined

$$\mathrm{RC}_t^{\mathrm{SS}} = \frac{m}{n(m-n+1)} \sum_{i=1}^{m-n+1} \tilde{\mathbf{r}}_{i,t}\tilde{\mathbf{r}}_{i,t}', \tag{4.27}$$

where $\frac{m}{n(m-n+1)}$ is a scaling factor that accounts for the overlap of the blocks. The forecast covariance is then $\boldsymbol{\Sigma}_{t+1} = \mathrm{RC}_t$ or $\boldsymbol{\Sigma}_{t+1} = \mathrm{RC}_t^{\mathrm{SS}}$.

Kyj et al. (2009) and Voev (2007) apply the shrinkage estimator of Ledoit and Wolf (2004a) to RC matrices. They find that shrinkage improves portfolio allocation problems when a subsampled RC is shrunk toward a realized version of the equicorrelation estimator. Oomen (2010) examines the performance of high dimensional covariance forecasts using UHF data with an emphasis on varying the forecast horizon from 1-min to 45-min, frequencies relevant for high frequency trading. Oomen finds that matching the measurement frequency to the forecast horizon is important, as is imposing a factor structure, but using lower frequency data reduces the performance in economic applications. Moreover, relatively simple covariance forecasts are capable of out-performing simple portfolio strategies such as no-short constraints or $1/k$ naïve diversification.

4.5.2 MIXED-FREQUENCY FACTOR MODEL COVARIANCE

Bannouh et al. (2009) impose a strict factor model to forecast high dimensional covariance matrices. The mixed-frequency factor model (MFFM) combines factor loadings estimated using daily data with a factor covariance estimated using RC. The precision of RC is adversely affected by trading frequency and so is unlikely to provide accurate forecasts for many assets that are not liquid. The MFFM avoids this issue by only estimating the factor covariance for a set of liquid factors and estimating the other parameters for the model using lower frequency data.

The MFFM model forecasts covariance using

$$\boldsymbol{\Sigma}_{t+1} = \boldsymbol{\beta}'_{t+1}\boldsymbol{\Sigma}^f_{t+1}\boldsymbol{\beta}_{t+1} + \boldsymbol{\Omega}_{t+1}.$$

The factor loadings are estimated using rolling OLS from daily data over $t - m$ to t, and the nonzero elements of $\boldsymbol{\Omega}_{t+1}$ are estimated using the residuals from the rolling regression, and so the estimators of $\boldsymbol{\beta}_{t+1}$ and $\boldsymbol{\Omega}_{t+1}$ are identical to those in the observable factor covariance forecast (Eq. (4.3)). In their empirical application, Bannouh et al. (2009) use 2.5 years of daily data to estimate these quantities. The MFFM differs from the observable factor covariance by estimating the covariance of the factors, $\boldsymbol{\Sigma}^f_{t+1}$, using UHF data. Let $\mathbf{f}_{i,t}$, $i = 1, 2, \ldots, m$, denote a set of m intradaily returns of the factors on day t. The factor covariance is estimated using the RC estimator on the factor returns,

$$\boldsymbol{\Sigma}^f_{t+1} = \sum_{i=1}^{m} \mathbf{f}_{i,t}\mathbf{f}'_{i,t}.$$

4.5.3 REGULARIZATION AND BLOCKING COVARIANCE

Hautsch et al. (2009) introduce the regularization and blocking (RnB) RC estimator. Unlike the MFFM, RnB is implemented using only intradaily returns over a single day. The RnB estimator is constructed in two steps. The first constructs a blocked covariance estimator in an effort to avoid discarding substantial amounts of the data and the second regularizes the initial covariance estimator.

Suppose the assets are ordered from most liquid (the highest number of transactions) to least. The first step in the RnB estimator is to estimate realized kernels using blocks. Multivariate realized kernels allow for estimation of the integrated covariance using tick-by-tick data when returns may not be synchronously traded and are defined

$$\mathrm{RK}_t = \mathbf{\Gamma}_0 + \sum_{i=1}^{H} K\left(\frac{i}{H+1}\right)\left(\mathbf{\Gamma}_i + \mathbf{\Gamma}_i'\right), \tag{4.28}$$

$$\mathbf{\Gamma}_j = \sum_{i=j+1}^{\tilde{m}} \tilde{\boldsymbol{r}}_{i,t}\tilde{\boldsymbol{r}}_{i-j,t},$$

where $\tilde{\boldsymbol{r}}_{i,t}$ are *refresh time returns*, $\tilde{m}$ is the number of refresh time returns, $K(\cdot)$ is a kernel weighting function , and H is a parameter that controls the ***bandwidth***. Refresh time returns are needed to ensure that prices are not overly stale and are computed by sampling all prices using last price interpolation only when all assets have traded. A simple bivariate example that illustrates the construction of refresh time returns is presented in Figure 4.1. Refresh time prices are only computed when both assets have traded, and refresh time returns are computed as the difference of refresh time log prices.[4]

The recommended kernel is Parzen's,

$$K(x) = \begin{cases} 1 - 6x^2 + 6x^3 & 0 > x \geq \frac{1}{2} \\ 2(1-x)^3 & \frac{1}{2} > x \geq 1 \\ 0 & x > 1 \end{cases}. \tag{4.29}$$

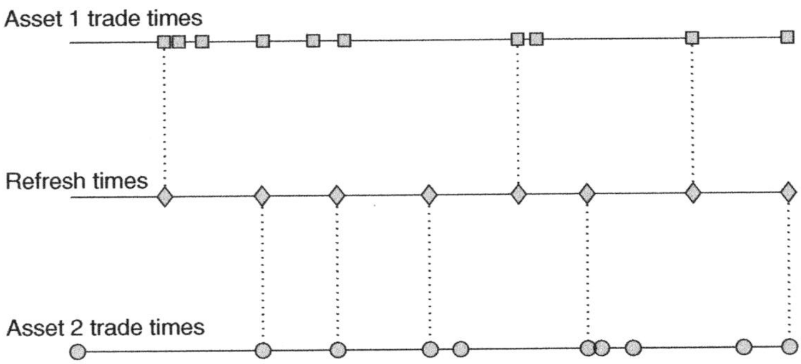

FIGURE 4.1 Refresh time sampling. The top and bottom bar indicate trade times of two assets, and the middle bar contains the refresh times. The dashed lines indicate the return which triggered the refresh, which occur after both assets have traded. When the number of assets is larger than 2, refresh times occur when all assets have traded.

[4]Consistency of multivariate realized kernels also requires preaveraging the first few prices of each series to eliminate end effects. In practice the number of prices which should be averaged is typically 1–3 when the number of observations is greater than 1000.

Selection of the bandwidth parameter, H, is an important choice when implementing realized kernels. For further details, see Barndorff-Nielsen et al. (2008) and Barndorff-Nielsen et al. (2010).

The realized blocked kernel attempts to minimize the amount of data discarded while remaining tractable in terms of the amount of estimation required in implementation. The implementation used three blocks, which requires estimating a total of six multivariate kernels. Let A represent the set of assets that are most liquid, B represent the assets with medium liquidity and C represent the assets with the lowest liquidity. Realized kernels are fit to A, B, C, A ∪ B, B ∪ C and A ∪ B ∪ C. Let RK_S denote the realized kernel fit to set S, then the blocked realized kernel (BRK) is assembled by layering the kernels. First, BRK = $\mathrm{RK}_{\mathrm{ABC}}$. Next, the corners are replaced with $\mathrm{RK}_{\mathrm{AB}}$ (upper left), and $\mathrm{RK}_{\mathrm{BC}}$ (lower right). Finally, BRK is completed by replacing the diagonal blocks with RK_{A}, RK_{B}, and RK_{C}. The output of the blocking approach is illustrated in Figure 4.2. Group membership is chosen using the k-means algorithm on the number of observations.

The second step in constructing the RnB covariance forecast is to regularize the BRK. Regularization is implemented using eigenvalue cleaning on the correlation matrix associated with the BRK,

$$\mathbf{R} = (\mathrm{BRK} \odot \mathbf{I}_k)^{-1/2}\, \mathrm{BRK}\, (\mathrm{BRK} \odot \mathbf{I}_k)^{-1/2}\,.$$

Let $\mathbf{R} = \mathbf{V}'\mathbf{\Lambda}\mathbf{V}$ be the singular value decomposition of the blocked correlation matrix where $\mathbf{V}$ the orthonormal matrix containing the eigenvectors and $\mathbf{\Lambda} = \mathrm{diag}\ (\lambda_1, \lambda_2, \ldots, \lambda_k)$ contains the eigenvalues ordered from the largest to the

FIGURE 4.2 The blocked realized kernel BRK is constructed from six realized kernels computed using three subsets of the assets, A, B, and C. This diagram indicates the subset of assets used in the realized kernels used to compute each section.

smallest. Eigenvalue cleaning is implemented by averaging all of the eigenvalues that are smaller than $\lambda_{\max} = \left(1 + k/\tilde{m} + 2\sqrt{k/\tilde{m}}\right)$ where $\tilde{m}$ is the number of refresh time returns in the full realized kernel RK_{ABC}. Eigenvalue cleaning is implemented by averaging the small eigenvalues,

$$\tilde{\lambda}_i = \frac{\sum_{j=n}^{k} \max\left(0, \lambda_j\right)}{n}, \quad i = n, n+1, \ldots, k,$$

where n is the index if the largest eigenvalue smaller than $\lambda_{\max}$. Eigenvalue cleaning replaces the small eigenvalue toward their grand average so that the matrix will be invertible and, in most cases, well conditioned. The RnB covariance forecast is then assembled

$$\mathbf{\Sigma}_{t+1} = \mathbf{V}'\tilde{\mathbf{\Lambda}}\mathbf{V},$$

where $\tilde{\mathbf{\Lambda}} = \mathrm{diag}\left(\lambda_1, \ldots, \lambda_{n-1}, \tilde{\lambda}_n, \ldots, \tilde{\lambda}_k\right)$ contains the regularized eigenvalues. In practice, Hautsch et al. (2009) recommend tightening the threshold by using $\lambda_{\max} = (1 - \lambda_1/k)\left(1 + k/\tilde{m} + 2\sqrt{k/\tilde{m}}\right)$ that allows for more nonzero eigenvalues to avoid the regularization procedure and reflects that returns often contain a correlation structure with a large, dominant factor.

Wang and Zou (2009) apply thresholding to RC matrices and show that if the true integrated covariance matrix is sufficiently sparse, then it can be consistently estimated in high dimensions as long as the number of intradaily returns grows sufficiently fast with the number of assets. While this is an interesting application of regularization to the problem of covariance estimation, the assumption that many of the covariances are zero is not consistent with the dependence structure found in financial data sets, for example, equity, where assets appear to be generated by a factor structure. Fan et al. (2010) use UHF data to estimate high dimensional covariance matrices. The covariance matrix is estimated using pairwise covariance estimators based on polarization where the covariance between two assets is the difference between the variance of a portfolio that holds both assets with weight 1 and a long-short portfolio with weights 1 and -1. This combined estimator, $\mathbf{\Sigma}_{t+1} = \mathbf{V}'\mathrm{diag}\left(\lambda_1, \lambda_2, \ldots, \lambda_k\right)\mathbf{V}$, is not positive semidefinite, and so use two methods to return the covariance to positive semidefinite, the first of which uses a singular value decomposition and then sets all negative eigenvalues to 0, $\ddot{\mathbf{\Sigma}}_{t+1} = \mathbf{V}'\mathrm{diag}\left(\lambda_1^+, \lambda_2^+, \ldots, \lambda_k^+\right)\mathbf{V}$ where $\lambda_j^+ = \max\left(\lambda_j, 0\right)$, and the second that shrinks using a scaled identity matrix,

$$\breve{\mathbf{\Sigma}}_{t+1} = \left(\mathbf{\Sigma}_{t+1} + \lambda_{\min}^{-}\mathbf{I}_k\right) / \left(1 + \lambda_{\min}^{-}\right),$$

where $\lambda_{\min}^{-} = \max\left(\min\left(\lambda_1, \lambda_2, \ldots, \lambda_k\right), 0\right)$. These covariance estimators are applied using gross portfolio constraints where the authors show that the pairwise estimator works better than large dimensional RKs that do not make efficient use of the information in all assets.

4.6 Forecast Evaluation

Virtually, all evaluation of covariance forecasts in high dimensional problems utilize "economic" loss functions, as opposed to statistical loss functions. The obvious rational for this choice is that the goal of high dimensional forecasts is to provide improvements over simple estimators such as the rolling window covariance estimator. A less obvious reason is that unbiased forecasts are often undesirable since other considerations, namely that the forecast is well conditioned and invertible, are more important. Moreover, unbiasedness of the covariance does not translate into unbiasedness of the inverse and so residual diagnostics based on $\hat{\mathbf{e}}_{t+1} = \hat{\boldsymbol{\Sigma}}_{t+1}^{-\frac{1}{2}}\boldsymbol{\varepsilon}_{t+1}$ may not have the expected properties when the dimension of the problem is large.

The most common evaluation framework makes use of Markowitz-type portfolio optimization (Campbell et al., 1997; pp. 184–185),

$$\begin{aligned}&\min_{\mathbf{w}} \ \mathbf{w}'\boldsymbol{\Sigma}_{t+1}\mathbf{w}\\ &\text{subject to } \mathbf{w}'\iota = 1\\ &\mathbf{w}'\boldsymbol{\mu}_{t+1} = \bar{\mu}.\end{aligned}$$

The solution to this problem depends on the expected return, and so, in many applications, a simpler problem is considered: finding the global minimum variance portfolio (GMVP). The GMVP weights depend on the forecast covariance through

$$\hat{\mathbf{w}} = \frac{\boldsymbol{\Sigma}_{t+1}^{-1}\iota}{\iota'\boldsymbol{\Sigma}_{t+1}^{-1}\iota}.$$

Recent examples of portfolio optimization-based evaluation of large dimensional covariance forecasts include Liu (2009b) and DeMiguel et al. (2009).

A closely related problem is to find the optimal tracking portfolio for an index or other asset. The problem is formulated as

$$\begin{aligned}&\min_{\mathbf{w}} \mathbf{w}'\boldsymbol{\Sigma}_{t+1}\mathbf{w}\\ &\text{subject to } \ w_1 = 1,\end{aligned}$$

where the index is located in position 1. The solution to this problem is the usual conditional regression coefficient

$$\mathbf{w} = \begin{bmatrix} 1 \\ -\boldsymbol{\Sigma}_{22,t+1}^{-1}\boldsymbol{\Sigma}_{21,t+1} \end{bmatrix},$$

where $\boldsymbol{\Sigma}_{22,t+1}$ is the lower block excluding the first asset and $\boldsymbol{\Sigma}_{21,t+1}$ is the covariance between the index and the assets used to track. It is also common to require that the amount invested in the tracking assets is identical to the amount invested in the index, which adds the additional constrain $\mathbf{w}'\iota = 0$.

Chan et al. (1999) benchmarked the sample covariance, observable factor covariance, and equicorrelation models in terms of asset allocation and tracking error minimization. They found that the standard three-factor model using the Fama and French (1992) factors performed well in asset allocation, while models with more factors were needed to minimize the tracking error. Briner and Connor (2008) benchmark the sample covariance estimator, a one-factor model using the market portfolio, and a multifactor model using the BARRA factors in UK equity data. They also modify the usual assumption of a rolling window estimator to allow for dynamics by using an EWMA similar to the RM1994 covariance estimator. They find that multifactor models outperform the one-factor model due to the misspecification and outperform the sample covariance estimator due to the excessive amount of noise when no structure is imposed. Clements et al. (2009b) provide a review of covariance forecast evaluation in the low dimensional case and find that statistical tests based on covariance forecasts or minimum variance portfolio problems are more powerful than tests that rely on expected returns or realized utility.

4.6.1 PORTFOLIO CONSTRAINTS

Jagannathan and Ma (2003) show that imposing no-short constraints is closely related to shrinking the sample covariance matrix and then using the minimum variance portfolio. This was the first article to suggest the gross exposure constraints can alleviate the need for an accurate and well weighted moving averageconditioned covariance matrix. Recent research on portfolio choice problems has highlighted the usefulness of gross portfolio weight constraints (L^1 constraints), which add an additional constraint to the usual Markowitz problem,

$$\sum_{i=1}^{k} |w_i| < \delta,$$

where δ is a number larger than 1. The case when $\delta = 1$ corresponds to a portfolio where short selling is not allowed. Larger values of δ allow for $(\delta - 1)/2$ of the portfolio to be held in short positions.

Fan et al. (2009) study gross portfolio constraints and find that adding gross portfolio constraints allows the sample covariance estimator to perform nearly as well as the true covariance in portfolios that have some short exposure. They show that as the gross exposure constraint is relaxed the variance of the constrained optimal portfolio improves until a point that involves little shrinkage and then rapidly deteriorates. In essence, even a small amount of constraint prevents a large amount of estimator errors in portfolio weights. Disatnik and Benninga (2007) conducted a horse race using monthly equity data between a large number of rolling window estimators including the sample covariance, one-factor model, and shrinkage estimators using the one-factor and equicorrelation as shrinkage targets. They found that the performance of all estimators is similar, at least in terms of performance in out-of-sample GMVP construction in portfolio allocation problems without short-sale constraints. When short positions are not allowed, shrinkage estimators outperformed the standard covariance estimator. DeMiguel et al. (2009) show that portfolio constraints, as well as shrinkage estimators such as Ledoit and Wolf (2003), can be interpreted as Bayesian estimators for a particular choice of prior. They study both gross exposure constraints and L^2 constraints that take the form

$$\sum_{i=1}^{k} w_i^2 < \delta,$$

and find that portfolio constraints outperform using standard portfolio optimization on shrinkage covariance estimators.

4.7 Conclusion

This chapter has reviewed the limited set of forecasting methods that are appropriate when the cross-sectional dimension is large. Three types of estimators were covered: simple, moving averages, and dynamics models, which make use of ARCH-type dynamics, and UHF-based estimator such as RC. This chapter has also described the dominant method for evaluating covariance forecasts and discussed recent developments in portfolio constraints that are particularly relevant when the number of assets is large.

Future developments in high dimensional covariance forecasting will come in three areas. First, estimators will continue to make use of UHF data. The increased availability of trade data, coupled with the simplicity of most estimators, makes estimators in this area highly desirable. Secondly, the recent developments in L^1 constraints on portfolio weights have demonstrated that there are gains to portfolio optimization over naïve diversification. This leads to the question of what properties should a good covariance forecast have when it will be used in constrained portfolio optimization. The optimal portfolio weights under L^1 constrains are simple to compute and remove the need to a well-conditioned covariance matrix. The third area will be more study of estimators when $k/T \to 1$, a framework that may be more useful in applications to high dimensional problems. Bickel and Levina (2008) use these asymptotics to regularizing covariance matrices by banding the covariance matrix or by tapering, which allows for consistency even when k is growing.

Acknowledgments

I thank Diaa Noureldin for comments which improved an earlier draft of this chapter.

CHAPTER FIVE

Mean, Volatility, and Skewness Spillovers in Equity Markets

AAMIR R. HASHMI and ANTHONY S. TAY

5.1 Introduction

A thorough understanding of the sources of risk in equity markets is useful for important financial market activities such as risk management, asset allocation, and the development and implementation of regulatory frameworks. These objectives have motivated much research into the interlinkages between stock markets, most of which have focused on comovements in the mean and volatility of returns across stock markets, and which in general have uncovered evidence of spillovers. For example, Eun and Shim (1989) find interdependence among the daily returns of major stock markets with the US stock market being the most influential. Kasa (1992) finds a common trend driving weekly and monthly returns from the US, Japanese, UK, German, and Canadian markets. Hamao et al. (1990) study the interdependence of returns volatility across the US, UK, and Japanese stock markets and find that volatility spills mainly from the US market over to the Japanese market but not the other way around, whereas Lin et al. (1994) find bidirectional dependency between the US and Japanese markets. Koutmos and Booth (1995) also study the US, UK, and Japanese markets but

Handbook of Volatility Models and Their Applications, First Edition.
Edited by Luc Bauwens, Christian Hafner, and Sebastien Laurent.

differentiate between good and bad news. They find, as did Booth et al. (1997) in a study of Scandinavian markets, that volatility spillovers are greater when news is bad, that is, when price falls in the latest market to trade before opening. More recently, Diebold and Yilmaz (2009) model stock market returns and stock market volatilities using VaRs (value-at-risks), and construct mean and volatility spillover indexes based on variance decompositions generated from these VaRs. They find that mean spillovers to have increased over time, whereas volatility spillovers spike whenever there is a crisis event.

Evidence of comovements in the mean and volatility of equity returns suggests that factor models, such as those developed in Bekaert and Harvey (1997) and Ng (2000), would be useful ways of modeling the behavior of stock returns. Specifying unexpected return as depending on a world factor as well as a local shock, Bekaert and Harvey (1997) find evidence that market volatility in emerging markets is affected by a world factor, and that the influence of the world factor varies considerably over time. Extending this approach to include both a world factor and a regional factor, Ng (2000) finds evidence of spillovers in volatility from the US and Japanese markets to six Asian markets, with the US market exerting a stronger influence, although the external shocks appear to explain only a small fraction of volatility in these markets. Both Bekaert and Harvey (1997) and Ng (2000) find that liberalization of equity markets changes the proportion of variance caused by external factors.

Past studies of mean and/or volatility spillovers generally assume that the conditional distribution of stock returns is symmetric about its conditional mean. Recent work, however, suggests that dynamics in the conditional third moment may be an empirically relevant feature of stock returns. Using a model that allows for autoregressive third moments, Harvey and Siddique (1999) present evidence of skewness in the conditional distributions of daily stock index returns in the US, German, Japanese, Chilean, Mexican, Taiwanese, and Thai markets and find that this asymmetry in the shape of the distribution depends on the degree of skewness in past periods. Harvey and Siddique (2000) and Chen et al. (2001) are detailed studies into the determinants and economic significance of skewness in stock returns; stocks that are experiencing relatively high turnover and/or unusually high returns over previous periods tend to be more negatively skewed. Stock capitalization also appears to be important in explaining the degree of skewness in stock returns. Perez-Quiros and Timmermann (2001) relate time-varying skewness to business cycle variation. The skewness in stock returns is economically significant: Chen et al. (2001) demonstrate this by showing that the asymmetry they find in stock returns changes option prices substantially; Harvey and Siddique (2000) incorporate time-varying conditional skewness into an asset pricing model and find that doing so helps to explain pricing errors in portfolio returns using other asset pricing models.

The presence of time-varying conditional skewness in equity returns raises a few interesting questions concerning the measurement of the importance of global, regional, and local factors on individual stock markets. For example, would incorporating time-varying skewness into an analysis of spillovers provide substantially different measurements of the relative importance of world and regional factors on the volatility of domestic equity returns? Also, can we improve our understanding of spillovers by also measuring spillovers in skewness? This would give us some insight into downside-risk and upside-"risk," where downside-risk is measured by the probability of large unexpected negative returns relative to the probability of similarly sized unexpected positive returns. Hashmi and Tay (2007) explore these questions using a factor model similar to those employed by Bekaert and Harvey (1997) and Ng (2000) in that unexpected returns comprise world, regional, and local shocks, but with the difference that these shocks are now characterized not only just by time-varying conditional volatility but also by time-varying conditional skewness. In an application to six Asian equity markets (Hong Kong, Korea, Malaysia, Singapore, Taiwan and Thailand) and using a sample period covering the 1997 Asian financial crisis, Hashmi and Tay (2007) showed that the incorporation of time-varying conditional skewness can alter estimates of volatility spillover and presented evidence concerning skewness spillovers.

In this chapter, we update the results in Hashmi and Tay (2007). We reapply our models to a different set of stock market data, and over a longer sample period that covers not just the Asian financial crisis but also more recent financial crises. We focus on the Hong Kong and Singapore markets. The objectives here are similar to those in Hashmi and Tay (2007)—to see if incorporation of time-varying skewness affects measurements of volatility spillovers (yes) and to obtain measurements of skewness spillovers (we find skewness to be primarily a local phenomenon). An important difference between the two studies, however, is the treatment here of possible structural change as a result of responses to the Asian financial crisis. Hashmi and Tay (2007) allow for structural change in a fairly limited fashion due to data limitations. Here, we repeat our analysis over two completely different subsamples and find substantial differences in interlinkages before and after the structural change. The models and the setup of the empirical study are presented in Section 5.2, empirical results are presented and discussed in Section 5.3, and Section 5.4 concludes.

5.2 Data and Summary Statistics

5.2.1 DATA

We use weekly equity market index returns from the first week of January 1990 to the last week of December 2009. All data are obtained from Datastream, and weekly percentage returns are calculated as the difference of log closing prices on Fridays (multiplied by 100). We focus on the Hong Kong and Singapore markets. For each of these countries, a market-capitalization weighted average of weekly returns of regional markets is computed to be used as a proxy for the regional factor. The countries included in the computation of the regional indexes are Australia, China (B-Market), Indonesia, Korea, Malaysia, New Zealand, Philippines, Hong Kong, Singapore, Taiwan, and Thailand, with the country under consideration left out. For instance, the regional index for the

Hong Kong market is computed as

$$r_{g(\mathrm{HK}),t} = \frac{\sum_j w_{j,t} r_{j,t}}{\sum_j w_{j,t}},$$

with j taken over the countries listed above, excluding Hong Kong, and where $r_{g(\mathrm{HK}),t}$ is the regional return excluding Hong Kong, $w_{j,t}$ is the market capitalization for country j, and $r_{j,t}$ is the return for country j. From this point on, we refer to the regional return as $r_{g,t}$ when referring to the regional factor generically. As a proxy for the world factor, we use a market-capitalization weighted average of weekly returns from the US, UK, and Japanese markets.

There are 1043 observations in our full sample. We estimate our models over the entire sample and over two separate subsamples, one from 1990 to 1998 (469 observations) and the other from 1999 to 2009 (574 observations). One of the lessons from a previous work on volatility spillover is that significant changes to the environment in which a stock market operates can influence the degree of spillovers from external factors into the market. Ng (2000), for instance, documents changes in the degree of linkages between stock markets as a result of events such as the introduction of country funds. Both markets in our study underwent significant changes, either as a result of or as a response to the financial crisis that began in July 1997 (Berg, 1999). Ignoring these developments might bias our measurement of the relative importance of world and regional factors. Hashmi and Tay (2007) took such structural changes into account in a limited manner, allowing only the factor loadings to change. Here, we allow for all parameters to change. By estimating our models over the two subsample periods, we can also compare spillovers during the 1997 crisis and the latest set of crises.

Table 5.1 contains summary statistics of the weekly returns on the world index, the two regional indexes, and the Hong Kong and Singapore country indexes over the two subsample periods. The Jarque-Bera statistic clearly indicates that the returns are nonnormal. The coefficient of skewness suggests that the index returns are significantly skewed to the left. All display statistically significant excess kurtosis, which is at least partly because of the presence of autoregressive conditional heteroskedasticity as indicated by the prominent autocorrelations in the square of all the returns series (with the exception of Hong Kong in the earlier sample period). Significant autocorrelation in the returns taken to the third power is sometimes taken as an indicator of the possible presence of autoregressive third moments. The first-order autocorrelation of returns to the third power would then indicate some autoregressive skewness in the first sample but not in the second sample. We present more comprehensive evidence of this in the next section. Table 5.1 also shows the correlation between the two individual markets with each other and with the world and regional indexes. In all cases, the correlations between the returns for the markets and the regional index are higher than those between the markets and the world index.

TABLE 5.1 Summary Statistics for Weekly Stock Returns

	World	$Region_{HK}$	$Region_{SG}$	HK	Sing.
Sample Period 1990–1998 (469 Observations)					
Mean	0.117	0.078	0.128	0.264	−0.006
Median	0.252	0.021	0.127	0.395	0.018
Standard Deviation	1.764	2.142	2.321	3.585	2.692
Skewness	−0.176	-0.208^c	-0.306^a	-0.694^a	-0.874^a
Kurtosis	4.606^a	5.552^a	5.388^a	7.497^a	10.401^a
JB	52.8^a	130.6^a	118.8^a	432.8^a	1130.1^a
$\rho_1(1)$	−0.002	0.064	0.087^a	0.060	−0.016
$\rho_2(1)$	0.241^a	0.298^a	0.209^a	0.035	0.122^a
$\rho_3(1)$	−0.082	-0.148^a	−0.036	0.013	−0.053
$\rho_4(1)$	0.174^a	0.132^a	0.070	−0.007	0.013
World	1.000	0.496	0.481	0.358	0.488
Region *j*	—	—	—	0.550	0.676
HK	—	—	—	1.000	0.603
Sample Period 1999–2009 (574 observations)					
Mean	−0.001	0.149	0.146	0.131	0.132
Median	0.287	0.390	0.372	0.326	0.266
Standard Deviation	2.540	2.444	2.603	3.380	2.882
Skewness	-1.168^a	-0.767^a	-0.645^a	-0.300^a	-0.396^a
Kurtosis	12.270^a	7.659^a	6.823^a	4.791^a	7.037^a
JB	2185.8^a	575.32^a	389.3^a	85.2^a	404.9^a
$\rho_1(1)$	−0.036	0.045	0.034	0.003	0.094^b
$\rho_2(1)$	0.231^a	0.168^a	0.164^a	0.141^a	0.207^a
$\rho_3(1)$	0.042	−0.029	−0.035	−0.053	−0.029
$\rho_4(1)$	0.034	0.017	0.018	0.024	0.051
World	1.000	0.687	0.699	0.632	0.613
Region *j*	—	—	—	0.799	0.795
HK	—	—	—	1.000	0.746

Notes: JB is the Jarque-Bera test of normality; $\rho_j(1)$ is the first-order autocorrelation of the returns to the *j*th power; HK stands for Hong Kong; Sing. for Singapore; Region refers to the weighted index of the country returns, excluding the market under consideration. For instance, in the second subsample, the unconditional correlation between Hong Kong returns and the regional index return (excluding Hong Kong) is 0.799.

[a]Statistical significance at 1%.

[b]Statistical significance at 5%.

[c]Statistical significance at 10%.

5.2.2 TIME-VARYING SKEWNESS (UNIVARIATE ANALYSIS)

To further explore if time-variation in conditional skewness is present in the data (and thus to assess the need for and potential gains from using a framework that permits this), we fit univariate models of time-varying conditional skewness to these returns: the stock returns are modeled as following an AR-GARCH process, with standardized residuals following a zero-mean unit-variance skewed-t distribution developed in Hansen (1994). Letting $r_{i,t}$ represent the time t return on the equity index of market i, with $i = w, g, 1, 2$ representing the world, regional, Hong Kong, and Singapore markets, respectively, we model returns as

$$r_{i,t} = \alpha_{i,0} + \alpha_{i,1} r_{i,t-1} + \varepsilon_{i,t}, \varepsilon_{i,t} = \sigma_{i,t} z_{i,t}, \tag{5.1}$$

$$\sigma_{i,t}^2 = \beta_{i,0} + \beta_{i,1}\sigma_{i,t-1}^2 + \beta_{i,2}\varepsilon_{i,t-1}^2 + \beta_{i,3}\left[\max\left(0, \varepsilon_{i,t-1}\right)\right]^2, \tag{5.2}$$

where the conditional distribution of the standardized residuals z_t is

$$g\left(z_{i,t}|\eta_i, \lambda_{i,t}\right) = \left\{ \begin{array}{ll} b_{i,t}c_i\left[1 + \frac{1}{\eta_i - 2}\left[\frac{b_{i,t}z_{i,t} + a_{i,t}}{1 - \lambda_{i,t}}\right]^2\right]^{-\frac{\eta_i+1}{2}}, & \text{when } z_{i,t} < \frac{-a_{i,t}}{b_{i,t}}; \\ b_{i,t}c_i\left[1 + \frac{1}{\eta_i - 2}\left[\frac{b_{i,t}z_{i,t} + a_{i,t}}{1 + \lambda_{i,t}}\right]^2\right]^{-\frac{\eta_i+1}{2}}, & \text{when } z_{i,t} \geq \frac{-a_{i,t}}{b_{i,t}}, \end{array} \right\} \tag{5.3}$$

with $a_{i,t}$, $b_{i,t}$, and c_i defined as

$$a_{i,t} = 4\lambda_{i,t}c_i\left[\frac{\eta_i - 2}{\eta_i - 1}\right], b_{i,t}^2 = 1 + 3\lambda_{i,t}^2 - a_{i,t}^2, c_i = \frac{\Gamma\left[\frac{\eta_i+1}{2}\right]}{\sqrt{\pi\left(\eta_i - 2\right)}\Gamma\left[\frac{\eta_i}{2}\right]}. \tag{5.4}$$

The distribution described in Equations 5.3 and 5.4 is obtained by modifying a standardized Student-t distribution (Hansen, 1994; Jondeau and Rockinger 2003). It is characterized by two parameters: $\lambda_{i,t} \in (-1, 1)$ determines the degree of asymmetry in the distribution and $\eta_i \in (2, \infty)$ is a degree of freedom parameter. The distribution is skewed to the left when $\lambda_{i,t}$ is less than 0, and skewed to the right when it is greater than 0. It reduces to the Student-t density when $\lambda_{i,t}$ is equal to 0. Time-varying conditional skewness is obtained by specifying $\lambda_{i,t}$ as following an autoregressive specification:

$$\lambda_{i,t} = f\left(\lambda_{i,t-1}, \varepsilon_{i,t-1}, \quad \max\left(0, \varepsilon_{i,t-1}\right)\right). \tag{5.5}$$

The autoregressive specification allows current skewness to depend on past skewness, thus allowing for persistence in the shape of the distribution. This follows previous work documenting time-varying conditional skewness, although the specification in Equation 5.5 does differ from previous applications of the model; in that, we allow for negative and positive shocks to have different effects not only just on volatility (the usual "leverage effect") but also on skewness. Note that while we sometime refer to $\lambda_{i,t}$ as the "skewness parameter," this parameter is not the same as the coefficient of skewness; the relationship between η_i and $\lambda_{i,t}$ and the skewness coefficient and kurtosis of $z_{i,t}$ is given in Jondeau and Rockinger (2003).

In fitting the model, we impose the restrictions $\lambda_{i,t} \in (-1, 1)$ and $\eta_i \in (2, 32)$ using the logistic transformations[1]

$$\lambda_{i,t} = -1 + \frac{2}{1 + \exp\left(-\lambda'_{i,t}\right)}, \quad \eta_i = 2 + \frac{30}{1 + \exp\left(-\eta'_i\right)} \tag{5.6}$$

with

$$\lambda'_{i,t} = \gamma_0 + \gamma_1 \lambda'_{i,t-1} + \gamma_2 \varepsilon_{i,t-1} + \gamma_3 \max\left(0, \varepsilon_{i,t-1}\right). \tag{5.7}$$

In principle, η_i should be allowed to take any value above 2. However, numerical maximization of the likelihood function is easier with an upper bound imposed on η_i. All the fitted values of η_i lie well within the imposed range.[2]

The results from this estimation exercise are shown in Table 5.2, where, to save on space, we omit the estimates from the mean and variance equations. The standard errors reported are the quasi-MLE "robust" standard errors. There is some evidence of time-varying conditional skewness despite the small sample sizes. There appears to be time-varying conditional skewness in both the Singapore returns and the Region$_{\text{HK}}$ index returns (which includes Singapore returns) in both sample periods. The Hong Kong returns series shows some evidence of time-varying conditional skewness in the first subsample but little in the second. The Region$_{\text{SG}}$ index returns (which includes Hong Kong but not Singapore) shows little time-varying conditional skewness in either period. At least in the univariate models, it appears that time-varying conditional skewness is a feature primarily of the Singapore market.

To gain some idea of the importance of the asymmetries implied by the model for various values of η_i and λ_t, we compare the probabilities of large negative returns when the distribution is skewed versus the corresponding probabilities when asymmetries are ignored. Figure 5.1 plots the value Prob($z_t \leq -2$), that is, the probability of an unexpected return falling more than two standard deviations below the mean, for various values of η_i and λ_t. A comparison of the value of Prob($z_t \leq -2$) over the entire range of λ_t against the same probability when $\lambda_t = 0$ suggests that when time-variation in conditional skewness is neglected, it is possible to severely underestimate (or overestimate) the probability of large negative changes in the value of a portfolio. In our application, the values of λ_t sometimes falls to just above -0.8, and the implication is

[1] The models are estimated by MLE using the BFGS Quasi-Newton method as implemented in the MATLAB function *fminunc*.

[2] The inclusion of γ_3 in the univariate models for the individual markets resulted either in very small and insignificant values for γ_3 or in numerical problems during maximization. We therefore decided to leave out γ_3 when estimating the univariate models for the individual markets.

TABLE 5.2 Univariate Model with Time-Varying Conditional Skewness

	World	Region$_{HK}$	Region$_{SG}$	Hong Kong	Singapore
Sample Period 1990–1998 (469 Observations)					
$\gamma_{i,0}$	−0.274	0.208	−0.156	−0.103	0.113
	(0.236)	(0.265)	(0.783)	(0.154)	(0.091)
$\gamma_{i,1}$	−0.001	0.275[b]	0.069	0.038	0.131[b]
	(0.119)	(0.126)	(0.091)	(0.029)	(0.059)
$\gamma_{i,2}$	−0.018	−0.257	0.002	0.330	0.322[a]
	(0.659)	(0.533)	(1.525)	(0.564)	(0.120)
$\gamma_{i,3}$	−0.005	−0.015	0.004	—	—
	(0.055)	(0.021)	(0.028)	—	—
η	23.684[a]	21.761	5.995[a]	5.787[a]	4.373[a]
	(5.255)	(15.762)	(2.173)	(1.497)	(1.098)
Wald	0.026	37.569[a]	1.753	10.185[a]	10.671[a]
Sample Period 1999–2009 (574 Observations)					
$\gamma_{i,0}$	−0.643	−0.388	−0.587	−0.310[c]	−0.103
	(1.143)	(0.840)	(0.870)	(0.177)	(0.098)
$\gamma_{i,1}$	0.014	−0.065	−0.040	−0.076[b]	0.065
	(0.160)	(0.045)	(0.473)	(0.038)	(0.086)
$\gamma_{i,2}$	−0.223	0.314	−0.280	0.377	0.333
	(2.066)	(1.706)	(5.604)	(0.233)	(0.422)
$\gamma_{i,3}$	−0.012	−0.015	−0.026	—	—
	(0.132)	(0.139)	(0.802)	—	—
η	8.320[a]	8.709[a]	13.176	20.168[b]	6.524[a]
	(2.608)	(3.300)	(19.543)	(7.945)	(1.980)
Wald	0.113	10.249[b]	1.352	2.198	7.717[b]

The estimated model is Equations 5.1 and 5.2 and the skewness equation: $\lambda'_{i,t} = \gamma_{i,0} + \gamma_{i,1}\lambda'_{i,t-1} + \gamma_{i,2}\varepsilon_{i,t-1} + \gamma_{i,3}\max(0, \varepsilon_{i,t-1})$, and where $z_{i,t} \sim g(z_{i,t}|\eta, \lambda_t)$ is specified in Equation 5.3. The standard errors are in parentheses. "Wald" refers to the Wald test statistic for the restriction $\gamma_{i,1} = \gamma_{i,2} = (\gamma_{i,3}) = 0$. Region$_{HK}$ refers to the weighted index of returns excluding Hong Kong.

[a]Statistical significance at 1%.

[b]Statistical significance at 5%.

[c]Statistical significance at 10%.

that $\text{Prob}(z_t \leq -2)$ could be underestimated by 0.5. $\text{Prob}(z_t \leq -2)$ can also potentially be severely overestimated if λ_t were positive. For instance, if λ_t were to be around 0.5 so that the conditional distribution is skewed to the right, the true value of $\text{Prob}(z_t \leq -2)$ would be just one-fifth of the value at $\lambda_t = 0$. These measurements highlight the importance of understanding the behavior of conditional third moments for risk management activities such as the calculation of VaR (see Duffie and Pan (1997), for an overview of VaR.)

Note that for values of η_i between 5 and 15 the value of $\text{Prob}(z_t \leq -2)$ does not differ much even at extreme values of λ_t. Our experience is that η_i tends to

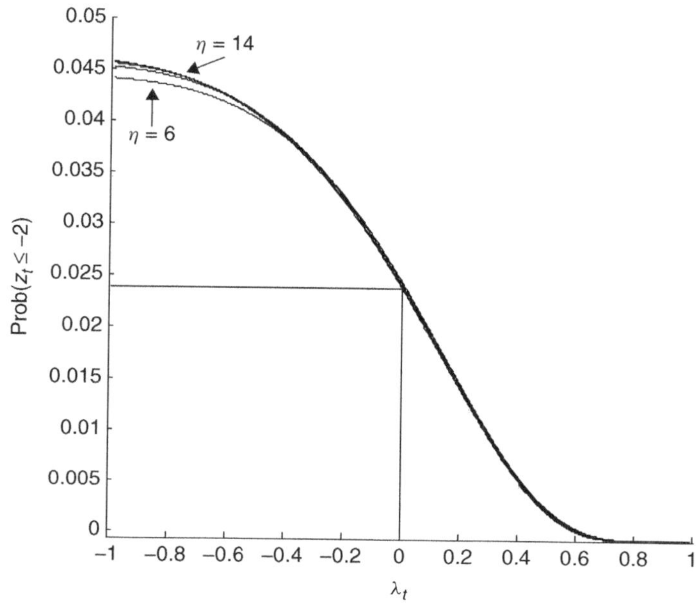

FIGURE 5.1 Prob ($z_t \le -2$) at various values of η and λ. Each Line is a plot of $\int_{-\infty}^{-2} g\,(z_t|\lambda_t, \eta)\,dz_t$ against λ_t for various values of η.

fall in this range, even when allowed to be time-varying. Thus, restricting η_i to be constant should be of limited consequence.

5.2.3 SPILLOVER MODELS

The results from the univariate models motivate the study of volatility spillovers using a factor model with time-varying conditional skewness. We construct, in the spirit of Bekaert and Harvey (1997) and Ng (2000), the following sequence of models for each of the two countries' indexes.[3] In each case, the world market returns series is assumed to follow the process described in Equations 5.1–5.5, and is assumed not to depend on any of the individual markets in this study or on the regional factor. The regional market returns series, on the other hand, is driven by a world shock, and a regional shock that is assumed to be independent of the world shock:

$$r_{g,t} = \alpha_{g,0} + \alpha_{g,1} r_{w,t-1} + \alpha_{g,2} r_{g,t-1} + \varepsilon_{g,t}, \tag{5.8}$$

$$\varepsilon_{g,t} = \phi_{g,1} \varepsilon_{w,t} + e_{g,t}, \; e_{g,t} = \sigma_{g,t} z_{g,t}, \tag{5.9}$$

[3]An alternative approach would be to model the individual market returns series using univariate conditional skewness models and link these using a copula, as in Rockinger and Jondeau (2001). However, the approach that we adopt allows us to directly measure the contribution of the world and regional factor to the variance and skewness of the individual returns series.

$$z_{g,t} \sim g\left(z_{g,t}|\eta_g, \lambda_{g,t}\right), \tag{5.10}$$

$$\sigma_{g,t}^2 = \beta_{g,0} + \beta_{g,1}\sigma_{g,t-1}^2 + \beta_{g,2}e_{g,t-1}^2 + \beta_{g,3}\left[\max\left(0, e_{g,t-1}\right)\right]^2, \tag{5.11}$$

$$\lambda'_{g,t} = \gamma_{g,0} + \gamma_{g,1}\lambda'_{g,t-1} + \gamma_{g,2}e_{g,t-1} + \gamma_{g,3}\max\left(0, e_{g,t-1}\right). \tag{5.12}$$

The unexpected returns on individual markets are, in turn, assumed to depend on the world shock, the idiosyncratic portion of the regional shock, $e_{g,t}$, and a country-specific shock that is independent of both $e_{g,t}$ and $\varepsilon_{w,t}$:

$$r_{i,t} = \alpha_{i,0} + \alpha_{i,1}r_{w,t-1} + \alpha_{i,2}r_{g,t-1} + \alpha_{i,3}r_{i,t-1} + \varepsilon_{i,t}, \tag{5.13}$$

$$\varepsilon_{i,t} = \phi_{i,1}\varepsilon_{w,t} + \phi_{i,2}e_{g,t} + e_{i,t}, e_{i,t} = \sigma_{i,t}z_{i,t}, \tag{5.14}$$

$$z_{i,t} \sim g\left(z_{i,t}|\eta_i, \lambda_{i,t}\right), \tag{5.15}$$

$$\sigma_{i,t}^2 = \beta_{i,0} + \beta_{i,1}\sigma_{i,t-1}^2 + \beta_{i,2}e_{i,t-1}^2 + \beta_{i,3}\left[\max\left(0, e_{i,t-1}\right)\right]^2, \tag{5.16}$$

$$\lambda'_{i,t} = \gamma_{i,0} + \gamma_{i,1}\lambda'_{i,t-1} + \gamma_{i,2}\varepsilon_{i,t-1}. \tag{5.17}$$

Throughout, the symbol ε is used to denote unexpected returns, while e denotes idiosyncratic shocks. The symbols σ^2 and λ always denote the conditional variance and skewness of an idiosyncratic shock. The parameters λ and λ' are connected through Equation 5.6. The world shock affects the volatility and skewness of unexpected regional returns only through Equation 5.9, while the world shock and idiosyncratic regional shock influence the volatility and skewness of unexpected country returns through Equation 5.14. Equations 5.9 and 5.14 are referred to as the factor equations.

For each market i, the multivariate likelihood function is given by $\prod_{t=1}^{T} f\left(r_{i,t}, r_{g,t}, r_{w,t}|I_{t-1}, \theta\right)$, where I_{t-1} represents past values of the returns and

$$\begin{aligned}
&f\left(r_{i,t}, r_{g,t}, r_{w,t}|I_{t-1}, \theta\right) \\
&= f\left(r_{i,t}|r_{g,t}, r_{w,t}, I_{t-1}, \theta_i, \theta_g, \theta_w\right) f\left(r_{g,t}|r_{w,t}, I_{t-1}, \theta_g, \theta_w\right) f\left(r_{w,t}|I_{t-1}, \theta_w\right) \\
&= f\left(e_{i,t}|e_{g,t}, \varepsilon_{w,t}, I_{t-1}, \theta_i, \theta_g, \theta_w\right) f\left(e_{g,t}|e_{w,t}, I_{t-1}, \theta_g, \theta_w\right) f\left(r_{w,t}|I_{t-1}, \theta_w\right),
\end{aligned}$$

while θ_w, θ_g, and θ_i are the parameters in Equations 5.1–5.7, 5.8–5.12, and 5.13–5.17, respectively. Owing to the large number of parameters, we maximize the likelihood sequentially, starting with the likelihood for the world model $\prod_{t=1}^{T} f\left(r_{w,t}|I_{t-1}, \theta_w\right)$ to obtain consistent estimates for θ_w, then maximize the regional likelihood $\prod_{t=1}^{T} f\left(e_{g,t}|\hat{\varepsilon}_{w,t}, I_{t-1}, \theta_g, \hat{\theta}_w\right)$, followed by the individual market likelihood $\prod_{t=1}^{T} f\left(e_{i,t}|\hat{e}_{g,t}, \hat{\varepsilon}_{w,t}, I_{t-1}, \theta_i, \hat{\theta}_g, \hat{\theta}_w\right)$. This process yields consistent (though inefficient estimates), and we do not correct for sampling error in having replaced θ_w, ε_w, θ_g, and e_g with $\hat{\theta}_w$, $\hat{\varepsilon}_w$, $\hat{\theta}_g$, and $\hat{e}_g$ in the second and third stages.

Equations 5.16 and 5.17 capture dynamics in the volatility and skewness due to each market's idiosyncratic shock. The factor loadings $\phi_{i,1}$ and $\phi_{i,2}$ capture the impact of the global and regional factors on the volatility and skewness of country i's return, and so in our analysis, we consider the relative size and significance of these two parameters. To understand the economic significance of these factors, however, we calculate the proportion of variance and skewness in the market returns that is explained by the global and regional factors. Since the conditional variance of country i's stock return is

$$E\left[\varepsilon_{i,t}^2 | I_{t-1}\right] = h_{i,t} = \phi_{i,1}^2 \sigma_{w,t}^2 + \phi_{i,2}^2 \sigma_{g,t}^2 + \sigma_{i,t}^2, \tag{5.18}$$

we estimate the proportion of country i's volatility accounted for by the factors by the average values of

$$\mathrm{VR}_{i,t}^{w} = \frac{\hat{\phi}_{i,1}^2 \hat{\sigma}_{w,t}^2}{\hat{h}_{i,t}} \text{ and } \mathrm{VR}_{i,t}^{g} = \frac{\hat{\phi}_{i,2}^2 \hat{\sigma}_{g,t}^2}{\hat{h}_{i,t}}. \tag{5.19}$$

Just as the estimated models generate a series of conditional volatilities for each country's stock return, they also generate a series of conditional skewness coefficients. Unlike variance, however, we do not have any neat analytical decompositions of the skewness coefficient into world, regional, and idiosyncratic components. We will instead use simulation methods to see how the world and regional factors contribute to the skewness in a country's stock return conditional density. We estimate the skewness coefficients at each period t of the country-specific shock $e_{i,t}$, the combination of the regional shock and the country-specific shock $\phi_{i,2} e_{g,t} + e_{i,t}$, and all the shocks combined $\varepsilon_{i,t} = \phi_{i,1}\varepsilon_{w,t} + \phi_{i,2} e_{g,t} + e_{i,t}$. We label the series of skewness coefficients as s_t^i, s_t^{i+g}, and s_t^{i+g+w}, respectively. The skewness coefficients are calculated by simulation: for each period t, we draw n observations $[n = 1000]$ of $z_{i,t} = e_{i,t}/\hat{\sigma}_{i,t}$ from $g\left(z_{i,t} | \hat{\eta}_i, \hat{\lambda}_{i,t}\right)$. Denoting the random numbers as $\left\{z_{i,t}^{(r)}\right\}_{r=1}^{n}$, the skewness coefficient of $e_{i,t}$ at time t is calculated as

$$s_t^i = \frac{1}{n} \sum_{r=1}^{n} \left(z_{i,t}^{(r)}\right)^3. \tag{5.20}$$

A similar procedure is used to obtain n draws $[n = 1000]$ from $z_{g,t} = e_{g,t}/\hat{\sigma}_{g,t}$ and $z_{w,t} = \varepsilon_{w,t}/\hat{\sigma}_{w,t}$, and the sample skewness coefficients for $\phi_{i,2} e_{g,t} + e_{i,t}$ and $\phi_{i,1}\varepsilon_{w,t} + \phi_{i,2} e_{g,t} + e_{i,t}$ calculated as

$$s_t^{i+g} = \frac{1}{n} \sum_{r=1}^{n} \frac{\left(\phi_{i,2} z_{g,t}^{(r)} \hat{\sigma}_{g,t} + z_{i,t}^{(r)} \hat{\sigma}_{i,t}\right)^3}{\left(\phi_{i,2}^2 \hat{\sigma}_{g,t}^2 + \hat{\sigma}_{i,t}^2\right)^{3/2}} \equiv \frac{1}{n} \sum_{r=1}^{n} \left(z_{i+g,t}^{(r)}\right)^3, \tag{5.21}$$

$$s_t^{i+g+w} = \frac{1}{n}\sum_{r=1}^{n} \frac{\left(\phi_{i,1} z_{w,t}^{(r)} \hat{\sigma}_{w,t} + \phi_{i,2} z_{g,t}^{(r)} \hat{\sigma}_{g,t} + z_{i,t}^{(r)} \hat{\sigma}_{i,t}\right)^3}{\left(\phi_{i,1}^2 \hat{\sigma}_{w,t}^2 + \phi_{i,2}^2 \hat{\sigma}_{g,t}^2 + \hat{\sigma}_{i,t}^2\right)^{3/2}}$$

$$\equiv \frac{1}{n}\sum_{r=1}^{n} \left(z_{i+g+w,t}^{(r)}\right)^3. \qquad (5.22)$$

A comparison of these three skewness series for a given country will show the cumulative effect of regional and global effects on the skewness of the conditional distribution of the individual market returns. For instance, if for country i, $s_t^i \approx s_t^{i+g}$ for all t, then this will indicate that the regional factor does not contribute to the skewness of the conditional density. If for this same country, s_t^{i+g} is very different from s_t^{i+g+w} for some t, then the world factor has an effect on the skewness of market i's conditional density. As the skewness coefficients vary over negative and positive values, we do not compute average skewness ratios. Instead, we use graphical methods to summarize these numbers, plotting s_t^{i+g} against s_t^i and s_t^{i+g+w} against s_t^{i+g}.

5.3 Empirical Results

5.3.1 PARAMETER ESTIMATES

Table 5.3 reports the results for the spillover models with time-varying, conditional skewness. The results are fairly different across the two sample periods. In the first sample period, there appears to be little significant mean spillover, except for the regional markets into the Singapore market. This continues into the second sample period. Mean spillover from the world returns into the individual markets, both increase substantially in the second period. The opposite remark holds, however, for the factor loadings. In the earlier sample, the factor loadings on both the world and regional factors are large, whereas in the second sample period, the size of the coefficients diminish substantially.[4] The estimates of the factor loadings in the full sample appear, unsurprisingly, to be more or less an average of the results in the two subperiods. Interestingly, the signs of the coefficients in the Hong Kong case are opposite, so while the regional factor reduces skewness, the world factor accentuates it. In the Singapore case, both coefficients are negative, so both the world factor and the regional factor reduce skewness in Singapore returns.

Table 5.4 shows similar parameter estimates in the spillover models with restrictions to constant conditional skewness and no skewness. The results for mean spillovers are similar in all three cases. The factor coefficients do differ a

[4]Only the estimates of the spillover coefficients in the mean and factor equation parameters are displayed to save space. The variance equation, which captures the evolution of the conditional variance of the idiosyncratic country shock, continues to display asymmetric effects of past shocks on variance.

TABLE 5.3 Spillover Model with Time-Varying Conditional Skewness

	1990–1998		1999–2009		1990–2009	
	HK	Sing.	HK	Sing.	HK	Sing.
Mean Equation						
$\alpha_{i,0}$	0.381^b	0.028	0.133	0.194^c	0.290^a	0.128^c
	(0.149)	(0.105)	(0.118)	(0.108)	(0.090)	(0.070)
$\alpha_{i,1}$	0.048	0.107	0.479^a	0.387	0.272^a	0.205^a
	(0.093)	(0.071)	(0.148)	(0.066)	(0.070)	(0.049)
$\alpha_{i,2}$	−0.015	0.112^b	−0.206	-0.214^a	−0.087	−0.002
	(0.097)	(0.054)	(0.131)	(0.076)	(0.069)	(0.047)
$\alpha_{i,3}$	0.029	−0.008	−0.112	0.018	−0.043	0.006
	(0.057)	(0.057)	(0.072)	(0.068)	(0.045)	(0.042)
Factor Equation						
$\phi_{i,1}$	0.921	-0.875^b	0.229	−0.198	0.091	-0.481^c
	(0.712)	(0.428)	(0.664)	(0.419)	(0.597)	(0.280)
$\phi_{i,2}$	−0.846	−0.679	−0.295	0.115	−0.007	−0.153
	(0.755)	(0.457)	(0.859)	(0.514)	(0.746)	(0.319)

The estimated model is in Equations 5.13–5.17. Only some of the parameters of Equations 5.13–5.17 are reported. HK stands for Hong Kong and Sing. for Singapore. The standard errors are in parentheses. The subscripts w and g refer to the world and regional indexes, respectively, while $i = 1, 2$ refers to the two individual markets.

[a]Statistical significance at 1%.

[b]Statistical significance at 5%.

[c]Statistical significance at 10%.

bit for Hong Kong, especially once time-varying skewness is incorporated into the model.

5.3.2 SPILLOVER EFFECTS IN VARIANCE AND SKEWNESS

To gain some insight into the economic significance of these results, we calculate, for each market, the proportion of the movements in the conditional variance and the amount of skewness in unexpected returns that can be attributed to the world and regional factors. We are also interested in the degree and pattern of spillovers of skewness.

5.3.2.1 Variance Ratios. Table 5.5 shows the average of period t variance ratios for the world and regional factors for each of the three spillover models (time-varying, constant and no conditional skewness) and for all three sample periods considered (1990–1998, 1999–2009, and the full sample). The rows labeled "World" and "Region," respectively, show the average value of $VR^{w}_{i,t}$ and $VR^{g}_{i,t}$ as described in Equation 5.19.

TABLE 5.4 Spillover Model with Constant and Zero Skewness

	1990–1998		1999–2009		1990–2009	
	HK	Sing.	HK	Sing.	HK	Sing.
			(i) The Model with Constant Conditional Skewness			
Mean Equation						
$\alpha_{i,0}$	0.389[b]	0.008	0.260	0.191[c]	0.307[a]	0.108
	(0.156)	(0.098)	(0.261)	(0.109)	(0.092)	(0.070)
$\alpha_{i,1}$	0.077	0.082	0.464[a]	0.361[a]	0.262[a]	0.217[a]
	(0.092)	(0.069)	(0.085)	(0.065)	(0.070)	(0.049)
$\alpha_{i,2}$	0.015	0.091[c]	−0.240[c]	−0.194[b]	−0.115	−0.021
	(0.088)	(0.052)	(0.144)	(0.076)	(0.070)	(0.044)
$\alpha_{i,3}$	0.006	−0.025	−0.097	0.015	−0.041	0.010
	(0.059)	(0.059)	(0.074)	(0.067)	(0.040)	(0.043)
Factor Equation						
$\phi_{i,1}$	0.505	−0.957	0.565	−0.192	0.229	−0.469
	(3.442)	(0.640)	(5.677)	(0.437)	(1.004)	(0.497)
$\phi_{i,2}$	−0.327	−0.563	−0.368	0.174	−0.048	−0.059
	(2.659)	(0.576)	(3.969)	(0.450)	(0.845)	(0.468)
			(ii) The Model with Conditional Symmetry			
Mean Equation						
$\alpha_{i,0}$	0.479[a]	0.009	0.242[c]	0.262[a]	0.347	0.137[b]
	(0.139)	(0.090)	(0.125)	(0.096)	(0.270)	(0.067)
$\alpha_{i,1}$	0.102	0.088	0.460[a]	0.342[a]	0.272	0.202[a]
	(0.092)	(0.070)	(0.084)	(0.066)	(0.273)	(0.049)
$\alpha_{i,2}$	−0.018	0.081	−0.254[b]	−0.204[a]	−0.093	−0.007
	(0.087)	(0.052)	(0.099)	(0.075)	(0.504)	(0.044)
$\alpha_{i,3}$	−0.000	−0.017	−0.076	0.044	−0.030	0.011
	(0.047)	(0.059)	(0.066)	(0.085)	(0.041)	(0.043)
Factor Equation						
$\phi_{i,1}$	0.440	−0.887	0.767	−0.359	0.147	−0.462
	(0.807)	(0.624)	(0.538)	(0.707)	(16.620)	(0.456)
$\phi_{i,2}$	−0.381	−0.520	−0.321	0.087	−0.088	−0.125
	(0.724)	(0.537)	(0.321)	(0.925)	(15.048)	(0.481)

The same comments apply as in the notes under Table 5.3. The only difference is that Equation 5.17 is given by $\lambda'_{i,t} = \gamma_{i,0}$ in the model with constant skewness and by $\lambda'_{i,t} = 0$ in the model with zero skewness. HK stands for Hong Kong and Sing. for Singapore.

[a]Statistical significance at 1%.

[b]Statistical significance at 5%.

[c]Satistical significance at 10%.

TABLE 5.5 Average Variance Ratios

	1990–1998		1999–2009		1990–2009	
	HK	Sing.	HK	Sing.	HK	Sing.
(i) *Spillover Model with Time-Varying Conditional Skewness*						
World	0.149	0.226	0.028	0.031	0.004	0.133
Regional	0.165	0.222	0.045	0.011	0.000	0.018
(ii) *Spillover Model with Constant Conditional Skewness*						
World	0.064	0.273	0.141	0.029	0.023	0.128
Regional	0.036	0.166	0.055	0.026	0.001	0.003
(iii) *Spillover Model with Conditional Symmetry*						
World	0.061	0.309	0.225	0.095	0.010	0.124
Regional	0.044	0.132	0.037	0.006	0.004	0.011

The variance ratios in this table are average values of the ratio of variance explained by the world and regional factors, and are computed using Equation 5.19 for various models. HK stands for Hong Kong and Sing. for Singapore.

The spillover model with time-varying conditional skewness shows both the world and regional factor playing an important role in explaining the variance of the unexpected returns for both the Hong Kong and Singapore markets but in the first sample period only. Both the world and the regional factors account for around 15% of the variance in the Hong Kong market and over 20% in the Singapore market. In the second subperiod, these ratios are reduced substantially in both markets. It is unclear why these figures should differ so much across the two samples. It may be because of regulatory changes put into place around this time. In the case of Hong Kong, this may be due to severe speculation activity in the Hong Kong financial markets that began following the crisis (Tse and Yip, 2003), and the following interventions in the Hong Kong stock market by the Government. It may also be that in the latter period the volatility experienced in the US market (which dominates the world index) was recognized within the Hong Kong and Singapore markets as due to factors specific to the US market. Panels (ii) and (iii) show the variance ratios computed from the constant skewness and no skewness versions of the spillover models. In some cases, these figures are quite different from the figures computed using the time-varying conditional skewness spillover model. However, there does not appear to be a regular pattern in the differences.

5.3.2.2 Pattern and Size of Skewness Spillovers. To evaluate the pattern and size of skewness spillover implied by our spillover models with time-varying skewness, we present for each market the series of skewness coefficients s_t^i, s_t^{i+g}, and s_t^{i+g+w} as computed in Equations 5.20–5.22. Recall that s_t^i is the skewness in the conditional density of a market's idiosyncratic shock, and s_t^{i+g+w} is the skewness of the conditional density of the market's unexpected return.

The differences going from s_t^i to s_t^{i+g}, and from s_t^{i+g} to s_t^{i+g+w} will show the contribution of the regional and world factor. We use graphical methods to compare s_t^i with s_t^{i+g} and s_t^{i+g} with s_t^{i+g+w}. In particular, we plot s_t^{i+g} against s_t^i and s_t^{i+g+w} against s_t^{i+g}.

Figures 5.2 and 5.3 show the scatterplots of s_t^{i+g} against s_t^i and s_t^{i+g+w} against s_t^{i+g} for the Hong Kong and the Singapore markets, respectively. The plots for each country comprise two columns of scatterplots. The left column shows the plot of s_t^{i+g} against s_t^i and the right column plots s_t^{i+g+w} against s_t^{i+g}. The first row for each country shows the figures for the first sample period, the second row shows the figures for the second sample period, and the third row shows

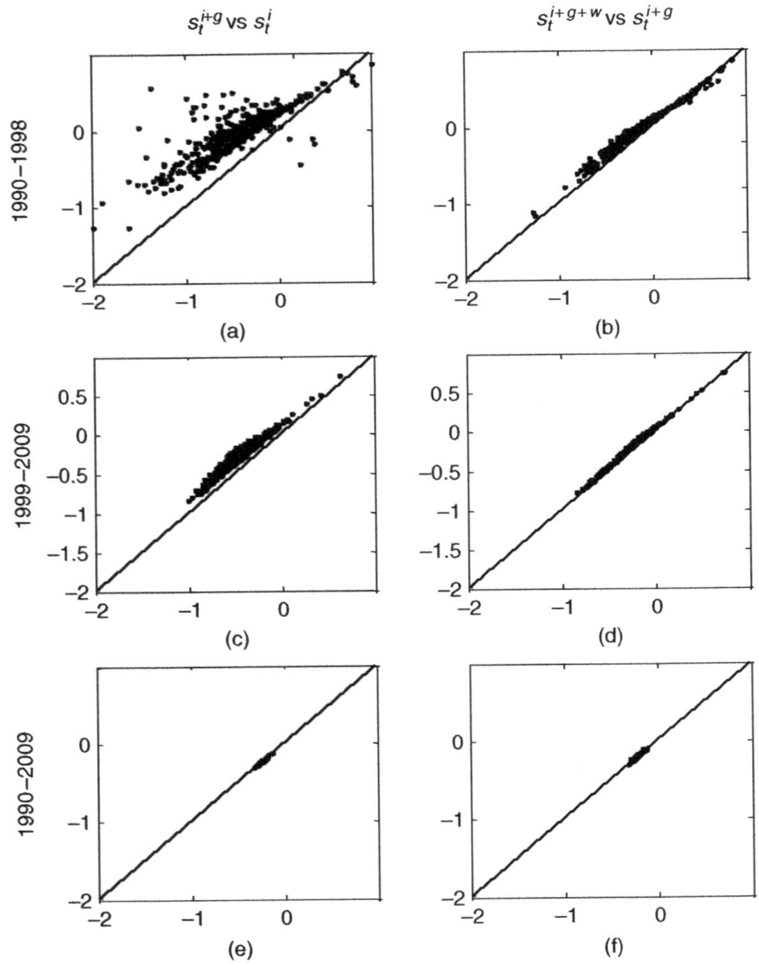

FIGURE 5.2 Scatterplots of skewness coefficients (Hong Kong).

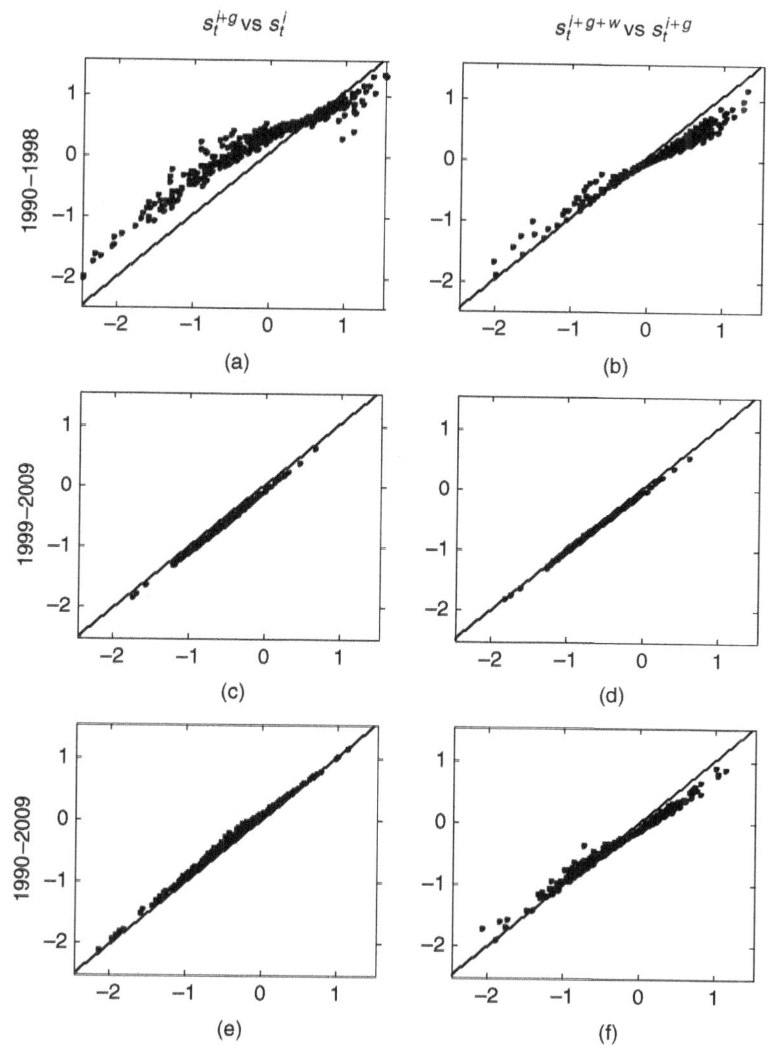

FIGURE 5.3 Scatterplots of skewness coefficients (Singapore).

the scatter diagrams for the full sample. Each scatterplot is augmented with a 45° line; a scatterplot with most of its points lying along this diagonal would indicate that the addition of the regional factor (for the diagrams in the left column) or the world factor (right column) contributes nothing to the shape of the distribution. Deviations from the diagonal will show the direction and strength of the influence of the regional or world factor in determining the shape of the distribution.

We begin with the Hong Kong market. The first row shows that skewness in local shocks in the Hong Kong market ranges from about −2 to 1 in the first sample period, but that the regional factor works to reduce the degree of skewness, especially when s_t^i is negative, so that most of the points lie above the 45° line. In some instances, the difference between s_t^i and s_t^{i+g} is large. The world factor appears to contribute little to the shape of the conditional distribution of Hong Kong returns. Both regional and world factors seem to have little contribution to the shape of the conditional distribution of Hong Kong returns in the second sample period. For the Singapore market, in the first sample period, both the regional and the world factors seem to contribute to the shape of the distribution, primarily by reducing the degree of skewness, more so the regional factor than the world factor, and the effect of both are generally quite small. In the second sample period, there does not appear to be any skewness spillovers at all; all points fall close to the 45° line.

To summarize, the influence of the world and regional factors for the two markets seem to have reduced substantially from the first sample period to the second, both in terms of variance spillovers and skewness spillovers. On the other hand, mean spillovers from the world factor increased substantially in the second sample period. The latter finding is consistent with the evidence in Diebold and Yilmaz (2009) that mean spillovers have been increasing slowly over time. The estimates obtained here suggest, in fact, a very dramatic increase in mean spillovers. Our results concerning volatility spillovers (and skewness spillovers), however, are somewhat at odds with the findings in Diebold and Yilmaz (2009). It would be very interesting to find an explanation for the changes in mean, variance, and skewness spillovers that we find here. An increase in mean spillovers can justifiably be attributed to increasing financial integration, although it is harder to explain the changes in volatility and skewness spillovers. It is, in fact, possible to view the reduction of volatility and skewness spillovers, together with increased mean spillover, as a reflection of *greater* financial integration among markets; whereas high variance and skewness spillovers would suggest an increased *probability* of large changes in individual markets following large movements in other markets, we find that movements in world and regional markets now affect more directly the *expected* returns in individual markets.

5.4 Conclusion

We present new measurements of the relative importance of global, regional, and local components of risk in equity markets, an issue with implications for important financial market activities, using factor models that allow for time-varying conditional skewness. The evidence is from two important Asian markets, Hong Kong and Singapore, using weekly data from 1990 to 2009, and using world and regional indexes as proxies for world and regional factors.

We explore spillovers in terms of mean, volatility, and skewness. We estimate a time-varying conditional skewness spillover model. To allow for possible structural change as a result of regulatory and other changes that took place during this period, we also estimate the models over two subsamples, 1990–1998 and 1999–2009. We compare our results with several alternative specifications, in particular, to a model with constant conditional skewness and to a model with no conditional skewness.

Our results suggest that (i) incorporating time-varying conditional skewness can alter measurements of variance spillovers and (ii) mean, variance, and skewness spillover into the Hong Kong and Singapore markets have changed substantially over the two sample periods: there are some variance and skewness spillovers in the first subperiod (1990–1998) but little mean spillover, whereas there are little variance and skewness spillovers in the second subperiod (1999–2009) but substantial mean spillover. We interpret this as a reflection of *greater* financial integration.

One interesting avenue for future research is to explore spillover effects with time-varying conditional skewness at the daily (or higher) frequencies. Also, more research into the economic reasons behind asymmetry in the conditional distribution of stock returns would be interesting. Despite our lack of knowledge of the causes of time-varying conditional skewness, the results in this chapter show that studies of spillovers and linkages between equity markets will benefit from incorporating predictability in conditional skewness. Finally, a closer examination into the changes in mean, variance, and skewness spillovers would be very useful.

Acknowledgments

Tay gratefully acknowledges financial support from the Singapore Management University. Vince Conti provided excellent research assistance. The usual disclaimer applies.

CHAPTER SIX

Relating Stochastic Volatility Estimation Methods

CHARLES S. BOS

6.1 Introduction

Interest in the volatility of returns dates back further than our capabilities of estimating such volatility sequences in a sensible manner. For example, Markowitz (1952), discussing the possibility of constructing a portfolio with an optimal expected return-variance trade-off, indicates that

> One suggestion as to tentative μ_i, σ_{ij} is to use the observed μ_i, σ_{ij} for some period of the past. I believe that better methods, which take into account more information, can be found. I believe that what is needed is essentially a "probabilistic" reformulation of security analysis.

Indeed, in his article, he explicitly claims to start from a set of beliefs on expected returns and volatility μ, σ, and does not consider the stage of forming the relevant beliefs on these moments on the basis of observations.

Part I of the present volume is largely directed at nonprobabilistic measures of volatility such as the (G)ARCH class of models, in which volatility depends in a deterministic way on past returns. These models have taken a large flight after the seminal publications of Engle (1982a) and Bollerslev (1986). The article of Clark (1973), on the other hand, is generally recognized as the first to explicitly

Handbook of Volatility Models and Their Applications, First Edition.
Edited by Luc Bauwens, Christian Hafner, and Sebastien Laurent.

refer to a probabilistic approach to variance estimation. In the article, log-prices are driven by two independent processes, one for the levels and one for the volatility. In discrete time, Taylor (1982) described a version of the product process, which later became known as the *stochastic volatility* (SV) model.

Taylor (1982) extracts the volatility of this product process by computing an exponentially weighted moving average of scaled absolute returns, where the weights are calibrated. Only a decade later, a series of more efficient estimation methods have been devised. Even though Ghysels et al. (1996) state that these estimation methods have made the SV model an attractive alternative to models such as GARCH, one cannot escape the impression that this attraction has not come to full fruition. While there are literally thousands of applications of GARCH, for SV, this number is far lower.

Two reasons for this relative lack of applied work using SV are apparent. First, there are as of yet no standard packages for estimating SV models, whereas for GARCH, most statistical packages have a wealth of options for incorporating GARCH effects. A second difference seems to be that GARCH has many variants of the model (Bollerslev, 2008), with basically a single estimation method for all of them. For SV, there are few variants of the model, but a full series of estimation methods. No estimation method has come out as clearly the simplest or most efficient, and the relations between the methods are not immediately clear.

Several reviews of the SV literature are available (see Ghysels et al., 1996; Broto and Ruiz, 2004; Shephard, 2005, to name a few). Instead of giving another review of the literature, this chapter focuses on the estimation of the basic univariate SV model, interrelating in detail the various estimation methods. In order to get a clear comparison and better understanding, only the most basic SV model is initially investigated here. Not all methods are equally adequate for incorporating extensions, and these extensions would hamper the understanding of the basics of estimating SV models. The methods covered are chosen to give a broad overview of the possible approaches for estimation, while still being relevant in that the methods have not been clearly surpassed by alternative estimation procedures.

Section 6.2 first introduces the basic SV model. It continues, using common notation, with a description of a series of estimation methods for the above model. First, the quasi-maximum likelihood method (Harvey et al. 1994b, QML) is introduced in Section 6.2.1, as it uses a linear approximation, which is in essence common to the other methods as well. This method is only a QML approach, as it does not adapt for the approximation error. The Gaussian mixture sampling (see Carter and Kohn, 1997; Kim et al., 1998, GMS) in Section 6.2.2, uses a Bayesian approach in which a mixture of normals decreases the approximation error. It is followed by the simulated method of moments (Section 6.2.3, see Gallant and Tauchen, 1996, among others, SMM), which provides a classical approach for extracting only the parameter estimates. Importance sampling for SV, as proposed by Durbin and Koopman (1997, IS), can be seen as an improvement on QML. It is, however, not fully efficient, and hence gave rise to both efficient importance sampling (Richard and Zhang, 2007, EIS) and improved importance sampling (Nguyen, 2007, IIS). These three methods are combined in Section

TABLE 6.1 Methods and Main References

Method (Acronym)	Central Reference	
Quasi-Maximum Likelihood (QML)	Harvey et al. (1994b)	C, f/s
Gaussian Mixture Sampling (GMS)	Kim et al. (1998)	B, s
Simulated Method of Moments (SMM)	Gallant and Tauchen (1996)	C, -
Importance Sampling (IS)	Durbin and Koopman (1997)	C, s
Efficient Importance Sampling (EIS)	Richard and Zhang (2007)	C, s
Improved Importance Sampling (IIS)	Nguyen (2007)	C, s
Single Site Sampler (SSS)	Carter and Kohn (1994)	B, s
MultiMove Sampler (MMS)	Shephard and Pitt (1997)	B, s

Note: The table reports the methods discussed, with one central reference, and indicates whether the approach is classical (C) or Bayesian (B) in background, resulting in a filtered (f) or smoothed (s) state, or none (-).

6.2.4. Last, the IS approach can also be turned into a Bayesian sampling scheme as described in Section 6.2.5. Sampling either a Single State at a time (Carter and Kohn 1994, SSS) or using a MultiMove Sampler (Shephard and Pitt, 1997, MMS) could provide more flexibility and/or efficiency. This set of methods is summarized in Table 6.1, indicating for each method the acronym used, one main reference, and whether the approach is classical or Bayesian in background, allowing for extracting either the filtered (f) or smoothed (s) state, or resulting in no state estimate at all (-).

The theory can be interesting by itself, although ultimately, the methods should be compared in their efficiency and ease of use in obtaining the estimates. Section 6.3 provides the results on a simulation exercise, where each method is used for estimating the volatility model on the same 1000 simulated data series. Results are presented on different aspects of efficiency. It is followed by Section 6.4, which looks at practical results on two financial returns series. These two return series are first estimated univariately, with the basic SV model. Afterward, a simple extension to a bivariate volatility model with stochastic correlation is introduced and estimated. A discussion of the methods with concluding remarks is found in Section 6.5.

6.2 Theory and Methodology

The following notation is used for the simple univariate SV model. Given a series of returns $Y \equiv \{y_1, \ldots, y_T\}$ with expectation zero,[1] the model is given by

$$y_t = \varepsilon_t, \qquad \varepsilon_t \sim \mathcal{N}(0, \sigma_\varepsilon^2 \exp(h_t)), \tag{6.1}$$

[1] Here, the model is kept as simple as possible on purpose for ease of exposition. Extensions to include either autocorrelation in the returns or non-Gaussianity could be taken up into the specification as well.

$$h_{t+1} = \phi h_t + \xi_t, \qquad \xi_t \sim \mathcal{N}(0, \sigma_\xi^2), \tag{6.2}$$

$$h_1 \equiv 0, \qquad t = 1, \ldots, T. \tag{6.3}$$

Here $H = \{h_1, \ldots, h_T\}$ is the latent SV, and $\theta = (\sigma_\varepsilon, \phi, \sigma_\xi)$ the vector of parameters. Interest is in estimating the parameters in the model, and preferably also extracting the volatility sequence, as this is useful for evaluating the uncertainty pertaining to the returns, and consequently, for financial decision making, which may use volatilities as input, for example, for option pricing.

The difficulty in estimating the SV model lies in the fact that the observation equation (6.1) depends nonlinearly on the states h_t. These states evolve according to the state equation (6.2). As the dependence in (6.1) is nonlinear, the Kalman filter (KF, see Harvey, 1989) equations cannot be used directly for obtaining the likelihood of the observations, or to extract filtered states. The estimation methods indicated in Table 6.1 each take their individual approach in solving this problem. However, those approaches are necessarily interrelated as the final model to estimate is the same. A commonality shared by most of the methods is the use of an approximating linear Gaussian state space model, approximating (6.1) by

$$c_t = h_t + u_t, \qquad u_t \sim \mathcal{N}(0, d_t), \tag{6.4}$$

for certain choices of c_t, d_t. In the remainder of this section, the relations between the methods, and their choice for the auxiliary data $y_t^* = (c_t, d_t)$ of the approximating linear model, are exposed.

6.2.1 QUASI-MAXIMUM LIKELIHOOD ESTIMATION

The most direct approach for estimating SV is found in Harvey et al. (1994b). As the nonlinearity of the observation equation is the main source of difficulty, the authors linearize the equation by writing

$$\ln y_t^2 = h_t + \ln \varepsilon_t^2 = h_t + \ln \sigma_\varepsilon^2 + \ln e_t^2, \quad e_t \sim \mathcal{N}(0, 1).$$

The density of $\ln e_t^2$ is approximated by a normal density, with expectation and variance given by

$$E(\ln e_t^2) = \left(\frac{\Gamma'(\frac{1}{2})}{\Gamma(\frac{1}{2})} - \ln\left(\frac{1}{2}\right) \right) \approx -1.2704,$$

$$\mathrm{Var}(\ln e_t^2) = \left. \frac{\partial^2 \ln \Gamma(\nu)}{\partial \nu^2} \right]_{\nu=\frac{1}{2}} = \frac{1}{2}\pi^2,$$

(see Abramowitz and Stegun (1972), Eq. 26.4.36). In terms of the linear approximating density (6.4) this gives parameters

$$c_t \approx \ln y_t^2 - \ln \sigma_\varepsilon^2 + 1.2704,$$
$$d_t = \frac{1}{2}\pi^2.$$

The resulting linear Gaussian state space model is amenable to evaluation using the Kalman filter equations, which deliver the likelihood of this model efficiently. No correction is made for approximating the density of $\ln e_t^2$ by a simple normal density, hence the resulting optimization delivers no true but only QML estimates.

6.2.2 GAUSSIAN MIXTURE SAMPLING

In Carter and Kohn (1997), Kim et al. (1998), and Omori et al. (2007), a similar linearization of the observation equation is used, but now the density of $\ln e_t^2$ is approximated using a Gaussian mixture (GM) density, as in

$$\ln e_t^2 \approx u_t \sim \sum_{i=1}^{C} p_i \mathcal{N}(m_i, s_i^2).$$

In this notation, p_i are the weights of the mixture components, and m_i, s_i^2 the respective means and variances. The distinction between the three articles is the number C of mixture components that is used (5, 7, and 10 respectively), where obviously, the mixture with the largest number of components delivers the closest match between the approximating and true density. The QML method would correspond to a one-component mixture in this notation.

With this extension to a GM, the full model is no longer an unconditionally linear and Gaussian state space (StSp) model, as it depends on the discrete unobserved states i_t. Instead of optimizing the likelihood directly, a Bayesian Markov chain Monte Carlo (MCMC) approach with data augmentation is used: If one assumes indices i_t indicating which element i of the mixture is used at time t, the model for $Y|I$ is *conditionally* linear and Gaussian, where $I = \{i_1, \ldots, i_T\}$. In terms of the general approximating linear Gaussian observation equation (6.4), conditional choices of

$$c_t|i_t = \ln y_t^2 - \ln \sigma_\varepsilon^2 - m_{i_t}, \qquad d_t|i_t = s_{i_t}^2$$

are used.

The simulation smoother (De Jong and Shephard, 1995; Durbin and Koopman, 2002) delivers a sample from the states H conditional on the data Y, state indices I, and parameters θ. Conditionally on the states H, on data Y, and on the parameters θ, each mixture node has a certain probability $P(i_t = i)$, which can be evaluated. From the resulting multinomial density, a sample of new indices i_t is drawn. Afterwards, conditional on states I, H, and data Y, new parameters θ are drawn as in a standard Gibbs scheme (Smith and Gelfand, 1992). A final sample from the parameters and states describes the posterior density of these, conditional on the full set of data. The posterior mean of the states is an estimate of the smoothed states.

6.2.3 SIMULATED METHOD OF MOMENTS

Where QML uses a likelihood approach, and GMS a Bayesian MCMC, the SMM approach (Gallant and Tauchen, 1996; Andersen et al., 1999) takes a third route to parameter estimation. If the log-likelihood function $\ln P_{SV}(Y;\theta)$ of the SV model were available in closed form, then it could be optimized by finding those parameters that set the average score to zero, with score function

$$s_{SV}(Y;\theta) = \frac{1}{T}\frac{\partial \ln P_{SV}(Y;\theta)}{\partial\theta}.$$

This true score function cannot be evaluated directly, as the likelihood function of SV models is not available in closed form. SMM instead uses an auxiliary model, which fits the most important characteristics of the data closely, and is easier to estimate. In this case, for the SV model, some GARCH model could be used as the auxiliary model. Suppose that this auxiliary model delivers auxiliary parameter estimates $\hat{\theta}_{Aux}$. Clearly, at these estimates, the score of the log-likelihood $\ln P_{Aux}(Y, \hat{\theta}_{Aux})$ of the auxiliary model for the current set of data equals zero. But if data were generated from the SV model, for the optimal set of parameters $\hat{\theta}$, the same $\hat{\theta}_{Aux}$ should provide a good fit for the auxiliary model as well. Hence SMM evaluates

$$s_{Aux}(Y^*(\theta), \hat{\theta}_{Aux}) = \frac{1}{T_{Aux}}\left.\frac{\partial \ln P_{Aux}(Y^*(\theta);\theta_{Aux})}{\partial\theta_{Aux}}\right]_{\theta_{Aux}=\hat{\theta}_{Aux}},$$

which is the score of the auxiliary model, at parameters $\hat{\theta}_{Aux}$, for T_{Aux} observations $Y^*(\theta)$ simulated from the SV model using parameters θ. Searching for those parameters θ that equate these scores to zero delivers estimates of the parameters of the SV model, through the detour of the auxiliary model.

As an auxiliary model, the QML-SV model of Harvey et al. (1994b) mentioned before could be used, although for this QML-SV model, the score function is not available analytically either. As mentioned before, a GARCH model, with either Gaussian or Student-t disturbances, or an EGARCH (Nelson, 1991b), provides an approximating model where the analytic scores can be derived. In those cases, the parameters of the auxiliary model are different in number and type from the those of the true model. Therefore, the score vector of the auxiliary model should be scaled by the inverse information matrix of the model, minimizing effectively

$$Q(\theta;\hat{\theta}_{\text{Aux}}) = s_{\text{Aux}}(Y^*(\theta),\hat{\theta}_{\text{Aux}})'\mathcal{I}^{-1}(\hat{\theta}_{\text{Aux}})s_{\text{Aux}}(Y^*(\theta),\hat{\theta}_{\text{Aux}}),$$

$$\mathcal{I}(\hat{\theta}_{\text{Aux}}) = \frac{1}{T}\sum \frac{\partial \ln P_{\text{Aux}}(y_t;\theta_{\text{Aux}})}{\partial\theta_{\text{Aux}}}\frac{\partial \ln P_{\text{Aux}}(y_t;\theta_{\text{Aux}})}{\partial\theta'_{\text{Aux}}}\bigg|_{\theta_{\text{Aux}}=\hat{\theta}_{\text{Aux}}}.$$

If the auxiliary model indeed covers the important characteristics of the data, and if the auxiliary sample size T_{Aux} is sufficiently large, then optimizing the function $Q(\theta;\hat{\theta}_{\text{Aux}})$ provides an efficient estimate of the parameters θ of the SV model (see also Andersen et al., 1999). SMM, however, never optimizes, or even calculates, a likelihood of the SV model, but arrives at a set of parameter estimates without even touching on the underlying states. If only parameter estimation is requested, it can be a good alternative to the other methods in this chapter.

6.2.4 METHODS BASED ON IMPORTANCE SAMPLING

All the three aforementioned methods have their drawbacks: QML is only approximative, GMS does not provide a classical maximum likelihood estimator, and SMM lacks an estimate for the state of the volatility. A set of methods based on the idea of IS provides alternative estimators. In the following discussion, three versions of IS will be differentiated: basic IS (Durbin and Koopman, 1997), efficient IS (Liesenfeld and Richard, 2006; Richard and Zhang, 2007), and an improved version of IS (Nguyen, 2007), which will be found to be as efficient as EIS.

For the basic method of IS, the likelihood $\mathcal{L}(Y;\theta)$ is approximated using simulation through

$$\begin{aligned}\mathcal{L}(Y;\theta) &= \int \frac{P(Y,H)}{G(H|Y^*)}G(H|Y^*)\partial H \\ &\approx \frac{1}{M}\sum \frac{P(Y,H^{(i)})}{G(H^{(i)}|Y^*)} = \frac{1}{M}\sum \omega_i \equiv \overline{\omega},\end{aligned} \tag{6.5}$$

where the $H^{(i)}$ are sampled volatilities from the approximating importance density $G(H|Y^*)$. The latter density depends on some auxiliary data Y^*, and is chosen such that it is a close approximation to $P(Y,H)$ (where dependence on parameters θ is skipped in the notation for simplicity). From this importance density, M series of $H^{(i)} = \{h_1^{(i)},\ldots,h_T^{(i)}\}$ are drawn and used for evaluating the likelihood.[2]

[2]In practice, it is often desired to estimate $\log\mathcal{L}(Y;\theta)$. Durbin and Koopman (1997) derive how an unbiased estimator for this quantity is

$$\log\mathcal{L}(Y;\theta) \approx \log\overline{\omega} + \frac{s_\omega^2}{2M\overline{\omega}^2},$$

with $\overline{\omega}$ the average weight and s_ω^2 the variance.

The approximation in (6.5) can be made as accurate as required by increasing the number M of sampled volatility sequences. If a common random seed is used for sampling $H^{(i)}$ when the likelihood is evaluated for different values of θ, the likelihood will be a smooth function of the parameters, and standard quasi-Newton optimization methods can be used.

The three methods IS, EIS, and IIS use the same setup (6.4) for the approximating linear observation equation. Where QML chose c_t, d_t only taking the $\ln \chi^2$ density into account, the IS methods also look at the values of h_t around the current observation to obtain an optimal fit between $P(Y, H)$ and $G(H|Y^*)$. The methods IS, EIS, and IIS differ in the way optimal $Y^* \equiv \{c_t, d_t, t = 1, \ldots, T\}$ and the sample of $H|Y^*$ are obtained.

6.2.4.1 Approximating in the Basic IS Approach. In the method of Durbin and Koopman (1997) full advantage of the linear Gaussian unobserved component structure of the approximating model (6.2) and (6.4) is taken. Notice that $G(H|Y^*)$ is the density of the linear states, dependent on the auxiliary data as represented by Y^*. A sample from this density can be drawn using the simulation smoother. The weights ω_i are evaluated by rewriting

$$G(H^{(i)}|Y^*) = \frac{G(Y^*|H^{(i)})G(H^{(i)})}{G(Y^*)},$$
$$P(Y, H^{(i)}) = P(Y|H^{(i)})P(H^{(i)}),$$

such that

$$\omega^{(i)} = \frac{P(Y, H^{(i)})}{G(H^{(i)}|Y^*)} = G(Y^*)\frac{P(Y|H^{(i)})P(H^{(i)})}{G(Y^*|H^{(i)})G(H^{(i)})}$$
$$= G(Y^*)\frac{P(Y|H^{(i)})}{G(Y^*|H^{(i)})} = G(Y^*)\prod_t \frac{P(y_t|h_t^{(i)})}{G(y_t^*|h_t^{(i)})}.$$

In these equations, $G(H^{(i)})$ represents the density of the states as defined by the transition equation (Eq. 6.2), and $G(Y^*|H^{(i)})$ the density corresponding with the approximating observation equation (Eq. 6.4). $G(Y^*)$ is the full unconditional likelihood of the auxiliary data according to the approximating model and can be evaluated using the KF equations. As the transition equations of the auxiliary and true models are the same, the factor $P(H^{(i)})/G(H^{(i)})$ cancels from the weight ω_i.

For finding the optimal $y_t^* = \{c_t, d_t\}$ of the approximating model, IS ensures that the densities relating to the observation equations (Eqs. 6.1 and 6.4) correspond in their first two moments. Define $p \equiv \ln P(y_t|h_t), g \equiv \ln P(y_t^*|h_t)$ with first and second derivatives with respect to h_t indicated as $\dot{p}, \dot{g}, \ddot{p}, \ddot{g}$, then

$$p = -\frac{1}{2}\left(\ln 2\pi + \ln \sigma_\varepsilon^2 + h_t + \frac{y_t^2}{\sigma_\varepsilon^2 \exp(h_t)}\right),$$
$$g = -\frac{1}{2}\left(\ln 2\pi + \ln d_t + \frac{(c_t - h_t)^2}{d_t}\right), \tag{6.6}$$

$$\dot{p} = -\frac{1}{2}\left(1 - \frac{y_t^2}{\sigma_\varepsilon^2 \exp(h_t)}\right), \quad \dot{g} = \frac{c_t - h_t}{d_t}, \tag{6.7}$$

$$\ddot{p} = -\frac{y_t^2}{2\sigma_\varepsilon^2 \exp(h_t)}, \quad \ddot{g} = -\frac{1}{d_t}. \tag{6.8}$$

For a given value of h_t, the corresponding optimal values of c_t, d_t can be solved from these equations by setting $\dot{p}_t \equiv \dot{g}_t, \ddot{p}_t \equiv \ddot{g}_t$.[3] Ideally, the approximating model would fit $\ln P(y_t|h_t)$ well around a plausible value of h_t, for all $t = 1, \ldots, T$. One such plausible value of $H = (h_1, \ldots, h_T)$ could be the smoothed state $\tilde{H}$ from the auxiliary model. By iterating back and forth between improving estimates of Y^* and extracting a new $\tilde{H}$, an optimal solution for the parameters can be found in what is usually a small number of iterations (Sandmann and Koopman, 1998).

6.2.4.2 Improving on IS with IIS. The IS method of estimating an SV model is flexible, relatively easy to implement, and not too computationally intensive in practice either. A weak spot of the IS method, first recognized in the EIS method (Liesenfeld and Richard, 2006) described below, is that the likelihood evaluation (Eq. 6.5) is based on M samples $H^{(i)}, i = 1, \ldots, M$ of the volatilities, whereas the auxiliary model is only fitted to the true SV model using a second order Taylor expansion at the mode $\tilde{H}$.

The Taylor expansion, however, provides the closest possible approximation only locally, where the error in the approximation increases with the order $O((h_t - \tilde{h}_t)^3)$, for the second-order Taylor expansion used here. Therefore, there is no guarantee that the current approximation is sufficiently close over the full range of possibly interesting values of H.

Nguyen (2007) proposes to take M samples from the approximating model, $H^{(i)}, i = 1, \ldots, M$, and minimize the distance between the two observation densities $P(y_t|h_t^{(i)})$ and $G(y_t^*|h_t^{(i)})$, following the example of the EIS sampler of Richard and Zhang (2007). As all dependence through time is taken up by the simulation smoother and incorporated into the sample $H^{(i)}$, optimizing the distance between the observation densities can be done at each time t, separately from other time points. A simple but effective approach is to minimize the variance of the log-weights $\ln \omega_t^{(i)}$, as in

$$Q_t(c_t, d_t) = \sum_i (\ln \omega_t^{(i)} - \overline{\ln \omega_t})^2 = \sum_i \left(p(y_t|h_t^{(i)}) - g(y_t^*|h_t^{(i)}) + \text{const}\right)^2$$
$$= \sum_i \left(-\frac{1}{2}h_t^{(i)} - \frac{y_t^2}{2\sigma_\varepsilon^2 \exp(h_t^{(i)})} + \frac{\ln d_t}{2} + \frac{(h_t^{(i)} - c_t)^2}{2d_t} + \text{const}\right)^2$$

[3]In general with IS, there is no guarantee that the second derivative $\ddot{p}$ is negative. For the present model, if the return y_t is close (equal) to zero, the corresponding variance $d_t \equiv -1/\ddot{p}_t$ becomes extremely large (infinite). Jungbacker and Koopman (2007) note that the simulation smoothing equations of De Jong and Shephard (1995) can be adapted to allow for this case, without influencing the effectiveness of the algorithm.

$$\equiv \sum_i \left(z^{(i)} - a_0 - a_1 h_t^{(i)} - a_2 (h_t^{(i)})^2 \right).$$

The optimal solution for c_t, d_t can be found using a linear regression of

$$z^{(i)} = -\frac{1}{2} h_t^{(i)} - \frac{y_t^2}{2\sigma_\varepsilon^2 \exp(h_t^{(i)})} \tag{6.9}$$

on $h_t^{(i)}$ and $(h_t^{(i)})^2$, solving for c_t, d_t from

$$a_1 = \frac{c_t}{d_t}, \qquad a_2 = -\frac{1}{2d_t}. \tag{6.10}$$

Note that the value of a_0 is not of interest, as it takes up $\overline{\ln \omega_t}$ and the integrating constants of the densities.

Given a new set of estimates $Y^* = \{c_t, d_t, t = 1, \ldots, T\}$, a more appropriate sample of H can be drawn, and the optimization repeated until convergence. As with the basic IS method, convergence will usually take place within a few iterations, and the final weights ω_t are expected to display lower variability.

6.2.4.3 Alternative Efficiency Gains with EIS. As seen with the IIS method, the fit of the auxiliary density could be improved compared to IS when the true and auxiliary density are matched for a sample $H^{(i)}$ of volatility sequences. IIS uses the simulation smoother to sample from the density of $H|Y^*$, whereas EIS chooses to sample from the predictive densities, that is, to sample each $h_t|y_t^*, h_{t-1}$. The final auxiliary sampling density will be indicated by $G^{\text{EIS}}(H|Y^*)$, where the notation explicitly indicates that the sampling density here is the predictive density only.

These predictive densities can be constructed from the combination of the information stemming from Gaussian transition equation (6.2) and observation equation (6.4), as

$$G(h_t|y_t^*, h_{t-1}) = \frac{G(h_t|y_t^*)G(h_t|h_{t-1})}{\chi_t(h_{t-1})} \propto G(h_t|y_t^*)G(h_t|h_{t-1}),$$

$$h_t|y_t^* \sim \mathcal{N}(c_t, d_t), \qquad h_t|h_{t-1} \sim \mathcal{N}(\phi h_{t-1}, \sigma_\xi^2).$$

This implies that $h_t|y_t^*, h_{t-1} \sim \mathcal{N}(m_t, s_t^2)$ with

$$s_t^2 = \left(\frac{1}{\sigma_\xi^2} + \frac{1}{d_t} \right)^{-1}, \qquad m_t = s_t^2 \left(\frac{\phi h_{t-1}}{\sigma_\xi^2} + \frac{c_t}{d_t} \right).$$

The integrating constant $\chi_t(h_{t-1})$ is

$$\chi_t(h_{t-1}) = \sqrt{\frac{2\pi\, d_t \sigma_\xi^2}{s_t^2}} \exp\left(\frac{c_t^2}{2d_t} + \frac{\phi^2 h_{t-1}^2}{2\sigma_\xi^2} - \frac{m_t^2}{2s_t^2} \right) \propto \exp\left(\frac{\phi^2 h_{t-1}^2}{2\sigma_\xi^2} - \frac{m_t^2}{2s_t^2} \right).$$

Note how $\chi_t(h_{t-1})$ depends on the previous value of the volatility, both directly through $\phi^2 h_{t-1}^2$ and indirectly through the value m_t^2. It is through the integrating constant that part of the information on the previous observation is handed over to the present.

EIS, like IIS, considers the variance of the log-weights

$$
\begin{aligned}
\ln \omega^{(i)} &= \sum_t \Big(p(y_t|h_t^{(i)}) + p(h_t^{(i)}|h_{t-1}^{(i)}) - g(h_t^{(i)}|y_t^*) \\
&\quad - g(h_t^{(i)}|h_{t-1}^{(i)}) + \ln \chi_t(h_{t-1}^{(i)}) \Big) \\
&= \sum_t \Big(p(y_t|h_t^{(i)}) - g(h_t^{(i)}|y_t^*) + \ln \chi_t(h_{t-1}^{(i)}) \Big) \\
&\equiv \sum_t \Big(p(y_t|h_t^{(i)}) - g(h_t^{(i)}|y_t^*) + \ln \chi_{t+1}(h_t^{(i)}) \Big) = \sum_t w_t(h_t^{(i)}).
\end{aligned}
$$

In the third step, the integrating constant is moved forward in time, in order to combine all elements concerning $h_t^{(i)}$ together in $w_t(h_t^{(i)})$. Defining $\chi_{T+1}(h_T) = 1$ takes care of the end point condition.

At each time point t, the sum-of-squares function to minimize becomes

$$
\begin{aligned}
Q_t(c_t, d_t) &= \sum_i (w_t(h_t^{(i)}) - \overline{w}_t)^2 \\
&= \sum_i \Bigg(-\frac{1}{2} h_t^{(i)} - \frac{y_t^2}{2\sigma_\varepsilon^2 \exp(h_t^{(i)})} + \frac{\ln d_t}{2} + \frac{(h_t^{(i)} - c_t)^2}{2d_t} \\
&\qquad + \frac{\phi^2 h_t^{(i)2}}{2\sigma_\xi^2} - \frac{m_{t+1}^{(i)2}}{2s_{t+1}^2} + \text{const} \Bigg)^2 \\
&\equiv \sum_i \left(z_i - a_0 - a_1 h_t^{(i)} - a_2 h_t^{(i)2} \right)^2,
\end{aligned}
$$

where now

$$
z^{(i)} = -\frac{1}{2} h_t^{(i)} - \frac{y_t^2}{2\sigma_\varepsilon^2 \exp(h_t^{(i)})} + \frac{\phi^2 h_t^{(i)2}}{2\sigma_\xi^2} - \frac{m_{t+1}^{(i)2}}{2s_{t+1}^2}. \tag{6.11}
$$

Note how this specification for $z^{(i)}$ in (6.11) corresponds to the IIS regressor in (6.9), apart from the added terms relating to the integrating constant $\ln \chi_{t+1}(h_t)$. Minimizing the sum of squares of $w_t(h_t^{(i)})$ then again corresponds to finding the solution of the linear regression model relating $z^{(i)}$ to $h_t^{(i)}$ and its square. From the regression output on a_1, a_2, the optimal values of (c_t, d_t) are extracted as in (6.10). This can be done recursively, starting at the end of the sample (as $\chi_{T+1}(h_t) \equiv 1$ is known), working backward toward $t = 1$.

At this stage, a theoretical comparison between the setup for IS, IIS, and EIS can be made. From the above description, it is clear how IS uses the simulation smoother for a linear approximating Gaussian model as auxiliary sampler. The approximating model is fitted such that at the smoothed estimate $\tilde{H}$, the true and approximating log-densities correspond in their first two moments. With IIS, the same approximating model is used, but the approximation is optimized not for an estimate $\tilde{H}$, but for a full sample. EIS changes the auxiliary sampler to contain only past and present information; future information is taken into account by adapting for the integrating constant in the sum-of-squares function, and hence it uses the same amount of information as IIS. Below, in Section 6.3, it is indeed seen that IIS and EIS are equally efficient, both surpassing the precision of the likelihood estimate of IS considerably.

6.2.5 ALTERNATIVE SAMPLING METHODS: SSS AND MMS

The IS-based methods effectively provide a sampling-based alternative to evaluating the exact log-likelihood function for the SV model (albeit by simulation), instead of the rough approximation of the QML method of Section 6.2.1. A different route discussed in Section 6.2.2 provided a Bayesian approach to a similar goal: improving the approximation of the density of $\ln e_t^2$ through a mixture density, and in turn, sampling from all full conditional densities. This latter approach, however exact the mixture density can be, is still an approximation, as the mixture density is theoretically not equal to the target density.[4]

Two alternative flexible methods are available for obtaining a theoretically exact Bayesian sampler for the SV model. These methods, the single site sampler (SSS) and the multimove sampler (MMS) can be described together, where the SSS is a special (and simpler) case of the MMS. Both methods provide a sampler of H from the true SV model. The methods follow the framework of GMS of Section 6.2.2 in that they try to sample H from the full conditional density. Instead of enlarging the parameter space with a set of mixture indices I, the problem of sampling $H = \{h_1, \ldots, h_T\}$ is broken up into smaller blocks. Say we have block sizes $k_1, \ldots, k_k, \sum k_j = T$, then successively, each block of k_j volatilities $H_{k_j} \equiv \{h_{t_j}, \ldots, h_{t_{j+1}-1}\}$ with $t_1 = 1, t_l = t_{l-1} + k_{l-1}, l > 1$ is sampled conditioning on Y and $(H \setminus H_{k_j}) = \{h_1, \ldots, h_{t_j-1}, h_{t_{j+1}}, \ldots, h_T\}$. With SSS, the block size $k_j = 1$, whereas with MMS, k_j is larger than 1.

To sample from the present block, a slightly enlarged approximating model is fitted to the data. (6.2) and (6.4) are extended with end point conditions for the auxiliary data outside the current block,

$$c_{t_j-1} \equiv h_{t_j}, \qquad d_{t_j-1} \equiv 0, \tag{6.12}$$

$$c_{t_{j+1}} \equiv h_{t_{j+1}}, \qquad d_{t_{j+1}} \equiv 0. \tag{6.13}$$

The knots outside the block are fixed at the current value of h_{t_j-1} and $h_{t_{j+1}}$. Within the block, again c_t, d_t can be chosen to provide a good fit for the

[4] In the original work of Kim et al. (1998), this is solved by performing an extra reweighting step. Here, we will forgo this possibility for simplicity.

approximating model to the true observation equation. As in Section 6.2.4, the first two derivatives of the log-densities are equated ($\dot{p} \equiv \dot{g}, \ddot{p} \equiv \ddot{g}$), for an estimate of the present set of volatilities. Again, one could use a smoothed estimate $\tilde{H}_{k_j}$, or even a full sample of $\tilde{H}_{k_j}^{(i)}$.

From the approximating model, a candidate sample $H_{k_j}^*$ is drawn using the simulation smoother. The candidate draw $H_{k_j}^*$ is accepted as the new value for $H_{k_j}^{(i)}$ with Metropolis–Hastings (MH) acceptance probability α, comparing the likelihood contributions of the true and approximating models:

$$\alpha\left(H_{k_j}^*, H_{k_j}^{(i-1)}\right) = \min\left[\frac{P(Y_{k_j}|H_{k_j}^*)G(Y_{k_j}^*|H_{k_j}^{(i-1)})}{P(Y_{k_j}|H_{k_j}^{(i-1)})G(Y_{k_j}^*|H_{k_j}^*)}, 1\right].$$

If the candidate draw is not accepted, one continues with $H_{k_j}^{(i)} \equiv H_{k_j}^{(i-1)}$, else $H_{k_j}^{(i)} \equiv H_{k_j}^*$. This approximating and sampling step is taken successively for all blocks, until a full new sample $H^{(i)}$ is obtained.

With SSS, constructing the optimal approximating density does not need to go through the full state space setup of the above equations, as the optimal Gaussian approximation sampler for $h_t|h_{t-1}, h_{t+1}, y_t$ can be found analytically. Notice that there are three sources of information on h_t, with

$$\begin{aligned}
h_t|h_{t-1} &\sim \mathcal{N}(\phi h_{t-1}, \sigma_\xi^2) \equiv \mathcal{N}(c^p, d^p), && \text{Past information,}\\
h_t|h_{t+1} &\sim \mathcal{N}\left(\frac{1}{\phi}h_{t+1}, \frac{1}{\phi^2}\sigma_\xi^2\right) \equiv \mathcal{N}(c^f, d^f), && \text{Future information,}\\
h_t|y_t^* &\sim \mathcal{N}(c_t, d_t) \equiv \mathcal{N}(-\ddot{p}^{-1}\dot{p} + \tilde{h}_t, -\ddot{p}^{-1}), && \text{Time } t \text{ information.}
\end{aligned}$$

The $\tilde{h}_t$ is an estimate of the present h_t, for which the last draw could be filled in. These three normal densities can be convoluted into one sampling density, with

$$h_t|h_{t-1}, h_{t+1}, y_t^* \sim \mathcal{N}(c^c, d^c), \qquad \text{Convoluted information,}$$

$$c^c = d^c\left(\frac{c^p}{d^p} + \frac{c^f}{d^f} + \frac{c_t}{d_t}\right), \qquad d^c = \left(\frac{1}{d^p} + \frac{1}{d^f} + \frac{1}{d_t}\right).$$

This manner of sampling, conditioning on the present and immediate past and future information, may lead to large correlation in the Markov chain of sampled volatilities, and of the sampled parameters. The MMS lowers the correlation by sampling larger blocks of volatilities at once. When the block size becomes too large, the acceptance rate of the MH step could become too low, again leading to an increase in sample correlation. Hence an intermediate choice for the average block size should be made.

As the elements h_t close to the knots are tied down more than elements in between two knots, it is advisable to change the location of the knots between iterations. The random procedure of Shephard and Pitt (1997) for choosing knots is used in this chapter.

6.3 Comparison of Methods

6.3.1 SETUP OF DATA-GENERATING PROCESS AND ESTIMATION PROCEDURES

From a theoretical point of view, the links between the estimation methods are described in Section 6.2. The practical implication of those differences for the estimation results is the topic of the present section. We consider a pure SV model (6.1)–(6.2), with parameters $\sigma_\varepsilon, \phi, \sigma_\xi$ as specified in Table 6.2. A value of $\phi = 0.95$ allows for a considerable amount of persistence in the volatility, while $\sigma_\xi = 0.1$ indicates a long-run variance of volatility of $\sigma_\xi^2/(1-\phi^2) \approx .1$. The σ_ε is a scaling parameter, and is set at 1. Note that the choices for these parameters are modeled to mimic the results of Section 6.4.

Further columns in the table indicate the prior densities for the parameters. For ϕ, a conjugate normal prior is taken, with expectation 0.9 and standard deviation 0.1. For $\sigma_\varepsilon, \sigma_\xi$, inverted gamma-1 (IG-1) priors are conjugate. The prior parameters are chosen such that the prior mean corresponds roughly with the value according to the data-generating process (DGP) value and the prior standard deviation allows for sufficient flexibility for the data to decide on the location of the posterior.

With these settings, 1000 data series of length $T = 1000$ are simulated from the SV model. The parameters of the SV model are estimated using each of the methods, for each of these data series, using a set of programs written in Ox (Doornik, 2009b) in combination with SsfPack (Koopman et al., 2008). Estimation is started at the values of the DGP and is continued until convergence for the QML, SMM, IS, EIS, and IIS methods. For the Bayesian methods GMS, SSS, and MMS, a sample of 10,000 draws from the posterior density is collected, after a burn-in sample of 1000 iterations for obtaining an initial estimate of H while fixing the parameters, followed by a further 1000 iterations where both H and parameters are sampled, but not stored. From the posterior sample, the mode is taken as the estimate of the parameters. The methods based on IS take $M = 250$ draws from the auxiliary density using antithetic sampling; therefore, effectively $M = 500$ weights are evaluated. For SMM, a GARCH(1, 1) auxiliary model with either normal (SMMn) or Student-t (SMMt) disturbances is used.

TABLE 6.2 DGP and Prior Specifications

	DGP	$\pi(\theta)$	r	a	$E(\theta)$	$s(\theta)$
σ_ε	1	IG-1(r, a)	2	1.5	1.09	0.57
ϕ	0.95	$N(\mu, \sigma^2)$			0.9	0.1
σ_ξ	0.1	IG-1(r, a)	1.3	0.006	0.1	0.1

From the estimated auxiliary model, $N = 100{,}000$ observations are generated for each evaluation of the criterion function.

6.3.2 PARAMETER ESTIMATES FOR THE SIMULATION

Table 6.3 displays results on the parameter estimates for the simulation. It reports the average parameter estimates (in the first three columns) together with the standard deviation of the estimates (in columns four to six), and the average time to completion in seconds. It can be seen that all methods estimate the standard deviation σ_ε close to the DGP value of 1. The overall level of volatility is relatively easy to extract from the data. For the persistence parameter ϕ, QML leads to a considerable downward bias, with SMM and the IS methods displaying a less severe bias. The Bayesian methods in the last three rows of the table seem to estimate ϕ closest to 0.95. In general, if ϕ is underestimated, the parameter σ_ξ tends to be overestimated. The bias on the long run variance $\sigma_\xi^2/(1-\phi^2)$ is generally smaller than the bias on the underlying parameters themselves.

The second set of columns displays the standard deviation of the parameter estimates. The Bayesian methods deliver the lowest uncertainty in the estimates. This effect can also be seen from Figure 6.1, which displays the density of the 1000 parameter estimates for each of the methods. Top panels (a1), (b1) and (c1) display results for σ_ε, ϕ and σ_ξ for the classical QML, SMM, IS, EIS, and IIS methods, whereas bottom panels (a2), (b2) and (c2) plot the density of the parameters for the Bayesian GMS, SSS, and MMS methods, together with the prior. From the figure, it is seen how the mode of the estimates of σ_ξ in panel (a1) corresponds closely with the DGP value of $\sigma_\xi = 0.1$, but the large right-hand tail leads to an upward bias for the estimates on average. The IS, EIS and IIS results are plotted separately, but are not distinguishable from each other in Figure 6.1 as the estimates are virtually equal. QML delivers only quasi maximum likelihood estimates, which are clearly distinct from the IS estimates.

TABLE 6.3 Parameter Estimates for SV Simulation

	$\overline{\sigma}_\varepsilon$	$\overline{\phi}$	$\overline{\sigma}_\xi$	$s(\sigma_\varepsilon)$	$s(\phi)$	$s(\sigma_\xi)$	Time
DGP	1	0.95	0.1				
QML	1.003	0.809	0.174	0.052	0.248	0.218	0.1
SMMn	0.996	0.934	0.113	0.049	0.065	0.114	38.9
SMMt	0.990	0.868	0.147	0.056	0.181	0.120	43.8
IS	0.998	0.914	0.116	0.041	0.115	0.063	63.0
EIS	0.998	0.913	0.117	0.041	0.116	0.064	133.0
IIS	0.998	0.914	0.117	0.041	0.112	0.064	300.7
GMS	0.997	0.944	0.086	0.040	0.030	0.027	14.1
SSS	0.999	0.945	0.088	0.041	0.032	0.031	13.1
MMS	1.000	0.944	0.088	0.038	0.030	0.030	253.9

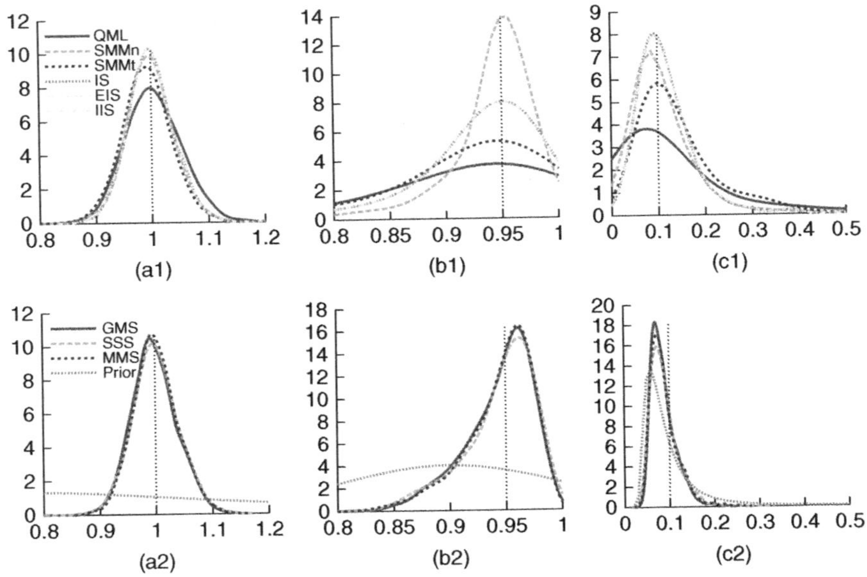

FIGURE 6.1 **Density of parameter estimates σ_ε (panels (a1) and (a2)), ϕ (panels (b1) and (b2)), and σ_ξ (panels (c1) and (c2)) for SV simulation exercise, for classical (panels (a1), (b1), and (c1)) and Bayesian (panels (a2), (b2), and (c2)) estimation methods.**

The SMM estimates should theoretically deliver the same efficient estimates as the maximum likelihood-based methods; the distinction in results in this case appears to be due to neither of the auxiliary models fitting the true model sufficiently well at the present sample size.[5]

With the Bayesian methods, estimates of σ_ξ in panel (c2) are seen to be spread around 0.1. The distribution of these estimates is close to the distribution of the prior for σ_ξ, indicating that the present DGP with 1000 observations provides little information on this parameter measuring volatility of volatility. The prior influences the location of the posterior mode estimates relatively strongly in such a case.

The last column of Table 6.3 reports the average optimization times in seconds. QML is clearly the fastest as it is only a simple and direct approximation. The speed of SMM depends fully on the length of the auxiliary sampler. For the IS methods, the basic IS is moderately quick as the approximating model needs only a single run from the volatility sequence, whereas EIS needs a full sample of runs for the approximating algorithm. EIS and IIS theoretically make a similar computational effort, although in practice, it is simpler to generate a sample from EIS's predictive density than from IIS's simulation smoother. For the Bayesian samplers, clearly MMS is computationally most intensive. For each block of

[5]As an additional auxiliary model, a semi-nonparametric GARCH model (Gallant and Nychka 1987) was tried. With $T = 1000$ observations, the data was not informative enough to obtain good convergence for the auxiliary parameters.

observations, an approximating model has to be found and a separate sample is drawn. For the SSS, the approximating model can be obtained using analytic closed-form expressions for the smoothed states, which tends to be quicker. GMS is comparable to SSS, at least in an effort that is needed for obtaining a similarly sized sample from the posterior density. Note how these computational times are roughly in line with the theoretical properties of the estimators: the procedures that are theoretically nicer, providing either a direct link with the likelihood or a full sample from the posterior density, take more time. While EIS may be slightly harder than IIS to set up, this extra effort is rewarded with a smaller computational effort.

6.3.3 PRECISION OF IS

Among the methods, IS, IIS, and EIS are based on idea of importance sampling, and the final likelihood estimate is calculated in (6.5) as the average of a set of weights, $L(Y;\theta) \approx \frac{1}{M}\sum \omega_i$. This estimator of the likelihood only converges if a central limit theorem holds for the average of weights ω_i (Koopman et al., 2009). Most importantly, the variance of the weights should converge to a finite constant. A lower variance then corresponds to a more precise likelihood estimate.

For one specific sample of the DGP, the three methods were used for estimation, and at the final estimates, the weights ω_i were collected. A sample of size $M = 250$ with antithetic sampling was used, resulting in a total of 500 weights for each method. The weights were standardized to have mean 1. Figure 6.2 plots the cumulative estimates of the average of the weights (panel (a)) and of the standard deviation (panel (b)).

From panel (a), it is seen that for IS the cumulative average converges slower than for the EIS and IIS approaches. Indeed, in panel (b), the final standard deviation of the weights for IS is found to be larger than for EIS and IIS. The latter two methods appear to have virtually equal standard deviations for their weights. Figure 6.2c compares the final standard deviations of IS, EIS, and IIS

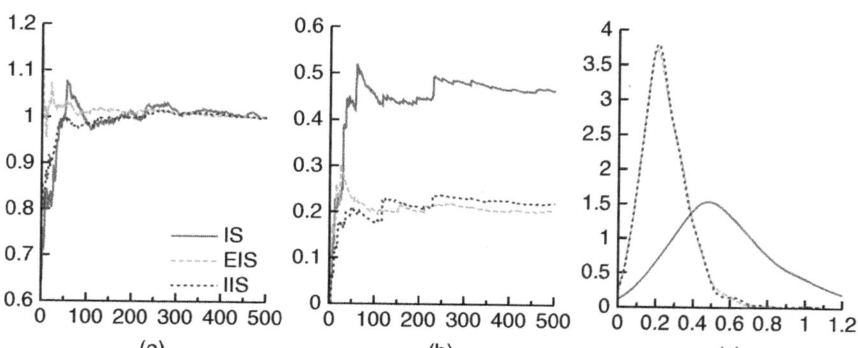

FIGURE 6.2 Cumulative average of standardized weights (a) and related standard deviation (b) for one iteration of IS, EIS, and IIS, and density of 1000 final weight standard deviations of full simulation (c).

over the $S = 1000$ simulations. Indeed, the IS is less efficient in general, and the EIS and IIS are indistinguishable. As EIS and IIS use exactly the same information for constructing the auxiliary density, they lead to similar draws of the weights with similar standard deviations.

6.3.4 PRECISION OF BAYESIAN METHODS

With the Bayesian methods GMS, SSS, and MMS, a final sample of size $S = 10{,}000$ of draws from the posterior was collected. For MMS, the average block size had to be chosen. A small block size leads to behavior similar to that of the SSS, sampling a single volatility at a time. Larger block sizes could decrease correlation in the chain, as a larger number of volatilities is updated in a single sweep. When the block size becomes too large, the MH acceptance probability drops, and correlation again increases when a candidate draw is rejected too often (see also the discussion in Shephard and Pitt (1997) and Liesenfeld and Richard (2008)).

In the above simulation, the volatility series of H was divided into seven blocks, resulting in a block size of around $k = T/7 \approx 143$ volatilities h_t on an average when using MMS. To judge the effect of the block size, Figure 6.3a displays the relative numerical inefficiency (Shephard and Pitt, 1997, $R_I(B)$) for different values of the average block size. The $R_I(B)$ compares the variance of the posterior sample when correcting for B lags of possible autocorrelation with the variance when no correction for autocorrelation is made. A bandwidth of $B = 1000$ lags is chosen.

In Figure 6.3a, it is seen how for very small block sizes, inefficiency is high. Starting at a block size of at least 10, inefficiency stabilizes, until it increases again when the block size reaches 250. These results correspond with the findings of Shephard and Pitt (1997), that the efficiency gains are fairly robust against the block size.

Figure 6.3b displays the related acceptance rate of the MH step. This acceptance rate is negatively related to the block size, and in this case, if the acceptance rate drops below around 0.9, the efficiency of the sampler starts to deteriorate with block size. Note that the insights of EIS/IIS could be combined with that of MMS as well: using the improved approximating density of EIS/IIS, the acceptance rate of MMS could be increased, allowing larger blocks to be sampled with lower inefficiencies as a result. See Liesenfeld and Richard (2008). This possibility is not pursued in this chapter.

Given a block size for the MMS sampler, the inefficiencies of the samplers can be compared. It must be kept in mind that the mixture sampler, GMS, theoretically only provides a sample for the model with the approximating Gaussian mixture as observation density (instead of using the true observation density). Table 6.4 compares the average inefficiencies of the GMS to that of the SSS (effectively the MMS, but with $k = 1$), and to the MMS with $k \approx 143$ in the last line of the table. In the present situation, the SSS delivers clearly higher correlation in the chain, and the MMS is roughly on par with the GMS. Notice, however, that the behavior of the samplers can also be affected by the sampling procedure

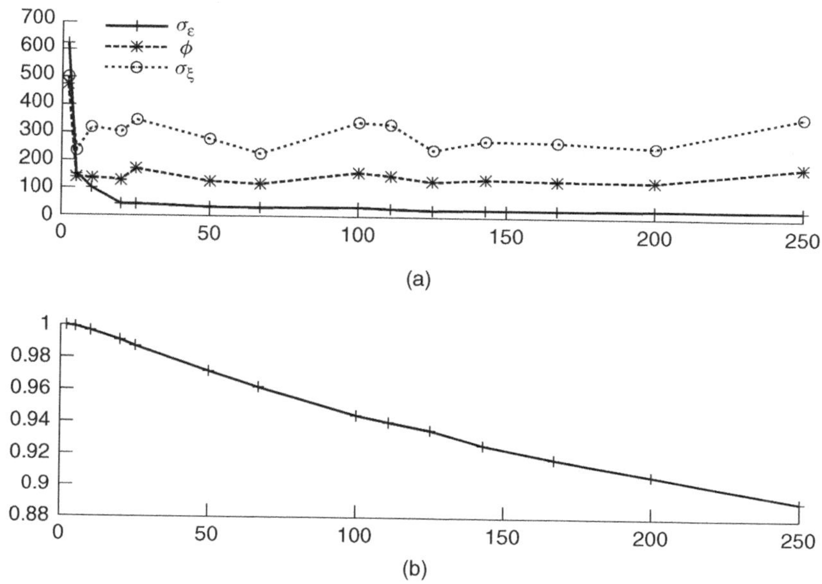

FIGURE 6.3 Inefficiency versus block size (a) and acceptance rate (b).

TABLE 6.4 Comparing Inefficiencies

	Average Relative Numerical Inefficiency			Acceptance Rate
	σ_ε	ϕ	σ_ξ	
GMS	27.72	143.42	332.10	
SSS	339.45	436.82	616.80	0.997
MMS	17.78	146.17	342.86	0.921

for the parameters θ, by their parameterization, and by the choice of those parameters in the DGP (cf. Bos and Shephard, 2006). In practical situations, the SSS sampler can still be of interest, as it is simpler to implement than the MMS, considerably quicker (such that a longer sample could be drawn, subsampling the draws from the posterior to reduce the correlation), and more flexible in combination with extended models; see also Section 6.4.4 for an example.

6.4 Estimating Volatility Models in Practice

6.4.1 DESCRIBING RETURN DATA OF GOLDMAN SACHS AND IBM STOCK

With simulated data, the DGP is fully under the control of the researcher, and estimation of the volatility models can be performed with few surprises. This section, however, compares the estimation results for the alternative estimation approaches for two series of financial stock returns, to judge their performance in a practical setting.

The data considered here are the stock returns on the adjusted closing prices of Goldman Sachs (GS) and IBM, measured over the period January 3, 2005, to December 31, 2009 for a total of 1,259 daily observations. These closing prices are available through Yahoo Finance. The period covers the financial crisis that has been affecting the economy since October 2007. For GS, this crisis led to large turmoil and great changes in the stock price. While the initial crisis delivered some large profits for GS (as they had invested in shorts on the subprime market before the major collapse, delivering them large gains), later the firm was hit by large losses and lawsuits. The uncertainty around the banking sector and the aftermath of the collapse of Lehman Brothers in September 2008 forced the firm to convert into a traditional bank, instead of the investment bank that they used to be.

The second stock, IBM, is chosen for its entirely different field of operation. As a computer firm, the financial crisis would have had far less of an effect on its stock price. Indeed, Figure 6.4a displays the stock price of GS and IBM, with strong gains and equally strong losses for GS, whereas comparatively little movement of the IBM stock over this five-year period.

Figure 6.4b displays the autocorrelation function (ACF) of the returns. Some of these autocorrelations are larger (in absolute value) than the 95% error bands. However, it should be kept in mind that these error bands are based on the assumption of underlying white noise data, whereas the variance of the returns is time-varying. These ACFs indicate that disregarding the autocorrelation in the return series is not at great odds with the data.

Figure 6.4c displays the autocorrelation of the squared returns. As usual, the squares of the returns are strongly correlated through time, and a model for volatility could help in fitting the return series correctly. Table 6.5 displays the moments of the returns. The kurtosis of the returns is around 15.3 for GS

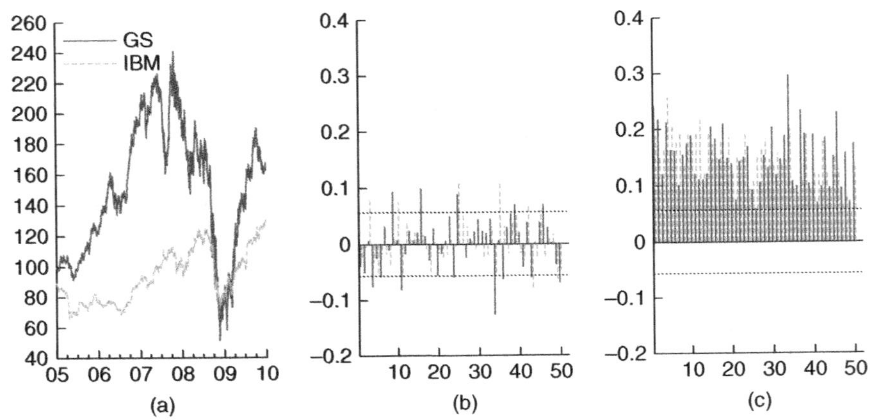

FIGURE 6.4 Daily Goldman Sachs and IBM stock price (a), ACF of returns (b), and ACF of squared returns (c) over the period 2005–2009.

TABLE 6.5 Moments of the Percentage Returns on Goldman Sachs and IBM stocks over the Period 2005–2009

Moments of the Returns	Goldman Sachs	IBM
n	1259	1259
Mean	0.04	0.03
Standard deviation	3.06	1.54
Skewness	0.44	0.06
Kurtosis	15.33	8.57

versus 8.6 for IBM. Although this could indicate either heavy tails in the return distribution or time-varying variance, for simplicity, we limit ourselves to the pure Gaussian SV model.

6.4.2 ESTIMATING SV MODELS

Table 6.6 displays the estimated parameters for the selection of methods. For each method, the optimal parameter is reported with its standard deviation. The results indicate a close correspondence between the group of IS, the group of Bayesian methods, and (mostly) the QML approach. The only estimates standing out are the SMM estimates. The choice of auxiliary density here seems to matter for the outcomes, with the GARCH model with normal disturbances delivering results that seem to be closer to other estimates. These results are in line with findings of Andersen et al. (1999). Trials to incorporate a semi-nonparametric density (Gallant et al., 1997) were not successful, as such an auxiliary model could not be optimized in a stable manner for the current sample size.

In Section 6.3, the methods based on IS were compared on their sampling efficiency through the standard deviations of the IS weights. These standard deviations are reported in Table 6.7. IS is found to be less efficient in its likelihood estimation than EIS and IIS. These latter methods deliver virtually the same efficiency, where the difference seems to be due to simulation error, as it was in Section 6.3.3.

Table 6.8 compares the inefficiencies in the posterior samples of the parameters from the three Bayesian estimation methods. Note that for these estimates, a sample of size 1,000,000 draws was collected after a burn-in period. The GMS method, through its approximation of the density of $\ln e_t^2$ by a mixture, delivers a well-mixing chain, in which a new draw from the full vector of volatilities is obtained through the simulation smoother. The SSS does not make the approximation, but instead, draws a single $h_t|h_{t-1}, h_{t+1}, y_t, \theta$, incurring far higher correlation in the sampling chain. The MMS, on the other hand, by sampling blocks of $k \approx 150$ volatilities at once, delivers efficiency values at least as good as those of GMS, at acceptance rates dropping toward 74–82%.

TABLE 6.6 **Parameter Estimates for Goldman Sachs and IBM, 2005–2009**

	$\hat{\sigma}_\varepsilon$	$s(\sigma_\varepsilon)$	$\hat{\phi}$	$s(\phi)$	$\hat{\sigma}_\xi$	$s(\sigma_\xi)$
			Goldman Sachs			
QML	1.1346	(0.304)	0.9975	(0.003)	0.1122	(0.023)
SMMn	1.6949	(0.353)	0.9861	(0.018)	0.1073	(0.058)
SMMt	1.2354	(0.071)	0.8257	(0.110)	0.3317	(0.123)
IS	0.8794	(0.210)	0.9976	(0.002)	0.1424	(0.022)
EIS	0.8878	(0.224)	0.9976	(0.002)	0.1427	(0.023)
IIS	0.8814	(0.211)	0.9976	(0.002)	0.1429	(0.023)
GMS	1.1460	(0.186)	0.9966	(0.003)	0.1406	(0.023)
SSS	0.7964	(0.223)	0.9982	(0.002)	0.1411	(0.022)
MMS	0.8829	(0.215)	0.9979	(0.003)	0.1378	(0.022)
			IBM			
QML	0.8523	(0.231)	0.9961	(0.004)	0.0994	(0.026)
SMMn	1.2016	(0.116)	0.9535	(0.030)	0.2279	(0.084)
SMMt	0.8636	(0.040)	0.7714	(0.116)	0.3925	(0.124)
IS	1.1005	(0.128)	0.9730	(0.011)	0.2176	(0.034)
EIS	1.1087	(0.127)	0.9725	(0.011)	0.2203	(0.035)
IIS	1.1012	(0.127)	0.9727	(0.011)	0.2200	(0.035)
GMS	0.8840	(0.129)	0.9903	(0.008)	0.1771	(0.031)
SSS	1.0808	(0.136)	0.9792	(0.010)	0.2004	(0.035)
MMS	1.0662	(0.148)	0.9797	(0.010)	0.1936	(0.033)

TABLE 6.7 **Standard Deviations $\sigma(\omega)$ of Importance Sampling Weights**

	IS	EIS	IIS
Goldman Sachs	2.152	0.709	0.652
IBM	3.585	1.049	1.119

6.4.3 EXTRACTING UNDERLYING VOLATILITY

All estimation methods, except for the SMM, deliver an estimate of the smoothed volatility together with the parameter estimates. These smoothed states of H are plotted in Figure 6.5. The line for QML-based volatility is clearly distinct from the others, running smoother than the other state estimates. The approximation of the nonlinear SV model by the linear Gaussian state space model influences the extracted state considerably. Close to the QML estimate of the state runs the GMS volatility estimate, both for GS and IBM data. Remember that the GMS uses a seven-component mixture density to approximate the $\ln e_t^2$ density, where

TABLE 6.8 Comparing Inefficiencies and Acceptance Rates

	Inefficiencies			Acceptance
	σ_ε	ϕ	σ_ξ	rate
		Goldman Sachs		
GMS	364.65	101.90	138.76	
SSS	1675.29	535.67	353.56	0.996
MMS	268.338	100.843	137.282	0.82
		IBM		
GMS	342.38	191.44	167.48	
SSS	1336.78	429.93	384.73	0.993
MMS	162.59	123.68	164.21	0.74

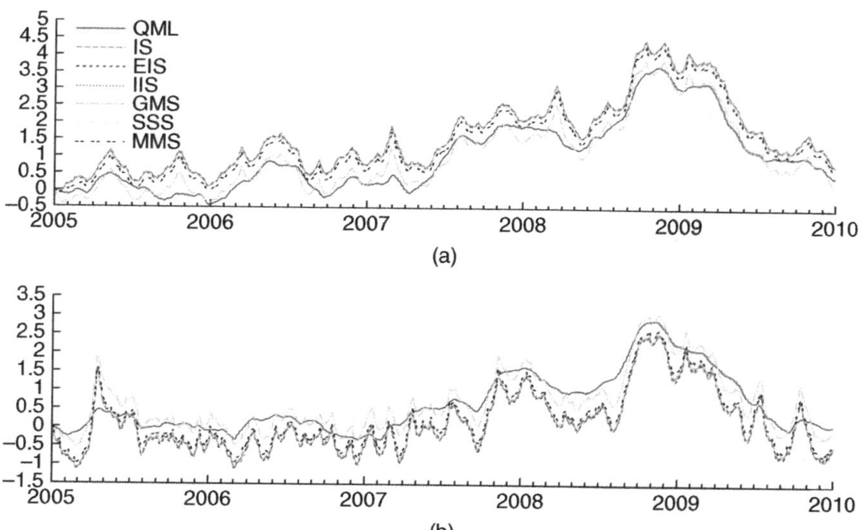

FIGURE 6.5 **Extracted smoothed volatility sequences h_t for Goldman Sachs (a) and IBM (b) returns.**

we did not perform any resampling to get rid of the remaining approximation error. The extracted state for GMS seems to run in-between the QML and the other estimates. Notice that the remaining methods were all theoretically exact, therefore it is no surprise that their state estimates are similar.

6.4.4 RELATING THE RETURNS IN A BIVARIATE MODEL

Both GS and IBM operate in the same market, and their stocks are traded in the same country on the same stock exchange. Therefore, one could expect that the returns on both stocks are related, as they both may react to the general atmosphere on the stock market. As an extension to the standard SV model, this section looks into the correlation between the stock returns. For this purpose, the vector of bivariate returns at time t can be modeled as

$$
\begin{aligned}
\mathbf{y}_t &= \varepsilon_t, & \varepsilon_t &\sim \mathcal{N}(\mathbf{0}, \Sigma_t),\\
\Sigma_t &= D_t R_t D_t',\\
D_t &= \begin{pmatrix} \sigma_{\varepsilon 1} \exp(\frac{1}{2}h_{1t}) & 0 \\ 0 & \sigma_{\varepsilon 2} \exp(\frac{1}{2}h_{2t}) \end{pmatrix}, & R_t &= \begin{pmatrix} 1 & \rho_t \\ \rho_t & 1 \end{pmatrix},\\
\rho_t &= \frac{\exp q_t - 1}{\exp q_t + 1},\\
q_{t+1} &= q_t + v_t, & v_t &\sim \mathcal{N}(0, \sigma_q^2).
\end{aligned}
$$

This dynamic correlation SV setup (DCSV, Yu and Meyer, 2006; Bos and Gould, 2007) allows the returns to be correlated, with the correlation ρ_t changing stochastically over time in a manner similar to the behavior of the SV component. As correlation is not easily estimated from the data, especially when it is time-varying, a simple specification like the present transformed random walk is preferred. For alternative specifications of multivariate SV models, see for example, Chapter 7 in this handbook.

With the likelihood or moments-based methods introduced above, estimating this extended model would require obtaining an approximating density for this full bivariate returns model, depending on the three underlying unobserved states. The Bayesian sampling methods, however, perform all sampling steps conditionally on other results. Adapting the model to include the correlation implies adding two steps to the sampling scheme, and adapting a third. First, the parameter σ_q is sampled conditionally on all the states and other parameters, which is comparable to drawing parameters σ_ξ or σ_ε. Second, $Q = \{q_1, \ldots, q_T\}$ is sampled conditionally on the parameters and the volatilities, in a manner fully comparable to the sampling of the H sequence. Last, the sampling of H has to be adapted to incorporate the information stemming from the correlation. With the GMS, this is not easily performed, as a fully new mixture sampling procedure has to be devised (cf. Omori et al., 2007). With SSS sampling, the volatilities $H_i | Y, H_j, \rho, \theta$, from the univariate volatility sequences conditioning on the parameters, correlation, second volatility, and the data implies using slightly altered conditional densities instead of Equations 6.6–6.8. If one uses $p = \ln P(y_{1t}, y_{2t}; H_t, \rho_t, \theta) \equiv \ln P(y_1, y_2; h_1, h_2, \rho, \theta)$ (skipping the dependence on time from the notation), then

$$
u_j = \frac{y_j}{\sigma_{\varepsilon_j}} \exp\left(-\frac{1}{2}h_j\right),
$$

$$p = -\frac{1}{2}\left(h_1 + h_2 + \log\sigma^2_{\varepsilon_1} + \log\sigma^2_{\varepsilon_2} + \frac{u_1^2 - 2\rho u_1 u_2 + u_2^2}{1-\rho^2}\right),$$

$$\dot{p}_1 = -\frac{1}{2}\left(1 - \frac{u_1^2 - \rho u_1 u_2}{1-\rho^2}\right),$$

$$\ddot{p}_1 = -\frac{1}{2}\frac{u_1^2 - \frac{1}{2}\rho u_1 u_2}{1-\rho^2},$$

where $\dot{p}_1$ and $\ddot{p}_1$ are the first and second derivatives of p with respect to the first volatility h_1. Derivatives with respect to h_2 are similar.

With these changes to the derivatives, the SSS is implemented on this extended model without further problems. The sampler can be started using the parameter estimates from the univariate samplers as initial values, initializing the correlation sequence at the fixed full-sample correlation. The prior for parameter σ_q was taken as IG-1(r, a), with expectation and standard deviation equal to 0.05. Results on the parameter estimates are reported in Table 6.9, with extracted volatilities and the correlation in Figure 6.6.

The parameter estimates of Table 6.9 are very similar to the estimates found for SSS in Table 6.6. The new parameter σ_q is estimated at 0.024, clearly below the prior mean of 0.05. In a plot of the posterior density of σ_q (not reported here), it is found that the mass of the posterior indeed is concentrated at the lower end of the range of the prior density, and hence the data is informative on the volatility of the correlation. The inefficiency measures are in general better than corresponding values for the SSS sampler in Table 6.8. It is commonly found that an alteration in the specification of the model can indeed alter the efficiency of the SSS strongly.

Figure 6.6 compares the volatilities as extracted from the univariate model with the results from the bivariate DCSV model in panels (a) and (b) for GS and IBM, respectively. Taking the second return series into the model does not alter

TABLE 6.9 Bivariate Goldman Sachs and IBM Volatility/Correlation results

Series	Parameter	$\hat{\theta}$	$s(\theta)$	Inefficiency
GS	σ_ε	0.9993	(0.027)	15.23
	ϕ	0.9977	(0.002)	29.39
	σ_ξ	0.1236	(0.019)	297.51
IBM	σ_ε	1.0028	(0.027)	46.35
	ϕ	0.9790	(0.009)	259.38
	σ_ξ	0.1953	(0.031)	469.18
Correlation	σ_q	0.0241	(0.006)	3551.96

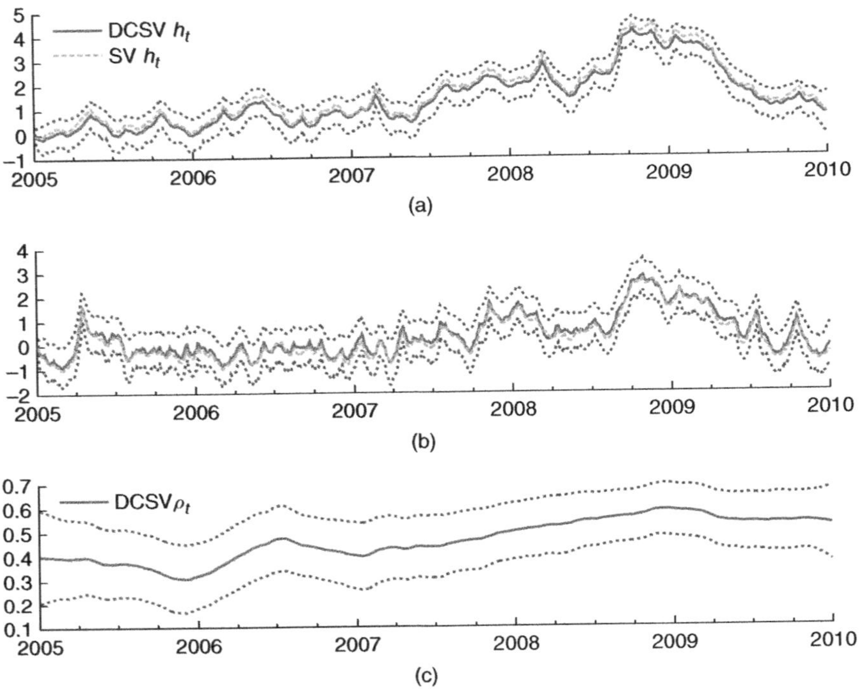

FIGURE 6.6 Extracted smoothed volatility sequences h_t for Goldman Sachs (a) and IBM stock returns (b) together with correlation ρ_t (c), with 95% confidence bands, using the bivariate DCSV model, and comparing with the univariate SV model.

the estimate of volatility, as the univariate return series themselves are sufficiently informative on the matter. Panel (c) displays the extracted correlation. Here, it is seen how correlation between stock returns for this bank and this information technology company are low, at around 0.4 at the start of the sample, to increase with the onset of the crisis, reaching a maximum of $\rho_t = 0.59$ in December 2008, within a month's distance from the moment when volatility peaked. Even though these two companies are very dissimilar in their field of operation, they both suffered from the financial crisis. In bad times, the comovement of their stocks increases slightly, which is valuable information for investors who plan on building a portfolio out of these assets.

6.5 Conclusion

This chapter set out as an investigation into the alternative estimation methods for basic SV models. A range of five classical and three Bayesian methods was described, using a common notation. While the SMM approach was found to stand apart, the others were found to share the basic idea of approximating the (nonlinear) observation equation (6.1) through a linear model, fitting the first two derivatives of the log-densities using (with most methods) a single parameter for the mean and a second for the variance at each time t.

Both QML and GMS made the approximation without taking the most likely volatility sequence into account, and without correcting for the approximation either. For QML, this was seen to lead to a bias in the parameter estimates. For GMS, the approximation was far more precise using a mixture of several normal densities, and the problem of the bias was mostly solved for parameter estimation. The extracted state, however, was seen to diverge from estimates of other, theoretically exact methods.

The basic IS method improves on QML by extracting the smoothed state of the QML approximation, and adapting the approximating model iteratively to take this most probable state of the volatility into account. EIS and IIS continue in this same direction by taking a full sample of probable volatilities instead of only a single smoothed state. This results in a better approximating model and less variance of the importance weights in the evaluation of the likelihood. EIS depended on deriving analytically the integrating constant of the auxiliary density, taking information on past volatilities into account when optimizing the parameters of the auxiliary model. For IIS, this integrating constant was not needed, as the information was taken along in the sampling of the volatilities, applying the simulation smoother for this purpose.

The remaining Bayesian approaches can be seen as also taking the IS approach as a starting point. Either for a single state, or for a block of volatilities, the approximating model is formed as in the IS method, and a single sample is drawn. Instead of using the importance weights of IS, now an MH-within-Gibbs acceptance probability is calculated. After deciding on acceptance, attention shifts to the next block of volatilities.

Simulation results were found to be in line with expectation, in that indeed QML can lead to quick but biased estimates, and that the IS, EIS, and IIS end up at virtually the same estimators. The advantage of highest efficiency is shared between EIS and the novel IIS, with the latter method requiring less input from the researcher in setting up the importance sampler. The SMM approach depends on the specification of the approximating model, although the mode of the estimates seems to be closely in line with the values of the DGP. It could be expected that SMM works better for larger samples, where a richer auxiliary model can be estimated with high precision. For the Bayesian approaches, SSS is found to be quick, and theoretically exact (in contrast to GMS if no resampling is applied), but the correlation in the resulting posterior sample is high. MMS, taking larger blocks of volatility for sampling at once, leads to less inefficiency in the posterior sample.

Extracting volatility for GS and IBM returns over the period 2005–2009 indicates that the estimates of parameters and volatility of both return series correspond largely between the methods. Mid-2007, when the first signs of the subprime crisis emerged, volatility started to creep up slowly. In September 2008, the big crisis hit the financial markets, and volatilities of both series went up further.

In an extension, the two stocks were modeled jointly, allowing for time-varying correlation between the returns. This was easily accommodated for in the SSS. For the volatilities, little difference was found compared to the univariate results. The extracted correlation indicated that these rather distinct companies display stock returns which are correlated at a level of around 0.4–0.6, where the amount of correlation is positively related to the uncertainty in the markets.

The GARCH model has the advantage that it can be estimated using a single, well-defined and simple, estimation method. There are, however, many variants of the GARCH model, which can make it cumbersome to choose the best specification for the data at hand. For the SV model, there is far less discussion about the preferred specification, and only the difficulty of estimation seems to hamper a larger uptake of the model in practical research. In this chapter, it was found that the estimation methods have many commonalities. These commonalities can help both in understanding in detail the algorithms, and also in the practical implementation and application of the stochastic volatility model.

CHAPTER SEVEN

Multivariate Stochastic Volatility Models

YASUHIRO OMORI and TSUNEHIRO ISHIHARA

7.1 Introduction

The stochastic volatility (SV) model has been widely discussed in the literature and shown to be useful to model the time-varying variance of asset returns in financial econometrics (see Chapter 1 by Bos (2011) in this handbook; Broto and Ruiz (2004)). Since the likelihood function in these models is difficult to evaluate to implement the maximum likelihood estimation, various efficient Bayesian estimation algorithms have been proposed using Markov chain Monte Carlo (MCMC) method (Omori et al., 2007; Omori and Watanabe, 2008; Shephard and Pitt, 1997; Watanabe and Omori, 2004).

Recently, more and more literature come to focus on modeling the multivariate time-varying volatilities by extending the univariate SV models and GARCH models (surveys by Asai et al., 2006; Bauwens et al., 2006; Chib et al., 2009; Silvennoinen and Teräsvirta, 2009). Such multivariate models for the multivariate asset returns have attracted attention in areas such as portfolio optimization and risk management (Della Corte et al., 2009; Fleming et al., 2001; Han, 2006). However, estimation methods have been proposed only for some simplified MSV models or bivariate SV models (Asai and McAleer, 2006; Chib et al., 2006; So

Handbook of Volatility Models and Their Applications, First Edition.
Edited by Luc Bauwens, Christian Hafner, and Sebastien Laurent.

and Choi, 2009). Thus, this chapter describes two major MSV models that are natural extensions of univariate SV models with leverage effects and shows how to estimate parameters of interest using an efficient MCMC algorithm.

First, we start with the notation using the univariate SV model. Let y_t and h_t denote an asset return and the corresponding log volatility at time t. Further, let $\alpha_t = h_t - \mu$ where μ is a mean of the log volatility. Then, the univariate SV model (Omori and Watanabe, 2008; Takahashi et al., 2009) is given by

$$y_t = \exp(\alpha_t/2)\varepsilon_t, \quad t = 1, \ldots, n, \tag{7.1}$$

$$\alpha_{t+1} = \phi\alpha_t + \eta_t, \quad t = 1, \ldots, n-1, \tag{7.2}$$

$$\alpha_1 \sim \mathcal{N}\left(0, \sigma_\eta^2/(1-\phi^2)\right), \tag{7.3}$$

$$\begin{pmatrix} \varepsilon_t \\ \eta_t \end{pmatrix} |\alpha_t \sim \mathcal{N}_2(\mathbf{0}, \Sigma), \quad \Sigma = \begin{pmatrix} \sigma_\varepsilon^2 & \rho\sigma_\varepsilon\sigma_\eta \\ \rho\sigma_\varepsilon\sigma_\eta & \sigma_\eta^2 \end{pmatrix}, \tag{7.4}$$

where $\mathcal{N}_p(\boldsymbol{\mu}, \Sigma)$ denotes a p-variate normal distribution with mean $\boldsymbol{\mu}$ and covariance matrix Σ. From the measurement Equations 7.1 and 7.4, we have $\text{Var}(y_t|\alpha_t) = \sigma_\varepsilon^2 \exp(\alpha_t)$, which implies that $h_t = \alpha_t + \mu, \mu = \log\sigma_\varepsilon^2$ may be understood as the log of the conditional variance of the outcome. To ensure that the evolution of these log-volatilities is stationary, one generally assumes that $|\phi| < 1$. The negative value of ρ, the correlation between ε_t and η_t, captures the leverage effects where the increase in volatility follows a drop in equity returns (Black, 1976; Nelson, 1991b; Omori et al., 2007; Omori and Watanabe, 2008; Yu, 2005).

Several efficient estimation methods have been proposed for the univariate SV models. A highly efficient method is the mixture sampler proposed in Kim et al. (1998) and Omori et al. (2007) where the measurement equation is linearized by the logarithm transformation of y_t^2 and the distribution of the log chi-square error ($\log\varepsilon_t^2$) is approximated by a mixture of normal distributions. An alternative efficient method is the so-called multimove sampler that samples a block of latent volatility variables given other parameters and latent volatilities (Omori and Watanabe, 2008; Shephard and Pitt, 1997; Watanabe and Omori, 2004; Takahashi et al., 2009). In the multivariate models, the mixture sampler is proposed for the factor MSV model (without leverage effects) in Chib et al. (2006), while the multimove sampler is described for the MSV model with cross leverage effects in Ishihara and Omori (2013).

In this chapter, we focus on two major MSV models, the MSV model and the factor MSV model, with (cross) leverage effects and describe an efficient MCMC algorithm using a multimove sampler in Sections 7.2 and 7.3. The proposed models are applied to the five S&P500 stock sector indices returns in Section 7.4.

7.2 MSV Model

7.2.1 MODEL

Let $\boldsymbol{y}_t = (y_{1t}, \ldots, y_{pt})'$ denote a set of observations at time t on p asset returns and let $\boldsymbol{\alpha}_t = (\alpha_{1t}, \ldots, \alpha_{pt})' = \boldsymbol{h}_t - \boldsymbol{\mu}$, where $\boldsymbol{h}_t = (h_{1t}, \ldots, h_{pt})'$ is the corresponding vector of log-volatilities and $\boldsymbol{\mu} = (\mu_1, \ldots, \mu_p)'$ is its mean vector. Then, the MSV model (Ishihara and Omori, 2013) is given by

$$\boldsymbol{y}_t = \mathbf{V}_t^{1/2} \boldsymbol{\varepsilon}_t, \qquad t = 1, \ldots, n, \tag{7.5}$$

$$\boldsymbol{\alpha}_{t+1} = \Phi \boldsymbol{\alpha}_t + \boldsymbol{\eta}_t, \quad t = 1, \ldots, n-1, \tag{7.6}$$

$$\boldsymbol{\alpha}_1 \sim \mathcal{N}_p(\mathbf{0}, \Sigma_0), \tag{7.7}$$

where

$$\mathbf{V}_t^{1/2} = \text{diag}(\exp(\alpha_{1t}/2), \ldots, \exp(\alpha_{pt}/2)),$$

$$\Phi = \text{diag}(\phi_1, \ldots, \phi_p),$$

and

$$\begin{pmatrix} \boldsymbol{\varepsilon}_t \\ \boldsymbol{\eta}_t \end{pmatrix} | \boldsymbol{\alpha}_t \sim \mathcal{N}_{2p}(\mathbf{0}, \Sigma), \quad \Sigma = \begin{pmatrix} \Sigma_{\varepsilon\varepsilon} & \Sigma_{\varepsilon\eta} \\ \Sigma_{\eta\varepsilon} & \Sigma_{\eta\eta} \end{pmatrix}.$$

We denote $\Sigma_{\varepsilon\varepsilon} = \{\rho_{ij,\varepsilon\varepsilon}\sigma_{i,\varepsilon\varepsilon}\sigma_{j,\varepsilon\varepsilon}\}$, $\Sigma_{\varepsilon\eta} = \{\rho_{ij,\varepsilon\eta}\sigma_{i,\varepsilon\varepsilon}\sigma_{j,\eta\eta}\}$, and $\Sigma_{\eta\eta} = \{\rho_{ij,\eta\eta} \sigma_{i,\eta\eta}\sigma_{j,\eta\eta}\}$, with correlation coefficients $\rho_{ij,\varepsilon\varepsilon} = \text{Corr}(\varepsilon_{it}, \varepsilon_{jt})$, $\rho_{ij,\varepsilon\eta} = \text{Corr}(\varepsilon_{it}, \eta_{jt})$, and $\rho_{ij,\eta\eta} = \text{Corr}(\eta_{it}, \eta_{jt})$, and with standard deviations $\sigma_{i,\varepsilon\varepsilon} = \sqrt{\text{Var}(\varepsilon_{it})}$ and $\sigma_{i,\eta\eta} = \sqrt{\text{Var}(\eta_{it})}$.

To enforce the stationarity of $\boldsymbol{\alpha}_t$, we assume $|\phi_j| < 1$ and the (i,j)-th element of Σ_0 is the (i,j)-th element of $\Sigma_{\eta\eta}$ divided by $1 - \phi_i\phi_j$ $(i,j = 1, \ldots, p)$, or equivalently,

$$\text{vec}(\Sigma_0) = \left(\mathbf{I}_{p^2} - \Phi \otimes \Phi\right)^{-1} \text{vec}(\Sigma_{\eta\eta}), \tag{7.8}$$

such that $\Sigma_0 = \Phi\Sigma_0\Phi + \Sigma_{\eta\eta}$, where $\otimes$ and vec(A) denote a Kronecker product and a vectorization of a matrix A. The expected value of the volatility evolution processes $\boldsymbol{\alpha}_t$ is set equal to $\mathbf{0}$ for identifiability.

The MSV model is often simplified to ignore the leverage effects, that is, $\Sigma_{\varepsilon\eta} = \mathbf{O}$ (Danielsson, 1998; Harvey et al., 1994; Smith and Pitts, 2006; So et al., 1997), or the cross leverage effects, that is, $\Sigma_{\varepsilon\eta}$ is diagonal (Asai and McAleer, 2006). We could use a nondiagonal matrix for Φ (So et al. 1997) but focus on the diagonal case for simplicity while allowing the cross leverage effects. We note that a similar setup of the model is described in Chan et al. (2006) where the correlation between $\boldsymbol{\varepsilon}_t$ and $\boldsymbol{\eta}_{t-1}$ is considered instead. In the analysis of financial time series, our setup corresponds to the leverage effects where the decrease in the asset return y_t is followed by the increase in the volatility h_{t+1}.

7.2.1.1 Likelihood Function. Let $\boldsymbol{\theta} = (\boldsymbol{\phi}, \Sigma)$, where $\boldsymbol{\phi} = (\phi_1, \ldots, \phi_p)'$, and let $\mathbf{1}_p$ denote a $p \times 1$ vector with all elements equal to one. Further, let $\boldsymbol{\alpha} = (\boldsymbol{\alpha}_1', \ldots, \boldsymbol{\alpha}_n')'$ and $Y_n = (\boldsymbol{y}_1, \ldots, \boldsymbol{y}_n)$. Then the likelihood function of the

MSV model outlined in Equations 7.5–7.7 is given by

$$f(\boldsymbol{\alpha}, Y_n|\boldsymbol{\theta}) \tag{7.9}$$

$$\begin{aligned}
&= f(\boldsymbol{\alpha}_1|\boldsymbol{\theta}) \prod_{t=1}^{n-1} f(\boldsymbol{y}_t, \boldsymbol{\alpha}_{t+1}|\boldsymbol{\alpha}_t, \boldsymbol{\theta}) f(\boldsymbol{y}_n|\boldsymbol{\alpha}_n, \boldsymbol{\theta}) \\
&\propto \exp\left\{\sum_{t=1}^{n} l_t - \frac{1}{2}\boldsymbol{\alpha}_1'\Sigma_0^{-1}\boldsymbol{\alpha}_1 - \frac{1}{2}\sum_{t=1}^{n-1}(\boldsymbol{\alpha}_{t+1} - \Phi\boldsymbol{\alpha}_t)'\Sigma_{\eta\eta}^{-1}(\boldsymbol{\alpha}_{t+1} - \Phi\boldsymbol{\alpha}_t)\right\} \\
&\quad \times |\Sigma_0|^{-\frac{1}{2}}|\Sigma|^{-\frac{n-1}{2}}|\Sigma_{\varepsilon\varepsilon}|^{-\frac{1}{2}},
\end{aligned} \tag{7.10}$$

where

$$l_t = \text{const} - \frac{1}{2}\mathbf{1}_p'\boldsymbol{\alpha}_t - \frac{1}{2}(\boldsymbol{y}_t - \boldsymbol{\mu}_t)'\Sigma_t^{-1}(\boldsymbol{y}_t - \boldsymbol{\mu}_t), \tag{7.11}$$

$$\boldsymbol{\mu}_t = \mathbf{V}_t^{1/2}\boldsymbol{m}_t, \quad \Sigma_t = \mathbf{V}_t^{1/2}\mathbf{S}_t\mathbf{V}_t^{1/2}, \tag{7.12}$$

$$\boldsymbol{m}_t = \begin{cases} \Sigma_{\varepsilon\eta}\Sigma_{\eta\eta}^{-1}(\boldsymbol{\alpha}_{t+1} - \Phi\boldsymbol{\alpha}_t), & t < n, \\ \mathbf{0}, & t = n, \end{cases} \tag{7.13}$$

and

$$\mathbf{S}_t = \begin{cases} \Sigma_{\varepsilon\varepsilon} - \Sigma_{\varepsilon\eta}\Sigma_{\eta\eta}^{-1}\Sigma_{\eta\varepsilon}, & t < n, \\ \Sigma_{\varepsilon\varepsilon} & t = n. \end{cases} \tag{7.14}$$

To implement the maximum likelihood estimation, we need to evaluate the likelihood function $f(Y_n|\boldsymbol{\theta}) = \int f(\boldsymbol{\alpha}, Y_n|\boldsymbol{\theta})d\boldsymbol{\alpha}$ analytically or by a very high dimensional numerical integration. However, it is difficult to compute because of many latent vectors $\boldsymbol{\alpha}_t$; thus, we take a Bayesian approach and employ a simulation method, namely, the MCMC method, to generate samples from the posterior distribution to conduct statistical inference with respect to the model parameters.

7.2.1.2 Prior Distribution. For prior distributions of $\boldsymbol{\theta}$, we assume

$$\frac{\phi_j + 1}{2} \sim \mathcal{B}(a_j, b_j), \quad j = 1, \ldots, p, \quad \Sigma \sim \mathcal{IW}(n_0, \mathbf{R}_0),$$

where $\mathcal{B}(a_j, b_j)$ and $\mathcal{IW}(n_0, \mathbf{R}_0)$ denote Beta and inverse Wishart distributions with probability density functions

$$\pi(\phi_j) \propto \left(1 + \phi_j\right)^{a_j - 1}\left(1 - \phi_j\right)^{b_j - 1}, \quad j = 1, 2, \ldots, p, \tag{7.15}$$

$$\pi(\Sigma) \propto |\Sigma|^{-\frac{n_0 + 2p + 1}{2}} \exp\left\{-\frac{1}{2}\text{tr}\left(\mathbf{R}_0^{-1}\Sigma^{-1}\right)\right\}. \tag{7.16}$$

7.2.1.3 Posterior Distribution. Using Equations 7.10, 7.15, and 7.16, we obtain the joint posterior density function of $(\boldsymbol{\theta}, \boldsymbol{\alpha})$ given by

$$\pi(\boldsymbol{\theta}, \boldsymbol{\alpha} | Y_n) \tag{7.17}$$

$$\propto f(\boldsymbol{\alpha}, Y_n|\boldsymbol{\theta})\pi(\boldsymbol{\Sigma}) \prod_{j=1}^{p} \pi(\phi_j) \tag{7.18}$$

$$\propto \exp\left\{\sum_{t=1}^{n} l_t - \frac{1}{2}\boldsymbol{\alpha}_1'\Sigma_0^{-1}\boldsymbol{\alpha}_1 - \frac{1}{2}\sum_{t=1}^{n-1}(\boldsymbol{\alpha}_{t+1} - \Phi\boldsymbol{\alpha}_t)'\Sigma_{\eta\eta}^{-1}(\boldsymbol{\alpha}_{t+1} - \Phi\boldsymbol{\alpha}_t)\right\}$$
$$\times \exp\left\{-\frac{1}{2}\mathrm{tr}\left(\mathbf{R}_0^{-1}\Sigma^{-1}\right)\right\} \times |\Sigma_0|^{-\frac{1}{2}}|\Sigma|^{-\frac{n_0+2p+n}{2}}|\Sigma_{\varepsilon\varepsilon}|^{-\frac{1}{2}}$$
$$\times \prod_{j=1}^{p}\left(1+\phi_j\right)^{a_j-1}\left(1-\phi_j\right)^{b_j-1}. \tag{7.19}$$

7.2.2 BAYESIAN ESTIMATION

To conduct Bayesian inference on the parameter $\boldsymbol{\theta}$, we generate random samples from its posterior distribution by implementing the following MCMC algorithm in five blocks:

1. Initialize $\boldsymbol{\alpha}, \boldsymbol{\phi}$ and Σ.
2. Generate $\boldsymbol{\alpha}|\boldsymbol{\phi}, \Sigma, Y_n$.
3. Generate $\Sigma|\boldsymbol{\phi}, \boldsymbol{\alpha}, Y_n$.
4. Generate $\boldsymbol{\phi}|\Sigma, \boldsymbol{\alpha}, Y_n$.
5. Go to Step 2.

7.2.2.1 Generation of $\boldsymbol{\alpha}$. The simple but inefficient way to generate $\boldsymbol{\alpha}$ is a so-called single-move sampler that samples one $\boldsymbol{\alpha}_t$ at a time given the other $\boldsymbol{\alpha}_j$s and parameters (Appendix 7.6). However, it tends to produce highly autocorrelated samples (Ishihara and Omori, 2013). An efficient way to generate $\boldsymbol{\alpha}$ is to use a multimove sampler that samples a block of state vectors, such as $(\boldsymbol{\alpha}_t, \ldots, \boldsymbol{\alpha}_{t+k})$, given the other state vectors and parameters.

First, we divide $\boldsymbol{\alpha} = (\boldsymbol{\alpha}_1', \ldots, \boldsymbol{\alpha}_n')'$ into $K+1$ blocks $(\boldsymbol{\alpha}_{k_{i-1}+1}', \ldots, \boldsymbol{\alpha}_{k_i}')'$ using $i = 1, \ldots, K+1$, with $k_0 = 0$, $k_{K+1} = n$, and $k_i - k_{i-1} \geq 2$. K knots $(k_1, \ldots, k_K)$ are generated randomly using

$$k_i = \mathrm{int}[n \times (i + U_i)/(K+2)], \quad i = 1, \ldots, K,$$

where U_is are independent uniform random variables on $(0, 1)$ (Shephard and Pitt, 1997) and K is a tuning parameter. These stochastic knots change the points of conditioning over the MCMC iterations and reduce the autocorrelation among the MCMC samples. Suppose that $k_{i-1} = s$ and $k_i = s + m$ for the ith block. Consider sampling this block from its conditional posterior distribution given other state vectors and parameters. We denote $\boldsymbol{x}_t = \mathbf{R}_t^{-1}\boldsymbol{\eta}_t$, where the matrix $\mathbf{R}_t$ denotes a Choleski decomposition of $\Sigma_{\eta\eta} = \mathbf{R}_t\mathbf{R}_t'$ for $t > 0$ and $\Sigma_0 = \mathbf{R}_0\mathbf{R}_0'$ for $t = 0$. To construct a proposal distribution for the Metropolis–Hastings (MH) algorithm, we focus on the distribution of the disturbance $\boldsymbol{x} \equiv (\boldsymbol{x}_s', \ldots, \boldsymbol{x}_{s+m-1}')'$, which is fundamental in the sense that it derives the distribution of $\boldsymbol{a} \equiv (\boldsymbol{\alpha}_{s+1}', \ldots, \boldsymbol{\alpha}_{s+m}')'$. Then, the logarithm of the full conditional joint density function of $\boldsymbol{x}$, excluding constant terms, is given by

$$\log f(\boldsymbol{x}|\boldsymbol{\alpha}_s, \boldsymbol{\alpha}_{s+m+1}, \boldsymbol{y}_s, \ldots, \boldsymbol{y}_{s+m}) = -\frac{1}{2}\sum_{t=s}^{s+m-1} \boldsymbol{x}_t'\boldsymbol{x}_t + L, \tag{7.20}$$

where

$$L = \sum_{t=s}^{s+m} l_t - \frac{1}{2}(\boldsymbol{\alpha}_{s+m+1} - \Phi\boldsymbol{\alpha}_{s+m})'\Sigma_{\eta\eta}^{-1}(\boldsymbol{\alpha}_{s+m+1} - \Phi\boldsymbol{\alpha}_{s+m})I(s + m < n).$$

Using the second-order Taylor expansion of the logarithm of the conditional posterior density of $\boldsymbol{x}$ around its mode $\hat{\boldsymbol{x}}$, we obtain the approximate normal density $f^*(\boldsymbol{x})$ as the posterior probability density function of $\boldsymbol{x}$ obtained from the state space model:

$$\hat{\boldsymbol{y}}_t = \mathbf{Z}_t\boldsymbol{\alpha}_t + \mathbf{G}_t\boldsymbol{u}_t, \quad t = s+1, \ldots, s+m, \tag{7.21}$$

$$\boldsymbol{\alpha}_{t+1} = \Phi\boldsymbol{\alpha}_t + \mathbf{H}_t\boldsymbol{u}_t, \quad t = s+1, \ldots, s+m-1, \tag{7.22}$$

where $\boldsymbol{u}_t \sim \mathcal{N}_{2p}(\mathbf{0}, \mathbf{I}_{2p})$, $\hat{\boldsymbol{y}}_t$, $\mathbf{Z}_t$, and $\mathbf{G}_t$ are defined in Appendix 7.6 and $\mathbf{H}_t = [\mathbf{0}, \mathbf{R}_t]$. First, to find a mode $\hat{\boldsymbol{x}}$, we repeat the following three steps until the convergence is reached,

1. Compute $\hat{\boldsymbol{a}}$ at $\boldsymbol{x} = \hat{\boldsymbol{x}}$ using Equation 7.6.
2. Obtain the approximate linear Gaussian state space model given by Equations 7.21 and 7.22.
3. Applying the disturbance smoother (Koopman, 1993) to the approximating linear Gaussian state space model in Step 2, compute the posterior mode $\hat{\boldsymbol{x}}$.

As an initial value of $\hat{\boldsymbol{x}}$, the current sample of $\boldsymbol{x}$ may be used in MCMC implementation. If the approximate linear Gaussian state space model is obtained using the mode $\hat{\boldsymbol{x}}$, we draw a sample $\boldsymbol{x}$ from the conditional posterior distribution by the AR-MH algorithm as in Ishihara and Omori (2013) or by the MH algorithm as follows.

Given the current value $\boldsymbol{x}$, propose a candidate $\boldsymbol{x}^\dagger \sim f^*$ using a simulation smoother (De Jong and Shephard, 1995; Durbin and Koopman, 2002) based on the approximate linear Gaussian state space model in Equations 7.21 and 7.22. Accept $\boldsymbol{x}^\dagger$ with probability

$$\min\left\{1, \frac{f(\boldsymbol{x}^\dagger)f^*(\boldsymbol{x})}{f(\boldsymbol{x})f^*(\boldsymbol{x}^\dagger)}\right\}.$$

7.2.2.2 Generation of ϕ. Let Σ^{ij} be a $p \times p$ matrix and denote the (i,j)-th block of Σ^{-1}. Furthermore, let $\mathbf{A} = \sum_{t=1}^{n-1} \boldsymbol{\alpha}_t \boldsymbol{\alpha}_t'$, $\mathbf{B} = \sum_{t=1}^{n-1} \{\boldsymbol{\alpha}_t \boldsymbol{y}_t' \mathbf{V}_t^{-1/2} \Sigma^{12} + \boldsymbol{\alpha}_t \boldsymbol{\alpha}_{t+1}' \Sigma^{22}\}$, and $\boldsymbol{b}$ denote a vector for which the i-th element is equal to the (i,i)-th element of $\mathbf{B}$. Then, the conditional posterior probability density function of $\boldsymbol{\phi}$ is

$$\pi(\boldsymbol{\phi}|\Sigma, \boldsymbol{\alpha}, Y_n) \propto h(\boldsymbol{\phi}) \times \exp\left\{-\frac{1}{2}(\boldsymbol{\phi} - \boldsymbol{\mu}_{\phi})'\Sigma_{\phi}^{-1}(\boldsymbol{\phi} - \boldsymbol{\mu}_{\phi})\right\},$$

$$h(\boldsymbol{\phi}) = |\Sigma_0|^{-\frac{1}{2}} \prod_{j=1}^{p} (1+\phi_j)^{a_j-1}(1-\phi_j)^{b_j-1} \exp\left\{-\frac{1}{2}\boldsymbol{\alpha}_1' \Sigma_0^{-1} \boldsymbol{\alpha}_1\right\},$$

where $\boldsymbol{\mu}_{\phi} = \Sigma_{\phi} \boldsymbol{b}$, $\Sigma_{\phi}^{-1} = \Sigma^{22} \odot \mathbf{A}$, and $\odot$ denotes a Hadamard product. To sample $\boldsymbol{\phi}$ based on its conditional posterior distribution using the MH algorithm, we generate a candidate from a truncated normal distribution over the region R, $\boldsymbol{\phi}^{\dagger} \sim \mathcal{TN}_R(\boldsymbol{\mu}_{\phi}, \Sigma_{\phi})$, and $R = \{\boldsymbol{\phi} : |\phi_j| < 1, j = 1, \ldots, p\}$ and accept it with probability $\min\{1, h(\boldsymbol{\phi}^{\dagger})/h(\boldsymbol{\phi})\}$ where $\boldsymbol{\phi}$ is a current sample.

7.2.2.3 Generation of Σ. The conditional posterior probability density function of Σ is

$$\pi(\Sigma|\boldsymbol{\phi}, \boldsymbol{\alpha}, Y_n) \propto |\Sigma|^{-\frac{n_1+2p+1}{2}} \exp\left\{-\frac{1}{2}\mathrm{tr}\left(\mathbf{R}_1^{-1}\Sigma^{-1}\right)\right\} \times g(\Sigma),$$

$$g(\Sigma) = |\Sigma_0|^{-\frac{1}{2}} |\Sigma_{\varepsilon\varepsilon}|^{-\frac{1}{2}} \exp\left\{-\frac{1}{2}\left(\boldsymbol{\alpha}_1'\Sigma_0^{-1}\boldsymbol{\alpha}_1 + \boldsymbol{y}_n'\mathbf{V}_n^{-1/2}\Sigma_{\varepsilon\varepsilon}^{-1}\mathbf{V}_n^{-1/2}\boldsymbol{y}_n\right)\right\},$$

where $n_1 = n_0 + n - 1$, $\mathbf{R}_1^{-1} = \mathbf{R}_0^{-1} + \sum_{t=1}^{n-1} \boldsymbol{v}_t \boldsymbol{v}_t'$ and

$$\boldsymbol{v}_t = \begin{pmatrix} \mathbf{V}_t^{-1/2}\boldsymbol{y}_t \\ \boldsymbol{\alpha}_{t+1} - \Phi\boldsymbol{\alpha}_t \end{pmatrix}.$$

Using the MH algorithm, we propose a candidate $\Sigma^{\dagger} \sim \mathcal{IW}(n_1, \mathbf{R}_1)$ and accept it with probability $\min\{1, g(\Sigma^{\dagger})/g(\Sigma)\}$ where Σ is a current sample.

7.2.3 MULTIVARIATE-*t* ERRORS

To describe the heavy tailed errors in the asset returns, the MSV model can be extended to have the multivariate t distribution, which is a scale mixture of normal distributions. For the MSV model with multivariate-t errors, the measurement equation is given by

$$\boldsymbol{y}_t = \lambda_t^{-1/2}\mathbf{V}_t^{1/2}\boldsymbol{\varepsilon}_t, \quad t = 1, \ldots, n, \tag{7.23}$$

$$\lambda_t \sim \mathcal{G}(\nu/2, \nu/2), \tag{7.24}$$

where $\mathcal{G}(a, b)$ denotes a gamma distribution with mean a/b and variance a/b^2.

The prior distribution for ν is assumed to be $\nu \sim \mathcal{G}(m_0^\nu, S_0^\nu)$, and we let $\pi(\nu)$ denote its prior probability density function. Let $\boldsymbol{\lambda} = \{\lambda_t\}_{t=1}^n$. Then the conditional joint posterior probability density function of $(\nu, \boldsymbol{\lambda})$ is given by

$$\pi(\nu, \boldsymbol{\lambda}|\boldsymbol{\phi}, \Sigma, \boldsymbol{\alpha}, Y_n)$$
$$\propto \pi(\nu)\left\{\frac{\left(\frac{\nu}{2}\right)^{\frac{\nu}{2}}}{\Gamma\left(\frac{\nu}{2}\right)}\right\}^n \prod_{t=1}^n \lambda_t^{\frac{p+\nu}{2}-1}$$
$$\times \exp\left[-\frac{1}{2}\sum_{t=1}^n \left\{\nu\lambda_t + \left(\sqrt{\lambda_t}\boldsymbol{y}_t - \boldsymbol{\mu}_t\right)' \Sigma_t^{-1} \left(\sqrt{\lambda_t}\boldsymbol{y}_t - \boldsymbol{\mu}_t\right)\right\}\right]. \quad (7.25)$$

To sample from the posterior distribution, we implement the MCMC simulation in five blocks.

1. Initialize $\boldsymbol{\alpha}, \boldsymbol{\phi}, \Sigma, \boldsymbol{\lambda}$, and ν.
2. Generate $(\boldsymbol{\alpha}, \boldsymbol{\phi}, \Sigma)$ as in Section 7.2.2 replacing $\boldsymbol{y}_t$ with $\lambda_t^{1/2}\boldsymbol{y}_t$.
3. Generate $\nu \sim \pi(\nu|\boldsymbol{\lambda})$.
4. Generate $\lambda_t \sim \pi(\lambda_t|\boldsymbol{\phi}, \boldsymbol{\Sigma}, \boldsymbol{\alpha}_t, \nu, \boldsymbol{y}_t)$ for $t = 1, \ldots, n$.
5. Go to Step 2.

7.2.3.1 Generation of ν. The conditional posterior probability density of ν is given by

$$\pi(\nu|\boldsymbol{\phi}, \Sigma, \boldsymbol{\lambda}, \boldsymbol{\alpha}, Y_n) \propto \pi(\nu)\left\{\frac{\left(\frac{\nu}{2}\right)^{\frac{\nu}{2}}}{\Gamma\left(\frac{\nu}{2}\right)}\right\}^n \left(\prod_{t=1}^n \lambda_t\right)^{\frac{\nu}{2}} \exp\left\{-\frac{\sum_{t=1}^n \lambda_t}{2}\nu\right\}. \quad (7.26)$$

To sample from this conditional posterior distribution, we transform ν such that $\vartheta_\nu = \log\nu$ and we let $\hat{\vartheta}_\nu$ denote a conditional mode of $\pi(\vartheta_\nu|\boldsymbol{\phi}, \Sigma, \boldsymbol{\lambda}, \boldsymbol{\alpha}, Y_n)$. Using the MH algorithm, we propose a candidate from the normal distribution $\vartheta_\nu^\dagger \sim \mathcal{N}(\mu_\nu, \sigma_\nu^2)$, where

$$\mu_\nu = \hat{\vartheta}_\nu + \sigma_\nu^2\left[\left.\frac{\partial \log\pi(\vartheta_\nu|\boldsymbol{\phi}, \Sigma, \boldsymbol{\lambda}, \boldsymbol{\alpha}, Y_n)}{\partial\vartheta_\nu}\right|_{\vartheta_\nu=\hat{\vartheta}_\nu}\right],$$
$$\sigma_\nu^2 = \left[-\left.\frac{\partial^2 \log\pi(\vartheta_\nu|\boldsymbol{\phi}, \Sigma, \boldsymbol{\lambda}, \boldsymbol{\alpha}, Y_n)}{\partial\vartheta_\nu^2}\right|_{\vartheta_\nu=\hat{\vartheta}_\nu}\right]^{-1}.$$

We accept the candidate with probability

$$\min\left[1, \frac{\pi(\vartheta_\nu^\dagger|\boldsymbol{\phi}, \Sigma, \boldsymbol{\lambda}, \boldsymbol{\alpha}, Y_n)f_N(\vartheta_\nu|\mu_\nu, \sigma_\nu^2)}{\pi(\vartheta_\nu|\boldsymbol{\phi}, \Sigma, \boldsymbol{\lambda}, \boldsymbol{\alpha}, Y_n)f_N(\vartheta_\nu^\dagger|\mu_\nu, \sigma_\nu^2)}\right],$$

where ϑ_ν is a current sample and $f_N(x|\mu, \sigma^2)$ denotes a normal density function with mean μ and variance σ^2.

7.2.3.2 Generation of $\boldsymbol{\lambda}$. The conditional posterior probability density function of λ_t is

$$\pi(\lambda_t|\boldsymbol{\phi}, \Sigma, \nu, \boldsymbol{\alpha}, Y_n) \propto \lambda_t^{\frac{\nu+p}{2}-1} \exp\left\{-\frac{c_t}{2}\lambda_t + d_t\sqrt{\lambda_t}\right\},$$

where $c_t = \nu + \boldsymbol{y}_t'\Sigma_t^{-1}\boldsymbol{y}_t$ and $d_t = \boldsymbol{y}_t'\Sigma_t^{-1}\boldsymbol{\mu}_t$. To sample λ_t using the MH algorithm, we generate a candidate $\lambda_t^\dagger \sim \mathcal{G}((\nu+p)/2, c_t/2)$ and accept it with probability,

$$\min\left[1, \exp\left\{d_t\left(\sqrt{\lambda_t^\dagger} - \sqrt{\lambda_t}\right)\right\}\right],$$

where λ_t is a current sample. Note that we generate $\lambda_n \sim \mathcal{G}((\nu+p)/2, c_n/2)$, since $\boldsymbol{\mu}_n = \mathbf{0}$ implies $d_n = 0$.

7.3 Factor MSV Model

7.3.1 MODEL

When p is very large, it would be computationally difficult to estimate the MSV model because of many parameters and latent variables. Also, in some cases, it is more appropriate to use common factors to describe comovements among many asset returns. We extend the factor MSV model discussed in Chib et al. (2006) to the model with leverage effects and propose an efficient MCMC algorithm. Our algorithm is based on the multimove sampler (Omori and Watanabe 2008; Takahashi et al., 2009), which does not need any approximation of the posterior distribution.

Let $\boldsymbol{y}_t = (y_{1t}, \ldots, y_{pt})'$ denote a set of observations at time t on p asset returns and $\boldsymbol{f}_t = (f_{1t}, \ldots, f_{qt})'$ denote a vector of factor variables at time t, with $q < p$. Let $\boldsymbol{\alpha}_t = (\alpha_{1t}, \ldots, \alpha_{p+q,t})' = \boldsymbol{h}_t - \boldsymbol{\mu}$ where $\boldsymbol{h}_t = (h_{1t}, \ldots, h_{p+q,t})'$ is the corresponding vector of log-volatilities and $\boldsymbol{\mu} = (\mu_1, \ldots, \mu_{p+q})'$ is its mean vector. Further, The factor MSV model with multivariate-t errors is given by

$$\boldsymbol{y}_t = \mathbf{B}\boldsymbol{f}_t + \lambda_t^{-1/2}\mathbf{V}_{1t}^{1/2}\boldsymbol{\varepsilon}_{1t}, \quad t = 1, \ldots, n, \tag{7.27}$$

$$\boldsymbol{f}_t = \mathbf{V}_{2t}^{1/2}\boldsymbol{\varepsilon}_{2t}, \quad t = 1, \ldots, n, \tag{7.28}$$

$$\boldsymbol{\alpha}_{t+1} = \Phi\boldsymbol{\alpha}_t + \boldsymbol{\eta}_t, \quad t = 1, \ldots, n-1, \tag{7.29}$$

$$\alpha_{j1} \sim \mathcal{N}(0, \sigma_{j\varepsilon}^2/(1-\phi_j^2)), \quad j = 1, \ldots, p+q, \tag{7.30}$$

where

$$\begin{pmatrix} \boldsymbol{\varepsilon}_t \\ \boldsymbol{\eta}_t \end{pmatrix} \sim \mathcal{N}_{2(p+q)}(\mathbf{0}, \boldsymbol{\Sigma}), \quad \boldsymbol{\Sigma} = \begin{pmatrix} \boldsymbol{\Sigma}_{\varepsilon\varepsilon} & \boldsymbol{\Sigma}_{\varepsilon\eta} \\ \boldsymbol{\Sigma}_{\varepsilon\eta} & \boldsymbol{\Sigma}_{\eta\eta} \end{pmatrix}, \tag{7.31}$$

$$\lambda_t \sim \mathcal{G}\left(\frac{\nu}{2}, \frac{\nu}{2}\right), \tag{7.32}$$

and $\boldsymbol{\varepsilon}_t = (\boldsymbol{\varepsilon}'_{1t}, \boldsymbol{\varepsilon}'_{2t})'$, $\mathbf{V}_t^{1/2} = \text{diag}\left(\mathbf{V}_{1t}^{1/2}, \mathbf{V}_{2t}^{1/2}\right)$ and

$$\mathbf{V}_{1t}^{1/2} = \text{diag}(\exp(\alpha_{1t}/2), \ldots, \exp(\alpha_{p,t}/2)), \tag{7.33}$$

$$\mathbf{V}_{2t}^{1/2} = \text{diag}(\exp(\alpha_{p+1,t}/2), \ldots, \exp(\alpha_{p+q,t}/2)), \tag{7.34}$$

$$\Phi = \text{diag}(\phi_1, \ldots, \phi_{p+q}), \tag{7.35}$$

$$\Sigma_{\varepsilon\varepsilon} = \text{diag}(\sigma_{1\varepsilon}^2, \ldots, \sigma_{p+q,\varepsilon}^2), \tag{7.36}$$

$$\Sigma_{\eta\eta} = \text{diag}(\sigma_{1\eta}^2, \ldots, \sigma_{p+q,\eta}^2), \tag{7.37}$$

$$\Sigma_{\varepsilon\eta} = \text{diag}\left(\rho_1\sigma_{1\varepsilon}\sigma_{1\eta}, \ldots, \rho_{p+q}\sigma_{p+q,\varepsilon}\sigma_{p+q,\eta}\right), \tag{7.38}$$

For the factor loading matrix **B**, we assume

$$\begin{aligned} b_{ij} &= 0, \quad i < j, \quad i = 1, \ldots, q, \\ b_{ii} &= 1, \quad i = 1, \ldots, q, \end{aligned}$$

for the identification (Chib et al., 2006) and we let $\boldsymbol{\beta}$ denote the free elements of **B**. In this model, we consider the multivariate t errors to describe the heavy tails in the asset returns and the results for the normal error can be obtained when we set $\lambda_t \equiv 1$ for $t = 1, \ldots, n$. We could further incorporate jump components as in Chib et al. (2006) but do not consider them for simplicity.

7.3.1.1 Likelihood Function.

Let $\boldsymbol{\theta} = (\boldsymbol{\phi}, \Sigma_1, \ldots, \Sigma_p, \boldsymbol{\beta}, \nu)$ where $\boldsymbol{\phi} = (\phi_1, \ldots, \phi_p)'$, $\boldsymbol{f} = \{\boldsymbol{f}_t\}_{t=1}^n$, $\boldsymbol{\lambda} = \{\lambda_t\}_{t=1}^n$, and

$$\boldsymbol{\Sigma}_j = \begin{pmatrix} \sigma_{j\varepsilon}^2 & \rho_j\sigma_{j\varepsilon}\sigma_{j\eta} \\ \rho_j\sigma_{j\varepsilon}\sigma_{j\eta} & \sigma_{j\eta}^2 \end{pmatrix}, \quad j = 1, \ldots, p+q.$$

Then the likelihood function of the factor MSV model outlined in Equations 7.27–7.30 is given by

$$\begin{aligned} &f(\boldsymbol{\alpha}, \boldsymbol{f}, \boldsymbol{\lambda}, Y_n|\boldsymbol{\theta}) \\ &\propto \left\{\frac{\left(\frac{\nu}{2}\right)^{\frac{\nu}{2}}}{\Gamma\left(\frac{\nu}{2}\right)}\right\}^n |\Sigma|^{-\frac{n-1}{2}} |\Sigma_{\varepsilon\varepsilon}|^{-\frac{1}{2}} \times \prod_{t=1}^n \lambda_t^{\frac{\nu+p}{2}-1} \times \exp -\frac{1}{2}\sum_{t=1}^n \nu\lambda_t \\ &\times |\Sigma_{\eta\eta}|^{-\frac{1}{2}} \prod_{j=1}^{p+q} (1-\phi_j^2)^{\frac{1}{2}} \times \exp -\frac{1}{2}\left\{\sum_{j=1}^{p+q}(1-\phi_j^2)\sigma_{j\eta}^{-2}\alpha_{j1}^2\right\} \\ &\times \exp -\frac{1}{2}\sum_{t=1}^n \left\{\left(\sum_{j=1}^{p+q}\alpha_{jt}\right) + \boldsymbol{w}_t'(\mathbf{P}_t\Sigma\mathbf{P}_t')^{-1}\boldsymbol{w}_t\right\}, \end{aligned} \tag{7.39}$$

where

$$\boldsymbol{w}_t = \begin{pmatrix} \boldsymbol{y}_t \\ \boldsymbol{f}_t \\ \boldsymbol{\alpha}_{t+1} - \Phi\boldsymbol{\alpha}_t \end{pmatrix}, \quad \mathbf{P}_t = \begin{pmatrix} \lambda_t^{-1/2}\mathbf{V}_{1t}^{1/2} & \mathbf{B}\mathbf{V}_{2t}^{1/2} & \mathbf{O} \\ \mathbf{O} & \mathbf{V}_{2t}^{1/2} & \mathbf{O} \\ \mathbf{O} & \mathbf{O} & \mathbf{I}_{p+q} \end{pmatrix}, \tag{7.40}$$

for $t = 1, \ldots, n-1$ and

$$\boldsymbol{w}_n = \begin{pmatrix} \boldsymbol{y}_n \\ \boldsymbol{f}_n \end{pmatrix}, \quad \mathbf{P}_n = \begin{pmatrix} \lambda_n^{-1/2}\mathbf{V}_{1n}^{1/2} & \mathbf{B}\mathbf{V}_{2n}^{1/2} & \mathbf{O} \\ \mathbf{O} & \mathbf{V}_{2n}^{1/2} & \mathbf{O} \end{pmatrix}. \tag{7.41}$$

7.3.1.2 Prior and Posterior Distributions. Let $\beta_2 = b_{21}, \boldsymbol{\beta}_3 = (b_{31}, b_{32})'$, $\ldots, \boldsymbol{\beta}_q = (b_{q1}, \ldots, b_{q,q-1})', \boldsymbol{\beta}_{q+1} = (b_{q+1,1}, \ldots, b_{q+1,q})', \ldots, \boldsymbol{\beta}_p = (b_{p1} \ldots, b_{pq})'$. Then, the prior distribution for $\boldsymbol{\theta}$ is assumed to be as follows:

$$\begin{aligned} \nu &\sim \mathcal{G}(m_0^{\nu}, S_0^{\nu}), \\ \boldsymbol{\beta}_j &\sim \mathcal{N}_{r_j}(\boldsymbol{\beta}_{0j}, \Gamma_{0j}), \quad j = 2, \ldots, p, \\ \frac{\phi_j + 1}{2} &\sim \mathcal{B}(a_j, b_j), \quad \Sigma_j \sim \mathcal{IW}(n_{0j}, \mathbf{R}_{0j}), \quad j = 1, \ldots, p+q, \end{aligned}$$

where r_j is the dimension of $\boldsymbol{\beta}_j$ for $j = 2, \ldots, p$. We let $\pi(\nu)$, $\pi(\boldsymbol{\beta}_j)$, $\pi(\phi_j)$, and $\pi(\Sigma_j)$ denote the corresponding prior probability densities. Then, the joint posterior density is given by

$$\pi(\boldsymbol{\theta}, \boldsymbol{\alpha}, \boldsymbol{f}, \boldsymbol{\lambda} | Y_n) \propto f(\boldsymbol{\alpha}, \boldsymbol{f}, \boldsymbol{\lambda}, Y_n | \boldsymbol{\theta}) \pi(\nu) \prod_{j=2}^{p} \pi(\boldsymbol{\beta}_j) \prod_{j=1}^{p+q} \pi(\phi_j) \pi(\Sigma_j). \tag{7.42}$$

7.3.2 BAYESIAN ESTIMATION

To conduct Bayesian inference on the parameter $\boldsymbol{\theta}$, we generate random samples from its posterior distribution by implementing the following MCMC algorithm in seven blocks:

1. Initialize $\boldsymbol{\alpha}, \boldsymbol{f}, \boldsymbol{\lambda}, \boldsymbol{\phi}, \Sigma, \boldsymbol{\beta}$, and ν.
2. Generate $\boldsymbol{\alpha}$, $\boldsymbol{\phi}$, and Σ as follows: for $j = 1, \ldots, p$,
   (a) Generate $\boldsymbol{\alpha}_j | \boldsymbol{f}, \boldsymbol{\lambda}, \phi_j, \Sigma_j, \boldsymbol{\beta}, Y_n$ where $\boldsymbol{\alpha}_j = (\alpha_{j1}, \ldots, \alpha_{jn})'$.
   (b) Generate $\phi_j | \boldsymbol{f}, \boldsymbol{\lambda}, \boldsymbol{\alpha}_j, \Sigma_j, \boldsymbol{\beta}, Y_n$.
   (c) Generate $\Sigma_j | \boldsymbol{f}, \boldsymbol{\lambda}, \boldsymbol{\alpha}_j, \phi_j, \boldsymbol{\beta}, Y_n$.
3. Generate $\boldsymbol{f} | \boldsymbol{\alpha}, \boldsymbol{\lambda}, \boldsymbol{\phi}, \Sigma, \boldsymbol{\beta}, Y_n$.
4. Generate $\boldsymbol{\lambda} | \boldsymbol{\alpha}, \boldsymbol{f}, \boldsymbol{\phi}, \Sigma, \boldsymbol{\beta}, \nu, Y_n$.
5. Generate $\boldsymbol{\beta} | \boldsymbol{\alpha}, \boldsymbol{f}, \boldsymbol{\lambda}, \boldsymbol{\phi}, \Sigma, Y_n$.
6. Generate $\nu | \boldsymbol{\lambda}$.
7. Go to Step 2.

7.3.2.1 Generation of $\boldsymbol{\alpha}$, $\boldsymbol{\phi}$, and Σ. Define

$$y_{jt}^* = \begin{cases} \lambda_t^{1/2}(y_{jt} - a_{jt}), & j = 1, \ldots, p, \\ f_{j-p,t}, & j = p+1, \ldots, p+q, \end{cases}$$

where a_{jt} is the j-th element of $\boldsymbol{a}_t = \mathbf{B}\boldsymbol{f}_t$. Then, given $\boldsymbol{f}$, $\boldsymbol{\lambda}$, $\boldsymbol{\beta}$, and ν, it can be shown that the conditional posterior distributions of $(\boldsymbol{\alpha}_j, \phi_j, \Sigma_j)$ are the same as those for the univariate SV model

$$y_{jt}^* = \exp(\alpha_{jt}/2)\varepsilon_{jt}, \quad t = 1, \ldots, n, \tag{7.43}$$

$$\alpha_{j,t+1} = \phi_j \alpha_{jt} + \eta_{jt}, \quad t = 1, \ldots, n-1, \tag{7.44}$$

$$\alpha_{j1} \sim \mathcal{N}(0, \sigma_{j\eta}^2/(1-\phi_j^2)), \tag{7.45}$$

$$\boldsymbol{u}_{jt} = \begin{pmatrix} \varepsilon_{jt} \\ \eta_{jt} \end{pmatrix} \sim \mathcal{N}\left(\mathbf{0}, \Sigma_j\right), \tag{7.46}$$

for $j = 1, \ldots, p+q$.

Generation of $\boldsymbol{\alpha}_j$. To generate $\boldsymbol{\alpha}_j$, we use a multimove sampler as in Section 7.2.2.1 with $p = 1$ for each j ($j = 1, \ldots, p+q$).

Generation of ϕ_j. The conditional posterior density of ϕ_j is given by

$$\pi(\phi_j | \boldsymbol{f}, \boldsymbol{\lambda}, \boldsymbol{\alpha}_j, \Sigma_j, \boldsymbol{\beta}, Y_n) \propto h(\phi_j) \times \exp -\frac{(\phi_j - \mu_j)^2}{2\sigma_j^2}, \tag{7.47}$$

where

$$\mu_j = \frac{\sum_{t=1}^{n-1} \alpha_{jt}\{\alpha_{j,t+1} - \rho_j \sigma_{j\eta}\sigma_{j\varepsilon}^{-1}\exp(-\alpha_{jt}/2)y_{jt}^*\}}{\rho_j^2\alpha_{j1}^2 + \sum_{t=2}^{n-1}\alpha_{jt}^2},$$

$$\sigma_j^2 = \frac{(1-\rho_j^2)\sigma_{j\eta}^2}{\rho_j^2\alpha_{j1}^2 + \sum_{t=2}^{n-1}\alpha_{jt}^2},$$

$$h(\phi_j) = (1+\phi_j)^{a_j - \frac{1}{2}}(1-\phi_j)^{b_j - \frac{1}{2}}.$$

Given the current value ϕ_j, generate a candidate $\phi_j^\dagger \sim \mathcal{TN}_{(-1,1)}(\mu_j, \sigma_j^2)$ and accept it with probability $\min\{1, h(\phi_j^\dagger)/h(\phi_j)\}$.

Generation of Σ_j. The conditional posterior density of Σ_j is given by

$$\pi(\Sigma_j | \boldsymbol{f}, \boldsymbol{\lambda}, \phi_j, \boldsymbol{\alpha}_j, \boldsymbol{\beta}, Y_n) \propto g(\Sigma_j) \times |\Sigma_j|^{-\frac{n_{1j}+3}{2}} \exp -\frac{1}{2}\mathrm{tr}\left(\mathbf{R}_{j1}^{-1}\Sigma_j^{-1}\right), \tag{7.48}$$

where $n_{1j} = n_{0j} + n - 1$ and

$$g(\Sigma_j) = \sigma_{j\eta}^{-1} \exp -\frac{\alpha_{j1}^2(1-\phi_j^2)}{2\sigma_{j\eta}^2} \times \sigma_{j\varepsilon}^{-1} \exp -\frac{y_{jn}^{*2}}{2\sigma_{j\varepsilon}^2 \exp(\alpha_{jn})},$$

$$\mathbf{R}_{j1}^{-1} = \mathbf{R}_{j0}^{-1} + \sum_{t=1}^{n-1} \boldsymbol{v}_{jt}\boldsymbol{v}_{jt}', \quad \boldsymbol{v}_{jt} = \begin{pmatrix} y_{jt}^* \exp(-\alpha_{jt}/2) \\ \alpha_{j,t+1} - \phi_j\alpha_{jt} \end{pmatrix}.$$

Given the current value Σ_j, generate a candidate $\Sigma_j^\dagger \sim \mathcal{IW}(n_{1j}, \mathbf{R}_{1j})$ and accept it with probability $\min\{1, g(\Sigma_j^\dagger)/g(\Sigma_j)\}$.

7.3.2.2 Generation of $\boldsymbol{f}$. The conditional posterior distribution of $\boldsymbol{f}_t$ is normal such that

$$\begin{aligned}
\boldsymbol{f}_t &\sim \mathcal{N}_q(\boldsymbol{\mu}_f, \Sigma_f), \\
\boldsymbol{\mu}_f &= \mathbf{P}_{1t}\Sigma\mathbf{P}_{2t}'(\mathbf{P}_{2t}\Sigma\mathbf{P}_{2t}')^{-1}\boldsymbol{w}_{2t}, \\
\Sigma_f &= \mathbf{P}_{1t}\Sigma\mathbf{P}_{1t}' - \mathbf{P}_{1t}\Sigma\mathbf{P}_{2t}'(\mathbf{P}_{2t}\Sigma\mathbf{P}_{2t}')^{-1}\mathbf{P}_{2t}\Sigma\mathbf{P}_{1t}',
\end{aligned} \tag{7.49}$$

where

$$\boldsymbol{w}_{2t} = \begin{cases} \begin{pmatrix} \boldsymbol{y}_t \\ \boldsymbol{\alpha}_{t+1} - \Phi\boldsymbol{\alpha}_t \end{pmatrix}, & t = 1, \ldots, n-1, \\ \boldsymbol{y}_n, & t = n, \end{cases}$$

$$\mathbf{P}_{1t} = \begin{pmatrix} \mathbf{O} & \mathbf{V}_{2t}^{1/2} & \mathbf{O} \end{pmatrix}, \quad t = 1, \ldots, n,$$

$$\mathbf{P}_{2t} = \begin{cases} \begin{pmatrix} \lambda_t^{-1/2}\mathbf{V}_{1t}^{1/2} & \mathbf{B}\mathbf{V}_{2t}^{1/2} & \mathbf{O} \\ \mathbf{O} & \mathbf{O} & \mathbf{I}_{p+q} \end{pmatrix}, & t = 1, \ldots, n-1, \\ \begin{pmatrix} \lambda_n^{-1/2}\mathbf{V}_{1n}^{1/2} & \mathbf{B}\mathbf{V}_{2n}^{1/2} & \mathbf{O} \end{pmatrix}, & t = n. \end{cases}$$

7.3.2.3 Generation of $\boldsymbol{\lambda}$. Let $c_{jt} = \rho_j\sigma_{j\varepsilon}\sigma_{j\eta}^{-1}(\alpha_{j,t+1} - \phi_j\alpha_{jt})\exp(\alpha_{jt}/2)I(t < n)$. The conditional posterior density of λ_t is given by

$$\pi(\lambda_t | \boldsymbol{f}, \boldsymbol{\alpha}_j, \phi_j \Sigma_j, \boldsymbol{\beta}, \nu, Y_n) \propto \lambda_t^{\frac{\nu+p}{2}-1} \exp\left\{-\frac{k_t}{2}\lambda_t + d_t\sqrt{\lambda_t}\right\},$$

where

$$d_t = \sum_{j=1}^{p} \frac{(y_{jt} - a_{jt})c_{jt}}{\sigma_{j\varepsilon}^2(1 - \rho_j^2)\exp(\alpha_{jt})},$$

$$k_t = \nu + \sum_{j=1}^{p} \frac{(y_{jt} - a_{jt})^2}{\sigma_{j\varepsilon}^2(1 - \rho_j^2 I(t < n))\exp(\alpha_{jt})}.$$

Given the current value λ_t, for $t < n$, generate a candidate $\lambda_t^\dagger \sim \mathcal{G}\left((\nu + p)/2, k_t/2\right)$ and accept it with probability,

$$\min\left[1, \exp\left\{d_t\left(\sqrt{\lambda_t^\dagger} - \sqrt{\lambda_t}\right)\right\}\right].$$

For $t = n$, generate $\lambda_n \sim \mathcal{G}\left((\nu + p)/2, k_n/2\right)$.

7.3.2.4 Generation of $\boldsymbol{\beta}$. The conditional posterior distribution of $\boldsymbol{\beta}_j$ is normal $\boldsymbol{\beta}_j \sim \mathcal{N}_{r_j}(\boldsymbol{\beta}_{1j}, \Gamma_{1j})$ where

$$\boldsymbol{\beta}_{1j} = \Gamma_{1j}\left[\Gamma_{0j}^{-1}\boldsymbol{\beta}_{0j} + \sum_{t=1}^{n} \frac{\lambda_t \boldsymbol{x}_{jt}\left\{y_{jt} - \lambda_t^{-\frac{1}{2}} c_{jt} - f_{jt} I(j \le q)\right\}}{\sigma_{j\varepsilon}^2(1-\rho_j^2 I(t<n))\exp(\alpha_{jt})}\right],$$

$$\Gamma_{1j} = \left\{\Gamma_{0j}^{-1} + \sum_{t=1}^{n} \frac{\lambda_t \boldsymbol{x}_{jt}\boldsymbol{x}_{jt}'}{\sigma_{j\varepsilon}^2(1-\rho_j^2 I(t<n))\exp(\alpha_{jt})}\right\}^{-1},$$

$$\boldsymbol{x}_{jt} = (f_{1t}, f_{2t}, \cdots, f_{\min(j-1,q),t})', \quad j = 2, \ldots, p.$$

7.3.2.5 Generation of ν. The conditional posterior density of ν is given by

$$\pi(\nu|\boldsymbol{\lambda}) \propto \pi(\nu) \left\{ \frac{\left(\frac{\nu}{2}\right)^{\frac{\nu}{2}}}{\Gamma\left(\frac{\nu}{2}\right)} \right\}^n \left(\prod_{t=1}^{n} \lambda_t \right)^{\frac{\nu}{2}} \exp\left\{ -\frac{\sum_{t=1}^{n} \lambda_t}{2} \nu \right\}. \tag{7.50}$$

To sample from this conditional posterior distribution, we conduct the MH algorithm as in Section 7.2.3.1.

7.4 Applications to Stock Indices Returns

7.4.1 S&P 500 SECTOR INDICES

We apply our MSV models to five S&P500 sector indices from January 2, 1995, to March 31, 2010, obtained from Thomson Reuters Datastream[1].

There are 3839 trading days after excluding the annual market holidays, September 11–14, 2001; July 3, 2006; and January 2, 2007, since the same values are recorded on those days as the value from the previous day. The returns are defined by the log-difference of each sector index multiplied by 100 for five series, namely, "Health Care" (Series 1), "Materials" (Series 2), "Financials" (Series 3), "Consumer Staples" (Series 4), and "Utilities" (Series 5), and the time series plots of the five return series with S&P500 index returns are shown in Figure 7.1. One clearly sees the comovement of volatilities among the five stock indices returns during this period.

[1]The Datastream codes of five series are SP5EHCR(PI), SP5EMAT(PI), SP5EFIN(PI), SP5ECST(PI), and SP5EUTL(PI).

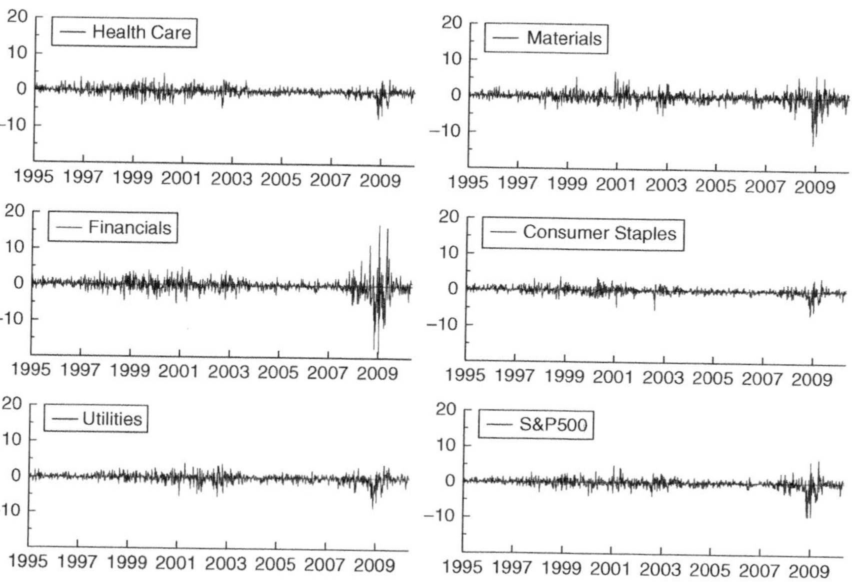

FIGURE 7.1 Returns of five S&P500 sector indices and the S&P500 index.

7.4.2 MSV MODEL WITH MULTIVARIATE t ERRORS

7.4.2.1 Prior Distributions . For the prior distributions, we assume

$$\nu \sim \mathcal{G}(0.01, 0.01), \quad \boldsymbol{\Sigma} \sim \mathcal{IW}(10, (10\boldsymbol{\Sigma}^*)^{-1}),$$

$$\frac{\phi_i + 1}{2} \sim \mathcal{B}(20, 1.5), \quad i = 1, \ldots, 5,$$

where

$$\boldsymbol{\Sigma}^* = \begin{pmatrix} 1.2^2(0.5\mathbf{I}_5 + 0.5\mathbf{1}_5\mathbf{1}_5') & 1.2 \times 0.2 \times (-0.1)\mathbf{I}_5 \\ & 0.2^2(0.2\mathbf{I}_5 + 0.8\mathbf{1}_5\mathbf{1}_5') \end{pmatrix},$$

and $E(\boldsymbol{\Sigma}^{-1}) = \boldsymbol{\Sigma}^{*-1}$. The hyperparameters are set to those typical values in the empirical studies.

7.4.2.2 Estimation Results. Using the MCMC algorithms described in Sections 7.2.2 and 7.2.3, we draw 100,000 samples after discarding 20,000 samples as a burn-in period. The tuning parameter K is set to 100 to obtain low autocorrelated samples, where the average size of one block is about 40.

TABLE 7.1 MSV Model: Posterior Means, Standard Deviations and 95% Credible Intervals

	i	Mean	Standard Deviation	95% Interval
ϕ_i	1	0.985	0.003	[0.979, 0.989]
	2	0.987	0.002	[0.983, 0.991]
	3	0.990	0.002	[0.987, 0.993]
	4	0.985	0.002	[0.980, 0.989]
	5	0.987	0.002	[0.982, 0.991]
$\sigma_{i,\varepsilon\varepsilon}$	1	1.184	0.079	[1.045, 1.358]
	2	1.416	0.103	[1.239, 1.649]
	3	1.580	0.134	[1.351, 1.872]
	4	0.970	0.058	[0.871, 1.100]
	5	1.106	0.086	[0.962, 1.300]
$\sigma_{i,\eta\eta}$	1	0.155	0.011	[0.135, 0.177]
	2	0.138	0.010	[0.120, 0.158]
	3	0.151	0.009	[0.133, 0.170]
	4	0.147	0.009	[0.130, 0.166]
	5	0.149	0.010	[0.130, 0.169]
$\rho_{ii,\varepsilon\eta}$	1	−0.425	0.054	[−0.526, −0.313]
	2	−0.400	0.058	[−0.509, −0.282]
	3	−0.507	0.051	[−0.601, −0.402]
	4	−0.475	0.050	[−0.569, −0.373]
	5	−0.298	0.061	[−0.414, −0.177]
ν		17.6	1.8	[14.5, 21.6]

$\sigma_{i,\varepsilon\varepsilon} = \sqrt{\text{Var}(\varepsilon_{it})}$, $\sigma_{i,\eta\eta} = \sqrt{\text{Var}(\eta_{it})}$, $\rho_{ii,\varepsilon\eta} = \text{Corr}(\varepsilon_{it}, \eta_{it})$.

Table 7.1 shows posterior means, standard deviations, and 95% credible intervals for $\phi_i, \sigma_{i,\varepsilon\varepsilon}, \sigma_{i,\eta\eta}, \rho_{ii,\varepsilon\eta}$, and ν. The estimated ϕ_i and $\sigma_{i,\varepsilon\varepsilon}$ are similar to typical values for the univariate model with high persistence in the log-volatilities. The absolute values of estimated $\rho_{ii,\varepsilon\eta}$ for the leverage effects seem to be smaller than expected, which may be because the variation of one series is partly explained by those of other series through the high correlations among ε_{it}s and η_{jt}s, as shown in Table 7.2.

Estimation results are shown in Table 7.2 for $\rho_{ij,\varepsilon\varepsilon}, \rho_{ij,\eta\eta}$, and $\rho_{ij,\varepsilon\eta}$. The correlations are high among ε_{it} (between 0.489 and 0.707) and among η_{it} (between 0.717 and 0.878), which may cause the low absolute values of $\rho_{ii,\varepsilon\eta}$ as mentioned above. The posterior means of $\rho_{ij,\varepsilon\eta}$ are all negative, and there is a strong evidence for the existence of cross asset leverage effects. It is interesting to notice that the cross leverage effects between series i and j are found to be asymmetric, that is, $\rho_{ij,\varepsilon\eta} \neq \rho_{ji,\varepsilon\eta}$ $(i \neq j)$. For example, in Table 7.2, $\rho_{i5,\varepsilon\eta}$s are between −0.415 and −0.353, while $\rho_{5j,\varepsilon\eta}$s are between −0.299 and −0.231. This means that the cross leverage effects from Series 1, 2, 3, and 4 on the volatility of Series 5 (i.e., Utilities) are relatively stronger than vice versa. The

TABLE 7.2 MSV Model: Posterior Means, Standard Deviations and 95% Credible Intervals

	ij	Mean	Standard Deviation	95% Interval
$\rho_{ij,\varepsilon\varepsilon}$	12	0.526	0.013	[0.500, 0.550]
	13	0.662	0.010	[0.642, 0.681]
	14	0.707	0.009	[0.689, 0.723]
	15	0.509	0.013	[0.483, 0.534]
	23	0.648	0.010	[0.628, 0.668]
	24	0.565	0.012	[0.542, 0.588]
	25	0.489	0.013	[0.463, 0.515]
	34	0.675	0.010	[0.657, 0.694]
	35	0.560	0.012	[0.537, 0.583]
	45	0.553	0.012	[0.529, 0.577]
$\rho_{ij,\eta\eta}$	12	0.773	0.041	[0.684, 0.845]
	13	0.781	0.040	[0.695, 0.851]
	14	0.878	0.024	[0.823, 0.919]
	15	0.742	0.048	[0.639, 0.823]
	23	0.829	0.034	[0.755, 0.886]
	24	0.802	0.036	[0.722, 0.862]
	25	0.792	0.041	[0.703, 0.861]
	34	0.814	0.033	[0.742, 0.872]
	35	0.717	0.050	[0.610, 0.806]
	45	0.785	0.041	[0.698, 0.855]
	12	−0.365	0.060	[−0.476, −0.240]
	13	−0.367	0.056	[−0.473, −0.252]
	14	−0.399	0.052	[−0.497, −0.294]
	15	−0.367	0.064	[−0.487, −0.238]
	21	−0.382	0.054	[−0.485, −0.275]
	23	−0.397	0.053	[−0.499, −0.289]
	24	−0.456	0.049	[−0.550, −0.358]
	25	−0.353	0.060	[−0.465, −0.229]
	31	−0.369	0.056	[−0.475, −0.256]
$\rho_{ij,\varepsilon\eta}$	32	−0.442	0.060	[−0.554, −0.316]
	34	−0.436	0.052	[−0.534, −0.332]
	35	−0.415	0.062	[−0.530, −0.287]
	41	−0.397	0.056	[−0.502, −0.284]
	42	−0.373	0.060	[−0.485, −0.250]
	43	−0.366	0.057	[−0.474, −0.250]
	45	−0.359	0.064	[−0.479, −0.228]
	51	−0.252	0.055	[−0.357, −0.139]
	52	−0.231	0.060	[−0.345, −0.111]
	53	−0.250	0.056	[−0.356, −0.137]
	54	−0.299	0.052	[−0.399, −0.195]

$\rho_{ij,\varepsilon\varepsilon} = \mathrm{Corr}(\varepsilon_{it}, \varepsilon_{jt})$, $\rho_{ij,\eta\eta} = \mathrm{Corr}(\eta_{it}, \eta_{jt})$, $\rho_{ij,\varepsilon\eta} = \mathrm{Corr}(\varepsilon_{it}, \eta_{jt})$.

volatility of the Utilities series is more influenced by decreases in returns of four other series, while those of the other series are less subject to changes in the returns of Utilities series. This suggests that market participants do not react so sharply when a decrease in the return is limited to Utilities series, but they do react in a more sensitive way if decreases occur in other series.

7.4.3 FACTOR MSV MODEL

7.4.3.1 Prior distributions. We assume the following prior distributions for the parameters:

$$\begin{aligned}
\nu &\sim \mathcal{G}(0.01, 0.01), \\
\boldsymbol{\beta}_j &\sim \mathcal{N}_{r_j}(\mathbf{0}, 10\mathbf{I}_{r_j}), \quad j = 2, \ldots, p, \\
\frac{\phi_j + 1}{2} &\sim \mathcal{B}(20, 1.5), \quad \Sigma_j \sim \mathcal{IW}(5, (5\boldsymbol{\Sigma}^*)^{-1}), \quad j = 1, \ldots, p+q,
\end{aligned}$$

where

$$\boldsymbol{\Sigma}^* = \begin{pmatrix} 1 & -0.1 \\ -0.1 & 0.04 \end{pmatrix},$$

and $E(\boldsymbol{\Sigma}_j^{-1}) = \boldsymbol{\Sigma}^{*-1}$. The hyperparameters are set to typical values of empirical studies.

7.4.3.2 Estimation Results. First, we determine the number of the factors and the order of the data as follows. We conducted a preliminary factor analysis and selected the number of factors equal to two. Then, for the first series, we chose Series 1 (Health Care), which has a high factor loading for the first factor but low factor loadings for the second factor. Similarly, we chose Materials (Series 2) as the second series and Financials (Series 3), Consumer Staples (Series 4), and Utilities (Series 5) for the rest of series. Thus, we fit the two-factor MSV model for the data series shown in Figure 7.1. To implement MCMC, we draw 100,000 samples after discarding 30,000 samples as a burn-in period. The tuning parameter K for the multimove sampler for $\boldsymbol{\alpha}_j$ is set to 100.

Figure 7.2 shows time series plots of the S&P500 index returns and posterior means of two factors, f_{jt} ($j = 1, 2$). The path of the first factor seems to represent the market movement in the usual time since the plot looks very similar to that of S&P500 index returns most of the time during the sample period. On the other hand, that of the second factor captures the sharp changes in the stock market, which corresponds to the periods after the internet bubble around the year 2000 and the financial crisis during which Lehman Brothers filed for Chapter 11 bankruptcy protection on September 15, 2008. Those fluctuations of the factors indicate that correlations among the five return series might vary over time.

Table 7.3 shows the estimation results for factor loadings, β_{ij} ($i = 2, \ldots, 5$, $j = 1, 2$), for the factor MSV model. All factor loadings are estimated to be positive; hence, correlations among series are positive. For the first factor, the posterior means are positive varying from 0.643 to 1.125, suggesting that it

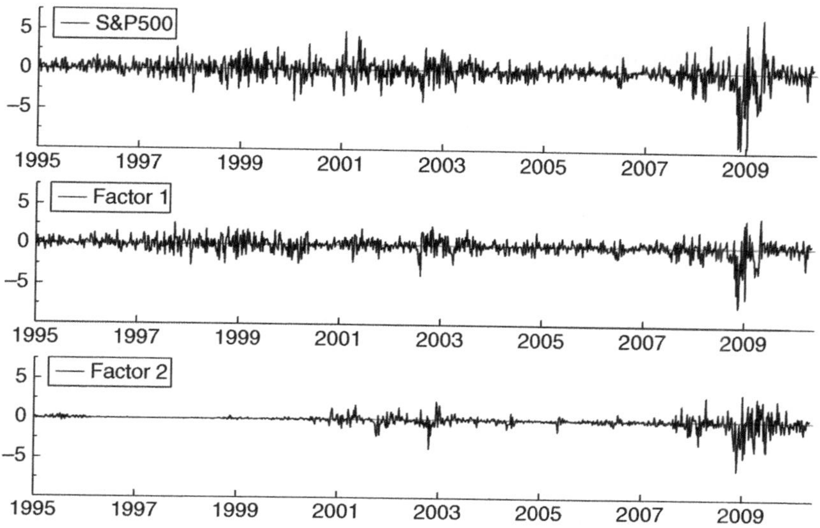

FIGURE 7.2 Factor MSV model. Time series plots of S&P500 index returns and posterior means of two factors, f_{jt} ($j = 1, 2$).

describes the comovement in the stock market. For the second factor, they vary from 0.085 to 0.767. The posterior mean of β_{42} for Consumer Staples (Series 4) is relatively small in comparison with other factor loadings, which implies that the series is relatively stable and is not so affected by those sharp changes in the stock market during the sample period. On the other hand, the factor loadings of the Financials series on both factors $\beta_{3j}, j = 1, 2$ are large and the series is found expectedly to be strongly affected by the stock market, taking into account that the sector includes banks, insurance companies, diversified financial companies, and real estate investment trusts.

Posterior means, standard deviations, and 95% credible intervals for ϕ_i, $\sigma_{i\varepsilon}$, $\sigma_{i\eta}$, ρ_i, and ν are shown in Table 7.4. Parameters for the two factors correspond to $i = 6, 7$. The estimated ϕ_is (between 0.978 and 0.997) show the

TABLE 7.3 Factor MSV Model: Posterior Means, Standard Deviations, and 95% Credible Intervals

	ij	Mean	Standard Deviation	95% Interval
	21	0.872	0.028	[0.818, 0.929]
	31	1.125	0.027	[1.072, 1.179]
	41	0.835	0.018	[0.801, 0.870]
β_{ij}	51	0.643	0.022	[0.601, 0.686]
	32	0.767	0.080	[0.625, 0.934]
	42	0.085	0.022	[0.043, 0.130]
	52	0.359	0.036	[0.292, 0.432]

TABLE 7.4 Factor MSV Model: Posterior Means, Standard Deviations, and 95% Credible Intervals

	i	Mean	Standard Deviations	95% interval
	1	0.992	0.003	[0.984, 0.997]
	2	0.984	0.005	[0.973, 0.993]
	3	0.996	0.001	[0.993, 0.999]
ϕ_i	4	0.995	0.003	[0.989, 0.999]
	5	0.991	0.003	[0.984, 0.996]
	6	0.978	0.004	[0.969, 0.985]
	7	0.997	0.002	[0.994, 0.999]
	1	0.629	0.093	[0.499, 0.850]
	2	0.720	0.055	[0.620, 0.836]
	3	0.848	0.176	[0.585, 1.260]
$\sigma_{i\varepsilon}$	4	0.596	0.115	[0.446, 0.893]
	5	0.715	0.085	[0.585, 0.920]
	6	0.856	0.054	[0.759, 0.975]
	7	1.114	0.352	[0.629, 1.958]
	1	0.138	0.019	[0.105, 0.179]
	2	0.130	0.019	[0.097, 0.171]
	3	0.146	0.015	[0.118, 0.178]
$\sigma_{i\eta}$	4	0.109	0.013	[0.086, 0.137]
	5	0.133	0.014	[0.107, 0.163]
	6	0.190	0.016	[0.160, 0.225]
	7	0.205	0.026	[0.158, 0.263]
	1	−0.224	0.102	[−0.416, −0.021]
	2	−0.065	0.099	[−0.252, 0.132]
	3	−0.409	0.092	[−0.578, −0.220]
ρ_i	4	−0.192	0.104	[−0.388, 0.024]
	5	−0.043	0.078	[−0.195, 0.112]
	6	−0.641	0.054	[−0.739, −0.528]
	7	−0.529	0.113	[−0.730, −0.289]
ν		11.97	1.099	[10.07,14.36]

high persistence in the log-volatilities for all series and two factors. We note that the absolute values of ρ_i ($i = 2, 4, 5$) are smaller than those in the MSV model and that their 95% credible intervals include zero. This may be because the leverage effects for these three series in the MSV model seem to be partly replaced by those of the common factors with $\rho_6 = -0.641$ and $\rho_7 = -0.529$.

The estimated $\sigma_{i\varepsilon}$ and $\sigma_{i\eta}$ for the two factors are found to be larger than those of individual series, which indicates that the movement of two factors is dominating those of individual series. Further, note that the estimates for the second factor are larger than those of the first factor. This corresponds to the large fluctuations of the second factor during the financial crisis.

Moreover, since the factor loadings $\beta'_{ij}s$ are all positive and the ρ_i's are all negative (hence, the leverage effects exist), the cross leverage effects are also found to exist in the factor MSV model. Finally, the posterior mean of ν is found to be much smaller than that in the MSV model, reflecting the fact that the factor MSV model is more parsimonious than the MSV model to describe the heavy tailed error distributions of the stock returns.

7.5 Conclusion

We have not discussed another general class of the MSV model, the dynamic correlation MSV model where the correlations among returns are also time-varying. These include the MSV model based on the Choleski decomposition of the time-varying correlation matrix in Tsay (2005), the matrix exponential transformation model mentioned in Asai et al. (2006); a class of Wishart processes in Asai and McAleer (2009), Philipov and Glickman (2006a), Philipov and Glickman (2006b), and Triantafyllopoulos (2008); and Wishart autoregressive processes in Gouriéroux (2006) and Gouriéroux et al. (2009), and positive semidefinite OU-type processes in Barndorff-Nielsen and Stelzer (2009) and Pigorsch and Stelzer (2009). These are very general and high dimensional models that are beyond our scope and their discussion is left for the future work. Thus, we focused on two major MSV models in this chapter, the MSV model and the factor MSV model with leverage effects. An efficient Bayesian estimation method without approximating errors is described and shown to be easy to implement. Empirical studies are given using five S&P500 sector indices returns with these models.

7.6 Appendix: Sampling α in the MSV Model

7.6.1 SINGLE-MOVE SAMPLER

Noting that the conditional posterior density of $\boldsymbol{\alpha}_t$ is

$$\pi(\boldsymbol{\alpha}_t|\{\boldsymbol{\alpha}_s\}_{s\neq t}, \boldsymbol{\phi}, \Sigma, Y_n) \propto \exp\left\{-\frac{1}{2}(\boldsymbol{\alpha}_t - \boldsymbol{m}_{\boldsymbol{\alpha}_t})'\Sigma_{\boldsymbol{\alpha}_t}^{-1}(\boldsymbol{\alpha}_t - \boldsymbol{m}_{\boldsymbol{\alpha}_t}) + g(\boldsymbol{\alpha}_t)\right\}$$

where

$$\boldsymbol{m}_{\boldsymbol{\alpha}_t} = \begin{cases} \Sigma_{\boldsymbol{\alpha}_1}\left(-\frac{1}{2}\mathbf{1}_p + \Phi\mathbf{M}_1\boldsymbol{\alpha}_2\right), & t = 1, \\ \Sigma_{\boldsymbol{\alpha}_t}\left(-\frac{1}{2}\mathbf{1}_p + \Phi\mathbf{M}_t\boldsymbol{\alpha}_{t+1} + \mathbf{M}_{t-1}\Phi\boldsymbol{\alpha}_{t-1} + \mathbf{N}_{t-1}\right), & 1 < t < n, \\ \Sigma_{\boldsymbol{\alpha}_n}\left(-\frac{1}{2}\mathbf{1}_p + \mathbf{M}_{n-1}\Phi\boldsymbol{\alpha}_{n-1} + \mathbf{N}_{n-1}\right), & t = n, \end{cases}$$

$$\Sigma_{\alpha_t} = \begin{cases} \left(\Sigma_0^{-1} + \Phi \mathbf{M}_1 \Phi\right)^{-1}, & t = 1, \\ (\mathbf{M}_{t-1} + \Phi \mathbf{M}_t \Phi)^{-1}, & 1 < t < n, \\ \mathbf{M}_{n-1}^{-1}, & t = n, \end{cases}$$

$$\mathbf{M}_t = \Sigma_{\eta\eta}^{-1} + \Sigma_{\eta\eta}^{-1} \Sigma_{\eta\varepsilon} \mathbf{S}_t^{-1} \Sigma_{\varepsilon\eta} \Sigma_{\eta\eta}^{-1},$$

$$\mathbf{N}_t = \Sigma_{\eta\eta}^{-1} \Sigma_{\eta\varepsilon} \mathbf{S}_t^{-1} \mathbf{V}_t^{-1/2} \boldsymbol{y}_t,$$

and

$$g(\boldsymbol{\alpha}_t) = -\frac{1}{2} \boldsymbol{y}_t' \Sigma_t^{-1} \boldsymbol{y}_t + \boldsymbol{y}_t' \Sigma_t^{-1} \boldsymbol{\mu}_t.$$

We sample from the conditional posterior distribution using the MH algorithm: generate a candidate $\boldsymbol{\alpha}_t^\dagger \sim \mathrm{N}(\boldsymbol{m}_{\alpha_t}, \Sigma_{\alpha_t})$ and accept it with probability

$$\min\left\{1, \exp\{g(\boldsymbol{\alpha}_t^\dagger) - g(\boldsymbol{\alpha}_t)\}\right\},$$

for $t = 1, \ldots, n$, where $\boldsymbol{\alpha}_t$ is a current value.

7.6.2 MULTI-MOVE SAMPLER

First, evaluate $\boldsymbol{d}_t$, $\mathbf{A}_t$, and $\mathbf{B}_t$ at $\hat{\boldsymbol{a}}$ to obtain $\hat{\boldsymbol{d}}_t$, $\hat{\mathbf{A}}_t$, and $\hat{\mathbf{B}}_t$, respectively. Let $\boldsymbol{z}_t = \mathbf{V}_t^{-\frac{1}{2}} \boldsymbol{y}_t$,

$$\begin{aligned} \boldsymbol{d}_t &= -\frac{1}{2}\mathbf{1}_p + \frac{1}{2}\left\{\mathrm{diag}(\boldsymbol{z}_t) - 2\Phi\Sigma_{\eta\eta}^{-1}\Sigma_{\eta\varepsilon} I(t < n)\right\} \mathbf{S}_t^{-1}(\boldsymbol{z}_t - \boldsymbol{m}_t) \\ &\quad + \Sigma_{\eta\eta}^{-1}\Sigma_{\eta\varepsilon}\mathbf{S}_{t-1}^{-1}(\boldsymbol{z}_{t-1} - \boldsymbol{m}_{t-1}) I(t > 1) \\ &\quad + \Phi\Sigma_{\eta\eta}^{-1}(\boldsymbol{\alpha}_{t+1} - \Phi\boldsymbol{\alpha}_t) I(t = s + m < n), \end{aligned}$$

$$\begin{aligned} \mathbf{A}_t &= \frac{1}{4}\left\{\mathbf{I}_p + \mathbf{S}_t^{-1} \odot (\mathbf{S}_t + \boldsymbol{m}_t\boldsymbol{m}_t')\right\} + \Phi\Sigma_{\eta\eta}^{-1}\Sigma_{\eta\varepsilon}\mathbf{S}_t^{-1}\Sigma_{\varepsilon\eta}\Sigma_{\eta\eta}^{-1}\Phi I(t < n) \\ &\quad - \frac{1}{2}\left(\Phi\Sigma_{\eta\eta}^{-1}\Sigma_{\eta\varepsilon}\mathbf{S}_t^{-1}\mathrm{diag}(\boldsymbol{m}_t) + \mathrm{diag}(\boldsymbol{m}_t)\mathbf{S}_t^{-1}\Sigma_{\varepsilon\eta}\Sigma_{\eta\eta}^{-1}\Phi\right) I(t < n) \\ &\quad + \Sigma_{\eta\eta}^{-1}\Sigma_{\eta\varepsilon}\mathbf{S}_{t-1}^{-1}\Sigma_{\varepsilon\eta}\Sigma_{\eta\eta}^{-1} I(t > 1) + \Phi\Sigma_{\eta\eta}^{-1}\Phi I(t = s + m < n), \end{aligned}$$

for $t = s + 1, \ldots, s + m$, $\mathbf{B}_{s+1} = \mathbf{O}$, and

$$\mathbf{B}_t = \frac{1}{2}\Sigma_{\eta\eta}^{-1}\Sigma_{\eta\varepsilon}\mathbf{S}_{t-1}^{-1}\left\{\mathrm{diag}(\boldsymbol{m}_{t-1}) - 2\Sigma_{\varepsilon\eta}\Sigma_{\eta\eta}^{-1}\Phi\right\},$$

for $t = s + 2, \ldots, s + m$. Next, set $\boldsymbol{b}_s = \mathbf{0}$ and $\hat{\mathbf{B}}_{s+m+1} = \mathbf{0}$, and compute

$$\mathbf{D}_t = \hat{\mathbf{A}}_t - \hat{\mathbf{B}}_t\mathbf{D}_{t-1}^{-1}\hat{\mathbf{B}}_t', \quad \boldsymbol{b}_t = \hat{\boldsymbol{d}}_t - \hat{\mathbf{B}}_t\mathbf{D}_{t-1}^{-1}\boldsymbol{b}_{t-1}, \quad \hat{\boldsymbol{\gamma}}_t = \hat{\boldsymbol{\alpha}}_t + \mathbf{D}_t^{-1}\hat{\mathbf{B}}_{t+1}'\hat{\boldsymbol{\alpha}}_{t+1},$$

for $t = s + 1, \ldots, s + m$ recursively. Finally, define auxiliary vectors and matrices

$$\hat{\boldsymbol{y}}_t = \hat{\boldsymbol{\gamma}}_t + \mathbf{D}_t^{-1}\boldsymbol{b}_t, \quad \mathbf{Z}_t = \mathbf{I}_p + \mathbf{D}_t^{-1}\hat{\mathbf{B}}'_{t+1}\Phi, \quad \mathbf{G}_t = [\mathbf{K}_t'^{-1}, \mathbf{D}_t^{-1}\hat{\mathbf{B}}'_{t+1}\mathbf{R}_t],$$

for $t = s + 1, \ldots, s + m$ where $\mathbf{K}_t$ denotes a Choleski decomposition of $\mathbf{D}_t$ such that $\mathbf{D}_t = \mathbf{K}_t\mathbf{K}_t'$. For details, see Ishihara and Omori (2013).

CHAPTER EIGHT

Model Selection and Testing of Conditional and Stochastic Volatility Models

MASSIMILIANO CAPORIN and MICHAEL McALEER

8.1 Introduction

Model selection and model comparison, especially of the conditional mean or first moment of a given random variable, have been widely considered in the sciences and social sciences for an extended period. The relevance and importance of such a topic comes from the recognized fact that the true data-generating processes are generally unknown. As a result, several approaches have been proposed to verify if a given model is able to replicate or capture the empirical features observed on sample data (the realization of the data-generating process) and to check if there is a preference across alternative models that might be considered given the sample data and the purposes of the analysis. In this chapter, we focus on model comparison and selection in a specific framework, namely univariate volatility models for financial time series. From the seminal work of Engle (1982a) and Bollerslev (1986), generalized autoregressive conditional heteroskedasticity (GARCH) models have become a very popular tool in empirical finance.

Handbook of Volatility Models and Their Applications, First Edition.
Edited by Luc Bauwens, Christian Hafner, and Sebastien Laurent.

They have been generalized in several ways (see, e.g., Bollerslev et al. (1992), Bollerslev et al. (1994), McAleer (2005), and the Chapters 2 of Teräsvirta (2012) and 3 of Haas and Paolella (2011) in this handbook). A companion family of models is that of stochastic volatility (SV), introduced by Taylor (1982) and Taylor (1986), and extended in several directions (Ghysels et al., 1996; Asai et al., 2006). Traditional methods for model selection and comparison could easily be extended and applied within specific families of models (for instance, within GARCH or within SV specifications). However, some model classes, or some specific models within a given model class, may be nonnested, thereby requiring appropriate approaches or novel techniques for the model selection step. In the following discussion, we consider separately the comparison of alternative specifications in-sample, thereby resorting to nested and nonnested model comparison, diagnostic checking, and out-of-sample model comparison based on the forecasts of given models. The discussion herein is based on univariate models that are capable of capturing financial time series asymmetry and/or leverage, but the results presented can be generalized to other model classes at the univariate level. The methods can also be generalized to the multivariate level, following Patton and Sheppard (2009a) and Caporin and McAleer (2009, 2010). The remainder of the chapter proceeds as follow. In Section 8.1.1, we introduce the models to be used. Section 8.2 discusses the model selection and testing methods, distinguishing between in-sample and out-of-sample approaches. Section 8.3 includes an empirical example on a set of stock market indices. Finally, Section 8.4 gives some concluding comments.

8.1.1 MODEL SPECIFICATIONS

In this chapter, we illustrate some approaches to model selection and comparison making use of simple and well-known univariate volatility models. We consider the traditional GARCH(1,1), its extension to capture asymmetry, the GJR(1,1) model of Glosten et al. (1993), Exponential GARCH(1,1) (EGARCH), and the Autoregressive SV(1) (also known as SV) specifications. We choose these three models for two simple reasons, namely, they are nonnested and can capture asymmetry and leverage (with the obvious exclusion of GARCH(1,1), which is a benchmark model).

In order to simplify model evaluation and comparison, we assume in the following discussion that the analyzed return series, r_t, has been filtered from its mean, so that we can focus on a zero-mean series, ε_t, that displays conditional heteroskedasticity, $\varepsilon_t = \sigma_t z_t$. Furthermore, the unit variance innovation, z_t, is a standardized residual.

If the conditional variances, σ_t^2, follow a GARCH(1,1) model, the following equation represents their law of motion:

$$\sigma_t^2 = \omega + \alpha\varepsilon_{t-1}^2 + \beta\sigma_{t-1}^2, \tag{8.1}$$

where $\omega > 0$, $\alpha \geq 0$, and $\beta \geq 0$ are sufficient conditions to guarantee positive conditional variances for all observations and $\alpha + \beta < 1$ ensures covariance stationarity.

If we introduce asymmetry to GARCH(1,1), we obtain the asymmetric or threshold model of Glosten et al. (1993), GJR(1,1):

$$\sigma_t^2 = \omega + \alpha \varepsilon_{t-1}^2 + \gamma \varepsilon_{t-1}^2 I\left(\varepsilon_{t-1} < 0\right) + \beta \sigma_{t-1}^2, \tag{8.2}$$

where the γ parameter captures asymmetry and $I\left(\varepsilon_{t-1} < 0\right)$ is an indicator function, which takes the value 1 when $\varepsilon_{t-1} < 0$ and 0 otherwise.

A clarification is needed here in order to avoid a common misconception between asymmetry and leverage: (i) asymmetry is a feature that is intended to capture the empirical regularity that positive and negative shocks of equal magnitude have different impacts on volatility and (ii) leverage is intended to capture the possibility that negative shocks increase volatility while positive shocks decrease volatility (or equivalently, a negative correlation between current returns and future volatility as discussed in Black (1976) and Christie (1982).

As a matter of model design, few conditional volatility models allow for leverage effects. For example, GARCH is symmetric and hence has no leverage. Despite comments to the contrary in various econometric software packages (for instance, EViews and Matlab), the GJR-GARCH model may be asymmetric, but it is unlikely to have leverage, as the ARCH effect must be negative, which is contrary to virtually every empirical finding in the financial econometrics literature.

The third model we consider is the EGARCH(1,1), where the conditional variance equation is defined in terms of log-variances:

$$\ln\left(\sigma_t^2\right) = \omega + \alpha \left|z_{t-1}\right| + \gamma z_{t-1} + \beta \ln\left(\sigma_{t-1}^2\right). \tag{8.3}$$

Note that the coefficients need not be positive, while $|\beta| < 1$ to avoid explosive variance patterns. Depending on α and γ, the parameters associated with the size and sign effect, the EGARCH model could display both asymmetry and leverage (for leverage to hold, $\gamma < 0$ and $\gamma < \alpha < -\gamma$, contrary to the single restriction stated in some econometric software). Finally, we consider the SV model, which assumes that the innovation term follows:

$$\varepsilon_t = \exp\left(\frac{1}{2} h_t\right) z_t, \tag{8.4}$$

where z_t is a unit variance innovation and the conditional variance $\sigma_t^2 = \exp\left(h_t\right)$ is driven by the following dynamic equation for h_t:

$$h_{t+1} = \phi_0 + \phi_1 h_t + \eta_t, \tag{8.5}$$

where the parameters are not required to be positive, $|\phi_1| < 1$ to avoid explosive patterns, and the innovation term, η_t, has variance σ_η^2. Chapter of this handbook gives an overview of estimation methods for the SV model.

As shown by Yu (2005), the SV model displays a leverage effect if the two innovation terms, η_t and z_t, are negatively correlated, while asymmetry may be included following, for instance, the approaches of Danielsson (1994), So et al. (2002), and Asai and McAleer (2005).

8.2 Model Selection and Testing

Selection of the best or the most appropriate model may be based on in-sample or out-of-sample criteria, or both. In the following discussion, we address these two approaches separately. Such a choice derives from purely illustrative purposes and should not be interpreted as a preference for one of the two methods. Indeed, identification of an optimal model would seem to require an optimal balance between these two approaches.

In empirical applications, we search for models that capture the features of the analyzed data and that provide accurate out-of-sample forecasts. Both elements may not be present over all models and thus, in empirical studies, a trade-off will likely exist. This possible inconsistency may be resolved in part by evaluating the purpose of an empirical exercise. Structural analysis may have greater emphasis on in-sample fit, while forecasting exercises will necessarily concentrate on out-of-sample outcomes. Nevertheless, both aspects need to be considered, as does the role of research expertise.

8.2.1 IN-SAMPLE COMPARISONS

This chapter examines conditional volatility (GARCH) models and SV processes. We focus on alternative model specifications that belong to the same family (either GARCH or SV). If the models we compare have known mathematical and asymptotic properties (such as strict stationarity of the underlying random process, and consistency and asymptotic normality of the estimators), we may compare them by checking if the conditions ensuring the existence of moments or asymptotic properties are satisfied. In principle, models where these conditions are not satisfied, or do not even exist, should be discarded. In practice, this is typically not the case.

For instance, log-moment conditions ensuring strict stationarity and ergodicity of GARCH models are reported in Nelson (1990) and Bougerol and Picard (1992), among others. These conditions are also sufficient for consistency and asymptotic normality of quasi-maximum likelihood estimators (QMLE) (Elie and Jeantheau, 1995; Boussama 2000). Stronger but simpler moment conditions for ergodicity, stationarity, consistency, and asymptotic normality of the QMLE have been provided in Ling and McAleer (2002) and McAleer et al. (2007). In practice, log-moment conditions are generally difficult to verify, especially for multivariate processes, while moment conditions may be considered as a useful diagnostic check. Notably, well-written software should implement these conditions (which are generally represented as nonlinear parametric restrictions) within the estimation step, thereby implicitly checking them.

As an example, consider the GJR-GARCH model of Equation 8.2. In this case, the stationarity and ergodicity condition, under the assumption that shocks follow a symmetric density, is given as $\alpha + \frac{1}{2}\gamma + \beta < 1$, while the condition for the existence of the fourth-order moment is $\beta^2 + 2\alpha\beta + 3\alpha^2 + \beta\gamma + 3\alpha\gamma + \frac{1}{2}\gamma^2 < 1$. The log-moment condition is given as $E\left[\ln\left(\alpha z_{t-1}^2 + \gamma z_{t-1}^2 I\left(z_{t-1} < 0\right) + \beta\right)\right] < 0$, but it could be difficult to verify as it requires the evaluation of the expectation of a function an unknown random variance and unknown coefficients.

From a different viewpoint, we may compare models with respect to the features they are supposed to be capturing. For example, we may prefer volatility models with asymmetry to specifications characterized by a symmetric news impact curve.

Model preference based on model flexibility should obviously be matched with the statistical significance of estimated parameters associated with a particular feature. For instance, referring to the GJR-GARCH model, it can capture asymmetry although not leverage and hence is more flexible than the symmetric GARCH(1,1) specification. However, GJR-GARCH should be preferred empirically to GARCH if the estimated asymmetry coefficient, γ, is statistically significant. Similarly, if we consider the SV model with leverage (this model can capture leverage and hence asymmetry), replacing (8.5) with (Danielsson, 1994):

$$h_t = \phi_0 + \phi_1 h_{t-1} + \delta_1 \varepsilon_{t-1} + \delta_2 |\varepsilon_{t-1}| + \eta_t. \tag{8.6}$$

Then tests of the coefficients δ_1 and δ_2 could be associated with the significance of both the size and sign of shocks.

Tests of significance associated with single parameters or model features are linked to diagnostic procedures based on the likelihood function. In fact, model comparison could also consider testing nested and/or nonnested models. In general, when we compare models belonging to the same family (such as within GARCH or SV), these are typically nested comparisons. Therefore, the validity of parametric restrictions could be evaluated by significance tests or, more appropriately, by likelihood ratio (LR) or Lagrange multiplier (LM) tests.

In order to present some simple examples, the GJR-GARCH(1,1) model nests the simple GARCH(1,1) model under a zero restriction on the parameter driving the asymmetry; APARCH nests GARCH that is obtained fixing the power coefficient to 2; SV model with asymmetry nests the simpler SV model under a zero parametric restriction similar to that of GJR-GARCH. In these cases, assuming correct specification of the model (particularly of the innovation density), LM and LR tests have the standard asymptotic properties, and the LM statistic can be evaluated when the analytic score is available (for an example, see Fiorentini et al. (1996)). As a further case, we mention the Augmented GARCH model of Duan (1997) that nests GARCH, GJR-GARCH , and EGARCH. Although these models cannot be directly compared, having to be tested against the more general Augmented GARCH specification, the model proposed by Duan (1997) may be used to determine which form of asymmetry and leverage better explains a given time series features. For a comparison of models belonging to separate (or nonnested) families of hypotheses, such as GARCH versus SV or EGARCH versus GARCH, nonnested tests are required. Ling and McAleer (2000) and McAleer et al. (2007) propose simple procedures to compare GARCH and GJR-GARCH models against the EGARCH model. Denote by $\hat{\sigma}^2_{\mathrm{GJR},t}$, the estimates of time t variance obtained from a GJR-GARCHmodel and consider the following EGARCH specification:

$$\ln\left(\sigma^2_{\mathrm{EGARCH},t}\right) = \omega + \alpha\left|z_{t-1}\right| + \gamma z_{t-1} + \beta\ln\left(\sigma^2_{\mathrm{EGARCH},t-1}\right) + \delta\ln\left(\hat{\sigma}^2_{\mathrm{GJR},t}\right), \tag{8.7}$$

where $\sigma^2_{\mathrm{EGARCH},t}$ are the EGARCH conditional variances and z_t are the standardized residuals. The test of the EGARCH null hypothesis against the GJR alternative corresponds to testing $\delta = 0$. Similarly, the test with GJR-GARCH as the null involves a test of $\delta = 0$ in the auxiliary model:

$$\sigma^2_{\mathrm{GJR},t} = \omega + \alpha\varepsilon^2_{t-1} + \gamma\varepsilon^2_{t-1} I\left(\varepsilon_{t-1} < 0\right) + \beta\sigma^2_{\mathrm{GJR},t-1} + \delta\hat{\sigma}^2_{\mathrm{EGARCH},t}, \tag{8.8}$$

where $\hat{\sigma}^2_{\mathrm{EGARCH},t}$ is the estimate of the conditional variance at time t obtained from an EGARCH model. The corresponding tests for GARCH against EGARCH can be obtained as special cases of those given above.

A different test for GARCH against EGARCH was proposed in Lee and Brorsen (1997). The authors suggested a test based on the likelihood of two competing nonnested models, based on the procedures developed in Cox (1961) and Cox (1962). The Cox test compares two parametric models by evaluating the difference between maximum likelihood values as a deviation from its expectation. Lee and Brorsen (1997) evaluate the test statistic by using Monte Carlo methods. However, it is not clear if the conditions underlying the Cox test are satisfied. In particular, the two likelihoods should belong to separate families, that is, for a given parameter choice, the null hypothesis cannot be arbitrarily closely approximated by the alternative. A further aspect that may affect the validity of the test of the EGARCH model as the null hypothesis is that the statistical properties of EGARCH are as yet not known.

The approach of Cox (1961) and Cox (1962) is also closely related to the comparison methods outlined in Kim et al. (1998), who suggest a LR test for nonnested models by obtaining the sampling distribution of the test statistic through Monte Carlo methods. In this case, the tested nonnested models are GARCH and SV, making the Cox test more appropriate.

The procedure outlined in Kim et al. (1998) involves the following steps:

1. Estimate the GARCH and SV model parameters and evaluate the corresponding likelihoods, denoted by $L_{\mathrm{GARCH}}\left(x; \hat{\theta}_{\mathrm{GARCH}}\right)$ and $L_{\mathrm{SV}}\left(x; \hat{\theta}_{\mathrm{SV}}\right)$ respectively, where the circumflex denotes estimated parameters, evaluate the LR statistics:

$$LR_{\mathrm{SV,GARCH}} = 2\left[\ln L_{\mathrm{SV}}\left(x; \hat{\theta}_{\mathrm{SV}}\right) - \ln L_{\mathrm{GARCH}}\left(x; \hat{\theta}_{\mathrm{GARCH}}\right)\right]$$
$$LR_{\mathrm{GARCH,SV}} = 2\left[\ln L_{\mathrm{GARCH}}\left(x; \hat{\theta}_{\mathrm{GARCH}}\right) - \ln L_{\mathrm{SV}}\left(x; \hat{\theta}_{\mathrm{SV}}\right)\right],$$

where the first model represents the null hypothesis, and the SV density is evaluated by simulation methods, following the procedure in Kim et al. (1998).

2. Simulate M paths under the null, estimate both models on each path, and evaluate the M LR statistics.
3. Test the null hypothesis using a Monte Carlo test, determining the p-value of the empirical LR statistics under the simulated density of the LR test statistic.

Note that the LR test statistic is not constrained to be positive as the two models are nonnested. Moreover, by reversing the null and alternative hypotheses, the test outcomes may lead to rejection or nonrejection of both models as the respective null hypotheses. Clearly, the procedure outlined in Kim et al. (1998) derives an approximate LR statistic density and is also influenced by the fact that the true parameters are not known. To state the obvious, this test is computationally intensive.

Kobayashi and Shi (2005) propose a closely related test for EGARCH against SV. Their approach differs from the previous method as they modify the SV model. In fact, they consider the following SV parameterization:

$$\varepsilon_t = \sigma_z \exp\left(\frac{1}{2} h_t\right) z_t, \tag{8.9}$$

$$h_t = \phi_0 + \phi_1 h_{t-1} + \alpha \frac{\varepsilon_{t-1}}{\exp(h_{t-1})} + \beta \left| \frac{\varepsilon_{t-1}}{\exp(h_{t-1})} \right| + \sigma_\eta \eta_t, \tag{8.10}$$

$$\begin{pmatrix} z_t \\ \eta_t \end{pmatrix} \sim D\left(\begin{pmatrix} 0 \\ 0 \end{pmatrix}, \begin{pmatrix} 1 & \rho \\ \rho & 1 \end{pmatrix}\right). \tag{8.11}$$

The model of Kobayashi and Shi (2005) is a slightly modified version of the model in Danielsson (1994), where the volatility equation includes a dependence on both the sign and size of the standardized innovations. Notably, the model includes both asymmetry and leverage as the parameters need not be positive.

In the context of the slightly modified SV model, EGARCH is associated with the parametric restriction, $\sigma_\eta^2 = 0$. Kobayashi and Shi (2005) propose a LM test for the null hypothesis $\sigma_\eta^2 = 0$ (EGARCH) against an alternative of positive variance for the volatility equation. The LM test has an advantage that only EGARCH needs to be estimated. The Monte Carlo simulations reported to verify the size and power of the test show that the LM test for EGARCH against SV has good size and reasonable power (but the results would seem to be heavily dependent on the values of the parameters).

In addition to hypothesis testing approaches, information criteria may also be considered to compare models by using their likelihood penalized by a function of the number of parameters and number of sample observations. These methods allow a comparison of models where the conditional variances depend on observable quantities, such as GARCH and EGARCH, but cannot be applied to compare GARCH and SV as the likelihood function for SV models differs from that of conditional variance specifications (for an example of the evaluation of the SV likelihood by simulation methods, see Kim et al. (1998)).

Alternative models of volatility may also be compared through their ability to capture the heteroskedasticity inherent in financial time series. The most common approach for diagnostic checking is the Ljung–Box test statistic applied to the squared standardized residuals, with the preferred model as the one that permits greater whitening of the residuals. Furthermore, distributional hypotheses could also be considered in order to evaluate which density is closer to the analyzed data. Standard tests such as the Jarque–Bera normality test, or the more general Kolmogorov–Smirnov, may be considered in this context.

In-sample comparisons, and the subsequent choice of the best model may be optimal for structural analysis, but it does not guarantee an optimal choice for out-of-sample forecasting. In this case, the literature provides a number of alternative approaches for model comparison. In the following section, we present some that are tailored for comparing conditional variance models.

8.2.2 OUT-OF-SAMPLE COMPARISONS

An out-of-sample comparison of SV and GARCH models may follow two different approaches: a direct comparison of variance forecasts, or an indirect comparison of variance models through the possible uses of the corresponding variance forecasts. This dichotomy follows from Patton and Sheppard (2009a), who present a number of alternative theoretical approaches.

8.2.2.1 Direct Model Evaluation. Within the direct comparison, alternative models are contrasted by tests directly based on variance forecasts. Denote by $\hat{\sigma}^2_{j,t}$ the time t variance forecast of model j and by σ^2_t the true and unknown variance at time t. For each model, we may evaluate, over a given forecast horizon, a set of standard quantities. Two well-known examples are the mean absolute error (MAE) and mean squared error (MSE):

$$\text{MAE}(j) = \frac{1}{m}\sum_{t=1}^{m}\left|\sigma^2_t - \hat{\sigma}^2_{j,t}\right|, \tag{8.12}$$

$$\text{MSE}(j) = \frac{1}{m}\sum_{t=1}^{m}\left(\sigma^2_t - \hat{\sigma}^2_{j,t}\right)^2. \tag{8.13}$$

Given these quantities for each model, the preferred model will typically have lower values of both MAE and MSE, meaning lower deviations from the true variance.

A closely related comparison method is the use of Mincer and Zarnowitz (1969) regressions, where the variance forecasts are used as explanatory variables for the true variance:

$$\sigma^2_t = \alpha + \beta\hat{\sigma}^2_{j,t} + \xi_t. \tag{8.14}$$

In this alternative framework, optimal models should have $\alpha = 0$ and $\beta = 1$, with a higher value of R^2. Therefore, models providing appropriate or similar coefficient values in Equation 8.14 could be ranked by means of R^2 values.

However, two problems arise both in the Mincer–Zarnowitz-type regressions and in the use of MSE or MAE: (i) the true variance is not known and (ii) ranking models on the basis of one or more statistical indicators is not necessarily a formal statistical test.

With respect to the first issue, unbiased estimates of the true variance could be recovered by realized volatility estimators (see Barndorff-Nielsen and Shephard (2002b), Barndorff-Nielsen and Shephard (2002a), and Barndorff-Nielsen et al. (2008), among others). When high frequency data are not available, the true variance could be approximated by the squared demeaned return observed at time t, at the cost of a large noise component. Nevertheless, in the case of the Mincer–Zarnowitz regressions, Meddahi (2002) shows that the rankings based on R^2 are consistent to the inclusion of noise in the proxy used for σ_t^2.

Model equivalence could be tested more formally, for instance, by the approach proposed by Diebold and Mariano (1995) and generalized by West (1996). These tests compare alternative models by means of loss function differentials (MAE and MSE could be considered as specific loss functions). As shown in Patton (2011), the use of proxies for the underlying true volatility induces distortions in the model ranking for some loss functions. Hansen and Lunde (2006a) provide the conditions for a loss function to be robust with respect to noisy volatility proxies, while Hansen and Lunde (2006a) and Patton (2011) prove that the class of homogeneous loss functions is robust and allows an unbiased model ordering. Two examples are the MSE and QLIKE loss functions, as given below:

$$\text{MSE}\left(j\right) = \frac{1}{m}\sum_{t=1}^{m}\left(s_t^2 - \hat{\sigma}_{j,t}^2\right)^2, \tag{8.15}$$

$$\text{QLIKE}\left(j\right) = \frac{1}{m}\sum_{t=1}^{m}\left(\ln\hat{\sigma}_{j,t}^2 + \frac{s_t^2}{\hat{\sigma}_{j,t}^2}\right), \tag{8.16}$$

where s_t^2 is a proxy for the true unobserved volatility σ_t^2. Alternative models for σ_t^2 can be compared by tests of equal predictive ability, which are associated with the null hypothesis of the unconditional expected null loss function differential:

$$\begin{aligned} H_0 : E\left[\text{MSE}\left(j\right)\right] - E\left[\text{MSE}\left(i\right)\right] &= E\left[\text{MSE}\left(j\right) - \text{MSE}\left(i\right)\right] \\ &= E\left[lf_{\text{MSE},t}\left(j,i\right)\right] = 0, \end{aligned} \tag{8.17}$$

where we may write a similar expression for QLIKE and the unconditional expectation is evaluated using the sample counterparts reported in Equations 8.15 and (8.16). Similarly to Patton and Sheppard (2009a), we take the forecasts as given, thereby not allowing for estimation error (for a testing framework including estimation error, see Giacomini and White (2006)). Building on the results in Diebold and Mariano (1995) and West (1996), under mild conditions on the loss function differentials, the test statistic is given as:

$$\tau_{\text{MSE}} = \frac{\overline{lf}_{\text{MSE}}\left(j,i\right)}{\sqrt{\text{Var}\left[\text{lf}_{\text{MSE,t}}\left(\text{j},\text{i}\right)\right]}}, \tag{8.18}$$

where

$$\overline{lf}_{\text{MSE}}(j,i) = \frac{1}{m}\sum_{t=1}^{m} lf_{\text{MSE},t}(j,i) = \frac{1}{m}\sum_{t=1}^{m}\left[\left(s_t^2 - \hat{\sigma}_{j,t}^2\right)^2 - \left(s_t^2 - \hat{\sigma}_{i,t}^2\right)^2\right],$$

and $\text{Var}[lf_{\text{MSE},t}(j,i)]$ is a heteroskedasticity and autocorrelation consistent variance estimator (with identical equivalence relations available for the QLIKE loss function). For nonnested models, the test statistic is asymptotically distributed as a standardized normal, which allows a simple evaluation of the null hypothesis. In fact, the test is equivalent to a significance test of the intercept in a regression of the loss function differentials $lf_{\text{MSE},t}(j,i)$ over a constant and is, thus, readily available in all computer software packages that implement robust linear regression methods. For nested specifications, a more appropriate test is given in Clark and McCracken (2001).

A relevant limitation of the comparisons based on Diebold–Mariano-type tests is that they represent pairwise comparisons, so that it is not possible to exclude a priori the possibility of having different model rankings associated with different robust loss functions. Furthermore, we note that the Diebold–Mariano test requires a Bonferroni bound correction when dealing with multiple comparisons. The literature contains several approaches that have attempted to resolve this issue, such as the reality check of White (2000), the superior predictive ability test of Hansen (2005), and the model confidence set (MCS) of Hansen et al. (2011).

We suggest the use of the MCS as this method provides a confidence set of statistically equivalent models. The approach developed in Hansen et al. (2011) constitutes a testing framework for the null hypothesis of equivalence across models, which is described by means of loss functions. By referring to the MSE loss function (similar quantities can be obtained for the QLIKE loss function), and assuming that the set $\mathcal{M}$ contains a number of different models used to produce forecasts in a given out-of-sample range, the null hypothesis of MCS is given as:

$$H_0 : E\left[lf_{\text{MSE},t}(j,i)\right] = 0, i > j, \forall i,j \in \mathcal{M}. \tag{8.19}$$

The null hypothesis can be tested by means of two test statistics proposed in Hansen et al. (2003), namely:

$$t_R = \max_{i,j\in\mathcal{M}} \left| \frac{\overline{lf}_{\text{MSE}}(j,i)}{\sqrt{\text{Var}\left[lf_{\text{MSE},t}(j,i)\right]}} \right|, \tag{8.20}$$

$$t_{SQ} = \sum_{i,j\in\mathcal{M}, j>i} \left(\frac{\overline{lf}_{\text{MSE}}(j,i)}{\sqrt{\text{Var}\left[lf_{\text{MSE},t}(j,i)\right]}} \right)^2. \tag{8.21}$$

Both test statistics are based on a bootstrap estimate of $\text{Var}\left[lf_{\text{MSE,t}}(j,i)\right]$ (the variance). As the distribution is nonstandard, the rejection region is determined using bootstrap p-values under the null hypothesis. If the null of equal predictive ability across all models is rejected, the worst performing model is excluded from the set $\mathcal{M}$. Such a model is identified using the elimination rule:

$$j = \arg\max_{j \in \mathcal{M}} \left(\sum_{i \in \mathcal{M}, i \neq j} \overline{lf}_{\mathrm{MSE}}(j,i) \right) \left(\mathrm{Var}\left[\sum_{i \in \mathcal{M}, i \neq j} \overline{lf}_{\mathrm{MSE}}(j,i) \right] \right)^{-\frac{1}{2}}, \tag{8.22}$$

where the variance is again determined through bootstrap techniques. The equal predictive ability of the remaining models should also be tested, thereby iterating the evaluation of the test statistics in Equations 8.20 and 8.21 and the identification of the worst performing model in Equation 8.22. The procedure stops when the null hypothesis of equal predictive ability of the models still included in the set is not rejected. Subsequently, the MCS method provides a set of statistically equivalent models (possibly even a single model) with respect to a given loss function. Additional details on the MCS method with further test statistics and elimination rules are included in Hansen et al. (2011).

8.2.2.2 Indirect Model Evaluation. Indirect evaluation methods consider the uses of alternative variance forecasts. For instance, conditional variances could be used to price derivatives or to define the market risk exposure of a portfolio. The literature has recently addressed the topic, focusing mainly on multivariate models (for example see Caporin and McAleer (2010), Clements et al. (2009a), Patton and Sheppard (2009a), and Laurent et al. (2009), among others). At the univariate level, the approaches are much more widespread and have generally focused on specific applications. Many studies dealt with the evaluation of alternative GARCH specifications within a Value-at-Risk (VaR) framework (Caporin, 2008; Berkowitz, 2001a; Lopez, 1999; Lopez, 2001). As distinct from direct model evaluation, these indirect methods generally require additional assumptions. Some examples are the choice of a pricing model in derivatives pricing frameworks, the definition of agent preferences, targets and constraints in portfolio allocation, and the choice of a distributional hypothesis in risk management. Therefore, when dealing with indirect evaluation, the economic motivation is fundamental as these approaches are not proper tests for comparing alternative variance models (Patton and Sheppard, 2009a).

Considerable empirical research has focused on tests for the evaluation of VaR forecasts. These are used to determine if a model is more appropriate with respect to competitors in determining the future expected risk of a financial instrument (such as a financial portfolio). In this framework, consider a variable displaying heteroskedasticity, possibly characterized by a time-varying mean, and with an unspecified conditional density (with additional parameters contained in the vector θ and with I^{t-1} denoting the information set up to time $t-1$):

$$x_t | I^{t-1} \sim f\left(x_t; \mu_t, \sigma_t^2, \theta\right). \tag{8.23}$$

The one-day VaR for x_t is defined as:

$$\alpha = \int_{-\infty}^{\mathrm{VaR}(x_{t+1};\alpha)} f\left(x_{t+1}; E\left[\mu_{t+1}|I^t\right], E\left[\sigma_{t+1}^2|I^t\right], \hat{\theta}\right) dx_{t+1}, \tag{8.24}$$

where the time-varying mean and variance are replaced by their conditional expectations, the additional parameters are estimated, and α is the VaR confidence level. Under normality, the VaR has a simpler expression, namely $\mathrm{VaR}(x_{t+1};\alpha) = E[\mu_{t+1}|I^t] + \Phi(\alpha)^{-1}\sqrt{E\left[\sigma_{t+1}^2|I^t\right]}$, where $\Phi(\alpha)^{-1}$ is the α-quantile of the standardized normal. Thus, VaR depends on the models used to capture the mean and variance dynamics.

The evaluation of alternative mean and variance specifications by using VaR could follow two approaches: (i) test if the VaR out-of-sample forecasts satisfy the condition $E[I(x_t < \mathrm{VaR}(x_t;\alpha))] = \alpha$, that is, if the expected number of VaR violations (namely, where returns are lower than the forecast VaR) is equal to the VaR confidence level and (ii) compare models by means of loss functions. Tests include the traditional method of Kupiec (1995) which, as shown in Lopez (1999), Lopez (2001), and Caporin (2008), have limited power in discriminating across alternative variance specifications. Thus, loss functions should be preferred, making an indirect comparison of GARCH and SV models very similar to the direct comparison. In the following section, we provide an interpretation of VaR model comparisons by means of the MCS, which, to the best of our knowledge, would seem to be novel.

Loss functions based on VaR forecasts have been proposed, for instance, by Lopez (1999) and Caporin (2008). We suggest the following:

$$\mathrm{IF} = I(x_t < \mathrm{VaR}(x_t;\alpha)), \tag{8.25}$$

$$\mathrm{PIF}_t = I(x_t < \mathrm{VaR}(x_t;\alpha))\left(1 + (x_t - \mathrm{VaR}(x_t;\alpha))^2\right), \tag{8.26}$$

$$\mathrm{AD}_t = \left||x_t| - |\mathrm{VaR}(x_t;\alpha)|\right| g(x_t), \tag{8.27}$$

$$\mathrm{SD}_t = \left(|x_t| - |\mathrm{VaR}(x_t;\alpha)|\right)^2 g(x_t), \tag{8.28}$$

$$\mathrm{ASD}_t = \mathrm{AD}_t + \lambda \mathrm{SD}_t, \tag{8.29}$$

$$\mathrm{RL}_t = \max\left(\mathrm{VaR}(x_t;\alpha); \frac{p_t}{60}\sum_{j=1}^{60}\mathrm{VaR}\left(x_{t-j};\alpha\right)\right). \tag{8.30}$$

In the previous list, the first function (the indicator loss function, IF) identifies exceptions, while the second penalizes exceptions by using the squared deviation (SD) between realized returns and VaR (penalized indicator function, $\mathrm{PIF_t}$). The third and fourth loss functions could be read as first-order and second-order losses, respectively, between VaR and realized returns (absolute deviation, AD_t, and squared deviation, SD_t, loss functions, respectively). They both depend on $g(x_t)$, a function of the observed variable, x_t, that focuses on the loss functions, for instance, only on negative returns $g(x_t) = I(x_t < 0)$, on VaR violations $g(x_t) = I(x_t < \mathrm{VaR}(x_t;\alpha))$, or, finally, on the entire returns path (if set equal to 1). In the fifth loss function, we combine the previous two, adding a parameter, λ, to modify the weight of a component (which can be used to increase or decrease the impact of squared deviations). Note that the fourth loss function is equivalent to the second if $g(x_t) = I(x_t < 0)$ and VaR $(x_t; \alpha)$ is always negative. Finally, the last loss function is also known as *regulatory loss*, and depends on a penalty term, p_t, which is calibrated over the number of exceptions in the last 250 days (3 up to 4 exceptions, 3.4, 3.5, 3.65, 3.75, 3.85 for 5, 6, 7, 8, and 9 exceptions, respectively, and 4 for more than 9 exceptions).

One striking advantage of these loss functions is that they are not based on the true volatility but still depend on the volatility forecasts. Thus, they could be used within an MCS framework to compare alternative models, without suffering from the problems associated with the replacement of the true variance by a noisy proxy. However, as noted in Patton and Sheppard (2009a), the choice of the standardized residual density is crucial as it enters in the evaluation of the VaR.

These methods could also be used in the multivariate framework and be applied to portfolios, in which the included asset variances follow a heteroskedastic density. In fact, within a risk management perspective, alternative covariance models could be compared through the portfolio VaR. In addition, the indirect comparison methods could be applied within an asset allocation framework in order to rank alternative models (Engle and Colacito (2006a); Patton and Sheppard (2009a)). Other multivariate applications where model comparison plays a role are the construction and evaluation of hedging strategies across different instruments and asset classes, the implementation of trading strategies involving many assets (pair trades), and the pricing of options involving more than one asset (for instance, product and quanto options).

8.3 Empirical Example

In this section, we present an empirical comparison of the methods discussed above. Daily stock market total return indices, as reported in Table 8.1, are examined for 2000–2009. We consider the large cap stock market indices of France (CAC40), Germany (DAX), Switzerland (SMI), Hong Kong (HS), and United States (S&P500). Returns are computed from index levels as $r_t = 100\,[\ln(I_t/I_{t-1})]$. For each series, in Table 8.1, we report the descriptive statistics and sample sizes, which differ across market indices as holidays have been removed from the data on a single series basis, and these are not common over the countries considered.

For each return series, we fit four specific models, namely GARCH(1,1), GJR-GARCH(1,1), EGARCH(1,1), and SV(1). The models are estimated on a rolling basis, using a window of 1000 observations, and under normality. The four models are then used to produce one-step-ahead variance forecasts, from January 1, 2004. The models are compared using some of the methods described in the previous section. In particular, we consider the Ling and McAleer (2000) test for comparing GJR and GARCH against EGARCH; the LR test in comparing GARCH against GJR; the Diebold–Mariano test using the MSE and QLIKE loss functions across all model pairs, and the MCS approach

TABLE 8.1 **Sample Statistics of Market Index Returns**

Market	T	Mean	Standard Deviation	Minimum	Maximum	Asymmetry	Kurtosis
CAC40	2552	−0.016	1.58	−9.47	10.60	0.026	7.95
DAX	2542	−0.005	1.67	−7.43	10.80	0.072	7.09
SMI	2522	−0.004	1.31	−8.11	10.79	0.072	8.97
HS	2489	0.009	1.71	−13.58	13.41	−0.038	10.61
S&P500	2514	−0.011	1.40	−9.47	10.96	−0.104	10.66

T, number of observations.

using the MSE and QLIKE loss functions, the loss functions in (8.25)-(8.29) with three VaR levels (1, 5, and 10%), and the loss function in Equation 8.30 with the 1% VaR level. For the absolute and squared deviation (ASD) loss function, we set $\lambda = 1$. Furthermore, in order to verify the stability of results over time, we compare the models over different out-of-sample periods and we consider annual comparisons from 2004 to 2009 (i.e., for five different years).

We start with the in-sample comparison of models using the Ling and McAleer (2000) and LR tests. As we estimated the models over a rolling sample of 1000 observations, we have a set of around 1500 estimates of all models (for estimation samples ending from 31 December 2003 to 30 December 2009). The number of estimates is not equal across all series as these differ with respect to national holidays. Table 8.2 reports the percentage of rejections of the null hypothesis at the 5% confidence level over the entire set of estimates available for each series.

Table 8.2 highlights that GJR(1,1) is always preferred to its GARCH(1,1) counterpart for the CAC40, DAX, SMI, and S&P500 indices, while only for the HS index does GJR not improve in-sample over GARCH in 32% of cases.

A different picture emerges when we compare nonnested models, namely GARCH and GJR-GARCH against EGARCH. We use the Ling and McAleer (2000) test and consider four possible comparisons, modifying the null and alternative models accordingly. The Ling and McAleer (2000) test adds the fitted variances under the alternative to the auxiliary regression equation for the conditional variance equation under the null. A significant coefficient of the added variable provides evidence against the null model. The results for DAX, SMI, and S&P500 are quite similar in that there is a large fraction of rejections when the null model is the GARCH and GJR-GARCH specification and a small fraction of rejections when the null model is EGARCH. Therefore, EGARCH is the preferred conditional volatility model. This finding is not surprising as EGARCH is more flexible than GARCH and GJR-GARCH, can exhibit asymmetry and leverage, and there are no restrictions on the parameters of the model.

However, for CAC40 and HS, the results do not support a particular model, suggesting that either any alternative model is an improvement over the null (CAC40) in a large fraction of cases or no model can improve the null (HS) (again in a large percentage of cases).

TABLE 8.2 **Rejection Percentages of the Null Hypothesis in the Full Sample**

Test	Null Alternative	CAC40	DAX	SMI	HS	S&P500
LR	GARCH GJR	100.00	100.00	100.00	68.36	99.80
Ling–McAleer	GARCH EGARCH	70.44	65.25	84.79	26.41	83.44
Ling–McAleer	GJR EGARCH	44.40	59.24	52.14	9.98	65.53
Ling–McAleer	EGARCH GARCH	63.60	36.12	23.30	39.05	32.58
Ling–McAleer	EGARCH GJR	55.66	21.68	22.84	39.78	39.47

The null hypothesis of the LR test is associated with a preference for the GARCH model against the GJR. For the Ling and McAleer (2000) test, the alternative model column denotes the model whose variances are used as additional explanatory variables in the dynamics governing the variances as given by the null model. The rejection of the null hypothesis is associated with a nonsignificant coefficient and signals a preference for the null model over the alternative one.

In order to shed some light on this result, we recomputed Table 8.2 over two subsamples, 2004–2006 and 2007–2009, and the outcome is reported in Table 8.3. We do not report the LR test as the outcomes are stable across the two subsamples, with the exception of the HS index (for this index, the rejection frequency is higher in the second subsample).

Table 8.3 suggests that EGARCH is optimal for the S&P500 index over the period 2004–2006, while asymmetry is significant for the period 2007–2009, that is, the GARCH estimates clearly improve when we include the EGARCH variances, there is little to choose between GJR and EGARCH.

For SMI, the empirical results are contrary to the above. GARCH is clearly rejected for 2004–2006, but there is no clear preference between the GJR and EGARCH models. In 2007–2009, EGARCH performs better as compared with GJR and GARCH. The results for the DAX and CAC40 indices are similar to those of SMI for 2007–2009, while for 2004–2006, there is no clear preference across the alternative models for DAX. The results for CAC40 suggest a mild preference for GJR.

Finally, for the HS index, the evidence suggests a small percentage of rejections of the null hypothesis, alluding to the fact that most models provide very similar conditional variance patterns.

Moving to the out-of-sample comparison, we start from the outcomes of the Diebold–Mariano test (direct evaluation method) using the MSE and QLIKE loss functions. In order to evaluate model performance across different market phases, we consider separately each out-of-sample year. Table 8.4 reports some salient empirical findings (the full set of empirical results is available from the authors on request).

TABLE 8.3 Rejection Percentages of the Null Hypothesis in Two Subsamples

		Market Index				
Test	Null Alternative	CAC40	DAX	SMI	HS	S&P500
2004–2006						
Ling–McAleer	GARCH					
	EGARCH	47.99	43.15	75.39	22.52	75.63
Ling–McAleer	GJR					
	EGARCH	10.89	34.79	13.55	18.10	61.46
Ling–McAleer	EGARCH					
	GARCH	63.81	13.95	10.53	42.36	10.86
Ling–McAleer	EGARCH					
	GJR	73.67	8.74	12.50	43.30	13.51
2007–2009						
Ling–McAleer	GARCH					
	EGARCH	92.95	87.66	94.20	30.25	88.08
Ling–McAleer	GJR					
	EGARCH	78.07	83.99	90.78	1.98	67.93
Ling–McAleer	EGARCH					
	GARCH	63.32	58.53	36.10	35.80	53.43
Ling–McAleer	EGARCH					
	GJR	37.47	34.78	33.20	36.33	64.49

In the Ling and McAleer (2000) test, the alternative model column denotes the model whose variances are used as additional explanatory variables in the dynamics governing the variances as given by the null model. The rejection of the null hypothesis is associated with a nonsignificant coefficient and signals a preference for the null model over the alternative one.

Focusing on the MSE loss function, all empirical models seem very similar for all stock market indices, with the null hypothesis of zero loss function differential being rejected only in few cases. When we consider the QLIKE loss function, the null hypothesis is rejected more frequently, with the finding seemingly independent of the sample used for model evaluation (the results are similar for 2006 and 2008, two years with very different volatility and returns). In this case, there are some differences across the stock market indices, but the outcomes suggest a preference of GJR-GARCH and EGARCH over SV. Furthermore, GJR-GARCH and EGARCH are generally equivalent (results for GARCH against GJR-GARCH are not reported, given the two models are nested).

Although some preference ordering across models may appear in some cases, the limitation of the Diebold–Mariano test is that it only considers pairwise comparisons. As suggested in Section 8.2, the MCS method overcomes this restrictive comparison.

A number of tables collect the results over the entire set of loss functions and over the out-of-sample years and stock market indices. Tables 8.5–8.9

TABLE 8.4 Diebold–Mariano Test Statistics for Selected Years

Index	EGARCH and GARCH	SV and GARCH	EGARCH and GJR	SV and GJR	SV and EGARCH
MSE loss function, out-of-sample period: 2004					
CAC40	−0.926	1.008	−0.215	1.239	1.191
DAX	−1.087	1.192	−1.334	1.085	1.848
SMI	0.934	1.496	−1.145	0.018	0.689
HS	−1.610	0.363	−0.758	1.082	1.246
S&P500	−0.658	−0.201	1.127	1.441	0.505
QLIKE loss function, out-of-sample period: 2004					
CAC40	−0.252	0.705	0.825	1.791	0.507
DAX	**−2.362**	1.158	−0.562	*3.038*	*2.840*
SMI	0.032	*2.177*	0.308	1.686	1.555
HS	−1.889	1.173	−0.283	*2.128*	*2.195*
S&P500	−0.621	0.089	1.019	1.953	0.637
MSE loss function, out-of-sample period: 2006					
CAC40	−0.610	1.309	0.150	1.005	1.136
DAX	0.057	*2.215*	1.674	1.857	1.534
SMI	−1.327	1.140	−0.307	0.977	1.254
HS	−1.845	0.652	−1.562	0.740	1.025
S&P500	1.464	0.743	1.614	1.921	−1.442
QLIKE loss function, out-of-sample period: 2006					
CAC40	−1.489	*2.025*	0.866	*2.280*	*2.351*
DAX	−0.178	*2.408*	1.505	*2.962*	*3.032*
SMI	**−3.555**	1.551	0.670	1.799	1.867
HS	−1.066	0.931	−0.906	0.979	1.080
S&P500	0.445	1.049	*2.082*	*2.510*	0.422
MSE loss function, out-of-sample period: 2008					
CAC40	**−2.082**	0.598	0.517	1.166	1.400
DAX	−1.746	0.990	1.347	1.493	1.482
SMI	−1.724	0.890	0.586	1.112	1.219
HS	**−2.013**	0.806	−0.251	1.210	1.436
S&P500	−1.046	1.826	0.574	1.892	1.844
QLIKE loss function, out-of-sample period: 2008					
CAC40	−0.746	1.940	0.765	*2.020*	1.641
DAX	−0.786	*2.570*	0.761	*2.549*	*2.355*
SMI	−0.594	1.734	1.310	1.948	1.865
HS	**−2.934**	1.963	−0.816	*2.015*	*2.048*
S&P500	0.616	*3.246*	*2.036*	*3.346*	*3.025*

The test evaluates the null of zero expected difference between the loss functions of the top row model and bottom row model. The test statistic is standard normal. Significant values (5% confidence level) indicate a preference for the first row model (if negative, in bold) or the second row model (if positive, in italics underlined).

TABLE 8.5 S&P500 Model Confidence Set

	MSE	QL	IF			PIF			AD			SD			ASD			RL
			1%	5%	10%	1%	5%	10%	1%	5%	10%	1%	5%	10%	1%	5%	10%	
Out-of-sample period: 2004																		
G	**0.15**	0.04	**0.31**	**1.00**	**1.00**	**0.27**	**1.00**	**1.00**	**0.16**	**0.19**	**0.27**	**0.24**	**0.28**	**0.33**	**0.24**	**0.27**	**0.30**	**0.69**
GJR	**1.00**	**1.00**	**1.00**	**0.34**	**0.62**	**1.00**	**0.55**	**0.84**	**0.42**	**0.45**	**0.70**	**0.71**	**0.78**	**0.88**	**0.55**	**0.59**	**0.77**	**0.40**
EG	**0.34**	**0.24**	**0.31**	**0.12**	**0.16**	**0.27**	**0.14**	**0.23**	**1.00**	**1.00**	**1.00**	**1.00**	**1.00**	**1.00**	**1.00**	**1.00**	**1.00**	**0.20**
SV	**0.34**	0.07	**0.31**	**0.12**	**0.25**	**0.27**	**0.14**	**0.40**	**0.78**	**0.76**	**0.70**	**0.97**	**0.94**	**0.88**	**0.88**	**0.84**	**0.77**	**1.00**
Out-of-sample period: 2006																		
G	0.06	0.06	**0.17**	0.06	**0.18**	**0.57**	**1.00**	**0.21**	0.02	0.01	0.01	0.02	0.03	0.04	0.02	0.02	0.01	**0.29**
GJR	**1.00**	**1.00**	**0.17**	**1.00**	**0.74**	**0.26**	**0.33**	**1.00**	**0.32**	**0.34**	**0.59**	**0.31**	**0.37**	**0.60**	**0.30**	**0.36**	**0.58**	0.04
EG	0.06	0.06	**1.00**	0.06	**1.00**	**1.00**	**0.33**	**0.94**	0.02	0.01	0.01	0.02	0.03	0.04	0.02	0.02	0.01	**1.00**
SV	0.06	0.06	**0.17**	0.04	0.06	**0.26**	0.08	0.03	**1.00**	**1.00**	**1.00**	**1.00**	**1.00**	**1.00**	**1.00**	**1.00**	**1.00**	0.01
Out-of-sample period: 2008																		
G	**0.27**	0.04	**0.46**	**0.56**	**1.00**	**0.43**	**0.48**	**1.00**	0.04	0.02	0.05	0.08	0.09	0.08	0.07	0.07	0.08	**0.63**
GJR	**1.00**	**1.00**	**1.00**	**1.00**	**0.47**	**1.00**	**1.00**	**0.37**	0.02	0.01	0.05	0.08	0.09	0.08	0.06	0.07	0.08	**1.00**
EG	**0.52**	0.04	0.07	0.04	0.01	0.06	0.03	**0.37**	**1.00**	**1.00**	**1.00**	**1.00**	**1.00**	**1.00**	**1.00**	**1.00**	**1.00**	0.01
SV	**0.22**	0.04	0.07	0.01	0.01	0.06	0.03	**0.12**	**0.73**	**0.41**	**0.26**	**0.47**	**0.27**	**0.11**	**0.54**	**0.39**	**0.15**	0.04

The table reports the model confidence set over different loss functions and periods. G is the GARCH model in Equation 8.1, GJR the model in Equation 8.2, EG the EGARCH model in Equation 8.3, and SV the stochastic volatility model in Equation 8.4. Bold values denote the models that are included at the 10% confidence level in the confidence set (these models are statistically equivalent if compared using the loss function reported in the first and second rows). The loss function QL corresponds to QLIKE in Equation 8.16, the other loss function names correspond to those in Equation 8.15 and Equations 8.25–8.30, and the second row reports the Value-at-Risk confidence level (when needed).

TABLE 8.6 CAC40 Model Confidence Set

	MSE	QL	IF			PIF			AD			SD			ASD			RL
			1%	5%	10%	1%	5%	10%	1%	5%	10%	1%	5%	10%	1%	5%	10%	
Out-of-sample period: 2004																		
G	**0.60**	**0.11**	**0.44**	0.08	**0.12**	**0.87**	**0.76**	**0.21**	0.02	0.02	0.02	0.03	0.04	0.04	0.03	0.02	0.04	**0.30**
GJR	**0.79**	**1.00**	**1.00**	0.08	**0.12**	**1.00**	**0.25**	**0.18**	0.02	0.02	0.03	0.04	0.04	0.04	0.03	0.02	0.04	**0.30**
EG	**1.00**	**0.45**	**0.44**	0.08	0.05	**0.58**	**0.13**	0.08	**1.00**	**1.00**	**1.00**	**1.00**	**1.00**	**1.00**	**1.00**	**1.00**	**1.00**	0.05
SV	**0.60**	**0.11**	**0.44**	**1.00**	**1.00**	**0.87**	**1.00**	**1.00**	0.02	0.02	0.03	0.04	0.04	0.04	0.03	0.02	0.04	**1.00**
Out-of-sample period: 2006																		
G	**0.68**	0.08	**1.00**	**0.63**	**0.79**	**1.00**	**0.68**	**0.94**	**0.11**	**0.31**	**0.12**	**0.24**	**0.28**	**0.43**	**0.15**	**0.30**	**0.24**	**0.78**
GJR	**1.00**	**1.00**	0.06	**1.00**	**1.00**	**0.49**	**1.00**	**1.00**	**0.18**	**0.31**	**0.12**	**0.24**	**0.28**	**0.35**	**0.15**	**0.30**	**0.24**	**1.00**
EG	**0.83**	**0.34**	0.06	**0.49**	**0.70**	**0.40**	**0.37**	**0.94**	**0.20**	**0.47**	**0.92**	**0.24**	**0.31**	**0.53**	**0.22**	**0.38**	**0.70**	**0.20**
SV	**0.38**	0.06	0.02	**0.49**	**0.40**	0.04	**0.37**	**0.44**	**1.00**	**1.00**	**1.00**	**1.00**	**1.00**	**1.00**	**1.00**	**1.00**	**1.00**	**0.10**
Out-of-sample period: 2008																		
G	0.08	**0.11**	**1.00**	**0.22**	**0.43**	**1.00**	**0.40**	**1.00**	0.01	0.01	0.02	0.04	0.04	0.03	0.04	0.03	0.04	**1.00**
GJR	**1.00**	**1.00**	0.05	**1.00**	**1.00**	**0.19**	**1.00**	**0.84**	0.01	0.02	0.02	0.05	0.05	0.05	0.06	0.05	0.04	**0.46**
EG	**0.45**	**0.42**	0.01	**0.13**	0.08	0.01	0.08	**0.73**	**1.00**	**1.00**	**1.00**	**1.00**	**1.00**	**1.00**	**1.00**	**1.00**	**1.00**	0.02
SV	**0.14**	**0.11**	0.05	**0.13**	0.04	0.09	0.08	**0.61**	**0.85**	**0.58**	**0.29**	**0.57**	**0.24**	0.05	**0.65**	**0.32**	**0.11**	0.02

The table reports the model confidence set over different loss functions and periods. G is the GARCH model in Equation 8.1, GJR the model in Equation 8.2, EG the EGARCH model in Equation 8.3, and SV the stochastic volatility model in Equation 8.4. Bold values denote the models that are included at the 10% confidence level in the confidence set (these models are statistically equivalent if compared using the loss function reported in the first and second rows). The loss function QL corresponds to QLIKE in Equation 8.16, the other loss function names correspond to those in Eqaution (8.15) and Equations 8.25–8.30, and the second row reports the Value-at-Risk confidence level (when needed).

TABLE 8.7 DAX Model Confidence Set

			IF			PIF			AD			SD			ASD			
	MSE	QL	1%	5%	10%	1%	5%	10%	1%	5%	10%	1%	5%	10%	1%	5%	10%	RL
Out-of-sample period: 2004																		
G	**0.26**	0.00	**0.70**	**1.00**	**1.00**	**0.90**	**1.00**	**1.00**	0.00	0.00	0.00	0.00	0.01	0.00	0.00	0.00	0.00	**0.93**
GJR	**0.26**	**0.54**	**0.30**	**0.55**	**0.22**	**0.81**	**0.64**	**0.11**	0.00	0.00	0.00	0.00	0.01	0.00	0.00	0.00	0.00	**0.93**
EG	**1.00**	**1.00**	**0.70**	0.02	**0.22**	**0.90**	0.01	**0.27**	**1.00**	**1.00**	**1.00**	**1.00**	**1.00**	**1.00**	**1.00**	**1.00**	**1.00**	0.05
SV	**0.26**	0.00	**1.00**	**0.55**	**0.22**	**1.00**	**0.64**	**0.11**	**0.36**	**0.30**	**0.17**	**0.55**	**0.49**	**0.37**	**0.51**	**0.40**	**0.26**	**1.00**
Out-of-sample period: 2006																		
G	**0.43**	0.08	0.06	**0.39**	**0.80**	**0.48**	**0.38**	**0.95**	0.04	**0.20**	**0.60**	**0.18**	**0.35**	**0.70**	**0.10**	**0.25**	**0.65**	**0.65**
GJR	**1.00**	**1.00**	0.06	**1.00**	**0.43**	**1.00**	**1.00**	**0.43**	0.04	**0.20**	**0.68**	**0.18**	**0.35**	**0.70**	**0.10**	**0.25**	**0.66**	**1.00**
EG	**0.13**	0.08	**1.00**	**0.39**	**1.00**	**0.17**	**0.38**	**1.00**	0.04	**0.20**	**0.68**	**0.18**	**0.35**	**0.70**	**0.10**	**0.25**	**0.66**	**0.39**
SV	**0.12**	0.01	0.06	**0.10**	**0.10**	**0.17**	**0.10**	**0.14**	**1.00**	**1.00**	**1.00**	**1.00**	**1.00**	**1.00**	**1.00**	**1.00**	**1.00**	0.03
Out-of-sample period: 2008																		
G	**0.10**	**0.10**	**0.69**	0.02	**1.00**	**0.70**	**0.13**	**0.74**	0.00	0.01	0.01	0.02	0.04	0.04	0.01	0.01	0.04	**1.00**
GJR	**1.00**	**1.00**	**1.00**	**1.00**	**0.69**	**1.00**	**1.00**	**1.00**	0.00	0.01	0.01	0.02	0.03	0.04	0.01	0.01	0.04	**0.40**
EG	**0.14**	**0.54**	**0.43**	0.01	0.04	**0.26**	0.02	**0.46**	0.03	**0.13**	**0.71**	0.02	**0.42**	**1.00**	0.01	**0.26**	**1.00**	0.02
SV	**0.10**	0.05	0.01	0.00	0.03	0.05	0.02	**0.34**	**1.00**	**1.00**	**1.00**	**1.00**	**1.00**	**0.33**	**1.00**	**1.00**	**0.49**	0.01

The table reports the Model Confidence Set over different loss functions and periods. G is the GARCH model in Equation 8.1, GJR the model in Equation 8.2, EG the EGARCH model in Equation 8.3, and SV the stochastic volatility model in Equation 8.4. Bold values denote the models that are included at the 10% confidence level in the confidence set (these models are statistically equivalent if compared using the loss function reported in the first and second rows). The loss function QL corresponds to QLIKE in Equation 8.16, the other loss function names correspond to those in Equation 8.15 and Equations 8.25–8.30, and the second row reports the Value-at-Risk confidence level (when needed).

TABLE 8.8 SMI Model Confidence Set

	MSE	QL	IF			PIF			AD			SD			ASD			RL
			1%	5%	10%	1%	5%	10%	1%	5%	10%	1%	5%	10%	1%	5%	10%	
Out-of-sample period: 2004																		
G	**1.00**	**0.95**	**0.14**	**1.00**	**0.80**	**0.22**	**1.00**	**0.82**	**0.69**	**0.69**	**0.81**	**0.98**	**0.98**	**0.95**	**0.93**	**0.91**	**0.81**	**0.94**
GJR	**0.43**	**1.00**	**0.14**	**0.44**	**1.00**	**1.00**	**0.46**	**1.00**	**0.69**	**0.69**	**0.81**	**0.71**	**0.71**	**0.79**	**0.67**	**0.70**	**0.79**	**0.46**
EG	**0.49**	**0.95**	**1.00**	**0.66**	**0.51**	**0.22**	**0.61**	**0.49**	**1.00**	**1.00**	**1.00**	**1.00**	**1.00**	**1.00**	**1.00**	**1.00**	**1.00**	0.09
SV	**0.43**	0.06	**0.14**	**0.66**	**0.51**	**0.22**	**0.58**	**0.49**	**0.78**	**0.74**	**0.81**	**0.98**	**0.98**	**0.95**	**0.93**	**0.91**	**0.79**	**1.00**
Out-of-sample period: 2006																		
G	**0.31**	0.00	**0.20**	**0.41**	**1.00**	**0.19**	**0.39**	**1.00**	0.03	0.01	0.02	0.07	0.06	**0.18**	0.05	0.03	0.05	**0.71**
GJR	**0.78**	**1.00**	**1.00**	**1.00**	**0.33**	**1.00**	**1.00**	**0.37**	**0.12**	**0.15**	**0.24**	**0.15**	**0.19**	**0.25**	**0.16**	**0.17**	**0.23**	**1.00**
EG	**1.00**	**0.57**	**0.20**	**0.41**	**0.33**	**0.20**	**0.39**	**0.37**	**0.12**	**0.16**	**0.26**	**0.15**	**0.19**	**0.39**	**0.16**	**0.17**	**0.30**	**0.22**
SV	**0.31**	0.00	**0.18**	**0.25**	**0.33**	**0.16**	**0.22**	**0.29**	**1.00**	**1.00**	**1.00**	**1.00**	**1.00**	**1.00**	**1.00**	**1.00**	**1.00**	0.05
Out-of-sample period: 2008																		
G	**0.14**	**0.14**	**0.28**	**0.86**	**0.93**	**0.42**	**1.00**	**1.00**	0.02	0.02	0.01	0.09	0.04	0.06	0.06	0.04	0.03	**1.00**
GJR	**1.00**	**1.00**	**1.00**	**0.46**	**1.00**	**1.00**	**0.68**	**0.98**	0.02	0.02	0.01	0.08	0.04	0.06	0.06	0.04	0.03	**0.64**
EG	**0.52**	**0.15**	**0.15**	**0.18**	**0.13**	0.06	**0.18**	**0.29**	**1.00**	**1.00**	**1.00**	**1.00**	**1.00**	**1.00**	**1.00**	**1.00**	**1.00**	0.03
SV	**0.21**	**0.14**	**0.15**	**1.00**	**0.93**	0.06	**0.60**	**0.79**	**0.19**	0.02	0.01	**0.24**	0.04	0.06	**0.22**	0.04	0.03	**0.48**

The table reports the model confidence set over different loss functions and periods. G is the GARCH model in Equation 8.1, GJR the model in Equation 8.2, EG the EGARCH model in Equation 8.3, and SV the stochastic volatility model in Equation 8.4. Bold values denote the models that are included at the 10% confidence level in the confidence set (these models are statistically equivalent if compared using the loss function reported in the first and second rows). The loss function QL corresponds to QLIKE in Equation 8.16, the other loss function names correspond to those in Equation 8.15 and Equations 8.25–8.30, and the second row reports the Value-at-Risk confidence level (when needed).

TABLE 8.9 HS Model Confidence Set

	MSE	QL	IF			PIF			AD			SD			ASD			RL
			1%	5%	10%	1%	5%	10%	1%	5%	10%	1%	5%	10%	1%	5%	10%	
Out-of-sample period: 2004																		
G	**0.36**	0.07	**0.69**	**0.71**	**1.00**	**0.74**	**0.77**	**1.00**	**0.28**	**0.47**	**0.46**	**0.39**	**0.43**	**0.42**	**0.31**	**0.43**	**0.46**	**1.00**
GJR	**0.45**	**0.76**	**0.31**	**0.83**	**0.43**	**0.70**	**1.00**	**0.13**	**0.28**	**0.47**	**0.46**	**0.39**	**0.43**	**0.42**	**0.31**	**0.43**	**0.46**	**0.55**
EG	**1.00**	**1.00**	**0.31**	**0.71**	**0.43**	**0.70**	**0.67**	**0.57**	**0.86**	**1.00**	**1.00**	**0.74**	**0.81**	**0.93**	**0.77**	**0.95**	**1.00**	**0.18**
SV	**0.41**	0.07	**1.00**	**1.00**	**0.43**	**1.00**	**0.81**	**0.13**	**1.00**	**0.85**	**0.82**	**1.00**	**1.00**	**1.00**	**1.00**	**1.00**	**0.92**	**0.10**
Out-of-sample period: 2006																		
G	**0.27**	**0.70**	**0.16**	**0.67**	0.01	**0.57**	**0.70**	**0.68**	0.01	0.01	0.02	0.03	0.03	0.02	0.01	0.01	0.03	**0.46**
GJR	**0.27**	**0.70**	**0.16**	**1.00**	0.01	**0.57**	**1.00**	**0.68**	0.01	0.01	0.02	0.03	0.03	0.02	0.01	0.01	0.03	**1.00**
EG	**1.00**	**1.00**	**1.00**	**0.67**	**1.00**	**1.00**	**0.70**	**1.00**	0.01	0.00	0.02	0.03	0.02	0.01	0.01	0.01	0.01	**0.74**
SV	**0.27**	**0.70**	**0.16**	**0.67**	0.01	**0.38**	**0.70**	0.02	**1.00**	**1.00**	**1.00**	**1.00**	**1.00**	**1.00**	**1.00**	**1.00**	**1.00**	0.02
Out-of-sample period: 2008																		
G	**0.24**	0.01	**0.31**	**1.00**	**0.81**	**0.13**	**1.00**	**0.26**	0.00	0.00	0.01	0.04	0.04	0.03	0.01	0.02	0.02	**1.00**
GJR	**0.73**	**0.36**	**1.00**	**0.19**	**1.00**	**1.00**	**0.93**	**1.00**	0.00	0.00	0.01	0.04	0.04	0.07	0.02	0.02	0.05	**0.20**
EG	**1.00**	**1.00**	**0.31**	**0.19**	**0.81**	**0.24**	**0.57**	**0.40**	0.00	0.00	0.01	0.04	0.04	**0.63**	0.02	0.02	**0.36**	0.03
SV	**0.24**	0.01	0.04	0.00	0.00	**0.13**	0.03	**0.10**	**1.00**	**1.00**	**1.00**	**1.00**	**1.00**	**1.00**	**1.00**	**1.00**	**1.00**	0.00

The table reports the Model Confidence Set over different loss functions and periods. G is the GARCH model in Equation 8.1, GJR the model in Equation 8.2, EG the EGARCH model in Equation 8.3, and SV the stochastic volatility model in Equation 8.4. Bold values denote the models that are included at the 10% confidence level in the confidence set (these models are statistically equivalent if compared using the loss function reported in the first and second rows). The loss function QL corresponds to QLIKE in Equation 8.16, the other loss function names correspond to those in Equation 8.15 and Equations 8.25–8.30, and the second row reports the Value-at-Risk confidence level (when needed).

report the MCS results based on the t_R statistic in Equation 8.20 for selected out-of-sample periods. The results for the statistic SQ are equivalent and are not reported (the entire set of results is available from the authors on request).

For each stock market index, we evaluate the four alternative models by using the MSE and QLIKE loss functions as well as the loss functions defined in Equations 8.25–8.30.

If we consider the S&P500 index (Table 8.5), the results differ across the out-of-sample evaluation periods. In 2004, all models are equivalent as they are all included in the confidence set independently of the loss function used for their evaluation. For 2006, some differences appear across the loss functions. For MSE and QLIKE, the optimal model is GJR-GARCH; IF and PIF exclude, in most cases, SV from the confidence set; AD, SD, and ASD suggest that the optimal models are GJR-GARCH and SV; finally, RL prefers the GARCH and EGARCH specifications. In summary, there is not a clear preference for a specific model. Model preference depends on the loss function under consideration and on the sample period used for model evaluation.

The last finding may be interpreted as confirmation of the in-sample and direct model comparison outcomes, which did not provide a clear indication of a single model. This interpretation is corroborated by the 2008 results for the S&P500 index: MSE considers all models as equivalent; QLIKE prefers GJR; IF, PIF, and RL indicate a preference for GARCH and GJR-GARCH; while AD, SD, and ASD suggest that the optimal models are EGARCH and SV.

Similar patterns are observed for the other stock market indices in that all models are equivalent under some specific out-of-sample periods and with model preferences changing with respect to the loss function used. Some behavior is, however, common. When the MCS includes fewer models than those that are available, the statistically equivalent models generally differ between the IF–PIF–RL loss functions and the AD–SD–ASD loss functions. The former indicate a preference for GARCH and GJR-GARCH, while the latter tend to support EGARCH and SV.

Thus, it seems that the second set of loss functions has a preference for more flexible models. Such behavior may depend on the structure of the loss functions themselves: AD and SD (and hence also ASD) monitor the entire evolution of conditional variances without focusing on the exceptions or without penalizing VaR with respect to past violations. The inevitable conclusion to be drawn is that when we give a large relevance to volatility spikes, most models appear relevant, and simple specifications may perform as well as their more flexible counterparts. If we consider the evolution over time of the conditional volatility, then more flexible models are to be preferred.

8.4 Conclusion

In this chapter, we reviewed some existing methods for model selection and testing of nonnested univariate volatility models. We first considered in-sample methods, such as nested and nonnested hypothesis testing, and diagnostic checking procedures (such as Ljung–Box and distributional hypotheses). We then focused on out-of-sample approaches based on model forecast evaluation. Starting from the traditional MSE and MAE criteria, we considered more general loss functions based on VaR forecasts, compared by means of the MCS approach. Finally, we presented an empirical example using the less common approaches for model comparison, namely nonnested hypothesis testing and VaR-based loss functions.

This chapter was based on simple univariate specifications focusing on volatility asymmetry and leverage. The proposed loss function approaches can easily be used on the forecasts produced by other univariate specifications as well as multivariate models.

PART TWO

Other Models and Methods

CHAPTER NINE

Multiplicative Error Models

CHRISTIAN T. BROWNLEES,
FABRIZIO CIPOLLINI, and GIAMPIERO M. GALLO

9.1 Introduction

Multiplicative error models (MEMs) are born out of the availability of financial data at a very fine detail. Examples are durations between trades or quotes, number of trades and volumes, number of buys and sells within (possibly fine) intervals, and volatility measures derived from ultrahigh frequency data (and measures of jumps) as detailed in the Part 3 of this handbook. All these variables share the feature of being nonnegative valued and exhibiting persistence features similarly to returns' variance modeled as GARCH. MEMs were first introduced as autoregressive conditional duration (ACD) models by Engle and Russell (1998) and were generalized to any nonnegative valued process by Engle (2002b). Early work is by Chou (2005) (for range) and Manganelli (2005) (in a multivariate setting).

In a univariate setting, the simplest MEM expresses the dynamics of the variable of interest as the product of two nonnegative terms, namely, a scale factor (evolving in a conditionally autoregressive way paralleling GARCH specifications) and an i.i.d. error term with unit mean. Thus, the scale factor represents the expectation of the process conditionally on the available information, and, as such, it can be used for forecasting purposes.

Handbook of Volatility Models and Their Applications, First Edition.
Edited by Luc Bauwens, Christian Hafner, and Sebastien Laurent.

There are several reasons why a direct specification of the dynamics of the variables is preferable to taking logarithms and adopt a linear model. There could be zeros in the data; even nonzero but small values may have a severe impact on estimation in a logarithmic model; deriving direct forecasts for the variable of interest is better than transforming forecasts expressed in logs; finally, as we will see in what follows, under nonrestrictive assumptions, the proposed estimator of the parameters in the conditional mean can be interpreted as a quasi-maximum likelihood estimator.

This chapter is structured as follows. In Section 9.2, we introduce the univariate specification, discussing the base choices for the conditional expectation and the error term. In the same section, we provide a general framework, allowing for richer specifications of the conditional mean. The outcome is a novel MEM (called *Composite MEM*), which is reminiscent of the short- and long-run component GARCH model by Engle and Lee (1999). Inference issues are discussed relative to maximum likelihood (ML) and generalized method of moments (GMM) estimation. Section 9.3 handles a univariate application with several kernel realized volatilities computed on Blue Chips traded on the NYSE. The estimated models are evaluated on the basis of the residual diagnostics and forecast performance. Section 9.4 briefly discusses some extensions handling the presence of components in the conditional mean with a different dynamics and multivariate extensions. Concluding remarks form the last section.

9.2 Theory and Methodology

9.2.1 MODEL FORMULATION

Let $\{x_t\}$ be a discrete time process defined on $[0, +\infty)$, $t \in \mathbb{N}$, and let $\mathcal{F}_{t-1}$ be the information available for forecasting x_t.[1] $\{x_t\}$ follows an MEM if it can be expressed as

$$x_t = \mu_t \varepsilon_t, \tag{9.1}$$

where, conditionally on $\mathcal{F}_{t-1}$: μ_t is a positive quantity that evolves deterministically according to a parameter vector $\boldsymbol{\theta}$,

$$\mu_t = \mu(\boldsymbol{\theta}, \mathcal{F}_{t-1}); \tag{9.2}$$

ε_t is a random variable (rv) with probability density function (pdf) defined over a $[0, +\infty)$ support, unit mean, and unknown constant variance,

$$\varepsilon_t | \mathcal{F}_{t-1} \sim D^+(1, \sigma^2). \tag{9.3}$$

[1]The occurrence of zeros is relevant for some financial variables observed at a very high frequency; for example, fixed short intervals or illiquid assets may deliver zero volumes; large trades against small orders may correspond to zero durations; and absolute returns may also be zero. Hautsch et al. (2010) discuss the issue at length.

Irrespective of the specification of the function $\mu(\cdot)$ and of the distribution D^+, Equations 9.1–9.3 entail (Engle, 2002b)

$$E(x_t|\mathcal{F}_{t-1}) = \mu_t \tag{9.4}$$

$$V(x_t|\mathcal{F}_{t-1}) = \sigma^2\mu_t^2. \tag{9.5}$$

9.2.1.1 Specifications for μ_t. Any practical specification of $\mu(\cdot)$ in Equation 9.2 depends on the available information $\mathcal{F}_{t-1}$: in what follows, we list some examples. In order to simplify the exposition, we discuss formulations including only one lag, at most, of the lagged effects appearing in the right-hand sides. Richer structures, useful in some applications, can be obtained in a trivial way.

When $\mathcal{F}_{t-1}$ includes only past values of the series, μ_t can be specified as

$$\mu_t = \omega + \beta_1\mu_{t-1} + \alpha_1 x_{t-1}, \tag{9.6}$$

which we label as baseline MEM model. The term $\beta_1\mu_{t-1}$ represents an inertial component, whereas $\alpha_1 x_{t-1}$ stands for the contribution of the more recent observation. Alternative representations are possible: defining the forecast error in the tth observation as $v_t = x_t - \mu_t$ and $\beta_1^* = \beta_1 + \alpha_1$, we can write

$$x_t = \omega + \beta_1^* x_{t-1} + v_t - \beta_1 v_{t-1},$$

which is an ARMA representation (with heteroskedastic errors).

Sometimes, an observed signed variable determines different dynamics in x_t according to its (lagged) sign. For example, we may want to consider lagged returns (e.g., r_{t-1}) in $\mathcal{F}_{t-1}$ and define $x_t^{(-)} \equiv x_t \mathrm{I}(r_t < 0)$, where $\mathrm{I}(\cdot)$ denotes the indicator function. To this end, we will assume that, conditionally on $\mathcal{F}_{t-1}$, r_t has a zero median and is uncorrelated with x_t: this implies $E(x_t^{(-)}|\mathcal{F}_{t-1}) = \mu_t/2$. Accordingly, μ_t can be specified as

$$\mu_t = \omega + \beta_1\mu_{t-1} + \alpha_1 x_{t-1} + \gamma_1 x_{t-1}^{(-)}, \tag{9.7}$$

which we refer to as the *Asymmetric MEM*. In applications where market microstructure is of interest, another relevant variable is signed trades where the sign can be attributed on the basis of whether they are "buy" or "sell."

If $\{x_t\}$ is mean stationary, then $E(x_t) = E(\mu_t) \equiv \mu$. In such a case, by taking the expectation of both members of Equation 9.7, one obtains

$$\omega = \mu - (\beta_1 + \alpha_1 + \gamma_1/2)\,\mu, \tag{9.8}$$

which is interesting for at least two reasons. The first one is related to inference. If μ is estimated by means of the unconditional mean $\bar{x}$, then ω is removed from the optimization algorithm and can be estimated in a second step by means of Equation 9.8, once estimates of α_1, γ_1, and β_1 are obtained. This strategy, that we can name *expectation targeting*, parallels the *variance targeting* approach within the GARCH framework proposed by Engle and Mezrich (1996) and investigated by Kristensen and Linton (2004) and Francq et al. (2009) from a theoretical point of view. The second reason deals with model interpretation. By means of Equation 9.8, Equation 9.7 can be rewritten as

$$\mu_t = \mu + \xi_t$$
$$\xi_t = \beta_1 \xi_{t-1} + \alpha_1 x_{t-1}^{(\xi)} + \gamma_1 x_{t-1}^{(\xi -)}, \tag{9.9}$$

where

$$x_t^{(\xi)} = x_t - \mu \qquad x_t^{(\xi -)} = x_t^{(-)} - \mu/2,$$

which shows μ_t as the sum of a long-run average level, μ, and a zero-mean stationary component, ξ_t, driven by the past values of the series (with asymmetries).

Such a representation inspires further formulations of the conditional mean, constructed by replacing the constant average level μ by time-varying structures. Considering the simplest case of just one time-varying component χ_t in the place of μ, the dynamics is given by

$$\mu_t = \chi_t + \xi_t, \tag{9.10}$$

with ξ_t defined in Equation 9.9 and, this time,

$$x_t^{(\xi)} = x_t - \chi_t \qquad x_t^{(\xi -)} = x_t^{(-)} - \chi_t/2. \tag{9.11}$$

Let us consider some possible choices for χ_t. In the presence of deterministic or predetermined variables ($\mathcal{F}_{t-1}$ is extended to include other indicators, calendar variables, etc. denoted as $\boldsymbol{z}_t$), we can write

$$\chi_t = \omega^{(\chi)} + \boldsymbol{\delta}' \boldsymbol{z}_t. \tag{9.12}$$

A direct inclusion of the $\boldsymbol{\delta}'\boldsymbol{z}_t$ term into the expression (Eq. 9.7) of the conditional mean may entail unwanted persistence effects, whereby a large value of $\boldsymbol{\delta}'\boldsymbol{z}_t$ would increase μ_t, driving the following values of the conditional mean. By contrast, expression (Eq. 9.12) allows for the distinct identification of the contribution of the past observations of x_t (together with asymmetric effects), keeping it separate from the predetermined variable(s), and preserving also its mean stationarity.

The second extension, inspired to Brownlees and Gallo (2010), is useful when the data show a pattern evolving around some slow moving trend. In such a case, χ_t can be structured as a smooth spline function, say (omitting technical details) $s(t)$. The methodology introduced by Engle and Rangel (2008) in the GARCH context lends itself to capturing an underlying average volatility that is not constant.

As an alternative to splines, but in the same vein as the component GARCH model proposed by Engle and Lee (1999) (see also Andersen et al. (2006, p. 806)), we suggest here a third type of specification, in which we specify the long-run component as

$$\chi_t = \omega^{(\chi)} + \beta_1^{(\chi)} \chi_{t-1} + \alpha_1^{(\chi)} x_{t-1}^{(\chi)}, \tag{9.13}$$

where

$$x_t^{(\chi)} = x_t - \xi_t. \tag{9.14}$$

We can reparameterize the short- and the long-run dynamics of the model, Equations 9.9 and 9.13, respectively, as

$$\begin{aligned}\xi_t &= \beta_1^* \xi_{t-1} + \alpha_1 v_{t-1} + \gamma_1 v_{t-1}^{(-)} \\ \chi_t &= \omega^{(\chi)} + \beta_1^{(\chi)*} \chi_{t-1} + \alpha_1^{(\chi)} v_{t-1},\end{aligned} \tag{9.15}$$

where

$$v_t = x_t - \mu_t \qquad v_t^{(-)} = x_t^{(-)} - \mu_t/2. \tag{9.16}$$

$\beta_1^* = \beta_1 + \alpha_1 + \gamma_1/2$ and $\beta_1^{(\chi)*} = \beta_1^{(\chi)} + \alpha_1^{(\chi)}$. This expression of the conditional mean emphasizes the role of the innovations v_t as the driving force behind μ_t, in both the short- and long-run components ξ_t and χ_t which can be interpreted as such only if we identify the model (on the interchangeability of the two components, cf. Engle and Lee (1999, p. 478)) by imposing

$$\beta_1^* < \beta_1^{(\chi)*}. \tag{9.17}$$

We name this model an Asymmetric *Composite* MEM[2] with the possibility to constrain γ_1 to be zero.

By following Lütkepohl (2005, Section 11.6), the conditional mean of such a model has the MEM-like representation

$$\begin{aligned}\mu_t = \omega^{(\mu)} &+ \beta_1^{(\mu)} \mu_{t-1} + \beta_2^{(\mu)} \mu_{t-2} \\ &+ \alpha_1^{(\mu)} x_{t-1} + \alpha_2^{(\mu)} x_{t-2} + \gamma_1^{(\mu)} x_{t-1}^{(-)} + \gamma_2^{(\mu)} x_{t-2}^{(-)},\end{aligned} \tag{9.18}$$

where

$$\begin{aligned}&\omega^{(\mu)} = (1 - \beta_1^*)\omega^{(\chi)} \qquad \alpha_1^{(\mu)} = \alpha_1 + \alpha_1^{(\chi)} \qquad \gamma_1^{(\mu)} = \gamma_1, \\ &\alpha_2^{(\mu)} = -(\beta_1^* \alpha_1^{(\chi)} + \beta_1^{(\chi)*} \alpha_1) \qquad \gamma_2^{(\mu)} = -\beta_1^{(\chi)*} \gamma_1, \\ &\beta_1^{(\mu)} = \beta_1^* + \beta_1^{(\chi)*} - \alpha_1^{(\mu)} - \gamma_1^{(\mu)}/2 \qquad \beta_2^{(\mu)} = -\beta_1^* \beta_1^{(\chi)*} - \alpha_2^{(\mu)} - \gamma_2^{(\mu)}/2.\end{aligned}$$

---

[2]We prefer the term *Composite*, since the *Component* MEM is one in which the dynamics of the conditional mean originates from elements entering multiplicatively in the specification: cf. for example, the MEM for intradaily volume in Brownlees et al. (2011a), discussed later in Section 9.4.

By means of Equation 9.18, necessary and sufficient conditions for $\mu_t \geq 0$ can be expressed, by following Nelson and Cao (1992, Section 2.2), as $\omega^{(\mu)} \geq 0$, $\alpha_1^* \geq 0$,

$$
\begin{aligned}
& -1 \leq \beta_2^{(\mu)} < 0,\ 2\sqrt{-\beta_2^{(\mu)}} \leq \beta_1^{(\mu)} < 1 - \beta_2^{(\mu)}, \\
& \beta_1^{(\mu)}\alpha_2^* + \left(\beta_1^{(\mu)2} + \beta_2^{(\mu)}\right)\alpha_1^* \geq 0,
\end{aligned}
$$

or

$$
0 \leq \beta_2^{(\mu)} < 1, \quad 0 \leq \beta_1^{(\mu)} < 1 - \beta_2^{(\mu)}, \quad \beta_1^{(\mu)}\alpha_2^* + \alpha_1^* \geq 0,
$$

where α_l^* indicate both $\alpha_l^{(\mu)}$ and $\alpha_l^{(\mu)} + \gamma_l^{(\mu)}$, $l = 1, 2$.

Stationarity conditions can be obtained by adapting the Corollary 2.2 (and the subsequent remark) in Bougerol and Picard (1992): if all the coefficients in (9.18) are nonnegative and $\beta_1^{(\mu)*} + \beta_2^{(\mu)*} \leq 1$ (where $\beta_l^{(\mu)*} = \beta_l^{(\mu)} + \alpha_l^{(\mu)} - \gamma_l^{(\mu)}/2$, $l = 1, 2$), then the Composite MEM (CM) is strictly stationary. A better insight can be gained by rewriting such a condition as $(1 - \beta_1^{(\chi)})(1 - \beta_1^*) \geq 0$: we note immediately that the Composite MEM is strictly stationary if $\beta_1^{(\chi)*}$, $\beta_1^* \leq 1$. If $\beta_1^{(\chi)}$, $\beta_1^{(\xi)} < 1$, then the process is also second-order stationary; otherwise if $\beta_1^{(\chi)*} = 1$ (remembering the identification condition (Eq. 9.17)), then the model is strictly stationary but not second-order stationary. Note that conditions in this discussion are weaker than in Engle and Lee (1999).

9.2.1.2 Specifications for $\boldsymbol{\varepsilon_t}$.

In principle, the conditional distribution of the error term ε_t can be specified by means of any pdf having the characteristics in Equation 9.3. Examples include gamma, log-normal, Weibull, inverted-gamma, and mixtures of them. Engle and Gallo (2006) favor a *Gamma*(ϕ, ϕ) (implying $\sigma^2 = 1/\phi$); Bauwens and Giot (2000), in an ACD framework, consider a *Weibull* $(\Gamma(1+\phi)^{-1}, \phi)$ (in this case, $\sigma^2 = \Gamma(1+2\phi)/\Gamma(1+\phi)^2 - 1$). De Luca and Gallo (2010) investigate (possibly time-varying) mixtures, while Lanne (2006) adopts mixtures and a conditional expectation specification with time-varying parameters.

An alternative strategy, leading to a semiparametric specification of the model, is to leave the distribution unspecified, except for the two conditional moments in Equation 9.3.

9.2.2 INFERENCE

9.2.2.1 Maximum Likelihood Inference.

We describe ML inference by assuming an MEM formulated as in Section 9.2.1, where ε_t has a conditional pdf expressed in generic terms by $f_\varepsilon(\varepsilon_t|\mathcal{F}_{t-1})$ (we suppress the dependence on parameters).

Because of such assumptions, $f_x(x_t|\mathcal{F}_{t-1}) = f_\varepsilon(x_t/\mu_t|\mathcal{F}_{t-1})/\mu_t$ so that the average log-likelihood function is

$$\bar{l}_T = T^{-1}\sum_{t=1}^{T} l_t = T^{-1}\sum_{t=1}^{T}\left[\ln f_\varepsilon(\varepsilon_t|\mathcal{F}_{t-1}) + \ln \varepsilon_t - \ln x_t\right],$$

where $\varepsilon_t = x_t/\mu_t$. The portions relative to $\boldsymbol{\theta}$ of the average score function, the average outer product of gradients (OPG), and the average Hessian are thus given by,

$$\bar{\boldsymbol{s}}_T = T^{-1}\sum_{t=1}^{T}\nabla_{\boldsymbol{\theta}} l_t = -T^{-1}\sum_{t=1}^{T}(\varepsilon_t b_t + 1)\boldsymbol{a}_t, \tag{9.19}$$

$$\bar{\boldsymbol{I}}_T = T^{-1}\sum_{t=1}^{T}\nabla_{\boldsymbol{\theta}} l_t \nabla_{\boldsymbol{\theta}'} l_t = T^{-1}\sum_{t=1}^{T}(\varepsilon_t b_t + 1)^2 \boldsymbol{a}_t \boldsymbol{a}_t', \tag{9.20}$$

$$\overline{\boldsymbol{H}}_T = T^{-1}\sum_{t=1}^{T}\nabla_{\boldsymbol{\theta}\boldsymbol{\theta}'} l_t = T^{-1}\sum_{t=1}^{T}\left[\varepsilon_t\left(b_t + \varepsilon_t \nabla_{\varepsilon_t} b_t\right)\boldsymbol{a}_t\boldsymbol{a}_t' - (\varepsilon_t b_t + 1)\nabla_{\boldsymbol{\theta}}\boldsymbol{a}_t'\right], \tag{9.21}$$

respectively, where

$$\boldsymbol{a}_t = \frac{1}{\mu_t}\nabla_{\boldsymbol{\theta}}\mu_t,$$
$$b_t = \nabla_{\varepsilon_t}\ln f_\varepsilon(\varepsilon_t|\mathcal{F}_{t-1}).$$

It is worth discussing the case when ε_t is taken to be conditionally distributed as *Gamma*(ϕ,ϕ) (Section 9.2.1.2). In such a case,

$$b_t = \frac{\phi - 1}{\varepsilon_t} - \phi \qquad \Rightarrow \qquad \varepsilon_t b_t + 1 = \phi(1 - \varepsilon_t), \tag{9.22}$$

and

$$\nabla_{\boldsymbol{\theta}} l_t = \phi(\varepsilon_t - 1)\boldsymbol{a}_t. \tag{9.23}$$

Plugging this result into Equations 9.17–9.19, one obtains the corresponding expressions for the three objects. In particular, the resulting average score

$$\bar{\boldsymbol{s}}_T = \phi T^{-1}\sum_{t=1}^{T}(\varepsilon_t - 1)\boldsymbol{a}_t, \tag{9.24}$$

leads to the first-order condition

$$\sum_{t=1}^{T}(\varepsilon_t - 1)\boldsymbol{a}_t = \boldsymbol{0}. \tag{9.25}$$

As a consequence, the solution $\widehat{\boldsymbol{\theta}}_T^{(ML)}$ does not depend on the dispersion parameter ϕ. This result also allows for a computational trick based on the similarity between an MEM and a GARCH model and the fact that any choice for ϕ leads to identical point estimates. Given that μ_t is the conditional expectation of x_t, its parameters can be estimated by specifying a GARCH for the conditional second moment of $\sqrt{x_t}$ while imposing its conditional mean to be 0. The wide availability of GARCH estimation routines (usually based on a normal distribution assumption) made this shortcut fairly convenient at the early stage of diffusion of MEMs: in fact, the point was raised by Engle and Russell (1998) for the case of the exponential ($\phi = 1$) in the context of ACDs but was then shown by Engle and Gallo (2006) to be valid for any other value ϕ.[3]

Moreover, under a correct specification of μ_t, Equation 9.24 guarantees that the expected score is 0 even when the *Gamma*(ϕ, ϕ) is not the true distribution of the error term. Note also that

$$E\left(\nabla_{\boldsymbol{\theta}} l_t \nabla_{\boldsymbol{\theta}'} l_t\right) = E\left(\phi^2 (\varepsilon_t - 1)^2 \boldsymbol{a}_t \boldsymbol{a}_t'\right) = \phi^2 \sigma^2 \boldsymbol{a}_t \boldsymbol{a}_t'$$

and

$$E\left(\nabla_{\boldsymbol{\theta}\boldsymbol{\theta}'} l_t\right) = E\left(-\phi \varepsilon_t \boldsymbol{a}_t \boldsymbol{a}_t' + \phi(\varepsilon_t - 1)\nabla_{\boldsymbol{\theta}} \boldsymbol{a}_t\right) = -\phi \boldsymbol{a}_t \boldsymbol{a}_t'.$$

As per Equations 9.20 and 9.21, Equation 9.22 leads to the corresponding limiting expressions,

$$\overline{\boldsymbol{I}}_\infty = \lim_{T\to\infty} \left[T^{-1} \sum_{t=1}^{T} E\left(\nabla_{\boldsymbol{\theta}} l_t \nabla_{\boldsymbol{\theta}'} l_t\right) \right] = \phi^2 \sigma^2 \boldsymbol{A}$$

$$\overline{\boldsymbol{H}}_\infty = \lim_{T\to\infty} \left[T^{-1} \sum_{t=1}^{T} E\left(\nabla_{\boldsymbol{\theta}\boldsymbol{\theta}'} l_t\right) \right] = -\phi \boldsymbol{A},$$

where

$$\boldsymbol{A} = \lim_{T\to\infty} \left[T^{-1} \sum_{t=1}^{T} E\left(\boldsymbol{a}_t \boldsymbol{a}_t'\right) \right].$$

Correspondingly, the OPG, Hessian, and Sandwich versions of the asymptotic variance matrix are,

$$\begin{aligned} \text{avar}_I(\widehat{\boldsymbol{\theta}}_T^{(\text{ML})}) &= \phi^{-2} \sigma^{-2} \boldsymbol{A}^{-1} \\ \text{avar}_H(\widehat{\boldsymbol{\theta}}_T^{(\text{ML})}) &= \phi^{-1} \boldsymbol{A}^{-1} \\ \text{avar}_S(\widehat{\boldsymbol{\theta}}_T^{(\text{ML})}) &= \sigma^2 \boldsymbol{A}^{-1}, \end{aligned} \tag{9.26}$$

respectively.

---

[3]However, the code for a direct estimation of the parameters assuming any conditional pdf for ε_t is fairly easy to implement.

Following the discussion above, the value of ϕ is irrelevant for point estimation; by the same token, from an inferential point of view, taking ϕ as fixed (e.g., $\phi = 0.5$ as in GARCH routines) leads to three different versions of the asymptotic variance matrix, up to a scale coefficient. Equivalence is ensured by taking $\phi = \sigma^{-2}$; hence, a consistent estimator is

$$\widehat{\text{avar}}(\widehat{\boldsymbol{\theta}}_T^{(ML)}) = \widehat{\sigma}_T^2 \left[T^{-1} \sum_{t=1}^{T} \widehat{\boldsymbol{a}}_t \widehat{\boldsymbol{a}}_t' \right]^{-1},$$

where $\widehat{\sigma}_T^2$ is a consistent estimator of σ^2 and $\widehat{\boldsymbol{a}}_t$ means $\boldsymbol{a}_t$ evaluated at $\widehat{\boldsymbol{\theta}}_T^{(ML)}$.

As per σ^2, in general, its ML estimator depends on the way it is related to the natural parameterization of $f_\varepsilon(\varepsilon_t|\mathcal{F}_{t-1})$. Considering again the *Gamma*(ϕ, ϕ) case, the ML estimator of ϕ solves

$$\ln \phi + 1 - \psi(\phi) + T^{-1} \sum_{t=1}^{T} [\ln \widehat{\varepsilon}_t - \widehat{\varepsilon}_t] = 0,$$

where $\psi(\cdot)$ denotes the *digamma* function and $\widehat{\varepsilon}_t$ indicates x_t/μ_t when μ_t is evaluated at $\widehat{\boldsymbol{\theta}}_T^{(ML)}$. This estimator, of course, is efficient if the true distribution is Gamma but it is unfeasible if zeros are present in the data, given that $\ln \varepsilon_t = \ln x_t - \ln \mu_t$.

9.2.2.2 Generalized Method of Moments Inference.

A different way to estimate the model, which does not need an explicit choice of the error term distribution, is to resort to GMMs. Let

$$u_t = \frac{x_t}{\mu_t} - 1. \tag{9.27}$$

Under model assumptions, u_t is a conditionally homoskedastic martingale difference, with conditional expectation 0 and conditional variance σ^2. As a consequence, let us consider any $(M, 1)$ vector $\boldsymbol{G}_t$ depending deterministically on the information set $\mathcal{F}_{t-1}$ and write $\boldsymbol{G}_t u_t \equiv \boldsymbol{g}_t$. We have

$$E(\boldsymbol{g}_t|\mathcal{F}_{t-1}) = \boldsymbol{0} \quad \forall t \Rightarrow E(\boldsymbol{g}_t) = \boldsymbol{0},$$

by the law of iterated expectations. This establishes that $\boldsymbol{G}_t$ and u_t are uncorrelated and that $\boldsymbol{g}_t$ is also a martingale difference. $\boldsymbol{G}_t$ satisfies the requirements to play the instrumental role in the GMM estimation of $\boldsymbol{\theta}$ (Newey and McFadden, 1994); should it depend on a nuisance parameter σ^2, we can assume for the time being that σ^2 is a known constant, postponing any further discussion about it to the end of this section.

If $M = p$, we have as many equations as the dimension of $\boldsymbol{\theta}$; hence, the moment criterion is

$$\bar{\boldsymbol{g}}_T = T^{-1}\sum_{t=1}^{T}\boldsymbol{g}_t = \boldsymbol{0}. \tag{9.28}$$

Under correct specification of μ_t and some regularity conditions, the GMM estimator $\widehat{\boldsymbol{\theta}}_T^{(\mathrm{GMM})}$, obtained solving Equation 9.28 for $\boldsymbol{\theta}$, is consistent (Wooldridge, 1994; th. 7.1). Furthermore, under additional regularity conditions, we have asymptotic normality of $\widehat{\boldsymbol{\theta}}_T^{(\mathrm{GMM})}$, with asymptotic covariance matrix (Wooldridge, 1994; th. 7.2)

$$\mathrm{avar}(\widehat{\boldsymbol{\theta}}_{Ts}^{(\mathrm{GMM})}) = (\boldsymbol{S}'\boldsymbol{V}^{-1}\boldsymbol{S})^{-1}, \tag{9.29}$$

where

$$\boldsymbol{S} = \lim_{T\to\infty}\left[T^{-1}\sum_{t=1}^{T}E\left(\nabla_{\boldsymbol{\theta}'}\boldsymbol{g}_t\right)\right] \tag{9.30}$$

$$\boldsymbol{V} = \lim_{T\to\infty}\left[T^{-1}V\left(\sum_{t=1}^{T}\boldsymbol{g}_t\right)\right] = \lim_{T\to\infty}\left[T^{-1}\sum_{t=1}^{T}E\left(\boldsymbol{g}_t\boldsymbol{g}_t'\right)\right]. \tag{9.31}$$

The last equality for $\boldsymbol{V}$ comes from the fact that the $\boldsymbol{g}_t$'s are serially uncorrelated given that they are a martingale difference. Moreover, the same property allows one to exploit a martingale central limit theorem and hence to some simplifications in the assumptions needed for asymptotic normality.

The martingale difference structure of u_t leads to a simple formulation of the *efficient* choice of the instrument $\boldsymbol{G}_t$, that is, having the "smallest" asymptotic variance within the class of GMM estimators considered here. Such an efficient choice is

$$_s\boldsymbol{G}_t^* = -E(\nabla_{\boldsymbol{\theta}}u_t|\mathcal{F}_{t-1})E(u_t^2|\mathcal{F}_{t-1})^{-1}. \tag{9.32}$$

Inserting $E(\boldsymbol{g}_t\boldsymbol{g}_t')$ into Equation 9.31 and $E(\nabla_{\boldsymbol{\theta}'}\boldsymbol{g}_t)$ into Equation 9.30, we obtain

$$E\left(\boldsymbol{g}_t\boldsymbol{g}_t'\right) = -E\left(\nabla_{\boldsymbol{\theta}'}\boldsymbol{g}_t\right) = \sigma^2 E\left(\boldsymbol{G}_t^*\boldsymbol{G}_t^{*\prime}\right),$$

so that

$$\boldsymbol{V} = -\boldsymbol{S} = \sigma^2\lim_{T\to\infty}\left[T^{-1}\sum_{t=1}^{T}E\left(\boldsymbol{G}_t^*\boldsymbol{G}_t^{*\prime}\right)\right] \tag{9.33}$$

and Equation 9.29 specializes to

$$\mathrm{avar}(\widehat{\boldsymbol{\theta}}_T^{(\mathrm{GMM})}) = (\boldsymbol{S}'\boldsymbol{V}^{-1}\boldsymbol{S})^{-1} = -\boldsymbol{S}^{-1} = \boldsymbol{V}^{-1}.$$

Considering the specific form of u_t in this model (Eq. 9.27), we have

$$\nabla_{\boldsymbol{\theta}} u_t = -(u_t + 1)\boldsymbol{a}_t,$$

so that Equation 9.32 becomes

$$\boldsymbol{G}_t^* = \sigma^{-2}\boldsymbol{a}_t.$$

Substituting it into $\boldsymbol{g}_t = \boldsymbol{G}_t u_t$ (and this, in turn, into Eq. 9.28) and Equation 9.33, we obtain that the GMM estimator of $\boldsymbol{\theta}$ solves the criterion Equation 9.25 and has the asymptotic variance matrix given in Equation 9.26. In practice, the same properties of $\widehat{\boldsymbol{\theta}}_T^{(ML)}$ assuming Gamma-distributed errors.

In the spirit of a semiparametric approach, a straightforward estimator for σ^2 is

$$\widehat{\sigma}_T^2 = T^{-1}\sum_{t=1}^{T}\widehat{u}_t^2,$$

where $\widehat{u}_t$ represents u_t evaluated at $\widehat{\boldsymbol{\theta}}_T^{(\mathrm{GMM})}$. Note that while this estimator does not suffer from the presence of zeros in the data, the corresponding model is not capable of predicting zero values. If such a property is needed, the model must be changed specifying a distribution of the error term as a mixture of a point mass at zero and an absolutely continuous component, following, for example, the suggestion of Hautsch et al. (2010). In our volatility framework, such a feature is irrelevant.

9.3 MEMs for Realized Volatility

We illustrate some features of a few MEM specifications by means of an application on *realized volatility*, that is, an ultrahigh-frequency-data-based measure of daily return variability, see, for example, this chapter by Park and Linton (2012) for an introduction to realized volatility. The list of estimators proposed in the literature is quite extensive (among others, Andersen et al. (2003), Aït-Sahalia et al. (2005), Bandi and Russell (2006), and Barndorff-Nielsen et al. (2008)). In this work, we use realized kernels (Barndorff-Nielsen et al. 2008), a family of heteroskedastic and autocorrelation consistent (HAC) type estimators robust to various forms of market microstructure frictions, known to contaminate high frequency data. For the sake of space, we do not discuss the important but somewhat intricate issues about data handling and the construction of the estimator (cf. Brownlees and Gallo 2006; Barndorff-Nielsen et al., 2009).

Realized volatility measurement delivers a positive valued time series characterized by empirical regularities of persistence and asymmetric behavior according to the sign of the lagged return of the corresponding asset (cf. Andersen et al. (2001), among others, for equities).

We analyze volatility dynamics of 10 stocks (constituents of the DJ30, as of December 2008, for which data exist between January 2, 2001, and December 31, 2008, corresponding to 1989 observations): BA (Boeing), CSCO (CISCO), DD (du Pont de Nemours), IBM (International Business Machines), JPM (JP Morgan Chase), MCD (McDonald's), PFE (Pfizer), UTX (United Technologies), WMT (Wal-Mart Stores), and XOM (Exxon Mobil). For illustration purposes, we choose BA as a leading example, synthesizing the results for the other tickers. We start by fitting the realized volatility series before the beginning of the credit crunch period (January 2, 2001, to June 29, 2007, 1612 observations), and we then perform a static out-of-sample forecasting exercise for the period between July 2, 2007, and December 31, 2008 (377 observations).

The time series plot of BA realized volatility in Figure 9.1 shows the customary strong persistence (the widely documented *volatility clustering*), alternating periods of great turmoil to others of great calm. We discern the steep surge in volatility following the 9/11 terrorist attacks, the crisis of confidence in 2002, the protracted period of low volatility between 2003 and 2007, and the financial crisis starting in August 2007 peeking in March 2008 with the Bear Sterns demise and in September 2008 with the collapse of Lehman Brothers.

Focusing for the moment on just Figure 9.2a,b (histogram and autocorrelogram of the raw series), the unconditional realized volatility distribution exhibits a strong positive asymmetry slowly tapering off. Table 9.1 reports summary descriptive statistics for the various tickers, with an average volatility ranging from 22.14 to 31.01, a volatility of volatility typically around 12, and a varying degree of occurrence of extreme values as indicated by the kurtosis. Interestingly, the inspection of the autocorrelations at daily, weekly, and monthly levels reveals a common slowly decaying pattern.

We employ four different specifications for the conditional expected volatility: the (baseline) MEM (M), the Asymmetric MEM (AM), the CM, and the Asymmetric Composite MEM (ACM). For each ticker and specification, the coefficients estimated over the period January 2, 2001, to June 29, 2007, are reported on the left-hand side of Table 9.2.

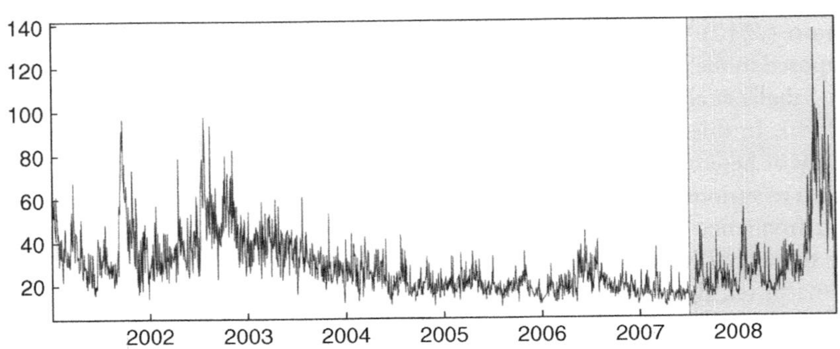

FIGURE 9.1 BA realized volatility expressed on a percent annualized scale. January 2, 2001, to December 31, 2008 (out-of-sample period starting July 2, 2007, is shaded).

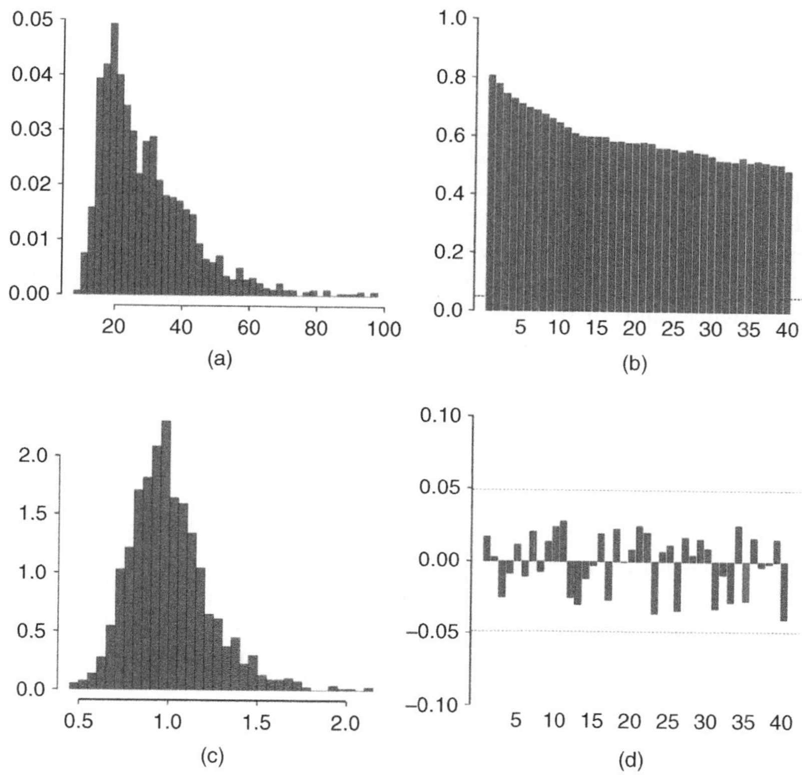

FIGURE 9.2 BA realized volatility: histogram and autocorrelogram of the raw data (a,b) and ACM residuals (c,d).

TABLE 9.1 Realized Volatility for 10 Constituents of the DJ30 Index

Ticker	Mean	Standard Deviation	Kurt	ρ_{1d}	ρ_{1w}	ρ_{1m}
BA	28.82	13.42	5.80	0.81	0.71	0.58
CSCO	31.01	16.71	14.20	0.86	0.75	0.61
DD	26.53	11.54	7.93	0.79	0.70	0.50
IBM	22.14	11.39	9.02	0.86	0.77	0.63
JPM	30.20	20.98	11.23	0.86	0.76	0.64
MCD	28.35	14.06	6.69	0.72	0.60	0.51
PFE	25.21	12.08	8.96	0.74	0.62	0.52
UTX	25.59	10.76	10.29	0.76	0.63	0.48
WMT	24.37	12.63	5.93	0.86	0.78	0.67
XOM	22.25	10.05	9.01	0.80	0.73	0.54

Descriptive statistics: means, standard deviations, kurtosis, as well as autocorrelations at daily, weekly and monthly levels.

All coefficients are statistically significant at 5% (details not reported) except for the asymmetric effect, for which there is a difference between the MEM and its Composite version: γ_1 is almost always significant in the AM (PFE is the only exception), but it is usually not significant in the ACM (for which only BA and XOM have a significant γ_1). We may note that the estimated coefficient values by specification are within a fairly narrow range providing evidence that volatility dynamics have a certain degree of homogeneity (see, among others, Bauwens and Rombouts (2007a), Shephard and Sheppard (2010), Pakel et al. (2010), Barigozzi et al. (2010), and Brownlees (2010)).

The baseline MEM exhibits a β_1^* very close to one, showing a high degree of persistence, and an α_1 coefficient usually between 0.25 and 0.30, which makes the dynamics more reactive to past realizations of the process than what is typically implied by past squared returns in a GARCH framework (cf. Shephard and Sheppard, 2010).

Similar comments hold for the AM estimates where the asymmetric effects have an impact on the corresponding α_1's (which become smaller), while not changing the persistence parameter β_1^*.

The CM enriches the specification in the direction of allowing us to confirm that the long-run component has a high degree of persistence ($\beta_1^{(\chi)*}$ is close to unity), which is coherent with its slow moving underlying pattern. The short-run component provides a very varied asset-specific response in the dynamics and, in particular, in the persistence β_1^* [which is lower than the other one as required by the identification condition (Eq. 9.17)].

Finally, in view of the generalized nonsignificance of the asymmetric effects, the ACM does not seem to add much to the CM.

Figure 9.3 illustrates the features of the ACM in producing the two components and the size of the multiplicative residual for the BA ticker (for which asymmetry is significant): the overall estimated conditional expectation reproduced in the panel (a) is split between the permanent component [panel (b)] and the transitory component [panel (c)]; the estimated multiplicative residuals are added in the panel (d). We can note that the most important events (e.g., 9/11 in 2001, the WorldCom scandal in mid-2002, Bear Sterns' demise in March 2008 and Lehman Brothers' bankruptcy in September 2008) are well recognizable in all panels, being captured by the expected volatility divided between a sudden change in the permanent component, some turbulence in the temporary component, and relatively high values of the residuals.

The right part of Table 9.2 reports the p-values associated with the 1-day, 1-week, and 1-month Ljung–Box test statistics for each ticker and specification. Only for UTX and XOM are the test statistics nonsignificant across specifications. For all the others, autocorrelation is a problem for the base specifications and is not solved by considering asymmetric effects. By contrast, the empirical significance levels are very high for the CMs (a typical correlogram for such a class is the one reported in Fig. 9.2d, next to a typical residual histogram—Fig. 9.2c—which shows a reduction in asymmetry relative to the raw data).

It is interesting to note that the consideration of a Composite specification solves the autocorrelation problem revealed in the base specification while, at the

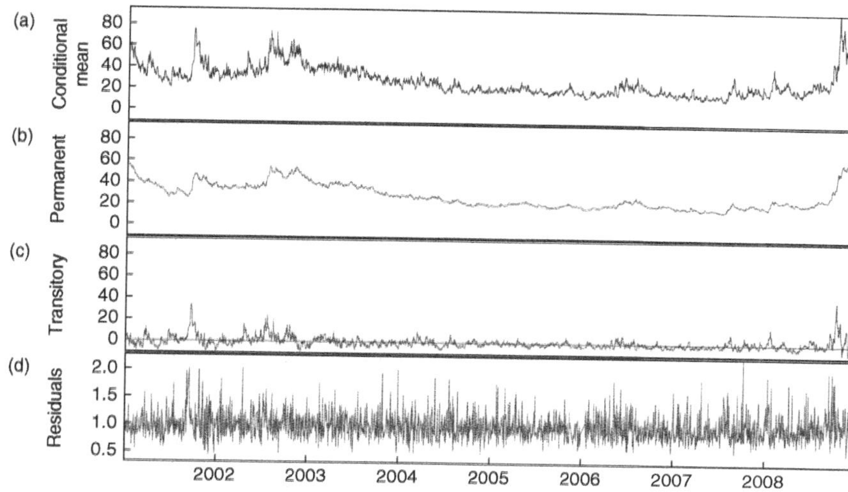

FIGURE 9.3 Panels on estimated components from the Asymmetric Composite MEM for BA (from a–d): overall conditional expectation, permanent component, transitory component, and multiplicative residuals. January 2, 2001 to December 31, 2008.

same time, it belittles the evidence about the presence of asymmetric effects in the short-run dynamics. Thus, taking the absence of autocorrelation as a lead into an improved specification, the CM would come out as the favored model. Our model provides yet another plausible "short memory" process capable of reproducing the "long memory" empirical features in the realized volatility data: for log-volatility, see Corsi (2009) who exploits dynamic components moving at different speeds as an alternative to the ARFIMA modeling of Giot and Laurent (2004).[4] Moreover, whether asymmetric effects are relevant or not in this context becomes an empirical question (in our case, in seven out of nine tickers, we lose relevance, for PFE, it is never relevant). For the BA ticker, Figure 9.3d allows for the appreciation of the uncorrelatedness of the residuals as providing no information on the volatility dynamics.

This strong result based on statistical significance is mitigated by the outcome of an out-of-sample static forecasting exercise of realized volatility between July 2007 and December 2008. For each day, we compute the predicted realized volatility for the next period using data up to the current observation and the in-sample parameter estimates. We choose the quasi log-likelihood loss function, defined as

$$\mathrm{QL} = \frac{1}{T^*} \sum_{t=T+1}^{T+T^*} \left(\frac{x_t}{\hat{\mu}_t} - \ln \frac{x_t}{\hat{\mu}_t} \right) - 1,$$

[4]For a comparison between the Component GARCH and the FIGARCH models having *n* similar decay of the volatility shocks, see Andersen et al. (2006, p. 807).

TABLE 9.2 Estimation Results for the Four Models Analyzed: the (baseline) MEM (M), the Asymmetric MEM (AM), the Composite MEM (CM), and the Asymmetric Composite MEM (ACM)

Ticker	Model	α_1	γ_1	β_1^*	$\alpha_1^{(\chi)}$	$\beta_1^{(\chi)*}$	Q_{1d}	Q_{1w}	Q_{1m}
BA	M	0.301		0.982			0.046	0.070	0.257
	AM	0.249	0.049	0.982			0.044	0.024	0.131
	CM	0.215		0.802	0.1154	0.9957	0.733	0.926	0.975
	ACM	0.151	0.100	0.830	0.1083	0.9957	0.489	0.864	0.947
CSCO	M	0.433		0.970			0.005	0.000	0.000
	AM	0.409	0.032	0.971			0.005	0.000	0.000
	CM	0.324		0.674	0.1554	0.9917	0.864	0.103	0.509
	ACM	0.302	0.044	0.682	0.1501	0.9917	0.941	0.099	0.514
DD	M	0.306		0.972			0.100	0.040	0.098
	AM	0.243	0.044	0.973			0.038	0.039	0.127
	CM	0.193		0.765	0.1335	0.9917	0.676	0.953	0.574
	ACM	0.186	0.073	0.868	0.0772	0.9948	0.240	0.532	0.347
IBM	M	0.349		0.979			0.008	0.001	0.038
	AM	0.285	0.059	0.980			0.010	0.000	0.011
	CM	0.248		0.863	0.1235	0.9932	0.206	0.047	0.324
	ACM	0.166	−0.032	0.380	0.2602	0.9864	0.980	0.420	0.525
JPM	M	0.323		0.988			0.038	0.011	0.009
	AM	0.278	0.049	0.988			0.058	0.004	0.004
	CM	0.256		0.853	0.1001	0.9962	0.707	0.785	0.341
	ACM	0.245	0.029	0.850	0.0947	0.9962	0.764	0.787	0.332
MCD	M	0.213		0.990			0.001	0.000	0.001
	AM	0.197	0.026	0.988			0.002	0.000	0.001
	CM	0.191		0.642	0.0955	0.9967	0.880	0.871	0.937
	ACM	0.164	0.045	0.644	0.0948	0.9968	0.913	0.879	0.934
PFE	M	0.256		0.979			0.000	0.000	0.000
	AM	0.252	0.004	0.979			0.000	0.000	0.000
	CM	0.233		0.385	0.1376	0.9920	0.679	0.677	0.376
	ACM	0.255	−0.043	0.376	0.1396	0.9920	0.722	0.697	0.383
UTX	M	0.311		0.976			0.464	0.803	0.046
	AM	0.261	0.053	0.978			0.497	0.838	0.028
	CM	0.229		0.849	0.0900	0.9956	0.924	0.689	0.226
	ACM	0.212	0.029	0.851	0.0880	0.9955	0.928	0.691	0.219
WMT	M	0.272		0.984			0.008	0.021	0.037
	AM	0.256	0.037	0.984			0.024	0.041	0.028
	CM	0.206		0.814	0.0978	0.9947	0.369	0.382	0.575
	ACM	0.205	0.003	0.815	0.0976	0.9947	0.364	0.380	0.574
XOM	M	0.281		0.978			0.134	0.475	0.286
	AM	0.237	0.052	0.974			0.362	0.651	0.435
	CM	0.200		0.930	0.0909	0.9940	0.306	0.439	0.376
	ACM	0.109	0.118	0.922	0.1064	0.9912	0.264	0.424	0.364

Coefficient estimates reported on the left-hand side (first five columns); Ljung–Box statistics at lag 1, 5, and 22 on the right-hand side. In-sample period: January 2, 2001, to June 29, 2007.

for its appealing theoretical properties (Hansen and Lunde, 2005a; Patton, 2011). In fact, it is a *consistent* loss function for ranking volatility models: as T^* grows, the model ranking based on the volatility proxy x_t approximates well the one based on the actual unobserved volatility. It reaches the value 0 when all forecasts coincide with the observed values and it is greater otherwise. Furthermore, the QL loss function is a natural choice in the MEM framework in that it is related to the out-of-sample log-likelihood function under the assumption of Gamma disturbances. It turns out that the QL values for each model are fairly similar to one another, with the AM model corresponding to the lowest value in 7 out of 10 cases and the ACM model in the remaining three. To appreciate the differences for comparison purposes, Table 9.3 shows a relative index constructed as follows:

$$\left(\frac{\mathrm{QL}_m}{\mathrm{QL}_{\mathrm{AM}}} - 1\right) \times 100 \qquad m = \mathrm{M}, \mathrm{CM}, \mathrm{ACM}. \tag{9.34}$$

The table indicates that the gains from the Composite model are of little relevance, while the gains from the AM are more substantial. Thus, judging on these results, in choosing a single best model in forecasting, that model should be the AM model. Not surprisingly, in the crisis period, the role of asymmetries becomes crucial for forecasting: in all cases, the best performing model contains an asymmetric component. On the other hand, even if the Composite specifications appear to improve significantly in-sample fit, in the crisis period, they improve performance only in three cases (only marginally so). This result is also in line with the findings (Brownlees et al. 2010) that the TGARCH model is the best performing specification in forecasting among several GARCH alternatives. The appealing features reported in Figure 9.3b,c make the Composite model one in which some additional insights on the evolution of the dynamics are possible.

TABLE 9.3 Static Forecasting Results: July 2007 to December 2008

Ticker	M	CM	ACM
BA	3.27	5.07	−0.61
CSCO	1.91	3.67	1.63
DD	0.62	3.82	−0.43
IBM	4.61	6.46	7.38
JPM	4.07	3.74	0.53
MCD	1.24	8.06	7.60
PFE	0.24	0.90	3.66
UTX	6.16	8.91	4.74
WMT	2.64	6.06	5.81
XOM	1.18	1.33	−0.06

The table reports the percentage difference in QL loss against the AM model (Eq. 9.34).

9.4 MEM Extensions

9.4.1 COMPONENT MULTIPLICATIVE ERROR MODEL

The *Component* MEM, proposed by Brownlees et al. (2011a), is an interesting representation of the model illustrated in Section 9.2.1. Built to reproduce the dynamics of (regularly spaced) intradaily volumes, the Component MEM is motivated by the salient stylized facts of such series: a clustering of daily averages, clear evidence that the overall series moves around a daily dynamic component; a regular U-shaped intradaily pattern that emerges once daily averages are removed; and, yet, a distinctive nonperiodic intradaily dynamics. The same framework can be adopted in all other contexts (volatility, number of trades, and average durations) where data aggregated by intradaily bins show some periodic features together with overall dynamics having components at different frequencies.

According to such empirical evidence, a Component MEM for $x_{t,i}$ (where $t \in \{1, \ldots, T\}$ indicates the day and $i \in \{1, \ldots, I\}$ denotes one of the I equally spaced time bins between market opening and closing times) is thus given by

$$x_{t,i} = \eta_t \, \phi_i \, \mu_{t,i} \, \varepsilon_{t,i},$$

where η_t is a daily component; ϕ_i is an intradaily periodic component, aimed at reproducing the time-of-day pattern; $\mu_{t,i}$ is an intradaily dynamic (nonperiodic) component; and, $\varepsilon_{t,i}$ is a nonnegative disturbance term assumed i.i.d. and, conditionally on the relevant information set $\mathcal{F}_{t,i-1}$, with mean 1 and constant variance σ^2. More specifically, the components entering in the conditional mean $E(x_{t,i}|\mathcal{F}_{t,i-1}) = \eta_t \, \phi_i \, \mu_{t,i}$ can be structured according to the following, relatively simple, specifications.

The daily component is specified as

$$\eta_t = \omega^{(\eta)} + \beta_1^{(\eta)} \eta_{t-1} + \alpha_1^{(\eta)} x_{t-1}^{(\eta)} + \gamma_1^{(\eta)} x_{t-1}^{(\eta-)}, \tag{9.35}$$

where

$$x_t^{(\eta)} = \frac{1}{I} \sum_{i=1}^{I} \frac{x_{t,i}}{\phi_i \mu_{t,i}}, \tag{9.36}$$

is the *standardized daily volume*, that is, the daily average of the intradaily volumes normalized by the intradaily components ϕ_i and $\mu_{t,i}$ and $x_t^{(\eta-)} \equiv x_t^{(\eta)} \mathrm{I}(r_{t,.} < 0)$ (where $r_{t,.}$ is the total return in day t) is a term built to capture the asymmetric effect.

The intradaily dynamic component is formulated as

$$\mu_{t,i} = \omega^{(\mu)} + \beta_1^{(\mu)} \mu_{t,i-1} + \alpha_1^{(\mu)} x_{t,i-1}^{(\mu)} + \gamma_1^{(\mu)} x_{t,i-1}^{(\mu-)}, \tag{9.37}$$

where

$$x_{t,i}^{(\mu)} = \frac{x_{t,i}}{\eta_t \phi_i}, \tag{9.38}$$

is the *standardized intradaily volume* and $x_{t,i}^{(\mu-)} \equiv x_{t,i}^{(\mu)} \mathrm{I}(r_{t,i} < 0)$ (where $r_{t,i}$ is the return at bin i of day t) is the corresponding asymmetric term. $\mu_{t,i}$ is constrained to have unconditional expectation equal to 1 in order to make the model identifiable, allowing us to interpret it as a pure intradaily dynamic component. If $r_{t,i}$ is assumed conditionally uncorrelated with $x_{t,i}$ and to have zero conditional mean (cf. Section 9.2.1.1), such a constraint implies $\omega^{(\mu)} = 1 - (\beta_1^{(\mu)} + \alpha_1^{(\mu)} + \gamma_1^{(\mu)}/2)$.

In synthesis, the system nests the daily and the intradaily dynamic components by alternating the update of the former (from η_{t-1} to η_t) and the latter (from $\mu_{t-1,I} = \mu_{t,0}$ to $\mu_{t,I}$): the time-varying η_t adjusts the mean level of the series, whereas the intradaily component $\phi_i \, \mu_{t,i}$ captures bin-specific (periodic, respectively, nonperiodic) departures from such an average level.

Finally, the intradaily periodic component ϕ_i can be specified in various ways. In Brownlees et al. (2011a), a Fourier (sine/cosine) representation (whose details are omitted here for the sake of space) is supported.

Parameter estimation of the Component MEM can be done via ML or GMM, along the lines outlined in Section 9.2.2. In Brownlees et al. (2011a), the GMM approach is discussed in detail.

There are two major differences in the Component MEM relative to the model defined in Section 9.2.1 above. The first is general: several components, each with a different meaning, are combined together multiplicatively, rather than additively as in the CM. The second aspect is related to the specific analysis of intradaily data: when markets close, the data are not equally spaced (the time lag between two contiguous bins of the same day is different from the lag occurring between the first bin of a day and the last one of the previous day). As a consequence, some adjustments may be needed in the formulation of the dynamic component for the first daily bin (for details, see Brownlees et al. (2011a).

9.4.2 VECTOR MULTIPLICATIVE ERROR MODEL

There are many instances where the joint consideration of several nonnegative processes is of interest. For example, different measures (realized volatility, daily range, and absolute returns) summarize information on return volatility but no individual one appears to be a sufficient measure (i.e., depending solely on its own past). Analyzing their joint dynamics may thus be of interest.

A second example concerns the dynamic interactions among volatilities in different markets (evaluated by means of a proxy, e.g., the daily range of the market indices) for analyzing the transmission mechanisms (spillovers, contagion) across markets (Engle et al., 2011).

A third example involves order-driven markets, in which there is a trade-off between the potential payoff of placing orders at a better price, against the risk of these orders not executing. Therefore, it is relevant to investigate the dynamics of the *quantity* of stock to be executed at a given distance from the current price in itself and also in the interaction with one another at different distances. In this framework, zeros are relevant because there are times when the quantity that could be executed at a certain distance from current price can be 0. Forecasts can be used for a trading strategy (Noss, 2007).

In an ultrahigh frequency framework, the market activity is evaluated by different indicators, such as the time elapsed since the last trade, the (possibly signed) volume, and the return associated with the trade. A model for the dynamic interrelationship between such variables can reveal the speed (in market and calendar time) at which private information is incorporated into prices (cf. Manganelli (2005) and Hautsch (2008)).

The MEM as defined in Section 9.4.2 can be extended to handle these situations (cf. Cipollini et al. 2007; 2009). Let $\{\boldsymbol{x}_t\}$ be the corresponding K-dimensional process with nonnegative elements.[5] Paralleling Equations 9.1–9.3, $\{\boldsymbol{x}_t\}$ follows a vector MEM (or vMEM for shortly) if it can be expressed as

$$\boldsymbol{x}_t = \boldsymbol{\mu}_t \odot \boldsymbol{\varepsilon}_t = \text{diag}(\boldsymbol{\mu}_t)\boldsymbol{\varepsilon}_t,$$

where $\odot$ indicates the Hadamard (element-by-element) product and diag($\cdot$) denotes a diagonal matrix with the vector in the argument on the main diagonal. Conditionally on the information set $\mathcal{F}_{t-1}$, $\boldsymbol{\mu}_t$ can be defined as

$$\boldsymbol{\mu}_t = \boldsymbol{\mu}(\mathcal{F}_{t-1}; \boldsymbol{\theta}),$$

except that now we are dealing with a K-dimensional vector depending on a (larger) vector of parameters $\boldsymbol{\theta}$. The innovation vector $\boldsymbol{\varepsilon}_t$ is a K-dimensional random variable defined over a $[0, +\infty)^K$ support, with unit vector $\mathbb{1}$ as its expectation and a general variance–covariance matrix $\boldsymbol{\Sigma}$,

$$\boldsymbol{\varepsilon}_t|\mathcal{F}_{t-1} \sim D_K^+(\mathbb{1}, \boldsymbol{\Sigma}). \tag{9.39}$$

From the previous conditions, we have

$$\begin{aligned} E(\boldsymbol{x}_t|\mathcal{F}_{t-1}) &= \boldsymbol{\mu}_t \\ V(\boldsymbol{x}_t|\mathcal{F}_{t-1}) &= \boldsymbol{\mu}_t\boldsymbol{\mu}_t' \odot \boldsymbol{\Sigma} = \text{diag}(\boldsymbol{\mu}_t)\boldsymbol{\Sigma}\text{diag}(\boldsymbol{\mu}_t), \end{aligned}$$

where the latter is a positive-definite matrix by construction (cf. the parallel Eqs. (9.4) and (9.5) in the univariate case).

[5]In what follows, we will adopt the following conventions: if $\boldsymbol{x}$ is a vector or a matrix and a is a scalar, then the expressions $\boldsymbol{x} \geq \boldsymbol{0}$ and $\boldsymbol{x}^a$ are meant element by element; if $\boldsymbol{x}_1, \ldots, \boldsymbol{x}_K$ are (m, n) matrices, then $(\boldsymbol{x}_1; \ldots; \boldsymbol{x}_K)$ means the (mK, n) matrix obtained stacking the matrices $\boldsymbol{x}_i$'s columnwise.

As far as the conditional mean is concerned, the generalization of Equation 9.7 becomes

$$\boldsymbol{\mu}_t = \boldsymbol{\omega} + \boldsymbol{\beta}_1 \boldsymbol{\mu}_{t-1} + \boldsymbol{\alpha}_1 \boldsymbol{x}_{t-1} + \boldsymbol{\gamma}_1 \boldsymbol{x}_{t-1}^{(-)}.$$

Among the parameters (whose nonzero elements are arranged in the vector $\boldsymbol{\theta}$), $\boldsymbol{\omega}$ has dimension $(K, 1)$, whereas $\boldsymbol{\alpha}_1$, $\boldsymbol{\gamma}_1$, and $\boldsymbol{\beta}_1$ have dimension (K, K). As above, the term $\boldsymbol{\gamma}_1 \boldsymbol{x}_{t-1}^{(-)}$ aims to capture asymmetric effects associated with the sign of an observed variable. For example, when different volatility indicators of the same asset are considered, such an indicator assumes value 1 when its previous day's return r_{t-1} is negative. In a market volatility spillover study, each market i would have its own indicator function built from the sign of its own returns $r_{t-1,i}$. Finally, in a microstructure context, we can think of assigning positive or negative values to volumes according to whether the trade was a buy or a sell.

As for the error term $\boldsymbol{\varepsilon}_t$, a completely parametric formulation of the vMEM requires a full specification of its conditional distribution: Ahoniemi and Lanne (2009) adopt a bivariate Gamma (and mixtures) for call and put volatilities. In Cipollini et al. (2007), marginals for the components $\varepsilon_{t,i}$ satisfying the unit mean constraint are linked together using copulas. Relying on the considerations of Section 9.2.2.1, a reasonable choice is to take $Gamma(\phi_i, \phi_i)$ $(i = 1, \ldots, K)$ marginals, whereas, for what concerns copulas, the Normal or t represents rather flexible choices. Alternatively, Cipollini et al. (2009) suggest a semiparametric formulation relying on the first two moments in Equation 9.39. In such a case, the estimation can be done via GMM along the lines illustrated in Section 9.2.2.2. The resulting estimator generalizes the one obtained in the univariate case (Eq. 9.25), in the sense of solving the criterion equation

$$\sum_{t=1}^{T} \boldsymbol{a}_t \boldsymbol{\Sigma}^{-1} (\boldsymbol{\varepsilon}_t - \mathbb{1}) = \mathbf{0}, \tag{9.40}$$

and having the asymptotic variance matrix

$$\mathrm{avar}(\widehat{\boldsymbol{\theta}}_T^{(GMM)}) = \left[\lim_{T \to \infty} T^{-1} \sum_{t=1}^{T} E\left[\boldsymbol{a}_t \boldsymbol{\Sigma}^{-1} \boldsymbol{a}_t'\right] \right]^{-1},$$

where

$$\boldsymbol{\varepsilon}_t = \boldsymbol{x}_t \oslash \boldsymbol{\mu}_t - \mathbb{1},$$

($\oslash$ denotes the element-by-element division) and

$$\boldsymbol{a}_t = \nabla_{\theta} \boldsymbol{\mu}_t' \mathrm{diag}(\boldsymbol{\mu}_t)^{-1}.$$

The main differences with respect to the univariate case are the dependence of the criterion Equation 9.40 on $\boldsymbol{\Sigma}$, and the fact that the same equation cannot be derived as a score function based on a known parametric distribution of the error term.

As a possible extension to univariate volatility modeling (cf. Section 9.3), we can analyze the joint dynamics of different measures within the vMEM framework. For example, let us consider absolute returns ($|r_t|$) and realized kernel volatility (rv_t), so that $\boldsymbol{x}_t = (x_{t,1}; x_{t,2}) = (|r_t|; rv_t)$ has conditional mean given by

$$\begin{pmatrix} \mu_{t,1} \\ \mu_{t,2} \end{pmatrix} = \begin{pmatrix} \omega_1 \\ \omega_2 \end{pmatrix} + \begin{pmatrix} \alpha_{1,1} & \alpha_{1,2} \\ \alpha_{2,1} & \alpha_{2,2} \end{pmatrix} \begin{pmatrix} x_{t-1,1} \\ x_{t-1,2} \end{pmatrix} + \begin{pmatrix} \beta_{1,1} & \beta_{1,2} \\ \beta_{2,1} & \beta_{2,2} \end{pmatrix} \begin{pmatrix} \mu_{t-1,1} \\ \mu_{t-1,2} \end{pmatrix},$$

where asymmetric effects are not included for the sake of space. This equation shows that the vMEM encompasses the GARCH model, when $\alpha_{1,2} = \beta_{1,2} = 0$; the GARCH-X model of Engle (2002b), when $\beta_{1,2} = 0$; and the HEAVY model of Shephard and Sheppard (2010), when $\alpha_{1,1} = \alpha_{2,1} = \beta_{1,2} = \beta_{2,1} = 0$. A vMEM formulation is thus preferable: substantial efficiency may be gained from the joint estimation of the equations (given the high contemporaneous correlation of errors) and from modeling the possible dynamic interdependence related to a nondiagonal $\boldsymbol{\beta}$; more specific models will result if testable restrictions are satisfied.

Other approaches for nonnegative joint processes are present in the literature. Manganelli (2005) proposes a model for durations, volumes, and volatility, which rests on factoring the conditional distribution $f(\boldsymbol{x}_t|\mathcal{F}_{t-1})$ as

$$f(x_{t,1}|\mathcal{F}_{t-1})f(x_{t,2}|x_{t,1}, \mathcal{F}_{t-1}) \ldots f(x_{t,K}|x_{t,1}, \ldots, x_{t,K-1}, \mathcal{F}_{t-1}).$$

Assuming uncorrelated errors, each factor can be formulated as a univariate MEM but is driven by contemporaneous information as well. Hautsch (2008) adopts a similar strategy for modeling the intraday dynamics of volatility, average volume per trade, and number of trades evaluated at equally spaced time intervals; in comparison with Manganelli (2005), the essential difference lies in the dependence of the univariate conditional distributions on a common latent component (assumed to represent the information flow). Hansen et al. (2011) propose the realized-GARCH model, where the unobservable conditional variance of returns is assumed to be driven just by the realized variance as in the HEAVY model. Since such a quantity is considered a noisy measure of the true latent variance, it ends up being indirectly dependent on the contemporaneous return as well.

A drawback of vMEMs is that the number of parameters tends to increase very rapidly with K, a fact that could potentially hinder the application domain. One possible solution is to resort to model selection techniques to isolate the elements of the coefficient matrices that could be 0 (off-diagonal or $\boldsymbol{\gamma}_1$ elements, in particular). In Cipollini and Gallo (2010), an automated general-to-specific selection procedure is proposed and investigated. Another solution is the one investigated by Barigozzi et al. (2010) for a vector of volatilities where each series follows univariate MEM dynamics around a common (systematic) component (estimated nonparametrically).

9.5 Conclusion

In this chapter, we have presented the main theoretical features of a class of models, called *multiplicative error models*, which are particularly suitable to represent the dynamics of nonnegative financial time series observed at daily or intradaily frequency. The main advantages are a direct modeling of the persistence in the conditional mean, without resorting to logarithmic transformations which could be unfeasible in the presence of zeros or introduce numerical problems, and the possibility of forecasting the variable of interest directly. In a univariate context, several components evolving at different speeds can be considered (e.g., long vs short run or daily vs intradaily components): in most cases, estimation proceeds in a fairly straightforward manner, either via an ML or a GMM approach. Multivariate specifications are possible, including those where some (factor-like) common features in the data can be exploited, allowing for full dynamic interdependence across several variables.

The application run for illustration purposes shows that an asymmetric specification is well suited in one-step ahead forecasting of volatility even if more sophisticated representations allow to better capture the dependence structure in the data.

CHAPTER TEN

Locally Stationary Volatility Modeling

SÉBASTIEN VAN BELLEGEM

10.1 Introduction

Volatility is a measure of variability of an economic time process. One challenging econometric problem is to understand and to model the heterogeneity of the volatility through time. In that respect, conditional models such as ARCH or ARCH-type models have received a lot of consideration during the past decades.

Conditional models have also been recently questioned because the volatility process is assumed to be covariance stationary. Several papers, some of them cited below, have suggested that one part of the time heterogeneity of volatility processes might be due to a lack of stationarity, which appears when the unconditional moments or distribution change over time.

The goal of this chapter is to present an overview of some approaches that have been proposed to model volatility processes by locally stationary time series. We focus on the modeling of a zero-mean discrete-time stochastic process, X_t ($t = 0, 1, 2, \ldots$), that sometimes results after removing the trend of an economic time series. One recurring empirical application in this survey is given by the analysis of the volatility of the Dow Jones industrial average (DJIA) index presented in Figure 10.1. The figure shows the observed index as well as its log-returns, which we assume to be zero-mean, as we do for X_t.

Handbook of Volatility Models and Their Applications, First Edition.
Edited by Luc Bauwens, Christian Hafner, and Sebastien Laurent.

In time series analysis, most existing models assume that the zero-mean process X_t is covariance stationary, meaning that the covariance between X_s and X_t depends on the time difference $|s - t|$ only. This assumption is useful to have some estimators for the autocovariance structure of the process with good statistical properties. It is also a fundamental assumption for forecasting purposes. However, many time series in the applied sciences are not covariance stationary and show a time-varying second-order structure. That is, variances and covariances can change over time. The returns of the DJIA index, shown in the second row of Figure 10.1, are likely to have such an inhomogeneous variance. By this, we mean that the variance of the process is possibly not constant over time. Later in this chapter, we apply a test of covariance stationarity to these data, confirming this intuition. Many other examples can be found in economics, as well as in many other fields of applied sciences.

Since the 1960s, gradually more and more attention has been paid to this challenging problem of how to model such processes with an evolutionary autocovariance structure. Among the pioneers, we would like to cite the work of Page (1952), Silverman (1957), Priestley (1965), and Loynes (1968). In his paper, Silverman proposed the approximation

$$\mathrm{Cov}(X_s, X_t) \approx m\left(\frac{s+t}{2}\right) c^X(s-t)$$

for some function $m(\cdot)$ that is, the covariance behaves locally as a typical stationary autocovariance function c^X but is allowed to vary from time to time depending on the midpoint between s and t. As in Silverman's definition, each

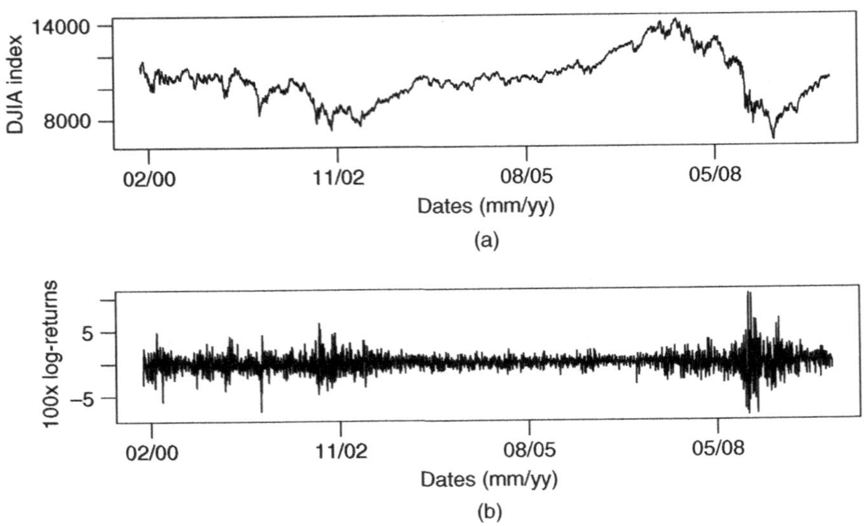

FIGURE 10.1 (a) Dow Jones industrial average (DJIA) index, from January 3, 2000, to December 31, 2009 (2528 daily observations). (b) Returns of the DJIA index.

model of nonstationary covariance has to define explicitly its departure from stationarity. However, constructing a statistical theory for these locally stationary processes is hampered by serious conceptual problems. For instance, with this lack of invariant second-order structure, how can one estimate the time-varying covariance accurately? Even if some regularity assumptions are imposed on the function m, a serious problem here is that one cannot build an asymptotic theory for the estimation of m. Consequently, the standard statistical concepts such as consistency, efficiency, or central limit theorems cannot be used to measure and compare the quality of different estimators.

To answer these questions, a decisive idea was introduced by Dahlhaus (1996, 1997) with his concept of "local stationarity." This concept allows the modeling of a time-varying autocovariance structure that can be estimated rigorously. An appropriate asymptotic theory can be developed for those processes, and the usual statistical properties of estimators can be derived.

This chapter is organized as follows. After presenting some economic justifications and empirical evidences for why volatility time series can sometimes be considered as nonstationary (Section 10.2), we present the definition of local stationarity in Section 10.3. The formal use of locally stationary processes to model volatility time series is a recent advance of the past decade and is considered in Section 10.4. Multivariate extensions of locally stationary models of volatility is an active topic of research, and we survey in Section 10.5, two recent approaches.

10.2 Empirical Evidences

10.2.1 STRUCTURAL BREAKS, NONSTATIONARITY, AND PERSISTENCE

In the early 1980s, the modeling of trends and business cycles in economic time series showed new developments. The common additive decomposition of a time series as a (linear) deterministic trend, a cyclical component, and a stationary stochastic process was questioned in both empirical and theoretical research (Hall, 1979; Nelson and Plosser, 1982; Perron, 1989; Rappoport and Reichlin 1989). Among the developments of this research,[1] an important branch of the macroeconomic literature emerged on testing the presence of structural breaks in time series. In this approach, the time series considered is supposed to be stationary over segments of time, and the limit of these segments define the breakpoints. Before and after a breakpoint, the process is not supposed to have the same parameter levels, or even not the same structure.

This debate on structural breaks naturally appeared in the literature on volatility modeling. Modeling structural changes has then been studied for example, by the Markov regime-switching models (see e.g., Hamilton and Susmel (1994) for ARCH and Gray (1996) for GARCH). Also, the literature on break identification in volatility processes has been very active

[1] A more complete historical view can be found for example, in Banerjee and Urga (2005).

during the past decade (Hillebrand, 2005; Franses et al., 2002; Andreou and Ghysels, 2009).

Models with structural changes in the variance or autocovariance provide a natural framework to analyze volatility if one considers the historical variations that have been observed in the volatility of many macroeconomic time series. A decline in volatility of the US output growth appeared in the mid-1980s, as documented in Kim and Nelson (1999) and McConnell and Quiros (2000), and breaks in the unconditional volatility have been detected in many macroeconomic time series over the past 60 years (Sensier and van Dijk, 2004). A volatility time series with one or more structural breaks is a particular case of a locally stationary process (a precise definition is to be found below). It is not a weakly stationary time series since its variance, or its autocorrelation function (ACF) changes between the breaks. Nonstationary models of volatility then have a strong empirical justification, and we recall below basic tests of stationarity that have been implemented to support this observation.

Another motivation for modeling volatility by means of nonstationary processes is related to the high persistence that is commonly observed in the squared or absolute returns. This persistence refers to the typical pattern for the ACF of the squared/absolute returns, that are positive and slowly decreasing. In a discussion on the IGARCH model of Engle and Bollerslev (1986), the point was raised that it may not be possible to separate persistence effects from structural changes; see Diebold (1986). An illustration for the Dow Jones index is given in Figure 10.2, in which the ACF of the absolute returns is given for two decades of the index. Panel (a) is for the years 1990–1999, and panel (b) is for the years 2000–2009. Both ACFs show persistence, although it is remarkable to see how the ACF has changed over the past two decades. The past decade shows higher persistence, while low order autocorrelations are smaller than those for the first decade.

One surprising feature of models with structural changes in their variance or ACF is their ability to capture the persistence in the absolute returns. This phenomenon has been pointed out in Mikosch and Stărică (2004) and is illustrated by means of a simulation in Figure 10.3. In this figure, we simulate the time series $X_t = \sigma_t Z_t$ with Z_t iid $N(0, 1)$, and σ_t is a piecewise constant function of t given in Figure 10.3b. The resulting process Y_t is not stationary since it contains three breaks in its unconditional variance. Between two successive breaks, the time series is a Gaussian white noise. The ACF of the resulting concatenation of white noises is empirically estimated in Figure 10.3c. The pattern of the ACF is similar to the pattern of long-range dependent data.

This observation is probably one of the most important motivations why it would be valuable to analyze volatility data using nonstationary models. In the above exercise, the nonstationary model has a very simple form with only three breakpoints in the unconditional variance. Before generalizing this approach to more involved models and to present a rigorous framework to construct nonstationary models, we briefly recall some useful tests to detect nonstationarity in volatility time series.

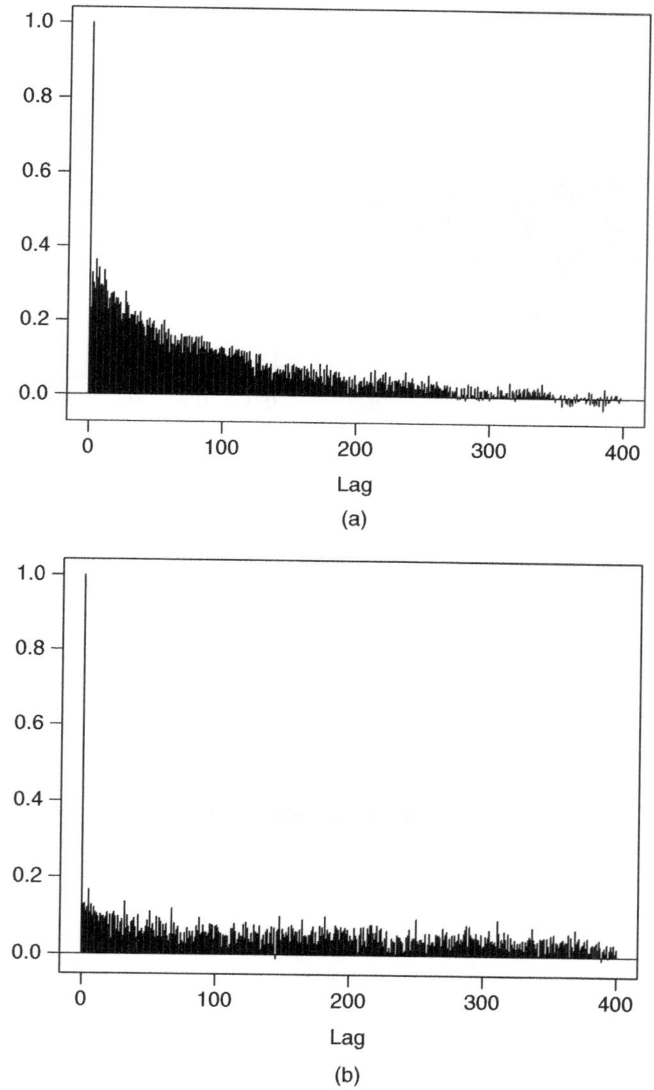

FIGURE 10.2 The empirical autocorrelation function of the Dow Jones industrial average (DJIA) absolute index returns, computed over two segments of time (a) from January 2, 1990, to December 31, 1999 and (b) from January 3, 2000, to December 31, 2009.

10.2.2 TESTING STATIONARITY

In this section, we review some tests of nonstationarity. A wide class of tests are based on the cumulative sum of squares. Certainly, the simplest version of this test is the *postsample prediction test*. Suppose we observe the zero-mean process

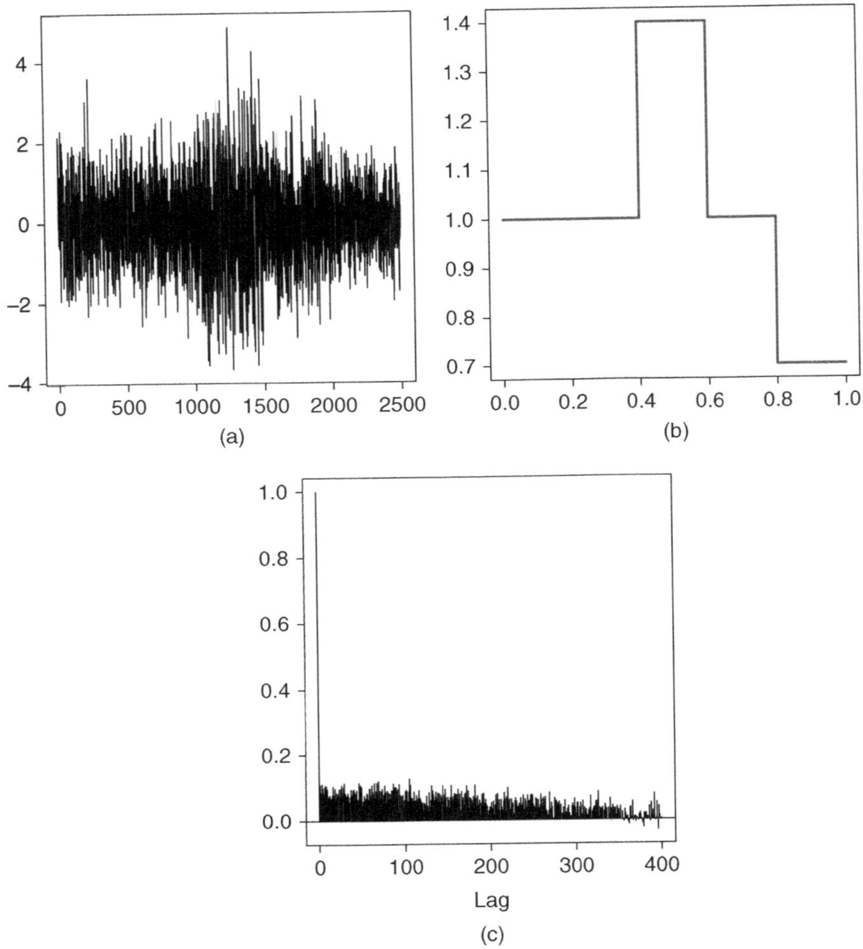

FIGURE 10.3 (a) Simulated time series of 2500 observations, which has a time-varying standard deviation as plotted in (b). (c)The empirical autocorrelation function of the absolute series.

$X_0, \ldots, X_{T-1}$ and split the time axis in $T = T_1 + T_2$ with $T_1 = T_2$. If we want to test the hypothesis that the variance on $X_0, \ldots, X_{T_1-1}$ is equal to the variance on $X_{T_1}, \ldots, X_{T-1}$, a suitable test statistic is

$$\hat{\tau} = \hat{\sigma}_1^2 - \hat{\sigma}_2^2$$

where $\hat{\sigma}_i^2$ is the sample variance on the ith segment. Under the null hypothesis, the distribution of $T_1^{1/2}\hat{\tau}$ is asymptotically normal if X_t^2 is a stationary process with autocovariance γ_j (Hoffman and Pagan, 1989):

$$T_1^{1/2}\hat{\tau} \xrightarrow{\text{d}} \mathcal{N}(0, 2\nu) \tag{10.1}$$

as T tends to infinity, where

$$\nu = \gamma_0 + 2\sum_{j=1}^{\infty} \gamma_j.$$

ν is estimated using the kernel-based estimate

$$\hat{\nu}_\ell = \hat{\gamma}_0 + 2\sum_{j=1}^{\ell}\left(1 - \frac{j}{\ell+1}\right)\hat{\gamma}_j$$

where $\hat{\gamma}_j$ is the jth serial covariance of X_t^2 and ℓ is a truncation number. A discussion on this estimator can be found in Newey and West (1987), where a consistency result is established when $\ell = \ell(T)$ tends to infinity with T and is such that $\ell(T) = O(T^{-1/4})$. Discussions about the choice of ℓ can be found in Phillips (1987) and White and Domowitz (1984).

Note that the postsample prediction test crucially depends on the time point where we split the series into two parts. As in practice this time point is arbitrary, we recall another test for covariance stationarity, the *CUSUM test*. This test does not require splitting of the time series into two parts. Let us define

$$\psi(r) = \frac{1}{\sqrt{T\nu}}\sum_{t=1}^{[Tr]}\left(X_t^2 - \hat{\sigma}_T^2\right) \tag{10.2}$$

where $0 < r < 1$ and $\hat{\sigma}_T^2$ is the classical variance estimate over the whole segment of length T. This test compares the global variance estimate with the partial sum of the squared process (recall that we assume the process to be zero-mean). If the X_t obey the moment and mixing conditions in Phillips (1987), then Lo (1991) proves that, under the null, $\psi(r)$ converges in distribution to a Brownian bridge.

Figure 10.4 illustrates the test (10.2) on three segments of the Dow Jones index [(a) from January 2, 1990 to December 31, 1999, (b) from January 3, 2000 to December 31, 2009; and (c) from January 3, 2000 to December 31, 2001]. For each segment, the curve $\psi(r)$ is displayed together with the percentiles of the Brownian bridge. The two first panels lead to a rejection of the covariance stationary hypothesis over the two decades. Panel (c) does not reject the hypothesis over the two years 2000–2001.

Tests for covariance stationarity are not limited to the above basic tests, and a survey of more recent approaches is beyond the scope of this study. We refer

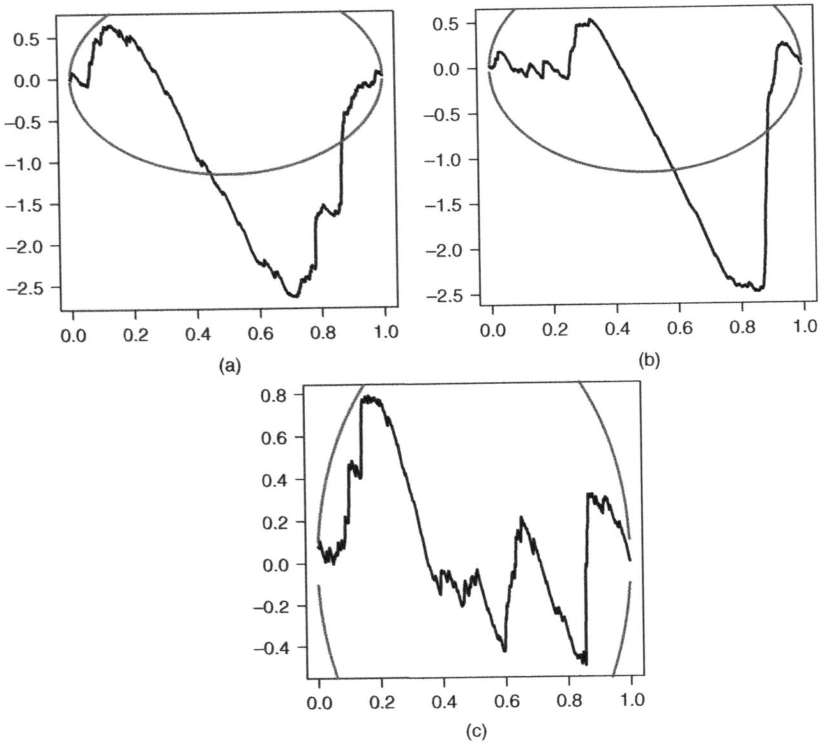

FIGURE 10.4 **The result of the CUSUM test (Eq. 10.2) for three segments of the DJIA index. (a) From January 2, 1990 to December 31, 1999; (b) from January 3, 2000 to December 31, 2009; and (c) from January 3, 2000 to December 31, 2001.**

the interested reader to Loretan and Phillips (1994); Dehay and Leškow (1996); Cavaliere (2004); and Xiao and Lima (2007) to cite but a few references on the topic.

10.3 Locally Stationary Processes and their Time-Varying Autocovariance Function

The first definition of locally stationary processes proposed by Dahlhaus (1996) and Dahlhaus (1997) was written in the frequency domain. In this definition, the spectral density is allowed to depend on time, with some degree of regularity with respect to time. Dahlhaus (1996) and Dahlhaus (1997) assume this variation to be smooth in time (existing second-order derivatives). This assumption has been relaxed in Neumann and von Sachs (1997) to allow jumps in the spectral density over time.

The definition presented below allows jumps and contains milder structural assumptions than the initial definition of locally stationary processes. It is written in the time domain and is taken from Dahlhaus and Polonik (2009).

To define the regularity of the (co)variance over time, we first recall the definition of the total variation divergence of a function g defined in the interval $[0, 1]$:

$$TV(g) = \sup\left\{\sum_{i=1}^{I} |g(x_i) - g(x_{i-1})| \ : \ 0 \leq x_0 < \cdots < x_I \leq 1, I \in N\right\}.$$

Functions with finite total variation can have a countable number of breaks of a limited size. For some $\kappa > 0$, we also need to define the function

$$\ell(j) := \begin{cases} 1 & |j| \leq 1 \\ |j|(\log |j|)^{1+\kappa} & |j| > 1. \end{cases} \quad (10.3)$$

DEFINITION 10.1 Dahlhaus and Polonik (2009)

The process $X_{t,T}$ $(t = 1, \ldots, T)$ is a locally stationary process if it is such that

$$X_{t,T} = \sum_{j=-\infty}^{\infty} a_{t,T}(j)\varepsilon_{t-j}$$

with the following conditions: for some finite generic constant K,

$$\sup_{t,T} |a_{t,T}(j)| \leq \frac{K}{\ell(j)}$$

and there exist functions $a(\cdot, j) : [0, 1) \to R$ such that

$$\sup_u |a(u, j)| \leq \frac{K}{\ell(j)}$$

$$\sup_j \sum_{t=1}^{n} \left|a_{t,n}(j) - a\left(\frac{t}{n}, j\right)\right| \leq K$$

$$TV(a(\cdot, j)) \leq \frac{K}{\ell(j)}.$$

The ε_t are assumed to be independent and identically distributed with all existing moments and such that $E(\varepsilon_t) = 0$ *and* $E(\varepsilon_t^2) = 1$.

According to this definition, locally stationary processes have an MA(∞) representation, with time-varying filters satisfying some regularity conditions.

In order to understand the above definition, it is useful to compute the autocovariance function of the resulting process. Consider the function $c_T(t,s) = \mathrm{Cov}(X_{[t-s/2],T}, X_{[t+s/2],T})$ for fixed T and $s \in \{0, 1, \ldots, T\}$. It can be shown that this covariance converges, in a sense defined below, to the function $c(u,s) = \sum_{j=-\infty}^{\infty} a(u, s+j)a(u,j)$ where $u \in [0,1)$. More precisely, Proposition 5.4 in Dahlhaus and Polonik (2009) implies that

$$\sum_{t=1}^{T} \left| c_T(t,s) - c\left(\frac{t}{T}, s\right) \right|$$

is uniformly bounded as $T \to \infty$. This result is important because it shows the uniqueness of the limit function $c(u,s)$, which can then be called the *time-varying autocovariance* of the locally stationary time series.

The class of locally stationary time series contains many processes of interest. It contains, of course, stationary MA(∞) for which the coefficients $a_{t,T}(j)$ in the definition do not depend on t. In such a case, the autocovariance function is the usual ACF for stationary processes. ARMA processes with time-varying coefficients are also in this family under some constraints on the regularity of their coefficients (Proposition 2.4 in Dahlhaus and Polonik, 2009). This fact is a reason why the definition of locally stationary processes involves two different objects $a_{t,T}(j)$ for $t = 1, \ldots, T$ and $a(u,j)$ for $u \in [0,1)$.

In the above definition, the process $X_{t,T}$ is doubly indexed, meaning that data arises in a triangular array. This setting is needed in order to study the asymptotic behavior of any estimator of the time-varying autocovariance function $c(u,k)$. Owing to the triangular device, growing T does not mean to look into the future of the process. Instead, it means that one observes another realization of the entire time series $X_{t,T}$ from which we can expect to construct a more accurate estimator of the time-varying autocovariance function $c(u,s)$. This phenomenon is illustrated in Figure 10.5 in the particular case of a process with a time-varying standard deviation. The standard deviation $\sqrt{c(u,0)}$ is plotted in the rescaled time $[0,1)$ in Figure 10.5a. This function is then used to construct the locally stationary process $X_{t,T} = \sqrt{c(t/T,0)}\varepsilon_t$ with a Gaussian white noise ε_t for three values of T. Each of the three simulated time series contains information about the entire time-varying variance of Figure 10.5a, with a starting constant variance, followed by a peak of volatility, and then a stepwise decline of the volatility. The advantage when T increases is that the variance curve from which the process is simulated, $c(t/T,0)$, is sampled on a finer grid, and therefore one can expect to construct estimators with more accuracy for larger sample sizes.

The introduction of rescaled time and triangular process is only theoretical and needed when asymptotic properties are considered. It is not a structural assumption on the observed process. Although it implies that future

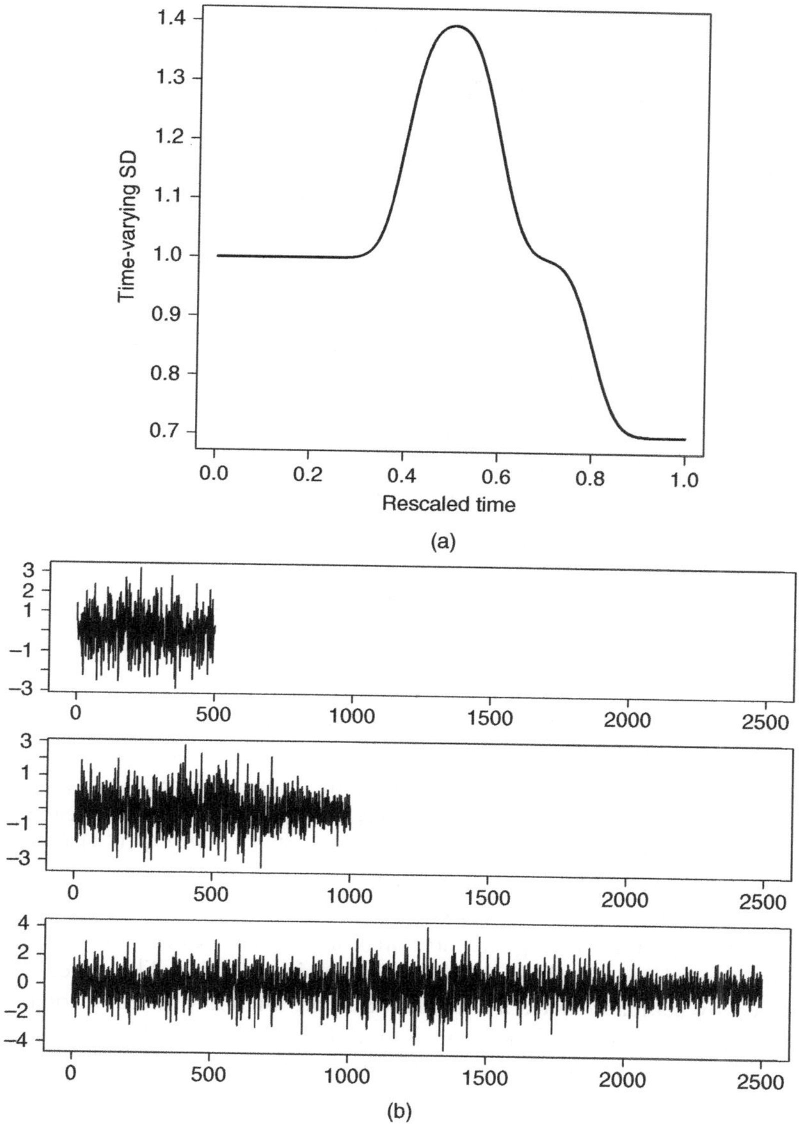

FIGURE 10.5 **(a) A given time-varying standard deviation (noted $c^{1/2}(u, 0)$ in the text) from which we give in (b) three variations of the locally stationary process to the right ($X_{t,T}$) with $T = 500$, 1000, and 2500.**

observations are not provided for growing T, it is nevertheless possible to reconcile this view with a prediction theory for locally stationary times series. This point has been formalized in Fryźlewicz et al. (2003) and Van Bellegem and von Sachs (2004).

10.4 Locally Stationary Volatility Models

10.4.1 MULTIPLICATIVE MODELS

A particular locally stationary model for volatility consists of a second-order stationary process that is modulated by a deterministic time-varying variance. If Y_t, $t = 1, 2, \ldots, T$, denotes a zero-mean stationary process (e.g., a GARCH process) and if $\sigma(\cdot)$ is a function in the interval $[0, 1)$, the time-modulated model is

$$X_{t,T} = \sigma\left(\frac{t}{T}\right) Y_t \,.$$

for $t = 1, 2, \ldots, T$. This model satisfies the definition of a locally stationary process, provided that the function $\sigma(\cdot)$ has a finite total variation norm, and all moments of Y_t exist. For identification reasons, we also assume that the unconditional variance of Y_t is normalized to 1. Let $c^Y(\cdot)$ be the autocovariance function of Y. Then the time-varying covariance of $X_{t,T}$ is

$$\begin{aligned} c^X(u,\tau) &= \lim_{T\to\infty} \mathrm{Cov}\left(X_{[uT-\tau/2]}, X_{[uT+\tau/2]}\right) \qquad u \in [0,1], \tau \in N \\ &= \lim_{T\to\infty} \sigma\left(\frac{[uT-\tau/2]}{T}\right)\sigma\left(\frac{[uT+\tau/2]}{T}\right)c^Y(\tau) \\ &= \sigma(u)^2 c^Y(\tau) \end{aligned}$$

if we assume the function $\sigma(\cdot)$ to be continuous.[2] Therefore, with the normalization $c^Y(0) \equiv 1$, $\sigma(u)^2$ models the time-varying unconditional variance.

The gain of this variance modulation in terms of forecasting economic data (stock returns and exchange rates) has been studied in Van Bellegem and von Sachs (2004), where various specifications of Y_t (ARMA, GARCH, and EGARCH) as well as two regularity conditions on the function $\sigma(\cdot)$ are tested (Lipschitz continuous or piecewise constant).

Modeling a time-varying unconditional variance can be beneficial to account for more permanent or slowly varying patterns in volatility. This aspect is not modeled by standard GARCH models, that are therefore more adequate for shorter run forecasts. In Engle and Rangel (2008), a multiplicative model is proposed, with more structural assumptions on the function $\sigma(\cdot)$ and on Y_t. They introduce a class of models, called spline-GARCH, that can be written with the following constraints:

$$\begin{aligned} X_{t,T} &= \sigma\left(\frac{t}{T}\right) g_t Z_t, \qquad \text{where } Z_t \text{ is conditionally } N(0,1), \\ g_t^2 &= (1-\alpha-\beta) + \alpha g_{t-1}^2 Z_{t-1}^2 + \beta g_{t-1}^2, \\ \sigma(u)^2 &= c\,\exp\left(w_0 u + \sum_{i=0}^{k} w_i((u-u_{i-1})_+)^2 + h(u)\gamma\right) \end{aligned} \tag{10.4}$$

[2]The argument can be extended to the case of noncontinuous functions $\sigma(u)$; see Van Bellegem and von Sachs (2004).

where h is a deterministic function and where $x_+ = x$ if $x > 0$ and 0 otherwise. The nodes $\{u_0 = 0, u_1, u_2, \ldots, u_k = 1\}$ denote a partition of $[0, 1]$ in k equally spaced segments. The original definition of Engle and Rangel (2008) is not written in rescaled time. Moreover, they allow the function h to depend on exogenous variables, a case that we do not discuss in this section. The function $\sigma(\cdot)$ is interpreted as the low frequency component of the volatility. If $\sigma(u)^2$ is a constant, then the process Y_t is a standard GARCH(1,1) process.

Figure 10.6 shows an estimator of $\sigma(u)^2$ for two segments of the DJIA index, with $k = 3$.[3] The spline-GARCH model can be viewed as a particular case of the time-modulated processes with a particular spline structure for $\sigma(u)$. In Engle and Rangel (2008), the dimension of the spline, k, is chosen by the Schwarz information criterion. An adaptive, data-driven procedure to select the dimensionality of a spline is studied in Van Bellegem and Dahlhaus (2006) in the general context of the approximation of time-varying parameters by the method of sieves.

Recent extensions of the spline-GARCH approach for modeling volatility include the use of large-dimensional B-splines as in Audrino and Bühlmann (2009) and the use of more flexible parametric forms for $\sigma(u)$ as in Amado and Teräsvirta (2011), see also Chapter 2. It is possible to go beyond this limitation and to estimate $\sigma(u)$ by arbitrary basis functions. In the context of locally stationary time series, Van Bellegem and Dahlhaus (2006) have developed a method of sieve to estimate a time-varying second-order structure. The dimensionality of the sieve is not known and adaptively inferred from the observed process.

10.4.2 TIME-VARYING ARCH PROCESSES

The class of ARCH(p) processes has been generalized to allow their parameters to change through time by Dahlhaus and Subba Rao (2006). The resulting time-varying ARCH(p) model, is defined as

$$X_{t,T} = \sigma_{t,T} Z_t,$$

$$\sigma_{t,T}^2 = a_0\left(\frac{t}{T}\right) + \sum_{j=1}^{p} a_j\left(\frac{t}{T}\right) X_{t-j,T}^2$$

$t = 1, 2, \ldots, T$, where Z_t are independent and identically distributed variables with zero-mean and such that $E(Z_t^2) = 1$. Analogous to the stationary ARCH model, the time-varying parameters need to satisfy some constraints: there exists positive, finite constants c, d such that $\inf_u a_0(u) > c$ and $\sup_u a_j(u) \leq d/\ell(j)$, where $\ell(j)$ is defined in Equation 10.3. The regularity of curves $a_j(\cdot)$ over time is also supposed to follow a Lipschitz constraint, that is, there exists constant K such that $|a_j(u) - a_j(v)| \leq K|u - v|/\ell(j)$ which, in particular, implies that the time-varying curves are continuous. The conditions on the coefficients also imply that $E(X_{t,T}^2)$ is uniformly bounded over t and T.

[3]Another example of a spline-GARCH estimation is provided in chapter 1 of this handbook.

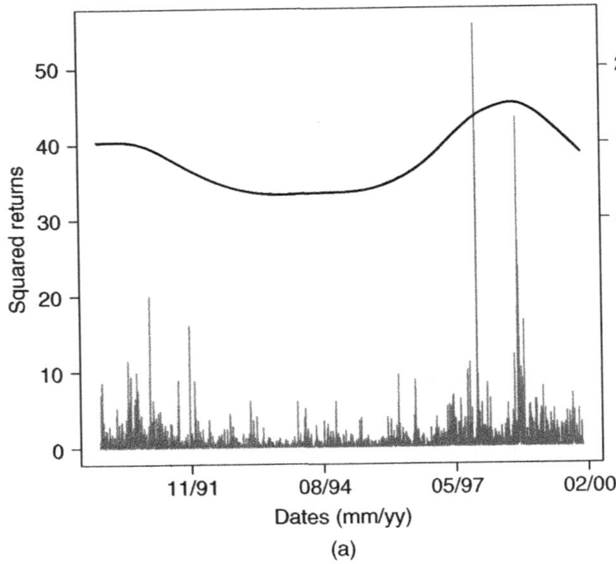

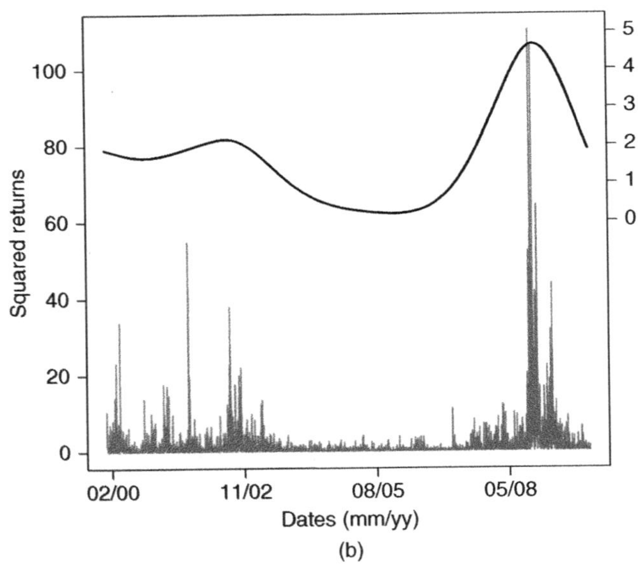

FIGURE 10.6 Spline-GARCH fits to two segments of the DJIA index. The squared returns (in gray) are superimposed with a cubic spline estimator of the time-varying unconditional variance (black curve and scale on the right side). (a) Index from January 2, 1990, to December 31, 1999. (b) Index from January 3, 2000 to December 31, 2009.

The persistence effect of time-varying ARCH(p) has been studied in detail by Fryźlewicz et al. (2008). In their Proposition 2 and under technical conditions, they establish that the sample autocovariance function of $X^2_{t,T}$ evaluated under the wrong premise of stationarity, that is,

$$\frac{1}{T-h}\sum_{t=1}^{T-h} X^2_{t,T}X^2_{t+h,T} - \left(\frac{1}{T-h}\sum_{t=1}^{T-h} X^2_{t,T}\right)^2$$

converges in probability, for fixed h and as $T \to \infty$, to

$$\int_0^1 c^{X^2}(u,h)\,du + \iint_{\{0\le u<v\le 1\}} \{\mu^{X^2}(u) - \mu^{X^2}(v)\}^2\,du dv$$

where $\mu^{X^2}(u)$ and c^{X^2} are, respectively, the time-varying mean and autocovariance function of the squared process. The ACF of the squares of a time-varying ARCH process is shown to exponentially decay to zero. The persistence effect appears from the second integral in the limit, which does not depend on the lag h and is typically nonzero (except for stationary ARCH, in which case μ^{X^2} is constant).

Advanced inference for time-varying ARCH(p) has been recently studied. In the seminal work Dahlhaus and Subba Rao (2006), a localized version of the quasi-maximum likelihood method is studied. A recursive online algorithm of estimation is proposed in Dahlhaus and Subba Rao (2007). An alternative least-squares type estimator is studied in Fryźlewicz et al. (2008). This estimator considers the following contrast function:

$$L_{t,T}(a_0,\ldots,a_p) = \sum_{k=p+1}^{T} W_{bT}(t-k)\frac{(X^2_{k,T} - a_0 - \sum_{j=1}^{p} a_j X^2_{k-j,T})^2}{g(u, X^2_{k-1,T},\ldots,X^2_{k-p,T})}$$

where $W_{bT}()$ is a given kernel function with bandwidth b and g is a weight function. If u is such that $|u - t/T| < 1/T$, then the weighted least-squares estimator of $(a_0(u),\ldots,a_p(u))$ is given by the arg min of $L_{t,T}(a_0,\ldots,a_p)$. The asymptotic normality of the estimator is established in Fryźlewicz et al. (2008), and it is shown that the performance of the estimator depends on the weight function g. Thus, a two-stage estimator is also studied, where in the first stage, the weight function is estimated.

An interesting connection between time-varying ARCH and spline-GARCH can be established if we restrict the latter to spline-ARCH processes (i.e., $\beta \equiv 0$ in Equation 10.4). Assuming that the conditional distribution is normal in both models, a simple calculation leads to

$$a_0\left(\frac{t}{T}\right) = (1-\alpha)\sigma_S\left(\frac{t}{T}\right)^2 \quad \text{and} \quad a_1\left(\frac{t}{T}\right) = \frac{\alpha\sigma_S(t/T)^2}{\sigma_S((t-1)/T)^2}. \qquad (10.5)$$

where σ_S denotes the low frequency component of the spline-ARCH. Spline-ARCH is therefore a specific case of time-varying ARCH in which the variation of a_0 is, up to a constant, given by the variation of $\sigma_S(\cdot)$. Since $\sigma_S(\cdot)$ is a smooth function of time, the curve $a_1(t/T)$ is not supposed to show high unconditional variations and is approximately equal to α.

Note that an extension of time-varying ARCH to time-varying GARCH, although straightforward, encounters theoretical problems. In particular, no inference theory is available on time-varying GARCH in the context of locally stationary time series.

The weighted least-squares estimator of time-varying ARCH curves is illustrated in Figure 10.7, where a time-varying ARCH(1) model is fitted on two segments of the DJIA index. In this estimation exercise, the bandwidth is set to $bT = 250$ data. The qualitative aspect of the curves do not vary when this bandwidth is taken between 150 and 800. The estimated $a_0(u)$ in Figure 10.7 behaves very similarly to what we obtained with the spline-GARCH in Figure 10.6. According to Equation 10.5 and under the assumption of spline-ARCH, they only differ in theory by a multiplicative constant.

10.4.3 ADAPTIVE APPROACHES

The above procedures are based on the structural assumption that the volatility belongs to a precise class of locally stationary models. The class of spline-GARCH provides the most restrictive formulation. An alternative approach to handle nonstationary volatilities is provided by adaptive approaches, in which one only assumes that volatility can be locally approximated by a constant volatility. Even if the volatility is locally constant, it is not so globally, and this new approach aims to evaluate pointwise estimators of volatility by fitting constant volatilities at each time point.

The root of this idea goes back to the paradigm of local polynomial inference in which a nonparametric estimator of a regression function is found when constants or polynomials are fitted locally at every point of the regression (Fan and Gijbels, 1996). One crucial aspect of this method is the definition at each estimation point of the neighborhood under which the regression can be supposed to be constant or polynomial. With that respect, a fundamental work by Lepski (1990) provides an automatic method to determine this neighborhood, which can have a different length from one estimation point to another.

The extension of local regression to estimate time-varying volatilities has been studied by Härdle et al. (2003) and Mercurio and Spokoiny (2004). Suppose X_t denotes some returns from which we want to infer a volatility function. The authors assume that the volatility function is *local time homogeneous* meaning that, at time t, there exists an interval $I = [t - m, t]$, with $m > 0$, such that the volatility can be estimated by the empirical average

$$\hat{\sigma}_I^2 = \frac{1}{|I|} \sum_{\tau \in I} X_\tau^2.$$

(Other forms of estimators are also considered in the above cited literature). Note that the parameter m defining the length of the interval I might differ for

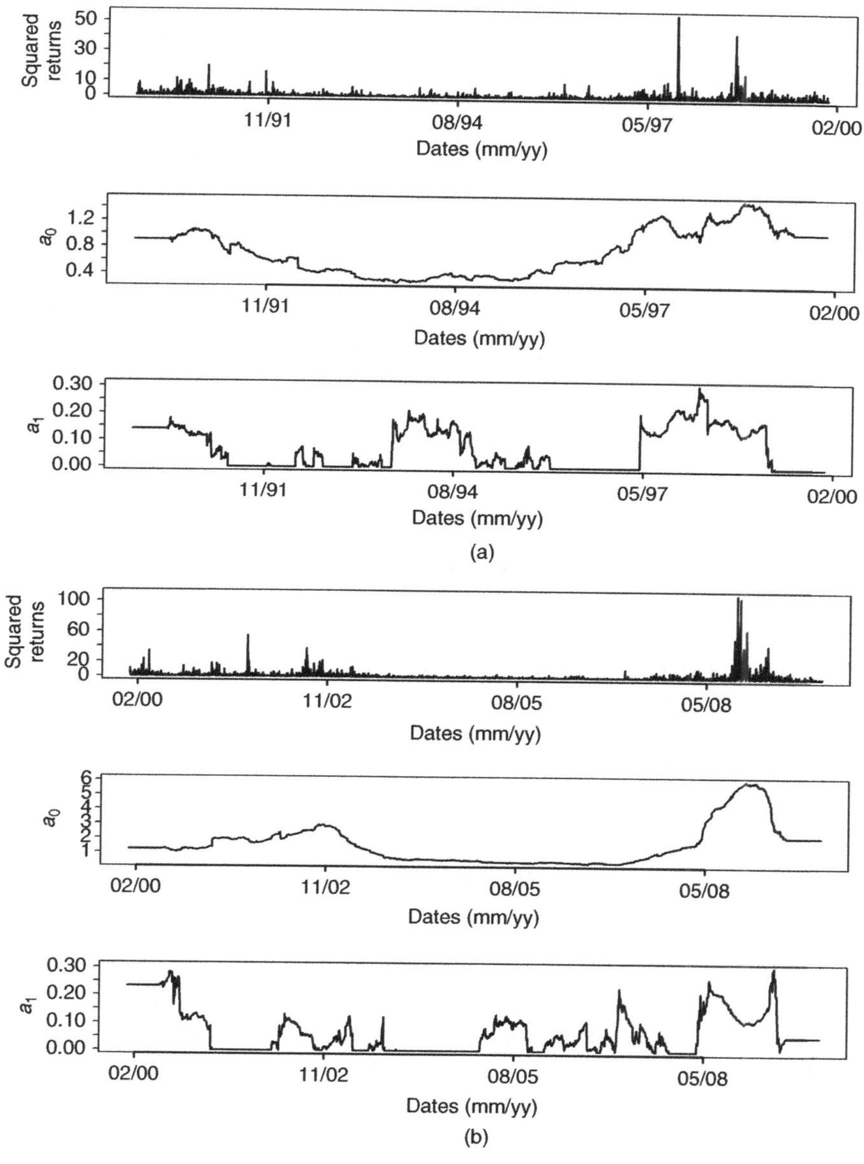

FIGURE 10.7 Time-varying ARCH(1) fits to two segments of the DJIA index. In each subfigure, the first row is the squared returns and the second and third rows are weighted least-squares estimators of $a_0(u)$ and $a_1(u)$ with bandwidth $b = 250$ data. (a) Index from January 2, 1990, to December 31, 1999. (b) Index from January 3, 2000, to December 31, 2009.

various time points t. Therefore the selection of m is the main statistical challenge and, based on the automatic selection of Lepski (1990), an adaptive procedure for choosing m has been developed by Härdle et al. (2003) and Mercurio and Spokoiny (2004). The procedure is a sequence of tests of stationarity on intervals $[t - m, t]$ for growing m. The adaptive interval is found to be the largest interval on which the observed time series is still compatible with the null of stationarity. To concretely implement the procedure, a choice of calibration parameters is needed such as the level of the stationarity tests. Under some assumptions, Mercurio and Spokoiny (2004) show that the necessary calibration parameters are time-invariant, and thus a procedure to find those parameters from some training sets of data can be developed.

Since the mentioned papers have been published, many extensions and improvements of the adaptive approach have been studied, see for example, Cížek et al. (2009) and Spokoiny (2009). Combining this approach with the above definition of locally stationary time series has been studied in Van Bellegem and von Sachs (2006).

10.5 Multivariate Models for Locally Stationary Volatility

The extension of locally stationary time series to multivariate time series has been formally studied by Dahlhaus (2000). In this first approach, the multivariate spectral density is allowed to vary with respect to the rescaled time, and this variation is supposed to be modeled by a vector of finite dimensional parameters.

The extension of multivariate locally stationary models of volatility is a very active topic of research at present, and a lot of work remains to be done. One challenge arises since the resulting process is very complex, difficult to interpret, and hard to estimate accurately. One ultimate aim in this context is to specify a multivariate model that achieves a reasonable trade-off between its flexibility (complexity), and the necessity to keep easy interpretation (or identification) and efficient estimation. In the context of stationary models, multivarate extension of volatility models are already challenging. Two surveys are available in this context: Bauwens et al. (2006) focus on parametric multivariate GARCH models and Silvennoinen and Teräsvirta (2009) also survey nonparametric and semiparametric multivariate GARCH models.

Below, we describe two successful extensions of the above univariate models for local stationarity. One is an extension of the multiplicative model, and the other is an extension of the adaptive approach.

10.5.1 MULTIPLICATIVE MODELS

A multivariate extension of the multiplicative model is found when the volatility process $X_{t,T} \in R^N$ satisfies the decomposition

$$X_{t,T} = \Sigma \left(\frac{t}{T}\right)^{1/2} Y_t,$$

where Σ now denotes a time-varying $N \times N$ deterministic definite positive matrix and $Y_t \in R^N$ is a stationary time series. Among the many possible specifications for Σ and Y_t, Hafner and Linton (2010) study the situation where $\Sigma(\cdot)$ is unknown, either smooth or with finite total variation norm components. They decompose Y_t as $G_t^{1/2}Z_t$ where Z_t is an N-dimensional strictly stationary martingale difference sequence satisfying $E(Z_t|\mathcal{F}_{t-1}) = 0$, $E(Z_tZ_t'|\mathcal{F}_{t-1}) = I_N$, $\mathcal{F}_{t-1}$ being the sigma algebra generated by $X_{t-1}, X_{t-2}, X_{t-3}, \ldots$, and $G_t \in R^N$ is a strictly stationary process adapted to $\mathcal{F}_{t-1}$. In the model of Hafner and Linton (2010),

$$X_{t,T} = \Sigma\left(\frac{t}{T}\right)^{1/2} G_t^{1/2}Z_t,$$

the process G_t is supposed to depend on a finite dimensional vector of parameters. Therefore, it can be viewed as a multivariate generalization of the spline-GARCH model above defined. Local maximum likelihood estimation is studied in Hafner and Linton (2010), who also establish the asymptotic properties of their estimators under the semistrong form specification of the errors and show that under the strong form Gaussian distributional specification, their estimators are semiparametrically efficient.

10.5.2 ADAPTIVE APPROACHES

In principle, the adaptive approach is not limited to one-dimensional volatility processes. Härdle et al. (2003) have considered this extension as follows. Suppose the volatility process $X_{t,T} \in R^N$ satisfies the decomposition

$$X_{t,T} = H\left(\frac{t}{T}\right)^{1/2} Z_t,$$

where Z_t is a standard Gaussian multivariate process and $H(\cdot)$ is an $\mathcal{F}_{t-1}$ measurable process that captures the entire dynamics of $X_{t,T}$. Under the assumption that at time t the volatility is local time homogenous over I (see above), an estimator of $H(t/T)$ is given by

$$\frac{1}{|I|}\sum_{\tau \in I} X_{t,T}X_{t,T}'.$$

As before, the main statistical challenge of the approach is to define a data-driven selection of the interval I such that the resulting estimator has good properties. To reduce the dimensionality, Härdle et al. (2003) use the idea of principal component analysis to transform the multivariate process to univariate processes.

10.6 Conclusions

This paper reviews the concept of local stationarity and its use for modeling volatility. Three main approaches have been discussed. The first approach is a multiplicative decomposition of the volatility as a time-varying unconditional variance that multiplies a stationary ARCH-type process. The time-varying unconditional variance models long-term patterns (such as cyclical patterns) of structural breakpoints in the volatility process. The second approach is to consider ARCH(p) models with time-varying coefficients. Feasible nonparametric estimators to estimate the coefficients have been studied in this context. Finally, a third approach, called *adaptive*, is purely nonparametric and approximates locally the volatility time series by a constant volatility.

Acknowledgments

This work was supported by the "Agence Nationale de la Recherche" under contract ANR-09-JCJC-0124-01 and by the SCOR Chair on "Market Risk and Value Creation." I thank Piotr Fryzlewicz for providing the R code to fit time-varying ARCH models to data and the editors of this volume for helpful comments on a preliminary version of this chapter.

CHAPTER ELEVEN

Nonparametric and Semiparametric Volatility Models: Specification, Estimation, and Testing

LIANGJUN SU, AMAN ULLAH, SANTOSH MISHRA, and YUN WANG

11.1 Introduction

In recent years, an extensive literature has developed on studying the volatility in financial markets. The simplest approach in this literature regards volatility as a time-invariant constant parameter σ. However, this is contradicted in some of the real world financial data, where a specific pattern of return variability is observed. These changes are often referred to as the *volatility clustering* and as first noted by Mandelbrot (1963), this is the property of prices that "large changes tend to be followed by large changes—of either sign—and small changes tend to be followed by small changes." As a consequence, there has been a concerted attempt to model this time-varying volatility. One of the distinct approaches

Handbook of Volatility Models and Their Applications, First Edition.
Edited by Luc Bauwens, Christian Hafner, and Sebastien Laurent.

to model time-varying volatility is to treat the conditional variance as a latent variable, and a suitable parametric, nonparametric (NP), or semiparametric (SP) structure is attributed to it. In this chapter, we focus mainly on modeling volatility as given in this case and present an overview of its developments. Owing to space limitation, we shall not survey alternative approaches to modeling volatility such as stochastic volatility (SV) and realized volatility (RV). The recent handbook edited by Andersen et al. (2009) has devoted seven articles to the former topic, most of which, however, focus on the parametric specification and estimation of SV models though. The handbook also devotes a whole chapter on the intuitive overview on RV and the associated applications. Also, see Chapter 1 for a general introduction on standard parametric volatility models, and Parts 2 and 3 in this handbook an SV and RV, respectively.

Our focus in this chapter is on NP and SP models of conditional variance in the discrete time setting. We find out that the majority of NP and SP works on volatility are focused on univariate models. For clarity, we will first consider the data generating process (DGP) of y_t as

$$y_t = m(x_t) + \sigma(z_t)\varepsilon_t, \; t = 1, \ldots, n, \tag{11.1}$$

where $E(\varepsilon_t|\mathcal{F}_{t-1}) = 0, E(\varepsilon_t^2|\mathcal{F}_{t-1}) = 1$, and x_t and z_t are d_x and d_z dimensional stochastic processes, respectively. Furthermore, assume that x_t and z_t are both $\mathcal{F}_{t-1}$ measurable and may include lagged y_t's. The above DGP states that $m(x_t)$ and $\sigma^2(z_t)$ are conditional mean and variance of the stochastic process y_t, respectively. It is well known that the conditional variance $\sigma^2(z_t)$ can be adaptively estimated (Fan and Yao, 1998). This implies that the conditional mean part $m(x_t)$ can be treated as if it were observed or assumed to be 0 in many cases. In the following, we keep our focus on the specification and estimation of $\sigma^2(z_t)$ and the density of ε_t. We study the estimation of $\sigma^2(z_t)$ when the process y_t is stationary. We distinguish the cases when there is no particular structure assumed for the functional form of $\sigma^2(\cdot)$ and when $\sigma^2(\cdot)$ is assumed to exhibit some particular structures, such as the additive, varying coefficient or single-index structure. For details on the NP and SP econometrics, see Pagan and Ullah (1999) and Li and Racine (2007). The dimension of z_t may be infinite as in ARCH(∞) model. The functional form of $\sigma^2(\cdot)$ can be semiparametrically specified such that it has both parametric and NP components. Then, we study estimation of volatility in nonstationary processes, such as the locally stationary multiplicative volatility processes of Feng (2004) and Engle and Rangel (2008) and the locally stationary varying coefficient generalized autoregressive conditional heteroskedasticity (GARCH) processes of Dahlhaus and Subba Rao (2006). Structural changes in volatility functions are also briefly addressed. Then, we focus on the issue related to the specification or estimation of the density of the standardized error term ε_t, which addresses the potential efficiency loss of the commonly used Gaussian quasi-maximum likelihood estimation (QMLE). Both adaptive estimation and estimating function (EF) approach are discussed. Finally, for the simple volatility model $y_t = \sigma_t\varepsilon_t$, we also review some papers on the estimation of the stationary density of the volatility σ_t^2 or $\ln(\sigma_t^2)$ when the density of ε_t is assumed to be known and the process $\{\sigma_t\}$ is left unspecified.

Despite the relatively few work on NP and SP discrete time multivariate volatility models, we also review the available literature on this aspect. We first review the papers for stationary multivariate volatility models and then move to the locally stationary ones. Specification of the multivariate error density are also addressed. To avoid the curse of dimensionality problem, both spherically symmetric density and SP copula-based density have been considered in the literature.

It is worth mentioning that there are two surveys on NP and SP GARCH models, namely, Linton (2009) and Linton and Yan (2011). Both papers provide a wide yet condensed view of the NP and SP volatility literature. However, although our coverage is narrower, it provides a more detailed explanation of major ideas compared to both the aforementioned papers.

The plan of our chapter is as follows. We survey the NP and SP univariate volatility models in Section 11.2. Then, in Section 11.3, we present the multivariate NP and SP volatility models. In Section 11.4, we conduct a small empirical analysis. Finally, Section 11.5 gives concluding remarks.

11.2 Nonparametric and Semiparametric Univariate Volatility Models

11.2.1 STATIONARY VOLATILITY MODELS

In this section, we first review the traditional NP volatility models that do not assume any particular structure and then focus on several special types of stationary volatility models that exhibit certain special structures. These include the widely used additive models, functional-coefficient models, index models, stationary SP ARCH(∞) models, SP combined volatility models, and SP GARCH-in-mean models. We present the specification, estimation, and related issues associated with these models.

11.2.1.1 The Simplest Nonparametric Volatility Model. To the best of our knowledge, the first significant work in NP modeling of conditional variance is due to Pagan and Ullah (1988), Pagan and Schwert (1990), and Pagan and Hong (1991) where a Nadaraya–Watson estimator of conditional variance is proposed. They also suggest a leave-one-out variation of the estimator to account for potential outliers. The estimation involves the squared residuals obtained from the conditional mean equation and the argument of the kernel function is the variable with respect to which the conditional variance is supposed to change. A theoretical formalization of their model can be found in Fan and Yao (1998), which we briefly discuss below. For the purpose of demonstration, we assume that $d_x = d_z = 1$ and $x_t = z_t = y_{t-1}$. Note that this can be easily extended to case when d_x and d_z are greater than 1 and when both x_t and z_t contain some other variables that are not the lagged variables of y_t. Assume that a strictly stationary stochastic process y_t is generated through the following DGP:

$$y_t = m(y_{t-1}) + \sigma(y_{t-1})\varepsilon_t, \qquad (11.2)$$

where $E(\varepsilon_t|\mathcal{F}_{t-1}) = 0, E(\varepsilon_t^2|\mathcal{F}_{t-1}) = 1$. Given $n+1$ observations $y_0, y_1, \ldots, y_n$, Fan and Yao (1998) propose the following two-stage approach to obtain the local linear estimator for the conditional variance.

1. Obtain the local linear estimator $\hat{m}(y)$ of $m(y)$ as the minimization intercept $\hat{\beta}_0(y)$ in the following minimization problem

$$\min_{\beta_0,\beta_1} n^{-1}\sum_{t=1}^{n}\{y_t - [\beta_0 + \beta_1(y_{t-1} - y)]\}^2 \kappa_{h_1}(y_{t-1} - y), \tag{11.3}$$

   where $k_{h_1}(\cdot) = k(\cdot/h_1)/h_1$, $k(\cdot)$ is a kernel function, and $h_1 \equiv h_1(n)$ is a bandwidth parameter that shrinks to 0 as the sample size $n \to \infty$. Obtain $\hat{m}(y) = \hat{\beta}_0(y)$ at $y = y_{t-1}$ for $t = 1, \ldots, n$. Obtain the squared residuals as $\hat{r}_t^2 = [y_t - \hat{m}(y_{t-1})]^2, t = 1, \ldots, n$.
2. The local linear estimator $\hat{\sigma}^2(y)$ of $\sigma^2(y)$ is obtained as the minimization intercept $\hat{\gamma}_0(y)$ in the following minimization problem

$$\min_{\gamma_0,\gamma_1} n^{-1}\sum_{t=1}^{n}\left\{\hat{r}_t^2 - [\gamma_0 + \gamma_1(y_{t-1} - y)]\right\}^2 k_{h_2}(y_{t-1} - y), \tag{11.4}$$

   where a different bandwidth h_2 is used.

The bandwidth choice in the first stage is not as crucial as the bandwidth choice in the second stage. So in the first stage, the rule of thumb bandwidth can be used but in the second stage, an "optimal" bandwidth (in the sense of minimizing the asymptotic mean integrated squared error, say) is recommended. Under some standard conditions, Fan and Yao (1998) show that

$$\sqrt{nh_2}\left\{\hat{\sigma}^2(y) - \sigma^2(y) - B_n(y)\right\} \xrightarrow{d} N(0, V(y)), \tag{11.5}$$

where the bias term is given by $B_n(y) = \frac{1}{2}h_2^2\mu_{2,1}\ddot{\sigma}^2(y) + o(h_1^2 + h_2^2)$, the asymptotic variance is given by $V(y) = \mu_{0,2}\sigma^4(y)E\{(\varepsilon_t^2 - 1)|y_{t-1} = y\}/f(y)$, $\ddot{\sigma}^2(y)$ is the second derivative of $\sigma^2(y)$ with respect to y, $f(\cdot)$ is the probability density function (PDF) of y_t, and $\mu_{s,t} = \int u^s\kappa(u)^t du$ for $s, t = 0, 1, 2$. It is straightforward to extend the local linear method to the general local polynomial method. Härdle and Tsybakov (1997) provide a joint estimation of conditional mean and conditional variance when both the functional forms are unknown.

A notable drawback of Fan and Yao's estimator of $\sigma^2(y)$ is that it can be negative. This is undesirable in applications. Observing this, Ziegelmann (2002) proposes a modified estimator that not only addresses this problem but also provides a potential improvement on the asymptotic bias of the Fan and Yao (1998) estimator. The first stage of Ziegelmann's approach is identical to that of

Fan and Yao (1998). In the second stage, he proposes to estimate the conditional variance $\sigma^2(y)$ by the following minimization problem:

$$\min_{\gamma_0,\gamma_1} n^{-1} \sum_{t=1}^{n} \left\{\hat{\gamma}_t^2 - \Psi(\gamma_0 + \gamma_1(y_{t-1} - y))\right\}^2 \kappa_{h_2}(y_{t-1} - y), \tag{11.6}$$

where $\Psi(x) = e^x$ is the exponential tilting function. Let $\hat{\gamma}_0$ be the minimization solution to γ_0. Then, the exponential tilting estimator of $\sigma^2(y)$ is given by $\tilde{\sigma}^2(y) = e^{\hat{\gamma}_0}$. As Ziegelmann (2002) demonstrates, $\tilde{\sigma}^2(y)$ shares the same asymptotic variance as $\hat{\sigma}^2(y)$, the Fan and Yao (1998) estimator, but the two estimators exhibit different asymptotic biases. Under some conditions on the second derivative of $\sigma^2(y)$, the asymptotic bias of the Ziegelmann (2002) estimator can be smaller than that of Fan and Yao (1998), thus achieving certain degree of bias reduction without sacrificing the variance. Of course, the exponential tilting function can be replaced by some other nonnegative monotone functions and similar conclusions can be drawn. However, we note that both the Fan and Yao (1998) and Ziegelmann (2002) estimators are valid for the ARCH (p)-type information set for small value of p, but they may not be useful for the GARCH-type information sets.

11.2.1.2 Additive Nonparametric Volatility Model. The NP volatility model in the previous subsection can be extended to the multivariate case where both x_t and z_t contain a vector of variables. But due to the notorious "curse of dimensionality" issue in the NP literature, an increase in the dimension d_z of z_t will decrease the convergence rate of the NP volatility estimators. In real applications, we should not use the model when d_z is larger than 3 if we do not have thousands of observations. Nevertheless, with the stylized fact that financial time series tend to exhibit high persistence, it is often useful to incorporate more lagged variables of y_t in z_t. One way to do this is to apply the additive volatility model of the following form

$$\sigma^2(z_t) = \mu + \sum_{i=1}^{d_z} \sigma_i^2(z_{it}), \tag{11.7}$$

where z_{it} is the ith element in z_t, $\sigma_i^2(\cdot)$, $i = 1, \ldots, d_z$ are unknown smooth functions, and μ is a normalizing constant. Clearly, without further restrictions, neither μ nor $(\sigma_1^2(\cdot), \ldots, \sigma_{d_z}^2(\cdot))$ is identifiable in the above model. There are two sets of conditions to identify these parameters. We can assume either $E[\sigma_i^2(z_{it})] = 0$ for $i = 1, \ldots, d_z$ or $\sigma_i^2(0) = \sigma_{i,0}^2$ for some prescribed value $\sigma_{i,0}^2$ for $i = 1, \ldots, d_z$. Below, we focus on the estimation of μ and $\sigma_i^2(\cdot)$ under the former set of identification conditions, under which we can estimate μ by $\hat{\mu} = n^{-1} \sum_{t=1}^{n} y_t^2$, say, at the usual parametric rate.

By assuming the target volatility function can be written as the sum of functions of covariates, the additive model in Equation 11.7 can effectively reduce the dimensionality of the multivariate regression problem and improve the convergence rate of the resulting volatility estimator. Most importantly, we can estimate $\sigma_i^2(\cdot)$ and thus $\sigma^2(\cdot)$ with the one-dimensional optimal rate of convergence regardless of d_z. Regarding the estimation of additive models, there are three approaches in the literature: the backfitting, marginal integration, and local instrumental variable estimation (LIVE) methods. We review each of them briefly.

The backfitting method is originally suggested by Breiman and Friedman (1985), Hastie and Tibshirani (1987), Hastie and Tibshirani (1990), and Buja et al. (1989). It estimates the additive functions through iterative calculations until certain convergence criterion is met. The intuition behind this method is clear, but its statistical properties were not clearly understood until Opsomer and Ruppert (1997) and Mammen et al. (1999). To see how the backfitting method works for volatility model, consider the stationary process $\{y_t\}$ generated by

$$\begin{aligned} y_t &= \sigma(z_t)\varepsilon_t, \\ \sigma^2(z_t) &= \mu + \sigma_1^2(y_{t-1}) + \sigma_2^2(y_{t-2}), \end{aligned} \tag{11.8}$$

where $z_t = (y_{t-1}, y_{t-2})'$ and ε_t is a martingale difference sequence with respect to the filter generated by past history of y_t. The backfitting estimation is carried out as follows:

1. Assume an initial estimate of $\sigma_1^2(y_1)$ and $\sigma_2^2(y_2)$ and call it $\sigma_1^{2(0)}(y_1)$ and $\sigma_2^{2(0)}(y_2)$ (e.g., both are 0).
2. Find $(\hat{\gamma}_0, \hat{\gamma}_1)$:

$$(\hat{\gamma}_0, \hat{\gamma}_1) = \arg\min_{\gamma_0, \gamma_1} \frac{1}{n}\sum_{t=1}^{n} \left\{y_t^2 - \sigma_2^{2(0)}(y_{t-2}) - [\gamma_0 + \gamma_1(y_{t-1} - y_1)]\right\}^2 \times k_{h_1}(y_{t-1} - y_1).$$

Set $\sigma_1^{2(1)}(y_1) = \hat{\gamma}_0$.

3. Find $(\hat{\delta}_0, \hat{\delta}_1)$:

$$(\hat{\delta}_0, \hat{\delta}_1) = \arg\min_{\delta_0, \delta_1} \frac{1}{n}\sum_{t=1}^{n} \left\{y_t^2 - \sigma_1^{2(0)}(y_{t-1}) - \left[\delta_0 + \delta_1(y_{t-2} - y_2)\right]\right\}^2 \times k_{h_2}(y_{t-2} - y_2).$$

Set $\sigma_2^{2(1)}(y_2) = \hat{\delta}_0$.

4. Repeat steps 2 and 3 until $\sum_{t=1}^{n} |\{\sigma_i^{2(m)}(y_{t-1}) - \sigma_i^{2(m-1)}(y_{t-1})\}| < \upsilon_i$ for $i = 1, 2$ for some previously defined small values υ_1 and υ_2.

After obtaining the estimators of $\sigma_1^2(y_1)$ and $\sigma_2^2(y_2)$ through the above method, we can normalize them according to the identification condition to obtain the final estimator $\hat{\sigma}_1^2(\cdot)$, $\hat{\sigma}_2^2(\cdot)$, and $\hat{\mu}$ of $\sigma_1^2(\cdot)$, $\sigma_2^2(\cdot)$, and μ, respectively. For more details and some extensions, see Hastie and Tibshirani (1990).

The marginal integration method was developed independently by Newey (1994), Tjøstheim and Auestad (1994), and Linton and Nielsen (1995). Its theoretical properties are easy to derive because it is based on averaging of multivariate kernel estimates. For the same reason, it requires high dimensional NP estimation that may play a role in finite samples. To see how the estimation works, we focus on Equation 11.8. One can first estimate $\sigma^2(y_{t-1}, y_{t-2})$ by using the usual local polynomial method without imposing the additive condition, say, by $\tilde{\sigma}^2(y_{t-1}, y_{t-2})$ for $t = 2, \ldots, n$. Then, we obtain preliminary estimates of $\sigma_1^2(y)$ and $\sigma_2^2(y)$ by $\tilde{\sigma}_1^2(y) = \frac{1}{n}\sum_{t=2}^{n} \tilde{\sigma}^2(y, y_{t-2})$ and $\tilde{\sigma}_2^2(y) = \frac{1}{n}\sum_{t=2}^{n} \tilde{\sigma}^2(y_{t-1}, y)$, respectively. These estimators are consistent with $\sigma_1^2(y)$ and $\sigma_2^2(y)$ up to a normalization constant. Linton (1997) suggests a method for fully efficient estimates of the individual component functions.

Noting that both the backfitting and marginal integration methods are computationally extensive, Kim and Linton (2004) propose an estimation tool called the *LIVE* for the components of additive models. Rewrite Equation 11.8 as

$$y_t^2 = \mu + \sigma_1^2(y_{t-1}) + \sigma_2^2(y_{t-2}) + v_t, \tag{11.9}$$

where $v_t = [\mu + \sigma_1^2(y_{t-1}) + \sigma_2^2(y_{t-2})](\varepsilon_t^2 - 1)$ satisfies $E(v_t|y_{t-1}, y_{t-2}) = 0$. Assume that the component functions satisfy the identification conditions $E[\sigma_1^2(y_{t-1})] = E[\sigma_2^2(y_{t-2})] = 0$. We continue to write Equation 11.9 as

$$y_t^2 = \mu + \sigma_1^2(y_{t-1}) + \eta_t, \tag{11.10}$$

where $\eta_t = \sigma_2^2(y_{t-2}) + v_t$. Equation 11.10 can be treated with a regression model with "omitted variable" problem, and one solution to this problem is to look for an instrumental variable (IV) w_t such that

$$E\left(w_t|y_{t-1}\right) \neq 0 \text{ and } E\left(w_t\eta_t|y_{t-1}\right) = 0. \tag{11.11}$$

In this case, we have

$$\sigma_1^2(y) = \frac{E\left(w_t y_t^2|y_{t-1} = y\right)}{E\left(w_t|y_{t-1} = y\right)} - \mu, \tag{11.12}$$

which suggests that we can estimate $\sigma_1^2(y)$ by the NP smoothing of $w_t y_t^2$ and w_t on y_{t-1}, respectively. If we assume that ε_t are i.i.d., we can follow Kim and Linton (2004) and show that a natural candidate for w_t is given by $w_t = p(y_{t-2})/p(y_{t-1}, y_{t-2})$, where $p(\cdot)$ is the marginal PDF of y_{t-1} and $p(\cdot,\cdot)$ is the joint PDF of y_{t-1} and y_{t-2}. [Alternatively, we can take $w_t = p(y_{t-1})p(y_{t-2})/p(y_{t-1}, y_{t-2})$.] Similarly, we have

$$\sigma_2^2(y) = \frac{E\left(\tilde{w}_t y_t^2|y_{t-2} = y\right)}{E\left(\tilde{w}_t|y_{t-2} = y\right)} - \mu, \tag{11.13}$$

by choosing $\tilde{w}_t = p(y_{t-1})/p(y_{t-1}, y_{t-2})$ or $p(y_{t-1})p(y_{t-2})/p(y_{t-1}, y_{t-2})$.

Clearly, none of the above three types of methods can ensure the nonnegativity of the volatility estimators. To avoid negative estimates of volatility, one can consider a variation of the additive volatility model, which specifies that the natural logarithm of $\sigma^2(z_t)$ is additively separable as follows:

$$y_t = \sigma(z_t)\varepsilon_t,$$
$$\ln\left(\sigma^2(z_t)\right) = \mu + \sigma_1^2(y_{t-1}) + \sigma_2^2(y_{t-2}). \tag{11.14}$$

This is the model first studied by Hafner (1998), also see Yang et al. (1999). Clearly, Equation 11.14 models $\sigma^2(z_t)$ as a multiplicatively separable model: $\sigma^2(z_t) = e^{\mu}e^{\sigma_1^2(y_{t-1})}e^{\sigma_2^2(y_{t-2})}$.

The additive volatility models have various extensions. For example, Kim and Linton (2004) consider the generalized additive nonlinear ARCH model (GANARCH), which includes the model of Hafner (1998) and Yang et al. (1999) as a special case by choosing F as the exponential function. Levine and Li (2007) generalize the additive model by considering NP interactions for any pair of lagged variables.

11.2.1.3 Functional-Coefficient Volatility Model. We start with the following functional-coefficient model

$$y_t = \sigma(z_t)\varepsilon_t$$
$$\sigma^2(z_t) = a_1(y_{t-\tau})y_{t-1} + a_2(y_{t-\tau})y_{t-2},$$

where $z_t = (y_{t-1}, y_{t-2}, y_{t-\tau})'$ and $y_{t-\tau}$ is the model-dependent variable to be determined later. The local linear estimators of $a_1(y)$ and $a_2(y)$ can be obtained by minimizing the following objective function

$$\underset{\{a_j,b_j\}_{j=1}^2}{\arg\min}\, n^{-1}\sum_{t=1}^{n}\left\{y_t^2 - \sum_{j=1}^{2}\left[a_j + b_j\left(y_{t-\tau} - y\right)\right]y_{t-j}\right\}^2 k_h(y_{t-\tau} - y).$$

Let $\{\hat{a}_j, \hat{b}_j\}_{j=1}^2$ denote the solution to the above problem. Then, $a_1(y)$ and $a_2(y)$ are estimated by $\hat{a}_1$ and $\hat{a}_2$, respectively, whose closed-form expressions are omitted here.

Below, we address two key issues for the above model, namely, the choice of bandwidth h and the choice of lag τ. For the choice of bandwidth, Cai et al. (2000) propose a modified multifold cross-validation criterion that aims to retain the stationary structure of the data. Let m and Q be two given positive integers such that $n > mQ$. The process involves the use of Q subseries of length $n - qm$ $(q = 1, \ldots, Q)$ to estimate the unknown coefficient functions and then to compute the one-step forecasting errors of the next section of the time series of length m based on the estimated model. Let $\hat{a}_{j,q}$ be the estimated coefficients using the qth $(q = 1, \ldots, Q)$ subseries with scaled bandwidth $= h \times (\frac{n}{n-qm})^{1/5}$

to account for the varying sample size. The average prediction errors are obtained as $\mathrm{APE}_\tau(h) = \frac{1}{Q}\sum_{q=1}^{Q}\mathrm{APE}_{\tau,q}(h)$, where

$$\mathrm{APE}_{\tau,q}(h) = \frac{1}{m}\sum_{t=n-qm+1}^{n-qm-m}\left\{y_t^2 - \sum_{j=1}^{2}\hat{a}_j(y_{t-\tau})\,y_{t-j}\right\}^2.$$

They propose to choose the bandwidth h to minimize APE(h). As they recommended, in practical implementations, it is common to use $m = [0.1n]$ and $Q = 4$.

For the choice of τ, the best strategy is to rely on economic intuition to obtain this lag. In the absence of this benefit, it is pertinent to choose τ in terms of some data-driven method. A useful method is to compute $\mathrm{APE}_\tau(h)$ as defined above for a given values of τ and h and minimize it simultaneously over both τ and h, say, by a grid search method.

Clearly, nothing in the above estimation procedure can ensure the nonnegativity of the volatility estimators.

11.2.1.4 Single-Index Volatility Model. Single-index model is another approach for modeling conditional variance. The single-index structure in the conditional mean has been developed by several authors, see Ichimura (1993) and Carroll et al. (1997), among others. Here, we follow Xia et al. (2002) and consider the single-index volatility model $\xi_t = \sigma(\theta' x_t)\varepsilon_t$, $t = 1, \ldots, n$, where ε_t is i.i.d. (0, 1), with bounded fourth moment, $x_t = (x_{1t}, \ldots, x_{pt})'$, and θ is a vector of unknown parameters with $\|\theta\| = 1$, and $\sigma(\cdot)$ is an unknown smooth link function. Note that $|\xi_t|^\tau = \sigma_\tau \sigma^\tau(\theta' x_t) + \sigma^\tau(\theta' x_t)(|\varepsilon_t|^\tau - \sigma_\tau)$, where $\tau > 0$ and $\sigma_\tau = E|\varepsilon_t|^\tau$. Standard literature on NP estimation of volatility is based on $\tau = 2$, which suffers from sensitivity to outliers. Carroll and Ruppert (1988) discuss how to choose τ in details. Here, we follow Xia et al. (2002) and consider the case where $\tau = 1$ and remind the readers that the other cases can be handled similarly. Assuming that $y_t = |\xi_t|$ the true value θ_0 of the parameter θ satisfies

$$\theta_0 = \arg\inf_{\|\theta\|=1} E\left\{\frac{y_t - E(y_t|\theta' x_t)}{\sigma(\theta' x_t)}\right\}^2. \tag{11.15}$$

Note that $E[\{y_t - E(y_t|\theta' x_t = \theta' x)\}^2|\theta' x_t = \theta' x]$ is the conditional variance that can be estimated by the following minimization

$$\left(\hat{a}, \hat{d}\right) \equiv \arg\min_{(a,d)} \frac{1}{n}\sum_{t=1}^{n}\left\{y_t - \left(a + d\theta'(x_t - x)\right)\right\}^2 w_{t0}(x), \tag{11.16}$$

where $w_{t0}(\cdot)$ is a set of weight functions that capture the local effect around x. Therefore, the sample version of the minimization given in Equation 11.15 is

$$\left(\hat{a}_s, \hat{d}_s, \hat{\theta}\right) \equiv \arg\min_{a_s, d_s, \theta} \frac{1}{n} \sum_{s=1}^{n} \frac{1}{\sigma^2(\theta' x_s)} \sum_{t=1}^{n} \left\{y_t - \left[a_s + d_s \theta'(x_t - x)\right]\right\}^2 w_{ts}(x_s),$$

where $w_{ts}(\cdot)$ is a set of weight functions that capture the local effect around x_s. Even though $\sigma(\cdot)$ is still unknown in the above equation, a_s is an estimate of it at x_s. Thus, we can replace $\sigma(\theta' x_s)$ by a_s and the estimate of θ is obtained by minimizing

$$n^{-1} \sum_{s=1}^{n} a_s^{-2} \sum_{t=1}^{n} \left\{y_t - \left[a_s + d_s \theta'(x_t - x)\right]\right\}^2 w_{ts}(x_s),$$

with respect to (a_s, d_s) and θ iteratively. For the implementation details as well as the asymptotic properties of the resulting estimators, see Xia et al. (2002).

11.2.1.5 Stationary Semiparametric ARCH(∞) Models. The models presented above are rather restrictive in the sense that they only take into account partial information allowed to affect volatility and they do not have the useful feature of GARCH-type models. More importantly, they may fail to capture the high persistence dynamics of GARCH models. So in this subsection we review several models that incorporate GARCH features.

Observe that the standard GARCH(1,1) model can be written as $y_t = \sigma_t \varepsilon_t$,

$$\sigma_t^2 = v(y_{t-1}) + \alpha v(y_{t-2}) + \alpha^2 v(y_{t-3}) + \cdots + \alpha^{t-1} v(y_0), \tag{11.17}$$

where $v(y) = \beta y^2 + \omega$ is the news impact curve defined by Engle and Ng (1993). Nevertheless, this symmetric news impact curve is not in accordance with the empirical behavior of stock returns due to leverage effect. A suitable modification is the Glosten et al. (1993) GJR-GARCH model that includes an additional term to allow for a stronger response of conditional variance to negative innovation as compared to positive innovation:

$$\sigma_t^2 = w + \alpha \sigma_{t-1}^2 + \beta \left\{y_{t-1}^2 + \delta y_{t-1}^2 1(y_{t-1} < 0)\right\},$$

where $1(\cdot)$ is the usual indicator function and the leverage effect is captured by the fact that $\delta > 0$. This model can also be put into the form of Equation 11.17 with $v(y) = \beta(y^2 + \delta y^2 I(y < 0)) + \omega$.

Motivated by the above observations, Yang (2006) proposes a model, where the conditional variance σ_t^2 is modeled as $\sigma_t^2 = g(\sum_{j=1}^{t} \alpha^{j-1} v(y_{t-j}; \delta))$ where $g(\cdot)$ is some smooth but unknown nonnegative link function defined on $\mathcal{R}^+ = [0, \infty]$, $\alpha \in (0, 1)$, and $v(y; \delta)$ is a known family of nonnegative functions that are continuous in y and twice continuously differentiable with respect to parameter δ. Clearly, Yang nests the GJR model as a special case by specifying

$g(x) = \beta x + \frac{\omega}{1-\alpha}$, $v(y;\delta) = y^2 + \delta y^2 1(y < 0)$ for the GJR model. If one further imposes $\delta = 0$, then we get back to the GARCH(1,1) model. Apparently, this approach has some similarity to the single-index model considered above. Yang (2006) proposes SP estimation of both the unknown link function $g(\cdot)$ and the unknown parameter vector (α, δ) and derives the asymptotic properties of these estimators.

Linton and Mammen (2005) propose the following ARCH(∞) model

$$\sigma_t^2(\theta, m) = \sum_{j=1}^{\infty} \psi_j(\theta)\, m\left(y_{t-j}\right), \tag{11.18}$$

where $m(\cdot)$ is an unknown smooth function, $\theta \in \Theta$ is a p-dimensional vector of parameters, the functional form of ψ_j is known, and the functional coefficients $\psi_j(\theta)$ at least satisfy the conditions $\psi_j(\theta) \geq 0\,\forall j$ and $\sum_{j=1}^{\infty} \psi_j(\theta) < \infty$ for all $\theta \in \Theta$. In the special case where $\psi_j(\theta) = \theta^{j-1}$ with $0 < \theta < 1$, the model (Eq. 11.18) can be written as $\sigma_t^2 = \theta\sigma_{t-1}^2 + m(y_{t-1})$, which is the model of Engle and Ng (1993). Taking $m(y) = \alpha + \gamma y^2$ or $\alpha + \gamma y^2 + \delta y^2 1(y < 0)$, the model nests the standard GARCH(1,1) model and the GJR model as special cases. We note that the idea behind the model stems from an interesting work in Carroll et al. (2002). The estimation method for model (Eq. 11.18) is based on iterative smoothing. The asymptotic properties of the estimators are quite complicated. We refer the reader directly to Linton and Mammen (2005).

Both the models of Yang (2006) and Linton and Mammen (2005) can capture the structure of GARCH models and allow for the leverage effect widely found in the volatility dynamics of financial returns. Nevertheless, in order to establish the asymptotic properties of the estimators for both models, they have to assume the process $\{y_t\}$ to be strictly stationary, which may not be the case in financial applications.

11.2.1.6 Semiparametric Combined Estimator of Volatility. While we have considered several papers that flexibly model conditional variances, none of them use the parametric models explicitly. Mishra et al. (2010) (MSU hereafter) take a different approach. They first model the conditional variance through a parametric model and then model nonparametrically the remaining nonlinearity in the squared standardized residuals from the parametric conditional variance model. By combining the two estimators multiplicatively, they obtain their final SP combined estimator of the volatility σ_t^2. The major advantage of their approach is that they do not need a correct specification for the parametric volatility model. The reason is that the parameters in the parametric model for σ_t^2 can be estimated at the usual parametric rate by the QMLE principle, and it plays asymptotically negligible role in the asymptotics for the combined estimator as long as the bandwidth used in the second-stage estimation shrinks to 0 as the sample size n passes to the infinity. If the first-stage parametric volatility model is misspecified, the parametric estimator of σ_t^2 is generally inconsistent, whereas the SP combined estimator is still consistent. If the first-stage parametric volatility model is correctly specified, the combined estimator can also achieve the parametric convergence rate by holding the bandwidth as fixed. The intuition for this approach comes from Hjort and Glad (1995) and Glad (1998) in which they provide similar combined estimators for density and conditional mean, respectively, also see Martins-Filho et al. (2008).

To demonstrate how the combined estimation works, we consider the DGP $y_t = \sigma_t \varepsilon_t$ and $\varepsilon_t \sim$ i.i.d. (0,1) with bounded fourth moment. Observing the identity

$$E(y_t^2|\mathcal{F}_{t-1}) = \sigma_{p,t}^2 E\left\{\left(\frac{y_t}{\sigma_{p,t}}\right)^2 |\mathcal{F}_{t-1}\right\}, \tag{11.19}$$

where $\sigma_{p,t}^2$ is the parametric component of the conditional variance that is $\mathcal{F}_{t-1}$-measurable, we can write σ_t^2 in the following product form

$$\sigma_t^2 = \sigma_{p,t}^2 \sigma_{np,t}^2,$$

where $\sigma_{np,t}^2 = E[(y_t/\sigma_{p,t})^2|\mathcal{F}_{t-1}]$. A crucial assumption in their paper is a certain form of information reduction. That is, $\sigma_{np,t}^2 = E\{(y_t/\sigma_{p,t})^2|\mathcal{F}_{t-1}\} = \sigma_{np}^2(x_t)$ where x_t is $\mathcal{F}_{t-1}$-measurable and is of finite dimension. For example, consider the simple ARCH(1) model for $\sigma_{p,t}^2 : \sigma_{p,t}^2 = \alpha_0 + \alpha_1 y_{t-1}^2$. The parameters α_0 and α_1 in this model can be estimated by $\hat{\alpha}_0$ and $\hat{\alpha}_1$ consistently under weak conditions. If we assume that $E\{(y_t/\sigma_{p,t})^2|\mathcal{F}_{t-1}\}$ is only a function of y_{t-1}, then we can estimate $\sigma_{np}^2(y_{t-1})$ by any NP technique by regressing $y_t^2/(\hat{\alpha}_0 + \hat{\alpha}_1 y_{t-1}^2)$ on y_{t-1}. Denote the estimate of $\sigma_{np}^2(y)$ as $\hat{\sigma}_{np}^2(y)$. Then, the final combined estimator of σ_t^2 is given by $\hat{\sigma}_t^2 = (\hat{\alpha}_0 + \hat{\alpha}_1 y_{t-1}^2)\hat{\sigma}_{np}^2(y_{t-1})$. MSU establish the asymptotic normality of the combined estimator and compare it with the parametric volatility estimator and the traditional NP estimator. They also develop a NP test of the correct functional form of the parametric volatility model.

11.2.1.7 Semiparametric Inference in GARCH-in-Mean Models. In our survey so far, we have focused on the specification and estimation of volatility itself, whereas it is often the case that the mean is of interest too. In finance, it is frequently expected that risk and return are related. This motivates the GARCH-in-mean (GARCH-M) model of the following form:

$$y_t = m\left(x_t, \sigma_t^2\right) + \sigma_t \varepsilon_t, \tag{11.20}$$

where x_t is an observable vector of regressors that enter the conditional mean model and the functional form $m(\cdot, \cdot)$ may be parametrically or nonparametrically specified. In a parametric setup, $m(x_t, \sigma_t^2)$ can be written as $m(x_t, \sigma_t^2, \gamma)$, where γ is a finite-dimensional vector of parameters to be estimated together with the parameters in the volatility process σ_t^2. Engle et al. (1987) first introduce such a parametric model where σ_t or $\log(\sigma_t)$ enters the conditional mean model linearly and σ_t^2 is specified as an ARCH(p) model. They also apply their models to the study of time-varying risk premia. In contrast, Pagan and Ullah (1988) and Pagan and Hong (1991) consider the case where σ_t^2 is modeled and estimated nonparametrically, but like the case of Engle et al. (1987), it (instead of σ_t) also enters the conditional mean linearly or log-linearly. Linton and Perron (2003) consider the model (Eq. 11.20) where x_t is absent so that $m(x_t, \sigma_t^2) = \mu(\sigma_t^2)$, the functional form of $\mu(\cdot)$ is left unspecified but σ_t^2 is parametrically specified. They apply their model to the study of monthly CRSP (Center for Research on Security Prices) value-weighted excess returns and find that the relationship between the two moments is nonlinear and nonmonotonic. But they do not provide any asymptotic properties for their estimators.

More recently, Conrad and Mammen (2008) consider Equation 11.20 where $m(x_t, \sigma_t^2) = \mu(\sigma_t^2)$ is nonparametrically specified. They propose an algorithm to estimate $\mu(\cdot)$ and a specification test for GARCH-in-mean effects by using the QMLE as a starting value in their iterative algorithm. But they do not provide the asymptotic theory for the QMLE, which, as Christensen et al. (2008) remark, is necessarily inconsistent if $\mu(\cdot)$ is indeed nonlinear. Christensen et al. (2008) consider Equation 11.20 where $m(x_t, \sigma_t^2) = x_t'\gamma + \mu(\sigma_t^2)$, $\sigma_t^2 = \omega + \alpha y_{t-1}^2 + \beta\sigma_{t-1}^2$, and ε_t is i.i.d. (0, 1). Note that it is not $\sigma_{t-1}^2\varepsilon_{t-1}^2$ but y_{t-1}^2 that enters the right-hand side in the above model. Using the profile likelihood approach, they show that their estimator of the finite dimensional parameters is asymptotically efficient in the sense that they can achieve the SP efficiency bound, and the NP component can be estimated consistently. They apply their model to the daily S&P 500 stock market returns and find evidence in support of the nonlinear relationship between the conditional expected return and the conditional variance of returns.

11.2.2 NONSTATIONARY UNIVARIATE VOLATILITY MODELS

Financial markets can experience many shorter or longer periods of instability such as the 1997 Asian crisis, 1998 Russian crisis, September 11 terrorist attack in 2001, and the ongoing 2007–2010 financial crisis. It has been recognized for a long time that the market and institutional changes can cause structural breaks in financial time series and ignoring these breaks can adversely invalidate statistical inference on volatility models. Such findings have led to the development of the change-point analysis in volatility models (Chu 1995; Chen and Gupta 1997; Chen et al. 2005) and the effort to develop some nonstationary volatility models. Polzehl and Spokoiny (2006) and Engle and Rangel (2008) present evidence against global stationarity and propose modifications of standard models. There are two basic approaches to develop nonstationary models. One approach is to allow some or all model parameters to vary over time, see Cai et al. (2000) and Fan et al. (2003) who do not consider the volatility models per se. The other is to augment the original GARCH-type models to allow nonstationarity. For a detailed review on locally stationary volatility models, see Chapter 10.

11.2.3 SPECIFICATION OF THE ERROR DENSITY

The specification of the innovation density is of equal significance while considering volatility models. It is well known that estimation of a strong GARCH process is typically carried out under the Gaussianity of the standardized error term. The lack of discussion of the error density is justified by the fact that even though the density functional form may be misspecified, the QMLE method continues to deliver consistent estimators despite the loss of efficiency. For further details on the theory of the QMLE, see White (1982) and Severini and Staniswalis (1994).

On the other hand, it is frequently observed in the empirical literature that the estimated standardized residuals are not normally distributed, which is particularly true for high frequency financial time series data. Thus, it is of interest to know the extent of efficiency loss associated with the misspecified density. For example, other parametric distributions than the Gaussian could be used in a consistent QMLE framework, as long as some restrictions (in particular, symmetry) hold, see, for example, Newey and Steigerwald (1997). It is also useful to explore estimation methods that take this unknown density information into account, which may lead to efficiency gains. In an ideal situation, we can estimate the finite dimensional parameters in the volatility models equally well as if we knew the true density function of the error term. This is the case that happens to adaptive estimators.

In the context of volatility models, Engle and Gonzalez-Rivera (1991) were the first to quantify the loss of efficiency of the QMLE that falsely assumes normality by using Monte Carlo simulations for two densities—one leptokurtic and the other positively skewed. They found the efficiency of the Gaussian QMLE for a Gamma distribution to be very low and proposed a more efficient estimator based on a NP estimated density and its score function. Let $y_t = \sigma_t \varepsilon_t$ where σ_t is $\mathcal{F}_{t-1}$-measurable and ε_t's are i.i.d. with zero-mean and variance 1. Assume the unknown density of ε_t is given by $g(\cdot)$ and σ_t can be parametrized to obtain a GARCH model. The conditional log-likelihood function takes the form

$$L_t(\theta) = -\frac{1}{2}\sum_{t=1}^{n} \log \sigma_t^2 + \sum_{t=1}^{n} \log g\left(\frac{v_t}{\sigma_t}\right), \tag{11.21}$$

where θ is the parameter vector built in the volatility process σ_t^2. The set of densities are restricted to the family with mean 0 and variance 1, and the estimation of the density is obtained independent of the location and scale parameters. Engle and Gonzalez-Rivera (1991) propose a four-step iterative algorithm to choose θ and $g(\cdot)$ to maximize the above objective function, during which they use NP estimates of the score function to estimate the parameter vector θ. Unfortunately, they did not establish the statistical properties of their estimators.

Linton (1993) studies the adaptive estimation in ARCH(p) models:

$$y_t = \gamma' x_t + u_t, u_t = \sigma_t \varepsilon_t,$$
$$\sigma_t^2 = \omega + \alpha_1 u_{t-1}^2 + \cdots + \alpha_p u_{t-p}^2,$$

where ε_t is i.i.d. with zero-mean, variance 1, and a common unknown density f. By reparametrizing the volatility process as $\sigma_t^2 = e^{\alpha}(1 + \lambda_1 u_{t-1}^2 + \cdots + \lambda_p u_{t-p}^2)$, he constructs an estimator of $(\gamma, \lambda_1, \ldots, \lambda_p)$ that achieves the SP efficiency bound. When f is symmetric about 0, he demonstrates that it is possible to adaptively estimate these parameters in the sense that one can achieve the same asymptotic efficiency as if one knew the true error density. For further work on the efficiency under a general framework for adaptive estimation, see Drost et al. (1997), Drost and Klaassen (1997), Sun and Stengos (2006), and Ling and McAleer (2003).

Also motivated by the observation that the QMLE procedure can produce inefficient and possibly biased estimates relative to the MLE when the true error density is known, Li and Turtle (2000) develop an EF approach for ARCH models that reduces bias and improves efficiency without assuming a known error density. Because the EF approach is based on finite samples from the outset, it does not suffer from the finite sample problem of the QMLE approach whose statistic properties are based on asymptotic theory. In general, the EF approach can partially recover the QMLE efficiency loss and displays less absolute bias than the QMLE approach.

11.2.4 NONPARAMETRIC VOLATILITY DENSITY ESTIMATION

Despite the many parametric, SP, and NP specifications for the volatility processes we have reviewed above, in general, it is not possible to compute, even in those parametric cases, the stationary density of the volatility process $\{\sigma_t^2\}$. On the other hand, it is desirable to obtain information on the properties of this hidden process as it allows us to look for its possible bimodality properties or to determine precisely the localization of the peaks.

Van Es et al. (2005) consider the following volatility model $y_t = \sigma_t \varepsilon_t$ where ε_t is an i.i.d. Gaussian sequence with mean 0 and variance 1 and, at each time, t the random variables σ_t and ε_t are independent. They square the above equation and take the natural logarithms on both sides to obtain $\ln(y_t^2) = \ln(\sigma_t^2) + \ln(\varepsilon_t^2)$. Under the given assumption, the density of $\ln(\varepsilon_t^2)$ is also known and given by $f_{\varepsilon}(x) = \frac{1}{\sqrt{2\pi}} e^{1/2x} e^{-1/2e^x}$ and the density of $\ln(y_t^2)$ can be estimated nonparametrically from the observed data, say, by the kernel method. Then, they use a deconvolution kernel density estimator to estimate the unknown density g of $\ln(\sigma_t^2)$. An estimator of the density of σ_t^2 or σ_t can then be obtained by a simple transformation. The joint density f of the p-vector $(\ln(\sigma_t^2), \ldots, \ln(\sigma_{t-p+1}^2))$ can also be estimated. They derive the expressions for the bias and bounds on the variance of the estimates of these densities by assuming that the process $\{y_t\}$ is strong mixing and f or g is twice continuously differentiable with bounded second-order partial derivatives. Comte et al. (2008) consider the adaptive estimation of g, the common density of $\ln(\sigma_t^2)$ when the noise process $\{\varepsilon_t\}$ is Gaussian, and consider general distributions for ε_t as heavier or thinner tails may be of interest. They also relax the requirement that the density g be twice continuously differentiable and prove that the rates of their NP estimator coincide with the rates obtained in the i.i.d. case when the two processes $\{\sigma_t\}$ and $\{\varepsilon_t\}$ are independent.

11.3 Nonparametric and Semiparametric Multivariate Volatility Models

The extension of volatility models from the univariate to the multivariate case is important. For asset allocation, risk management and hedging, and asset pricing, we frequently need to model volatility and covolatility of multiple financial assets jointly. This gives rise to the need for multivariate volatility models, where multivariate GARCH (MGARCH) models play a fundamental role. Many recent works have been done in the area of parametric MGARCH models, such as the VECH model, the BEKK model, the dynamic conditional correlation (DCC) model, the factor GARCH model, to name just a few. These parametric MGARCH models often share two common features: the normality assumption on the error's distribution and the linearity of the dynamic conditional covariance matrix, either of which may be violated in empirical studies.

SP and NP methods offer an alternative way to model multivariate volatility without the need to impose a particular structure on the data or a particular distribution on the multivariate innovation. Here, we review only the recent works on SP and NP multivariate volatility models in discrete time.

We consider a vector time series $\mathbf{y}_t = (y_{1,t}, ..., y_{N,t}) \in \mathcal{R}^N$ that is generated through

$$\mathbf{y}_t = \mathbf{H}_t^{1/2}\varepsilon_t, \tag{11.22}$$

where $\varepsilon_t \equiv (\varepsilon_{1,t}, \ldots, \varepsilon_{N,t})'$ is an $N \times 1$ vector of martingale difference sequence satisfying that $E(\varepsilon_t|\mathcal{F}_{t-1}) = 0$, $E(\varepsilon_t\varepsilon_t'|\mathcal{F}_{t-1}) = I_N$, $\mathcal{F}_{t-1}$ is the information set (σ-field) at time $t-1$, I_N is an $N \times N$ identity matrix, and $\mathbf{H}_t$ is a symmetric positive-definite matrix. Clearly, $\mathbf{H}_t$ is the conditional covariance matrix. Traditionally, ε_t is assumed to follow the standard normal distribution: $\varepsilon_t \sim$ i.i.d. $N(0, \mathbf{I}_N)$ and $\mathbf{H}_t$ is parametrically specified. Alternatively, we can specify the conditional covariance matrix $\mathbf{H}_t$ through the specification of the volatility process for each component $y_{j,t}$ of $\mathbf{y}_t$ and the conditional correlation matrix $\mathbf{R}_t$ of $\mathbf{y}_t$:

$$\mathbf{H}_t = \mathbf{D}_t\mathbf{R}_t\mathbf{D}_t, \tag{11.23}$$

where $\mathbf{R}_t$ is the conditional correlation matrix with the (i,j)th element denoted as $\rho_{ij,t}$, which stands for the conditional correlation between $y_{i,t}$ and $y_{j,t}$ and can be time-varying; $\mathbf{D_t} = \text{diag}(\sigma_{1,t}, \ldots, \sigma_{N,t})$ is a diagonal matrix and $\sigma_{j,t}^2 = E(y_{j,t}^2|\mathcal{F}_{t-1})$. An obvious advantage of Equation 11.23 is that the positive-definiteness of $\mathbf{H}_t$ can be easily ensured. It is well known that the conditional correlation matrix $\mathbf{R}_t$ is also the conditional covariance matrix of the standardized residuals $\varepsilon_t = \mathbf{D}_t^{-1}\mathbf{y}_t$, that is, $E(\varepsilon_t\varepsilon_t'|\mathcal{F}_{t-1}) = \mathbf{R}_t$. In the parametric setup, both $\mathbf{D}_t$ and $\mathbf{R}_t$ are parameterized through a parameter vector θ and thus we can write them as $\mathbf{D}_t(\theta)$ and $\mathbf{R}_t(\theta)$, respectively.

To proceed, it is worth mentioning that two surveys are available on the development of MGARCH models. The first survey is done by Bauwens et al. (2006) who focus only on parametric MGARCH models. The second survey is by Silvennoinen and Teräsvirta (2009) who also discuss NP and SP MGARCH models. In contrast, our survey in this part focuses on the NP and SP volatility models, which are not be limited to MGARCH models.

11.3.1 MODELING THE CONDITIONAL COVARIANCE MATRIX UNDER STATIONARITY

Like in the parametric setup, there are two fundamental problems associated with the NP and SP MGARCH models. First, as the dimension N increases, the number of parameters in MGARCH models increases rapidly so that the specification of an MGARCH model has to be parsimonious enough. But owing to the curse of dimensionality in the NP literature, a pure NP MGARCH model is doomed to lose its attraction. A common approach is to specify a SP MGARCH or volatility model that has both parametric and NP components, and the dimension of the NP component is usually small in order to facilitate the estimation and inference procedure. Second, one has to impose symmetry and positive definiteness on the covariance matrix or correlation matrix. This can be handled by formulating the model in a way such that positive definiteness is implied by the model structure as in Equation 11.23.

11.3.1.1 Hafner, van Dijk, and Franses' Semiparametric Estimator. Hafner et al. (2006) (HDF hereafter) propose a semiparametric conditional covariance (SCC) estimator by modeling the conditional variance matrix $\mathbf{D}_t$ parametrically as $\mathbf{D}_t(\theta)$ and the conditional correlation matrix $\mathbf{R}_t$ nonparametrically. Motivated by the idea that the conditional correlations depend on exogenous factors such as the market return or volatility, HDF propose the following SP model for $\mathbf{y}_t$:

$$\mathbf{y}_t = \mathbf{D}_t(\theta)\,\varepsilon_t, E(\varepsilon_t|\mathcal{F}_{t-1}) = 0, E\left(\varepsilon_t\varepsilon_t'|\mathcal{F}_{t-1}\right) = \mathbf{R}(\mathbf{x}_t), \tag{11.24}$$

where $\mathbf{x}_t \in \mathcal{F}_{t-1}$. Assuming that θ can be estimated by $\hat{\theta}$ at the usual parametric $\sqrt{n}$-rate, they define the standardized residuals by $\tilde{\boldsymbol{\varepsilon}}_t \equiv \boldsymbol{\varepsilon}_t(\hat{\theta}) = \mathbf{D}_t(\hat{\theta})^{-1}\mathbf{y}_t$. Then, they regress $\tilde{\boldsymbol{\varepsilon}}_t\tilde{\boldsymbol{\varepsilon}}_t'$ on $\mathbf{x}_t$ nonparametrically to obtain $\tilde{\mathbf{Q}}(\mathbf{x})$, the Nadaraya–Watson kernel estimator of $E(\tilde{\boldsymbol{\varepsilon}}_t\tilde{\boldsymbol{\varepsilon}}_t'|\mathbf{x}_t = \mathbf{x})$. Their SP conditional correlation matrix estimator is defined by $\tilde{\mathbf{R}}(\mathbf{x}) = (\tilde{\mathbf{Q}}^*(\mathbf{x}))^{-1}\tilde{\mathbf{Q}}(\mathbf{x})(\tilde{\mathbf{Q}}^*(\mathbf{x}))^{-1}$, where $\tilde{\mathbf{Q}}^*(\mathbf{x})$ is a diagonal matrix with the square roots of the diagonal elements of $\tilde{\mathbf{Q}}(\mathbf{x})$ on its diagonal. Their SP estimator of $\mathbf{H}_t$ can be written as $\tilde{\mathbf{H}}_t = \mathbf{D}_t(\hat{\theta})\tilde{\mathbf{R}}(\mathbf{x}_t)\mathbf{D}_t(\hat{\theta})$.

Clearly, HDF's estimator requires correct specification of the conditional variance process in order to obtain a final consistent conditional correlation or covariance estimator. This is unsatisfactory since it is extremely hard to know a priori the correct form of the conditional variance process.

11.3.1.2 Long, Su, and Ullah's Semiparametric Estimator. Following Mishra et al. (2010), Long et al. (2011) propose an alternative SCC estimator, which combines in a multiplicative way the parametric conditional covariance (PCC) estimator from the first stage with the NP conditional covariance estimator from the second stage. Essentially, this estimator nonparametrically adjusts the initial PCC estimator.

Let $\{\mathbf{H}_{p,t}(\theta)\}$ be a parametrically specified time-varying conditional covariance process for $\mathbf{y}_t$, where $\theta \in \Theta \subset \mathcal{R}^p$ and $\mathbf{H}_{p,t}(\theta) \in \mathcal{F}_{t-1}$. The estimation strategy of Long et al. (2011) builds on the simple identity

$$\mathbf{H}_t = \mathbf{H}_{\mathrm{p},t}(\theta)^{1/2} E\left[\boldsymbol{\varepsilon}_t(\theta)\boldsymbol{\varepsilon}_t(\theta)'|\mathcal{F}_{t-1}\right] \mathbf{H}_{\mathrm{p},t}(\theta)^{1/2},$$

where $\mathbf{H}_{\mathrm{p},t}(\theta)^{1/2}$ is the symmetric square root matrix of $\mathbf{H}_{\mathrm{p},t}(\theta)$ and $\boldsymbol{\varepsilon}_t(\theta) = \mathbf{H}_{\mathrm{p},t}(\theta)^{-1/2}y_t$ is the standardized residual from the parametric model. Under some standard conditions, the parametric estimator $\hat{\theta}$ of θ converges to some pseudo-true value θ^*. Like HDF, they assume that the conditional expectation of $\boldsymbol{\varepsilon}_t(\theta^*)\boldsymbol{\varepsilon}_t(\theta^*)'$ depends on the information set $\mathcal{F}_{t-1}$ only through a $q \times 1$ observable vector $\mathbf{x}_t = (x_{1,t}, \ldots, x_{q,t})'$. That is,

$$E\left[\boldsymbol{\varepsilon}_t(\theta^*)\boldsymbol{\varepsilon}_t(\theta^*)'|\mathcal{F}_{t-1}\right] = \mathbf{G}_{\mathrm{np}}(\mathbf{x}_t) \text{ a.s.},$$

where $\mathbf{x}_t \in \mathcal{F}_{t-1}$ and $\mathbf{G}_{\mathrm{np}}$ is a smooth but unknown function. Unlike HDF, whose results rely on the correct specification of $\mathbf{D}_t(\theta)$, Long et al. (2011) do not need $\mathbf{H}_{\mathrm{p},t}(\theta)$ to be correctly specified. Their final SCC estimator of $\mathbf{H}_t$ takes the form

$$\hat{\mathbf{H}}_{\mathrm{sp},t} = \mathbf{H}_{\mathrm{p},t}(\hat{\theta})^{1/2}\hat{\mathbf{G}}_{\mathrm{np},t}\mathbf{H}_{\mathrm{p},t}(\hat{\theta})^{1/2},$$

where $\hat{\mathbf{G}}_{\mathrm{np},t}$ is a NP kernel estimator of $\mathbf{G}_{\mathrm{np}}(\mathbf{x}_t)$ by regressing $\boldsymbol{\varepsilon}_t(\hat{\theta})\boldsymbol{\varepsilon}_t(\hat{\theta})'$ on $\mathbf{x}_t$.

11.3.1.3 Test for the Correct Specification of Parametric Conditional Covariance Models. In the parametric setup, there are a few tests that are developed to test for the correct specification of parametric MGARCH models. For example, Ling and Li (1997) develop a χ^2 test statistic to test whether a parametric MGARCH model is correctly specified by testing whether the standardized error terms are i.i.d. $(0, I_N)$. Tse (2000) constructs a Lagrange multiplier (LM) test of the CCC-GARCH model against some particular alternatives to check the adequacy of the CCC-GARCH model. Bera and Kim (2002b) propose an information-matrix-based test for a bivariate CCC-GARCH model against the alternative that the correlation coefficient is stochastic. A common feature of these tests is that they are all of parametric nature.

A great advantage of the approach of Long et al. (2011) (Section 11.3.1.2) is that a natural testing strategy arises from their approach to test for the correct specification of PCC models. Observing that $\mathbf{G}_{\text{np}}(\mathbf{x}_t) = I_N$ a.s. if the first-stage parametric model $\mathbf{H}_{\text{p},t}(\theta)$ is correctly specified, Long et al. (2011) propose to test the correct specification of the initial PCC model by testing the null hypothesis

$$H_0 : \mathbf{G}_{\text{np}}(\mathbf{x}_t) = I_N \text{ a.s.} \tag{11.25}$$

The alternative hypothesis H_1 is the negation of H_0. Let $\sigma_{ij}(\mathbf{x})$ denote the (i, j) element of $\mathbf{G}_{\text{np}}(\mathbf{x})$, $i, j = 1, \ldots, N$. Then, the null can be written as

$$H_0 : P\left(\sigma_{ij}(\mathbf{x}_t) = \delta_{ij}\right) = 1 \text{ for all } i, j = 1, \ldots, k, \tag{11.26}$$

where δ_{ij} is Kronecker's delta, that is, $\delta_{ij} = 1$ if $i = j$ and 0 otherwise. A convenient test statistic can be based on the observation

$$\Gamma = \sum_{i=1}^{N} \sum_{j=i}^{N} \int \left(\sigma_{ij}(\mathbf{x}) - \delta_{ij}\right)^2 f^2(\mathbf{x})\, d\mathbf{x} \geq 0 \tag{11.27}$$

where $f(\mathbf{x})$ denotes the density function of $\mathbf{x}_t$ and $\Gamma = 0$ if and only if H_0 holds. Long et al. (2011) propose a test statistic based on a kernel estimator $\hat{\Gamma}$ of Γ, which, after being appropriately scaled, is asymptotically normally distributed under the null hypothesis and a sequence of local alternatives. They also establish the global consistency of their test and propose a bootstrap procedure to enhance the finite sample behavior of their test. Clearly, the Long et al. (2011) test is in the spirit of Ling and Li (1997), and both tests can also be applied to test the correct specification of univariate volatility models ($N = 1$).

Alternative research can be done along the lines of Kroner and Ng (1998) who base their misspecification test on the fact that $E(\mathbf{y}_t\mathbf{y}_t' - \mathbf{H}_t|\mathcal{F}_{t-1}) = 0$ a.s. under the correct specification of PCC models. This reduces to the problem of testing the martingale difference sequence property, which has been widely studied in the literature.

11.3.2 SPECIFICATION OF THE ERROR DENSITY

Owing to the notorious curse of dimensionality problem in the NP literature, NP modeling and estimation of the error density in the multivariate case have been done with great care. Two popular approaches have emerged, one is to restrict the class of multivariate densities to a class of spherically symmetric density functions, and the other is to apply a copula to model the multivariate density.

Hafner and Rombouts (2007) consider a model for a multivariate time series where the conditional variance matrix is a function of a finite-dimensional parameter and the innovation density f is unspecified. Clearly, this approach extends that of Engle and Gonzalez-Rivera (1991) to the multivariate case. Hafner and Rombouts (2007) characterize the semiparametric efficiency lower bound (SPELB) for the estimation of the finite-dimensional parameters and show that adaptive estimation without reparametrization is generally not possible, although one can achieve the SPELB. They also note that one major issue with the unrestricted SP multivariate volatility model is the curse of dimensionality: as the number of assets N increases, the estimate of the multivariate error density performs worse and worse. So, they restrict the multivariate density to the class of univariate spherically symmetric densities and propose an estimator that attains the SPELB.

Chen and Fan (2006) introduce a new class of semiparametric copula-based multivariate dynamic (SCOMDY) models, which specify the conditional mean and variance of a multivariate time series parametrically, but specify the multivariate distribution of the standardized innovations semiparametrically as a parametric copula evaluated at NP marginal distributions. For more details on this topic, see Chapter 12 in this handbook and Patton (2009).

11.4 Empirical Analysis

In this section, we apply some of the above discussed NP and SP univariate and multivariate volatility models to real data and compare them with some of the parametric models. In addition, a NP test is conducted for testing the correct specification of PCC model.

In order to illustrate the use of NP/SP univariate volatility models, we examine the Dow Jones Industrial Average Index (DJIA) and Standard & Poor's 500 Index (SPX) daily returns from January 2, 2003, through December 31, 2007, a total of 1257 observations. The whole sample dataset is splitted at day R, June 30, 2007. Therefore, the in-sample (IS) estimation is based on the samples from 2003 to the middle of 2007, and one-day-ahead conditional variance forecast is implemented throughout the end of year 2007. The out-of-sample (OoS) forecasting length is 128 days. The data employed here is demeaned log returns. The start-up model considered here is $y_t = m(x_t) + \sigma_t(x_t)\varepsilon_t$, since the plot of fitted $m(x_t)$ showed nonzero values at some points of data, especially around the fourth quarter of year 2003. However, we also did our analysis with the start-up model $y_t = \sigma_t(x_t)\varepsilon_t$. The details are omitted here, but the results remain similar. For the purpose of comparison, we fit conventional ARCH(1), GARCH(1,1) to the empirical dataset, apply nonparametric Nadaraya–Watson (NPNW), additive NP local instrument variable estimation (ANPLIVE) of Section 11.2.1.2, NP functional-coefficient volatility (NPFC) models of Section 11.2.1.3, and SP combined estimators of volatility (SPARCH, SPGARCH) of Section 11.2.1.6 to the same dataset as well. All estimation and forecasting are conditional on one-day-lagged variable except for ANPLIVE and NPFC models in which both one-day-lagged and two-day-lagged variables are used. The second-order Epanechnikov kernel is used for all NP and SP estimation and forecasting. In the first step, we fit NP regression to obtain the realized volatility, and Silverman's rule of thumb bandwidth is adopted at this stage. In the second step, we fit various NP and SP models, and least squares cross-validation bandwidth is used. Using the squared returns as a proxy of the unobservable volatility, the mean squared errors (MSEs) are calculated for comparison in various models. The results are reported in Table 11.1.

From Table 11.1, we have some interesting findings as below. First, all NP/SP models can always reduce both the IS and OoS MSE loss values. The reason behind may be that ARCH(1) and GARCH(1,1) may suffer misspecification problems. Second, among all the models with one lagged variable, SPARCH and SPGARCH generally have extremely lower IS and OoS MSE loss values compared to the rest of models, namely, ARCH(1), GARCH(1,1), and NPNW. Thus, the SP combined estimator is adjusting the estimation bias arising from misspecification of parametric model estimation. Also, the SP estimators perform better than the NP estimator perhaps because the NP adjustment of a parametric model is easy to carry out compared to the direct NP smoothing of the original data. Third, we also report the results of ANPLIVE and NPFC models in which there are two lagged variables. We find NPFC perform better than ANPLIVE. It is not appropriate to directly compare the results of ANPLIVE and NPFC with others, since they contain only one lagged variable.

To illustrate the use of multivariate volatility models, we consider $y_t = \mathbf{H}_t^{1/2}\varepsilon_t$. NPNW, parametric DCC model, and SP combined estimator of covariance are implemented. For the SP estimation, we combine the DCC model from the first step and Nadaraya–Watson estimation from the second step (SP-DCC, hereafter). The second-order Gaussian kernel and least squares cross-validation bandwidth are used for the conditional covariance analysis. The data period used here is slightly different from the univariate volatility models, since we would like to show the forecasting performance of SP-DCC for the recession period. The data from January 2003 through November 2007 is

TABLE 11.1 MSE Loss for Various Volatility Models

	DJIA		SPX	
	IS	OoS	IS	OoS
ARCH(1)	1.3824	4.1726	2.0659	6.3009
GARCH(1,1)	4.8557	4.1894	3.8759	6.3860
NPNW	1.0442	3.2274	1.1539	5.0468
SPARCH	0.3039	1.5214	0.4497	2.9487
SPGARCH	0.5170	1.9248	0.5830	4.1464
ANPLIVE	0.8570	3.0967	0.9671	3.3680
NPFC	0.8479	2.5117	0.9686	2.7145

used for the IS estimation, the recession period from December 2007 through June 2009 is used for the one-step-ahead OoS forecasting. For the purposes of model comparisons, we calculate the MSE loss for both equal weight (EW) and minimum variance weight (MVW) portfolios. The results are summarized as below. First, the SP-DCC performs best in the sense of having the lowest MSEs for both the IS estimation and OoS forecasting no matter which weight is used. The efficiency gains of SP-DCC over DCC in terms of MSE loss values are 40.69% for the IS with EW, 45.12% for the IS with MVW, 3.14% for the OoS with EW, and 2.73% for the OoS with MVW. Comparing NP and DCC, we find out that NP model has better performance than DCC in terms of MSE loss of IS estimation for both EW and MVW.

Figure 11.1 plots the DJIA volatility and its estimated and forecasted ones by parametric and SP methods based on bivariate volatility models. It clearly shows the relative superiority of SP-DCC over DCC. The shaded area indicates the recession period during which the volatilities are forecasted by SP-DCC and DCC. Apparently, SP forecasted volatility matches with the true volatility much better than DCC. Especially, during the recession period, the forecasted volatility by SP-DCC captures well the structure in true volatility. However, DCC forecasted volatility is too smooth compared with the structure of the true one. Also, we calculate the MSE of forecasts for DJIA in the recession period and find out that the SP method gives 3.30% of gain over the DCC model.

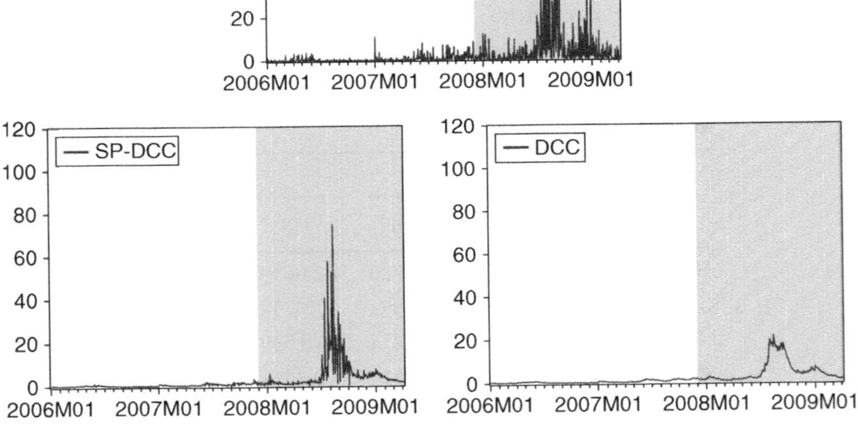

FIGURE 11.1 Parametric and semiparametric estimation and forecasting of DJIA volatility.

In addition, we implement the NP test in Long et al. (2011) for the correct specification of the PCC model. Conditioning on the one-day-lagged percentage return, the standardized residuals used for testing are calculated from the IS estimation. The null of correct specification of DCC model is rejected at 1% level. Therefore, we conclude that the DCC model may suffer from misspecification for this multivariate volatility analysis and that is perhaps the explanation for the better behavior of the SP-DCC model.

11.5 Conclusion

In this chapter, we review the development of univariate and multivariate NP and SP volatility. Owing to space limitation, we omit some of the important areas in the literature that include the work on SV and realized volatility models, for an extensive coverage of these areas, see, however, Parts 2 and 3 of this handbook. Another area which is not covered here is the NP or SP estimation of the continuous time volatility models (Aït-Sahalia, 2002; Bandi and Phillips, 2003). In the panel data NP models, no estimator has been proposed to deal with the conditional variance models. A systematic development of the nonstationarity cases is another interesting yet challenging research topic.

Acknowledgments

The authors thank Christian Hafner for his many constructive comments on this chapter.

CHAPTER TWELVE

Copula-Based Volatility Models

ANDRÉAS HEINEN and ALFONSO VALDESOGO

12.1 Introduction

Copulas are a statistical tool that capture the dependence structure of a joint distribution, independent of the features of the marginal distributions; see Nelsen (1999) and Joe (1997). This makes them ideally suited for combining univariate volatility models into flexible multivariate distributions that can offer a good description of the distribution of stock returns. Copulas provide an alternative to multivariate GARCH models based either on the Constant Conditional Correlation (CCC) model of Bollerslev (1990) when the copulas are constant or on the Dynamic Conditional Correlation (DCC) of Engle (2002a) when the copula dependence parameters are allowed to be time-varying. While traditional multivariate GARCH models use correlation as a measure of dependence, correlation is only a good measure of dependence in the elliptical world, for instance, when returns are multivariate Gaussian or Student-t. In that case returns are dependent whenever there exist linear relations between them. When there exist nonlinear relations between variables, correlation can be misleading, as has been widely documented, see for instance, Embrechts et al. (2001).

Given the stylized facts about financial returns such as the prevalence of skewness and kurtosis, it is clear that elliptical distributions can be viewed only

Handbook of Volatility Models and Their Applications, First Edition.
Edited by Luc Bauwens, Christian Hafner, and Sebastien Laurent.

as a very crude approximation, and therefore, correlation might miss some types of dependence that can be important from a financial point of view. The great advantage of copulas is that they permit the construction of flexible joint distributions by combining different types of marginals with dependence structures that are able to take into account nonlinear relations between variables. There exists a large collection of bivariate copulas with different features that can match stylized facts of dependence. One such feature is asymmetric dependence, the fact that negative returns tend to be more dependent than positive ones. Another one is tail dependence, the fact that the dependence between returns does not vanish when returns become extreme.

Asymmetric dependence has been reported by Longin and Solnik (2001), who use extreme value theory and the method of Ledford and Tawn (1997) to show that exceedance correlation, defined as the correlation that exists between returns that are above or below a certain threshold, are different for positive and negative returns. Ang and Chen (2002) developed a test for asymmetric correlation that is based on comparing empirical and model-based conditional correlations. Amongst the models they compare, regime-switching models are best at replicating this phenomenon. Ang and Bekaert (2002) estimated a Gaussian Markov-switching model for international returns and identify two regimes, a bear regime with negative returns, high volatilities, and correlations and a bull regime with positive mean, low volatilities, and correlations. Asymmetric dependence and tail dependence have important consequences in finance. For instance, Patton (2004) shows that ignoring asymmetric dependence can lead to significant costs for a risk-averse utility-maximizing investor. Chollete et al. (2009) use a regime-switching copula model to show that taking into account asymmetric dependence leads to better asset allocation and Value-at-Risk (VaR) estimation in a multivariate setting.

The remainder of this chapter is organized as follows. Section 12.2 is devoted to the main concepts of copulas, such as the Sklar theorem, conditional copula, as well as dependence measures based on copulas, and we illustrate them with four commonly used copulas in finance. Section 12.3 discusses estimation of copula models. Section 12.4 reviews dynamic copula models in the bivariate case. Section 12.5 compares VaR estimates derived from static and dynamic copula models. Section 12.6 discusses the recent developments in multivariate copulas, but we restrict attention to the static case. Section 12.7 concludes the discussion.

12.2 Definition and Properties of Copulas

Modeling the dependence between different risk factors is one of the key issues in most applications in finance such as VaR and portfolio selection. Even though the notion of dependence has been traditionally linked to Pearson's correlation, it has some limitations. Consider, for example two random variables X and Y, where $X \sim \mathcal{N}(0,1)$ and $Y = X^2$. In this setup, $\text{Cov}(X,Y) = \text{Cov}(X,X^2) = \text{Skewness}(X)$. Therefore X and Y are uncorrelated, since their covariance is equal to the skewness of X, which is 0, by normality of X. Yet, clearly, these variables are perfectly dependent. This simple example shows that correlation is not a good measure of dependence in all cases.[1] Pearson's correlation is only a good measure of dependence in the elliptical distributions, such as the multivariate Gaussian or Student-t distributions. Given the stylized facts about financial returns, it is clear that elliptical distributions can be viewed only as a very crude approximation, and the same holds for correlation. In order to create more appropriate multivariate models, one can use the notion of copula.[2]

12.2.1 SKLAR'S THEOREM

Copula theory goes back to the work of Sklar (1959), who showed that a joint distribution can be decomposed into its n marginal distributions and a copula, which fully characterizes the dependence between the variables. Copulas provide an easy way to form valid multivariate distributions from known marginals that need not be of the same class. For example, it is possible to use a normal, Student-t or any other marginal, combine them with a copula, and get a suitable joint distribution that reflects the kind of dependence that is present in the series.[3] Specifically, let $F(y_1, \ldots, y_n)$ be a continuous n-variate cumulative distribution function with univariate margins $F_i(y_i)$, $i = 1, \ldots, n$, where $F_i(y_i) = F(\infty, \ldots, y_i, \ldots, \infty)$. According to Sklar (1959), there exists a function C, called a *copula*, mapping $[0, 1]^n$ into $[0, 1]$, such that

$$F(y_1, \ldots, y_n) = C(F_1(y_1), \ldots, F_n(y_n)). \tag{12.1}$$

The joint density function is obtained by differentiating once with respect to all arguments, and it is given by the product of the marginals and the copula density

$$\frac{\partial^n F(y_1, \ldots, y_n)}{\partial y_1, \ldots, \partial y_n} = \prod_{i=1}^{n} f_i(y_i) \frac{\partial^n C(F_1(y_1), \ldots, F_n(y_n))}{\partial F_1(y_1), \ldots, \partial F_n(y_n)}. \tag{12.2}$$

This allows to define the copula as a multivariate distribution with uniform [0, 1] margins

$$C(u_1, \ldots, u_n) = F(F_1^{-1}(u_1), \ldots, F_n^{-1}(u_n)), \tag{12.3}$$

where $u_i = F_i(y_i) \sim U[0, 1]$, $i = 1, \ldots, n$ are the probability integral transformations (PIT) of the marginal models. With the use of copulas, one can map the univariate marginal distributions of n random variables, each supported in the $[0, 1]$ interval, to their n-variate distribution, supported on $[0, 1]^n$. This method applies, regardless of the type and degree of dependence among the variables.

---

[1] For further examples, see Embrechts et al. (2001).

[2] For related work on copulas as a modeling tool for returns, see Embrechts et al. (1997) and Dias and Embrechts (2004).

[3] A more detailed account of copulas can be found in Joe (1997), in Nelsen (1999), and in Cherubini et al. (2004), who provide a more finance-oriented presentation.

12.2.2 CONDITIONAL COPULA

Sklar's theorem, as presented above, works essentially for constant marginal distributions and copula functions. Patton (2006b) introduces the concept of *conditional copula*, which adapts this framework to the time series case by allowing for time-variation in the parameters of the marginal distributions. This is particularly useful for returns, since volatility models imply that marginal distributions have time-varying means and volatilities. The conditional copula is defined as

$$F_t(y_{1t}, \ldots, y_{nt}|\mathbf{Y}^{t-1}) = C_t(F_{1t}(y_{1t}|\mathbf{Y}^{t-1}), \ldots, F_{nt}(y_{nt}|\mathbf{Y}^{t-1})|\mathbf{Y}^{t-1}), \qquad (12.4)$$

where $Y_s = \{y_{1s}, y_{2s}, \ldots, y_{ns}\}$ denotes the time s observations of all series, and $\mathbf{Y}^{t-1} = \{Y_s\}_{s=1}^{t-1}$ is the history of the multivariate process up to time $t-1$. In principle, to apply Sklar's theorem to conditional distributions, the conditioning information needs to be the same for all marginals and the copula. It is common practice to assume that each marginal distribution only depends on its own history and that the copula can depend on the history of all series. In principle, this assumption should be checked, even though it is often neglected.[4]

12.2.3 SOME COMMONLY USED BIVARIATE COPULAS

There are an almost unlimited number of bivariate copulas, but we limit our attention to the four most commonly used copulas in finance, which are the Gaussian, the Student-t, the Gumbel, and the Clayton. Table 12.1 shows the density functions of these copulas, and Figure 12.1 shows contour plots for different distribution functions constructed using these copulas but with the same standard normal marginals and a linear correlation of 0.5. Both the Gaussian and Student-t copulas are symmetric, but the Student-t has more weight in the tails than the Gaussian, which translates into contours that are more elongated along the 45° line. Symmetry is an undesirable feature for the purpose of modeling financial returns, which are typically more dependent in the left than in the right tail, due to the occurrence of market crashes.

The Clayton and Gumbel copulas are better suited for financial returns, since they are asymmetric. The Clayton has only lower tail dependence, while the Gumbel copula has only upper tail dependence. Since financial markets are more likely to crash together than enjoy booms together, the Gumbel copula is generally used in its rotated version[5]. Both the Clayton and Gumbel are examples of *Archimedean* copulas. Archimedean copulas can be constructed from a *generator function*, which is a continuous, strictly decreasing, convex function $\psi : [0, \infty] \to [0, 1]$, such that $\psi(0) = 1$ and $\psi(\infty) \equiv \lim_{t\to\infty} \psi(t) = 0$, and

---

[4]The same is true for models such as the Dynamic Conditional Correlation (DCC) of Engle (2002a).

[5]A rotated copula is the survival copula $\hat{C}(u_1, u_2) = u_1 + u_2 - 1 + C(1 - u_1, 1 - u_2)$, and its contour plot is obtained by symmetry of the original copula with respect to the −45-degree line. Essentially, it exchanges the upper and lower tails.

TABLE 12.1 Density Functions of Some Common Copulas

Copula	Density
Gaussian	$\frac{1}{\sqrt{1-\rho^2}} \exp\left[\frac{-(q_1^2+q_2^2-2\rho q_1 q_2)}{2(1-\rho^2)} + \frac{q_1^2+q_2^2}{2}\right]$ where $q_i = \Phi^{-1}(u_i)$
Student-*t*	$\frac{\Gamma\left(\frac{\nu+2}{2}\right)}{\Gamma(\frac{\nu}{2})\nu\pi\sqrt{1-\rho^2} f_\nu(q_1) f_\nu(q_2)} \left(1 + \frac{q_1^2+q_2^2-2\rho q_1 q_2}{\nu(1-\rho^2)}\right)^{-\left(\frac{\nu+2}{2}\right)}$ where $q_i = T_\nu^{-1}(u_i)$
Clayton	$(1+\theta)(u_1 u_2)^{-\theta-1}(u_1^{-\theta} + u_2^{-\theta} - 1)^{-2-1/\theta}$
Gumbel	$(\log u_1 . \log u_2)^{\theta-1} \frac{((-\log u_1)^\theta + (-\log u_2)^\theta)^{1/\theta} + \theta - 1}{u_1 u_2((-\log u_1)^\theta + (-\log u_2)^\theta)^{2-1/\theta}} C_G(u_1, u_2, \theta)$ where $C_G(u_1, u_2, \theta) = \exp\left[-((-\log(u_1))^\theta + (-\log(u_2))^\theta)^{1/\theta}\right]$
rotated Gumbel	Same as Gumbel but replacing u_i by $1 - u_i$, for $i = 1, 2$

$\Phi(.)$ denotes the cumulative distribution of the standard normal. $f_\nu(.)$ and $T_\nu(.)$ are, respectively, the density and the cumulative distribution function of the Student-*t* distribution with ν degrees of freedom.

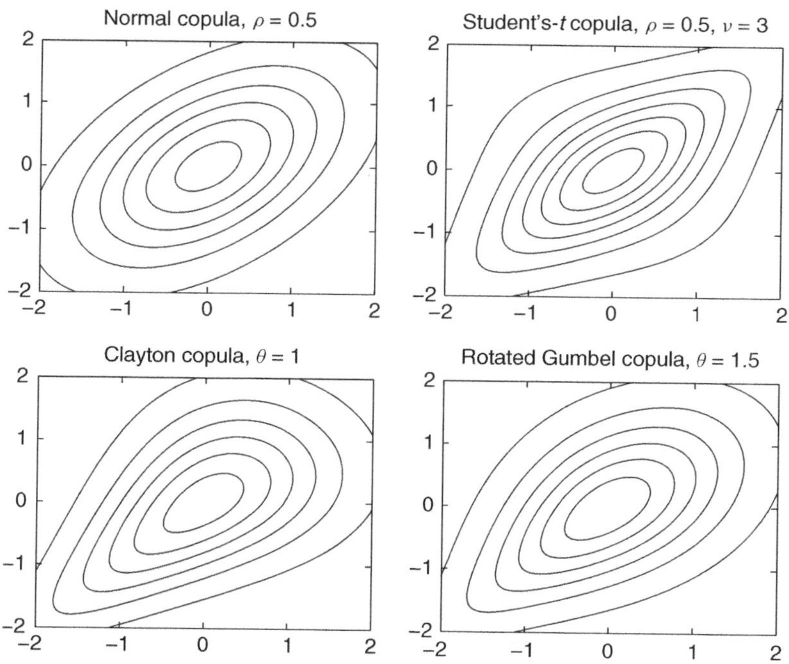

FIGURE 12.1 Contour plots for the Gaussian, Student-*t*, Clayton and rotated Gumbel copulas with standard normal marginal distributions and linear correlation coefficients of 0.5.

whose inverse is $\psi^{-1}(u) = \inf\{t : \psi(t) \leq u\}$. A bivariate Archimedean copula distribution obtains as

$$C(u_1, u_2) = \psi(\psi^{-1}(u_1) + \psi^{-1}(u_2)). \tag{12.5}$$

The Clayton can be derived from the generator $\psi(t) = (1 + t)^{-1/\theta}$, while the Gumbel is obtained from $\psi(t) = \exp(-t^{1/\theta})$.

12.2.4 COPULA-BASED DEPENDENCE MEASURES

In order to describe dependence that exists amongst variables that are not in the class of elliptical distributions, there exist several measures, based on the ranks of the variables. These measures are invariant with respect to any strictly increasing transformation of the data. *Rank correlations* are popular distribution-free measures of the association between variables. Unlike the traditional Pearson correlation, they are also relevant outside the range of the spherical and elliptical distributions and can detect certain types of nonlinear dependence. One of the most commonly used coefficient of rank correlation is Kendall's τ. It relies on the notion of concordance. Intuitively, a pair of random variables is *concordant* whenever large values of one variable are associated with large values of the other variable. More formally, if (y_i, x_i) and (y_j, x_j) are two observations of random variables (Y, X), we say that the pairs are *concordant* whenever $(y_i - y_j)(x_i - x_j) > 0$ and *discordant* whenever $(y_i - y_j)(x_i - x_j) < 0$.

Kendall's τ is defined as the difference between the probability of concordance and the probability of discordance. Kendall's τ is a copula-based dependence measure in the sense that it does not depend on the marginal distribution, but is exclusively a function of the copula:

$$\tau = 4 \int_{[0,1]^2} C(u_1, u_2) dC(u_1, u_2) - 1. \tag{12.6}$$

While Kendall's τ measures overall dependence, there exist copula-based measures of dependence that focus on dependence between extremes. *Quantile dependence* focuses on the tails of the distribution. If X and Y are random variables with distribution functions F_X and F_Y, there is quantile dependence in the lower tail at threshold α, whenever $P[Y \leq F_Y^{-1}(\alpha) | X \leq F_X^{-1}(\alpha)]$ is different from zero. Finally, *tail dependence* is obtained as the limit of this probability, as we go arbitrarily far out into the tails. The coefficient of lower tail dependence of X and Y is

$$\lim_{\alpha \to 0^+} P[Y \leq F_Y^{-1}(\alpha) | X \leq F_X^{-1}(\alpha)] = \lambda_{\mathrm{L}}, \tag{12.7}$$

provided a limit $\lambda_L \in [0, 1]$ exists. If $\lambda_L \in (0, 1]$, X and Y are said to be asymptotically dependent in the lower tail; if $\lambda_{\mathrm{L}} = 0$, they are asymptotically independent. If the marginal distributions of random variables X and Y are continuous, their tail dependence is only a function of their copula, and hence, the amount of tail dependence is invariant under strictly increasing transformations. If a bivariate copula C is such that the limit

$$\lim_{u \to 0^+} C(u, u)/u = \lambda_L$$

exists, then C has lower tail dependence if $\lambda_L \in (0, 1]$ and no lower tail dependence if $\lambda_L = 0$. Similarly, if a bivariate copula C is such that

$$\lim_{u \to 1^-} \bar{C}(u, u)/(1 - u) = \lambda_U \tag{12.8}$$

exists, then C has upper tail dependence if $\lambda_U \in (0, 1]$ and no upper tail dependence if $\lambda_U = 0$. $\bar{C}(u_1, u_2) = 1 - u_1 - u_2 + C(u_1, u_2)$ denotes the survivor function of copula C.

Table 12.2 shows the tail dependence and Kendall rank correlation for the four standard copulas. As can be seen from Table 12.2, the Gaussian copula has no tail dependence, which means that extreme returns are independent. This is an undesirable property for the purpose of modeling stock returns, which are typically subject to crashes. The Student copula has some tail dependence, which is a function of the correlation coefficient and the degrees of freedom, but unfortunately, like the Gaussian, it is symmetric, which implies that financial returns have an equal probability of enjoying very extreme positive and negative returns together, which, again, does not fit the stylized facts. The Clayton and rotated Gumbel have negative tail dependence and no positive tail dependence, which makes them good candidates for financial returns.

TABLE 12.2 Range of Parameters, Tail Dependence, and Kendall's τ for Some Common Copulas

Copula	Coefficient	λ_L	λ_U	Kendall's τ
Gaussian	$\rho \in [-1, 1]$	0	0	$\frac{2}{\pi} \arcsin(\rho)$
Student-t	$\rho \in [-1, 1]$, $\nu \in (2, +\infty]$	$2T_{\nu+1}(x)$ where $x = -\sqrt{\nu+1}\sqrt{\frac{1-\rho}{1+\rho}}$	$= \lambda_L$	$\frac{2}{\pi} \arcsin(\rho)$
Clayton	$\theta \in (0, \infty)$	$2^{-1/\theta}$	0	$\frac{\theta}{2+\theta}$
Gumbel rotated	$\theta \in [1, \infty)$	$2 - 2^{1/\theta}$	0	$1 - \frac{1}{\theta}$
Gumbel	$\theta \in [1, \infty)$	0	$2 - 2^{1/\theta}$	$1 - \frac{1}{\theta}$

$T_\nu(v)$ is the cumulative distribution function of the Student-t distribution with ν degrees of freedom.

12.3 Estimation

Sklar's theorem opens the way for two alternative estimation methods for copulas based on the likelihood. From Equation 12.4, one can obtain the density by differentiating, and taking logs leads to the joint likelihood of the marginals and the copula

$$L(\mathbf{Y}; \theta_{\mathrm{m}}, \theta_{\mathrm{c}}) = \sum_{t=1}^{T} \log f(Y_t|\mathbf{Y}^{\mathbf{t-1}}; \theta_{\mathrm{m}}, \theta_{\mathrm{c}}), \tag{12.9}$$

where θ_{m} denotes the parameters of the marginals and θ_{c} the copula parameter. This likelihood can be decomposed as per Equation 12.2 into one part, L_{m}, that contains the marginal densities and another part, L_{c}, that contains the dependence structure

$$L(\mathbf{Y}; \theta_{\mathrm{m}}, \theta_{\mathrm{c}}) = L_{\mathrm{m}}(\mathbf{Y}; \theta_{\mathrm{m}}) + L_c(\mathbf{Y}; \theta_{\mathrm{m}}, \theta_{\mathrm{c}}), \tag{12.10}$$

$$L_{\mathrm{m}}(\mathbf{Y}; \theta_{\mathrm{m}}) = \sum_{t=1}^{T} \sum_{i=1}^{n} \log f_i(y_{i,t}|y_i^{t-1}; \theta_{\mathrm{m},i}), \tag{12.11}$$

$$L_{\mathrm{c}}(\mathbf{Y}; \theta_{\mathrm{m}}, \theta_{\mathrm{c}}) = \sum_{t=1}^{T} \log c\left(F_1(y_{1,t}|y_1^{t-1}; \theta_{\mathrm{m},1}), \ldots, F_n(y_{n,t}|y_n^{t-1}, \theta_{\mathrm{m},n}); \mathbf{Y}^{t-1}\theta_{\mathrm{c}}\right), \tag{12.12}$$

where we now assume that each variable i only depends on its own history, $y_i^{t-1} = (y_{i,1}, \ldots, y_{i,t-1})$. The likelihood of the marginal models, L_m, is a function of the parameter vector $\theta_{\mathrm{m}} = (\theta_{\mathrm{m},1}, \ldots, \theta_{\mathrm{m},n})$ that collects the parameters of each one of the n marginal densities f_i, but the copula likelihood directly depends on the copula parameter θ_{c}, and indirectly on the parameters of the marginal densities, through the distribution function F_i.

12.3.1 EXACT MAXIMUM LIKELIHOOD

The first estimation method consists of maximizing the joint likelihood with respect to all parameters. The maximum likelihood estimator is:

$$\hat{\theta}_{\mathrm{m}}^{ML}, \hat{\theta}_{\mathrm{c}}^{ML} = \underset{\theta_{\mathrm{m}}, \theta_{\mathrm{c}}}{\operatorname{argmax}}\ L(\mathbf{Y}; \theta_{\mathrm{m}}, \theta_{\mathrm{c}}) \tag{12.13}$$

Under the usual regularity conditions for maximum likelihood, the following result holds for the collection of the marginal and copula parameters $\hat{\theta}^{\mathrm{ML}} = (\hat{\theta}_{\mathrm{m}}^{\mathrm{ML}}, \hat{\theta}_{\mathrm{c}}^{\mathrm{ML}})$:

$$\sqrt{T}(\hat{\theta}^{\mathrm{ML}} - \theta_0) \rightarrow N(0, F^{-1}(\theta_0)), \tag{12.14}$$

where $F(\theta_0)$ is the Fisher information matrix and θ_0 is the true value of the parameter.

12.3.2 IFM

Exact maximum likelihood is a "brute force" method, which is not feasible in many practically relevant cases because of the computational difficulties that can arise when the number of parameters is large. Joe and Xu (1996) propose a two-step estimation procedure, called *inference for the margins* (*IFM*), which first consists of estimating the margins:

$$\hat{\theta}_{\mathrm{m}} = \underset{\theta_{\mathrm{m}}}{\operatorname{argmax}} \sum_{t=1}^{T} \sum_{i=1}^{n} \log f_i(y_{i,t} | y_i^{t-1}; \theta_{\mathrm{m},i}). \tag{12.15}$$

Whenever the marginals models are independent of each other, for instance, when univariate ARMA-GARCH models are used, this can be simplified further into a set of n separate estimations for each one of the margins i:

$$\hat{\theta}_{\mathrm{m},i} = \underset{\theta_{\mathrm{m},i}}{\operatorname{argmax}} \sum_{t=1}^{T} \log f_i(y_{i,t} | y_i^{t-1}; \theta_{\mathrm{m},i}). \tag{12.16}$$

These coefficients are then collected in a vector $\hat{\theta}_{\mathrm{m}} = (\hat{\theta}_{\mathrm{m},i}, \ldots, \hat{\theta}_{\mathrm{m},n})$, and in a second step, the parameters of the copula are estimated taking as given the parameter estimates of the marginal models:

$$\hat{\theta}_{\mathrm{c}} = \underset{\theta_{\mathrm{c}}}{\operatorname{argmax}} L_{\mathrm{c}}(\mathbf{Y}; \hat{\theta}_{\mathrm{m}}, \theta_{\mathrm{c}}). \tag{12.17}$$

All parameters are then collected into a vector $\hat{\theta} = (\hat{\theta}_m, \hat{\theta}_c)$. Under regularity conditions, we have

$$\sqrt{T}(\hat{\theta} - \theta_0) \rightarrow N(0, G^{-1}(\theta_0)), \tag{12.18}$$

where the Godambe information matrix takes the form $G(\theta_0) = D^{-1}V(D^{-1})'$ with $D = E\left[\frac{\partial s(\theta)}{\partial \theta}\right]$ and $V = E[s(\theta)s(\theta)']$, where $s(\theta) = \left(\frac{\partial L_m}{\partial \theta_{\mathrm{m}}}, \frac{\partial L_c(\hat{\theta}_m, \theta_c)}{\partial \theta_{\mathrm{c}}}\right)$. This method entails a loss of efficiency compared to exact maximum likelihood, but it is the most frequently used in practice. Joe (2005) studies the properties of the IFM procedure in the more challenging multivariate copula case and finds only limited losses in efficiency compared to exact maximum likelihood, except in cases in which the dependence is very strong.

12.3.3 BIVARIATE STATIC COPULA MODELS

We illustrate copulas by estimating the five bivariate copulas that we presented, on a data set of returns of Latin American and European stock markets. The data set consists of four daily MSCI equity indices: Brazil, Mexico, France, and Germany, downloaded from Datastream. All price series are in US dollars from August 15, 1990 to July 28, 2010, which gives a sample of 1042 weekly returns.

TABLE 12.3 Descriptive Statistics of the Data

	Mean	Std. Dev.	Skewness	Kurtosis	Min	Max
Brazil	14.36	44.35	−0.95	7.97	−44.53	20.83
Mexico	11.92	32.68	−0.81	9.23	−37.31	18.08
France	4.96	22.30	−0.59	5.95	−17.58	12.83
Germany	4.18	23.79	−0.75	6.16	−17.50	13.98

This table shows descriptive statistics of the annualized Wednesday-to-Wednesday stock index returns for Brazil, Mexico, France, and Germany (multiplied by 100).

We use Wednesday-to-Wednesday returns, because of the difference in opening and closing times of the different stock exchanges. Summary statistics of the data are shown in Table 12.3. The annualized means and standard deviations are quite different for Latin American and European countries. While Brazil and Mexico have high means and standard deviations, France and Germany enjoy lower but less volatile returns. With skewness and excess kurtosis, all series present clear signs of nonnormality. This is particularly the case for Brazil and Mexico, and to a lesser extent for France and Germany. As a result, the range of observed returns is larger for Brazil and Mexico than for France and Germany, with lows around −.40, compared to minimal returns around −.17 for France and Germany.

We estimate GARCH(1,1) models for the marginals using the skew-t distribution of Hansen (1994). Specifically, the returns are modeled as $y_{i,t} = \mu_i + \eta_{i,t}$, where $\eta_{i,t} = \sqrt{h_{i,t}} \cdot \varepsilon_{i,t}$, $h_{i,t} = \omega_i + \alpha_i \eta^2_{i,t-1} + \beta_i h_{i,t-1}$, and $\varepsilon_{i,t} \sim$ *skewed-t*(ν_i, λ_i), where the skewed-*t* density is given by[6]

$$g(z|\nu,\lambda) = \begin{cases} bc\left(1 + \dfrac{1}{\nu-2}\left(\dfrac{bz+a}{1-\lambda}\right)^2\right)^{-(\nu+1)/2} & z < -a/b \\ bc\left(1 + \dfrac{1}{\nu-2}\left(\dfrac{bz+a}{1+\lambda}\right)^2\right)^{-(\nu+1)/2} & z \geq -a/b. \end{cases}$$

A negative λ corresponds to a left-skewed density, which means that there is more probability of observing large negative than large positive returns. This is what we expect when we work with equity returns, since it captures the large negative returns associated with market crashes that are responsible for the skewness.

The results of the univariate skewed-*t* GARCH models are presented in the second to fifth columns of Table 12.4. The coefficients of the lagged conditional variance, β, are around 0.85, which implies a reasonable amount of persistence, especially because we are considering weekly returns. The estimated asymmetry coefficients of the conditional distribution, λ, are negative, consistent with our expectation. The degrees of freedom parameters of the Student-*t* distribution are low for Brazil and Mexico, which corresponds to the high kurtosis of these returns.

[6]The constants a, b, and c are defined as $a = 4\lambda c\left(\frac{\nu-2}{\nu-1}\right)$, $b^2 = 1 + 3\lambda^2 - a^2$ and $c = \frac{\Gamma\left(\frac{\nu+1}{2}\right)}{\sqrt{\pi(\nu-2)}\Gamma\left(\frac{\nu}{2}\right)}$.

TABLE 12.4 Parameter Estimates of the GARCH Models for Weekly Returns for Brazil, Mexico, France, and Germany

	α	β	ν	λ	KS=	KS+	KS−	AD	K
Brazil	0.16	0.82	7.42	−0.23	0.95	0.67	0.58	0.82	0.86
Mexico	0.09	0.86	5.93	−0.14	0.55	0.28	0.29	0.74	0.12
France	0.12	0.84	12.26	−0.20	0.99	0.70	0.69	1.00	0.96
Germany	0.12	0.87	9.12	−0.22	0.64	0.87	0.33	0.90	0.81

This table shows estimates of the GARCH models for Brazil, Mexico, France, and Germany. The parameters of the GARCH dynamics are shown in the second and third columns, the degrees of freedom of the Student-t are shown in the fourth column, while the asymmetry parameter is shown in column 5. Columns 6–10 show p-values of tests of the null hypothesis of uniformity of the PITs implied by the GARCH models. Columns 6–8 show results of different versions of the Kolmogorov–Smirnov, while the Anderson–Darling and the Kuiper tests are shown in columns 9 and 10.

We check that the marginal models are well specified and subject them to a battery of goodness of fit tests. We include three versions of the Kolmogorov–Smirnov test, as well as the Anderson–Darling and Kuiper tests of uniformity of the PIT of the marginal models. The p-values of the tests are reported in the sixth to tenth columns of Table 12.4. All models pass all the tests. It is very important that the marginal models be well specified, since otherwise, the copula estimation that is conditional on the marginal models would be affected, see Fermanian and Scaillet (2005).

We illustrate the properties and estimation of the bivariate copulas by focusing on the stock market returns of Brazil and Mexico. Figure 12.2 displays the upper and lower quantile dependence for thresholds α and $1-\alpha$ between .2 and .01, and this shows very clear signs of asymmetry, with much higher quantile dependence in the lower tail (solid line) than in the upper tail (crosses). Therefore, one can expect that copulas with lower tail dependence would fit best. According to Figure 12.2, the upper tail dependence is close to zero, since the curve is decreasing as one moves further out in the tail, while the upper quantile dependence remains about constant and seems to end up somewhere between 0.4 and 0.5 in the limit. Table 12.5 shows estimates of the bivariate static copulas. The copulas were estimated conditionally on the estimates of the GARCH models for the margins, which corresponds to using the IFM estimation method. Those models can be viewed as more general versions of the CCC model of Bollerslev (1990). Although all copulas lead to a rank correlation of about 0.35, their likelihoods are very different. The best model is the rotated Gumbel, with a lower tail dependence coefficient of 0.36. The Gaussian copula has no tail dependence at all and does significantly worse. The Student-t copula improves over the Gaussian, but it struggles with tail dependence because of its symmetry. It therefore exaggerates upper and underestimates lower tail dependence with a compromise value of 0.22. The Clayton implies a little too much lower tail dependence (0.5) for a rank correlation of 0.33, in the sense that it implies a lower tail dependence that is too extreme for this data. The Gumbel copula has

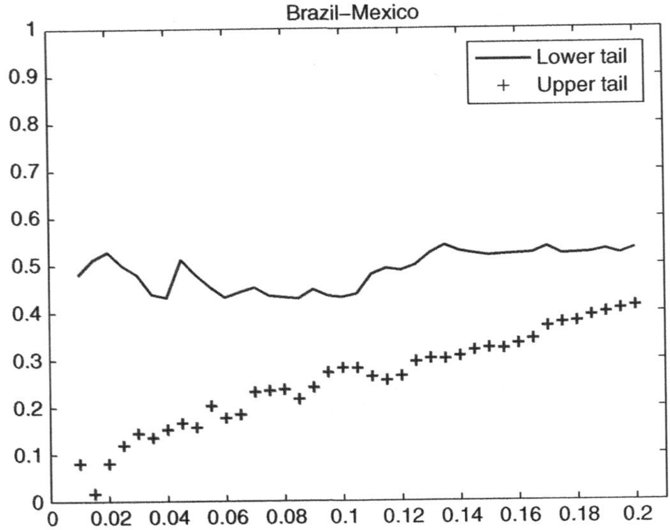

FIGURE 12.2 **Quantile dependence for Brazil and Mexico The solid line shows the lower quantile dependence, while the crosses are for upper quantile dependence. The quantile dependence has been computed for thresholds of 0.01–0.2.**

TABLE 12.5 **Estimates of Several Static Copulas for the Brazilian and Mexican Stock Markets**

	Parameter	DoF	LL	BIC	τ	λ_L	λ_U
Gaussian	0.52		166.83	−326.70	0.35		
Student-*t*	0.53	5.19	184.97	−356.05	0.36	0.22	0.22
Clayton	0.99		192.97	−378.98	0.33	0.50	
Gumbel	1.47		133.83	−260.72	0.32		0.40
rotated Gumbel	1.57		202.34	−397.72	0.36	0.44	

This table shows estimates of the static copulas for the Brazil–Mexico pair, in columns 2 and 3, along with the log-likelihood (LL) in column 4, the Bayesian information criterion (BIC) in column 4, Kendall's rank correlation (τ) in column 5, and the upper and lower tail dependence in columns 5 and 6. DoF refers to the degrees of freedom parameter of the Student-*t* copula.

the lowest Kendall's τ of all copulas, since it implies a positive relation between Kendall's τ and upper tail dependence and there is no upper tail dependence in the data. It also does the poorest of all models in terms of likelihood.

12.4 Dynamic Copulas

A recent literature in empirical finance initiated by Longin and Solnik (1995) has shown that correlations between financial returns are not constant over time and some models have been proposed to take this into account. The model that has achieved the highest level of popularity in this literature is certainly the DCC model of Engle (2002a) and the model of Tse and Tsui (2002). This idea was adapted to the copula context and led to a recent development of alternative approaches, surveyed by Manner and Reznikonva, forthcoming.

12.4.1 EARLY APPROACHES

Time-varying copula models have been pioneered by Patton (2004), Patton (2006b), Patton (2006a) and Jondeau and Rockinger (2006). The difficulty in specifying such models is to come up with a forcing variable in the evolution equation of the dependence parameter. Patton (2006b) proposes to model the parameter of the Gaussian copula as

$$\rho_t = \Lambda_1 \left(\omega + \beta\rho_{t-1} + \alpha\frac{1}{m}\sum_{i=1}^{m} \Phi^{-1}(u_{1,t-i})\Phi^{-1}(u_{2,t-i}) \right), \tag{12.19}$$

where $\Lambda_1 = \frac{1-\exp(-x)}{1+\exp(-x)}$ is a normalized version of the inverse Fisher transformation, which maps the real line into the interval $[-1, 1]$ and the u_{it}s are the PITs of the marginals. For non-elliptical copulas, he uses

$$\theta_t = \Lambda_2 \left(\omega + \beta\theta_{t-1} + \alpha\frac{1}{m}\sum_{i=1}^{m} |u_{1,t-i} - u_{2,t-i}| \right), \tag{12.20}$$

where $m = 10$, $\Lambda_2(x) = (1 + \exp(-x))^{-1}$ and θ_t is the tail dependence parameter. The forcing variable in Equation 12.20 is inversely related to the dependence, since it is zero under perfect dependence, $1/3$ under independence and $1/2$ under perfect negative dependence.

These models introduce dynamics by specifying a law of motion for the copula parameter or the tail dependence. This makes comparison across models difficult, since the elliptical models have a time-varying copula parameter, and the other ones have time-varying tail dependence. Another drawback of models such as the one of Equation 12.20 is that their MA(∞) form will involve terms like $\Lambda_2 \circ \Lambda_2 \cdots \circ \Lambda_2()$, which are highly nonlinear and make it difficult to understand their mathematical properties.

12.4.2 DYNAMICS BASED ON THE DCC MODEL

It is also possible to use the dynamic equation of the DCC to model non-elliptical copulas. Recently, Heinen and Valdesogo (2009) propose a dynamic evolution of the parameter of a bivariate copula that is an extension of the DCC equations. As the inputs for the dynamic correlation in the DCC model are standardized residuals, they first apply the inverse CDF of the normal to the uniform PITs of the marginals, the u_{it}, which are the inputs of the bivariate copula, in order to transform them to a bivariate vector of standard normals:[7]

$$\varepsilon_{i,t} = \Phi^{-1}(u_{i,t}). \tag{12.21}$$

$$\varepsilon_t = [\varepsilon_{1,t}, \varepsilon_{2,t}]. \tag{12.22}$$

Then they use the dynamic equations of the DCC model for the bivariate case:

$$Q_t = \Omega(1 - \alpha^C - \beta^C) + \alpha^C \varepsilon_{t-1}\varepsilon_{t-1}^{'} + \beta^C Q_{t-1}, \tag{12.23}$$

$$R_t = (Q_t \odot I_2)^{-1/2} Q_t (Q_t \odot I_2)^{-1/2}, \tag{12.24}$$

where Ω is a symmetric 2×2 matrix, with ones on the diagonal, and the off-diagonal element equal to ω^C, while α^C and β^C are the autoregressive parameters. They then define the dynamic Kendall's τ as:

$$\tau_t = 2 \ \arcsin(\rho_t)/\pi. \tag{12.25}$$

where ρ_t is the time-varying off-diagonal element of the matrix R_t which makes Kendall's τ time-varying. Using the relation between copula parameter and Kendall's τ from Table 12.2, one can transform the Kendall's τ coefficient τ_t for every period t, into the coefficient θ_t of the corresponding copula. Denote $g(.)$ the function that maps the Kendall's τ into the copula parameter θ_t:

$$\theta_t = g(\tau_t). \tag{12.26}$$

Together, Equations 12.21–12.24, along with the copula likelihood L_c of Equation 12.12, where θ_c has been replaced by its time-varying version θ_t of Equation 12.26, constitute the model. This specification implies that ρ_t is the parameter of the Gaussian copula that would prevail, if the copula were indeed Gaussian. One should emphasize that, while Equation 12.25 holds exactly in the case of an elliptical copula, it becomes an identifying assumption of the model in the non-elliptical case. For those copulas that only allow positive dependence, the off-diagonal element, q_t, of Q_t is replaced by $max(q_t, 0)$, which ensures a well-defined model.

To illustrate copulas based on DCC dynamics, we estimate a Gaussian, Student-t, Clayton, Gumbel, and rotated Gumbel version of each of these copulas. The results, displayed in Table 12.6 show very similar coefficients for the dynamics, with very high persistence.[8] Not surprisingly, this means that the dynamic evolution of Kendall's τ, shown in Figure 12.3 for the rotated Gumbel copula does not actually depend very much on the type of copula. This is comparable to the fact that the estimated volatility does not change very

[7]With the exception of the Student-t copula where they apply the inverse CDF of the Student-t distribution with the corresponding degrees of freedom.

[8]The sum of the dynamic coefficients, $\alpha^C + \beta^C$ in Table 12.6 only look like they sum to 1 because of rounding.

TABLE 12.6 Parameter Estimates of Several Dynamic Copulas for the Brazilian and Mexican Stock Markets

	ω^C	α^C	β^C	DoF	LL	BIC
Gaussian	0.18	0.04	0.96		233.51	−446.17
Student-t	0.17	0.04	0.96	8.75	240.01	−452.23
Clayton	0.40	0.03	0.96		234.06	−447.27
Gumbel	0.01	0.03	0.97		193.57	−366.30
rotated Gumbel	0.09	0.04	0.96		252.84	−484.83

This table shows estimates of the dynamic copulas for the Brazil Mexico pair, in columns 2 to 6, along with the log-likelihood (LL) in column 6 and the Bayesian information criterion (BIC) in column 7. DoF refers to the degrees of freedom parameter of the Student-t copula.

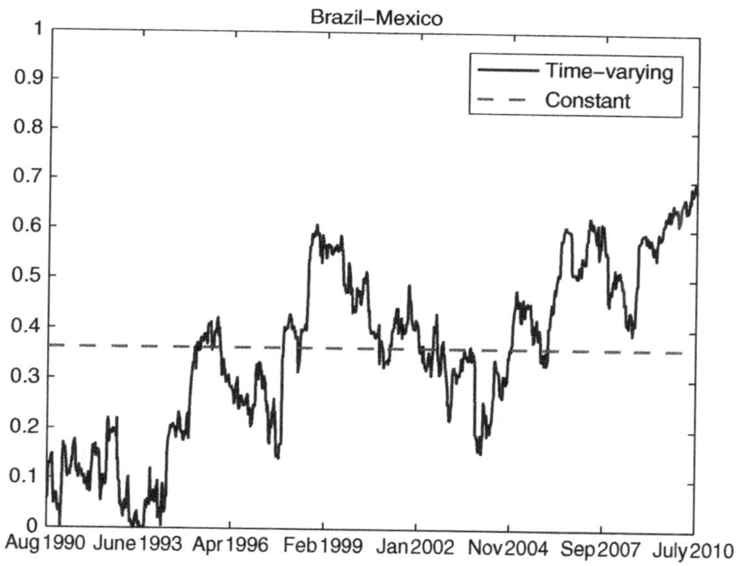

FIGURE 12.3 Kendall's tau for time-varying and constant rotated Gumbel copulas between Brazil and Mexico.

much depending on the type of marginal distribution that is used in estimating a GARCH model. By far, the best model is the one given by the rotated Gumbel, which can accommodate the lower tail dependence that is present in the data.

12.4.3 ALTERNATIVE METHODS

A lot of recent research has dealt with different ways of introducing dynamics in copulas. We briefly review some of them:

1. Structural breaks. Dias and Embrechts (2004) propose a test for a break in the dependence parameter of the copula. They adapt to the copula framework the procedure of Andrews (1993) based on the supremum over all possible break dates of the likelihood ratio test of the null hypothesis of no break versus the alternative of a break.
2. GAS model. Creal et al. (2008) introduce a general method to deal with time-varying parameters for any distribution, where the autoregressive parameters are updated with the score of the likelihood of the model. This method is shown to adapt more rapidly to changes in the parameter, but at the cost of more volatility in the trajectory of the dependence parameter.
3. Regime-switching copulas: Rodriguez (2007) and Okimoto (2008) estimate regime-switching copulas for pairs of international stock indices. Okimoto (2008) focuses on the US–UK pair, whereas Rodriguez (2007) works with pairs of Latin American and Asian countries. They follow the tradition of Ramchand and Susmel (1998) to impose a structure where variances, means, and dependence all switch together. They show that the best performance is obtained when the copula switches between a symmetric and an asymmetric regime. Markwat et al. (2009) propose a model in which both the shape of the dependence and the magnitude of the dependence are allowed to switch.
4. SCAR. Hafner and Manner (2010) transpose the method of "stochastic volatility" to the dependence parameter of a copula. They assume that there is a latent Gaussian process, and they use link functions to map it to a copula parameter with the appropriate domain. The estimation is quite demanding and relies on simulation methods to integrate out the latent process in the evaluation of the likelihood. As in an Expectation-Maximization (EM) algorithm, one can get a smoothed estimate of the dependence parameter based on the whole data.
5. Hafner and Reznikova (2010a) propose a semiparametric approach where the dependence parameter is the result of the maximization of a likelihood weighted locally in time.
6. Giacomini et al. (2009) assume that the dependence parameter is constant locally. They use the local change point (LCP) method of Mercurio and Spokoiny (2004) to determine the interval over which the parameter is constant. This method has the advantage of being able to detect breaks, as well as smooth changes in the dependence parameter.

12.5 Value-at-Risk

In order to compare the implications of using copulas in practice, we compute VaR for long and short positions of an equally weighted portfolio of Brazil and Mexico, with the CCC model of Bollerslev (1990), the DCC model of Engle (2002a), which are benchmark models, as well as a static and dynamic model based on the rotated Gumbel copula, which we found to perform best according to a likelihood criterion. VaR is one of the most commonly used risk measures for a portfolio. For a given threshold α, $VaR(\alpha)$ is the α percentile point of the portfolio loss function, and the expected shortfall $ES(\alpha)$ is the expected loss conditional on observing a return below the VaR. Formally, the VaR of a portfolio at the confidence level α is defined as the minimum return such that the probability that the loss in portfolio value over some period of time is greater than the VaR is $1-\alpha$, or

$$VaR(\alpha) = -\inf\{l : \text{Prob}(R > l) \leq 1-\alpha\} ,$$

where R is the portfolio return.

We evaluate the performance of the different estimates of VaR in-sample using the likelihood ratio test of correct conditional coverage of Christoffersen (1998). The comparison of the VaR forecast and the realized returns of the portfolio defines a sequence of binary variables, I_t, called *hits*. A hit occurs whenever the observed return is lower than the predicted VaR, resulting in a violation of the threshold. A successful VaR model at a threshold α should have close to a fraction α of violations in sample, and these violations should be independently distributed. The likelihood ratio test of conditional coverage of Christoffersen (1998) is a combination of the unconditional coverage and the independence tests. For the unconditional coverage, Kupiec (1995) proposes to test $H_0 : f = \alpha$ against $H_1 : f \neq \alpha$, where f is the failure rate (estimated by $\hat{f}$, the empirical failure rate). Under the null hypothesis, the Kupiec likelihood ratio statistic $LR = 2ln[\hat{f}^N(1-\hat{f})^{T-N}] - 2ln[\alpha^N(1-\alpha)^{T-N}]$ is asymptotically distributed as a $\chi^2(1)$, where N is the number of VaR violations, T is the total number of observations (1042 in our case) and α is the failure rate of the null hypothesis. For the independence test, Christoffersen (1998) considers a binary first-order Markov chain for the hits, with transition probability matrix Π_1

$$\Pi_1 = \begin{bmatrix} 1-\pi_{01} & \pi_{01} \\ 1-\pi_{11} & \pi_{11} \end{bmatrix},$$

where $\pi_{i,j} = Pr(I_t = j|I_{t-1} = i)$. Under the null hypothesis, $H_0 : \pi_{01} = \pi_{11} = \alpha$, the likelihood ratio test of conditional coverage

$$LR = 2ln[(1-\hat{\pi}_{01})^{n_{00}}\hat{\pi}_{01}^{n_{01}}(1-\hat{\pi}_{11})^{n_{10}}\hat{\pi}_{11}^{n_{11}}] - 2ln[\alpha^N(1-\alpha)^{T-N}],$$

is asymptotically distributed as a $\chi^2(2)$, where n_{ij} is the number of hits with value i followed by j, $\hat{\pi}_{01} = n_{01}/(n_{00}+n_{01})$ and $\hat{\pi}_{11} = n_{11}/(n_{10}+n_{11})$.

Table 12.7 shows the p-values of the tests for the four models and different levels of the quantile. Both the CCC and the static rotated Gumbel perform very poorly. Introducing dynamics with the DCC model does not necessarily improve the results, and it sometimes leads to even worse results than the CCC, its static counterpart. The dynamic rotated Gumbel offers an improvement with

TABLE 12.7 **Value-at-Risk**

	Long Positions				Short Positions			
	10%	5%	2.5%	1%	10%	5%	2.5%	1%
CCC	0.12	0.10	0.11	0.00	0.00	0.00	0.00	0.01
RG	0.02	0.04	0.79	0.63	0.04	0.73	0.09	0.01
DCC	0.29	0.07	0.18	0.02	0.00	0.00	0.00	0.02
DRG	0.03	0.13	0.52	0.63	0.21	0.97	0.27	0.03

This table shows p-values from the conditional coverage test of of Christoffersen (1998) for VaR estimates from the CCC model of Bollerslev (1990), a static rotated Gumbel model, the DCC model of Engle (2002a), and a dynamic rotated Gumbel copula model.

respect to the previous models except for a failure at the 10% threshold for long positions. All models are rejected at the 1% threshold for short positions.

12.6 Multivariate Static Copulas

While there is a very large catalog of bivariate copulas, the choice is much more restricted in the multivariate case. In applied work, the two most widely used multivariate copulas are the Gaussian and Student-t copulas. They have the advantage of describing the dependence between a set of variables with a correlation matrix, without imposing any further restrictions on the dependence across pairs of variables. However, these copulas have some limitations in that they do not allow asymmetric dependence, one of the desirable features of a copula, and they are restrictive in the tail behavior, since the Gaussian does not allow tail dependence, while the Student-t implies that the upper and lower tail dependence be equal, a contradiction of the stylized facts.

12.6.1 MULTIVARIATE ARCHIMEDEAN COPULAS

Multivariate exchangeable Archimedean copulas are a natural extension of their bivariate counterparts, and they provide an alternative to multivariate elliptical copulas. They are obtained from a generator function according to

$$C(u) = \psi\left(\sum_{i=1}^{n} \psi^{-1}(u_i)\right), \tag{12.27}$$

where $u = (u_1, u_2, \ldots, u_n)$ and ψ is a generator function; see Section 10.2.3. They are the subject of intensive research, and many of their theoretical properties have been established recently by McNeil and Nešlehová (2009), including the fact that multivariate Archimedean copulas obtain as survival copulas of simplex distributions.[9] Moreover, they show the relation between the radial distribution of the simplex distribution and the generator of the copula. This connection gives rise to methods for simulation as well as methods for generating new families of Archimedean copulas. While such copulas allow for asymmetric dependence between more than two variables, they impose that all pairs of variables have the exact same dependence, characterized by a single parameter, which limits their applicability to financial returns.

We compare estimates of the multivariate elliptical and Archimedean copulas for our full data set of stock index returns for Brazil, Mexico, France, and Germany. Panel A of Table 12.8 shows estimates of the Gaussian and Student-t copula. The correlation coefficients are very similar for the Gaussian and the Student-t, but the log-likelihood is much higher for the Student-t, which is the preferred model, according to the BIC. Panel B shows estimates of exchangeable Archimedean copulas with Clayton, Gumbel, and rotated Gumbel copulas. The rotated Gumbel performs best, but it has a much lower likelihood than the elliptical copulas. The deterioration in the fit of the Archimedean copulas is less than fully compensated by the reduction in the number of parameters. This is due to the strong dependence between France and Germany, with estimated copula correlation of 0.83, whereas all other pairs happen to have copula correlation close to 0.5.

There exist some alternatives to multivariate exchangeable Archimedean copulas that partially alleviate the very strong constraints imposed on the data by exchangeable Archimedean copulas. Fully nested Archimedean copulas (FNAs) were originally proposed by Joe (1997), and they consist of building an n-variate copula from $n-1$ bivariate Archimedean copulas. In the case of four variables, the distribution can be written as

$$C(u_1, u_2, u_3, u_4) = C_1(u_1, C_2(u_2, C_3(u_3, u_4))), \qquad (12.28)$$

or with the Archimedean copulas written out in terms of their generators

$$\psi_1(\psi_1^{-1}(u_1) + \psi_1^{-1} \circ \psi_2(\psi_2^{-1}(u_2) + \psi_2^{-1} \circ \psi_3(\psi_3^{-1}(u_3) + \psi_3^{-1}(u_4)))), \qquad (12.29)$$

where C_i, $i = 1, 2, 3$ are bivariate Archimedean copulas with generators ψ_i. These copulas were studied, amongst others, by Savu and Trede (2006), Whelan (2004), Morillas (2005), and McNeil et al. (2006). While FNAs are less restrictive than their fully exchangeable counterparts, they still impose identical dependence for many pairs of variables, which in general, from a financial point of view, seems difficult to interpret or justify. For instance, the copula in Equation 12.28 implies that pairs (u_1, u_2), (u_1, u_3), and (u_1, u_4) have the same dependence captured by copula C_1, while (u_2, u_3) and (u_2, u_4) are modeled with copula C_2 and C_3 captures the dependence of the pair (u_3, u_4). Moreover, in order to produce a

[9] Simplex distributions are uniform distributions of vectors on the simplex $\mathcal{S}_n = \{y \in \mathcal{R}_+^n : \|y\|_1 = 1\}$, and they were introduced by Fang and Fang (1988).

TABLE 12.8 Estimation of Multivariate Copulas

Panel A: Multivariate Elliptical Copulas

Copula		Parameters			LL	BIC
Gaussian		ME	FR	GE		
	BR	0.52	0.44	0.45		
	ME		0.48	0.46		
	FR			0.81	913.24	−1784.79
Student-*t*		ME	FR	GE		
	BR	0.54	0.45	0.46		
	ME		0.51	0.49		
	FR			0.83		
	DoF	6.08			1003.39	−1958.14

Panel B: Multivariate Archimedean Copulas

Copula	Parameter	Kendall's τ	LL	BIC
Clayton	0.83	0.29	651.92	−1296.90
Gumbel	1.49	0.33	598.10	−1189.25
rotated Gumbel	1.49	0.33	675.07	−1343.19

Panel C: Canonical vine

	Copula	Parameter	DoF	LL	BIC
BR-ME	rotated Gumbel	1.57			
BR-FR	rotated Gumbel	1.40			
BR-GE	rotated Gumbel	1.41			
ME-FR|BR	Student-*t*	0.34	11.09		
ME-GE|BR	Student-*t*	0.31	11.96		
FR-GE|BR,ME	Student-*t*	0.76	4.42	1028.95	−1995.37

Panel D: D-vine

	Copula	Parameter	DoF	LL	BIC
BR-ME	rotated Gumbel	1.57			
ME-FR	Student-*t*	0.50	6.41		
FR-GE	Student-*t*	0.83	3.16		
BR-FR|ME	Student-*t*	0.24	8.59		
ME-GE|FR	rotated Gumbel	1.10			
BR-GE|ME,FR	Gumbel	1.07		1025.68	−1988.82

This table shows estimates of multivariate copulas for Brazil (BR), Mexico (ME), France (FR), and Germany (GE). Panel A displays the correlation matrix of the Gaussian and Student-*t* copulas, panel B shows parameter estimates and implied Kendall's τ of the multivariate Clayton, Gumbel, and rotated Gumbel. Panels C and D show estimates, respectively, of a canonical vine and a D-vine. The last two columns of the table contain the log-likelihood (LL) and the Bayesian Information Criterion (BIC). DoF stands for the degrees of freedom of the Student-*t* copula.

well-defined distribution, an FNA with n variables requires constraints on its generator functions: $\psi_i^{-1} \circ \psi_{i+1}$ must have completely monotone derivatives for $i = 1, n-2$. When all copulas are in the same family, this implies that the dependence needs to decrease with the level of nesting ($\theta_1 \geq \cdots \geq \theta_n$), but when the copulas are allowed to be from different families, these constraints can become even more stringent and difficult to verify, see Aas and Berg (2009). Partially Nested Archimedean copulas (PNAs) provide alternative ways of grouping pairs of variables, but they are also subject to the limitation of modeling $n(n-1)/2$ interactions between n variables with only $n-1$ different copulas.

12.6.2 VINES

Recently Bedford and Cooke (2002) introduced vine copulas, which are multivariate copulas based on graphical methods. These very flexible multivariate copulas are obtained by a hierarchical construction. The main idea is that a multivariate copula can be decomposed into a cascade of iteratively conditioned bivariate copulas. Vine copulas were introduced in the financial literature by Aas et al. (2009), who also provide an estimation method. The great advantage of vine copulas is that they make the large choice of bivariate copulas available in the multivariate situation, therefore providing an incredible amount of flexibility.

In the case of three uniform variables (u_1, u_2, u_3), the density of a vine copula can be written as

$$c(u_1, u_2, u_3) = c_{23|1}(F_{2|1}(u_2|u_1), F_{3|1}(u_3|u_1))c_{12}(u_1, u_2)c_{13}(u_1, u_3) ,$$

where conditional distribution functions are computed using Joe (1996):

$$F(u|v) = \frac{\partial C_{u,v_j|v_{-j}}(F(u|v_{-j}), F(v_j|v_{-j}))}{\partial F(v_j|v_{-j})} .$$

v_j denotes the jth element of vector v, and v_{-j} denotes all elements of vector v, excluding the jth element. In the development above, we have implicitly chosen to condition on u_1. This choice is arbitrary, and other ways of ordering the data when conditioning are also possible. Different types of vines are obtained depending on how the variables are ordered. The two most prominent types of vines are the canonical vine and the D-vine. Figure 12.4 represents the dependence structure of a canonical vine copula graphically. In the first stage of the copula, we model the bivariate copulas of u_1 with all other variables in the system. Then we condition on u_1, and consider all bivariate conditional copulas of u_2 with all other variables in the system. For an n-dimensional set of variables, assuming uniform marginals, this leads to a density $c(u_1, \ldots, u_n)$ of an n-dimensional canonical vine copula

$$\prod_{j=1}^{n-1} \prod_{i=1}^{n-j} c_{j,j+i|1,\ldots,j-1}(F(u_j|u_1, \ldots, u_{j-1}), F(u_{j+i}|u_1, \ldots, u_{j-1})) .$$

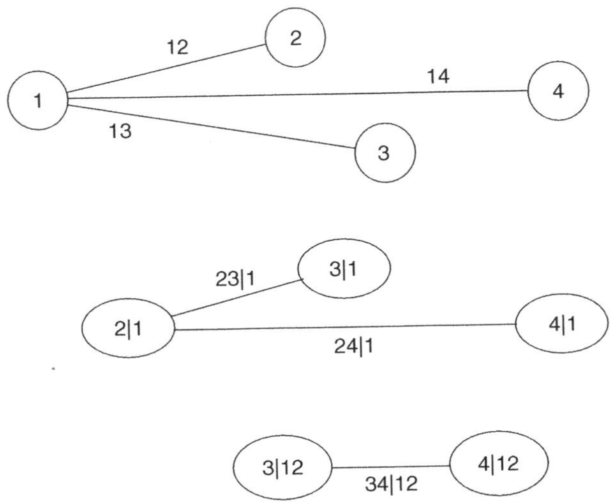

FIGURE 12.4 Dependence structure of a canonical vine. This figure shows the structure of a canonical vine copula with four variables. In the first tree, the dependence between variable 1 and all the other variables in the system is modeled with bivariate copulas. The second tree consists in modeling the dependence of variables 2 with variables 3 and 4, conditionally on variable 1. In the last layer, one uses a bivariate copula to model the dependence between variables 3 and 4, conditionally on variables 1 and 2. In the case of this system with 4 variables, the dependence is modeled with 6 bivariate copulas.

Canonical vines can be viewed as factor models with one variable playing the role of pivot (factor) in every tree of the dependence structure.

The dependence structure of a D-vine is represented graphically in Figure 12.5 for four variables. Its density $c(u_1, \cdots, u_n)$ may be written as

$$\prod_{j=1}^{n-1}\prod_{i=1}^{n-j} c_{i,i+j|i+1,\cdots,i+j-1}(F(u_i|u_{i+1},\cdots,u_{i+j-1}), F(u_{i+j}|u_{i+1},\cdots,u_{i+j-1})).$$

The advantages of vine copulas are immediately apparent: there are only very few general multivariate copulas, whereas there exists an almost unlimited number of bivariate copulas. When specifying vine copulas, we can therefore choose each one of the building blocks involved from a very long list, which allows a very large number of possible copulas.

We specify and estimate a canonical vine and a D-vine for our data set of four countries. In the vines, we use the structures of Figures 12.4 and 12.5, where the order of the variables is Brazil (u_1), Mexico (u_2), France (u_3), and Germany (u_4). We did not try to optimize over different orderings. As a general principle, one tries to capture as much dependence as possible in the first trees.

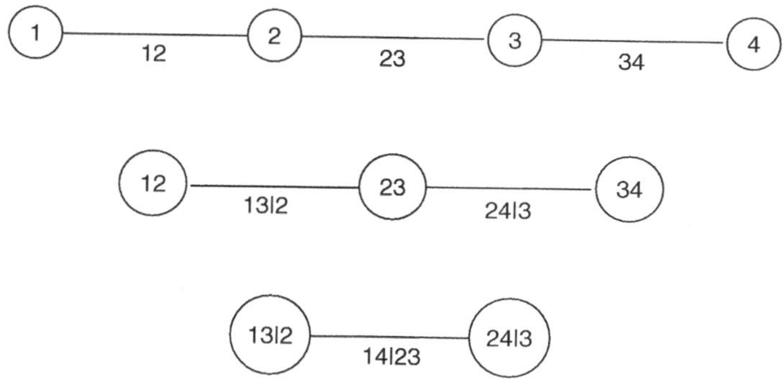

FIGURE 12.5 Dependence structure of a D-vine. This figure shows the structure of a D-vine copula with four variables. In the first tree, the dependence between pairs of adjacent variable 1 (1 with 2, 2 with 3, and 3 with 4) is modeled with bivariate copulas. The second tree consists in modeling the dependence of variables 1 with 3, conditionally on 2 and 2 with 4, conditionally on 3. In the last layer, one uses a bivariate copula to model the dependence between variables 1 and 4, conditionally on variables 2 and 3. In the case of this system with 4 variables, the dependence is modeled with 6 bivariate copulas.

When asymmetric dependence is important, an alternative strategy is to put the more asymmetric pairs in lower trees. We select each bivariate copula from the list of four copulas that we consider in this chapter (Gaussian, Student-*t*, Clayton, and rotated Gumbel) according to the BIC, for each tree in succession. In this section, we only consider static copulas. However, one could use bivariate dynamic copulas at each tree or even combine static and dynamic copulas. This could modify the preference between the copulas presented in Table 12.8. Panels C and D of Table 12.8 show the results of the canonical vine and the D-vine. The canonical vine model is made up of rotated Gumbel models in the first tree with Brazil and Student-*t* models for all conditional copulas. This model has the best performance of all multivariate copula models. The D-vine is the second best multivariate model, and it is made up of rotated Gumbel and Student-*t* copulas, with one Gumbel copula in the last tree.

12.7 Conclusion

In this chapter, we reviewed copula-based volatility models and illustrated their uses with a VaR exercise. Research in this field seems to have taken two main directions: introducing time-variation in copula models and developing flexible copula methods for the multivariate case. A few recent papers combine time-variation with multivariate copulas. Garcia and Tsafack (2007) and Chollete et al. (2009) estimate regime switches between a symmetric copula and an asymmetric copula. Garcia and Tsafack (2007) use mixture copulas, while

Chollete et al. (2009) use a canonical vine for the asymmetric regime to show that the asymmetry matters for VaR and for the formation of portfolios. Härdle and Okhrin (2010) adapt the method of Mercurio and Spokoiny (2004) to make a hierarchical copula time-varying both in the coefficients and in the structure of the hierarchical copula. Heinen and Valdesogo (2009) use a truncated canonical vine for a large-dimensional factor copula-multivariate GARCH model and show that it delivers good forecasts of VaR.

PART THREE

Realized Volatility

CHAPTER THIRTEEN

Realized Volatility: Theory and Applications

SUJIN PARK and OLIVER LINTON

13.1 Introduction

This chapter reviews some recent developments in the theory and practice of volatility measurement. Volatility is a fundamental quantity for investment decisions. Its measurement is necessary for the implementation of most economic or financial theories that guide such investment. Volatility is also important for assessing the quality of performance of financial markets, with very volatile markets being perceived as not functioning effectively as a way of channeling savings into investment. Despite its importance, volatility is not an easy quantity to measure, and there are many approaches to do that. From the point of view of the investor facing investment opportunities with returns r_t at time t and information $\mathcal{F}_s$ at time $s < t$, one might be interested in the matrix $\mathrm{var}(r_t|\mathcal{F}_s)$. This represents a challenge because the time horizon $t - s$ might be unknown or be stochastic; the information set $\mathcal{F}_s$ might be extremely large, containing current and past values of many variables; and the probability distribution $f(r_t|\mathcal{F}_s)$ may be unknown. The recent emphasis on continuous time methods of volatility measurement addresses in some way all of these concerns.

We review the basic theoretical framework and describe the main approaches to volatility measurement in continuous time. In this chapter, the central

Handbook of Volatility Models and Their Applications, First Edition.
Edited by Luc Bauwens, Christian Hafner, and Sebastien Laurent.

parameter of interest is the integrated variance and its multivariate counterpart. We describe the measurement of these parameters under ideal circumstances and when the data are subject to measurement error. We discuss the main types of measurement error models that apply and how they may arise from the way the market operates at the fine grain, that is, microstructure issues. We also describe some common applications of this literature. Our review is necessarily selective, and there are many topics and papers that we do not cover.

13.2 Modeling Framework

13.2.1 EFFICIENT PRICE

We start by setting the modeling framework. Under the standard assumptions that the return process does not allow for arbitrage and has a finite instantaneous mean, the asset price process, as well as smooth transformations thereof, belong to the class of special semimartingale processes, as detailed by Back (1991). If, in addition, it is assumed that the sample paths are continuous, we have the Martingale Representation Theorem (e.g., Protter, 1990; Karatzas and Shreve, 2005). Specifically, there exists a representation for the log-price Y_t, such that for all $t \in [0, T]$,

$$Y_t = \int_0^t \mu_u \mathrm{d}u + \int_0^t \sigma_u \mathrm{d}W_u, \tag{13.1}$$

where μ_u is a predictable locally bounded drift, σ_u is a cádlág volatility process and W_u is an independent Brownian motion, and the integral is of the Itô form. Let Y_{t_j} denote an observed log-price on the time grid, $0 = t_0 < \cdots < t_n = T$, where we take $T = 1$ for simplicity. Note that $\{t_i\}$ is usually assumed to be a nondecreasing deterministic sequence. Crucial to semimartingales, and to the economics of financial risk, is the quadratic variation (QV) process. Let Γ_t be a set of points that partition the interval $[0, t]$ with $\Gamma = \Gamma_1$. The QV of Y over the time interval $[0, t]$ is given by

$$[Y, Y]_t = \lim_{\sup_{t_j \in \Gamma_t} |t_j - t_{j-1}| \to 0} \sum_{0 \le t_j \le t} (Y_{t_j} - Y_{t_{j-1}})^2, \tag{13.2}$$

with $[Y, Y] = [Y, Y]_1$. This quantity is a measure of ex-post volatility. As per Equation 13.1, the following holds almost surely

$$[Y, Y] = \int_0^1 \sigma_u^2 \mathrm{d}u. \tag{13.3}$$

The QV is also called the *integrated variance*, for obvious reasons. It is the key parameter of interest that this survey focuses on. It is an integral over the sample path of the stochastic process σ_u^2, and hence is itself a random variable. The specification of the process σ_u^2 is very general and nonparametric, that is, it may depend on the entire past of Y_t and additional sources of randomness. The averaging inherent in Equation 13.3 suggests gains in terms of estimability.

We now relate the parameter of interest to other concepts of volatility. A natural theoretical notion of ex-post return variability in this setting is notional volatility (Andersen et al., 2000). Under the maintained assumption of continuous sample path, the notional volatility equals the integrated volatility. The notional volatility over an interval $[t-h, t]$, is

$$\upsilon^2(t,h) \equiv [Y,Y]_t - [Y,Y]_{t-h} = \int_{t-h}^{t} \sigma_u^2 \mathrm{d}u.$$

Let $\mathcal{F}_t$ denote information on Y up to and including time t. Now, in the above setting, the conditional volatility, or expected volatility, over $[t-h, t]$, is defined by

$$\begin{aligned}
\operatorname{var}(Y_t|\mathcal{F}_{t-h}) &\equiv E\left[\{Y_t - E(Y_t|\mathcal{F}_{t-h})\}^2 |\mathcal{F}_{t-h}\right] \\
&= E\left[\left\{\int_{t-h}^{t} \mu_u \mathrm{d}u - E\left(\int_{t-h}^{t} \mu_u \mathrm{d}u|\mathcal{F}_{t-h}\right) + \int_{t-h}^{t} \sigma_u \mathrm{d}W_u\right\}^2 |\mathcal{F}_{t-h}\right] \\
&= E\left[\left\{\int_{t-h}^{t} \{\mu_u - E(\mu_u|\mathcal{F}_{t-h})\}\mathrm{d}u\right\}^2 |\mathcal{F}_{t-h}\right] && (13.4) \\
&\quad + E\left[\left\{\int_{t-h}^{t} \sigma_u \mathrm{d}W_u\right\}^2 |\mathcal{F}_{t-h}\right] && (13.5) \\
&\quad + 2E\left[\int_{t-h}^{t} \{\mu_u - E(\mu_u|\mathcal{F}_{t-h})\}\mathrm{d}u \int_{t-h}^{t} \sigma_u \mathrm{d}W_u|\mathcal{F}_{t-h}\right]. && (13.6)
\end{aligned}$$

Let us denote $A_h = O_{a.s.}(B_h)$ when A_h/B_h converges almost surely to a finite constant as $h \to 0$. We have that Equation 13.4 $= O_{a.s.}(h^2)$, Equation 13.5 $= \int_{t-h}^{t} \sigma_u^2 \mathrm{d}u = O_{a.s.}(h)$, and Equation 13.6 $= O_{a.s.}(h^{3/2})$, so that Equation 13.5 is the dominant term. Therefore, we have

$$\operatorname{var}(Y_t|\mathcal{F}_{t-h}) \simeq E[\upsilon^2(t,h)|\mathcal{F}_{t-h}].$$

In other words, the conditional variance of returns volatility is well approximated by the expected notional volatility, that is, it is an approximately unbiased proxy. The above approximation is exact if the mean process $\mu_u = 0$, or if μ_u is measurable with respect to $\mathcal{F}_{t-h}$. However, the result remains approximately valid for a stochastically evolving mean return process over relevant horizons, as long as the returns are sampled at sufficiently high frequencies. This gives further justification for $[Y, Y]$ as a parameter of interest.

Notional volatility or integrated volatility is latent. However, it can be estimated consistently using the so-called realized volatility. The realized variance

(RV) for the time interval [0, 1] is the discrete sum in Equation 13.2;

$$[Y, Y]^n = \sum_{j=1}^{n} (Y_{t_j} - Y_{t_{j-1}})^2, \tag{13.7}$$

where $t = 1$.

Barndorff-Nielsen and Shephard (2002a) showed that the RV is a $\sqrt{n}$ consistent estimator of the QV and is asymptotically mixed Gaussian under infill asymptotics. We can also generalize the above specification for the process driven by Lévy process. In this case, the RV converges in probability to the QV of the process, which includes contributions from the jumps. We discuss estimation further below.

13.2.2 MEASUREMENT ERROR

Empirical evidence suggests that the price process deviates from the semimartingale assumption in Equation 13.1. The "volatility signature plot" (which shows Equation 13.7 against sampling frequency, i.e., $1/n$) in Figure 13.5 suggests a component in observed price that has an infinite QV. Earlier, authors have identified this component as microstructure noise, meaning that it is due to the fine grain structure of how observed prices are determined in financial markets. A common way of modeling this is as follows. Let X_{t_j} be an observed log-price and Y_{t_j} be discretely sampled from the process in Equation 13.1. Then suppose that

$$X_{t_j} = Y_{t_j} + \varepsilon_{t_j}, \tag{13.8}$$

where ε_{t_j} is a random error term. The simplest case is where the microstructure noise ε_{t_j} is i.i.d. with zero mean, independent of the process Y. This model was first considered in Zhou (1996). In this case, Zhang et al. (2005) showed that $RV = 2nE(\varepsilon^2) + O_p(n^{1/2})$, which implies that RV is inconsistent and that when divided by $2n$, it is an asymptotically unbiased estimator of the variance of the microstructure noise. The noise can also be assumed to be serially correlated, and there are some theoretical results for this case, which we discuss below. One may want to allow for heteroscedasticity in the noise (Eq. 13.8), which has been taken up by Kalnina and Linton (2008). This is motivated by the stylized fact in market microstructure literature that intradaily spreads and intradaily stock price volatility are typically described by a U-shape (or a reverse J-shape). See Andersen and Bollerslev (1997b), Gerety and Mulherin (1994), Harris (1986), Kleidon and Werner (1996), Lockwood and Linn (1990), and McInish and Wood (1992).

Also, to closely mimic the high frequency transaction data, authors considered rounding error noise or nonadditive noise that is generated from specific model of order book dynamics. Li and Mykland (2007) discuss the rounding model,

$$X_{t_j} = \log(\delta[\exp(Y_{t_j} + \varepsilon_{t_j})/\delta]) \vee \log \delta, \tag{13.9}$$

where $\delta[s/\delta]$ denotes the value of s rounded to the nearest multiples of δ, which is a small positive number. This is consistent with the market that has a minimum price change, tick sizes for stocks and futures, and pips for foreign exchange. The rounding model (Eq. 13.9) is much more complex to work with than Equation 13.8, because of the nonlinear way in which the efficient price enters. For example, even assuming no microstructure noise, the QV of X_t is given by $[f(Y), f(Y)]_t$ where $f(Y) = E(X|Y)$ is a complicated nonlinear function, even though we are interested in estimating $[Y, Y]_t$. Li and Mykland (2007) showed that when var(ε) is large, we have $f(Y_t) \sim Y_t$, whereas for a small noise variance, the divergence of two QVs can be large. In any case, under the presence of such microstructure noise the RV is no longer a consistent estimator of the integrated variance. We explore the impact of different microstructure noise assumptions on RV and the class of consistent estimators under Equations 13.1 and 13.8 in Section 13.4.

13.3 Issues in Handling Intraday Transaction Databases

Before examining volatility estimators based on high frequency data, it is important to understand the basic statistical features of such a dataset. In this section, we provide a brief summary of the stylized features of intraday transaction data. Goodhart and O'Hara (1997) and Guillaume et al. (1997) provide early reviews. The distributional properties of high frequency returns varies with sampling frequency. At higher frequency, there is a stronger evidence of return distribution being non-Gaussian. The empirical evidence suggests that high frequency returns are approximately symmetric, with finite second moment but large fourth moment, and that the tail of the distribution declines according to a power law. In fact, prices are discrete, taking values that are integer multiples of tick sizes, which vary according to assets and time period (in the US stock market, tick size changed from being 1/8 of a dollar to 1/100 of a dollar during a few years at the beginning of the past decade); see Figure 13.1, which plots the intraday price of the Dell stock over a single day. The data we use in this paper is a National Best Bid and Offer (NBBO) trade and quote (TAQ) consolidated dataset. This puts together the best available quotes from multiple venues and matches the trades to NBBO quotes. Therefore, TAQ price dynamics should be indicative of that from a single order book. However, returns, whether defined logarithmically or exactly, are less discrete, since the normalization changes over time; so this comment mostly just affects the study of prices within a single day.

The returns of executed trade prices (trade returns) are negatively serially correlated. This is due to bid-ask bounce: at the tick level, buy orders are likely to be followed by sell orders and vice versa. Absolute returns and trade activity variables such as volume, spread, and trade duration exhibit strong serial correlation. Andersen and Bollerslev (1997a) showed that the absolute trade returns, after eliminating the short-term periodic component, have a hyperbolic decaying autocorrelation function. This can affect the construction of

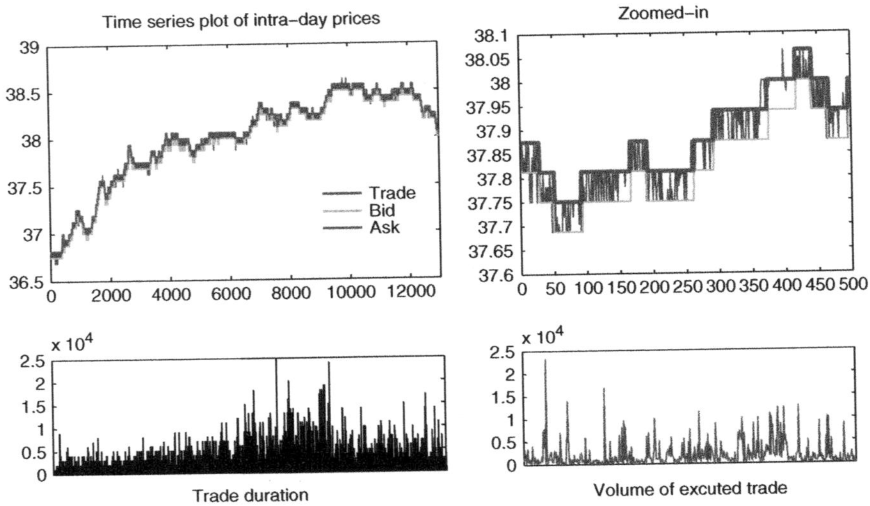

FIGURE 13.1 Time series plot of intraday price over a day.

the standard errors and forecasting. Variables associated with transaction activity show periodic patterns due to trading convention. Activities are high at the start and at the end of the trading session, and this induces a particular pattern in activity variables. See bottom left of Figure 13.1. The presence of periodicity has an important implication for modeling intraday series. For example, Andersen and Bollerslev (1997b), Andersen and Bollerslev (1997a) showed that absolute returns exhibit clear long memory structure only after adjusting for the periodic pattern. Periodicity can be modeled by introducing periodic dummies, frequency domain filtering, and analysis at the activity time scale. The intraday periodicity and long memory structure can be explained by the presence of the information arrival process that drives the price formation process. See Hansen and Lunde (2005b) for how to treat the problem of intermittent data, such as in stock markets.

13.3.1 WHICH PRICE TO USE?

In intraday, we typically have different types of prices. We briefly describe workings of stock market order book. Order book is a collection of sell and buy orders at any point of time, recording a price, time stamp, and volume associated with each order. The bid is the maximum buy price, and the ask is the minimum selling price. The spread is defined by ask minus bid. Depending on the type of the order sent, it either adds to the order book, gets canceled, or generates a trade. For example, a buy limit order with price above the current bid but below the current ask tightens the spread. The same order with price below the current bid joins the queue. Buy order with price specified at the current ask, assuming that the order is filled, takes off the liquidity. This is always the case for a market order. Orders that are stored in the order book are referred as quotes. The quote return is defined by the change in the midquote, which is an average of bid

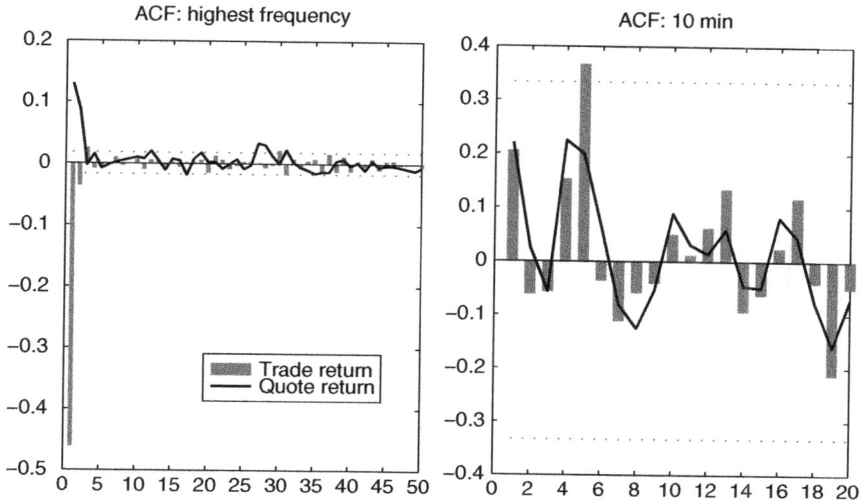

FIGURE 13.2 ACF (autocorrelation function) of trade and quote return depending on sampling frequency.

and ask. Trade returns is the return associated with the price of the executed trade. In terms of time series behavior, trade returns show significant negative first-order autocorrelation due to bid-ask bounce. In comparison, quote returns show positive first-order autocorrelation in a short interval (Figure 13.2). If the data is based on the higher frequency sampling, for example, at a tick time or one second, the quote and trade price have distinctively different features in returns and in absolute values. The difference disappears in lower frequency sampling. See Figure 13.3, which also shows that absolute returns are quite persistent. In certain cases, we may want to construct a price series that reflects the information at the deeper level of order book and also the volumes of these orders. We may construct such price as a weighted sum of quote prices at different levels of order book, where weight is given by the associated volume. Such price construction has the advantage that it uses more information available regarding investor's anticipation of price movement and that its discreteness is less severe by construction. Related but not the same VWAP (volume-weighted average price) can also be used. Over the specified period, it is constructed by taking the sum of executed trade price weighted by its volume. This quantity is used in a common strategy for execution of large transactions (See e.g., Almgren and Chriss, 2001).

One of the important conclusions that we can draw from the analysis is that in ultrahigh frequency, the choice of quote or trade price will sometimes affect the results of empirical modeling. For example, in calculating the naive RV measure of integrated variance based on low frequency returns, at 10–20 min, which is a popular choice, the choice of quote or trade returns will not have a discernible impact on the final quantity. However, for the more recently proposed methods that use unsampled tick data, we should compare the results using quote and trade returns. See Barndorff-Nielsen et al. (2009) for such studies.

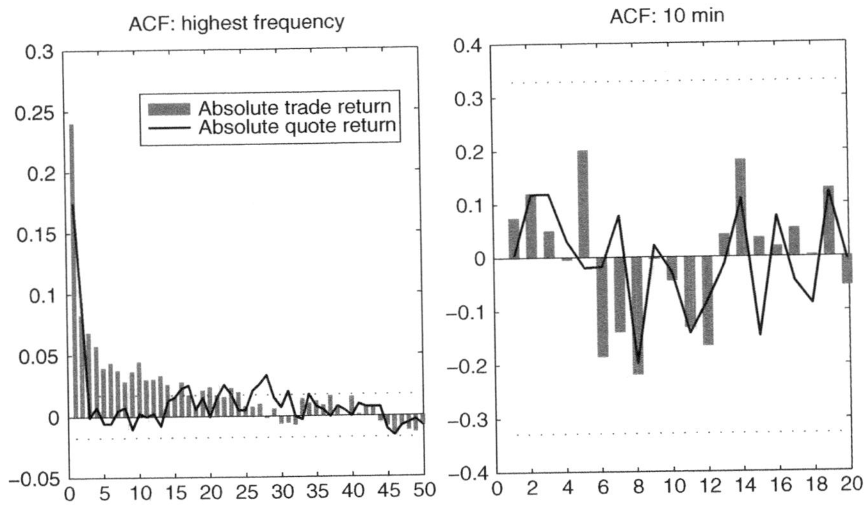

FIGURE 13.3 ACF of absolute trade and quote returns at different sampling frequency.

13.3.2 HIGH FREQUENCY DATA PREPROCESSING

Before analysis, the tick data has to be preprocessed to remove nonsensible prices and duplicated transaction data points. Barndorff-Nielsen et al. (2009) provide a guideline to do this for equity intraday data. Brownlees and Gallo (2006) summarize the structure of the TAQ high frequency dataset and address various issues in high frequency data management including outlier detection and how to treat nonsimultaneous observations, irregular spacing, issues of bid-ask bounce, and methods for identifying exact opening and closing prices. The authors also present the effect of data handling on the result of empirical analysis.

For the market where there is a centralized exchange and trading is electronic, the intraday transaction data should be available easily. The example of such market is equities and commodity futures market. Most empirical work has so far concentrated on NYSE-traded stocks and major currencies. Empirical application in other markets—geographically and other fixed income markets also—will be of interest.

13.3.3 HOW TO AND HOW OFTEN TO SAMPLE?

Intraday prices are observed at the discrete and irregular intervals. For volatility estimation, one can ask what is the effect of using all the data versus using sparsely sampled data, for example, at 10–20 min. For covariance estimation, the problem is more substantial. Naturally, the estimation of covariance involves the cross product of returns. How should we align the data points observed at a different times, and what is the statistical impact of the synchronization method on the estimators? This section discusses two data sampling/alignment methods: *fixed clock time* and *refresh time* methods. We present the synchronization method for d number of assets. The sampling method for univariate series is a special case for $d = 1$. In a given interval (for simplicity, 1 day) $[0, 1]$, we observe intraday transaction prices of the ith asset, X_i at discrete time points $\{t_{i,j}; j = 0, \ldots, n_i\}$ where n_i is the total number of observations on that interval. The set of

$$\{X_{i,t_{i,j}}, t_{i,j}; i = 1, \ldots, d, j = 1, \ldots, n_i\}$$

gives us the tick database of prices for d numbers of assets. We can associate the counting process to $\{t_{i,j}\}$

$$N_i(t) := \sum_{j=1}^{n_i} 1(t_{i,j} \leq t),$$

recording the number of transactions that occurred for the ith asset up to and including the time t. Let $0 = \tau_0 < \cdots < \tau_n = 1$ be an artificially created time grid and let $\{s_{i,j}\}$ be the actual time points of the data for ith asset to be aligned on the $\{\tau_j\}$'s grid. Regardless of how τ is defined, we take the data that is closest to this artificial grid,

$$s_{i,j} = \max_{0 \leq l \leq n_i} \{t_{i,l} \leq \tau_j\}. \tag{13.10}$$

We denote an aligned dataset as

$$\{X_{i,\tau_j}, \tau_j; i = 1, \ldots, d, j = 1, \ldots, n\}$$

with $X_{i,\tau_j} := X_{i,s_{i,j}}$. If no observation is available during the given interval, we repeat the previous data point.

First, consider the problem of sampling scheme for univariate time series of intraday prices. One can use the raw tick data of prices observed at $\{t_{i,j}\}$ or instead, work with sparser sampling. One method of sparse sampling is called *fixed clock time*. For example, we might want to create 1-min returns from the irregularly spaced tick data

$$\tau_j = jh, h = 1/60., \tag{13.11}$$

so that $\tau_j - \tau_{j-1} = h$, for all i. Empirical work shows that the effect of microstructure noise becomes attenuated when returns are sparsely sampled. Aït-Sahalia et al. (2005) derived the optimal sampling rate h minimizing the mean square of the RV under the presence of i.i.d. microstructure noise. When market microstructure noise is present but unaccounted for, they showed that the optimal sampling frequency is finite and derived its closed-form expression. The optimal sampling frequency is often found to be between 1 and 5 min. See Bandi and Russell (2008) for further discussion of the optimal sampling rate in estimating integrated variance. However, modeling the noise and using all the data should yield a better solution; see Section 13.4.1.1 on the noise robust estimators.

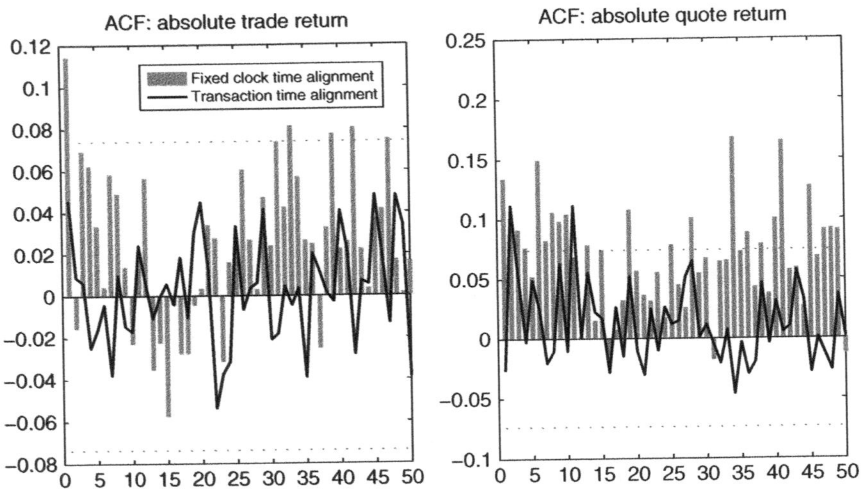

FIGURE 13.4 ACF of absolute trade and quote return sampled by fixed clock time and transaction time.

The second method for sparse sampling is to sample the price per given number of transactions. For example, data sampled per h number of transactions is

$$\tau_{j+1} = t_{i,N_i(\tau_j)+h}. \tag{13.12}$$

Griffin and Oomen (2008) argued that under the transaction time sampling, returns are less serially correlated and microstructure noise is closer to i.i.d. They note that the bias correction procedures that rely on the noise being independent are better implemented in transaction time. Figure 13.4 shows the ACF of absolute returns at a different sampling scheme—verifying that the transaction time sampling scheme reduces the serial correlation and that the process is closer to i.i.d.

For the multivariate case, the additional issue of synchronicity arises, whereby trading for different assets occurs at different times. It is necessary to align the returns of asynchronously traded assets to calculate the covariance estimator that involves the cross product of returns. One method is to use the *fixed clock time* as given in Equation 13.11. Another method, called the *refresh time*, proposed by Barndorff-Nielsen et al. (2010) can be thought as the multivariate version of the transaction time alignment given in Equation 13.12. It is constructed by

$$\tau_{j+1} = \max_{1 \leq i \leq d} \{t_{i,N_i(\tau_j)+1}\}. \tag{13.13}$$

As we sample the returns at higher frequency, zero returns (stale price) induce the downward bias in covariance estimators. This is known as the Epps effect. Hayashi and Yoshidam (2005) analytically showed the bias induced by the *fixed clock time*, assuming independent homogenous Poisson process for $N_i(t)$. The *refresh time* also induces synchronization bias, and the problem is more severe for

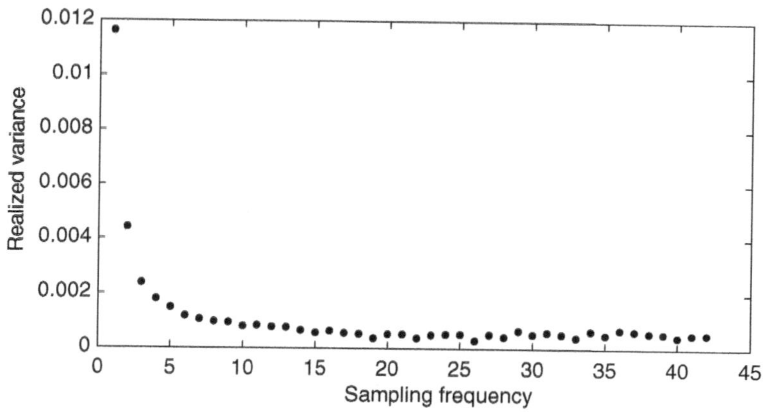

FIGURE 13.5 Realized variance calculated at different calendar time frequencies.

a high dimension covariance estimation since the method effectively collects the transaction time of the most illiquid asset. See Zhang (2011) for further studies on the refresh time bias and its effect on the time-domain-based estimator of integrated covariance matrix. See Section 13.4.2 for a discussion of covariance estimator robust to the synchronization bias.

13.4 Realized Variance and Covariance

13.4.1 UNIVARIATE VOLATILITY ESTIMATORS

We first present the results for realized volatility in the perfect world where there is no measurement error. The case of no noise is dealt with by Andersen et al. (2001a), Barndorff-Nielsen and Shephard (2002a), Barndorff-Nielsen and Shephard (2004a), and Mykland and Zhang (2006). Barndorff-Nielsen and Shephard (2002a) showed that the error using the RV to estimate the QV is asymptotically normal with rate $\sqrt{n}$, that is,

$$\sqrt{n}\frac{\sum_j y_{t_j}^2 - \int_0^1 \sigma_u^2 \mathrm{d}u}{\sqrt{2\int_0^1 \sigma_u^4 \mathrm{d}u}} \Longrightarrow N(0,1),$$

where $y_{t_j} = Y_{t_j} - Y_{t_{j-1}}$ is the observed return and $\Longrightarrow$ denotes convergence in distribution. We remark that their proof does not require that $Ey_{t_j}^4 < \infty$ or even $Ey_{t_j}^2 < \infty$ as would generally be the case for a central limit theorem (CLT) to hold. The reason is that the data-generating process assumes a different type of structure, namely, that locally, the process is even Gaussian, and it is this feature that permits the arrival of the normal distribution in the limit. Note that this CLT is statistically unfeasible since it involves a random unknown quantity called *integrated quarticity* (IQ), $\int_0^1 \sigma_u^4 du$. However, we can consistently estimate this by the following sample quantity

$$\widehat{IQ} = \frac{n}{3}\sum_j y_{t_j}^4 \to_p IQ.$$

Therefore, the feasible CLT is given by

$$\sqrt{n}\frac{\sum_j y_{t_j}^2 - \int_0^1 \sigma_u^2 du}{\sqrt{2\widehat{IQ}}} \Longrightarrow N(0,1).$$

This implies that $\sum_j y_{t_j}^2 \pm z_{\alpha/2}\sqrt{\frac{2}{3}\sum_j y_{t_j}^4}$ gives a valid α-level confidence interval for $\int_0^1 \sigma_u^2 du$.

13.4.1.1 Measurement Error. Motivated by some of the issues observed in the intraday financial time series largely to do with the presence of microstructure noise, authors have proposed competing estimators of the QV. The assumption on a microstructure noise has been generalized from a white noise to a noise process with some of following characteristics: autocorrelation, heteroskedasticity, and rounding models. McAleer and Medeiros (2008b) provide a summary of the theoretical properties of different estimators of QV under different assumptions of microstructure noise.

Suppose that the efficient prices process is given by Equation 13.1 and we observe Equation 13.8. In this case, the RV is inconsistent. The first consistent estimator under this scheme was the two time scale estimator (TSRV) of Zhang et al. (2005). Let us split the sample of size n into K subsamples, with the ith subsample containing n_i observations. Let $[X,X]^{n_i}$ denote the ith subsample estimator based on a K-spaced subsample of size n_i, and let $[X,X]^{\text{avg}}$ denote the averaged estimator

$$[X,X]^{n_i} = \sum_{j=1}^{n_i-1}\left(X_{t_{jK+i}} - X_{t_{(j-1)K+i}}\right)^2, \; i = 1,\ldots,K, \tag{13.14}$$

$$[X,X]^{\text{avg}} = \frac{1}{K}\sum_{i=1}^{K}[X,X]^{n_i}. \tag{13.15}$$

To simplify the notation, we assume that n is divisible by K and hence the number of data points is the same across subsamples, $n_1 = n_2 = \cdots = n_K = n/K$. Let $\overline{n} = n/K$. Let us define the adjusted TSRV estimator as

$$\widehat{[X,X]} = [X,X]^{\text{avg}} - \left(\frac{\overline{n}}{n}\right)[X,X]^n. \tag{13.16}$$

Zhang et al. (2005) show that this estimator is consistent and that

$$\frac{n^{1/6}\left(\widehat{[X,X]} - [X,X]\right)}{\sqrt{8c^{-2}E^2\varepsilon^2 + \frac{4}{3}cIQ}} \Longrightarrow N(0,1)$$

provided that $K = cn^{2/3}$ for any $c \in (0,\infty)$. Zhang (2006a) extended this work to the multiscale estimator (MSRV). She shows that this estimator is more efficient than the two time scale estimator and achieves the best convergence rate of $O_p(n^{1/4})$ (i.e., the same as the MLE with complete specification of the observed process).

Kalnina and Linton (2008) proposed a modification of the TSRV estimator that is consistent under heteroskedasticity and endogenous noise. Aït-Sahalia et al. (2012) modified TSRV and MSRV estimators and achieve consistency in the presence of serially correlated microstructure noise.

An alternative class of estimators is given by the so-called, realized kernel estimators. The motivation for this class of estimators is to recognize the connection between the problem of estimating the long-run variance of a discrete time process, Bartlett (1946). Let us define the symmetric realized autocovariance sequence

$$\gamma_h(X) := \sum_{j=h+1}^{n} x_{t_j} x_{t_{j-h}}, \tag{13.17}$$

for $h \in \mathbb{Z}^+$ and $\gamma_{-h}(X) = \gamma_h(X)$. At a zero lag, $\gamma_0(X)$ gives us the usual sum-of-squared high frequency returns, that is, RV. The kernel estimators smooth the realized autocovariances with the weight function given by $k(\cdot)$, where $k(0) = 1$, $k(s) \to 0$ as $s \to \infty$, and the bandwidth H controls the bias-variance trade-off. Specifically, let us consider

$$\widehat{[X,X]} = \sum_{|h|<n} k\left(\frac{h}{H+1}\right)\gamma_h(X). \tag{13.18}$$

Zhou (1996) was the first to consider the use of the kernel method to deal with the problem of microstructure noise. Hansen and Lunde (2006b) examined the properties of Zhou's estimator and showed that, although unbiased under the presence of i.i.d. microstructure noise, the estimator is not consistent. However, they advocated that, while inconsistent, Zhou's kernel method is able to uncover several properties of the microstructure noise.

Barndorff-Nielsen et al. (2010) proposed an estimator of the form in Equation 13.18 with a second-order kernel $k(\cdot)$. Their important contribution is to show that it is consistent under the presence of second-order stationary noise, and that furthermore, it is asymptotically normal with rate $O_p(n^{1/5})$ and

$$\frac{n^{1/5}\left(\widehat{[X,X]} - [X,X] - c^{-2}|k''(0)|w^2\right)}{\sqrt{4c||k||^2 IQ}} \Longrightarrow N(0,1), \tag{13.19}$$

provided that $H = cn^{3/5}$ for any $c \in (0, \infty)$, where $||k||^2 := \int k(s)^2 ds$ and $w^2 = \sum_h E(\varepsilon_t \varepsilon_{t-h})$, a long-run variance of the noise process. The estimator is guaranteed to be positive-definite, and note that the limiting distribution has an asymptotic bias component. For inference, Zhang et al. (2005) showed that $\frac{[X,X]^n}{2n}$ is $\sqrt{n}$ consistent estimator of $E\varepsilon^2$. The IQ can be estimated by the bipowertype estimator of Barndorff-Nielsen and Shephard (2004b), which is guaranteed to be positive-definite but rate inefficient at $O_p(n^{1/5})$. Barndorff-Nielsen et al. (2008) had a realized kernel estimator with a flat-top kernel that is, $k(0) = k(|1|/H) = 1$, and the realized autocovariance γ_h was defined such that the sum runs from 1 not $h + 1$. Their flat-top realized kernel is unbiased under the presence of i.i.d. microstructure noise and achieves the optimal convergence rate, $O_p(n^{1/4})$. The drawback of the earlier version, however, is that the resulting estimator is not guaranteed to be p.s.d.

We should briefly mention the promising preaveraging method analyzed for an example in Jacod et al. (2009), which involves averaging observed prices over a moderate number of time points to reduce the measurement error. Consider

$$\overline{X}_t = \frac{1}{n_t} \sum_{|t-t_j|<\varepsilon_T} X_{t_j}; \qquad \overline{x}_t = \frac{1}{n_t} \sum_{|t-t_j|<\varepsilon_T} x_{t_j},$$

where n_t is the number of time points with $|t - t_j| < \varepsilon_T$ for some small $\varepsilon_T \to 0$. Then $\overline{X}_t = n_t^{-1} \sum_{|t-t_j|<\varepsilon_T} Y_{t_j} + O_p(n_t^{-1})$ and $\overline{x}_t = n_t^{-1} \sum_{|t-t_j|<\varepsilon_T} y_{t_j} + O_p(n_t^{-1})$, so that now the noise is small provided n_t is large. The preaveraged data can then be used in a variety of the above procedures.

The final method involves a little departure. Parkinson (1980) and Alizadeh et al. (2002) proposed a range-based volatility proxy defined by the extreme prices over the predetermined interval. Specifically, let

$$\mathcal{R} = \sup_{0 \le t \le 1} X_t - \inf_{0 \le t \le 1} X_t.$$

This is an alternative measure of volatility to QV. In some special cases, it has a known positive relationship with QV. Specifically, if $X_t = \sigma W_t$, then $\mathcal{R}$ is a stochastic variable, while the quadratic variation is the constant σ^2. In fact, $\mathcal{R} = \sigma \left[\sup_{0 \le u \le 1} W(u) - \inf_{0 \le u \le 1} W(u)\right]$, from which one can compute $E\mathcal{R}^\kappa = \lambda_\kappa \sigma^{\kappa/2}$ for $\kappa \ge 1$, where λ_κ are known constants. More generally, the relationship between $\mathcal{R}$ and QV is likely to be rather complex. In practice, one may compute

$$\mathcal{R}_n = \max_{1 \le j \le n} X_{t_j} - \min_{1 \le j \le n} X_{t_j},$$

from a given sample of data observed at times $t_1, \ldots, t_n$. One can expect that $\mathcal{R}_n \to \mathcal{R}$ with probability 1 under quite general conditions. The most rigorous analysis of the realized range has been in Christensen and Podolskij (2007), except that they only compute $\mathcal{R}$ over small subintervals, which is like assuming that locally $X_t = \sigma W_t$ for some σ, and then average the resulting values of $\mathcal{R}_n$ over these subintervals. Alizadeh et al. (2002) recommend using the log of the sample range, as it is closer to a normally distributed random variable.

The realized range has the significant advantage that one can find the daily value in the newspapers for a variety of financial instruments, and so one has a readily available volatility measure without recourse to analysis of the intraday price path. Alizadeh et al. (2002) also argue that the method is relatively robust to a measurement error of a bid-ask bounce variety, since the intraday maximum is likely to be at the ask price and the daily minimum at the bid price of a single quote, and so, one expects a bias only corresponding to an average spread. By contrast, in computing the realized variance, one can be cumulating these biases over many small periods, thereby greatly expanding the total effect.

A number of authors have carried out empirical studies to rank the performance of competing estimators of QV. One way to do this is by simulating the process given in Equation 13.1. To test for the robustness of the estimator, we may introduce jumps in the price or in the volatility and assume different settings for microstructure noise or sampling scheme. Gatheral and Oomen (2010) took a different approach to this and simulated the order book directly. They compared QV estimators under the realistic microstructure setting and compared if the theoretical prediction matches well with actual small sample properties. They found that subsampling estimator, realized kernel, and maximum likelihood estimator deliver superior performance in terms of efficiency and robustness to different parameterizations of microstructure noise.

The actual data may deviate from the assumed model. Then, to directly test the competency of the estimators when population quantity is unknown, a popular method is to look at the volatility signature plot, which plots the $\widehat{[X,X]}$ against the sampling frequencies. The estimator prone to a microstructure bias will show upward sloping pattern as data is sampled increasingly frequently. See Barndorff-Nielsen et al. (2009) for example. The authors also compared forecasts of QV estimators under different scenarios of underlying stochastic volatility process and the distribution of microstructure noise. Ait-Sahalia and Mancini (2008) found that TSRV in Equation 13.16 outperforms the RV under varying degree of assumptions. Bandi et al. (2008) considered comparison in the context of option pricing and Voev (2009) in the context of an unconditional measure of portfolio performance.

13.4.2 MULTIVARIATE VOLATILITY ESTIMATORS

In this section, we discuss estimators of integrated covariance matrix. We present a framework for the bivariate case, as this allows treatment of the main issues. We suppose that the efficient price process follows a Brownian semimartingale. For the ith asset, $i = 1, 2$, we have

$$Y_{i,t} = \int_0^t \mu_{i,u} \mathrm{d}u + \int_0^t \sigma_{i,u} \mathrm{d}W_{i,u}, \tag{13.20}$$

where $\mu_{i,u}$ is a predictable locally bounded drift, $\sigma_{i,u}$ is a cádlág volatility process, and $W_{i,u}$ is a Brownian motions with $E[\mathrm{d}W_{1t}\mathrm{d}W_{2t}] = \rho_t \mathrm{d}t$. The time span we consider is fixed and scaled to vary between [0, 1]. We observe a (log) price at discrete time points, $0 = t_{i,0} < \cdots < t_{i,n_i} = 1$. Let Υ be a set of points that partition the interval [0, 1]. Let us define $m_i(n) := \sup_{j:t_{i,j}\in\Upsilon} |t_{i,j} - t_{i,j-1}|$ and assume that as $n \to \infty$, $m(n) := m_1(n) \vee m_2(n) \to 0$, so that the observation grid is becoming finer and finer. Let us denote by $Y_{i,t_{i,j}}$ the discretely sampled log-prices. Suppose that the two prices series are observed on the synchronous time points $\{\tau_j, j = 1, \ldots, n\}$. The quadratic covariation of Y_1 and Y_2 over a time interval [0, 1] is defined by

$$[Y_1, Y_2] = \lim_{m(n)\to 0} \sum_{j=1}^{n} (Y_{1,\tau_j} - Y_{1,\tau_{j-1}})(Y_{2,\tau_j} - Y_{2,\tau_{j-1}}) = \int_0^1 \sigma_{1,u}\sigma_{2,u}\rho_u \mathrm{d}u, \tag{13.21}$$

where the last equality holds with probability one. We may denote the QV of general $d \times 1$ vector of Y as $[Y, Y]_t = \int_0^t \Sigma(u)\mathrm{d}u$ where $\Sigma_{i,j}(t)$ denotes the instantaneous covariation between i-th and j-th element of Y. The natural estimator of quadratic covariation is the discrete sum in Equation 13.21, called the *realized covariance*

$$[Y_1, Y_2]^n = \sum_{j=1}^{n} (Y_{1,\tau_j} - Y_{1,\tau_{j-1}})(Y_{2,\tau_j} - Y_{2,\tau_{j-1}}). \tag{13.22}$$

Under perfect synchronization, Barndorff-Nielsen and Shephard (2004a) showed that the Realized Covariance is a $\sqrt{n}$ consistent estimator of the integrated covariance and is asymptotically mixed normal according to Equation 13.20. Let us denote the returns for the ith asset by $y_{i,\tau_j} := Y_{i,\tau_j} - Y_{i,\tau_{j-1}}$. Then, we have

$$\sqrt{n}\frac{\sum_{j=1}^{n} y_{1,\tau_j} y_{2,\tau_j} - \int_0^1 \Sigma_{1,2}(u)\mathrm{d}u}{\sqrt{\int_0^1 \Sigma_{1,1}(u)\Sigma_{2,2}(u) + \left(\Sigma_{1,2}(u)\right)^2 \mathrm{d}u}} \Longrightarrow N(0, 1).$$

The corresponding feasible CLT is given by

$$\frac{\sum_{j=1}^{n} y_{1,\tau_j} y_{2,\tau_j} - \int_0^1 \Sigma_{1,2}(u)\mathrm{d}u}{\sqrt{\sum_j y_{1,\tau_j}^2 y_{2,\tau_j}^2 - \sum_j y_{1,\tau_j} y_{1,\tau_{j+1}} y_{2,\tau_j} y_{2,\tau_{j+1}}}} \Longrightarrow N(0, 1).$$

Compare this with the univariate case in the previous section. A similar asymptotic argument can be carried out for the realized regression coefficient or the realized betas in the capital asset pricing model (CAPM).

The time stamp for transactions of two different securities rarely matches, and so some data synchronization method is typically employed. This will have an impact on the finite sample as well as on the asymptotic behavior of the resulting covariance estimate. The well-known Epps effect (1979) refers to the phenomenon that the sample correlation tends to have a strong bias toward zero as the sampling interval progressively shrinks. Hayashi and Yoshidam (2005) showed that the realized covariance calculated from the aligned data using the *fixed clock time* alignment method described in the Section 13.3.3 is biased. They proposed a modified covariance estimator

$$\widehat{[Y_1, Y_2]} = \sum_{i=1}^{n} \sum_{j=1}^{n} y_{1,t_{1,i}} y_{2,t_{2,j}} 1_{\{\Delta t_{1,i} \cap \Delta t_{2,j} \neq \emptyset\}},$$

which they showed is unbiased and $\sqrt{n}$ consistent. In the presence of asynchronicity but with no microstructure noise, this estimator is theoretically the best one. Essentially, their estimator takes the cross product of returns only if the portion of transaction time intervals of two assets overlaps.

Malliavin and Mancino (2009) proposed an estimator of the integrated covariance that does not require synchronization. They establish the relationship between the Fourier transform of returns and the Fourier transform of spot volatility. As per Equation 13.20, their estimator is consistent and asymptotically normal. Their estimator is defined by

$$\widehat{[Y_1, Y_2]} = \frac{1}{2m+1} \sum_{|k| \leq m} \mathcal{F}_n(Y_1)(k) \mathcal{F}_n(Y_2)(-k),$$

where $\mathcal{F}_n(Y_i)(\cdot)$ denotes the discretized Fourier transform of ith asset returns. For $k \in \mathbb{Z}$ and assuming that the time interval is rescaled to vary $[0, 2\pi]$,

$$\mathcal{F}_n(Y_i)(k) := \sum_{j=1}^{n} e^{ikt_{i,j}} (Y_{i,t_{i,j}} - Y_{i,t_{i,j-1}}) \to_p \int_0^{2\pi} e^{ikt} dY_t.$$

In fact, they have a stronger result where the Fejer Fourier inversion of the above estimator gives a consistent estimator of the instantaneous (co)volatility.

Finally, we should mention some work on the multivariate range-based estimation. Brandt and Diebold (2006) extended the work on the realized range to the multivariate case. It is not immediately obvious how to extend such notion to the multivariate case, and indeed their cunning idea relies on the specific structures that arise in a number of settings, notably exchange rates. Suppose we observe the exchange rates between three currencies: A, B, and C, denoted $X_{A:B}$, $X_{B:C}$, and $X_{A:C}$, then we know that in the absence of arbitrage $X_{A:C} = X_{A:B}X_{B:C}$. Taking logs and differentiating, we obtain

$$\text{cov}(\Delta \ln X_{A:B}, \Delta \ln X_{A:C}) = \frac{1}{2} [\text{var}(\Delta \ln X_{A:C}) + \text{var}(\Delta \ln X_{A:B}) - \text{var}(\Delta \ln X_{B:C})].$$

Therefore, using the relationship between the variance and the range, they obtain an estimate of the covariance between the two exchange rates. The advantage of this method as before is that it does not require high frequency data so that the effect of measurement error is minimized.

13.4.2.1 Measurement Error. So far we have considered the case where the only source of error is observation error, that is, discretization error of the continuous semimartingale and the nonsynchronicity of the observed price. We next consider the presence of an infinite QV component in the observed prices due to a further measurement issue, microstructure noise. There has not been a uniform approach to modeling multivariate microstructure noise, perhaps due to the confounding effects of asynchronicity. Furthermore, it is not clear if the microstructure noise between two assets should be correlated and if so, how to parameterize this quantity. Let us assume an additive noise for each asset

$$X_{i,t_{i,j}} = Y_{i,t_{i,j}} + \varepsilon_{i,t_{i,j}} \text{ for } i = 1, \ldots, d, 0 = t_{i,0} < t_{i,1} < \cdots < t_{i,n_i} = 1.$$

Zhang (2011) assumed that $\{\varepsilon_{1,t_{1,j}}, \varepsilon_{2,t_{2,j}}\}$ are stationary and exponentially alpha mixing. She proposed a two-scales realized covariance (TSCV) estimator, which is defined as the bivariate version of Equation 13.16 applied to an aligned data,

$$\widehat{[Y_1, Y_2]} = [Y_1, Y_2]^K - \left(\frac{\overline{n_K}}{\overline{n_J}}\right)[Y_1, Y_2]^J,$$

where the average lag K realized covariance is defined by

$$[Y_1, Y_2]^K = \frac{1}{K}\sum_{j=K}^{n}(Y_{1,\tau_j} - Y_{1,\tau_{j-K}})(Y_{2,\tau_j} - Y_{2,\tau_{j-K}}).$$

for $1 \leq J \ll K$. Let the summation of sample sizes of two assets be $N = n_1 + n_2$, and recall that the number of points for the aligned time stamp τ is n. Define $\overline{n_K} = n - K + 1)/K$ and similarly for $\overline{n_J}$. Then the above estimator is $O_p(n^{1/6})$ consistent and asymptotically normal under the presence of noise and asynchronous trading, provided that $K = O(N^{2/3})$.

Barndorff-Nielsen et al. (2010) proposed to synchronize the high frequency prices using *refresh time* explained in Section 13.3.3. They assumed that the microstructure noise $\{\varepsilon_{i,\tau_j}, i = 1, \ldots, d\}$ is a second-order stationary process with respect to refresh time $\{\tau_j\}$. Their multivariate realized kernels (MRK) is given in Equation 13.18 with realized autocovariance defined by

$$\gamma_h(X) = \sum_j x_{\tau_j} x_{\tau_{j-h}}^T, \quad h = 0, \pm 1, \pm 2, \cdots$$

where $\sum_j = \sum_{h<j\leq n}$ for $h \geq 0$, and $\sum_j = \sum_{1\leq j\leq n+h}$ for $h < 0$ and $x = [x_1 : \cdots : x_d]$ is a matrix of *refresh time* aligned returns for d number of assets. The MRK is $O_p(n^{1/5})$–consistent and asymptotically normal and its asymptotic distribution is given in Equation 13.19 modified with relevant multivariate quantities, under the second-order kernel. It is also guaranteed to be positive semidefinite at the cost of asymptotic bias. Note that the asymptotic rate is based on the sample size of the aligned time stamp. Aït-Sahalia et al. (2010) proposed an $O(n^{1/4})$ consistent estimator based on the QMLE and a generalized time synchronization method. An advantage of their estimator over TSCV and MRK is that it does not involve choosing or estimating tuning parameters such as bandwidth. However, they adopt a somewhat restrictive assumption on the microstructure noise—it is a white noise that is mutually independent across assets.

Christensen et al. (2010) proposed a multivariate preaveraging estimator. Voev and Lunde (2007) proposed a modified Hayashi and Yoshida estimator to bias-correct for the microstructure noise. Park and Linton (2012) proposed a covariation estimator that is robust to both microstructure noise and asynchronicity based on the Fourier analysis of returns, extending Malliavin and Mancino (2009). Griffin and Oomen (2011) ranked the performance in terms of efficiency of the three estimators: realized covariance, realized covariance plus lead and lag adjustments, and the Hayashi and Yoshida estimator. They found that the performance of competing estimators depends on the level of microstructure noise as well as on the magnitude of correlation.

13.5 Modeling and Forecasting

We designate the class of estimators of quadratic (co) variation based on the high frequency data as "realized measures". In this section, we review how realized measures can be used to model and forecast the (co)variances. We summarize the studies that compare these competing models in terms of forecasting power where the forecasting variable is a general function of volatility such as Value-at-Risk and portfolio performance. We also consider extensions to a dynamic model of the realized covariance matrix. See other chapters of this handbook for more detailed surveys on this area.

13.5.1 TIME SERIES MODELS OF (CO) VOLATILITY

There is a large literature on time series models of volatilities. In the well-known GARCH and stochastic volatility family of models, volatility is treated as a latent variable. The method we discuss here takes a different stance. We treat the RV as ex-post observed variance. Given the sequence of RVs (or the robust estimator discussed in Section 13.4.1.1), we use traditional time series techniques such as autoregressive moving average (ARMA) to fit a model and carry out forecasts. The key feature of the time series of the RV is that it is highly persistent. To account for this, Andersen et al. (2003) proposed an autoregressive fractionally integrated moving average (ARFIMA) to model the time series of the RV. Let h_t denote an estimator of integrated variance for tth day, $t = 1, \ldots, T$. The ARFIMA model for h_t is given by

$$\Phi(L)(1 - L)^{\nu}(h_t - \mu) = \Theta(L)\varepsilon_t, \varepsilon_t \sim \mathrm{WN}(0, 1), \tag{13.23}$$

where $\Theta(L)$ is a polynomial of lag operators and ν is a real-valued parameter that measures the degree of fractional integration. The model can be estimated by maximum likelihood method. Lanne (2006) modified Equation 13.23 by making parameters in $\Theta(\cdot)$ time-varying and letting ε_t be a non-Gaussian. In practice, these methods can be problematic as estimation of ν is nontrivial and influential on other features of the model. A simpler model that seems to capture lag dependencies well is the heterogenous autoregressive model of Corsi (2009);

$$h_{t+1} = \theta_0 + \theta_D h_t + \theta_W h_t^{(W)} + \theta_M h_t^{(M)} + \varepsilon_{t+1}, \qquad (13.24)$$

where $h_t^{(W)} := \frac{1}{5}(h_t + \cdots + h_{t-4})$ is the RV over a week, and the similarly defined $h_t^{(M)}$ denotes the RV over a month. Other approaches include the unobserved component model by Barndorff-Nielsen and Shephard (2002a) and Koopman et al. (2005). Shephard and Sheppard (2010) proposed a model which is a hybrid of GARCH augmented with a realized measure and a reduced form time series model for the RV. See similar approach in Hansen et al. (2011) who jointly modeled returns and realized measures of volatility. Liu and Maheu (2009) carried out Bayesian averaging over both different measures of integrated variance and different time series models.

In the multivariate setting, a key issue is that the fitted model should produce a positive-definite covariance matrix. Also, if we were to model a high dimensional covariance matrix, we need to address the dimension issue, which grows rapidly with the number of assets considered. Voev (2007) proposed a method to combine volatility and bivariate covolatility forecasts to produce a positive-definite matrix. The problem with this method is that interaction between elements of covariance matrix is not taken into account. The full joint modeling of covariance matrix is an important issue. For example, the variance of one asset and covariance with another asset have significant dependencies, especially during episodes of market crashes and large economic events. Compared with the univariate volatility modeling literature, such multivariate models have been sparsely researched mainly due to the fact that consistently estimating a general $d \times d$ covariance matrix for $d > 2$ has been difficult, plagued by bias induced by synchronization as well as microstructure noise. However, with recent work in Section 13.4.2.1, this area of research can progress further.

Let $H_t, t = 1, \ldots, T$, be a time series of such estimates of the integrated covariance matrix. A natural way to model the persistency and lead-lag dependencies in the elements of matrix H_t is to fit a multivariate version of model given in Equation 13.23, called *vector ARFIMA model*. We fit a model for $h_t = vech(g(H_t))$ where $vech(\cdot)$ operation stacks the lower triangular matrix of an argument. The dimension of h_t is given by $m = d(d+1)/2$. A range of transformation functions $g(\cdot)$ is considered for the purpose of dimension reduction and to guarantee a p.s.d. matrix forecast. We discuss this in a moment. First, we consider the vector ARFIMA model

$$\Phi(L)D(L)(h_t - BZ_t) = \Theta(L)\varepsilon_t, \varepsilon_t \sim \mathrm{WN}(0, I_m), \qquad (13.25)$$

where $\Theta(L) = I_m - \Theta_1 L \cdots - \Theta_q L^q$ is a matrix lag polynomial of degree $q \in \mathbb{Z}$ for the MA component, $\Phi(L)$ is defined similarly for autoregressive (AR) component. $D(L) = \mathrm{diag}\{(1-L)^{\nu_1}, \ldots, (1-L)^{\nu_m}\}$ is a matrix fractional difference operator with $\nu_1, \ldots, \nu_m$ the degrees of fractional integration for each element of h_t. Z_t are exogenous variables that affect the dynamics of volatility; candidate variables are trading activity variables and macroeconomic state variables. B is a restriction matrix. We can estimate such a model by maximum likelihood. The one-step-ahead prediction is then $\widehat{h_{t+s}} = E(h_t | h_s, s \leq t)$. We obtain a covariance matrix forecast by $\widehat{H}_{t+s} = vech^{-1}(\widehat{h}_{t+s}))$ where the $vech^{-1}(\cdot)$ restacks the vector into a symmetric matrix. See the Chapter 15 for more detail.

Bauer and Vorkink (2011) fitted the vech of $\log(H_t)$ (rather like a matrix E-GARCH (exponential generalized autoregressive conditional) model) to an AR model where the right-hand side lagged variables are dimension reduced by principal component analysis. Chiriac and Voev (2010) carried out a Cholesky decomposition of the covariance matrix and modeled the lower-dimensional factors by a vector ARFIMA model. They showed that this method outperforms in terms of root mean square error, a number of models including the heterogeneous autoregressive model, a multivariate version of Equation 13.24, Wishart autoregressive (WAR) model of Gouriéroux et al. (2009) , and the dynamic conditional correlation model. We may use the RV to proxy true H_{t+s} and compare the Frobenius norm of the bias $\|\widehat{H}_{t+s} - H_{t+s}\|$, across different models and different horizons s. Authors also compare minimum variance portfolio-efficient frontiers using different covariance matrix forecast.

13.5.2 FORECAST COMPARISON

Since volatility itself is unobservable, the comparison of volatility forecasts relies on an observable proxy for the latent volatility process. In the previous section, we presented how we can compare root-mean squared error (MSE) of covariance forecasts. We might be interested in economically meaningful loss functions. Brownlees and Gallo (2010) compared the Value-at-Risk forecasts from different time series models of RV. Bandi et al. (2008) considered the forecast comparison in the context of option pricing.

An important research question is whether there is a gain in using the high frequency data over traditional daily volatility models. We can compare the dynamic model of estimators of ex-post variation calculated from the high frequency data against the latent volatility models such as GARCH and stochastic volatility. Koopman et al. (2005) found that the ARFIMA model of RV delivers the best out-of-sample forecast compared with the GARCH or the stochastic volatility (SV) model fitted to a daily S&P500 index. Shephard and Sheppard (2010) showed that their hybrid model using the realized measures outperforms the daily GARCH model in terms of various criteria. Siu and Okunev (2009) compared historical, realized, and implied volatility measures for predicting over multiple horizons.

We are also interested in ranking the competing realized measures in Section 13.4. Ghysels et al. (2006c) proposed a framework to do this, called *the mixed data sampling* (MIDAS) regression, comparing measures of ex-post variation in terms of their forecasting ability at various horizons. Ghysels and Sinko (2011) found that the microstructure-robust realized measures deliver better forecasts.

Likewise, Ait-Sahalia and Mancini (2008) reach similar conclusion where the TSRV estimator in Equation 13.16 outperforms the RV under diverse setting of volatility process and assumptions on the noise.

13.6 Asset Pricing

13.6.1 DISTRIBUTION OF RETURNS CONDITIONAL ON THE VOLATILITY MEASURE

Authors found evidence that the devolatized returns by the class of RV estimators are Gaussian or approximately so. Andersen et al. (2001a) found that daily returns standardized by the realized volatility approximate the Gaussian distribution. Thomakos and Wang (2003) also found such evidence for a futures market.

Peters and de Vilder (2006) studied the volatility and return dependence by sampling the returns in financial time. They tested if the return series are a realization of a local martingale using the theorem by Dubins and Schwartz (1965), who stated that any continuous local martingale $Y_t \in \mathcal{F}_t$ is a time-changed Brownian motion. Formally stated,

$$B_s = Y_{T_s},\ T_s = \inf\{t|[Y]_t \geq s\}, \tag{13.26}$$

where $B_s \in \mathcal{F}_{T_s}$ is an independent Brownian motion and T_s is the stopping time. It is the first time the QV reaches a specified level. Equivalently, the theorem implies that

$$Y_t = B_{[Y]_t}, \tag{13.27}$$

which states that every continuous martingale is a time-changed Brownian motion where the time change is given by the QV. In empirical analysis, Equation 13.26 is more useful, since it states that between the unit interval of the transformed time, $[T_{(j-1)a}, T_{ja}]$, Y has a constant QV at a. Given an interval of physical time, Y is sampled more frequently when QV is large. More precisely, the (discretized) transformed time is constructed by $T_0 = 0$, $T_{(j+1)a} = T_{ja} + \Delta T_{(j+1)a}$,

$$\Delta T_{(j+1)a} = \inf\{t|[Y]_{[T_{ja},T_{ja}+t)} \geq a\}, \tag{13.28}$$

where $[Y]_{[T_{ja},T_{ja}+t)}$ denotes the QV in the interval $[T_{ja}, T_{ja} + t)$. The standardized increment in financial time

$$\xi = \frac{Y_{T_{ja}} - Y_{T_{(j-1)a}}}{\sqrt{a}}, \tag{13.29}$$

is i.i.d. standard normal. Observe the trade-off between having large and small a. We need to have a large a to have many data points to consistently estimate QV by a realized measure, but large a means sparse sampling of Y. Note also that we can explicitly derive the distributional features of the stopping time T when the Y process is completely specified. Testing for the hypothesis that Y_t is a local martingale is then equivalent to testing for i.i.d. standard normality of the return series that is spaced by T_s. Peters and de Vilder (2006) tested if the S&P500 intraday return is a local martingale where they constructed the stopping time T_s based on the RV. They concluded that we cannot reject the null hypothesis that returns are the realization of a martingale process at various time scales (>1 day) based on the tests for Gaussianity, independence, and serial correlation.

13.6.2 APPLICATION TO FACTOR PRICING MODEL

We next discuss applications to asset pricing models for cross sections of returns. Let us denote a stock return for i-th firm at time t by $y_{i,t}$, with $i = 1, \ldots, d$ and $t = 1, \ldots, T$. The K factor pricing model for stock returns is given by

$$y_{i,t} = \beta_i^\top f_t + \varepsilon_{i,t}, \tag{13.30}$$

where the factor loadings $\beta_i = (\beta_{i,1}, \ldots, \beta_{i,K})^\top$ are unrestricted (Ross, 1976). The sampling unit t is typically a low frequency, such as monthly. In some cases, f_t are unobserved statistical factors, while in others, they are the returns on carefully constructed portfolios (Fama and French 1993). In the latter case, $\beta_{i,k}$ can be given by the interpretation of the covariance between return on portfolio k and asset i divided by the variance of the return on portfolio k. The continuous time framework allows us to measure the time-varying beta between two assets using the high frequency data. The realized beta between asset i and k in period $[t-1, t]$ calculated from high frequency returns $\{y_{\cdot,t}\}$ is given by,

$$\hat{\beta}_{i,k}(t) = \frac{\sum_j y_{i,j} y_{k,j}}{\sum_j y_{k,j}^2} \rightarrow_p \frac{\int_{t-1}^{t} \Sigma_{i,k}(s)ds}{\int_{t-1}^{t} \Sigma_{k,k}(s)ds} := \beta_{i,k}(t),$$

where the convergence in probability holds according to Equation 13.20 and as the mesh goes to zero. For studies on the relationship between returns and volatility, see Gosh and Linton (2007). They showed that estimating the risk-return trade-off parameters can be posed as a generalized method of moments (GMM) estimation problem. They used the RV as a conditional volatility proxy and showed that there is a significant time-variation in the risk-return slope coefficient. Bali and Peng (2006) found a positive and statistically significant relation between the conditional mean and conditional volatility of market returns at a daily level, where volatility is proxied by RV. Bollerslev et al. (2006) made use of the time aggregation formula between lower and high frequency covariance. They found that the correlations between absolute high frequency returns and current and past high frequency returns are significantly negative for several days.

Andersen et al. (2005) and Bandi and Russell (2005) estimated the beta in CAPM by a realized covariation. Bandi and Russell (2005) provided the MSE-based optimal sampling frequency for calculating the realized beta designed to reduce the effect of market microstructure noise. Bollerslev and Zhang (2003) estimated the factor loadings in the three-factor Fama-French model using the high frequency data, adopting a simple adjustment procedure to account for nonsynchronous trading effects. Bannouh et al. (2009) and Kyj et al. (2009) used a mixed frequency framework, using the high frequency data to obtain an estimate of the factor covariance matrix and using the daily data to estimate the factor loadings. This method avoids the nonsynchronicity between an individual stock and usually more liquid factor prices.

The economic value of using the realized covariance in portfolio management is discussed by Fleming et al. (2003) and Liu (2009b). Fleming et al. (2003) found that a risk-averse investor is willing to pay between 50 and 200 basis points per annum to switch from a covariance measurement based on the daily data to the one based on intraday data, whereas Liu (2009b) found that the benefits depend on the rebalancing frequency and estimation horizon of portfolio optimization decision. See Fan et al. (2010) for estimating high dimensional covariance matrix using high frequency data and its benefit in portfolio selection.

13.6.3 EFFECTS OF ALGORITHMIC TRADING

Recently, the effects of high frequency or algorithmic trading have been the focus of policy discussions, arising part from the flash crash of May 2010, where the US market suffered rapid price decreases ultimately followed by a recovery. Chaboud et al. (2009) investigated the effects of algorithmic trading on volatility in the foreign exchange market. They considered the following regression equation:

$$RV_{it} = \alpha_i + \beta_i AT_{it} + \gamma_i^{\top} \tau_{it} + \sum_{k=1}^{22} \delta_{ik} RV_{i,t-k} + \varepsilon_{it},$$

where RV_{it} is the log of realized volatility of currency i during day t computed using 1-min returns, AT_{it} is the fraction of algorithm trading in that day and currency, which was recorded by the trade matching engine, and τ_{it} are dummy and time trend variables. The latter are included because the AT series has a pronounced upward trend, while volatility appears to be stationary. They recognized that AT is endogenous an variable since high frequency automated trading algorithms may trade more in volatile times. They therefore instrument it with a variable that measures the capacity for computer trading in a given currency–period combination. The estimation strategy matters here, so that using OLS yields a positive effect, $\beta_i > 0$, but the instrumental variable estimator finds $\beta_i < 0$ but not statistically significant. They conclude that intraday algorithmic trading does not by itself lead to higher daily volatility. For other studies that use realized measure of volatility to determine the effects of high frequency trading, see Hendershott et al. (2010) and Hendershott and Riordan (2009). Finally, we should mention the related work of Ait-Sahalia and Yu (2009), who investigated the relationship between the noise component of the RV and various measures of liquidity.

13.6.4 APPLICATION TO OPTION PRICING

In recent years, volatility has been thought of as an asset class in its own right. One can trade volatility through a position in puts and calls, but this has an additional exposure to a price movement. Swaps and options on QV have been developed for a pure exposure on the volatility. For a discussion on the volatility as an asset class, see Demeterfi et al. (1999). An investor of volatility swap is swapping a fixed volatility $SW_{t,T}$ for a floating (actual) volatility $[Y]_{t,T}$, denoting QV accumulated over $[t, T]$. The floating leg is usually given by the sum-of-squared daily log-returns over the relevant time interval. Given N notional amount in dollar terms per annualized volatility point, its payoff at expiration is equal to

$$([Y]_{t,T} - SW_{t,T})N.$$

Let us denote r a risk-free discount rate corresponding to an expiration date T. The value of such forward contract is given by the expected present value of the future payoff under a risk-neutral measure $\mathbb{Q}$, a probability measure such that the discounted price of traded asset is a martingale,

$$E^{\mathbb{Q}}[e^{rT}([Y]_{t,T} - SW_{t,T})].$$

Then the strike for which the contract has zero present value is

$$SW^{*}_{t,T} = E^{\mathbb{Q}}([Y]_{t,T}).$$

Carr et al. (2005) proposed a method of pricing options on QV via Laplace transform when returns follow pure jump Lévy process. Itkin and Carr (2010) considered a pricing problem when returns are time-changed Lévy processes. Britten-Jones and Neuberger (2000) proposed a method to estimate $E^{\mathbb{Q}}([Y]_T)$, an option-implied (i.e., risk-neutral) integrated variance over the life of the option contract, assuming that price follows stochastic volatility diffusion process. Jiang and Tian (2005) showed the accuracy of this method when prices have jumps. $SW^{*}_{t,T}$ can be labeled as a model-free implied variance as well as being a no-arbitrage variance swap rate. Carr and Wu (2009) showed that the variance swap rate is well approximated by the value of a particular portfolio of options. They established that the difference between the RV and this synthetic variance swap rate, given by

$$[Y]_{t,T} - SW^{*}_{t,T},$$

quantifies the variance risk premium. They have analyzed the variance swaps for stocks and found it to be significantly negative. This means that investors are willing to pay a premium to hedge away upward movement in the return variance.

Bollerslev et al. (2010) proposed a method for constructing a volatility risk premium relying on sample moments of the RV and an option-implied volatility estimator. Wu (2010) studied the variance risk premium using both variance swap rates constructed from the option prices and the quadratic variance estimates using the high frequency data and found a strong evidence for negative variance risk premium in the equity market. For the research studying the pricing of volatility risk in individual stock options, see Driessen et al. (2009). They found that cross-sectional differences in the exposure to market-wide correlation risk can account for differences in the expected option returns. For how QV estimators are used in pricing options on a cash instrument, see Stentoft (2008) and Christoffersen et al. (2010). For correlation swap valuation, see Jacquier and Slaoui (2007).

13.7 Estimating Continuous Time Models

In this section, we review how realized measures can be used to estimate the parameters of a continuous time model. Consider a diffusion model for financial prices X_t,

$$dX_t = \mu(X_t, \theta)dt + \sigma(X_t, \theta)dB_t, \tag{13.31}$$

where B_t is an independent Brownian motion, $\mu(X_t, \theta)$ is a drift function, and $\sigma(X_t, \theta)$ is a given diffusion coefficient function. We are interested in estimating vector of parameters θ. X_t is nonhomogenous in the sense that the diffusion coefficient is not constant. This specification includes geometric Brownian motion, Ornstein–Uhlenbeck process, and Cox-Ingersoll-Ross process as special cases. Since X_t in Equation 13.31 is Markov, we can write down a log-likelihood in terms of transition density if a closed form for this exists. For discretely observed data $\{X_{t_i}\}_{0\leq i\leq n}$ on the equally spaced grid, $\Delta t_i = 1/n$, the transition density is given by $\mathbb{P}[X_{\frac{i}{n}} \mid X_{\frac{i-1}{n}}; \theta]$. Such exact maximum likelihood method yields a consistent and efficient estimator under usual regularity conditions.

When transition density does not have a closed-form expression, we may use Euler scheme and its higher order refinement to approximate the process or use a closed-form approximation to the transition density itself. See Phillips and Yu (2009b) for a survey on maximum likelihood estimation of a model in Equation 13.31. If X_t can be observed continuously, the likelihood function for the continuous record can be obtained via the Girsanov theorem.

However, in practice we observe the data at discrete time points, and even for densely sampled high frequency data, it deviates from the model in Equation 13.31 due to the presence of microstructure noise. Phillips and Yu (2009a) proposed a two-stage estimation method based on the RV to estimate parameters in diffusion coefficient $\sigma(X_t, \theta)$ and using the infill likelihood to estimate the drift parameters, $\mu(X_t, \theta)$. Yu and Phillips (2001) also showed that the time-changed Brownian motion given in Equation 13.26 can be used to construct an exact Gaussian maximum likelihood for a nonhomogeneous Itô-processes.

Once the model departs from the Markovian property, we cannot decompose the likelihood into a transition density involving just observable quantities. There is a large amount of literature on computationally intensive estimation method; however, the availability of high frequency data gives us an alternative route to estimate such a model. Consider the stochastic volatility specified by the OU process and assume that there is an additive measurement error in the RV. Then the realized volatility has an ARMA representation, and the parameter can be estimated by the quasi-maximum likelihood constructed using the output of the Kalman filter. Barndorff-Nielsen and Shephard (2002a) showed that the method yields quite precise estimates even for non-Gaussian-driven volatility processes. See also Barndorff-Nielsen and Shephard (2006c) for related approach for estimating a time-deformed Lévy processes. In this case, the source of stochastic volatility is through a deformation of time, and we are interested in estimating the parameter for the autocovariance function of a deformed time process.

Bollerslev and Zhou (2002) proposed a generalized-method-of-moment-type estimator for parameters of a Brownian-motion-driven stochastic volatility model under no microstructure noise. Their method is by matching the sample moments of the realized volatility to the population moments of the integrated volatility implied by an assumed continuous time model. Corradi and Distaso (2006) provided a theoretical justification for such estimator. Todorov et al. (2010) proposed a method, first integrating intraday data into the realized Laplace transform (Todorov and Tauchen (2010b)) of volatility and then matching moments of the integrated joint Laplace transform with those implied by the assumed stochastic volatility model. This method is robust to the presence of jumps in the price. See also Todorov (2009) for estimating the SV model under price jumps, using realized multipower variation statistics.

CHAPTER FOURTEEN

Likelihood-Based Volatility Estimators in the Presence of Market Microstructure Noise

YACINE AÏT-SAHALIA and DACHENG XIU

14.1 Introduction

Driven by the need for accurate measurement of financial risk using intraday data, high frequency econometric methods have been evolving rapidly, bringing into focus a range of issues that were otherwise unobservable or, in many cases, irrelevant from the perspective of daily and weekly data or lower frequency data. The huge amount of intraday tick-by-tick data provides rich and timely information regarding fluctuations of traded assets and their comovements, which may yield more accurate measurements of volatility and covariance over relatively short horizons than estimates based on years of historical data at low frequency.

However, statistical inference with high frequency data presents many challenges. Closer scrutiny of the data reveals the pervasive presence of market microstructure noise, including frictions such as the existence of bid-ask spreads and bounces, the discreteness of price changes, the price impact of some transactions, and informational effects, all of which add volatility to the observed price process. When measuring correlation, the fact that the two assets may not trade or otherwise be observed at exactly the same times, known as *observation*

Handbook of Volatility Models and Their Applications, First Edition.
Edited by Luc Bauwens, Christian Hafner, and Sebastien Laurent.

asynchronicity, is another issue that may distort the covariance and correlation estimates, unlike the synchronous daily and lower frequency data.

For example, the popular realized volatility estimator, that is, the sum of squared log-returns,[1] diverges when the sampling frequency increases to beyond approximately every 5 min, a fact that was well recognized empirically in the realized volatility literature in the form of "signature plots" (Andersen et al., 2000) and was first analyzed theoretically in Aït-Sahalia et al. (2005) in the presence of market microstructure noise. Noise clearly has the potential to generate an increase of the realized volatility, and, in turn, bias the correlation estimates, since the realized volatility appears in the denominator when calculating the correlation. When it comes to estimating the correlation between two assets' returns, the estimate is known to be biased toward 0 as the sampling interval progressively shrinks. This puzzling phenomenon is known as the *Epps effect* after Epps (1979). In view of this, we start in the univariate case with a decomposition of the observed transaction log-price, Y, into the sum of an unobservable efficient log-price, X, and a noise component due to the frictions induced by the trading process, ε:

$$Y_t = X_t + \varepsilon_t, \tag{14.1}$$

where the efficient log-price process follows a general Itô process:

$$\mathrm{d}X_t = \mu_t \, \mathrm{d}t + \sigma_t \, \mathrm{d}W_t \tag{14.2}$$

and W is a Brownian motion. The goal is to disentangle the quadratic variation of the efficient price process, $\int_0^T \sigma_t^2 \, \mathrm{d}t$, on a fixed time interval $[0, T]$, from the variance of the noisy observations, $E[\varepsilon^2]$, using high frequency discrete observations on Y. A pair of assets (X_{1t}, X_{2t}) can be modeled in the same way when considering correlation estimation.

Initially, the literature focused on sampling sparsely to address the issue of noise; even though the data may be available every few seconds, one would sample every 15 min or so as a means of limiting the damaging impact of the noise. More recently, however, the focus has shifted toward developing noise-robust statistics. For instance, such estimators in the univariate variance case include two scales realized volatility of Zhang et al. (2005), the first consistent estimator for integrated volatility in the presence of noise, multiscale realized volatility, a modification that achieves the best possible rate of convergence proposed by Zhang (2006), realized kernels by Barndorff-Nielsen et al. (2008), and the preaveraging approach by Jacod et al. (2009), both of which contain sets of nonparametric estimators that can also achieve the best convergence rate. In terms of covariance estimator, Zhang (2011) proposes a consistent two scales realized covariance estimator using the previous tick method that is capable of dealing with asynchronous and noisy data. Barndorff-Nielsen et al. (2010) suggest multivariate realized kernels with a refresh time synchronization scheme to provide a consistent and semidefinite estimator of the covariance matrix,

[1] Which should therefore be more accurately termed *realized variance*.

while Kinnebrock and Podolskij (2008) proposed a multivariate preaveraging estimator. Related works also include, among others, Hayashi and Yoshidam (2005), Hansen and Lunde (2006b), Li and Mykland (2007), Kalnina and Linton (2008), Bandi and Russell (2008), Audrino and Corsi (2010), Aït-Sahalia et al. (2011), Zhang et al. (2011), and Kalnina (2011). A model consisting of a pure rounding error has been studied by Gloter and Jacod (2000).

In this chapter, we review one particular class of methods that have been developed to address these issues. The class of method we review are based on maximum-likelihood estimators (MLEs) and have been proposed and analyzed in Aït-Sahalia et al. (2005), Xiu (2010), and Aït-Sahalia et al. (2010). Likelihood-based methods, when available, are often the privileged parametric type of inference method for an econometrician, because of their statistical efficiency and ease of implementation. But, especially when vast quantities of high frequency observations are available, it is tempting to conduct inference that is nonparametric in nature, including, in particular, stochastic volatility of an unrestricted form, and this might seem to invalidate maximum-likelihood based on a parametric volatility structure, in fact a constant volatility parameter, and a Gaussian distribution for the noise term. We see that this is not the case, and that maximum-likelihood based on a constant volatility parameter is in fact a robust estimation method that produces consistent and even rate-efficient estimators in the cases of essentially arbitrary stochastic volatility and noise distributions.

We are also interested in estimating consistently the variance of the noise, which can be regarded as a measure of the liquidity of the market, or the quality of the trade execution in a given exchange or market structure. Measuring the impact of the bid-ask spread dates back to as early as Roll (1984). A recent study by Aït-Sahalia and Yu (2009) employ the likelihood-based noise estimators to decompose the transaction prices of NYSE stocks into a fundamental component and a microstructure noise component, and relates the two components to observable financial characteristics of these stocks and, in particular, to different observable measures of their liquidity.

This chapter is organized as follows: Section 14.2 discusses the volatility estimators, including both the constant volatility and the stochastic volatility case. Section 14.3 extends the previous method to covariance estimation. Section 14.4 illustrates the implementation of the method by providing an empirical application to measuring the volatility and correlation of stock and commodity financial returns. Section 14.5 concludes.

14.2 Volatility Estimation

14.2.1 CONSTANT VOLATILITY AND GAUSSIAN NOISE CASE: MLE

We first consider the benchmark case where volatility is a constant, and where the noise is Gaussian, which permits the straightforward use of likelihood methods. Even though the constant volatility assumption sounds implausible in practice, we shall see later that the estimator constructed under this assumption retains desirable properties in a stochastic volatility environment, and where the noise is not necessarily Gaussian.

For now, under these unrealistic assumptions, the efficient log-price X satisfies $dX_t = \sigma dW_t$. If there were no market microstructure noise, that is, $\varepsilon \equiv 0$, the log-returns $R_i = Y_{\tau_i} - Y_{\tau_{i-1}}$ would be i.i.d. $N(0, \sigma^2\Delta)$. The MLE for σ^2 then coincides with the realized variance estimator of the process,

$$\hat{\sigma}^2 = \frac{1}{T}\sum_{i=1}^{n} R_i^2. \tag{14.3}$$

Moreover, the estimator achieves the optimal convergence rate $n^{1/2}$, where $n = T/\Delta$, with the following central limit result:

$$n^{\frac{1}{2}}(\hat{\sigma}^2 - \sigma_0^2) \xrightarrow{\mathcal{L}} N(0, 2\sigma^4). \tag{14.4}$$

When the observations are contaminated by i.i.d. noise $\varepsilon's$ with mean 0 and variance a^2, the log-returns R_i's now exhibit the structure of an MA(1) process, since

$$R_i = \sigma\left(W_{\tau_i} - W_{\tau_{i-1}}\right) + \varepsilon_{\tau_i} - \varepsilon_{\tau_{i-1}} \equiv u_i + \eta u_{i-1}, \tag{14.5}$$

where the u's are mean 0 and variance γ^2 with

$$\gamma^2(1+\eta^2) = \text{Var}[R_i] = \sigma^2\Delta + 2a^2 \tag{14.6}$$

$$\gamma^2\eta = \text{Cov}(R_i, R_{i-1}) = -a^2. \tag{14.7}$$

If we assume that the noise distribution is Gaussian, then the log-likelihood function for the vector of observed log-returns $R = [R_1, \ldots, R_n]'$ is

$$l(\sigma^2, a^2) = -\frac{1}{2}\log det(\Omega) - \frac{n}{2}\log(2\pi) - \frac{1}{2}R'\Omega^{-1}R, \tag{14.8}$$

where

$$\Omega = \begin{pmatrix} \sigma^2\Delta + 2a^2 & -a^2 & 0 & \cdots & 0 \\ -a^2 & \sigma^2\Delta + 2a^2 & -a^2 & \ddots & \vdots \\ 0 & -a^2 & \sigma^2\Delta + 2a^2 & \ddots & 0 \\ \vdots & \ddots & \ddots & \ddots & -a^2 \\ 0 & \cdots & 0 & -a^2 & \sigma^2\Delta + 2a^2 \end{pmatrix}. \tag{14.9}$$

The MLE $(\hat{\sigma}^2, \hat{a}^2)$ is consistent with different rates of convergence for its volatility part and noise part:

$$\begin{pmatrix} n^{\frac{1}{4}}(\hat{\sigma}^2 - \sigma_0^2) \\ n^{\frac{1}{2}}(\hat{a}^2 - a_0^2) \end{pmatrix} \xrightarrow{\mathcal{L}} N\left(\begin{pmatrix} 0 \\ 0 \end{pmatrix}, \begin{pmatrix} 8a_0\sigma_0^3 T^{-\frac{1}{2}} & 0 \\ 0 & 2a_0^4 + \text{Cum}_4[\varepsilon] \end{pmatrix}\right). \tag{14.10}$$

As ε has mean 0, its fourth cumulant can be written as

$$\mathrm{Cum}_4[\varepsilon] = E[\varepsilon^4] - 3(E[\varepsilon^2])^2. \tag{14.11}$$

In the special case where ε is Normally distributed, $\mathrm{Cum}_4[\varepsilon] = 0$.

14.2.2 ROBUSTNESS TO NON-GAUSSIAN NOISE

A key result here is that Equation 14.10 holds even if the noise term ε is *not* Normally distributed, as long as the noise is still i.i.d. with mean 0 and variance a^2. This is because the estimator using the log-likelihood function $l(\sigma^2, a^2)$ in Equation 14.8 is now a generalized method of moments (GMM) estimator, using the scores $\dot{l}_{\sigma^2}$ and $\dot{l}_{a^2}$ as moment functions.

Since the expected values of $\dot{l}_{\sigma^2}$ and $\dot{l}_{a^2}$ only depend on the first- and second-order moment structure of the log-returns, R, which is unchanged by the absence of normality, the moment functions are unbiased

$$E_{\text{true}}[\dot{l}_{\sigma^2}] = E_{\text{true}}[\dot{l}_{a^2}] = 0,$$

where "true" denotes the expected value computed under the true distribution of the Y's (where the ε's are not necessarily Gaussian).

Hence the estimator $(\hat{\sigma}^2, \hat{a}^2)$ based on these moment functions remains consistent. The effect of misspecification therefore lies in their asymptotic variance. By using the cumulants of the distribution of ε, we express this asymptotic variance in terms of deviations from normality.

We see from Equation 14.10 that the estimator $(\hat{\sigma}^2, \hat{a}^2)$ is consistent and its asymptotic variance is given by

$$\mathrm{AVAR}_{\text{true}}(\hat{\sigma}^2, \hat{a}^2) = \mathrm{AVAR}_{\text{normal}}(\hat{\sigma}^2, \hat{a}^2) + \mathrm{Cum}_4[\varepsilon] \begin{pmatrix} 0 & 0 \\ 0 & 1 \end{pmatrix},$$

where $\mathrm{AVAR}_{\text{normal}}(\hat{\sigma}^2, \hat{a}^2)$ is the asymptotic variance in the case where the distribution of ε is Normal, whereas $\mathrm{AVAR}_{\text{true}}(\hat{\sigma}^2, \hat{a}^2)$ is the asymptotic variance under the true distribution of ε whatever that may be. That is, $\mathrm{AVAR}_{\text{normal}}(\hat{\sigma}^2, \hat{a}^2)$ coincides with $\mathrm{AVAR}_{\text{true}}(\hat{\sigma}^2, \hat{a}^2)$ for all but the (a^2, a^2) term.

So, not only do we retain consistency of the estimator but we in fact also retain rate efficiency for the estimation of both (σ^2, a^2) and actual efficiency for the estimation of σ^2. Aït-Sahalia et al. (2005) show how to interpret this in terms of the profile likelihood and the second Bartlett identity.

14.2.3 IMPLEMENTING MAXIMUM LIKELIHOOD

As can be seen from Equation 14.10, the optimal rate of convergence for volatility estimation turns out to be $n^{1/4}$ in the presence of noise, as opposed to $n^{1/2}$ in its absence (recall Equation 14.4). To be precise, it is not whether noise is present or not that matters, but whether it is incorporated or not in the estimation. The

MLE based on Equation 14.8 would still produce a rate $n^{1/4}$ for σ^2 even if ε were identically 0, as long as we actually did as if ε could have been present.

Given a typical 6.5 h trading day, if we model the noise and sample as high as every 1 s, we have the normalization constant $n^{1/4}$ around 12.4, whereas sampling every 5 min and ignoring the noise lead to a normalization constant $n^{1/2}$ that approximately equals 8.8. It appears that the gain in efficiency is marginal when sampling at highest frequency. However, if we further compare the asymptotic variances, $8a_0\sigma_0^3 T^{-1/2}$ is much smaller than $2\sigma_0^4$, since the standard deviation a_0 of the microstructure noise is usually very small in practice.

Implementing the MLE is more convenient than it appears. In fact, the likelihood function for the observed log-returns can be expressed in the following computationally efficient form, as a function of the transformed parameters (γ^2, η) by triangularizing the matrix Ω:

$$l(\eta, \gamma^2) = -\frac{1}{2}\sum_{i=1}^{N} \ln(2\pi d_i) - \frac{1}{2}\sum_{i=1}^{N} \frac{\tilde{Y}_i^2}{d_i}, \tag{14.12}$$

where

$$d_i = \gamma^2 \frac{1 + \eta^2 + \cdots + \eta^{2i}}{1 + \eta^2 + \cdots + \eta^{2(i-1)}},$$

and the $\tilde{Y}_i' s$ are obtained recursively as $\tilde{Y}_1 = Y_1$ and for $i = 2, \ldots, N$:

$$\tilde{Y}_i = Y_i - \frac{\eta\left(1 + \eta^2 + \cdots + \eta^{2(i-2)}\right)}{1 + \eta^2 + \cdots + \eta^{2(i-1)}} \tilde{Y}_{i-1}.$$

This algorithm avoids the brute-force computation of the inverse of the variance–covariance matrix Ω^{-1}, and hence significantly accelerates the optimization procedure in practice.

14.2.4 ROBUSTNESS TO STOCHASTIC VOLATILITY: QMLE

What happens to this MLE if the volatility is in fact not constant but is instead either deterministic and time-varying or stochastic? There is of course a vast theoretical literature on nonconstant volatility models initiated by Engle (1982a) and Bollerslev (1986), and empirical studies have documented a U-shaped intraday volatility pattern (Wood et al., 1985; Andersen and Bollerslev, 1997b; Boudt et al., 2011) and an implied volatility "smile" or "smirk" (Jackwerth and Rubinstein, 1996; Aït-Sahalia and Lo, 1998). Under such circumstances, simulation studies by Aït-Sahalia and Yu (2009) and Gatheral and Oomen (2010) suggest that the MLE defined above may perform well in practice as an estimator of the integrated volatility of the process, $T^{-1}\int_0^T \sigma_t^2\, dt$ instead of the constant σ^2. Intuitively, the conjecture that the estimator remains consistent is plausible in that when volatility becomes stochastic, the integrated volatility, the parameter of interest, happens to be the average of the volatility process, which is expected to be a legitimate candidate as an estimator.

In the absence of microstructure noise, the MLE has a closed-form (Eq. 14.3), which is of course an ideal estimator even with a nonparametric stochastic volatility model. However, the consistency of the MLE is no longer straightforward in the presence of noise, because there may not be a closed form available for this estimator. Its asymptotic variance is far more complicated because of heteroskedasticity and autocorrelation, as mentioned by Hansen et al. (2008).

Theoretically, the MLE under this new setting can be regarded as a quasi-MLE constructed under misspecified assumptions such as constant volatility, zero drift, and Gaussian microstructure noise. For this reason, we give the MLE an alias Quasi-Maximum Likelihood Estimator (QMLE) in such situation, in order to emphasize model misspecification and keep the notation in line with the classic results of likelihood-based estimation under misspecified models (White, 1982; Domowitz and White, 1982). In view of this, the consistency of the QMLE can be proved by extending the theory to cases where random parameters are allowed.

As shown by Xiu (2010), it turns out to be possible to establish consistency and derive the following central limit theorem (where $\mathcal{L}-s$ denotes stable convergence in law, a stronger form of convergence than the usual convergence in law) for the QMLE:

$$\begin{pmatrix} n^{\frac{1}{4}}(\hat{\sigma}^2 - \frac{1}{T}\int_0^T \sigma_t^2\, dt) \\ n^{1/2}(\hat{a}^2 - a_0^2) \end{pmatrix} \xrightarrow{\mathcal{L}-s} N\left(\begin{pmatrix} 0 \\ 0 \end{pmatrix}, V\right),$$

where

$$V = \begin{pmatrix} \frac{5a_0\int_0^T \sigma_t^4\, dt}{T(\int_0^T \sigma_t^2\, dt)^{\frac{1}{2}}} + \frac{3(\int_0^T \sigma_t^2\, dt)^{\frac{3}{2}} a_0}{T^2} & 0 \\ 0 & 2a_0^4 + \mathrm{Cum}_4\,[\varepsilon] \end{pmatrix}.$$

Stochastic volatility therefore does not affect the efficiency of the noise variance estimator, which remains the same as in the previous case. Although the volatility estimator may not achieve the optimal efficiency except in the constant volatility case, it achieves the optimal rate of convergence $n^{1/4}$ for σ^2 and $n^{1/2}$ for a^2.

An intuitive way to understand how the QMLE $(\hat{\sigma}^2, \hat{a}^2)$ works theoretically is to rewrite it as an iterative quadratic estimator:

$$\hat{\sigma}^2 T = R' W_1(\hat{\sigma}^2, \hat{a}^2) R \qquad (14.13)$$

$$\hat{a}^2 = R' W_2(\hat{\sigma}^2, \hat{a}^2) R. \qquad (14.14)$$

The weighting matrices satisfy:

$$W_1(\sigma^2, a^2) = \frac{n \cdot tr(\Omega^{-2}\Lambda) \cdot \Omega^{-1}\Lambda\Omega^{-1} - n \cdot tr(\Omega^{-2}\Lambda^2) \cdot \Omega^{-2}}{(tr(\Omega^{-2}\Lambda))^2 - tr(\Omega^{-2}) \cdot tr(\Omega^{-2}\Lambda^2)} \qquad (14.15)$$

$$W_2(\sigma^2, a^2) = \frac{tr(\Omega^{-2}\Lambda) \cdot \Omega^{-2} - tr(\Omega^{-2}) \cdot \Omega^{-1}\Lambda\Omega^{-1}}{(tr(\Omega^{-2}\Lambda))^2 - tr(\Omega^{-2}) \cdot tr(\Omega^{-2}\Lambda^2)}, \qquad (14.16)$$

where Ω is given by Equation 14.9, and

$$\Lambda = \begin{pmatrix} 2 & -1 & 0 & \cdots & 0 \\ -1 & 2 & -1 & \ddots & \vdots \\ 0 & -1 & 2 & \ddots & 0 \\ \vdots & \ddots & \ddots & \ddots & -1 \\ 0 & \cdots & 0 & -1 & 2 \end{pmatrix}.$$

Also, $W_1(\sigma^2, a^2)$ and $W_2(\sigma^2, a^2)$ depend on σ^2 and a^2 only through $\lambda^2 = a^2/(\sigma^2 T)$. Figure 14.1 plots the weighting matrices.

The quadratic representation also sheds light on the estimation procedure. Unlike a nonparametric estimator, the QMLE is fully parametric without any tuning parameters. Nevertheless, it seems reasonable (in view of the following comparison with Realized Kernels) to regard $\hat{\lambda} \cdot n^{\frac{1}{2}}$ as the "bandwidth" of the QMLE, which is automatically updated by the optimization algorithm, or more intuitively, by iterating Equations 14.13 and 14.14. Therefore, it is natural to construct a one-step alternative for the QMLE, which, instead of running nonlinear optimization, employs a consistent plug-in of $\hat{\lambda}$ for Equations 14.13 and 14.14.

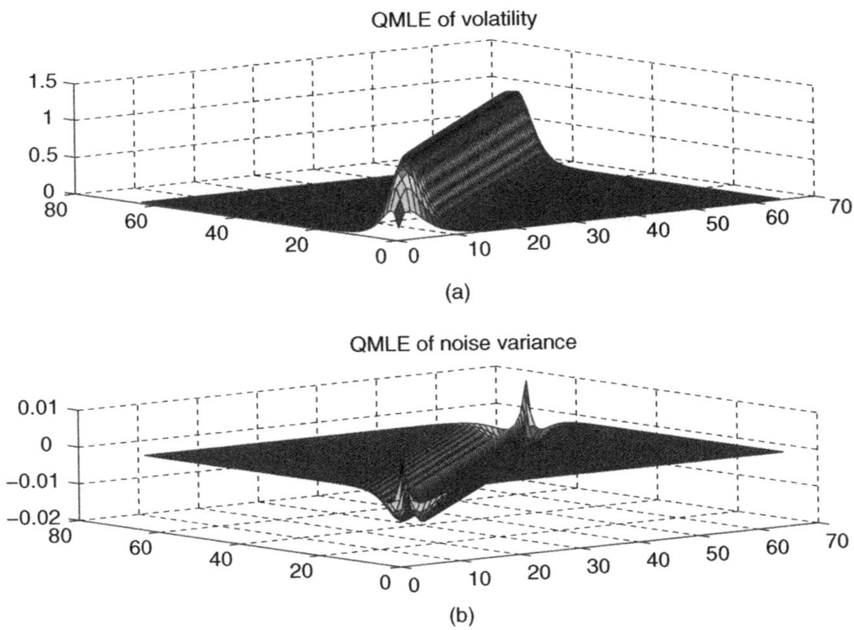

FIGURE 14.1 The weighting matrices of the quadratic representation of the QMLE.

14.2.5 COMPARISON WITH OTHER ESTIMATORS

How does the QMLE of volatility compare with other nonparametric estimators, such as realized kernels, given by Barndorff-Nielsen et al. (2008)? Realized kernels include a series of nonparametric estimators designed for volatility estimation in the presence of noise. Flat-top realized kernels with kernel weight $k(\cdot)$ take on the following form:

$$K(Y_\tau) = \gamma_0(Y_\tau) + \sum_{h=1}^{n-1} k\left(\frac{h-1}{H}\right)(\gamma_h(Y_\tau) + \gamma_{-h}(Y_\tau)),$$

where the hth sample autocovariance function is

$$\gamma_h(Y_\tau) = \sum_{j=1}^{n}(Y_{\tau_j} - Y_{\tau_{j-1}})(Y_{\tau_{j-h}} - Y_{\tau_{j-h-1}}).$$

A major drawback of realized kernels is that they require a number of out-of-period intraday returns because of the construction of the autocovariance estimator $\gamma_h(Y_\tau)$. For this reason, a feasible finite-lag realized kernel is constructed using a feasible autocovariance estimator and its quadratic representation is

$$K(\tilde{X}_\tau) = Y'WY, \tag{14.17}$$

where W is determined by the kernel $k(\cdot)$ and bandwidth H.

$$W_{i,i} = 1_{\{1+H \le i \le n-H\}}$$

$$W_{i,j} = k\left(\frac{|i-j|-1}{H}\right) \cdot 1_{\{1 \le |i-j| \le H\}} \cdot 1_{\{1+H \le j \le n-H\}}.$$

Infinite-lag kernels, which have nonzero weights on every autocovariance function, are not implementable empirically, although in theory with appropriate bandwidth, they may achieve the optimal efficiency among all kernel estimators. The following exponential kernel is the optimal infinite-lag kernel:

$$k_{opt}(x) = (1+x)e^{-x}.$$

In view of the quadratic representation, the QMLE is asymptotically equivalent to the optimal kernel with implicit bandwidth:

$$H = \hat{\lambda} \cdot n^{1/2} = a_0 \left(\int_0^T \sigma_t^2 \, dt\right)^{-\frac{1}{2}} n^{\frac{1}{2}}.$$

In other words, for any $K = n^{1/2+\delta}$, $0 < \delta < \frac{1}{2}$, and any $K \le i,j \le n-K$, we have

$$W_{1,i,j}(\sigma^2, a^2) \approx k_{\text{opt}}\left(\frac{|i-j|}{\lambda \cdot n^{1/2}}\right).$$

Therefore, the QMLE, in some sense, implements the exponential optimal kernel except for the implicit bandwidth, which is suboptimal. In addition, its weighting matrix $W_1(\sigma^2, a^2)$ is approximately a symmetric Toeplitz matrix with equal weight along the diagonal, barring the boundary. The weights on the boundary along the diagonal decrease gradually, in contrast, with a discontinuous cut-off boundary for most kernel estimators, which may lead to a better finite sample performance for the QMLE.

In regard to asymptotic efficiency, realized kernels can achieve the same optimal convergence rate as the QMLE with appropriate kernels and bandwidths. When volatility is constant, the asymptotic variance of finite-lag kernels can only approximate the parametric variance bound, which, by contrast, can be obtained by the QMLE and the optimal kernel. If volatility is stochastic, the relative efficiency of the QMLE and realized kernels depends on the extent of heteroskedasticity, as measured by $\rho = \int_0^T \sigma_u^2 \, du / \sqrt{T \int_0^T \sigma_u^4 \, du}$. Apparently, the QMLE tends to be more favorable than finite-lag kernels as ρ becomes larger, whereas realized kernels are better when ρ is small. Intuitively, the smaller ρ is, the further the misspecified model deviates from the truth.

14.2.6 RANDOM SAMPLING AND NON-I.I.D. NOISE

If the sampling intervals between two consecutive observations are random, but i.i.d., and independent of the price process, we may pretend that the data are regularly spaced, and employ the same estimator as before. In fact, this estimator can be regarded as the pretend fixed MLE discussed in Aït-Sahalia and Mykland (2003). In light of this, the full information maximum likelihood or integrated out MLE may be preferred, if information concerning the distribution of the random sampling intervals is available.

If the microstructure noise exhibits autocorrelation such as an MA(1) structure, it may be better to divide the whole sample into two subsamples such that the noises within each subsample are uncorrelated, apply the QMLE to each subsample and aggregate the estimates. Such method is parsimonious, and easy to implement, as opposed to performing the maximum-likelihood estimation using the whole sample with one more parameter.

14.3 Covariance Estimation

We now extend the previous results to covariance estimation with a two-dimensional log-price process $\boldsymbol{X}_t = (X_{1t}, X_{2t})$, discretely observed over the interval $[0, T]$. The latent log-price processes satisfy

$$dX_{it} = \mu_{it} \, dt + \sigma_{it} \, dW_{it},$$

with $E(dW_{1t} \cdot dW_{2t}) = \rho_t \, dt$. Suppose that the observations are recorded at times $0 = t_{i,0} \leq t_{i,1} \leq t_{i,2} \leq \cdots \leq t_{i,n_i} = T$, respectively, where $i = 1, 2$. As in the univariate case, one can only observe $Y_{i,t}$, contaminated by an additive error $\varepsilon_{i,t}$, associated at each observation point. The noise $\boldsymbol{\varepsilon}_t$ is an i.i.d. two-dimensional vector with mean 0, diagonal covariance matrix $\boldsymbol{\Theta}$, and has a finite fourth moment.

On the basis of the identity that expresses covariance in terms of variances, Aït-Sahalia et al. (2010) proposed the following covariance and correlation estimators:

$$\widehat{\mathrm{Cov}}(Y_1, Y_2) = \frac{1}{4}\left(\widehat{\mathrm{Var}}(Y_1 + Y_2) - \widehat{\mathrm{Var}}(Y_1 - Y_2)\right) \tag{14.18}$$

$$\widehat{\mathrm{Cov}}(Y_1, Y_2) = \frac{\widehat{\mathrm{Cov}}(Y_1, Y_2)}{\sqrt{\widehat{\mathrm{Var}}(Y_1)}\sqrt{\widehat{\mathrm{Var}}(Y_2)}}, \tag{14.19}$$

where $\widehat{\mathrm{Cov}}(\cdot, \cdot)$ is the covariance estimator, $\widehat{\mathrm{Var}}(\cdot, \cdot)$ denotes the QMLE in the univariate case, and $\cdot$ indicates the data we are actually using.

In order to compute the prices $Y_1 + Y_2$ and $Y_1 - Y_2$, we need the two assets to be synchronically traded. Nevertheless, this is not the case in practice, at least for high frequency financial data. Instead, high frequency transactions for two assets occur at times that are not synchrone. This practical issue may induce a large bias for the estimation, and may be (at least partly) responsible for the Epps effect. The remaining question is what kind of data synchronization procedure one should use. Clearly, if we apply the QMLE to estimate the diagonal elements in the covariance matrix, it would be better to cross out a small number of data points rather than adding more through an interpolation method, because the former strategy may suffer from efficiency loss, while the latter one may result in inconsistency due to the change in the autocorrelation structure.

We define a *generalized sampling time*, which we then use to propose a general synchronization scheme. A sequence of time points $\{\tau_0, \tau_1, \tau_2, \ldots, \tau_n\}$ is said to be the generalized sampling time for a collection of M assets, if they form a partition of the time interval $[0, T]$, and there exists at least one observation for each asset between consecutive τ_js. In addition, the time intervals, $\{\Delta_j = \tau_j - \tau_{j-1}, 1 \leq j \leq n\}$, satisfy $\sup_i \Delta_i \xrightarrow{\mathrm{P}} 0$, as n increases to ∞.

The generalized synchronization method is then built on the generalized sampling time by selecting an arbitrary observation $Y_{i,\check{t}_j}$ for the ith asset between the time interval $(\tau_{j-1}, \tau_j]$. The synchronized data sets are, therefore, $\{Y^{\tau}_{i,\tau_j}, 1 \leq i \leq M, 1 \leq j \leq n\}$ such that $Y^{\tau}_{i,\tau_j} = Y_{i,\check{t}_j}$.

The concept of generalized synchronization method is more general than that of the Previous Tick approach discussed in Zhang (2011), and the Refresh Time scheme proposed by Barndorff-Nielsen et al. (2010), namely, the Replace All scheme in deB. Harris et al. (1995).

More precisely, if we require $\{\tau_j\}$ to be equally spaced on $[0, T]$, and the previous tick for each asset before τ_j to be selected, we are back to the Previous Tick approach. Or, if we choose τ_j recursively as

$$\tau_{j+1} = \max_{1 \leq i \leq M} \{t_{i,N_i(\tau_j)+1}\},$$

where $\tau_1 = \max\{t_{1,1}, t_{2,1}, \ldots, t_{M,1}\}$ and $N_i(t)$ measures the number of observations for asset i before time t, and if we select those ticks that occur right before or at τ_js, we return to the Refresh Time scheme. In both cases, the previous ticks of the assets, if needed, are regarded as if they were observed at the sampling time τ_js. By contrast, we advocate choosing an arbitrary tick for each asset within each interval. In practice, it may happen that the order of consecutive ticks is not recorded correctly. Because our synchronization method has no requirement on tick selection, the estimator is robust to data misplacement error, as long as these misplaced data points are within the same sampling intervals.

It is apparent that the Refresh Time scheme is highly dependent on the relatively illiquid asset. On the one hand, the number of synchronized pairs is smaller than the number of observations of this asset, inducing an inevitable loss of data for the other asset. More importantly, it is very likely that the Refresh Time points are determined by the occurrence of the relatively more illiquid asset, rendering the selected observations of the other asset always ahead of the corresponding illiquid asset. This hidden effect may induce some additional bias in the estimation.

Alternatively, we can design the synchronization scheme requiring each asset to lead in turn. For example, take two assets. If we require the first asset to lead, we choose $\tau_1 = t_{2,N_2(t_{1,1})+1}$. Recursively,

$$\tau_i = t_{2,N_2(t_{1,N_1(\tau_{i-1})+1})+1}.$$

Literally, it means that right after τ_{i-1}, we find the first observation of Y_{1t}, which should happen at $t_{1,N_1(\tau_{i-1})+1}$, and then the next generalized sampling time is defined to be the point when the first Y_{2t} is observed right after $t_{1,N_1(\tau_{i-1})+1}$. In this case, at all sampling time points, the second asset would always have records. The previous tick of the first asset, if needed, is regarded as if it were observed a bit later at the sampling time. Hence, in the synchronized pairs, the first asset always leads the second.

If the generalized sampling time $\{\tau_j\}$ is independent of the price process, the volatility process and the noise, and the time intervals, $\{\Delta_j = \tau_j - \tau_{j-1}, 1 \le j \le n\}$, are i.i.d. with mean $\bar{\Delta}$, then replacing the idealized data with the products of the generalized sampling time maintains the consistency and rate efficiency of the estimators:

$$\widehat{\mathrm{Cov}}(Y_1^\tau, Y_2^\tau) - 1/T \int_0^T \rho_t \sigma_{1t} \sigma_{2t} = O_P(\bar{\Delta}^{\frac{1}{4}})$$

$$\widehat{\mathrm{Corr}}(Y_1^\tau, Y_2^\tau) - \frac{\int_0^T \rho_t \sigma_{1t} \sigma_{2t}\, dt}{\sqrt{\int_0^T \sigma_{1t}^2\, dt}\sqrt{\int_0^T \sigma_{2t}^2\, dt}} = O_P(\bar{\Delta}^{\frac{1}{4}}).$$

In other words, the proposed estimators are robust with respect to asynchronous data.

14.4 Empirical Application: Correlation between Stock and Commodity Futures

To assess the empirical relevance of these likelihood-based estimators, we estimate the volatilities of S&P 500 futures and crude oil futures as well as their correlation. The S&P 500 futures are traded on the Chicago Mercantile Exchange (CME) from 8:30 AM to 3:15 PM central time. The regular-size contracts are liquidly traded via the open outcry market, whereas the electronic market is in charge of mini-contracts. The crude oil futures used to be the most popular energy contract in the New York Mercantile Exchange (NYMEX), which has become part of the CME group recently. Since June 2006, the 24-h electronic market for crude oil has started to take over the open outcry market. Nevertheless, the most active trading period is between 9:00 AM and 2:30 PM Eastern Time (after February 2007), when the open outcry market is open. We only consider the liquid S&P500 futures traded via open outcry and the crude oil futures traded electronically. It is plausible to assume that the two microstructure noise terms, reflecting markets with little cross-trading or cross-arbitrage, are uncorrelated across the two markets. The sample period ranges from February 1, 2007 to December 18, 2009, therefore including the height of the financial crisis during the fall of 2008 and the winter of 2008–2009.

Figure 14.2 plots the daily realized volatility for S&P 500 and crude oil, and Figure 14.3 plots their daily correlation, estimated from high frequency data over the sampling period. The results shows that crude oil, which incidentally is the primary component of most commodity indices, is more volatile than the

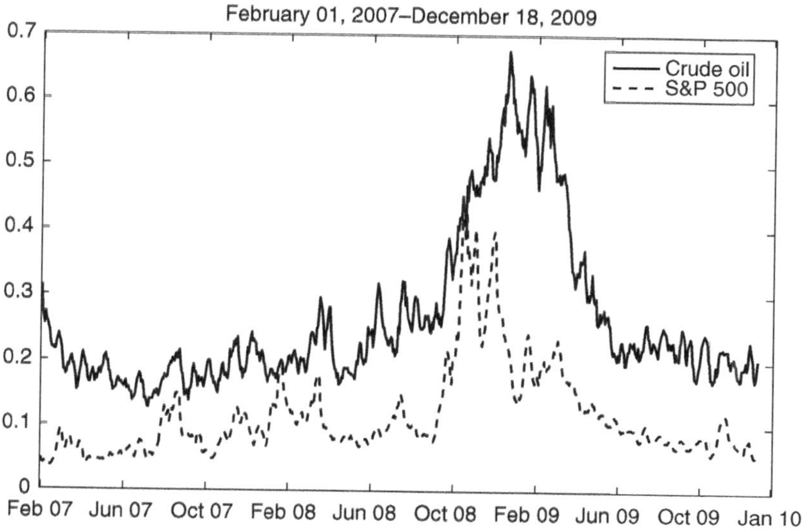

FIGURE 14.2 The 5-day moving average of the daily annualized volatilities of the S&P 500 and crude oil futures.

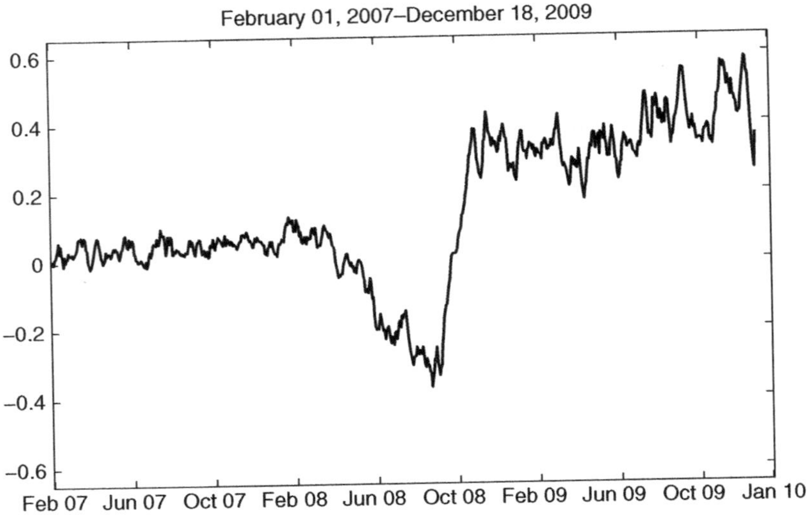

FIGURE 14.3 The 5-day moving average of the daily correlation between the S&P 500 and crude oil futures.

aggregate stock market, confirming that the commodity markets are generally riskier than the equity markets. With commodities representing a relatively new trading avenue for investors, as an asset class, the price of an individual commodity is not only simply determined by its own supply and demand but also by overall portfolio considerations, which may lead to larger correlations between the aggregate financial markets for the standard asset classes such as U.S. equities and commodity markets (Tang and Xiong (2010)). We find that the correlation is time-varying and may sometimes behave differently for a short period. For instance, at the beginning of the financial crisis, commodities appeared to be considered as a relatively safe hedge against the stock market downturn, hence the returns of the two markets were negatively correlated. Shortly, after October 2010, however, which may be viewed as after the heightened phase of the crisis, both markets started to move at the same pace, leading to a positive correlation of the returns. Although such short-term pattern is important to investors, it may not be captured, at least punctually, using lower frequency data, since years of historical data may dilute the short-term abnormality.

14.5 Conclusion

This chapter reviews the likelihood-based parametric methods designed to estimate the volatility and covariance of asset returns in the presence of market microstructure noise. Compared to nonparametric estimators, the major advantage of such estimators is their convenience and robustness; there is no need to choose any tuning parameters such as kernel functions, bandwidths, or number of subsamples. Moreover, being parametric in this circumstance does not lead to loss of robustness or generality. As we have seen, these estimators are consistent and achieve the optimal rate of convergence even in situations where their "construction hypotheses" of constant volatility and Gaussian noise are no longer satisfied, and in practice have good finite sample performance. All these features make them good choices for empirical applications.

Acknowledgments

Financial support from the NSF under grants DMS-0532370 (Aït-Sahalia) is gratefully acknowledged.

CHAPTER FIFTEEN

HAR Modeling for Realized Volatility Forecasting

FULVIO CORSI, FRANCESCO AUDRINO, and ROBERTO RENÒ

15.1 Introduction

The importance of financial market volatility has generated a very large literature in which volatility dynamics has been modeled in order to take into account its most salient features: clustering, slowly decaying autocorrelation, and nonlinear responses to previous market information of a different type.

In the literature, these phenomena have typically given rise to models in which volatility is generated by a long-memory process, characterized by fractional integration, and a hyperbolic decay of the autocorrelation function. However, in this chapter, we follow an alternative direction that generates very similar stylized facts for volatility series using the superposition of short-memory frequencies. This framework turns out to be easier to handle, with a straightforward economic interpretation and an excellent fit to the data.

Originally, this framework was inspired by the work of Muller et al. (1997) and Dacorogna et al. (1998). We view volatility persistence as the result of the aggregation of the heterogeneous components present in the financial market (the so-called heterogeneous market hypothesis). Heterogeneity among participants in the financial market may be of a different nature: differences in the endowments,

Handbook of Volatility Models and Their Applications, First Edition.
Edited by Luc Bauwens, Christian Hafner, and Sebastien Laurent.

institutional constraints, risk profiles, information, geographical locations, and so on. The proposed model concentrates on the heterogeneity that originates from (or materializes in) the difference in time horizons. Typically, a financial market is composed of participants having a large spectrum of trading frequencies. At one end of the spectrum are dealers, market makers, and intraday speculators with an intraday trading horizon. At the other end, there are institutional investors, such as insurance companies and pension funds trading much less frequently and possibly for larger amounts. The key idea is that agents with different time horizons perceive, react to, and cause different types of volatility components.

In addition, it has been recently observed that volatility over longer time intervals has stronger influence on volatility over shorter time intervals than conversely.[1] This can be economically explained by noticing that for short-term traders the level of long-term volatility matters because it determines the expected future size of trends and risk. The overall pattern that emerges can be statistically described by a cascade of heterogeneous volatility components (generated by the action of market participants of different natures) from low frequencies to high frequencies.

This idea has been pursued in Corsi (2009), who proposed an additive cascade model of realized volatility aggregated at different time horizons. This cascade of heterogeneous volatility components leads to a simple AR-type model in the realized volatility that considers volatilities realized over different time horizons and is thus called ***heterogeneous autoregressive*** (HAR). In spite of its simplicity and the fact that it does not formally belong to the class of long-memory models, the HAR model for realized volatility is able to reproduce the volatility persistence revealed by the empirical analysis on financial markets. The combination of ease of implementation with a very accurate fit of financial volatility time series has made the HAR models very popular in the financial econometrics community.

In this chapter, we survey the HAR model for realized volatility forecasting and its extensions. After reviewing some stylized facts of realized volatility, we present the derivation and possible interpretations of the heterogeneous structure of the HAR model. We then discuss different extensions of the univariate HAR model aiming at modeling the forecasting power of jumps, leverage effect, and structural breaks.

In particular, we provide evidence for the contention that jumps have significant impact on future realized volatility and that the impact of negative returns (the so-called *leverage effect*) is highly persistent and also presents an HAR structure, confirming the view of the existence of an heterogeneous structure in the financial market. Moreover, we also provide empirical evidence of the existence of other nonlinear effects of past market information on volatility on the top of the leverage effect by introducing a flexible HAR-type model able to explicitly take into account structural breaks and regime switches. Finally, we provide a brief review of multivariate models for realized variance–covariance matrix dynamics.

[1]See Muller et al. (1997), Arneodo et al. (1998), and Lynch and Zumbach (2003).

15.2 Stylized Facts on Realized Volatility

Summarized from the vast literature on the empirical analysis of financial markets, the main characteristics of financial market volatility are as follows:

1. Long-range dependence: (hourly, daily, weekly, and monthly) realized volatility displays significant autocorrelations even at very long lags. This property is often ascribed to a long-memory data-generating process. In this chapter, we take another approach by using a superposition of autoregressive processes with different timescales.
2. Leverage effect: it is empirically observed that returns are negatively correlated with (realized) volatility. In particular, volatility bursts are more likely associated with negative past returns.
3. Jumps: financial prices are subject to abrupt variations. Jumps are not very frequent and practically unpredictable, but they have a strong positive impact on future volatility.

To illustrate these stylized facts of realized volatility (RV_t), let us now consider historical data on the S&P 500 stock index over the period 1982–2009. Figure 15.1 plots Corr(RV_t, Z_{t-h}), that is, the correlation between RV_t and Z_{t-h}, for $h = 1, \ldots, 50$. Z_t corresponds to RV_t, negative daily returns ($r_t^- = \min(r_t, 0)$,

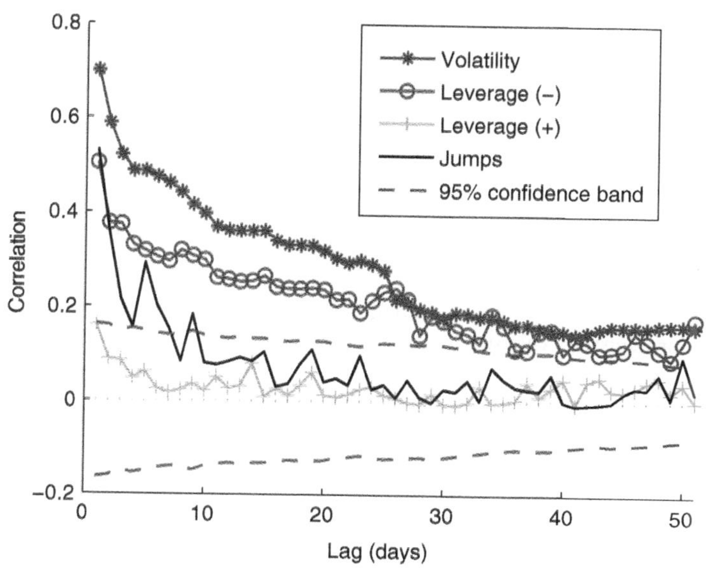

FIGURE 15.1 $Corr(RV_t, Z_{t-h})(h = 1, \ldots, 50)$ for the S&P 500 series for the period January 1990 to February 2009. Z_t corresponds either to RV_t, negative daily returns ($r_t^- = \min(r_t, 0)$, where r_t is the return on day t), positive returns ($r_t^+ = \max(r_t, 0)$) or jumps (J_t). The displayed 95% confidence bands (dashed lines) are computed with the generalized Bartlett's formula of Francq and Zakoian (2009).

where r_t is the return on day t), positive returns ($r_t^+ = \max(r_t, 0)$), or jumps (J_t). More details on the data and the estimation of RV_t and J_t are given in Section 15.3. $Corr(RV_t, RV_{t-h})$ is the autocorrelation function (ACF) of RV_t. Figure 15.1 clearly suggests the presence of long memory in the realized volatility. This figure also suggests that while past positive daily returns (r_{t-h}^+) are not significantly correlated with RV_t, past negative returns (r_{t-h}^-) have a significant impact on futures volatilities, and negative shocks take a long time to die out (which might also be viewed as long memory). Interestingly, jumps seem also to have a positive impact on future values of RV_t, although their effect decays at a faster rate than RV_t and r_{t-h}^-. This motivates the analysis in the following sections.

15.3 Heterogeneity and Volatility Persistence

The appearance of long-range dependence might be due to a genuine long-memory data-generating process, or, alternatively, it can be explained as a combination of different short-memory processes (as discussed further below). Although a true long-memory process requires the aggregation of an infinite number of short-memory processes (as shown by Granger (1980)), an approximated long-memory process (practically indistinguishable from a true one) can be obtained by aggregating only few heterogeneous timescales (LeBaron (2001)).

The need for multiple components in the volatility process has been advocated by (among others) Muller et al. (1997), Engle and Lee (1999), Bollerslev and Wright (2001), Barndorff-Nielsen and Shephard (2001), and Calvet and Fisher (2004) and has been reconsidered by making the use of the concept of an additive cascade of realized volatility aggregated over different time horizons in Corsi (2009). In what follows, we briefly review this latter approach.

We assume that the state variable X (typically the log price) is driven by the stochastic process:

$$dX_t = \mu_t dt + \sigma_t dW_t + c_t dN_t, \tag{15.1}$$

where μ_t is predictable, σ_t is càdlàg, W_t is a Brownian motion, and N_t is a doubly stochastic Poisson process[2] whose intensity is an adapted stochastic process λ_t, the random times of the corresponding jumps are $(\tau_j)_{j=1,\ldots,N_T}$, and c_j are i.i.d.-adapted random variables measuring the size of the jump at time τ_j. In practice, for example, for risk management purposes, we are interested in forecasting the quadratic variation defined as:

$$\widetilde{\sigma}_t^2 = \int_t^{t+1} \sigma_s^2 ds + \sum_{t \le \tau_j \le t+1} c_{\tau_j}^2,$$

where the time unit is 1 day.

[2]We could also consider a wider class of jumps, such as Lévy, in the case in which they have a finite quadratic variation process.

This quantity is not directly observable and therefore has to be estimated. Let us denote by $\hat{V}_t$ a consistent estimator of $\widetilde{\sigma}_t^2$, that is:

$$\log \widetilde{\sigma}_t^2 = \log \hat{V}_t + \omega_t,$$

where ω_t is i.i.d. noise.[3] In the ideal case of no microstructure noise, RV_t is the most natural choice for $\hat{V}_t$. In the presence of microstructure noise, other estimators are preferable such as the two-scale estimator proposed by Zhang et al. (2005), the realized kernels method of Barndorff-Nielsen et al. (2008), the pre-average approach of Jacod et al. (2009), or the multiscales discrete sine transform (DST) estimator of Curci and Corsi (2010). In our empirical analysis in Section 15.6, we use the DST estimator.

Consider the aggregated values of $\log \mathrm{V}_t$, defined as:

$$\log \mathrm{V}_t^{(n)} = \frac{1}{n} \sum_{j=1}^{n} \log \mathrm{V}_{t-j+1}, \tag{15.2}$$

and assume two different timescales, of length n_1 and n_2, with $n_1 > n_2$ (e.g., weekly and daily). For the largest timescale, assume that $\widetilde{\sigma}_t^2$, once aggregated as in Equation 15.2, is determined by:

$$\log \widetilde{\sigma}_{t+n_1}^{2,(n_1)} = c^{(n_1)} + \beta^{(n_1)} \log \mathrm{V}_t^{(n_1)} + \varepsilon_{t+n_1}^{(n_1)}, \tag{15.3}$$

where $\varepsilon_t^{(n_1)}$ is an i.i.d. random variable with mean 0 and unit variance, which is independent of the estimation error ω_t and $c^{(n_1)}$ and $\beta^{(n_1)}$ are unknown parameters.

This can be explained by assuming that the level of short-term volatility does not affect the trading strategies of long-term traders.[4] On the other hand, for short-term traders, the level of long-term volatility matters because it determines the expected future size of trends and risk. Hence, the shorter timescale (n_2) is assumed to be influenced by the expected future value of the largest timescale (n_1), so that:

$$\log \widetilde{\sigma}_{t+n_2}^{2,(n_2)} = c^{(n_2)} + \beta^{(n_2)} \log \mathrm{V}_t^{(n_2)} + \delta^{(n_2)} \mathbf{E}_t \left[\log \widetilde{\sigma}_{t+n_1}^{2,(n_1)} \right] + \varepsilon_{t+n_2}^{(n_2)}, \tag{15.4}$$

where $\varepsilon_t^{(n_2)}$ is an i.i.d. random variable with mean 0 and unit variance, independent of $\varepsilon_t^{(n_1)}$ and ω_t, and $\delta^{(n_2)}$ is a constant. The economic interpretation of this mechanism is that each volatility component corresponds to a market component

[3]The model can also be specified in terms of V_t and for $\sqrt{\mathrm{V}_t}$, as in Corsi (2009), Andersen et al. (2007), and Corsi et al. (2010). However, the log specification has the double advantage of avoiding imposing positivity constraints and making the distribution closer to normality (Gonçalves and Meddahi, 2011).

[4]The HAR model would hold even if we allow the short-term volatility to affect the long-term volatility.

whose expectation on next period volatility is formed looking at, beyond the current realized volatility value, the forecast on the longer time horizon. The basic idea is that agents with different time horizons perceive, react to, and cause different types of volatility components. By substitution, this gives

$$\log V_{t+n_2}^{(n_2)} = c + \beta^{(n_2)} \log V_t^{(n_2)} + \beta^{(n_1)} \log V_t^{(n_1)} + \varepsilon_{t+n_2}; \tag{15.5}$$

where ε_t is i.i.d. noise depending on $\varepsilon_t^{(n_1)}$, $\varepsilon_t^{(n_2)}$, and ω_t. The model (Eq. 15.5) can be easily extended to d horizons of length $n_1 > n_2 > \cdots > n_d$. Typically, three components are used with length $n_1 = 22$ (monthly), $n_2 = 5$ (weekly), and $n_3 = 1$ (daily).

The HAR model is then a parsimonious AR model reparameterized by imposing different sets of restrictions (one for each volatility component) on the autoregressive coefficients of the AR model. Each set of restrictions takes the form of equality constraints among the autoregressive coefficients constituting a given time horizon, so that once combined they lead to a step function for the autoregressive weights. In this sense, the HAR can be related to the MIDAS regression of Ghysels et al. (2006a), Ghysels et al. (2006), and Forsberg and Ghysels (2007), although the standard MIDAS with the estimated Beta function lag polynomial cannot reproduce the HAR step function weights.

In practice, the HAR model provides a simple and flexible method to fit the partial autocorrelation function of the empirical data with a step function that has predefined tread depth and estimated (by simple OLS) rise height. More generally, however, nothing prevents the use of different types of kernel in the aggregation of V_t instead of the rectangular one used in the simple moving average; in this case, we would no longer have a step function for the coefficients but a more general function given by a mixture of kernels (e.g., mixture of exponentials for exponentially weighted moving averages), which can still be easily estimated by simple OLS.

Even if the HAR model does not formally belong to the class of long-memory processes, it fits the persistence properties of financial data as well as (and potentially better than) true long-memory models, such as the fractionally integrated one, which, however, are much more complicated to estimate and to deal with (see the review of Banerjee and Urga (2005)). For these reasons, the HAR model has been employed in several applications in the literature, of which an incomplete list is: Ghysels et al. (2006a) and Forsberg and Ghysels (2007) compare this model with the MIDAS model; Andersen et al. (2007) use an extension of this model to forecast the volatility of stock prices, foreign exchange rates, and bond prices; Clements et al. (2008) implement it for risk management withValue-at-Risk (VaR) measures; Bollerslev et al. (2008) use it to analyze the risk-return tradeoff; and Bianco et al. (2009) use it to study the relation between intraday serial correlation and volatility.

In the literature dealing with HAR models, it is commonly assumed that the innovations of the log-realized volatility are identically and independently distributed. However, volatility clustering in the residuals of the HAR model (as well as in other realized volatility models) are often observed in practical applications. The presence of time-varying conditional distributions in realized volatility models can distort risk assessment and, thus, impair risk management analysis. To account for the observed volatility clustering in realized volatility, Corsi et al. (2008) extend the HAR model by explicitly modeling the volatility of realized volatility. The proposed model adds GARCH-type innovations to the standard HAR model, giving rise to an HAR-GARCH(p, q) model which, with the three commonly used frequencies, reads:

$$\log \mathrm{V}_{t+1}^{(1)} = c + \beta^{(1)} \log \mathrm{V}_t^{(1)} + \beta^{(5)} \log \mathrm{V}_t^{(5)} + \beta^{(22)} \log \mathrm{V}_t^{(22)} + \sqrt{h_{t+1}}\varepsilon_{t+1} \quad (15.6)$$

$$h_t = \omega + \sum_{j=1}^{q} a_j u_{t-j}^2 + \sum_{j=1}^{p} b_j h_{t-j} \quad (15.7)$$

$$\varepsilon_t | \Omega_{t-1} \sim (0, 1), \quad (15.8)$$

where Ω_{t-1} denotes the σ-field generated by all the information available up to time $t-1$ and $u_t = \sqrt{h_t}\varepsilon_t$.

15.3.1 GENUINE LONG MEMORY OR SUPERPOSITION OF FACTORS?

Assessing whether volatility persistence is generated by a data-generating process with genuine long memory or from a superposition of factors as illustrated above may appear an impossible task. Clearly, the two possibilities might generate very similar empirical features that would make them indistinguishable. In this case, analytical tractability becomes the most important feature to take into account. However, as we discuss here, some specific data-generating processes can be ruled out on the basis of the statistical features of the realized volatility time series.

Such an investigation is carried out in Corsi and Renò (2010). They propose two competing continuous time models for the volatility dynamics which belong to the class (Eq. 15.1). The first one is a genuine long-memory model with constant volatility of volatility:

$$\mathrm{d}\log \sigma_t = k(\omega - \log \sigma_t)\mathrm{d}t + \eta \mathrm{d}W_t^{(d)}, \quad (15.9)$$

where $\mathrm{d}W_t^{(d)}$ is a *fractional Brownian motion* with memory parameter $d \in [0, 0.5]$ (Comte and Renault, 1998). The value $d = 0$ corresponds to the standard Brownian motion, while higher d correspond to higher memory in the time series. Model (Eq. 15.9) (or its discrete counterpart) is usually advocated as the source of long memory in volatility, even if it is very difficult to deal with mathematically and econometrically. It is important to note that in this model persistence comes both from the mean-reverting term $k(\omega - \log \sigma_t)$ and from the fractional Brownian motion $\mathrm{d}W_t^{(d)}$. Corsi and Renò (2010) estimate model (Eq. 15.9) via indirect inference, using the HAR model as auxiliary model. The advantage of indirect inference is that, beyond providing an estimate of the parameters k, ω, η, and d, it provides overall statistics of the goodness of fit of the model. They find unambiguously that the model (Eq. 15.9) is unable to reproduce the time series of volatilities in the S&P500 index.

The second model they test is an affine two-factor model

$$\begin{aligned}
\sigma_t^2 &= V_t^1 + V_t^2 \\
\mathrm{d}V_t^1 &= \kappa_1(\omega_1 - V_t^1) + \eta_1\sqrt{V_t^1}\mathrm{d}W_t^1 \\
\mathrm{d}V_t^2 &= \kappa_2(\omega_2 - V_t^2) + \eta_2\sqrt{V_t^2}\mathrm{d}W_t^2,
\end{aligned} \tag{15.10}$$

where W^1 and W^2 are two independent Brownian motions. In this case, even imposing the restriction $\omega_1 = \omega_2$ to identify the model,[5] the two-factor model is perfectly able to reproduce the statistical features of the volatility of the S&P500 index. The obtained estimates of $\hat{\kappa}_1 = 2.146$ and $\hat{\kappa}_2 = 0.004$ imply the presence of a fast mean-reverting factor and a slowly mean-reverting factor with a half-life of nearly 200 days, which is usually suggested in the empirical literature on stochastic volatility and option pricing.

Clearly, a more complicated long-memory model (e.g., with two factors) might also reproduce the volatility time series, so it would be wrong to conclude that these results rule out the presence of genuine long memory in the volatility series. However, these results show that the superposition of volatility factors is able to reproduce the long-range dependence displayed by realized volatility, for which a genuine long-memory data-generating process is unnecessary (and certainly not mathematically convenient).

These results can also help explaining the good performance of multifactor model in the option pricing (Bates, 2000). They also suggest that two factors might be unnecessary if the volatility dynamics is specified directly with a model similar to HAR: an attempt in this direction is the study proposed by Corsi et al. (2010) where a realized volatility option-pricing model is developed based on the HAR structure. Such a model is found to provide good pricing performances.

15.4 HAR Extensions

15.4.1 JUMP MEASURES AND THEIR VOLATILITY IMPACT

The importance of jumps in financial econometrics is rapidly growing. Recent research focusing on jump detection and volatility measuring in the presence of jumps includes Barndorff-Nielsen and Shephard (2004b), Mancini (2009), Lee and Mykland (2008), Jiang and Oomen (2008), Ait-Sahalia and Mancini (2008), Aït-Sahalia and Jacod (2009), Christensen et al. (2010b), Mancini and Renò (2011), and Boudt et al. (2010). Andersen et al. (2007) suggested that the continuous volatility and jump component have different dynamics and should thus be modeled separately. In this section, we closely follow Corsi

[5] The structural model (Eq. 15.10) has six free parameters, while the auxiliary three-component HAR model has five (including the parameter of the variance of the innovations).

et al. (2010) using the $\mathsf{C}-\mathsf{Tz}$ test[6] for jumps detection, and TBPV_t, that is, the threshold bipower variation, to estimate the continuous part of integrated volatility, defined as:

$$\mathsf{TBPV}_t = \frac{\pi}{2}\sum_{j=0}^{n-2} |\Delta_{t,j}X| \cdot |\Delta_{t,j+1}X| I_{\{|\Delta_{t,j}X|^2 \leq \vartheta_{j-1}\}} I_{\{|\Delta_{t,j+1}X|^2 \leq \vartheta_j\}}, \qquad (15.12)$$

where $I_{\{\cdot\}}$ is the indicator function and ϑ_t is a threshold function which we estimate as in Corsi et al. (2010). It can be proved that, under model (Eq. 15.1), $\mathsf{TBPV}_t \to \int_t^{t+1} \sigma_s^2 ds$ as the interval between observations goes to 0. This continuous volatility estimator has much better finite sample properties than standard bipower variation and provides more accurate jump tests, which allows for a corrected separation of continuous and jump components. For this purpose, we set a confidence level α and estimate the jump component as:

$$\mathsf{J}_t = I_{\{\mathsf{C}-\mathsf{Tz} > \Phi_\alpha\}} \cdot (\mathrm{V}_t - \mathsf{TBPV}_t)^+, \qquad (15.13)$$

where Φ_α is the value of the standard Normal distribution corresponding to the confidence level α and $x^+ = \max(x, 0)$. The corresponding continuous component is defined as

$$\mathsf{C}_t = \mathrm{V}_t - \mathsf{J}_t, \qquad (15.14)$$

which is equal to V_t if there are no jumps in the trajectory, while it is equal to TBPV_t if a jump is detected by the $\mathsf{C}-\mathsf{Tz}$ statistics.

As for $\log \mathrm{V}_t$, we define aggregated values of $\log \mathsf{C}_t$ as

$$\log \mathsf{C}_t^{(n)} = \frac{1}{n}\sum_{j=1}^{n} \log \mathsf{C}_{t-j+1}.$$

For the aggregation of jumps, given the presence of a large number of zeros in the series, we prefer to simply take the sum of the jumps over the window h instead of the average, that is

$$\mathsf{J}_t^{(n)} = \sum_{j=1}^{n} \mathsf{J}_{t-j+1}.$$

[6] The $\mathsf{C}-\mathsf{Tz}$ statistics is defined as:

$$\mathsf{C}-\mathsf{Tz}_t = \delta^{-\frac{1}{2}} \frac{(\mathsf{RV}_t - \mathsf{C}-\mathsf{TBPV}_t) \cdot \mathsf{RV}_t^{-1}}{\sqrt{\left(\frac{\pi^2}{4} + \pi - 5\right) \max\left\{1, \frac{\mathsf{C}-\mathsf{TTriPV}_t}{(\mathsf{TBPV}_t)^2}\right\}}},$$

where δ is the time between high frequency observations, $\mathsf{C}-\mathsf{TBPV}_t$ is a correction of Equation 15.13 devised to be unbiased under the null, and $\mathsf{C}-\mathsf{TTriPV}$ is a similar estimator of integrated quarticity $\int_t^{t+1} \sigma_s^4 ds$ (for details, see Corsi et al., 2010).

Consistent with the above section, in the volatility cascade, we assume that C_t and J_t enter separately at each level of the cascade, that is

$$\log \widetilde{\sigma}^{2,(n_1)}_{t+n_1} = c^{(n_1)} + \alpha^{(n_1)} \log\left(1 + \mathsf{J}_t^{(n_1)}\right) + \beta^{(n_1)} \log \mathsf{C}_t^{(n_1)} + \varepsilon^{(n_1)}_{t+n_1}$$

$$\log \widetilde{\sigma}^{2,(n_2)}_{t+n_2} = c^{(n_2)} + \alpha^{(n_2)} \log\left(1 + \mathsf{J}_t^{(n_2)}\right) + \beta^{(n_2)} \log \mathsf{C}_t^{(n_2)}$$
$$+ \delta^{(n_2)} \mathbf{E}_t\left[\log \widetilde{\sigma}^{2,(n_1)}_{t+1}\right] + \varepsilon^{(n_2)}_{t+n_2},$$

originating the model:

$$\log \mathsf{V}^{(n_2)}_{t+n_2} = c + \alpha^{(n_1)} \log\left(1 + \mathsf{J}_t^{(n_1)}\right) + \alpha^{(n_2)} \log\left(1 + \mathsf{J}_t^{(n_2)}\right) \quad (15.15)$$
$$+ \beta^{(n_2)} \log \mathsf{C}_t^{(n_2)} + \beta^{(n_1)} \log \mathsf{C}_t^{(n_1)} + \varepsilon_{t+n_2}.$$

Note that we use $\log(1 + \mathsf{J}_t)$ instead of $\log \mathsf{J}_t$ since J_t can be 0. This model has been introduced as the HAR-CJ model by Andersen et al. (2007).

15.4.2 LEVERAGE EFFECTS

It is well known that volatility tends to increase more after a negative shock than after a positive shock of the same magnitude: this is the so-called leverage effect (see Christie (1982), Campbell and Hentschel (1992), Glosten et al. (1993) and more recently Bollerslev et al. (2006)).

Given the stylized facts presented in Section 15.2, it is then natural to extend the heterogeneous market hypothesis approach to leverage effects. We assume that realized volatility reacts asymmetrically not only to previous daily returns but also to past weekly and monthly returns. We model such heterogeneous leverage effects by introducing asymmetric return-volatility dependence at each level of the cascade considered in the above section. Define daily returns $r_t = X_t - X_{t-1}$ and aggregated returns as

$$r_t^{(n)} = \frac{1}{n} \sum_{j=1}^{n} r_{t-j+1}.$$

To model the leverage effect at different frequencies, we define

$$r_t^{(n)-} = \min\left(r_t^{(n)}, 0\right).$$

We assume that integrated volatility is determined by the following cascade:

$$\log \widetilde{\sigma}^{2,(n_1)}_{t+n_1} = c^{(n_1)} + \beta^{(n_1)} \log \mathsf{V}_t^{(n_1)} + \gamma^{(n_1)} r_t^{(n_1)-} + \varepsilon^{(n_1)}_{t+n_1}$$

$$\log \widetilde{\sigma}^{2,(n_2)}_{t+n_2} = c^{(n_2)} + \beta^{(n_2)} \log \mathsf{V}_t^{(n_1)} + \gamma^{(n_2)} r_t^{(n_2)-}$$
$$+ \delta^{(n_2)} \mathbf{E}_t\left[\log \widetilde{\sigma}^{2,(n_1)}_{t+n_1}\right] + \varepsilon^{(n_2)}_{t+n_2},$$

where $\gamma^{(n_1,n_2)}$ are constants. This now gives

$$\log V_{t+n_2}^{(n_2)} = c + \beta^{(n_2)} \log V_t^{(n_2)} + \beta^{(n_1)} \log V_t^{(n_1)} + \gamma^{(n_2)} r_t^{(n_2)-} + \gamma^{(n_1)} r_t^{(n_1)-} + \tilde{\varepsilon}_{t+n_2}. \quad (15.16)$$

We then postulate that leverage effects influence each market component separately and that they appear aggregated at different horizons in the volatility dynamics.

Combining heterogeneity in realized volatility, leverage, and jumps, we construct the *leverage heterogeneous autoregressive with continuous volatility and jumps* (LHAR-CJ) model. As is common in practice, we use three components for the volatility cascade: daily, weekly, and monthly. Hence, the proposed model reads

$$\begin{aligned}\log V_{t+h}^{(h)} &= c + \beta^{(d)} \log C_t + \beta^{(w)} \log C_t^{(5)} + \beta^{(m)} \log C_t^{(22)} \\ &\quad + \alpha^{(d)} \log(1 + J_t) + \alpha^{(w)} \log\left(1 + J_t^{(5)}\right) + \alpha^{(m)} \log\left(1 + J_t^{(22)}\right) \\ &\quad + \gamma^{(d)} r_t^{-} + \gamma^{(w)} r_t^{(5)-} + \gamma^{(m)} r_t^{(22)-} + \varepsilon_{t+h}^{(h)}. \end{aligned} \quad (15.17)$$

Model (Eq. 15.17) nests the other models introduced in this chapter. When $\alpha^{(d,w,m)} = \gamma^{(d,w,m)} = 0$ and $C_t = V_t$, the model reduces to the HAR model (Eq. 15.5). When $\gamma^{(d,w,m)} = 0$, we get the HAR-CJ model (Eq. 15.15).

Model (Eq. 15.17) can be estimated by OLS with the Newey–West covariance correction for serial correlation. In order to make multiperiod predictions, we will estimate the model considering the aggregated dependent variable $\log V_{t+h}^{(h)}$ with h ranging from 1 to 22, that is, from 1 day to 1 month.

15.4.3 GENERAL NONLINEAR EFFECTS IN VOLATILITY

Another question of interest is to investigate whether the leverage effects introduced in the previous section are the only relevant nonlinear (in that case asymmetric) behaviors present in the realized volatility dynamics in response to past shocks in the market and, more in general, in the whole (macro)economy. In fact, in the last 5 years, several empirical studies published in the literature applied different (parametric and nonparametric) methodologies to the problem of estimating and forecasting realized volatilities, covariances, and correlation dynamics. These showed that they are subject to structural breaks and regime switches driven by shocks of a different nature (see, among others, McAleer and Medeiros (2008a), Scharth and Medeiros (2009), and Audrino and Corsi (2010)).

To investigate this, we generalize the LHAR-CJ model introduced in Equation 15.17 to estimate leverage effects. We propose a tree-structured local HAR-CJ model (Tree HAR-CJ), which is able to take into account both long-memory and possible general nonlinear effects in the (log-) realized volatility dynamics. Tree-structured models belong to the class of threshold regime models, where regimes are characterized by some threshold for the relevant predictor variables. The class of tree-structured GARCH models was introduced by Audrino and Bühlmann (2001) in the financial volatility literature, and was recently generalized to capture simultaneous regime shifts in the first- and second-conditional moment dynamics of returns series (Audrino and Trojani (2006)). The proposed model reads

$$\log \mathrm{V}_{t+h}^{(h)} = \mathbf{E}_t[\log \mathrm{V}_{t+h}^{(h)}] + \varepsilon_{t+h}^{(h)}, \tag{15.18}$$

where $\mathbf{E}_t[\cdot]$ denotes (as usual) the conditional expectation given the information up to time t. The conditional dynamics of the realized (log-) volatilities are given by

$$\begin{aligned} \mathbb{E}_t[\log \mathrm{V}_{t+h}^{(h)}] = \sum_{j=1}^{k} \Big[& c_j + \beta_j^{(d)} \log \mathbf{C}_t + \beta_j^{(w)} \log \mathbf{C}_t^{(5)} + \beta_j^{(m)} \log \mathbf{C}_t^{(22)} \\ & + \alpha_j^{(d)} \log(1+\mathsf{J}_t) + \alpha_j^{(w)} \log(1+\mathsf{J}_t^{(5)}) + \alpha_j^{(m)} \log\left(1+\mathsf{J}_t^{(22)}\right) \\ & + \gamma_j^{(d)} r_t + \gamma_j^{(w)} r_t^{(5)} + \gamma_j^{(m)} r_t^{(22)} \Big] I_{[\mathbf{X}_t^{\text{pred}} \in \mathcal{R}_j]}, \end{aligned} \tag{15.19}$$

where $\theta = (c_j, \alpha_j^{(d,w,m)}, \beta_j^{(d,w,m)}, \gamma_j^{(d,w,m)}, j = 1, \ldots, k)$ is a parameter vector that parameterizes the local HAR-CJ dynamics in the different regimes, k is the number of regimes (endogenously estimated from the data), and $I_{[\cdot]}$ is the identity function that defines regime shifts.[7]

The regimes are characterized by partition cells $\mathcal{R}_j$ of the relevant predictor space G of $\mathbf{X}_t^{\text{pred}}$:

$$G = \bigcup_{j=1}^{k} \mathcal{R}_j, \mathcal{R}_i \cap \mathcal{R}_j = \emptyset (i \neq j).$$

For modeling (log-)realized volatilities, the relevant predictor variables in $\mathbf{X}_t^{\text{pred}}$ are past-lagged realized volatilities (considering the estimated ones as well as the continuous and the jump parts alone) and past-lagged returns of the underlying instrument under investigation to allow explicitly for leverage effects. In taking volatility cascades into account, all such predictor variables are considered at three different time horizons: daily, weekly, and monthly. We also consider time as an additional predictor variable to investigate the relevance of structural breaks in time.[8]

[7]The drastic 0-1 rule to define regime switches can be relaxed to allow for more smooth regime transitions using, for example, a logistic function instead of the identity function (McAleer and Medeiros, 2008a).

[8]The predictor set can be easily expanded to incorporate information included in any other relevant (endogenous or exogenous) explanatory variable.

To completely specify the conditional dynamics given in Equation 15.19 of the realized volatilities, we determine the shape of the partition cells $\mathcal{R}_j$, which are admissible in the Tree HAR-CJ model. Similar to the standard classification and regression tree (CART) procedure (Breiman et al., 1984), the only restriction we impose is that regimes must be characterized by (possibly high dimensional) rectangular cells of the predictor space, with edges determined by thresholds on the predictor variables. Such partition cells are practically constructed using the idea of binary trees. Introducing this restriction has two major advantages: it allows a clear interpretation of the regimes in terms of relevant predictor variables and it also allows an estimation of the model using large-dimensional predictor spaces G.

The Tree HAR-CJ model introduced above can be estimated for any fixed sequence of partition cells using quasi-maximum likelihood (QML). The choice of the best partition cells (i.e., splitting variables and threshold values) involves a model choice procedure for nonnested hypotheses. Similar to CART, the model selection of the splitting variables and threshold values can be performed using the idea of binary trees (for all details, see Audrino and Trojani (2006), Section 2.3 and Appendix A). Within any data-determined tree structure, the best model is selected using information criteria or a more formal sequence of statistical tests to circumvent identification problems (McAleer and Medeiros, 2008a).

15.5 Multivariate Models

We now turn to a multivariate setting, in which an $\mathbb{R}^N$-valued stochastic process X_t evolves over time according to the dynamics:

$$dX_t = \mu_t dt + \Sigma_t dW_t + dJ_t$$

where μ_t is an $\mathbb{R}^N$-valued predictable process, Σ_t is an $\mathbb{R}^{N\times N}$-valued cádlág process, $W_1, \ldots, W_N$ is an N-dimensional Brownian motion, and dJ_t is an $\mathbb{R}^N$-valued jump process. Modeling and forecasting asset returns (conditional) covariance matrix Σ_t is pivotal to many prominent financial problems such as asset allocation, risk management, and option pricing. However, the multivariate extensions of the realized volatility approach pose a series of difficult challenges that are still the subject of active research.

First, in addition to the common microstructure effect biasing realized volatility measures (i.e., bid-ask spread, price discreteness, etc.), the so-called nonsynchronous trading effect (Lo and MacKinlay, 1990) strongly affects the estimation of the realized covariance and correlation measures. In fact, since the sampling from the underlying stochastic process is different for different assets, assuming that two time series are sampled simultaneously when, indeed, the sampling is nonsynchronous gives rise to the nonsynchronous trading effect. As a result, standard covariance and correlation measures constructed by imposing an artificially regularly spaced time series of high frequency data will possess a bias toward 0, which increases as the sampling frequency increases.[9] This effect of a consistent drop of the absolute value of correlations when increasing the sampling frequency was first reported by Epps (1979) and hence called "the Epps effect." To solve this problem, various approaches have been proposed in the literature: incorporate lead and lag cross returns in the estimator (Scholes and Williams 1977; Cohen et al., 1983; Bollerslev and Zhang 2003; Bandi and Russell, 2005), avoid any synchronization by directly using tick-by-tick data (De Jong and Nijman, 1997; Hayashi and Yoshidam, 2005; Griffin and Oomen, 2011; Palandri, 2006; Sheppard, 2006; Voev and Lunde, 2007; Corsi and Audrino, 2008), multivariate realized kernel (Barndorff-Nielsen et al., 2010), and the multivariate Fourier method (Renò, 2003; Mancino and Sanfelici, 2010). Given the high level of persistence present in both realized covariances and correlations, the HAR model has also been employed to model the univariate time series dynamics of realized correlations as in Audrino and Corsi (2010).

Second, when realized volatility and covariance measures apply any kind of correction for microstructure effects, the resulting variance–covariance matrix is not guaranteed to be positive semidefinite (psd). Exceptions are the multivariate realized kernel with refresh time of Barndorff-Nielsen et al. (2010) and the multivariate Fourier method of Mancino and Sanfelici (2010). In both cases, however, the frequency at which all the realized variance–covariance estimates are computed is dictated by the asset having the lowest liquidity, hence discarding, in practice, a considerable amount of information especially for the most liquid assets.

Third, in order to have a valid multivariate forecasting model, it is necessary to construct a dynamic specification for the stochastic process of the realized covariance matrix that produces symmetric and psd covariance matrix predictions. In the still relatively scarce but growing literature on multivariate modeling of realized volatilities, three types of approaches have been proposed thus far: modeling the Cholesky factorization of Σ (Chiriac and Voev, 2010), its matrix-log transformation (Bauer and Vorkink, 2011), and directly modeling the dynamics of Σ as a Wishart autoregressive model (WAR) (Bonato et al., 2009) and Jin and Maheu, 2010).

Fourth, as with all other types of multivariate models, the multivariate modeling of realized volatilities is prone to the curse of dimensionality in the number of parameters of the model. This problem is made particularly severe by the high persistence of the variance–covariance processes, which requires consideration of a large number of variance–covariance elements in the conditioning set. To precisely deal with this problem, the HAR modeling approach has also been adopted in the multivariate framework and, because of its simplicity, is often preferred to multivariate long-memory models.

[9] This is because, in addition to the problem of 0 returns, any difference in the time stamps between the last ticks for the two assets in each regularly spaced interval will correspond to a portion of the cross product returns that will not be accounted for in the computation of the covariance. This is itself due to the fact that the returns corresponding to this time difference will be ascribed to two different time intervals and hence no longer matched in the cross product summation.

For instance, after decomposing the realized covariance matrix into Cholesky factors P_t, where

$$P_t'P_t = \Sigma_t,$$

Chiriac and Voev (2010) apply both a vector fractionally integrated model (where the same fractional difference parameter is imposed) and an HAR specification with scalar coefficients to the vector of the lower triangular elements of the Cholesky factorization (i.e., to $U_t = vech(P_t)$). In their HAR specification, they also include the biweekly frequency, in addition to the commonly used daily, weekly, and monthly frequencies. The authors find that, in comparison with the more involved vector fractionally integrated model, "the HAR specification shows very good forecasting ability".[10]

For Σ_t, Bauer and Vorkink (2011) chose the bipower covariance of Barndorff-Nielsen and Shephard (2005), but the same principle can be applied to any other covariance estimator. Then, they apply a multivariate extension of the HAR-RV model to the principal components of $\text{logm}(\Sigma_t)$.[11] They also include negative past returns to model asymmetric responses and other prediction variables that have been shown to forecast stock returns (such as interest rates, dividend yields, and credit spreads). In their empirical application, they find that "lagged principal components of realized weekly and monthly bipower covariation have a strong predictive power" on the covariance matrix dynamics of size-sorted stock returns.

Bonato et al. (2009) propose capturing the persistence properties in the realized variances and covariances with a Wishart-based generalization of the HAR model. The HAR structure is then obtained by direct temporal aggregation of the daily covariance matrices over different window lengths. The authors propose a restricted parametrization of their Wishart HAR-type model that is able to deal with large asset cross-sectional dimensions. In a four-dimensional application using two US treasury bills and two exchange rates, they show that the restricted specification of the model provides results similar to the fully parameterized model for variance forecasting and risk evaluation.

In the same direction, Jin and Maheu (2010) propose a Wishart specification having HAR-type components (i.e., defined as sample averages of past realized covariance matrices). Two types of time-varying Wishart models are considered by the authors: one in which the components affect the scale matrix of the Wishart distribution in a multiplicative way and the second with the components entering in an additive way. Both models are estimated using standard Bayesian techniques

[10]The authors find a slightly superior performance of the fractionally integrated model at a longer horizon. However, this result could be due to the authors' choice to neglect, in the long horizon direct forecast, the forecasting contribution coming from the higher frequency volatility components.

[11]If Σ_t is a $(N \times N)$ psd matrix, we have by the spectral decomposition theorem that $\Sigma_t = E_t \Lambda_t E_t'$, where the columns of the $(N \times N)$ orthonormal matrix E_t correspond to the eigenvectors of Σ_t and Λ_t is a $(N \times N)$ diagonal matrix diagonal elements are equal to the N eigenvalues of Σ_t. Then, the matrix logarithm of Σ_t, denoted $\text{logm}(\Sigma_t)$, is defined by $\text{logm}(\Sigma_t) = E_t \log(\Lambda_t) E_t'$. Recall that the logarithm of a diagonal matrix is a diagonal matrix whose diagonal elements are taken in log.

with Markov Chain Monte Carlo (MCMC) methods for posterior simulation, given that the posterior distribution is unknown. In their empirical analysis on five-assets stock prices, the additive specification showed better performance in terms of density forecasts of returns up to 3 months ahead.

15.6 Applications

The purpose of this section is first to empirically analyze the performance of the LHAR-CJ model (Eq. 15.17) and then investigate the presence of other nonlinear effects in the dynamics of the S&P500 futures volatilities in addition to the leverage effects.

Our data set covers a long time span of almost 20 years of high frequency data for the S&P 500 futures from January 1990 to February 2009, for a total of 4766 daily observations. In order to reduce the impact of microstructure effects, the estimator for the daily volatility V_t is computed with the multiscales DST estimator of Curci and Corsi (2010). The multiscales DST estimator combines the DST orthogonalization of the volatility signal from the microstructure noise with a multiscales estimator similar to that proposed by Zhang (2006)[12] but constructed with a simple regression-based approach.

The (significant) jump component $\mathbf{J}_t$ in Equation 15.13 and the continuous volatility $\mathbf{C}_t$ in Equation 15.14 are computed at the 5-min sampling frequency (corresponding to 84 returns per day). The confidence level α in Equation 15.13 is set to 99.9%. All the quantities of interest are computed on an annualized base.

The results of the estimation of the LHAR-CJ on the S&P500 sample from January 1990 to February 2009, with $h = 1, 5, 10, 22$, are reported in Table 15.1, together with their statistical significance, evaluated with the Newey–West robust t-statistic with 44 lags.

As usual, all the coefficients of the three continuous volatility components are positive and highly significant. We observe that the coefficient measuring the impact of monthly volatility on future daily volatility (i.e., 0.203) is more than twice as big as the one of daily volatility on future monthly volatility (i.e., 0.105). This finding is consistent with the hierarchical asymmetric propagation of the volatility cascade formalized in Section 15.3.

A similar hierarchical structure, although less pronounced, is present in the impact of jumps on future volatility. The daily and weekly jump components remain highly significant and positive especially when modeling realized volatility at short horizons. In addition, their impact declines when the frequency at which RV is modeled declines. The jumps aggregated at the monthly level, however, turn out to be insignificant on the considered data set.

Interestingly, estimation results for model (Eq. 15.17) reveal the strong significance (with the economically expected negative sign) of the negative

[12]A generalization of the two-scales estimator of Zhang et al. (2005) to many realized volatilities computed at different frequencies.

TABLE 15.1 OLS Estimates of the LHAR-CJ Model (Eq. 15.17), for S&P500 Futures from January 1990 to February 2009 (4766 Observations)

Variable	One Day	One Week	Two Weeks	One Month
c	0.765*	0.847*	0.954*	1.096*
	(11.416)	(7.888)	(6.327)	(4.941)
C	0.248*	0.172*	0.132*	0.105*
	(13.169)	(11.720)	(10.182)	(8.215)
$C^{(5)}$	0.317*	0.299*	0.285*	0.243*
	(11.210)	(8.516)	(7.027)	(5.110)
$C^{(22)}$	0.230*	0.315*	0.361*	0.398*
	(8.577)	(7.951)	(6.720)	(5.497)
J	0.016*	0.012*	0.012*	0.010*
	(3.135)	(2.914)	(3.606)	(2.654)
$J^{(5)}$	0.058*	0.055*	0.047*	0.027
	(4.573)	(3.330)	(2.282)	(1.171)
$J^{(22)}$	0.010	0.011	0.008	0.028
	(0.544)	(0.413)	(0.222)	(0.522)
r^-	−0.736*	−0.526*	−0.411*	−0.337*
	(−8.620)	(−10.154)	(−8.226)	(−5.436)
$r^{(5)-}$	−1.070*	−0.685*	−0.739*	−0.644*
	(−4.602)	(−3.054)	(−3.491)	(−2.685)
$r^{(22)-}$	−0.899*	−1.111	−0.985	−0.668
	(−2.116)	(−1.809)	(−1.411)	(−0.778)

The LHAR-CJ model is estimated with $h = 1$ (1 day), $h = 5$ (1 week), $h = 10$ (2 weeks), and $h = 22$ (1 month). The significant jumps are computed using a critical value of $\alpha = 99.9\%$. Reported in parenthesis are t-statistics based on Newey–West correction.

returns at (almost) all frequencies, which unveils the presence of a heterogeneous structure in the leverage effect as well. In fact, the daily volatility is significantly affected not only by the daily negative return of the day before (the well-known leverage effect) but also of the week and of the month before. This result suggests that the market aggregates information at the daily, weekly, and monthly levels and reacts to shocks happening at these three levels/frequencies. Thus, these findings further confirm the views of the heterogeneous market hypothesis.

To evaluate the performance of the LHAR-CJ model, we compare it with the standard HAR (with only heterogeneous volatility) and the HAR-CJ model (with heterogeneous jumps) on the basis of a genuine out-of-sample analysis. For the out-of-sample forecast of V_t on the $[t, t+h]$ interval, we keep the same forecasting horizons (1 day, 1 week, 2 weeks, and 1 month) and reestimate the model at each day t on a moving window of length 2500 days. Table 15.2 reports the out-of-sample forecasts of the different models evaluated on the basis of the

TABLE 15.2 R^2 of Mincer-Zarnowitz Regressions for Out-of-Sample Forecasts for Horizons $h = 1$ (1 Day), $h = 5$ (1 Week), $h = 10$ (2 Weeks), and $h = 22$ (1 Month) of the S&P500 from January 1990 to February 2009 (4766 Observations, the First 2500 Observations Are Used to Initialize the Models

Variable	One Day	One Week	Two Weeks	One Month
HAR	0.8073	0.8351	0.8162	0.7573
HAR-CJ	0.8107	0.8397	0.8188	0.7597
	(1.994)	(1.808)	(0.835)	(0.115)
LHAR-CJ	0.8238	0.8487	0.8279	0.7651
	(4.663)	(2.854)	(2.023)	(1.169)

The forecasting models are the standard HAR, the HAR-CJ, and the LHAR-CJ model. In parentheses is reported the Diebold–Mariano test for the out-of-sample RMSE with respect to the standard HAR model.

R^2 of Mincer–Zarnowitz forecasting regressions and the Diebold–Mariano test for the out-of-sampleroot mean square error (RMSE).[13]

The superiority of the HAR-CJ model over the HAR model is mild, since it has to be ascribed preeminently to days that follow a jump, and thus on a very small sample; conditioning on days following the occurrence of a jump would show a sharper improvement (as shown in Corsi et al. (2010)). However, the superiority of the LHAR-CJ model at all horizons, with respect to the HAR (and the HAR-CJ model), is much stronger, validating the importance of including both the heterogeneous leverage effects and jumps in the forecasting model.

In the second part of our empirical analysis, we estimate the Tree HAR-CJ model introduced in Equation 15.19 to investigate whether additional nonlinear effects are present in the dynamics of the S&P500 futures volatilities on the top of the leverage effect and whether the explicit modeling of structural breaks and regime shifts is able to improve the accuracy of the estimates and forecasts. To simplify the interpretations and reduce the number of parameters in the model, we assume that the cascade is present only in the volatility continuous component C_t (i.e., we set the parameters $\alpha_j^{(w,m)}$ and $\gamma_j^{(w,m)}$, $j = 1, \ldots, k$, to 0). Estimated coefficients, as well as the estimated regimes, are reported in Table 15.3 for $h = 1$. Classical model-based bootstrapped standard errors are given in parentheses.

Table 15.3 shows that almost all coefficients in the local dynamics of realized volatilities are highly significant, with a couple of interesting exceptions. As discussed previously, the leverage effect is found to be the most important asymmetry and yields the first binary split in the procedure. The optimal threshold is found to be around 0, highlighting the different reaction of realized volatilities to past positive and negative S&P 500 returns. A second relevant nonlinear behavior of realized volatility dynamics is found in response to past

[13] Diebold–Mariano test should be applied with care when competing models are nested; however, Giacomini and White (2006) showed that if the window size is bounded (e.g., computed over a fixed moving window as in our setting) the test is still valid.

TABLE 15.3 Tree HAR-CJ Estimated Parameters and Regimes for the S&P 500 Realized (log-) Volatilities with $h = 1$

Regime Structure	Local Parameters					
$\mathcal{R}_j$	c_j	$\alpha_j^{(d)}$	$\beta_j^{(d)}$	$\beta_j^{(w)}$	$\beta_j^{(m)}$	$\gamma_j^{(d)}$
$r_t \leq 0.05$,	0.658	0.057	0.186	0.406	0.258	−0.198
$\log C_t \leq 5.34$	(0.041)	(0.012)	(0.035)	(0.043)	(0.037)	(0.025)
$r_t \leq 0.05$,	0.563	−0.010	0.392	0.418	0.078	−0.133
$\log C_t > 5.34$	(0.030)	(0.013)	(0.038)	(0.042)	(0.039)	(0.014)
$r_t > 0.05$	0.185	0.060	0.326	0.396	0.234	−0.006
	(0.052)	(0.008)	(0.027)	(0.040)	(0.030)	(0.012)

The sample period is from January 1990 to February 2009, for a total of 4766 daily observations. r_t and $\log C_t$ denote the past-lagged daily S&P 500 return and past-lagged daily (log-) continuous components of the realized volatility, respectively. Model-based bootstrap standard errors computed using 1000 replications are given in parentheses.

low and moderate versus high (continuous part) volatilities when past S&P 500 returns are negative. In fact, the threshold value $d_2 = 5.34$ corresponds to the 70% quantile of the estimated $\log C_t$ series.

In these three regimes, local volatility dynamics show significant differences. In particular, it is worth mentioning the following two results: first, past-lagged S&P 500 returns are significant only in the regimes where they are negative, yielding to an increase in the realized volatilities. When past-lagged S&P 500 returns are positive (last regime), their impact in estimating future volatility dynamics is negligible. Second, the impact of jumps highly changes depending on the regime in which they occur: it is positive and significant in regimes characterized by (somehow) stable financial markets (regimes 1 and 3), yielding to an increase of realized volatility. By contrast, in times of market turbulence (measured by past negative returns and high past volatilities), jumps are found to have no particular impact in driving future realized volatility dynamics. These interesting results confirm and extend previous empirical findings shown in this section.

Similarly to what has been shown above for the LHAR-CJ model, in a preliminary series of forecasting experiments for h equal to 1, the Tree HAR-CJ model has been found to be able to significantly improve the out-of-sample performance of the classical HAR and HAR-CJ models. A more detailed and complete investigation of how the introduction of regimes (threshold-based or of a Markovian type) may improve predictions in a general HAR setting is left for the future.

15.7 Conclusion

By projecting a dynamic process on its own past values aggregated over different time horizons, the HAR model is a general and flexible approach to fit the autocorrelation function of any persistent process in a very simple and tractable way. In this chapter, we have briefly surveyed the nature, construction, and properties of the HAR class of models for realized volatility estimation and prediction. We discussed some of the extensions of the standard HAR model that have been recently proposed to explicitly take into account the predictive power of jumps, leverage effects, and other nonlinearities (i.e., structural breaks and regime switches driven by the different sources acting on the financial market) for the time-varying dynamics of realized volatilities. We also reviewed some recent studies generalizing the HAR model for predicting univariate realized volatilities to the multivariate setting of realized covariance matrices. This is a fast-growing field and the list of references will no doubt need updating in the near future.

In our review of the extant literature on HAR models, a number of topics stand out as possible avenues for future research. The most obvious, and perhaps difficult, is to generalize the univariate flexible HAR model with jumps, leverage effects, and other nonlinear behaviors due to regime changes to the multivariate context. Existing models do not take these effects into account and are not well designed to deal with (possibly) high dimensional realized covariance matrices. What is needed are flexible yet parsimonious multivariate HAR-type extensions that remain computationally feasible in large dimensions. This task may be accomplished using recent techniques coming from the computational statistics community, similar to what was done 10 years ago in Audrino and Bühlmann (2003) for the estimation of a flexible volatility matrix in a multivariate GARCH setting.

CHAPTER SIXTEEN

Forecasting Volatility with MIDAS

ERIC GHYSELS and ROSSEN VALKANOV

16.1 Introduction

We focus on the issues pertaining to mixed frequencies that arise typically because we would like to consider multistep volatility forecasts while maintaining information in high frequency data. For example, when we forecast daily volatility, we want to preserve the information in the intradaily data without computing daily aggregates such as realized volatility (RV). Likewise, when we focus on, say, weekly or monthly volatility forecasts, we want to use daily returns or daily RV measures.

The focus on multistep forecasting is natural even if we do not consider the case of using intradaily returns for the purpose of daily volatility forecasts as it features prominently in the context of Value-at-Risk (VaR) within the risk management literature. In the context of forecasting the 10-day VaR, required by the Basle accord, using daily or even intradaily information, MIDAS (mixed data sampling) models can be used to directly produce multistep forecasts.

Econometric methods involving data sampled at different frequencies have been considered in recent work by Ghysels et al. (2005) in a likelihood-based setting and by Ghysels et al. (2002), Ghysels et al. (2006b), and Andreou et al. (2010a) using regression-based methods. The mixed frequency setting has been labeled MIDAS, meaning Mi(xed) Da(ta) S(ampling).

Handbook of Volatility Models and Their Applications, First Edition.
Edited by Luc Bauwens, Christian Hafner, and Sebastien Laurent.

The original work on MIDAS focused on volatility predictions, see Alper et al. (2008), Aragó and Salvador (2010), Chen and Ghysels (2010), Engle et al. (2008), Brown and Ferreira (2003), Chen et al. (2009a, 2009b), Clements et al. (2008), Corsi (2009), Forsberg and Ghysels (2007), Ghysels et al. (2005, 2006b), Ghysels and Sinko (2006, 2011), Ghysels et al. (2008), León et al. (2007), among others.

Armesto et al. (2010) provide a user-friendly introduction to MIDAS regressions. A Matlab Toolbox for MIDAS regressions is also available (Sinko et al., 2010). A topic not covered, since we deal with volatility, but noteworthy is the fact that MIDAS regressions can be related to Kalman filters and state space models (Bai et al., 2009).

In the first section, we cover MIDAS regressions in the context of volatility forecasting. The second section covers likelihood-based models, which means we cover MIDAS as it relates to ARCH (autoregressive conditional heteroskedasticity)-type models. The final section covers multivariate extensions.

16.2 MIDAS Regression Models and Volatility Forecasting

In order to analyze the role of MIDAS in forecasting volatility, let us introduce the relevant notation. Let $V_{t+1,t}$ be a measure of volatility in the next period. We focus on predicting future conditional variance, measured as increments in quadratic variation (or its log transformation), due to the large body of existing recent literature on this subject. The increments in the quadratic variation of the return process, $Q_{t+1,t}$, is not observed directly but can be measured with some discretization error. One such measure would be the sum of (future) m intradaily squared returns, namely, $\sum_{j=1}^{m}[r_{j,t}]^2$, which we will denote by $\mathrm{RV}_{t+1,t}$. We can also consider multiple periods, which will be denoted by $\mathrm{RV}_{t+h,t}$, for horizon h. Note that the case where no intradaily data is available corresponds to $m = 1$ and RV becomes a daily squared return. In the first subsection, we cover MIDAS regressions, followed by the subsection that elaborates on direct versus iterated volatility forecasting. The next subsection discusses variations on the theme of MIDAS regressions, and the final subsection deals with microstructure noise and MIDAS regressions.

16.2.1 MIDAS REGRESSIONS

We start with MIDAS regressions involving daily regressors for predictions at horizon h :

$$\mathrm{RV}_{t+h,t} = \mu + \phi \sum_{k=0}^{k^{\max}} w(k, \theta) X_{t-k} + \varepsilon_t. \tag{16.1}$$

The volatility specification (Eq. 16.1) has a number of important features.

MIDAS regressions typically do *not* exploit an autoregressive scheme, so that X_{t-k} is not necessarily related to lags of the left-hand side variable. Instead, MIDAS regressions are first and foremost regressions and therefore the selection of X_{t-k} amounts to choosing the best predictor of future quadratic variation from the set of several possible measures of past fluctuations in returns. Examples of X_{t-k} are past daily squared returns (that correspond to the ARCH-type of models with some parameter restrictions, Engle (1982a) and Bollerslev (1986)), absolute daily returns (that relate to the specifications of (Ding et al., 1993), realized daily volatility (Andersen et al., 2010), realized daily power of (Barndorff-Nielsen and Shephard, 2003; Barndorff-Nielsen et al., 2004), and daily range (Alizadeh et al., 2002; Gallant et al. 1999).

Since all of the regressors are used within a framework with the same number of parameters and the same maximum number of lags, the results from MIDAS regressions are directly comparable. Moreover, MIDAS regressions can also be extended to study the joint forecasting power of the regressors. The weight function or the polynomial lag parameters are parameterized via Almon, Exponential Almon, Beta, linear step-functions (see below), etc., see Ghysels et al. (2006), and they are especially relevant in estimating a persistent process parsimoniously, such as volatility, where distant X_{t-k} are likely to have an impact on current volatility. In addition, the parameterization allows us to compare MIDAS regressions at different frequencies as the number of parameters to estimate will be the same even though the weights on the data and the forecasting capabilities might differ across horizons. Most importantly, one does not have to adjust measures of fit for the number of parameters; and in most situations with one predictor, one has a MIDAS model with either one or two parameters determining the pattern of the weights. Note also that in the above equation, we specify a slope coefficient as the weights are normalized to add up to 1. Such a restriction will not always be used in the sequel. The selection of $k^{\max}$ can be done conservatively (by taking a large value) and letting the weights die out as determined by the parameter estimation. The only cost to taking large $k^{\max}$ is the loss of initial data in the sample, which should be inconsequential in large samples.

Related to the MIDAS volatility regression is the heterogeneous autoregressive realized volatility (HAR-RV) regressions proposed by Corsi (2009). The HAR-RV model is given by

$$\mathrm{RV}_{t+1,t} = \mu + \beta^{\mathrm{D}}\mathrm{RV}_t^{\mathrm{D}} + \beta^{\mathrm{W}}\mathrm{RV}_t^{\mathrm{W}} + \beta^{\mathrm{M}}\mathrm{RV}_t^{\mathrm{M}} + \varepsilon_{t+1}, \tag{16.2}$$

which has a simple linear prediction regression using RV over heterogeneous interval sizes, daily (D), weekly (W), and monthly (M). As noted by Andersen et al. (2007) (footnote 16) and Corsi (2009) (discussion, p. 181), the above equation is in a sense a MIDAS regression with step-functions (in the terminology of Ghysels et al. (2006)). In this regard, the HAR-RV can be related to the MIDAS-RV in Equation 16.1 of Ghysels et al. (2006b) and Forsberg and Ghysels (2007), using different weight functions such as the Beta, exponential Almon, or step-functions and different regressors not just autoregressive with mixed frequencies. Note also that both models exclude the jump component of quadratic variation. Simulation results reported in Forsberg and Ghysels (2007) also show that the difference between HAR and MIDAS models is very small for RV. For other regressors, such as the realized absolute variance, the MIDAS model performs slightly better.

It should also be noted that one can add lagged RV to the above specifications, for example, for $h = 1$ and using intradaily data for day t, denoted $X_{j,t}$ assuming we pick only 1 day of lags:

$$\mathrm{RV}_{t+1,t} = \mu + \alpha \mathrm{RV}_{t,t-1} + \phi \sum_{k=1}^{m} w(k, \theta) X_{j,t} + \varepsilon_t. \tag{16.3}$$

The above equation is reminiscent of the ADL-MIDAS regression models used extensively in the context of macro forecasting by Andreou et al. (2010b). The above equation will also relate to the HYBRID GARCH (generalized autoregressive conditional heteroskedasticity) class of models discussed later.

16.2.2 DIRECT VERSUS ITERATED VOLATILITY FORECASTING

The volatility measure on the left-hand side and the predictors on the right-hand side are sampled at different frequencies. As a result, the volatility in Equation 16.1 can be measured at different horizons (e.g., daily, weekly, and monthly frequencies), whereas the forecasting variables X_{t-k} are available at daily or higher frequencies. Thus, this specification allows us not only to forecast volatility with data sampled at different frequencies but also to compare such forecasts and ultimately evaluate empirically the continuous asymptotic arguments. In addition, Equation 16.1 provides a method to investigate whether the use of high frequency data necessarily leads to better volatility forecasts at various horizons.

The existent literature has placed most of the emphasis on the accuracy of one-period-ahead forecasts (Engle, 1982a; Bollerslev, 1986; Andersen and Bollerslev, 1998; Hansen and Lunde, 2005a). Long-horizon volatility forecasts have received significantly less attention. Yet, financial decisions related to risk management, portfolio choice, and regulatory supervision are often based on multiperiod-ahead volatility forecasts. The preeminent long-horizon volatility forecasting approach is to scale the one-period-ahead forecasts by $\sqrt{k}$, where k is the horizon of interest. Christoffersen and Diebold (2000) and others have shown that this "scaling" approach leads to poor volatility forecasts at horizons as short as 10 days. The lack of a comprehensive and rigorous treatment of multiperiod volatility forecasts is linked to the more general theoretical difficulty to characterize the trade-off between bias and estimation that exists in multiperiod forecasts (Findley, 1983, 1985; Lin and Granger, 1994; Clements and Hendry, 1996; Bhanzali, 1999; Chevillon and Hendry, 2005). The paucity of new results on this topic has lead researchers to conclude that, in general, volatility is difficult to forecast at long horizons (Christoffersen and Diebold, 2000; West and Cho, 1995).

In a recent paper, Ghysels et al. (2008) undertake a comprehensive empirical examination of multiperiod volatility forecasting approaches, beyond the simple $\sqrt{k}$-scaling rule. They consider two alternative approaches—direct and iterative—of forming long-horizon forecasts (Marcellino et al. 2006). The "direct" forecasting method consists of estimating a horizon-specific model of the volatility at, say, monthly or quarterly frequency, which can then be used to form direct predictions of volatility over the next month or quarter. An "iterative" forecast obtains by estimating a daily autoregressive volatility forecasting model and then iterate over the daily forecasts for the necessary number of periods to obtain monthly or quarterly predictions of the volatility. In addition to the direct and iterated approaches, Ghysels et al., 2008 consider a third, novel way of long-horizon forecasts, which is based on MIDAS regressions. A MIDAS method uses daily data to produce directly multiperiod volatility forecasts and can thus be viewed as a middle ground between the direct and the iterated approaches. The results of their study suggest that long-horizon volatility is much more predictable than previously suggested at horizons as long as 60 trading days (about 3 months).

The direct and iterated methods that Ghysels et al. (2008) use are based on three volatility models: GARCH (Engle, 1982a; Bollerslev, 1986), autoregressive models of RV (Andersen and Bollerslev, 1998; Andersen et al., 2001, 2003), and integrated volatility. Ghysels et al. (2008) point out that a long-horizon forecast is implicitly a joint decision of choosing the appropriate volatility model and the appropriate forecasting method. A similar distinction between a method and a model has also been made implicitly by Andersen et al. (2003) and, in a different context, by Giacomini and White (2006). The three volatility models that Ghysels et al. (2008) consider in conjunction with the iterated and direct forecasting methods give rise to six different ways to produce long-horizon forecasts. The MIDAS approach, which in essence combines the forecasting model and the long-horizon method into one step, offers a seventh way of producing multiperiod-ahead forecasts of volatility.

To establish the accuracy of the seven long-term forecasts, Ghysels et al. (2008) use a loss function that penalizes deviations of predictions from the ex-post realizations of the volatility (similar to French et al. (1987) and Andersen and Bollerslev (1998)) and a test for predictive accuracy that allows them to compare the statistical significance of competing forecasts. They use the mean square forecasting error (MSFE) as one loss function, because of its consistency property, that is, it delivers the same forecast ranking with the proxy as it would with the true volatility (Hansen and Lunde 2006a; Patton 2011). They use a VaR as an alternative metric of forecast accuracy. To test the statistical significance in predictive power, Ghysels et al. (2008) use two tests. The first one, proposed by West (1996), takes into account the parameter uncertainty, which is of particular concern in the volatility forecasting literature. The second test, proposed by Giacomini and White (2006), can be viewed as a generalization or a conditional version of the West (1996) test. Rather than comparing the difference in average performance, Giacomini and White (2006) consider the conditional expectation of the difference across forecasting models. This conditioning approach allows not only for parameter uncertainty (as in West (1996)) but also uncertainty in a number of implicit choices made by the researcher when formulating a forecast, such as what data to use, the windows of in-sample estimation period, the length of the out-of-sample forecast, among others.

Using the above setup, Ghysels et al. (2008) investigate whether multihorizon forecasts of the volatility of US stock market returns are more accurate than the naive but widely used scaling approach. They consider volatility forecasts of the US market portfolio returns as well as of 5 size, 5 book-to-market, and 10 industry portfolio returns. They find that the scaling-up method performs poorly relative to the other methods for all portfolios and horizons. This result is consistent with Diebold et al. (1997) and other papers, who have documented the poor performance of this approach. More surprisingly, however, they find that the direct method does not fair much better. At horizon longer than 10 days ahead, the approach of scaling one-period-ahead forecasts performs significantly better than the direct method. Hence, if the direct method were the only alternative to the scaling approach, and since scaling is a poor forecaster of future volatility, one might come to the hasty conclusion that the volatility is hard to forecast at long horizons by any model.

Ghysels et al. (2008) find that for the volatility of the market portfolio, iterated and MIDAS forecasts perform significantly better than the scaling and the direct approaches. At relatively short horizons of 5- to 10-days ahead, the iterated forecasts are quite accurate. However, at horizons of 10 days ahead and higher, MIDAS forecasts have a significantly lower MSFE relative to the other forecasts. At horizons of 30- and 60-days ahead, the MSFE of MIDAS is more than 20% lower than that of the next best forecast. These differences are statistically significant at the 1% level according to the West (1996) and Giacomini and White (2006) tests. Hence, they find that suitable MIDAS models produce multiperiod volatility forecasts that are significantly better than other widely used methods.

Ghysels et al. (2008) also link predictive accuracy to portfolio characteristics. They note that the superior performance of MIDAS in multiperiod forecasts is also observed in predicting the volatility of the size, book-to-market, and industry portfolios. Similar to the market volatility results, the relative precision of the MIDAS forecasts improves with the horizon. At horizons of 10-periods and higher, the MIDAS forecasts of 8 out of the 10 size and book-to-market portfolios dominate the iterated and direct approaches. At horizons of 30-periods and higher, the MIDAS has the smallest MSFEs amongst all forecasting methods for all 10 portfolios. They observe that the volatility of the size and book-to-market portfolios is significantly less predictable than that of the entire market. Also, the predictability of the volatility increases with the size of the portfolio. The volatility of the largest-cap stocks is the most predictable, albeit still less forecastable than the market's. They fail to observe such a discernible pattern for the book-to-market portfolios.

From the MSFE results, it might be tempting to generalize that the MIDAS forecasts are more accurate than the iterated forecasts, which in turn dominate the direct and scaling-rule approaches. However, Ghysels et al. (2008) caution that a general ranking of forecast accuracy is difficult, since it is ultimately predicated on the loss function and application at hand. As an illustration, they note that when they use the VaR as a measure of forecast accuracy, then the direct method not only dominates the iterated method but for most portfolio returns, its coverage is close to that of the MIDAS model. Overall, however, they find that MIDAS forecasts strike a good balance between bias and estimation efficiency.

16.2.3 VARIATIONS ON THE THEME OF MIDAS REGRESSIONS

The MIDAS approach can also be used to study various other interesting aspects of forecasting volatility. Chen and Ghysels (2010) provide a novel method to analyze the impact of news on forecasting volatility. The following semiparametric (SP) regression model is proposed to predict future RV with past high frequency returns:

$$\mathrm{RV}_{t+1,t} = \psi_0 + \sum_{j=1}^{\tau}\sum_{i=1}^{m} \psi_{i,j}(\theta)\mathrm{NIC}(r_{j,t}) + \varepsilon_{t+1}, \tag{16.4}$$

where $\psi_{i,j}(\theta)$ is a polynomial lag structure parameterized by θ, NIC(.) is the news impact curve (NIC) and $r_{t/m}$ is the log-asset price difference (return) over some short-time interval i of length m on day t. Note $i = 1, \ldots, m$ of intervals on day t.

The regression model in Equation 16.4 shows that each intradaily return has an impact on future volatility measured by $\mathrm{NIC}(r_{j,t}^{\mathrm{ID}})$ and fading away through time with weights characterized by $\psi_{i,j}(\theta)$. One can consider Equation 16.4 as the SP model that nests a number of volatility forecasting models and, in particular, the benchmark RV forecasting equation below:

$$\mathrm{RV}_{t+1,t} = \psi_0 + \sum_{j=0}^{\tau} \psi_j(\theta)\mathrm{RV}_{t-j,t-j-1} + \varepsilon_{t+1}. \tag{16.5}$$

Equation 16.4 nests Equation 16.5 when we set $\psi_{i,j} \equiv \psi_i \; \forall\, j = 1, \ldots, m$, and $\mathrm{NIC}(r) \equiv r^2$. This nesting emphasizes the role played by both the NIC and the lag polynomial $\psi_{i,j}$.

The reason it is possible to nest the RV AR structure is due to the multiplicative specification for $\psi_{i,j}(\theta) \equiv \psi_j^{\mathrm{D}}(\theta) \times \psi_i^{\mathrm{ID}}(\theta)$, with the parameter θ containing subvectors that determine the two polynomials separately. The polynomial $\psi_j^{\mathrm{D}}(\theta)$ is a daily weighting scheme, similar to $\psi_i(\theta)$ in the regression model appearing in Equation 16.5. The polynomial $\psi_i^{\mathrm{ID}}(\theta)$ relates to the intradaily pattern. With equal intradaily weights, one has the RV measure when NIC is quadratic. Chen and Ghysels (2010) adopt the following specification for the polynomials:

$$\psi_j^{\mathrm{D}}(\theta)\psi_i^{\mathrm{ID}}(\theta) = \beta(j, \tau, \theta_1, \theta_2) \times \beta(i, 1/m, \theta_3, \theta_4), \tag{16.6}$$

where τ and $1/m$ are the daily (D) and intradaily (ID) frequencies, respectively. The restriction is imposed that the intradaily patterns wash out across the entire day, that is, $\sum_i \beta(i, 1/m, \theta_3, \theta_4) = 1$, and also impose without loss of generality, a similar restriction on the daily polynomial, in order to identify a slope coefficient in the regressions.

The multiplicative specification (Eq. 16.6) has several advantages. First, as noted before, it nests the so-called flat aggregation scheme, that is, all intradaily weights are equal, which yields a daily model with RV when the NIC is quadratic. Or more formally, when $\theta_3 = \theta_4 = 1$, and $\text{NIC}(r) = r^2$, one recovers RV-based regression appearing in Equation 16.5. Second, by estimating $\beta(i, 1/m, \theta_3, \theta_4)$, one lets the data decide on the proper aggregation scheme, which is a generic issue pertaining in MIDAS regressions as discussed in Andreou et al. (2010a). Obviously, the intradaily part of the polynomial will pick up how news fades away throughout the day and this, in part, depends on the well-known intradaily seasonal pattern.

Finally, the MIDAS-NIC model can also nest existing parametric specifications of NICs adopted in the ARCH literature, namely, the daily symmetric one when $\text{NIC}(r) = br^2$, the asymmetric GJR-GARCH model when $\text{NIC}(r) = br^2 + (cr^2)\mathbf{1}_{r<0}$ (Glosten et al., 1993) and the asymmetric GARCH model when $\text{NIC}(r) = (b(r-c)^2)$ (Engle, 1990).

16.2.4 MICROSTRUCTURE NOISE AND MIDAS REGRESSIONS

Ghysels and Sinko (2011) study a regression prediction problem with volatility measures that are contaminated by microstructure noise and examine optimal sampling for the purpose of volatility prediction. The analysis is framed in the context of MIDAS regressions with regressors affected by microstructure noise. They consider univariate MIDAS regressions for the prediction performance evaluation and several RV measures. Their general framework also leads us to the study of optimal sampling issues in the context of volatility prediction with microstructure noise.

The topic of their paper has been studied by a variety of authors independently and simultaneously. Garcia and Meddahi (2006) and Ghysels and Sinko (2006) discussed forecasting volatility and microstructure noise. Ghysels et al. (2006) provided further empirical evidence expanding on Ghysels and Sinko (2006). Ait-Sahalia and Mancini (2008) consider a number of stochastic volatility and jump diffusions, including the Heston and log-volatility models, and study the relative performance of the two-scales realized volatility (henceforth TSRV) estimator versus RV estimators. They provide simulation evidence showing that TSRV largely outperforms RV.

Discussions about the impact of microstructure have mostly focused so far on *measurement* and therefore mean squared error and bias of various adjustments. Ghysels and Sinko (2011) instead focus on prediction in a regression format, and therefore can include estimators that are suboptimal in mean square error (MSE) sense, since covariation with the predictor is what matters. Previously, the optimal sampling frequency was studied in terms of *MSE of estimators* in an asymptotic setting (Zhang et al., 2005) and for finite samples (Bandi and Russell,

2010). They derive theoretical results for RV, TSRV, average over subsamples, and Zhou (1996) estimators and study theoretically optimal sampling as well.

Ghysels and Sinko (2011) also conduct an extensive empirical study of forecasting with microstructure noise, using the same data as in Hansen and Lunde (2006b), namely, the 30 Dow Jones industrial average (DJIA), from January 3, 2000 to December 31, 2004. The purpose of the empirical analysis is twofold. First, they verify whether the predictions from the theory hold in actual data samples. They find that is indeed the case. Secondly, they also implement optimal sampling schemes empirically and check the relevance of the theoretical derivations using real data. They distinguish between "conditional" and "unconditional" optimal sampling schemes, as in Bandi and Russell (2006). They find that "conditional" optimal sampling seems to work reasonably well in practice.

16.3 Likelihood-Based Methods

The initial work on MIDAS and volatility involved a likelihood-based on risk-return trade-offs. In the first subsection, we discuss this approach, followed by recent model specifications involving mixture of ARCH-type and MIDAS specifications. These recent extensions are covered in two subsections.

16.3.1 RISK-RETURN TRADE-OFF

The Merton (1973) ICAPM suggests that the conditional expected excess return on the stock market should vary positively with the market's conditional variance:

$$E_t[r_{t+1}] = \mu + \gamma \mathrm{Var}_t[r_{t+1}], \tag{16.7}$$

where γ is the coefficient of relative risk aversion of the representative agent—which should obviously be positive and take plausible values—and, according to the model, μ should be equal to 0. The expectation and the variance of the market excess return are conditional on the information available at the beginning of the return period, time t.

Baillie and DeGennaro (1990), French et al. (1987), Chou (1992), and Campbell and Hentschel (1992) do find a positive albeit mostly insignificant relation between the conditional variance and the conditional expected return. In contrast, Campbell (1987) and Nelson (1991b) find a significantly negative relation. Glosten et al. (1993), Harvey (2001), and Turner et al. (1989) find both a positive and a negative relation depending on the method used. The main difficulty in testing the ICAPM relation is that the conditional variance of the market is not observable and must be filtered from past returns. The conflicting findings of the above studies are mostly due to differences in the approach to modeling the conditional variance.

Ghysels et al. (2005) take a different look at the risk-return trade-off with a MIDAS forecast of the monthly variance specified as a weighted average of lagged daily squared returns and estimated via a QMLE—similar to the GARCH-in-mean approaches of Engle et al. (1987) and Glosten et al. (1993). Namely, they estimate the coefficients of the conditional variance process jointly with μ and γ from the expected return equation (Eq. 16.7) with quasi-maximum likelihood. Hence, this approach is very different from the MIDAS regressions discussed in the previous section. The similarity, however, is that in both MIDAS regressions and in the likelihood-based MIDAS, one uses the same type of parsimoniously specified lag-polynomials. In particular, Ghysels et al. (2005) use an exponential Almon lag specification.

Using monthly and daily market return data from 1928 to 2000 and, with a MIDAS specification for the conditional variance, Ghysels et al. (2005) find a positive and statistically significant relation between risk and return. The estimate of γ is 2.6, which lines up well with economic intuition about a reasonable level of risk aversion. The MIDAS volatility estimator explains about 40% of the variation of realized variance in the subsequent month and its explanatory power compares favorably to that of other models of conditional variance such as GARCH. The estimated weights on the lagged daily squared returns decay slowly, thus capturing the persistence in the conditional variance process. More impressive still is the fact that, in the ICAPM risk-return relation, the MIDAS estimator of conditional variance explains about 2% of the variation of next month's stock market returns (and 5% in the period since 1964). This is quite substantial, given the previous results about forecasting the stock market return. Finally, the above results are qualitatively similar when one splits the sample into two subsamples of approximately equal sizes, 1928–1963 and 1964–2000. These results are obtained when extreme outliers are winsorized.

It should be noted that the ICAPM risk-return relation has also been tested using several variations of GARCH-in-mean models. However, the evidence from that literature is inconclusive and sometimes conflicting. Using simple GARCH models, Ghysels et al. (2005) confirm the findings of French et al. (1987) and Glosten et al. (1993), among others, of a positive but insignificant γ coefficient in the risk-return trade-off. The absence of statistical significance comes both from GARCH's use of *monthly* returns in estimating the conditional variance process. The use of daily data and the flexibility of the MIDAS estimator provides the power needed to find statistical significance in the risk-return trade-off.

A comparison of the time series of conditional variance estimated according to MIDAS, GARCH, and rolling windows reveals that while the three estimators are correlated, there are some differences that affect their ability to forecast returns in the ICAPM relation. Ghysels et al. (2005) find that the MIDAS variance process is more highly correlated with both the GARCH and the rolling windows estimates than these two estimates are with each other. This suggests that MIDAS combines some of the unique information contained in the other two estimators. They also find that MIDAS is particularly successful at forecasting realized variance both in high and low volatility regimes. These features explain the superior performance of MIDAS in finding a positive and significant risk-return relation.

It has long been recognized that volatility tends to react more to negative returns than to positive returns. Nelson (1991b) and Engle and Ng (1993) show that GARCH models that incorporate this asymmetry perform better in forecasting the market variance. However, Glosten et al. (1993) show that when such asymmetric GARCH models are used in testing the risk-return trade-off, the γ coefficient is estimated to be negative (sometimes significantly so). This stands in sharp contrast with the positive and insignificant γ obtained with symmetric GARCH models and remains a puzzle in empirical finance. To investigate this issue, Ghysels et al. (2005) also extend the MIDAS approach to capture asymmetries in the dynamics of conditional variance by allowing lagged positive and negative daily squared returns to have different weights in the estimator. Contrary to the asymmetric GARCH results, they still find a large positive estimate of γ that is statistically significant. In particular, they find that what matters for the tests of the risk-return trade-off is not so much the asymmetry in the conditional variance process but rather its persistence. In this respect, asymmetric GARCH and asymmetric MIDAS models prove to be very different. Consistent with the GARCH literature, negative shocks have a larger immediate impact on the MIDAS conditional variance estimator than do positive shocks. However, Ghysels et al. (2005) find that the impact of negative returns on variance is only temporary and lasts no more than 1 month. Such evidence is also consistent with the findings reported in Andersen et al. (2007) showing that (negative?) jumps have no or little impact on future volatility. Positive returns, on the other hand, have an extremely persistent impact on the variance process. In other words, while short-term fluctuations in the conditional variance are mostly due to negative shocks, the persistence of the variance process is primarily driven by positive shocks. This is an intriguing finding about the dynamics of the variance process. Although asymmetric GARCH models allow for a different response of the conditional variance to positive and negative shocks, they constrain the persistence of both types of shocks to be the same. Since the asymmetric GARCH models "load" heavily on negative shocks and these have little persistence, the estimated conditional variance process shows little to no persistence.

16.3.2 HYBRID GARCH MODELS

The volatility specification in Ghysels et al. (2005) involves a single polynomial applied to daily data. Similar to the specification of the MIDAS regression (Eq. 16.3), one could think of introducing lagged volatilities. We do not operate in a regression format, so this approach would be similar to the specification of a GARCH model.

This insight has recently been pursued by Chen et al. (2009a) and (2009b). A key ingredient of conditional volatility models is that more weight is attached to the most recent returns (i.e., information). In the case of the original ARCH model (Engle, 1982a), that means that the most recent (daily) squared returns have more weight when predicting future (daily) conditional volatility. While intradaily data are used to construct RV, prediction models put more weight on recent (daily) RV, but despite the use of intradaily data—do not differentiate among intradaily returns. If volatility is a persistent process, it would be natural to weight intradaily data differently, as pointed out recently by

Malliavin and Mancino (2009). This is one example of the class of models Chen et al. (2009b), the so-called HYBRID GARCH models. They are a unifying framework, based on a generic GARCH-type model, which addresses the issue of volatility forecasting involving forecast horizons of a different frequency than the information set. Hence, Chen et al. (2009b) propose a class of GARCH models that can handle volatility forecasts over the next 5 business days and use past daily data, or tomorrow's expected volatility while using intradaily returns. The models are called *HYBRID GARCH*, which stands for *h*igh Frequenc*y* data-*b*ased p*r*ojecti*o*n-*d*riven GARCH models as the GARCH dynamics are driven by what Chen et al. (2009b) call HYBRID processes.

Compared to Malliavin and Mancino (2009), they go beyond linear projections—albeit in a discrete time setting. The HYBRID GARCH models do have a connection with continuous time models as well when one restricts attention to linear projections. Chen et al. (2009b) study three broad classes of HYBRID processes: (i) parameter-free processes that are purely data-driven; (ii) structural HYBRIDs, where one assumes some explicit data structure for the high frequency data; and finally (iii) HYBRID filter processes. In case (i), the HYBRID process H_τ does not depend on parameters. The obvious case would be a simple return process such that $V_{\tau+1|\tau}$ is the conditional volatility of the next period. More recently, however, other purely data-driven examples of what we call *generic HYBRID processes* have been suggested. For example, Engle and Gallo (2006), de Vilder and Visser (2008), Visser (2008), and Shephard and Sheppard (2010) suggest the use of (daily) realized volatilities, high–low range or realized kernels or generic realized measures as they are called by Shephard and Sheppard (2010). Structural HYBRID processes appear in the context of temporal aggregation—a topic discussed extensively in the (weak) GARCH literature, see Drost and Nijman (1993) and Drost and Werker (1996), among others. Finally, the HYBRID process $H_\tau \equiv H(\phi, \vec{r}_\tau)$, where $\vec{r}_\tau = (r_{\tau-1+1/m}, r_{\tau-1+2/m}, \ldots, r_{\tau-1/m}, r_\tau)^T$ is $\mathbf{R}^m$–valued random vector, which can involve parameters that are *not* explicitly related to α, β, and γ appearing in Equation 16.8 below. There is no underlying high frequency data DGP that is being assumed, unlike in the structural HYBRID case. One can view this as a GARCH model driven by a filtered high frequency process—where the filter weights—(hyper-)parameterized by ϕ are estimated jointly with the volatility dynamics parameters. A generic HYBRID GARCH model has the following dynamics for volatility:

$$V_{t+1|t} = \alpha + \beta V_{t|t-1} + \gamma H_t, \tag{16.8}$$

where H_t will be called a *HYBRID process*. When H_t is simply a daily squared return, we have the volatility dynamics of a standard daily GARCH(1,1), or H_t a weekly squared return those of a standard weekly GARCH(1,1). However, what would happen if we want to attribute an individual weight to each of the 5 days in a week? In this case, we might consider a process $H_t \equiv \sum_{j=0}^{4} \omega_j r_{t-j/5}^2$, where we use the notation $r_{t-j/5}$ to indicate intraperiod returns—in the this case daily observations of week t (when days spill over into the previous week, we assume $r_{t-j/m} \equiv r_{t-1-(j-5)/m}$). This is an example of a parameter-driven HYBRID process $H_t \equiv H(\phi, \vec{r}_t)$, where $\vec{r}_t = (r_{t-1+1/m}, r_{t-1+2/m}, \ldots, r_{t-1/m}, r_t)^T$ with in this case

$m = 5$. In addition, the weights $(\omega_j(\phi), j = 0, \ldots, m-1)$ are governed by a low dimensional parameter vector ϕ. One can think of at least two possibilities: (i) the weights are treated as additional parameters and estimated as such (with m small this is possible, but not as m gets large), or (ii) anchor the weights ω_j to an underlying daily GARCH(1,1) in which case the parameters α, β, and γ and the weights in ϕ are jointly related to the assumed daily DGP. The discussion so far implicitly relates to many issues we elaborate on next.

The HYBRID process H_t may be purely data-driven and not depend on parameters. The obvious case would be a simple return process such that $V_{t+1|t}$ has the typical GARCH(1,1) dynamics. More recently, however, other purely data-driven examples of what we call *generic HYBRID processes* have been suggested. For example, Engle and Gallo (2006), de Vilder and Visser (2008), Visser (2008), and Shephard and Sheppard (2010), among others, suggest the use of (daily) realized volatilities, high–low range, or realized kernels or generic realized measures. It is important to note that typically parameter-free HYBRID processes do not differentiate intraperiod returns, that is, an equal weighting scheme is supposed—although some kernel-weighting or preaveraging may take place to eliminate microstructure noise.

To study structural HYBRIDs, consider a daily weak GARCH(1,1), as defined by Drost and Nijman (1993), then the implied weekly prediction, using past daily returns is

$$V_{t+1|t} = \alpha_m + \beta_m V_{t|t-1} + \gamma_m \sum_{j=0}^{m-1} \beta_m^{j/m} r_{t-j/m}^2, \quad t \in \mathbf{Z}, \tag{16.9}$$

with $m = 5$, and where α_m, β_m, and γ_m depend on the daily GARCH(1,1) parameters α_1, β_1, and γ_1, respectively. Note that all the parameters are driven by the daily parameters. Therefore, while the HYBRID process is parameter-driven, it is in principle an integral part of the volatility dynamics and $H(\phi, \vec{r}_t)$ in Equation 16.8 does not involve stand-alone parameters ϕ. This will have consequences when we elaborate on the estimation of HYBRID GARCH models. Indeed, the context of temporal aggregation precludes us from using, say standard QMLE methods, a topic that is discussed later.

Finally, consider a HYBRID filtering process. Here, the HYBRID process $H(\phi, \vec{r}_t)$ in Equation 16.8 involves parameters that are *not* explicitly related to α, β, and γ appearing in Equation 16.8. There is no underlying high frequency data DGP that is being assumed, unlike in the structural HYBRID case. One can view this as a GARCH model driven by a filtered high frequency process—where the filter weights—(hyper-)parameterized by ϕ are estimated jointly with the volatility dynamics parameters. The choice of the parameterizations of the HYBRID process weighting scheme is inspired by Chen and Ghysels (2010). The commonly used specifications are exponential, beta, linear, hyperbolic, and geometric weights. This approach has implications too as far as estimation is concerned. Unlike the structural HYBRID case, we can now consider likelihood-based methods, although the regularity conditions required are novel and more involved as those of the usual QMLE approach to GARCH estimation, for instance, in Bollerslev and Wooldridge (1992).

So far we have done the same as Malliavin and Mancino (2009) in terms of the formulation of HYBRID processes in the context of discrete time GARCH dynamics. At this stage, we start to deviate from the linear projection paradigm and continue the logic of GARCH modeling. In light of these findings, we consider HYBRID GARCH models that feature intradaily NICs—similar to the framework of Chen and Ghysels (2010)—except that the latter use a MIDAS regression format. The HYBRID processes are of the following type:

$$H_t(\phi) = \sum_{j=0}^{m-1} \Psi_j(\phi_1)\mathrm{NIC}(\phi_2, r_{t-j/m}), \quad \sum_{j=0}^{m-1} \Psi_j(\phi_1) = 1, \tag{16.10}$$

where $\mathrm{NIC}(\phi_2, \cdot)$ stands for a high frequency data NIC discussed earlier.

Various estimation procedures can be considered—some tailored to specific cases of HYBRID processes. Let us first collect all the parameters of the model appearing in Equation 16.8 in a parameter vector called $\theta \in \Theta$, with the (pseudo-) true parameter being denoted θ_0. One has to keep in mind that specific cases—notably involving structural HYBRID processes—may involve constraints across the parameters in Equation 16.8 or the filtering weights of the HYBRID process may also be hyper-parameterized, so that the dimension of θ (denoted as d) depends on the specific circumstances considered. For this generic setting, we have the following estimators:

$$\hat{\theta}_T^{mdrv} = \arg\min_{\theta \in \mathcal{C}} \frac{1}{T} \sum_{t=1}^{T} (\mathrm{RV}_t - V_{t|t-1}(\theta))^2,$$

where $\mathcal{C}$ is a convex compact subset of Θ such that θ_0 is in the interior of $\mathcal{C}$. This minimum distance estimator involves observations about RV or possibly a realized measure that corrects for microstructure effects, etc. This estimator applies to volatility models involving all possible HYBRID processes, including structural ones for which a weak GARCH assumption is required. Note that this means that $V_{t|t-1}(\theta)$ in the above estimator is based on a best *linear predictor*, not the conditional variance—a technical issue that will be discussed in the next section.

A companion estimation procedure involves a single-squared-return process, namely:

$$\hat{\theta}_T^{mdr2} = \arg\min_{\theta \in \mathcal{C}} \frac{1}{T} \sum_{t=1}^{T} (R_t^2 - V_{t|t-1}(\theta))^2.$$

The above estimator has a likelihood-based version, namely:

$$\hat{\theta}_T^{llr2} = \arg\min_{\theta \in \mathcal{C}} \frac{1}{T} \sum_{t=1}^{T} \left(\log V_{t|t-1}(\theta) + \frac{R_t^2}{V_{t|t-1}(\theta)} \right),$$

requiring far more stringent in terms of regularity conditions, notably because $V_{t|t-1}(\theta)$ is a conditional variance, and in fact does not apply to all types of HYBRID processes, in particular, structural ones. The estimator $\hat{\theta}_T^{mdr2}$ is reminiscent of QMLE estimators for semistrong GARCH models—yet the mixed data frequencies add an extra layer of complexity discussed later in the paper. One can again replace daily squared returns by, say RV and consider the following estimator:

$$\hat{\theta}_T^{llrv} = \arg\min_{\theta \in \mathcal{C}} \frac{1}{T} \sum_{t=1}^{T} \left(\log V_{t|t-1}(\theta) + \frac{\mathrm{RV}_t}{V_{t|t-1}(\theta)} \right).$$

The choice of R^2 versus RV in $\hat{\theta}_T^{mdr2}$ versus $\hat{\theta}_T^{mdrv}$ and $\hat{\theta}_T^{llr2}$ versus $\hat{\theta}_T^{llrv}$ has efficiency implications that will be discussed as well.

Inspired by the multiplicative error model (MEM) of Engle (2002b) and the subsequent work by Engle and Gallo (2006), Lanne (2006), Cipollini et al. (2006) also consider the following model

$$\mathrm{RV}_{t+1} = \sigma_{t+1|t}^2 \eta_{t+1}, \tag{16.11}$$

where conditional on $\mathcal{F}_t$, η_{t+1} is independent and identically distributed with mean 1. Suppose the cumulative distribution function of η is F. The choice of F could be a unit exponential (Engle, 2002b), or a Gamma distribution as suggested in Engle and Gallo (2006), or a mixture of two gamma distributions of Lanne (2006). The resulting class of estimators will be denoted by $\tilde{\theta}_T^{\mathrm{MEM}}$.

Chen et al. (2009b) provide further detail regarding the theoretical properties of the various estimators and various HYBRID processes. They also conduct a Monte Carlo simulation study, which shows that the estimator that appears to have the best finite sample properties is $\hat{\theta}_T^{llrv}$. It is typically vastly better than the estimators based on R^2, either minimum distance or likelihood based. It should also be noted that the MEM-type estimator—which is asymptotically equivalent to $\hat{\theta}_T^{llrv}$—is occasionally in small samples the most efficient for one parameter, in particular, namely, α. This means that the most efficient estimation of the unconditional mean of the volatility dynamic process can be achieved with the MEM principle that estimates directly the volatility process. As far as empirical specification goes, the jury is still out. At the time this chapter was being written, a thorough empirical investigation was still being conducted looking at the various types of HYBRID processes and their forecast performance at different horizons. Chen et al. (2009a) used the HYBRID GARCH class of models to predict volatility at daily horizons using intradaily returns. The use of such returns forces one to think about how to treat intradaily seasonality. Chen et al. (2009a) considered four approaches which we called: (i) (Unconstrained) HYBRID GARCH; (ii) Periodic HYBRID GARCH; (iii) (Unconstrained) SA HYBRID GARCH; and (iv) Constrained SA HYBRID GARCH. The former two apply to raw returns, and the latter two to rescaled returns using intradaily unconditional volatility patterns. Overall, they find that the use of seasonally adjusted returns is inferior both in-sample and out-of-sample. This means that we have essentially a relatively simple class of models that handle intraday seasonality well.

16.3.3 GARCH-MIDAS MODELS

So far, we did not cover component models of volatility. Empirical evidence suggests that volatility dynamics is better described by component models. Engle and Lee (1999) introduced a GARCH model with a long- and short-run component.[1] The volatility component model of Engle and Lee decomposed the equity conditional variance as the sum of the short-run (transitory) and long-run (trend) components.

So far, we considered MIDAS filters that applied to high frequency data. Here, we use the same type of filters to extract low frequency components. Hence, it is again a MIDAS setting, using different frequencies, but this time we use the polynomial specifications to extract low frequency movements in volatility.

In anticipation of the material in the next section, we consider multiple returns, although we study here still one single return series at the time. Namely, we consider a set of n assets and let the vector of returns be denoted as $\mathbf{r}_t = \left[r_{1,t}, \ldots, r_{n,t}\right]'$.

The new class of models is called *GARCH-MIDAS*, since it uses a mean reverting unit *daily* GARCH process, similar to Engle and Rangel (2008), and a MIDAS polynomial that applies to *monthly, quarterly,* or *biannual* macroeconomic or financial variables. In what follows, we will refer to g_i and m_i as the short- and long-run variance components, respectively, for asset i. Engle et al. (2008) consider various specifications for g_i, and we select only a specific one where the long-run component is held constant across the days of the month, quarter, or half-year. Alternatively, one can specify m_i based on rolling samples that change from day to day. The findings in Engle et al. (2008) show that they yield very similar empirical fits—so we opted for the simplest to implement, which involves locally constant long-run components. We will denote by N_v^i the number of days that m_i is held fixed. The superscript i indicates that this may be asset specific. The subscript v differentiates it from a similar scheme that will be introduced later for correlations. It will be convenient to introduce two time scales t and τ. In particular, while $g_{i,t}$ moves daily, $m_{i,\tau}$ changes only once in every N_v^i days.

More specifically, we assume that for each asset $i = 1, \ldots, n$, univariate returns follow the GARCH-MIDAS process:

$$r_{i,t} = \mu_i + \sqrt{m_{i,\tau} \cdot g_{i,t}}\xi_{i,t}, \quad \forall t = \tau N_v^i, \ldots, (\tau + 1)N_v^i, \tag{16.12}$$

where $g_{i,t}$ follows a GARCH(1,1) process:

$$g_{i,t} = (1 - \alpha_i - \beta_i) + \alpha_i \frac{(r_{i,t-1} - \mu_i)^2}{m_{i,\tau}} + \beta_i g_{i,t-1}, \tag{16.13}$$

[1] Several authors have proposed related two-factor volatility models, see Ding and Granger (1996), Gallant et al. (1999), Chernov et al. (2003), and Adrian and Rosenberg (2008) among many others.

while the MIDAS component $m_{i,\tau}$ is a weighted sum of K_v^i lags of realized variances (RV) over a long horizon:

$$m_{i,\tau} = \overline{m}_i + \theta_i \sum_{l=1}^{K_v^i} \varphi_l(\omega_v^i)\mathrm{RV}_{i,\tau-l}, \tag{16.14}$$

where the realized variances involve N_v^i daily squared returns, namely:

$$\mathrm{RV}_{i,\tau} = \sum_{j=(\tau-1)N_v^i+1}^{\tau N_v^i} (r_{i,j})^2.$$

Note that N_v^i could, for example, be a quarter or a month. The above specification corresponds to the block sampling scheme as defined in Engle et al. (2008), involving so-called Beta weights defined as

$$\varphi_l(\omega_v^i) = \frac{\left(1 - \frac{l}{K_v^i}\right)^{\omega_v^i - 1}}{\sum_{j=1}^{K_v^i}\left(1 - \frac{j}{K_v^i}\right)^{\omega_v^i - 1}}. \tag{16.15}$$

In practice, we will consider cases where the parameters N_v^i and K_v^i are independent of i, that is, the same across all series. Similarly, we can also allow for different decay patterns ω_v^i across various series, but once again we will focus on cases with common ω_v (see the next subsection for further discussion). Obviously, despite the common parameter specification, we expect that the $m_{i,\tau}$ substantially differ across series, as they are data-driven.

Engle et al. (2008) study long historical data series of aggregate stock market volatility, starting in the nineteenth century, as in Schwert (1989b). Their empirical findings show that for the full sample the long-run component accounts for roughly 50% of predicted volatility. During the Great Depression era, even 60% of expected volatility is due to the long-run component. For the most recent period, the results show roughly a 40% contribution. Finally, they also introduce refinements of the GARCH-MIDAS model, where the long-run component is driven by macroeconomic series.

16.4 Multivariate Models

The estimation of multivariate volatility models with mixed sampling frequencies is a relatively unexplored area. In this final section, we present one approach that appears promising. It was proposed by Colacito et al. (2011) and also applied by Baele et al. (2010) to the determinants of stock and bond return comovements.

Colacito et al. (2011) address the specification, estimation, and interpretation of correlation models that distinguish short- and long-run components.

They show that the changes in correlations are indeed very different. Dynamic correlations are a natural extension of the GARCH-MIDAS model to Engle (2002a) DCC model. The idea captured by the DCC-MIDAS model is similar to that underlying GARCH-MIDAS. In the latter case, two components of volatility are extracted, one pertaining to short-term fluctuations and the other pertaining to a secular component. In the GARCH-MIDAS, the short-run component is a GARCH component, based on daily (squared) returns, that moves around a long-run component driven by realized volatilities computed over a monthly, quarterly, or biannual basis. The MIDAS-weighting scheme helps to extract the slowly moving secular component around which daily volatility moves. Engle et al. (2008) explicitly link the extracted MIDAS component to macroeconomic sources. It is the same logic that is applied here to correlations. Namely, the daily dynamics obey a DCC scheme, with the correlations moving around a long-run component. Short-lived effects to correlations will be captured by the autoregressive dynamic structure of DCC, with the intercept of the latter being a slowly moving process that reflects the fundamental or long-run causes of time variation in correlation.

To estimate the parameters of the DCC-MIDAS model, Colacito et al. (2011) follow the two-step procedure of Engle (2002a). They start by estimating the parameters of the univariate conditional volatility models. The second step consists of estimating the DCC-MIDAS parameters with the standardized residuals. Moreover, they also discuss the regularity conditions we need to impose on the *MIDAS-filtered* long-run correlation component, as models of correlations are required to yield positive-definite matrices.

Using the standardized residuals $\xi_{i,t}$ of the previous section, it is possible to obtain a matrix $\boldsymbol{Q}_t$ whose elements are

$$q_{i,j,t} = \overline{\rho}_{i,j,t}(1-a-b) + a\xi_{i,t-1}\xi_{j,t-1} + bq_{i,j,t-1}, \tag{16.16}$$

$$\overline{\rho}_{i,j,t} = \sum_{l=1}^{K_c^{ij}} \varphi_l\left(\omega_r^{ij}\right) c_{i,j,t-l},$$

$$c_{i,j,t} = \frac{\sum_{k=t-N_c^{ij}}^{t} \xi_{i,k}\xi_{j,k}}{\sqrt{\sum_{k=t-N_c^{ij}}^{t} \xi_{i,k}^2}\sqrt{\sum_{k=t-N_c^{ij}}^{t} \xi_{j,k}^2}},$$

where the weighting scheme is similar to that appearing in Equation 16.14. Note that in the above formulation of $c_{i,j,t}$, one could have used simple cross products of $\xi_{i,t}$. One can regard $q_{i,j,t}$ as the short-run correlation between assets i and j, whereas $\overline{\rho}_{i,j,t}$ is a slowly moving long-run correlation. Rewriting the first equation of system (Eq. 16.16) as

$$q_{i,j,t} - \overline{\rho}_{i,j,t} = a\left(\xi_{i,t-1}\xi_{j,t-1} - \overline{\rho}_{i,j,t}\right) + b\left(q_{i,j,t-1} - \overline{\rho}_{i,j,t}\right), \tag{16.17}$$

conveys the idea of short-run fluctuations around a time-varying long-run relationship. The idea captured by the DCC-MIDAS model is similar to that underlying GARCH-MIDAS. In the latter case, two components of volatility are extracted, one pertaining to short-term fluctuations and the other pertaining to a secular component. In the GARCH-MIDAS, the short-run component is a GARCH component, based on daily (squared) returns, that moves around a long-run component driven by realized volatilities computed over a monthly, quarterly, or biannual basis. The MIDAS-weighting scheme helps one to extract the slowly moving secular component around which daily volatility moves. It is the same logic that is applied here to correlations. Namely, the daily dynamics obey a DCC scheme, with the correlations moving around a long-run component. Short-lived effects on correlations will be captured by the autoregressive dynamic structure of DCC, with the intercept of the latter being a slowly moving process that reflects the fundamental or secular causes of time variation in correlation.

In terms of empirical implementation, Colacito et al. (2011) and Baele et al. (2010) consider examples involving stocks and bonds. Both papers show the usefulness of the component specification in correlations and, in particular, the appeal of using MIDAS filters to specify long-run component of correlations. Formal testing reported in both papers show that the DCC-MIDAS models outperform standard DCC models. Colacito et al. (2011) also study asset allocation with multiple international equities (five international stock markets) and a single MIDAS filter. Using the methodology proposed by Engle and Colacito (2006) pertaining to minimum variance portfolio management, they document the economic significance of using the DCC-MIDAS specification as well.

16.5 Conclusion

We focused on the issues pertaining to mixed frequencies that arise typically because we would like to consider multistep volatility forecasts while maintaining information in high frequency data. We expect this topic to get more attention, as high frequency data becomes more widely available while the forecast horizons of interest are mostly low frequency.

CHAPTER SEVENTEEN

Jumps

CECILIA MANCINI and FRANCESCO CALVORI

17.1 Introduction

In what follows, we review all the nonparametric methods in the literature we are aware about estimating the *integrated variance* (IV) and testing for the presence of jumps in asset prices models, when the prices are assumed to be *Itô semimartingales* (SM) and are observed discretely on a finite time horizon T. All the terms in italic style are explained in this chapter, while the definition of terms such as 'finite variation' (fV) is not given here but can be found in the cited books or papers.

17.1.1 SOME MODELS USED IN FINANCE AND OUR FRAMEWORK

The models mostly used in finance for describing the log-price of an asset or a spot interest rate fall within the class of the Itô SMs. An *SM* can be represented as $X_t = X_0 + A_t + L_t$, where A is a process[1] with paths of "fV" and L is a "local martingale" (this is a little bit more general than a "martingale," see

[1] A indicates the whole process $\{A_t\}_{t\in\mathbb{R}}$, $\mathbb{R}$ being the set of the real numbers, while A_t denotes the random variable describing the state of the process at time t.

Handbook of Volatility Models and Their Applications, First Edition.
Edited by Luc Bauwens, Christian Hafner, and Sebastien Laurent.

Protter (2005)). This model is consistent with the assumption that in the market no arbitrage opportunities are allowed (Madan, 2001). Part A includes drift components of X and jump components with fV, while L typically involves Brownian parts and *compensated* small jumps. Itô SMs as in Equations 17.1 and 17.2 below are especially used: the drift component and the *compensator* of the jump part are absolutely continuous with respect to Lebesgue measure, and the "continuous local martingale part" of L (Protter, 2005) is the stochastic integral of some process σ with respect to (wrt) a Brownian motion (BM). In fact, many features of Itô SMs are now known (Jacod and Shiryaev, 2003) and make for mathematical tractability. Nevertheless, some authors use models lying outside the mentioned classes, as, for example, 'fractional Brownian motion' (which is not an SM, see Shiryaev, 1999) or 'multifractal' models (which are SMs but not of Itô type, see Bacry et al., 2010).

Let us consider a unidimensional Itô SM X defined on a filtered probability space $(\Omega, (\mathcal{F}_t)_{t\in[0,T]}, \mathcal{F}, X)$. X can be described by a process starting at a r.v. X_0 at time 0 and evolving in time as (Jacod, 2007)

$$dX_t = a_t\,dt + \sigma_t\,dW_t + dJ_t + dM_t,\ \ t \in [0, T], \tag{17.1}$$

where W is a standard Brownian motion, a and σ are adapted càdlàg[2] processes and J, M are jump components describing, respectively, the "large" and the "small" jumps of X. With the SM representation given previously, we would have $A_t = \int_0^t a_s ds + J_t, L_t = \int_0^t \sigma_s dW_s + M_t$. Assuming Equation 17.1 means that the evolution of X is driven by a drift component $\int_o^t a_s ds$, with instantaneous positive or negative rate a_t, which is perturbed by Brownian zero-mean shocks and also by the occurrence of, usually unforeseeable, jumps. The Brownian perturbations, which are "predictable," are usually small and represent the uncertainty underlying the markets. The inclusion of the jumps has been shown to be largely consistent with various financial return series (see the references in Dobrev, 2007): large jumps reflect the arrival of surprising news, of abnormally large orders, or also of asset liquidity shocks, while for some assets small jumps seem to be necessary to better explain the observed data (see Lahaye et al. (2011) and the references therein for analyses of the determinants of the jumps in specific assets) and the jump component appears to account for a significant proportion of the sum of the squared available returns (Andersen et al., 2007). In specific models, a and σ can in turn be described by SMs (as, e.g., in the Heston model, in the trivariate Cox Ingersoll Ross model, or in model 2 simulated below).

The key tool to model the arrival of jumps is a *random measure* $\mu(\omega, dx, ds)$ defined on $\Omega \times \mathbb{R} \times \mathbb{R}_+$ and with values in $I\!N \cup \{0\}$, $I\!N$ being the set of the natural numbers. Each jump size that the model is allowed to realize is labeled by a *mark* $x \in \mathbb{R}$, while $\mathbb{R}_+$ contains time indices. The number

[2]Having right continuous paths with left limits at each time t; *càdlàg* is the French acronym of continu à droite avec limite à gauche; càdlàg processes fall within the class of "optional" processes mentioned in Jacod (2007); this latter class is in turn a subset of the class of "progressively measurable" processes mentioned in Mancini (2009).

$\mu(\omega, B, [0, t])$ reveals how many jumps the path $X(\omega)$ did up to time t and with sizes marked by labels within B. For instance, a process described by $\int_0^t \int_{|x|>1} x\mu(\omega, \mathrm{d}x, \mathrm{d}s)$ is a *pure jump* process with marks coinciding with the jump sizes, which are larger than 1. More generally, the jump sizes γ of an SM can depend on ω and time, for example, a pure jump process with jumps larger than 1 can be expressed by $J_t(\omega) = \int_0^t \int_{x:\,:\gamma(\omega,x,s)|>1} \gamma(\omega, x, s)\mu(\omega, \mathrm{d}x, \mathrm{d}s)$. Given that we have a jump at time t, the possibility that the size labeled by x occurs is regulated by the "Lévy measure" $\nu_t(\omega, \mathrm{d}x)$ of X. Denote by $\Delta X_t \doteq X_t - X_{t-}$ the jump size at t. On a given ω only one jump size, say the size labeled by $\bar{x}$, is realized (it holds that $\forall t, \mu(\omega, \mathbb{R}, \{t\}) \in \{0, 1\}$), thus $\Delta X_t = \gamma(\omega, \bar{x}, t) = \int_{\{t\}} \int_{\mathbb{R}} \gamma(\omega, x, s)\mu(\omega, \mathrm{d}x, \mathrm{d}s)$. As usual, also for μ, ν, and γ, the ω dependence is suppressed in what follows, for brevity.

Using $\{\int_0^t \int_{\mathbb{R}} \gamma(x, s)\mu(\mathrm{d}x, \mathrm{d}s), t \in [0, T]\}$ allows us only to describe pure jump Itô SMs with fV, that is, satisfying a.s. $\sum_{s\leq T} |\Delta X_s| < \infty$, while in general the above integral might not converge. Particular fV jump processes are the *finite activity* (FA) ones, where a.s. for any finite time interval $[a, b]$ the number $N_b - N_a = \int_a^b \int_{\mathbb{R}} 1\mu(\mathrm{d}x, \mathrm{d}s)$ of jumps that have occurred within it is finite. When this condition is violated (i.e., on some paths we have that, up to some time instant t, $\int_0^t \int_{\mathbb{R}} 1\mu(\mathrm{d}x, \mathrm{d}s) = \infty$), the jump process is said to have *infinite activity* (IA). For any SM, for any fixed $\varepsilon > 0$, the jumps with size larger than ε make an FA jump process (Cont and Tankov, 2004). When infinite variation (iV) jumps can occur, then in order to make $\int_0^t \int_{\mathbb{R}} \gamma(x, s)\mu(\mathrm{d}x, \mathrm{d}s)$ converge, we need to *compensate* the small jumps of X (e.g., the ones smaller than 1). For Itô SMs, it is always possible to choose a representation as in Equation 17.1, where μ is a "Poisson random measure" (Jacod, 2007; Jacod and Shiryaev, 2003; Cont and Tankov, 2004), the Lévy measure does not depend on t or ω

$$J_t = \int_0^t \int_{x:|\gamma(x,s)|>1} \gamma(x, s)\mu(\mathrm{d}x, \mathrm{d}s),$$

$$M_t = \int_0^t \int_{x:|\gamma(x,s)|\leq 1} \gamma(x, s)[\mu(\mathrm{d}x, \mathrm{d}s) - \nu(\mathrm{d}x)\mathrm{d}s]. \tag{17.2}$$

The measure $\nu(\mathrm{d}x)\mathrm{d}s$ is called *compensator* of X, as whenever γ is a bounded predictable function then its integral in $\mu(\mathrm{d}x, \mathrm{d}s) - \nu(\mathrm{d}x)\mathrm{d}s$ is a martingale. Equation 17.2 specifies that the jump part is given by the sum of the rare FA jumps larger than 1 and a compensated sum of possibly IA jumps smaller than 1. All SMs are such that a.s. $\int_{x:|\gamma(x,s)|\leq 1} \gamma^2(x, s)\nu_s(\mathrm{d}x)$ is finite, which guarantees the a.s. convergence of the compensated small jumps. Technical conditions for the existence of a unique strong solution of Equation 17.1 on $[0, T]$, which is "adapted" and càdlàg, are given, for example, in Ikeda and Watanabe (1981), Protter (2005), and Jacod and Shiryaev (2003). Other representations are possible for a unidimensional Itô SM (Jacod, 2007). For instance, when X has FA jumps, it has also a representation where $M \equiv 0$ and a.s. $J_t = \int_0^t \int_{\mathbb{R}} \gamma(x, s)\mu(\mathrm{d}x, \mathrm{d}s) = \sum_{j=1}^{N_t} \gamma_j$, where the Poisson process $N_t(\omega)$ counts the number of jumps that have occurred for path ω from 0 to time t, and

γ_j is the size of the jth jump, as in the Merton or Kou models (for the models, we mention without giving a reference see the references in Cont and Tankov, 2004). When $\sigma \equiv 0$, the model is said to be a *pure jump* process, which moves only through jumps, other than an eventual drift, as, for instance, the "normal inverse Gaussian" (NIG), the "variance gamma" (VG), and the "Car, Geman, Madan, and Yor" (CGMY) processes.

Fundamental examples included in Equations 17.1 and 17.2 are the *Lévy processes*, where a and σ are constants, $\gamma(\omega, x, s) \equiv x$. In particular, when the jumps are of FA, the sizes γ_j are i.i.d. and independent of N. In this last subclass, we mention the Bachelier model with $a = 0, J = M \equiv 0$, the Black and Scholes model where $J = M \equiv 0$, and the Merton and Kou models. On the other hand, the NIG, VG, and CGMY models are examples of Lévy processes with IA jumps. Other Itô SM models outside the Lévy class are the *Brownian semimartingales* (BSMs), where $J = M \equiv 0$ but a and σ are allowed to be stochastic ("stochastic volatility models," such as the Heston model) and the "diffusion models," where $J = M \equiv 0$ and $a_t \equiv a(t, X_t)$ and $\sigma_t = \sigma(t, X_t)$ with deterministic functions $a(t,x), \sigma(t,x)$ ensuring that X is Markov. Models resulting by adding FA jumps to diffusions are called *jump-diffusions*. In general, the Itô SM assumption allows for dependency among the jump sizes, the number of jumps that have occurred, and the other X components. Many models of the form $X_t = B_{\tau_t}$ (obtained as a BM B computed at the 'business-time clock' τ_t, see references in Cont and Tankov, 2004; Dobrev, 2007) fall in the class (Eq. 17.1) (e.g., NIG, VG, and CGMY are such).

A finer important measure of the jump activity of an SM X is the "generalized Blumenthal Getoor (BG) index." For Lévy processes, which are, in particular, SMs, $x^2 I_{\{|x|\leq 1\}}$ is always ν-integrable; however, it is possible that for lower powers of x this is not the case, meaning that a high power δ is needed to render $x^\delta I_{\{|x|\leq 1\}}$ sufficiently small to be summable. This indicates that ν allows μ to produce relatively big and very frequent jumps. The BG index was defined (Cont and Tankov, 2004) as $\beta := \inf\{\delta > 0 : \int_{x \in \mathbb{R}} |x|^\delta \wedge 1 \nu(dx) < \infty\}$. The higher the β, the more frenetic the jump activity. β belongs to [0,2], for instance, FA jump processes have always $\beta = 0$, while a Lévy process with positive β has IA jumps. The VG process is an example of an IA jump process still with $\beta = 0$, meaning that it has infinite but mild activity. The α stable processes have BG index equal to α, for CGMY processes, the BG index coincides with the parameter Y (see below). When $\beta < 1$, we have fV jumps while when $\beta > 1$ the jumps are of iV. In the case $\beta = 1$, we can have either fV or iV jumps (Barndorff-Nielsen et al., 2006). In the SM framework, the BG index has been generalized in different directions (in Woerner, 2006b; Aït-Sahalia and Jacod, 2011; Todorov and Tauchen, 2010a) and generally depends on ω, T. However, in many central limit theorems (CLTs), we need to control the behavior of the small jumps of X and in such cases assumptions on the model are made in order to ensure that the generalized BG index is constant, thus coinciding with the BG index.

We can observe one path $X(\omega)$ on a finite and fixed time horizon $[0, T]$, and realistically, we only have a discrete record $\{X_0, X_{t_1}, \ldots, X_{t_{n-1}}, X_{t_n}\}$ of $n + 1$ data.

X is called a *data generating process* (DGP). In most of the methods we exposit, the observations are *evenly spaced*, with $t_i = ih$ for a given temporal mesh h, and $n = [T/h]$, the integer part of T/h. We indicate different magnitudes of h by using LF, HF, or UHF to mean that the data is sampled at *low frequency* (more or less $h > 15$ min), *high frequency* ($h \in [1 \text{ min}, 15 \text{ min}]$), or *ultrahigh frequency* ($h < 1$ min), respectively. The huge variety of (presented and not presented) models existing in the literature allows for very different path properties (e.g., with fV/iV, being continuous/discontinuous, allowing for finite/infinite jump activity), which turn out to have deeply different implications, for instance, for option pricing (Carr and Wu, 2003; Cont and Tankov, 2004). This makes relevant the problem of model selection and coefficient estimation.

17.1.2 SIMULATED MODELS USED IN THIS CHAPTER

We illustrate specific features of the data and of the estimators we present by using real and simulated observations. We now describe the models we simulate, which are common in the financial and econometric literature. X stands for the log-price of an asset; in models 1 and 2 the parameters are given on a daily basis, and are such that the generated returns are expressed in percentage form, while in model 3 they are annual and the returns are in absolute form, t varies within *[0, T]*. The number n of generated observations is either 1000 or 25,200 for the different applications below. The simulation of each path is obtained by discretizing the SDE giving the considered model with the Euler scheme and 1 second (s) temporal step; the increments of the jump parts are simulated as explained in Cont and Tankov (2004); data is then aggregated to obtain the desired constant mesh h (which can be 5 min or something else, as specified below). For each model, $X_0 \equiv 0$.

Model 1, called *HT1FJ*, is taken from Huang and Tauchen(2005), and has stochastic volatility (correlated with the Brownian motion driving X) and FA jumps:

$$dX_t = 0.03\, dt + e^{0.125 v_t}\, dW_t^{(1)} + dJ_t,$$

where

$$dv_t = -0.1 v_t dt + dW_t^{(2)}, \tag{17.3}$$

$v_0 = 0$, $W^{(1)}$, and $W^{(2)}$ are standard correlated Brownian motions with correlation coefficient $\operatorname{corr}(W_1^{(1)}, W_2^{(2)}) = -0.62$, and $J_t = \sum_{i=1}^{N_t} \gamma_i$ is an FA compound Poisson process with i.i.d. $\mathcal{N}(0, 0.5^2)$ sizes of jumps, where $\mathcal{N}$ indicates a Gaussian random variable (r.v.) and N has constant jump intensity $\lambda = 0.014$. The volatility factor v is a mean reverting Ornstein–Uhlenbeck process tending to push σ toward its "steady state," $e^0 = 1$.

Model 2, called HT2F, also is taken from Huang and Tauchen (2005). It has continuous paths and the stochastic volatility is determined by two factors. This allows σ to have an erratic behavior such as to produce a rugged appearance of the price series and consequently high values of the returns $\Delta_i X \doteq X_{t_i} - X_{t_{i-1}}$.

Thus, this model represents an interesting challenge for the methods aiming at recognizing returns where jumps have occurred.

$$\begin{aligned} dX_t &= 0.03\,dt + \text{sexp}[-1.2 + 0.04v_t^{(1)} + 1.5v_t^{(2)}]dW_t^{(0)}, \\ dv_t^{(1)} &= 0.00137v_t^{(1)}\,dt + dW_t^{(1)}, \\ dv_t^{(2)} &= -1.386v_t^{(2)}dt + [1 + 0.250v_t^{(2)}]dW_t^{(2)}, \end{aligned}$$

where $v_0^{(1)} = v_0^{(2)} = 0$, $d < W^{(0)}, W^{(1)} >_t = d < W^{(0)}, W^{(2)} >_t = -0.3dt$, $W^{(1)}$ and $W^{(2)}$ are independent and the function $\text{sexp}(x) = e^x I_{\{x \le k\}} + e^k \sqrt{k - k^2 + x^2}/\sqrt{k} I_{\{x>k\}}$, with $k = \ln\sqrt{10{,}000/252}$, is built in order to ensure that the coefficients of the SDE for X satisfy growth conditions such that a solution of the system exists and the Euler scheme works well.

Model 3, called Gauss-CGMY, is taken from Carr et al. (2002), with the parameter values estimated for the SPX index.

$$dX_t = \sigma dW_t + dM_t,$$

where M is a CGMY process, which is a martingale of compensated jumps with Lévy measure density $k(x) = C\frac{e^{-G|x|}}{|x|^{1+Y}} I_{\{x<0\}} + C\frac{e^{-L|x|}}{|x|^{1+Y}} I_{\{x>0\}}$, $C = 24.8$, $G = 94.5$, $L = 95.8$, and $Y = 0.25$. Also this model represents a difficult challenge for the methods we present for estimating $\text{iV}_T := \sigma^{2T}$, because the process contains a negligible Brownian part, thus in finite samples, the jumps can be easily confused with the movements of a BM.

The first row of Figure 17.1 displays the log-prices of the SPX (futures on the S&P500 index) for the period 23/12/1994–9/3/1999, and one path

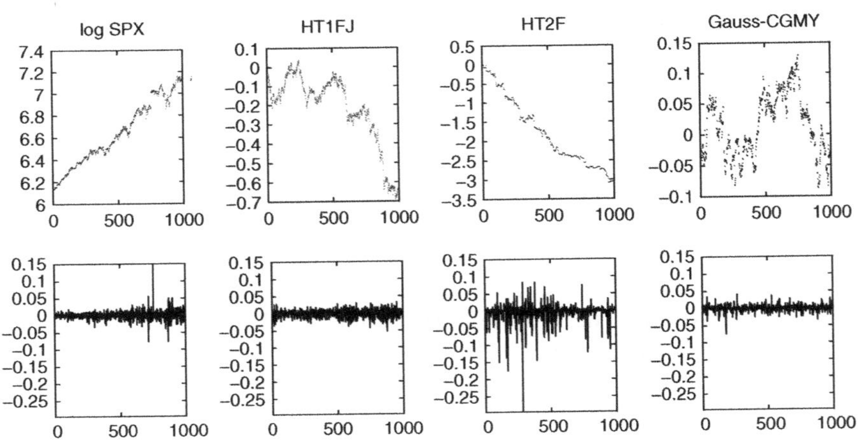

FIGURE 17.1 Realized paths of log-price (first row) and log-return $X_{t_i} - X_{t_{i-1}}$ (second row) for 1000 daily observations (about 3 years) of SPX (first column) and simulated data from the models HT1FJ (second column), HT2F (third column), and Gauss-CGMY (third column).

of simulated data for the three presented models. The second row shows the corresponding returns series. This figure suggests that the three simulated DGPs produce realistic time series of log-prices.

17.1.3 REALIZED VARIANCE AND QUADRATIC VARIATION

The *realized variance* of $X = \log S$ is defined as $\mathrm{RV}_n \doteq \sum_{i=1}^{n}(\Delta_i X)^2$ and is a way of measuring the risk of S, the price of an asset. In fact, let us think of the case where $J + M \equiv 0$, then as $h \to 0$, $\mathrm{RV}_n \xrightarrow{P} \mathrm{IV}_T \doteq \int_0^T \sigma_t^2\,\mathrm{d}t$, the *integrated variance* up to time T, where σ modulates how W impacts on X. More generally, with X as in Equation 17.1, we have

$$\mathrm{RV}_n \xrightarrow{P} [X,X]_T \doteq \mathrm{IV}_T + [J,J]_T, \tag{17.4}$$

where $[J,J]_T = \sum_{s\le T}(\Delta X_s)^2 = \int_0^T \int_{\mathbb{R}} \gamma^2(x,s)\mu(\mathrm{d}x,\mathrm{d}s)$ is the sum of the squared jump sizes realized by X on ω within the time horizon $[0,T]$ and modulates how the jump risk μ impacts on X. Note that for any SM, while the sum of the jumps need not converge, the sum of their squares does a.s.. $[X,X]_T$ is called the *quadratic variation* (QV) of X and has been adopted, since 1998, in the literature as a measure of the impact of the global risk that X undergoes (Andersen and Bollerslev, 1998). Before then, risks were quantified by some parameters within a specific model for X (e.g., by the constant σ in the Black and Scholes model; by σ and the standard deviation σ_J of the jump sizes in the Merton model). $[X,X]_T$ is defined path by path, so that it can be assessed simply by looking at one trajectory of X and has the advantage of being a model-free notion. $[X,X]$ is uniquely determined, any mathematical decomposition of X being adopted and under any probability Q equivalent to P.

If, for instance, X is a simple Poisson process N, then the N_T jumps that have occurred up to T all have size 1, and the sum of their squares is the same N_T, i.e., $[N,N]_T = N_T$. If X is a Lévy process then $[X,X]_T = \sigma^2 T + \int_0^T \int_{\mathbb{R}} x^2 \mu(\mathrm{d}x,\mathrm{d}s)$. Many properties of the QV of an SM can be found in Cont and Tankov (2004) and Jacod and Shiryaev (2003). $[X,X]_T$ has a very important role in the development of the SM theory. For instance, it appears within the Itô formula when expressing the dynamic evolution in time of $F(X_t,t)$ for some deterministic functional $F(x,t)$; secondly, the expectation of QV gives a norm in the space of the squared integrable martingales (to which, e.g., the estimation error of IV_T belongs), and as such it allows us to establish criteria for the convergence of sequences of them.

In the literature, $\sqrt{\sum_{i=1}^{n}(\Delta_i X)^2}$ is usually called *realized volatility*, while by *volatility* we indicate the, possibly stochastic, coefficient σ of Equation 17.1. As RV_n is a consistent estimator of QV, $\sqrt{\mathrm{RV}_n}$ estimates $\sqrt{\mathrm{QV}}$. The smaller the h, the closer we expect $\sqrt{\mathrm{RV}_n}$ to be to $\sqrt{\mathrm{QV}}$. The plot of $\sqrt{\mathrm{RV}_n}$ of an asset against the step h between the observations is called the *signature plot* (SP, see Fig. 17.2d to f) and is used in the econometric literature to visualize at which fine scale h

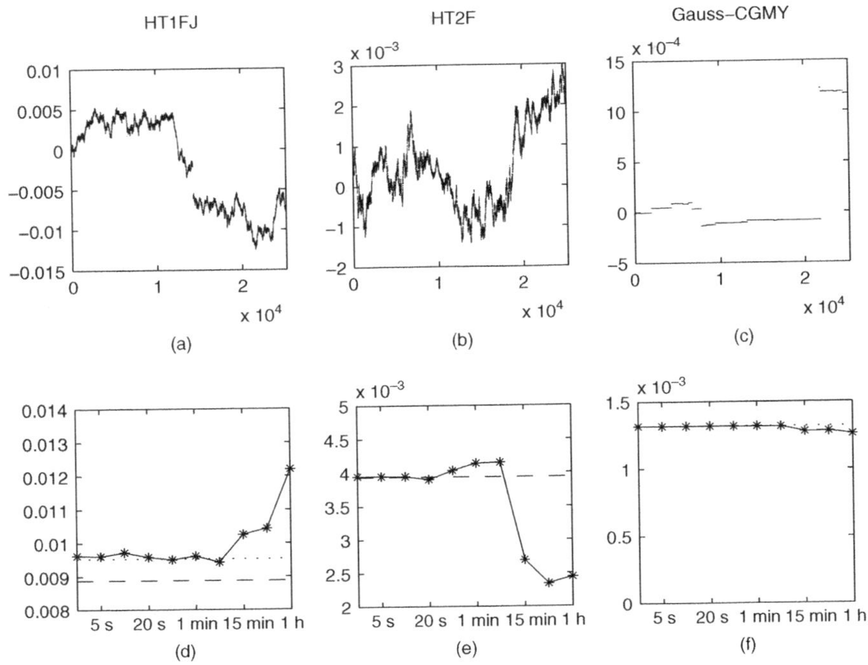

FIGURE 17.2 (a–c) Simulated 1-day paths of models HT1FJ, HT2F, and Gauss-CGMY for the evolution of the log-price of an asset, built from 25,200 1-s observations; (d–f) relative signature plots of $\sqrt{\mathrm{RV}_n}$ at the frequencies of $h = 1$ h; 30, 15, 5, 1 min, and 30, 20 ,10, 5, 1 s.

the estimated values $\sqrt{\mathrm{RV}_n}$ stabilize. The mesh h at which stability begins (e.g., $h = 10$ min in Fig. 17.2d) is considered a proper mesh at which the estimate of $\sqrt{\mathrm{QV}}$ is reliable.

17.1.4 IMPORTANCE OF DISENTANGLING

$\sum_i (\Delta_i X)^2$ is a measure of the global risk affecting an asset. However, Brownian risk and jump risk are amplified by different coefficients. In particular, the price of a derivative product written on a jumping asset needs different risk premia for the two components, and, assuming stationarity of X, capturing and measuring IV_T and $[J, J]_T$ separately allows premia assessment and a more precise hedge of risk (Wright and Zhou, 2009; Brownlees and Gallo, 2010). Secondly, a separate estimation of IV_T serves for model selection purposes, e.g., for testing the necessity of a jump component in a model, as in Barndorff-Nielsen and Shephard (2006b); or for testing the necessity of a BM component, as in Cont and Mancini (2011). Thirdly, including separate measures for the contributions of IV_T and $[J, J]_T$ in econometric models for the future evolution of X significantly improves the accuracy of volatility forecasts, especially in periods following the occurrence of jumps (Andersen et al., 2007; Corsi et al., 2010).

17.1.5 FURTHER NOTATION

$\sigma \cdot W$ indicates the process given by the stochastic integral of σ wrt W; given the representation (Eqs. 17.1 and 17.2), we indicate $D_{\cdot} = \int_0^{\cdot} a_s ds + \sigma \cdot W$; $\text{IV}_t = \int_0^t \sigma_s^2 ds$, while for brevity IV_T is also indicated by IV; given two deterministic functions f and g, $f(h) \sim g(h)$ means that both $f = O(g)$ and $g = O(f)$ as $h \to 0$; given two random functions $f(\omega, h), g(\omega, h)$, $f = o_P(1)$ means that f tends to 0 in probability as $h \to 0$, $f = O_P(1)$ means that f is bounded in probability, $f \sim g$ means that both $f = O_P(g)$ and $g = O_P(f)$; when not ambiguous we suppress the n-dependence of the estimators we present below, for example, RV_n is also indicated by RV; *rhs* stands for *right hand side*.

17.2 How to Disentangle: Estimators of Integrated Variance and Integrated Covariance

If we can observe a process only every h units of time, data will appear discrete and thus as a succession of jumps. However, there are different degrees of discontinuity and some discrete data is compatible with continuous sample paths but some is not (Aït-Sahalia, 2002). Many methods have been proposed for disentangling IV from the jumps contribution in the QV of a given asset model. When we assume a parametric model for the evolution of an asset (for instance, a Heston model or CGMY model), we are uncertain whether the DGP in fact belongs to the selected class of models. Thus, nonparametric approaches are particularly important, as they are applicable to many subclasses of SMs. Anyway, even nonparametric methods usually need some assumptions restricting the model classes the DGP is allowed to belong to. Trying to generalize as much as possible the framework where it is possible to obtain a consistent estimator $\hat{\text{IV}}_n$ and to evaluate its efficiency (the speed at which it converges) is thus not merely the passion of mathematicians for theoretical disquisitions but serves a genuine need to limit the risk of excluding models for our DGP. For instance, the question is open as to whether FA jumps are sufficient to describe the evolution of an asset price or IA jumps have to be considered. Most models in finance, including jumps, consider an FA jump component. However, Lee and Hannig (2010) and Aït-Sahalia and Jacod (2011) show that for some assets the BG index is strictly positive and even larger than 1. Aït-Sahalia and Jacod (2011) propose a test to check finiteness versus infiniteness of jump activity. We cannot exclude, in general, the presence of IA jumps at the moment, so it is important to check whether a proposed estimator of IV is robust to them or not. We concentrate only on nonparametric methods allowing of considering rather general stochastic coefficients.

Some methods (such as threshold, wavelet, outlyingness, and hard rejection weighting) aim to recognize the jump occurrences so as to eliminate the jump contaminated returns and to apply methods proper for a BSM. On the other hand, other methods (such as the *multipower variations*, MPVs) keep all the returns but aim to dampen the jumps' impact. We repeat that we consider here only the case of equally spaced observations as most of the proposed estimators of IV adopt such an assumption. In what follows, we have tried to unify the notation from the different cited papers, so the names we give to the important variables do not always correspond to the names in the original articles.

Remark: Estimation of Spot Volatility and of Integrated Powers of $\boldsymbol{\sigma}$.

We concentrate on estimating IV in the presence of jumps, however, in practice also the estimation of $\text{IP}_T(p) \doteq \int_0^T \sigma_s^p \, ds$ with $p \neq 2$ and of spot volatility σ_s is sometimes needed. For instance, for a given estimator $\hat{\text{IV}}_n$, through a CLT, it is typically shown that the asymptotic variance of the estimation error $\hat{\text{IV}}_n - \text{IV}$ involves the *integrated quarticity* $\text{IQ} \doteq \text{IP}_T(4) = \int_0^T \sigma_s^4 ds$ (Eq. 17.6) and in some cases also sums of the type $Z(g) \doteq \sum_{s \leq T} g(\Delta X_s)(\phi_s \sigma_{s-} + \phi'_s \sigma_s)$, with some deterministic functions g and proper random variables ϕ and ϕ' (Vetter, 2010). For testing purposes, for instance, we need to concretely construct confidence intervals and their amplitude is computed using estimates of the mentioned asymptotic variances. In fact also the estimation of the jump sizes may be needed, other than those of IQ and spot σ. When $p \in (0, 2)$, it is possible to estimate $\text{IP}_T(p)$ using realized *power variations*

$$\text{PV}_n(p, kh) \doteq \sum_{i=1}^{n-k} |X_{t_i+kh} - X_{t_i}|^p$$

of X, after scaling by $\mu_p(kh)^{1-p/2}$, where $\mu_p = E(|u|^p) = 2^{p/2}\Gamma(\frac{p+1}{2})/\Gamma(1/2)$ and $u(P) = \mathcal{N}(0, 1)$, with *staggering* fixed integer constant $k \geq 1$, (see Jacod, 2008, Theorem 2.4 ii; Aït-Sahalia and Jacod, 2009). Otherwise, for any $p > 0$, we can use the MPVs, or the *threshold power variations*, which are treated below.

When $p > 2$, then (Lepingle, 1976)

$$\text{PV}_n(p, h) \xrightarrow{P} \sum_{s \leq T} |\Delta X_s|^p. \tag{17.5}$$

This is easy to understand in the simple case of constant σ. The Gaussian increments $|\sigma \Delta_i W|^p$ have in probability the magnitude order of $h^{p/2} = o(h)$, as $h \to 0$. Because $\text{PV}_n(p)$ is a sum of n terms, when $p > 2$, it asymptotically neglects the Brownian component of X. On the contrary, on the given path the jumps contribution does not vanish when $h \to 0$.

Nonparametric estimation of spot volatility in the presence of jumps in the returns (even allowing σ to jump) given discrete observations has been done using: kernels (Bandi and Renò, 2010; Bandi and Nguyen, 2003; Mancini and Renò, 2011) or more general delta sequences (Mancini et al., 2011); MPVs within local windows (Ngo and Ogawa, 2009); *threshold realized variance* (TRV) in local windows (Aït-Sahalia and Jacod, 2009); and a duration-based technique (Andersen et al., 2009). We only report here the last method, as the others are not used for IV estimation, while the duration-based one approximates the spot volatility as a first step with the final aim of obtaining IV estimation.

Finally, in principle, we could obtain an IV estimate also starting from the estimation of $(\int_0^t |\sigma|_s^p ds)_{t>0}$. We could in fact numerically differentiate in t, erase the result to the power $2/p$ and then numerically integrate, however, this procedure would induce a further bias so a direct approximation of IV seems preferable.

RV is the privileged measure of IV in the absence of jumps (Andersen et al., 2003) as the sum of the squared increments represents a natural way to measure the variability of X, it is simple to be computed and efficient (in the Cramer–Rao inequality lower bound sense, see Aït-Sahalia and Jacod (2008) for the efficiency rates in a Lévy model framework and Jacod and Protter (1998) for BSMs), as it is the maximum-likelihood estimator of QV in the parametric framework. As, by Equation 17.4, in the presence of jumps RV mixes up IV information and jump information, modifications of it in many different directions have been proposed to filter the jumps out.

17.2.1 BIPOWER VARIATION

The estimator of IV most widely used is the realized *bipower variation* of Barndorff-Nielsen and Shephard

$$\mathrm{BPV}_n(T) = \frac{\pi}{2}\sum_{i=2}^{n} |\Delta_i X||\Delta_{i-1}X|,$$

introduced in Barndorff-Nielsen and Shephard (2004b). When not ambiguous, we will suppress the time T dependence. If no jumps occur within $[t_{i-1}, t_{i+1}]$ and $\Delta_i X$, $\Delta_{i+1}X$ are i.i.d. Gaussian $\mathcal{N}(0, \sigma^2 h)$ with constant σ, then $E[|\Delta_i X| |\Delta_{i+1}X|] = \frac{2}{\pi}\sigma^2 h$. Therefore, each term in the above sum, if divided by h, is an unbiased estimator of the local spot variance $\sigma_{t_i}^2 \equiv \sigma^2$ and the sum of the terms $|\Delta_i X||\Delta_{i-1}X|$ approaches in probability $\sum_{i=1}^n \sigma_{t_i}^2 h$, a Riemann sum converging to IV when $h \to 0$. If the jumps have FA, for sufficiently small h, within each $[t_{i-1}, t_{i+1}]$ at most one single jump will occur, affecting only one of the two returns $\Delta_i X$, $\Delta_{i+1}X$. Suppose the jump occurs within $[t_{i-1}, t_i]$, then the multiplication of $|\Delta_i X|$ with the adjacent $|\Delta_{i+1}X| = O_P(\sqrt{h})$ will dampen the jump's impact. As a.s. for the given ω only $N_\omega < \infty$ jumps occur within $[0, T]$, the total contribution of the terms involving jumps is $O_P(N_T(\omega)\sqrt{h})$ and tends to 0 in probability as $h \to 0$. In fact in Barndorff-Nielsen and Shephard (2006b), it is shown that BPV_n converges to IV in probability, when the jumps have FA and the drift and volatility processes (a, σ) are jointly independent of W (Theorem 2). If further $J \equiv 0$, it is also shown that (Theorem 3) conditionally on (a, σ), we have the following convergence in distribution

$$\frac{\mathrm{BPV}_n - \mathrm{IV}}{\sqrt{h}\sqrt{\vartheta_{\mathrm{BPV}}\mathrm{IQ}}} \xrightarrow{d} \mathcal{N}(0, 1), \tag{17.6}$$

where $\vartheta_{\text{BPV}} \doteq \frac{\pi^2}{4} + \pi - 3 \approx 2.609$. Denoting by $\text{AVar}_{\hat{\text{IV}}}$, the asymptotic variance of $(\hat{\text{IV}}_n - \text{IV})/\sqrt{h}$, the above CLT means that the estimation error $\text{BPV}_n - \text{IV}$ tends to 0 as $h \to 0$ with the same speed of $\sqrt{h}$ and that AVar_{BPV} is given by $\vartheta_{\text{BPV}}\text{IQ}$, which depends on σ^4 in a way indicating that, as with all the other estimation methods, volatility estimation is more difficult when the level reached by σ is higher. Unfortunately, the magnitude of ϑ_{BPV} indicates an inefficiency of BPV in estimating IV even in the absence of jumps, as an efficient estimator would have $\text{AVar} = 2\text{IQ}$. Even if small, the inefficiency of BPV can be quite important in the applications (see the figures in Mancini, 2009), especially when the data is given at HF or LF. However, in practice returns at UHF undergo *microstructure noises* (see below), which invalidate the consistency of all the estimators presented in this section. Further, for some assets or commodities, observations are not so frequently available. In all the estimation methods we mention here, $\text{AVar}_{\hat{\text{IV}}}$ has the form $\vartheta_{\hat{\text{IV}}}\text{IQ}$, with a proper constant term $\vartheta_{\hat{\text{IV}}}$, so the efficiency comparisons are simply done through the $\vartheta_{\hat{\text{IV}}}$s (Table 17.1).

Assuming σ independent of W excludes the possibility of leverage (dependence between the returns $\Delta_i X$ and the volatility process), which on the contrary is documented empirically (Bollerslev et al., 2009). In Barndorff-Nielsen et al. (2006) and Kinnebrock and Podolskij (2008), an asymptotic analysis is conducted for generalized bipower measures of the variation of BSMs, where the absolute values are more generally replaced by smooth functions. The authors show that at least in the absence of jumps, Equation 17.6 holds even unconditionally and in the presence of leverage. For that they need to assume that σ is in turn a, possibly jumping, Itô SM. Such an assumption, denoted here by (Ito σ), allows us to rigorously approximate the increments $\int_{t_{i-1}}^{t_i} \sigma_u \, dW_u$ by $\sigma_{t_i}\Delta_i W$, and thus to apply criteria for the convergence of triangular arrays of increments of martingales. The assumption amounts to saying that σ is well approximated by a time constant σ_{t_i} within all the time interval $]t_{i-1}, t_i]$. We do not know whether this is realistic, but it is assumed in most of the models used in finance, and it allows the development of extremely powerful tools for the analysis of asset prices. In Andersen et al. (2010) the sensitivity of many IV estimators to time variation of sigma is studied. In the presence of fV jumps, AVar_{BPV} is given by

TABLE 17.1 Asymptotic Efficiency Comparison of the Presented Estimators

Rate	Estimator	Efficiency	Estimator	Efficiency	Estimator	Efficiency
$\sqrt{n}$	TRV	2.00	$\text{QRV}^{k=5}_{m=100}$	2.19	$\text{QRV}_{\text{overl.}}$	2.32
	$\text{QRV}^{k=4}_{m=20}$	2.42	TBV	2.61	MedRV	2.96
	RV*	2.00	ROWV*	2.00	BPV*	2.61
$\sqrt{n/m}$	$\text{RBV}^*_{m\to\infty}$	0.36	$\text{RBV}^*_{m\to 1}$	2.61		
$\sqrt{m}$	$\text{DV}^*_{\text{first range}}$	0.41	$\text{DV}^*_{\text{first exit}}$	0.77		

The AVar of each estimator equals ϑ.IQ. For GR no CLT is available. * means that a CLT for the considered method is available only in the absence of jumps. For $\text{QRV}_{\text{overl}}$ we considered $k = 4$ and $m = 100$ and for ROWV the weight w_{HR} has $\beta = 1$.

the sum of $\vartheta_{\mathrm{BPV}}\mathrm{IQ}$ and a jumps term with the effect that the larger the jumps, the slower the convergence speed of BPV_n (Vetter, 2010).

Further measures of how $\sigma \cdot W$varies in time. W are the *multipower variations* (mentioned in Barndorff-Nielsen and Shephard (2006b) and subsequently developed):

$$\mathrm{MPV}_n^{r_1,\ldots,r_k} \doteq \prod_{i=1}^{k} \mu_{r_i}^{-1} h^{1-\frac{\sum_i r_i}{2}} \sum_{i=k+1}^{n} |\Delta_i X|^{r_1} |\Delta_{i-1} X|^{r_2} \cdots |\Delta_{i-k} X|^{r_k}.$$

When the returns are i.i.d. Gaussian then each scaled summand gives an unbiased estimator of $|\sigma|^{\sum_i r_h}$. In Woerner (2006b), it is shown that $\mathrm{MPV}_n^{r_1,\ldots,r_k}$ consistently estimates $\int_0^T |\sigma_s|^{\sum_{j=1}^k r_j} ds$ under path regularity and independence from W of the drift and volatility coefficients, as soon as $r_i > 0$ for all $i = 1, \ldots, k$ and $\max_i r_i < 2$. Without the latter condition, the big jumps would not be sufficiently dampened anymore, and the normalization by $h^{1-\sum_i r_i/2}$ would cause the explosion of MPV_n to infinity. If further X has generalized BG index $\beta < 1$, $\max_i r_i < 1$, and $\sum_i r_i > \beta/(2-\beta)$, then as $h \to 0$ the convergence speed of $MPV_n^{r_1,\ldots,r_k}$ is $\sqrt{h}$ with $\mathrm{AVar}_{\mathrm{MPV}} = \vartheta_{\mathrm{MPV}} \mathrm{IP}_T(2\sum_{j=1}^k r_j)$, with an explicitly given constant ϑ_{MPV}. A similar result in the presence of leverage and when J is Lévy is obtained by combining the outcomes in Barndorff-Nielsen et al. (2006) and in Barndorff-Nielsen et al. (2006). More general jumps are allowed in Jacod (2008). Note that the integral $\mathrm{IP}_T(2\sum_{j=1}^k r_j)$ can be estimated using in turn the multipower variations, for instance, the multipower most used to estimate IQ is $\mathrm{MPV}_n^{4/3,4/3,4/3}$.

The results in Vetter (2010) show that $\max_i r_i < 1$ is a necessary condition to obtain that an MPV estimator of IV converges at speed $\sqrt{h}$. That forces us to use at least three powers. An upper estimation bias is caused when a large jump is present, as the adjacent return is not really vanishing in finite samples. That bias would be even worse in the presence of jumps in contiguous returns, which, however, has a low probability of happening. In Huang and Tauchen (2005), it is shown that $\log(\mathrm{BPV}_n)$ has a slightly better performance than BPV_n. Thirdly, if we choose $r_1 = \cdots = r_k$ with $\sum_{i=1}^k r_i = 2$, the inefficiency of $\mathrm{MPV}_n^{r_1,\ldots,r_k}$ increases as k increases, as shown in plot Figure 17.3a. So to estimate IV using MPVs, it is convenient to use tripower variation.

Considering equal powers r_i is now of common use (Huang and Tauchen, 2005), but $\vartheta_{\mathrm{MPV}_n^{2/3,2/3,2/3}} = 3.06$. On the contrary, unequal powers would be a better choice toward efficiency, as $\inf_{r_i > 0: \sum_i r_i = 2} \vartheta_{\mathrm{MPV}_n^{r_1,r_2,r_3}} = \vartheta_{\mathrm{BPV}}$ and is approached when r_1 and r_2 are close to 1.

BPV has been widely applied (see Andersen et al. (2007), for instance). A further drawback found in finite samples is that MPVs are sensitive to the presence of zero returns arising from stale quotes and rounding to a discrete price grid (Andersen et al., 2010, p. 1). In practice, zero returns are quite numerous at UHF if the considered asset is not very liquid, as, for example, US bonds. The

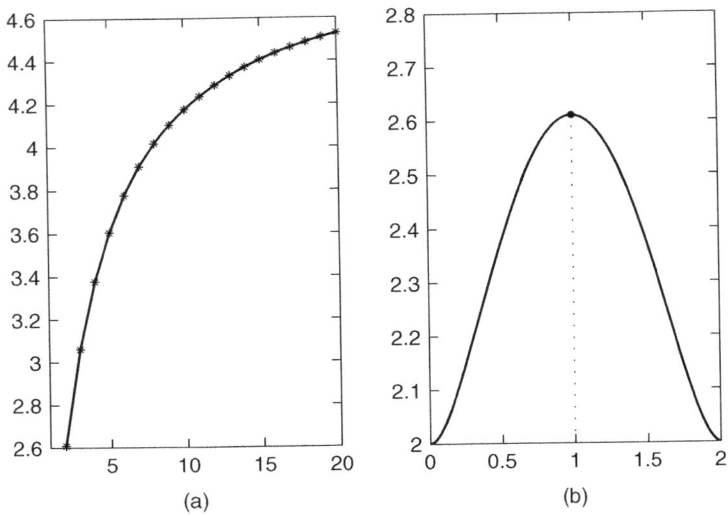

FIGURE 17.3 (a) Plot of ϑ_{MPV} when $r_1 = r_2 = \cdots = r_k$ as we increase the number k (in the x-axis) of powers used to estimate IV, that is, with the constraint $\sum_{j=1}^{k} r_k = 2$. (b) Plot of ϑ_{BPV} when r_1 in the x-axis varies within $[0, 2]$ and $r_2 = 2 - r_1$.

occurrence of a zero return in $[t_{i-1}, t_i]$ affects two consecutive terms in BPV_n, as such destroying information about σ.

Much effort has been expended to estimate IV, seeking to improve the efficiency, finite sample performance, and robustness even to IA jumps and to noise. Extensions of the BPV in different directions (in the present framework) are, for instance, the threshold-BPV, the MinRV, the MedRV, the bipower-type estimator, and the bipower range, all of which are treated below. Very recently, in Mykland and Shephard (2010), it has been proved that replacing $|\Delta_i X|$ with the square root of the realized variance of m blocked returns, and properly scaling, improves the efficiency of BPV, as $\vartheta_{\mathrm{BPV},m} \to 2$, as $m \to \infty$. We conclude this part by mentioning that further properties of MPVs have also been studied for processes not belonging to the SM class (see Barndorff-Nielsen et al. (2011) and references therein), which gives tools to study a similar notion of variability (intermittency) in models needed for turbulent fluids.

17.2.2 THRESHOLD ESTIMATOR

An alternative estimator is the *threshold realized variance* (also called *truncated RV*) of (Mancini 2001, 2009)

$$\mathrm{TRV}_n(T) = \sum_{i=1}^{n} (\Delta_i X)^2 I_{\{\Delta_i X^2 \leq r_{t_i}(h)\}},$$

where $r_t(h) = c_t R(h)$, c_t is a stochastic process that is a.s. bounded and bounded away from 0, and $R(h)$ is any deterministic function of the step h between the observations such that $\lim_{h\to 0} R(h) = 0$ and $\lim_{h\to 0} (h \log \frac{1}{h})/R(h) = 0$. $r_t(h)$ is called *threshold*. The method originated in Mancini (2001) for a simple Gauss–Poisson model with $c_t \equiv 1$. It was then further studied in Mancini (2004, 2009) and Jacod (2008), and developed and applied to obtain a variety of tools to study the characteristics of DGPs. TRV_n is a consistent estimator of IV, which, when $c_t \equiv 1$, is asymptotically Gaussian for a very general class of models.

The intuition of why TRV_n approaches IV is based on the result of Lévy (Karatzas and Shreve, 2005, Theorem 9.25) stating that a.s. the absolute value of the maximal increment $\Delta_i W$ on $[0, T]$ tends to 0 at the same speed as the deterministic function $\sqrt{2h \ln \frac{1}{h}}$, as $h \to 0$. An analogous property holds for the maximal absolute increment of $\int a_s\,\mathrm{d}s + \int \sigma_s\,\mathrm{d}W_s$ (Mancini (2009), note that the drift part increments tend to 0 at the higher speed h). For any t the threshold function tends a.s. to 0, but more slowly than the function $2h \ln \frac{1}{h}$, consequently, if for small h, we find that the squared increment $(\Delta_i X)^2$ is larger than $r_{t_i}(h)$, which in turn is higher than $2h \ln \frac{1}{h}$, then it is likely that some jumps have occurred. In fact, we have that in the presence of only FA jumps with $P\{\Delta N_t \neq 0, \Delta X_t = 0\} = 0$ then a.s. for a sufficiently small h, depending on the selected ω, we have

$$\forall i = 1, \ldots, n, \quad I_{\{\Delta_i X^2 \leq r_{t_i}(h)\}}(\omega) = I_{\{\Delta_i N = 0\}}(\omega). \tag{17.7}$$

Therefore TRV_n a.s. for sufficiently small h excludes from RV_n the finitely many returns where a jump occurred, allowing estimation of IV. In the presence of also IA jumps, then for all $\delta > 0$ a.s. for sufficiently small h the threshold $r_{t_i}(h)$ cuts off all the jumps of J and the jumps of M larger, in absolute value, than $\delta + 2\sqrt{r_{t_i}(h)}$. However, as a.s. $\max_i r_{t_i}(h) \to 0$, since δ is arbitrary, then every jump of M is cutoff.

The consistency of TRV_n is shown in Mancini (2009) when $c_t \equiv 1$, J is any FA jump process but M is Lévy; and in Jacod (2008), when $c_t \equiv 1$, $R(h) = ch^{\alpha}$, $c \in \mathbb{R}$, $\alpha \in [0, 1]$ and $J + M$ is a general SM jump component. The consistency when c_t is stochastic is remarked in Mancini and Renò (2011) and is obtained by repeating the proof of Theorem 1 in Mancini (2009). CLTs are obtained with $c_t \equiv 1$: in Cont and Mancini (2011) for any càdlàg σ and $J + M$ Lèvy; in Jacod (2008), under (Itô σ) but with the most general SM jump process $J + M$ considered so far (Jacod, 2008). It turns out that the convergence speed of TRV_n is $\sqrt{h}$ when the jumps of X have fV (BG index < 1), while when $\beta \geq 1$ and $J + M$ is symmetric β-stable the speed is the not efficient $r(h)^{1-\beta/2}$ (Mancini, 2011a).

The main advantage of TRV is its efficiency when the jumps have fV, as $\vartheta_{\text{TRV}} = 2$. A comparison of the finite sample performances of log BPV, $\text{MPV}^{2/3,2/3,2/3}$, $\text{MPV}^{0.99,0.02,0.99}$, and TRV is shown in Mancini (2009). Further, TRV is immune from the zero returns issue.

The increment $\int_{t_{i-1}}^{t_i} \sigma_s\,\mathrm{d}W_s$ is the slowest part of $\Delta_i D$ when $h \to 0$. As $\sigma \cdot W$ is a time changed Brownian motion, that is, $\int_0^t \sigma_s\,\mathrm{d}W_s = B_{\text{IV}_t}$, where B is a standard BM (Revuz and Yor, 2001; Theorems 1.9, 1.10), then a.s. for small h, we approximately have $|\int_{t_{i-1}}^{t_i} \sigma_s\,\mathrm{d}W_s| \leq \sqrt{2\Delta_i \text{IV} \log \frac{1}{\Delta_i \text{IV}}} \leq \bar{\sigma}_i \sqrt{2h \log \frac{1}{h}}$, $\bar{\sigma}_i$

being an upper bound for σ within $[t_{i-1}, t_i]$ (see Equation 14 in Mancini (2009) for a more precise statement). Thus, the magnitude of σ has an impact on determining whether $(\Delta_i X)^2 \leq r_{t_i}(h)$ or not, and thus on the TRV_n finite sample performance. So in principle the choice of the terms $r_{t_i}(h)$ would have to depend on a preliminary rough estimate of $\bar{\sigma}_i$ or of $\sigma_{t_{i-1}}$. The fact that the estimator depends on unobservable characteristics of the DGP is a typical issue in nonparametric estimation. Further, each model has its own finite sample optimal threshold. An analogous problem arises even for the MPVs, where the exponents r_i have to be chosen depending on the unknown BG index of X, if we want a CLT to be guaranteed to hold. However, in principle, in order to construct TRV, we need some preliminary information about the same σ. The formal study of methods for optimal threshold selection in a given model is the object of further research (Mancini, 2008); however, it is now common to use power functions ch^α as mentioned above. In Mancini (2009) $r(h) = h^{0.99}$ is used, allowing for a good estimation performance on simulated HF data generated by a model with parameters given in annual units of measure. This can be explained by the fact that the chosen (realistic) DGP (taken from Huang and Tauchen (2005)) is such that σ does not move away too much from the standard value of 0.3, so $h^{0.99}$ is about 10 times the expected squared variation $\sigma^2 h$ of the Gaussian increment $\Delta_i(\sigma \cdot W)$. In Figure 17.4, the sensitivity of TRV_n to the choice of c in $r(h) = ch^{0.99}$ is checked on simulations of model 1 for fixed observation steps of $h = 5$ min and 1 s. On the other hand, allowing $r_t(h)$ to be stochastic as specified above permits us to use an adaptive threshold accounting for volatility persistence: in Mancini and Renò (2011), $h = 1$ day, $r_{t_i}(h)$ is nine times a GARCH forecast of the future $\sigma^2_{t_i} h$ made at time t_{i-1}; in Corsi et al. (2010), an iterative estimation of σ_{t_i} is implemented (see below). Another common choice is $r_t(h) = 9\text{BPV}_n h^{0.98}/T$ for all $t \in [0, T]$ (Jacod and Todorov, 2009). In Table 17.2, we call BTV, *bipower threshold variation*, the threshold estimator with the choice $r_t(h) = 9\text{BPV}_n h^{0.99}/T$.

The second advantage of the threshold technique is that, in the presence of only FA jumps, a.s. for h sufficiently small identification of the location of the jumps is possible with high precision (Mancini, 2004). Estimation of the jump sizes and evaluation of the convergence rate is done in Mancini (2009). On the contrary, using MPVs, the identification of jump locations and sizes is not straightforward. Such a property of the threshold method has important consequences. For example, after removing the time intervals where some jumps occurred, we can adapt known estimation methods for diffusion processes also to jump-diffusion processes (Mancini and Renò, 2011).

TRV is applied in Cont and Mancini (2011) to devise a test for the presence of a Brownian component in asset prices, while *threshold power variations* $B(p, u, kh) = \sum_{i=1}^{[n/k]} |X_{t_{i+k}} - X_{t_i}|^p I_{\{|X_{t_{i+k}} - X_{t_i}| \leq u\}}$ have been applied in Aït-Sahalia and Jacod (2010a) to obtain a variety of tools to investigate the characteristics of the DGP by separately varying p, u, and k. $B(p, u, h)$ is also used in Podolskij and Ziggel (2010) to test for the presence of jumps in asset prices.

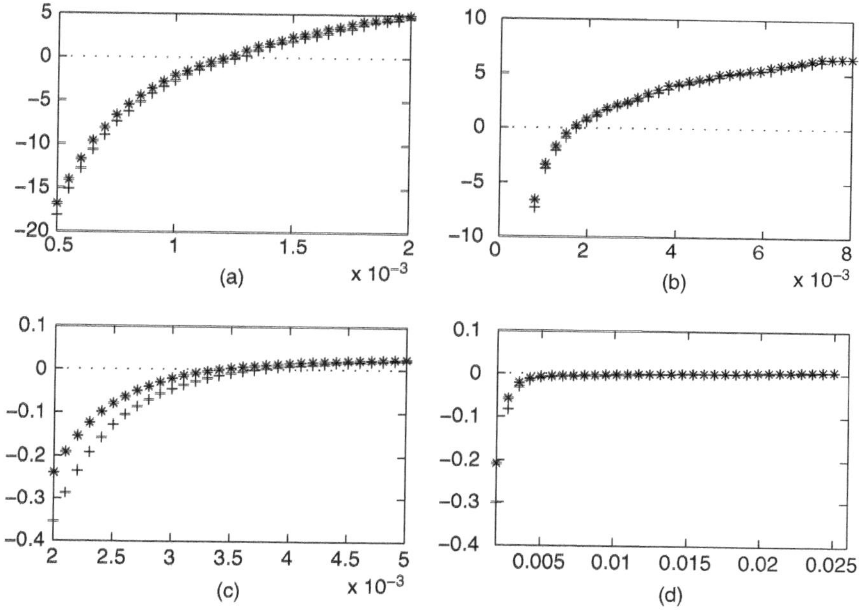

FIGURE 17.4 Mean of the relative percentage estimation bias $100(\hat{IV} - IV)/IV$ for TRV and TBV as the c within the thresholds $r(h) = ch^{0.99}$ (*) and $r(h) = ch^{0.999}$ (+) varies. (a) TRV with $h = 5$ min; (b) TBV_n with $h = 5$ min; (c) TRV with $h = 1$ s; (d) TBV with $h = 1$ s. For any c in the x-axis, 1000 daily paths of model 1 are simulated, where J is constrained to have one jump each day. The daily estimation bias is then averaged.

17.2.3 THRESHOLD BIPOWER VARIATION

By combining the threshold and bipower criteria, we improve both the robustness to the threshold selection and the finite sample efficiency of BPV_n in estimating IV in the presence of jumps. In Corsi et al. (2010), Corsi, Pirino, and Renò define

$$TBV_n \doteq \frac{\pi}{2} \sum_{i=1}^{n-1} |\Delta_i X| I_{\{(\Delta_i X)^2 \le r_{t_i}(h)\}} |(\Delta_{i+1} X)^2| I_{\{\Delta_{i+1} X \le r_{t_{i+1}}(h)\}} \tag{17.8}$$

which is consistent to IV under general predictable drift coefficient a, càdlàg volatility σ, $M \equiv 0$, FA jumps with i.i.d. sizes and 'doubly stochastic' Poisson counting process N_t. The threshold function can be stochastic and different in different intervals $[t_{i-1}, t_i]$, as soon as it satisfies the boundedness requirements mentioned above. The entire class of the MPVs is generalized by replacing the returns by thresholded returns. In practical applications, for h fixed at the level of 5 min, $r_{t_i}(h) = c^2 \hat{\sigma}_{t_i}^2 h$ is chosen, where $c = 3$ and the spot σ is recursively estimated by averaging 22 thresholded returns in a bilateral local

TABLE 17.2 Mean Relative Percentage Estimation Error $100(\hat{IV} - IV)/IV$ of the presented Estimators in the Three Simulated Models

	5 min			1 s		
	HT1FJ	HT2F	CGMY	HT1FJ	HT2F	CGMY
RV	28.543	0.015	3.03e+7	28.160	−0.006	3.04e+7
	(51.495)	(22.438)	(8.20e+7)	(47.467)	(1.319)	(8.21e+7)
BPV	7.840	−2.707	6.34e+5	0.629	−0.008	248.449
	(21.081)	(25.190)	(5.37e+6)	(1.243)	(1.546)	(5.64e+3)
TRV°	0.003	−0.004	0.462	$-3.14e^{-4}$	−0.006	0.125
	(15.843)	(22.419)	(49.614)	(0.931)	(1.319)	(50.122)
TRV	0.003	−9.892	2.68e+6	$-3.14e^{-4}$	−4.770	5.65e+4
	(15.843)	(24.962)	(3.00e+6)	(0.931)	(15.114)	(4.50e+4)
BTV	−0.836	−19.795	5.77e+4	−2.013	−19.193	−99.730
	(16.099)	(21.731)	(5.75e+5)	(0.939)	(10.593)	(4.496)
TBV°	0.009	−2.707	4.467	$-2.00e^{-5}$	−0.008	8.266
	(17.748)	(25.190)	(816.980)	(1.034)	(1.546)	(2.60e+3)
TBV	0.009	−7.378	5.24e+3	$-2.00e^{-5}$	−0.008	−99.949
	(17.748)	(24.637)	(3.82e+4)	(1.034)	(1.546)	(0.002)
QRV°	−4.556	−27.852	1.64e+4	0.014	−1.267	10.109
	(16.119)	(19.126)	(1.02e+5)	(1.003)	(1.441)	(2.04e+3)
MinRV	3.002	−2.334	3.00e+5	−0.003	$3.462e^{-4}$	−9.604
	(21.873)	(30.439)	(2.40e+6)	(1.246)	(1.856)	(2.19e+3)
MedRV	3.304	−2.968	5.00e+5	0.021	0.003	96.350
	(19.400)	(26.183)	(3.67e+6)	(1.118)	(1.637)	(3.92e+3)
ROWV°	0.387	1.301	−48.234	−0.045	−0.384	−99.967
	(16.922)	(22.726)	(566.590)	(0.940)	(1.393)	($2.08e^{-8}$)
RBV*	−0.523	−2.865	5.95e+5	0.466	−0.170	247.883
	(32.755)	(25.149)	(3.15e+6)	(1.241)	(1.544)	(5.63e+3)
GR°	9.381	0.729	1.14e+6	0.413	−0.033	3.80e+3
	(19.389)	(68.872)	(2.79e+6)	(1.125)	(15.661)	(9.48e+3)
GR	9.934	−18.507	1.24e+6	0.561	−16.783	4.99e+3
	(20.421)	(18.497)	(3.04e+6)	(1.266)	(10.265)	(1.24e+4)
DV	−67.3538	—	—	−4.5711	—	—
	(8.5205)			(7.3432)		

Model 1 contains FA jumps, model 2 contains no jumps, model 3 has IA jumps of fV. For all the other details see section 17.2.6

window containing t_i and excluding the returns at times t_{i-1}, t_i, t_{i+1}, so to avoid having an eventual jump occurring close to t_i impacting on $\hat{\sigma}^2_{t_i}$. In Figure 17.4, we instead implement both TRV and TBV with threshold $ch^{0.99}$, and we show how the robustness to the choice of c increases by using TBV in place of TRV. Note that, on the contrary, Figure 17.1 in Corsi et al. (2010) compares such robustness when selecting for both TBV and TRV the recursive threshold function mentioned above.

On the other hand, assuming $r_t(h) \equiv R(h)$, as a.s. asymptotically TBV_n cuts off all the discontinuities, the CLT for TBV_n has convergence speed $\sqrt{h}$ and $\text{AVar} = \vartheta_{\text{TBV}}\text{IQ}$ with $\vartheta_{\text{TBV}} = \vartheta_{\text{BPV}}$, as for BPV_n in the no-jumps case. Vetter (2010) finds the same CLT for TBV even allowing the jumps to have IA but fV. In Corsi et al. (2010), a finite sample performance comparison is reported among TRV, BPV, *staggered* BPV, TBV, and a corrected version of TBV. It is shown that in fact for the purposes of estimation of IV, the less-biased estimator is TBV. Very interestingly, the authors show that using the latter measure of IV significantly improves volatility forecast power over the Andersen et al. (2007) approach. In the latter paper, contrary to Corsi et al. (2010), the authors conclude that jumps have a negative or nonsignificant impact in determining the future volatility; however, to measure the contribution of IV, they use the nonefficient BPV.

17.2.4 OTHER METHODS

All methods below, apart from GR, similarly as the threshold method, are based on the sum of properly selected or weighted squared returns. For all the methods, asymptotic properties are shown (theoretically and/or numerically) only in the presence of FA jumps in returns, so for the moment the only estimators that have been shown to be robust to IA jumps are the MPVs, TRV and the thresholded MPVs. This last turns out to be the only efficient one but only when jumps have fV.

17.2.4.1 Realized Quantile. In Christensen et al. (2010b), a **quantile-based** approach is proposed by Christensen, Oomen, and Podolskij. $T = 1$ and data is divided into n/m non overlapping blocks of m adjacent returns; $k + 1$ percentage numbers $\lambda_1, \ldots, \lambda_k \in (1/2, 1)$ are chosen and the estimator of IV is defined by

$$\text{QRV}_n \doteq \sum_{j=1}^{k+1} \alpha_j \frac{m}{n} \sum_{i=1}^{n/m} \frac{(\Delta_{\ell_{i,\lambda_j}} X)^2/h + (\Delta_{\bar{\ell}_{i,\lambda_j}} X)^2/h}{\nu(m, \lambda_j)},$$

where the selected returns are empirical quantiles of the ith block, of returns, $\Delta_{\ell_{i,\lambda_j}} X$ being the $(\lambda_j \cdot m)$th order statistic and $\Delta_{\bar{\ell}_{i,\lambda_j}} X$ the $(m - \lambda_j m + 1)$th order statistic of the returns in group i. Each scaling factor $\nu(m, \lambda_j)$ is the expectation of the term at its numerator when all the normalized returns $\Delta_j X/\sqrt{h}$ are Gaussian, k is fixed and α_j are optimally chosen weights to minimize the AVar. Large returns not consistent with Gaussian realizations are ignored as soon as all λ_j are < 1, which enables the estimator to be robust both to large jumps and to the presence of data outliers. For small observation step h, each block contains at most one jump, and each term $[(\Delta_{\ell_{i,\lambda_j}} X)^2/h + (\Delta_{\bar{\ell}_{i,\lambda_j}} X)^2/h]/\nu(m, \lambda_j)$ estimates the $\sigma^2_{t_{i-1}}$ of the ith block. Special cases in this class of estimators are *MinRV* and *MedRV*. In the presence of FA jumps, for any fixed m, the estimator is consistent as $n \to \infty$ and, assuming σ to be an Itô continuous SM, it converges at speed $\sqrt{h}$ with AVar coefficient ϑ_{QRV}. This last is close to 2.4 when $k = 4$ $m = 20$

and the λ_j are in the range $[0.8, 0.95]$. Efficiency is improved by allowing for higher k, or for overlapping blocks (*subsampled* QRV), but it deteriorates when m increases. A finite sample performance comparison on simulated data among QRV, RV, BPV, TRV, and MedRV can be found in the paper, where about two observations per minute are used.

17.2.4.2 MinRV and MedRV. In Andersen et al. (2010), Andersen, Dobrev, and Schaumburg propose **MinRV** and **MedRV**, defined by

$$MinRV_n = \frac{\pi}{\pi - 2}\frac{n}{n-1}\sum_{i=1}^{n-1} \min(|\Delta_i X|, |\Delta_{i+1} X|)^2,$$

$$MedRV_n = \frac{\pi}{6 - 4\sqrt{3} + \pi}\frac{n}{n-2}\sum_{i=2}^{n-1} \text{median}(|\Delta_{i-1} X|, |\Delta_i X|, |\Delta_{i+1} X|)^2,$$

where in each case the first factor makes each summand an unbiased proxy of $\sigma^2\, h$ if the involved returns are i.i.d. Gaussian (thus with the same σ). As, for sufficiently small h, jumps in contiguous intervals $]t_{i-1}, t_i]$ will not occur, the returns affected by large jumps are completely ignored, which improves the estimators finite sample performances over the BPV. The consistency of both estimators is proved in the presence of FA jumps, as soon as σ is a.s. bounded away from 0. Under the further assumption (Itô σ), a CLT holds with $\vartheta_{\text{MinRV}} = 3.81$, $\vartheta_{\text{MedRV}} = 2.96$. The better efficiency of MedRV is due to the fact that large returns contain more information about σ than small returns, but they are thrown away in MinRV. Further, in finite samples, contrarily to MedRV, MinRV still suffers from a similar exposure to zero returns as BPV. Very recently, a two-step quantile-based generalization of MinRV and MedRV has been proposed (Andersen, et al., 2011) and seems promising on simulated data. In the first step of the procedure, spot volatility estimation is required, and this can be made by any available spot volatility estimation method.

17.2.4.3 Realized Outlyingness Weighted Variation. In Boudt et al. (2011), Boudt, Croux, and Laurent modify RV by considering weighted returns, with small or zero weight given to local outliers, that is, returns that are extreme in amplitude with respect to the neighbors within a local window. The following estimator

$$\text{ROWV}_n \doteq c_w \sum_{i=1}^{n} w(d_{i,h})(\Delta_i X)^2$$

is defined, where w is a weight function, the preferred one is the *hard rejection function* $w_{\text{HR},\beta}(z) = I_{\{z \leq k_\beta\}}$, k_β being the β quantile of the χ^2 law, the recommended β value being 0.999; c_w is a correction factor explicitly given in terms of w and ensuring consistency in the considered framework; $d_{i,h} \doteq \Delta_i X^2/(h\hat{\sigma}_{t_i}^2)$ measures the distance of the squared normalized return from 0; $\hat{\sigma}_{t_i}^2$ is a first step *least trimmed squares* (LTS) estimator of spot $\sigma_{t_i}^2$ obtained using the returns in a local window around $\Delta_i X$, so that $d_{i,h}$ would be asymptotically χ^2-distributed if the underlying model was Gaussian with constant σ. More precisely, $[0, T]$ is divided into local windows containing $[\lambda/h]$ returns; in order to estimate $\sigma^2_{t_i}$, the local window containing $\Delta_i X$ is considered; for each subsample of $H = [0.5 \times \lambda/h] + 2$ standardized returns $\Delta_j X/\sqrt{h}$ within the window, RV is computed; LTS is $c_{w_{\mathrm{HR}},\beta=0.5}$ times the minimal RV of such subsamples. Under the assumptions of FA jumps, regular w function, smoothness conditions on σ, and the independence of J on W, the authors argue (in a web appendix) that ROWV_n is consistent as $\lambda \to 0$ with $\lambda n \to \infty$. The convergence speed is shown to be $\sqrt{h}$ when furthermore: $J \equiv 0$ and no leverage is present. The AVar constant $\vartheta_{\mathrm{ROWV}}$ is explicitly given and tabulated in the web appendix in terms of the weight function w: $\vartheta_{\mathrm{ROWV}}$ is decreasing in β, $\vartheta_{\mathrm{ROWV},w_{\mathrm{HR}},\beta=0.999} = 2.152$ and $\vartheta_{\mathrm{ROWV},w_{\mathrm{HR}},\beta=1} = 2$ is minimal. However, $\beta = 1$ is an infeasible choice in the presence of jumps, because in that case ROWV would coincide with RV, which is not consistent to IV. The extension of this estimator to the multivariate asset context has nice properties, which motivates proposing the outlyingness measure. In the bivariate case, the finite sample performance on simulated data is good already at HF, which in principle allows us to bypass the distortions connected with the presence of microstructure noise in the data.

17.2.4.4 Range Bipower Variation. In Christensen and Podolskij (2010), Christensen, and Podolskij modify BPV by replacing each $\Delta_i X$ by the maximum return between two any time instants of a predefined time grid within $]t_{i-1}, t_i]$. More precisely the available n observations are divided into N non overlapping blocks of m data, so that each $[t_{i-1}, t_i]$ contains m observed returns. For the ith block

$$s_{X,i,h,m} \doteq \max_{t_{i-1} \le t_\ell < t_u \le t_i} |X_{t_\ell} - X_{t_u}|$$

is taken. Considering the range $s_{W,0,1} \doteq \max_{s,u:0\le s<u\le 1} |W_s - W_u|$ of a BM continuously observed on $[0, 1]$ for financial modeling purposes goes back to the 1980s (see the references in Dobrev (2007)). We consider here the feasible discretized version. With constant σ and $X = \sigma W$, we have $E[s^r_{\sigma W,i,h,m}] = \sigma^r h^{r/2} \lambda_{r,m}$, with $\lambda_{r,m} = E[s^r_{W,0,1,m}]$ (Christensen and Podolskij, 2007), and the *realized range variation* $\mathrm{RRV}_n \doteq \lambda^{-1}_{2,m} \sum_{i=1}^N s^2_{X,i,h,m}$ consistently estimates the IV of an Itô BSM X, for any m, taking $N \to \infty$, and the convergence *rate* (i.e. the reciprocal of the speed, times some multiplicative constants) is $\sqrt{N} = \sqrt{\frac{n}{m}}$. The constant $\lambda_{2,m}$ does not have an explicit form but can be obtained numerically with arbitrary precision, a plot of $\lambda_{2,m}$ letting m vary is displayed in Christensen and Podolskij (2007). However, in the presence of FA jumps, RRV_n is shown to tend to $\mathrm{IV} + \lambda^{-1}_{2,m}[J]_T$ (Christensen and Podolskij, 2010), so in order to estimate IV, the following *range-based bipower variation* is computed:

$$\mathrm{RBV}_{n,m} \doteq \frac{1}{\lambda^2_{1,m}} \sum_{i=1}^{N-1} s_{X,i,h,m} s_{X,i+1,h,m}. \tag{17.9}$$

This is shown to be consistent, for any m, as $N \to \infty$, while a CLT is shown to hold only in the absence of jumps. As $n \to \infty$ and m tends to a finite integer c or to $c = +\infty$, the convergence rate is shown to be $\sqrt{n/m}$, which is strictly less than $\sqrt{n}$ if $m > 1$. The $\vartheta_{\text{RBV},c} \doteq \text{AVar}(\sqrt{n/m}(\text{RBV}_n - \text{IV})/\sqrt{\text{IQ}})$ equals $\vartheta_{\text{BPV}} = 2.6091$ if $m = c = 1$, while it decreases in c and equals 0.3631 if $c = \infty$ (see Figure 1 in Christensen and Podolskij, 2010). However $c = +\infty$ corresponds to the unfeasible situation, where we can observe continuously X over $[0, T]$. In sum, as we refine the partition within each $]t_{i-1}, t_i]$ (c increases) $\vartheta_{\text{RBV},c}$ decreases, but the convergence rate decreases as well.

17.2.4.5 Generalization of the Realized Range. In Dobrev (2007), Dobrev proposes the following alternative **generalization of the realized range** of X. The n observed returns are here not necessarily evenly spaced, and we set $h = \max_i |t_i - t_{i-1}|$. A fixed number $k < n$ of returns is selected and the maximal variation

$$\text{GR}_{X,n} \doteq \max_{0 \le t_1 \le t_2 \cdots \le t_{2k} \le T} \sum_{i=1}^{k} |X_{t_{2i}} - X_{t_{2i-1}}|$$

is looked for, where the times $t_1, \ldots, t_k, t_{k+1}, \ldots, t_{2k}$ vary within the grid of the n available returns. This formulation allows for nonadjacent returns ($X_{t_{2i}} - X_{t_{2i-1}}$ is adjacent to $X_{t_{2(i-1)}} - X_{t_{2(i-1)-1}}$ only if $t_{2(i-1)} = t_{2i-1}$). Only k terms are considered above, but in order to establish where the maximum is attained, all the n absolute returns have to be checked. As already mentioned, we have $\int_0^T \sigma_s \text{d}W_s = B_{\text{IV}}$, where B is a BM. Using then the scaling property of the BM we have that, for $X = \sigma \cdot W$ with càdlàg $\sigma > 0$ bounded away from 0, then $\text{GR}_{X,n} = \sqrt{\text{IV}}\text{GR}_{B,n}$. The number k has to be carefully chosen, in fact the variation $\sum_{i=1}^{k} |X_{t_{2i}} - X_{t_{2i-1}}|$ increases as k does, for fixed n, but taking $k = n$ would make the variation explode in the limit, as soon as X contains a BM component. In Dobrev (2007) k is taken such that $k, n \to \infty$ with the condition $kh \log(1/h) \to 0$. This implies that $n/k \to \infty$, and we are excluding from the variation so many terms that we can hope for convergence. In fact, we have that $\text{GR}_{B,n}/E[\text{GR}_{B,n}] \overset{a.s.}{\to} 1$. It follows that a strongly consistent and asymptotically unbiased estimator of $\sqrt{\text{IV}}$ is obtained by $\frac{\text{GR}_{X,n}}{E[\text{GR}_{B,n}]}$. IV is then asymptotically correctly estimated by

$$\frac{\text{GR}^2_{X,n}}{E[\text{GR}^2_{B,n}]}.$$

The behavior of the scaling factor $E[\text{GR}^2_{B,n}]$ is fully determined by the Brownian paths and is shown to have the same a.s. limit as $1/(2\sqrt{k})$, under the requirements mentioned on h. Robustness of $\text{GR}_{X,n}$ to the presence of a drift and of FA jumps is given by the fact that, as these terms have fV, their contribution to $\text{GR}_{X,n}$ is bounded as $k, n \to \infty$, thus the normalization by the Brownian range expectation makes the impact of the drift and jumps negligible. We expect that robustness to IA jumps would have to be kept, as soon as they are of fV. No CLT is given, so we do not know the convergence speed; however, a performance comparison on simulated data is done with RBV, BPV, and an averaged BPV, and the GR estimator seems to be able to compete.

17.2.4.6 Duration-Based Variation. As a dual approach to the modified RV measures mentioned, a duration-based estimator is proposed in Andersen et al. (2009) by Andersen, Dobrev, and Schaumburg. For the modifications of RV the time step h between the observations is given, and we look at the level reached by the returns, while in the duration-based approach what is given is a barrier level r and we look at the first time τ_r when X exits from $[-r, r]$ (or the first time $\tau_r^{(2)}$ when X hits the barrier r or the first time $\tau_r^{(3)}$ when the range $\max_{s\in[0,\tau_r]} X_s - \min_{s\in[0,\tau_r]} X_s$ exceeds r). For $X = \sigma W$ with constant σ, we have $E[\tau_r] = r^2/\sigma^2$, which offers that $\hat{\sigma}^2 \doteq \frac{r^2}{2C\tau_r}$, with $C \approx 0.92$ being the 'Catalan constant,' is an unbiased estimator of σ^2. Similar estimators are constructed with $\tau_r^{(2)}$ and $\tau_r^{(3)}$. Each estimator variance turns out to be $\nu\sigma^4$. When σ is stochastic (and still $X = \sigma \cdot W$) and a discrete grid $\{t_i, i = 1, \ldots, N\}$ of not necessarily evenly spaced observations is considered,

$$\hat{\sigma}_{t_i}^2 \doteq \frac{r^2}{2C\hat{\tau}_r}$$

is defined, where the exit time is estimated using a subgrid $\{t_{i,j}, j = 1, \ldots, m\}$ in each $]t_{i-1}, t_i]$. Similarly is done using $\tau_r^{(2)}$ or $\tau_r^{(3)}$. The Riemann sum $\mathrm{DV}_n \doteq \sum_{i=1}^{N} \hat{\sigma}_{t_i}^2 h_i$ with $h_i = t_{i+1} - t_i$ and $N = n/m$ is then constructed to estimate IV, where n is the total number of needed observations. When the paths of σ have specified regularity properties, σ is independent of W, $\forall i = 1, \ldots, N, h_i = O(1/N)$ and $r = o(1/\sqrt{N})$ then the estimators are consistent as $N, m \to \infty$ with $m = o(N)$. For each estimator the convergence rate is $\sqrt{m} = \sqrt{n/N}$, and the AVar constant factor is $\vartheta_{\mathrm{DV}} = \nu$. Robustness to FA jumps, to (even autocorrelated) microstructure noise, and to leverage effects is argued via a simulation study, where also a comparison with BPV and subsampled BPV is made.

17.2.4.7 Irregularly Spaced Observations. Allowing for nonevenly spaced observations to estimate IV is important, in fact on the one hand, especially at UHF, it is more realistic; on the other hand, it can be more convenient, for instance, Hansen and Lunde (2006b) prove that "business-time sampling" allows us to minimize the finite sample estimation error variance of RV when $X = \sigma \cdot W$.

The consistency of RV to IV in a BSM and finite time horizon framework is straightforward, as soon as the observation times are stopping times tending to infinity and with maximal distance tending to 0 (Protter, 2005). In the presence of jumps in the returns, using irregular but nonrandom data, IV is consistently estimated with TRV Mancini (2009), GR Dobrev (2007), and DV Andersen et al. (2009).

On the contrary, proving the validity of a CLT is more complicated, as the observation steps enter in the AVar of the estimation error. For the moment, only results in the absence of jumps are available. Considering irregularly spaced data for IV estimation using RV originated in Mykland and Zhang (2006) with nonrandom observation times. If $\bar{h}$ is the average step between the data, assuming that $\max_i h_i/\bar{h} = O(1)$ and $\sum_{t_i \le t} h_i^2/\bar{h}$ has a limit $H(t)$ as $n \to \infty$, then the convergence speed of RV is $\sqrt{\bar{h}}$ and the AVar becomes $2\int_0^t H'_u \sigma_u^4 du$, which depends on the speed at which the sampling is done, and which can be estimated using the fourth power variation of X. When the data is evenly spaced then $H(t) = t$, and we find again the usual AVar of RV. Alternatively, the range RRV has also been considered with deterministic irregularly spaced data (Christensen and Podolskij, 2007). Allowing for random observation times, possibly dependent on the BSM asset price process, CLTs for RV have also been found (see Fukasawa (2010) and the references therein), while CLTs for a wider class of power variations of X are studied in (Hayashi et al., 2009).

17.2.5 COMPARATIVE IMPLEMENTATION ON SIMULATED DATA

Table 17.2 compares the indicated estimators, which are implemented on the three simulated models. For each model, 1000 paths are generated and the mean relative percentage estimation error $100(\hat{IV} - IV)/IV$ is reported, when either 5 min or 1 s observations are used within a 1-day time horizon. In parentheses, the empirical standard error of each such bias is reported. As mentioned, RV is not consistent for IV in the presence of jumps, but it is important to understand how wrong the estimate is when RV is not properly used T is set equal to 1 day.

For TRV, the chosen threshold is $ch^{0.99}$ and c is calibrated for all three models, so that it minimizes the absolute value of the estimation error in model 1 (if $h = 5$ min then $c = 0.0012$, if $h = 1$ s, $c = 0.0034$; these c values correspond to about 12 and 34 times the average squared spot volatility 0.0098^2). On the contrary, for TRV°, c is optimally chosen in each model (in model 2: if $h = 5$ min, $c = 0.12$, if $h = 1$ s, $c = 0.4$; in model 3: if $h = 5$ min, $c = 9.00 \times 10^{-9}$; if $h = 1$ s, $c = 2.34 \times 10^{-6}$). For TBV, the chosen threshold is $c^2\hat{\sigma}_{t_i}^2 h$, as described after Equation 17.8. Also in this case, c is chosen optimally only for model 1 (if $h = 5$ min then $c = 4.1$, if $h = 1$ s, $c = 12.6$), while for TBV°, it is optimally chosen in each model (in model 2: if $h = 5$ min, $c = 10$; if $h = 1$ s, $c = 7$; in model 3: if $h = 5$ min, $c = 0.276$; if $h = 1$ s, $c = 2.8800579 \times 10^{+5}$). We recall that BTV is the special case of TRV with $r_t(h) = 9\text{BPV}_n(T)h^{0.99}/T$.

For QRV°, non overlapping blocks are used, the number m of returns per block is optimally chosen in each model (in model 1: if $h = 5$ min, $m = 84$; if $h = 1$ s, $m = 2520$; in model 2: if $h = 5$ min, $m = 84$; if $h = 1$ s, $m = 200$; in model 3: if $h = 5$ min, $m = 84$; if $h = 1$ s, $m = 8$), $\lambda = [0.8, 0.85, 0.9, 0.95]$ and the optimal α is calculated for each model numerically using the algorithm described in (Christensen et al., 2010b). For instance, in model 1, if $h = 5$ min, $\alpha = [0.1821, 0.1353, 0.2141, 0.4685]$. ROWV° is computed using $w_{\text{HR},\beta=99.9\%}$. The factor c_ω equals 1.013. For the first step estimation of spot variance the MAD (median absolute deviation) method is used, in place of LTS, because it is much more simply implemented, while Boudt confirmed (in a private conversation) that this change only marginally influences the results. The local window length parameter λ is optimally calibrated in each model (in model 1: if $h = 5$ min, $\lambda = 1/4$; if $h = 1$ s, $\lambda = 1$; in model 2: if $h = 5$ min, $\lambda = 1/42$; if $h = 1$ s, $\lambda = 1/126$; in model 3: if $h = 5$ min, $\lambda = 1/7$; if $h = 1$ s, $\lambda = 1$). For RBV*, the number m of increments per window is chosen in each model so as to strike a balance between bias and efficiency, since, the efficiency decreases as m increases (in model 1: if $h = 5$ min, $m = 12$; if $h = 1$ s, $m = 1$; in model 2: if $h = 5$ min, $m = 1$; if $h = 1$ s, $m = 15$; in model 3: if $h = 5$ min, $m = 2$; if $h = 1$ s, $m = 1$). The implementation of GR has been done using an algorithm by Calvori, which is much simpler than the one described in Dobrev (2007). However, Dobrev kindly provided the results obtained with his algorithm on our simulated data, and these coincide with ours. For GR°, the number k of increments included in the estimation procedure is optimally chosen in each model (in model 1: if $h = 5$ min, $k = 44$; if $h = 1$ s, $k = 12,600$; in model 2: if $h = 5$ min, $k = 1$; if $h = 1$ s, $k = 14$; in model 3: if $h = 5$ min, $k = 83$; if $h = 1$ s, $k = 12,600$), while for GR, k is set for all the three models to values giving acceptable results in terms of the bias and efficiency of the estimator (if $h = 5$ min, $k = 30$ and if $h = 1$ s, $k = 6000$). Finally, for DV, the time when the range of X exceeds the barrier $r = 5 \times 0.03 \times 0.01$ is considered, as indicated in Dobrev (2007), where 0.01 is the expected daily volatility and 0.03×0.01 gives a proxy for the log-bid-ask spread of an asset. In models 2 and 3, the range of the observed time series never passes r.

The optimal choices we considered are only possible in a simulation framework and not with empirical data, but allow us to evaluate the potential precision the estimators could reach. We report the estimation errors also when $h = 1$ s in order to assess the performance of the estimators: this is not feasible with empirical data, due to the high relevance of the microstructure noise in the 1-s returns, but it gives useful indications in ideal conditions.

Note how in the presence of IA jumps, all the estimators but TRV°; TBV°; QRV° with 1 s data; MinRV with 1 s data, and MinRV with one second data give huge estimation errors. Note, however, that TBV°, QRV°, and MinRV have high dispersions across the different paths. We recall that the development of the asymptotic properties of the estimators when IA jumps are present has only been done for TRV, BPV (and MPVs), and TBV.

17.2.6 NOISY DATA

Estimation of IV is done with $h \to 0$. In practice, the smaller the step, the better the estimate. Because, nowadays, we have access to databases of prices that are recorded at each transaction, we can consider extremely small h.

Figure 1 in Park and Linton (2012) reports all transaction, bid and ask prices of a representative asset during a representative day. If we compare the picture with a one-day path of the commonly used model HT1FJ (Fig. 17.2a), we note that at such a fine level, the two pictures seem qualitatively different. The most striking characteristic of the empirical prices is the discreteness, as a price movement cannot be smaller than one tick. A strand of the literature still keeps SM price models (such as HT1FJ), motivated by the hypothesis of the absence of arbitrage opportunities in efficient markets. However, the behavioral discrepancy $\varepsilon \doteq X - Y$ between the observed path X and the model path Y is also accounted for. ε is called *microstructure noises* process (see Park and Linton (2012); Barndorff-Nielsen and Shephard (2006a) and references therein) and Y is called the *efficient* log-price. We are interested in the IV of Y, Y however is unobservable. Simulated noisy prices (Fig. 17.5a) seem to display a local strip (which is more evident for higher values of the noise variance), similar to the bid-ask spread, indicating an interval where the efficient price is placed. Note in Figure 1 in Park and Linton (2012) the important feature that the noisy prices X_{ti} observed at UHF display many zero returns.

Section 2.2 of Park and Linton (2012) reports how the ε behavior has been modeled in the literature. The most common framework considers *additive i.i.d. noise* (also called *additive white noise*). Even if not completely realistic (as pointed out in Hansen and Lunde (2006b)), such an assumption is accepted at moderate observation frequencies and, in general, as a first approximation to the real phenomenon. For a comprehensive discussion of the noise models and the effect of noise on the inference for the underlying process, see also Li and Mykland (2007). Most of the theoretical developments in estimating IV in the presence of noise have been conducted for continuous stochastic processes (Aït-Sahalia et al., 2005; Bandi and Russell, 2008; Jacod et al., 2009; Podolskij

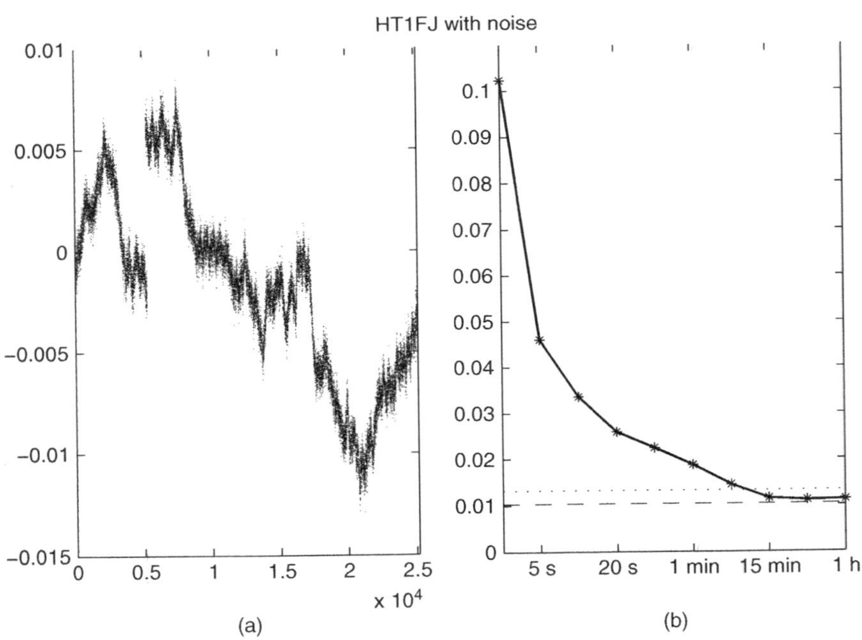

FIGURE 17.5 (a) One-day simulated path of HT1FJ model with i.i.d. Gaussian noise $\mathcal{N}(0, (4.5 * 10^{-4})^2)$, the variance being estimated from the J&J series, and $n = 25,200$; (b) SP of $\sqrt{\text{RV}_n}$ relative to the observations in (a).

and Vetter, 2009a; Zhang, 2006), but as this chapter is about jumps, we give some details only for the results on estimating IV obtained in the presence of jumps.

X is not an SM anymore in that as $h \to 0$, while the increment $|\Delta_i Y|$ of any SM tends to 0 in probability, we have for small $\varepsilon > 0$ that $P\{|\Delta_i X| > \varepsilon\}$ is close to 1, due to the fact that $P\{|\Delta_i \varepsilon| > \tilde{\varepsilon}\}$ does, for small $\tilde{\varepsilon} > 0$, for example, under the additive i.i.d. noise assumption, for the commonly used model distributions (Gaussian or uniform) for ε_{t_i}. On the other hand, when we observe prices at LF, they seem much more compatible with an SM DGP. Figure 17.1 shows that observing the SPX prices only once per day over 4 years, the true price path and the simulated paths have similar characteristics and produce similar returns. So microstructure effects have a substantial impact on data only at UHF.

When including i.i.d. centered noises, denoted $\sigma_\varepsilon^2 \doteq \mathrm{Var}[\varepsilon_{t_i}]$, because

$$\sum_i (\Delta_i Y)^2 \sim \sum_i (\Delta_i X)^2 + \sum_i (\Delta_i \varepsilon)^2 \sim [X]_T + 2n\sigma_\varepsilon^2 \qquad (17.10)$$

explodes to infinity as $h \to 0$, RV_n is not adequate anymore to estimate QV (and thus to estimate IV when X is continuous). This is reflected in Figure 17.5b, showing the SP of $\sqrt{\mathrm{RV}_n}$ of simulated log-prices generated by the HT1FJ model plus an independent Gaussian i.i.d. noise process. Note that the real data SP displayed in Figure 5 in Park and Linton (2012) shows a qualitatively similar feature.

Specific devices have been designed to robustify estimators of IV in the presence of both jumps and noise. The most common approach is *sparse sampling* that which avoids sampling too frequently. Criteria for optimal frequency selection are given in Bandi and Russell (2008) and Aït-Sahalia et al. (2005), in a BSM framework and are under study in Mancini (2011b) in the presence of jumps. The optimal frequency depends on the specific asset we need to analyze; however, 5 min is commonly considered as a watershed: for data observed at lower frequencies, noise is usually considered negligible. However, some consistent IV estimators still have significantly nonzero estimation bias for $h = 5$ min.

Andersen et al. (2007) propose *staggered versions of BPV*. As i.i.d. noise induces a first-order autocorrelation in the adjacent returns $\Delta_i X$, $\Delta_{i-1} X$ (Aït-Sahalia et al., 2005), by considering the staggered returns $\Delta_i X$, $\Delta_{i-q} X$ one breaks the correlation and $\mathrm{BPV}_n^s \doteq \sum_{i=2+q}^n |\Delta_i X||\Delta_{i-q} X|$ was defined, for fixed $q \geq 2$. The performance of such a modification of BPV, still for HF data, is shown in Huang and Tauchen (2005).

Other robust estimators of IV have been proposed, trying to use all the available data, thus facing noise but making bias corrections. The most used methods are *subsampling* (Zhang, 2006; Zhang et al., 2005) the "kernel method" (Barndorff-Nielsen et al., 2008; Zhou, 1996), and *preaveraging* (Jacod et al., 2009; Podolskij and Vetter, 2009a). Other approaches are cited in Christensen et al. (2010b). In the presence of jumps, subsampling and kernels give consistent estimators of the whole $[Y, Y]$ but not of IV. However, Fan and Wang (2007) implement subsampling on the path of an SM with FA jumps after the estimated jumps have been removed, while preaveraging is robust to jumps. We concentrate on the last two approaches.

In Gloter and Jacod (2001), it is shown that the optimal convergence rate for the IV estimation error in a noisy parametric diffusion model, with i.i.d. noise, is $n^{-1/4}$, meaning that the convergence is slower than in the absence of noise, as expected (the intuition for this is explained later). When σ is constant the minimal reachable $\text{AVar}\big(n^{1/4}(\hat{\text{IV}}_n - \text{IV})\big)$ is $8\sigma^3\sigma_\varepsilon$, which is attained by the maximum-likelihood estimator. Note that, as for extremely small h noise is the predominant term in Equation 17.10, one of the most used estimates of σ_ε^2 is $\hat{\sigma}_\varepsilon^2 = \text{RV}_n/(2n)$. Two alternative estimators are reported in Christensen et al. (2010b, p. 20).

The *subsampling* method is based on staggered RV, $[X,X]^{(\bar{n})}$, as explained in Park and Linton (2012), Equation 14. This allows us to decrease the impact of the noise on RV, because $X_{t_{jK+i}} - X_{t_{(j-1)K+i}}$ contains only one noise increment $\varepsilon_{t_{jK+i}} - \varepsilon_{t_{jK+i}}$, which has variance $2\sigma_\varepsilon^2$, in contrast $\sum_{\ell=0}^{K-1} X_{t_{jK+i-\ell}} - X_{t_{jK+i-\ell-1}}$ involves K noise increments and the variance of their sum is $2K\sigma_\varepsilon^2$. Asymptotically, $[X,X]^{(\bar{n})} \sim [Y,Y] + 2\sigma_\varepsilon^2\bar{n}$. In order to get rid of the last term, $\hat{\sigma}_\varepsilon^2$ (which equals $[X,X]^{(1)}/(2n)$) is used and the *two-scales estimator* (Equation 16 in Park and Linton, 2012) is defined (Zhang et al., 2005), where RV is computed at the two-scale levels 1 and K. As this has been shown to converge at the nonoptimal rate $n^{1/6}$, Zhang (2006) proposed a *multiscale estimator* given by a weighted sum of staggered RVs computed at different scales, $\text{MSRV} \doteq \sum_{\ell=1}^{m} a_\ell [X,X]^{(\bar{n}_\ell)}$, with $\bar{n}_\ell \to \infty, m \sim \sqrt{n} \to \infty$. By properly choosing the coefficients a_ℓ, such an estimator may be written as $\sum_{\ell=1}^{m} a_\ell [Y,Y]^{(\bar{n}_\ell)} + \sum_{\ell=1}^{m} a_\ell u_{(\bar{n}_\ell)} + o_P(1)$, where $u_{(\bar{n}_\ell)}$ are asymptotically independent, centered, r.v.s, so their weighted sum converges to their expected value 0. The MSRV estimator is rate-optimal. In Fan and Wang (2007), the *wavelets method* has been directly designed to remove jumps from the Y path and then to apply MSRV. Wavelets are real deterministic functions on $\mathbb{R}$ and give many classes of orthonormal bases for the space of the Lebesgue square integrable functions on $\mathbb{R}$. In Fan and Wang (2007), FA jumps are allowed, which preserves the Lebesgue square integrability of any path of Y on $[0, T]$. Each path $Y(\omega)$ can then be represented as a combination of elements of a chosen wavelets basis. The coefficients are time dependent and, at the times when some jumps occur, such coefficients turn out to be significantly higher than at the other times. A threshold R_n is chosen to discriminate when a coefficient has to be considered large and allows the identification of the jump times. This method allows us to remove jumps and thus to estimate the D part of Y, in the framework of FA jumps, and then (in the same spirit as Mancini and Renò (2011) for the estimation of spot volatility) to apply known methods designed to estimate IV in the BSM framework. In the absence of noise, in order to eliminate the jumps the wavelet method is nonoptimal, because, under the continuity of a and σ and the independence of D on J, the convergence rate of the estimator of $[J,J]$ is $n^{-1/4}$ rather than $n^{-1/2}$, but the method becomes interesting in the presence of noise. Under additive i.i.d. noise, jump identification remains robust, because for ultrasmall h, the Y path representation coefficients dominate the coefficients for the noise process near jump locations, while they are dominated otherwise. The jump sizes are estimated by averaging the observations X_{t_i} on local windows of amplitude $k_n \sim n^{1/2}$. MSRV is then applied to the estimated D and the IV estimation error due to jumps does not worsen the one due to noise, in fact, the final rate is optimal. The exact AVar of the estimation error is not explicitly given.

The *preaveraging method*, initiated in Podolskij and Vetter (2009b), exploits more directly the fact that the noise is centered, as instead of each noisy return $\Delta_i X$, it considers averaged (and staggered) returns $\bar{X}_m^{(K)}$, which, by the law of large numbers, asymptotically (to first order) lose the noise component (see after Equation 2.5 in Podolskij and Vetter (2009b)). More precisely, under the i.i.d. additive noise assumption, the preaveraged returns $\bar{X}_m^{(K)}$ are defined by the empirical mean of $n/L - K + 1$ staggered returns $X_{t_{i+K}} - X_{t_i}$; $m = 1, \ldots, L$ and $K, L \sim \sqrt{n}$. The *modulated bipower variation* $\mathrm{MBV}_n(X, r, \ell)$ is then defined as the scaling factor $n^{\frac{r+\ell}{2} - \frac{1}{2}}$ times the sum of L bipower variation terms $|\bar{X}_m^{(K)}|^r |\bar{X}_{m+1}^{(K)}|^\ell$. It turns out that the mean of the MBV terms involves the second moment of the preaveraged returns, and in Podolskij and Vetter (2009a) it is shown that in the presence of FA jumps, taking $r \vee \ell < 2$ then $\mathrm{MBV}_n(X, r, \ell) \xrightarrow{P} C_0 \int_0^T (C_1 \sigma_u^2 + C_2 \sigma_\varepsilon^2)^{\frac{r+\ell}{2}} du$, with known constants C_i, so combining MBV with $\hat{\sigma}_\varepsilon^2$ allows us to estimate IV. Analogously, *modulated multipower variations* $\mathrm{MMV}(X, r_1, \ldots, r_k)$ are defined and are shown to be robust to FA jumps when $\max_i r_i < 2$. Their combination with MBV and $\hat{\sigma}_\varepsilon^2$ allows us to estimate also the integrals of arbitrary positive powers of σ. Under the further assumptions (Itô σ) and that the noise terms ε_{t_i} are realizations of an independent scaled BM, then, for specified ranges of the powers to be used and in the absence of jumps, the convergence rate of MBV and MMV is $n^{-1/4}$. The choice of L and K is such as to optimize the estimation error AVar, which however turns out to be higher than the AVar of the kernel estimator of Barndorff-Nielsen et al. (2008).

In Podolskij and Vetter (2009b), MBV is generalized, in that the preaveraged returns $\tilde{X}_i^{(K)}$ are given by weighted sums of K returns $\Delta_i X$ with more general weights. The *bipower-type estimator* $\mathrm{BT}_n(\ell, r)$ is built as the K-staggered BPV of the $\tilde{X}_i^{(K)}$ with $K \sim \sqrt{n}$ and scaling factor $n^{(r+\ell)/4-1}$. What the authors gain is that IV is then consistently estimated allowing for also IA jumps, in the presence of additive i.i.d. noise. More precisely, Theorem 2 shows that $\mathrm{BT}_n(2, 0) \xrightarrow{P} \int_0^T C_1 \sigma_u^2 du + C_2 \sigma_\varepsilon^2 + C_3 \sum_{s \le T} |\Delta Y_s|^2$ and $\mathrm{BT}_n(\ell, r) \xrightarrow{P} \mu_\ell \mu_r \int_0^T (C_1 \sigma_u^2 + C_2 \sigma_\varepsilon^2)^{(r+\ell)/(2)} du$ as soon as $\ell \vee r < 2$. A consistent estimator of IV is thus obtained by combining $\mathrm{BT}_n(1, 1)$ with $\hat{\sigma}_\varepsilon^2$. When jumps are absent and σ is a never 0 Itô BSM then IV is estimated at the optimal rate $n^{-1/4}$.

When preaveraging, it is particularly clear why the optimal convergence rate is $n^{-1/4}$. $\sqrt{n}$ data of the whole sample is used for "denoising" the returns, and the remaining $\tilde{n} = \sqrt{n}$ "denoised" data is used to construct the estimator, so the convergence rate is $\sqrt{\tilde{n}} = n^{1/4}$. A similar phenomenon happens with the kernel and the multiscaling methods.

Finally, we mention the robustification of two other estimators of IV to the presence of additive i.i.d. noise, still in models with FA jumps. By applying the quantile-based QRV to the preaveraged returns, in Christensen et al. (2010b), an estimation of IV is obtained with convergence rate $n^{-1/4}$; $\vartheta = 8.5\sigma^3\sigma_\varepsilon$ in the constant σ case. In Christensen et al. (2009), robustification of the range bipower variation is done by considering $\sum_{i_1}^{N} |s_{Y,i,m} - 2\hat{\sigma}_\varepsilon||s_{Y,i+1,m} - 2\hat{\sigma}_\varepsilon|$. Only consistency is stated in the paper.

17.2.7 MULTIVARIATE ASSETS

When X is a d-dimensional Itô SM, it can be represented as in Equation 17.1 with $a_s \in \mathbb{R}^d$ at all times s, a multidimensional standard BM $W_s \in \mathbb{R}^{d'}$, $\sigma_s \in \mathbb{R}^{d\times d'}$, jump sizes $\gamma(x,s) \in \mathbb{R}^d$, where the space of the marks x is $\mathbb{R}$ and the counting measure $\mu(\{x\}\times[0,t])$ still takes values in $\mathbb{N}\cup\{0\}$. In this case, we have that as $h \to 0$

$$\mathrm{RV}_n \doteq \sum_i \Delta_i X \Delta_i X' \xrightarrow{P} \int_0^T \Sigma_s \mathrm{d}s + \sum_{s\in[0,T]} \Delta X_s \Delta X_s',$$

where X' means the transpose of X and $\Sigma = \sigma\sigma' \in \mathbb{R}^{d\times d}$. RV_n is now a matrix, the *realized variance–covariance* matrix, and to fix ideas we concentrate on its (ℓ, r)th component $\mathrm{RC} \doteq \sum_i \Delta_i X^\ell \Delta_i X^r$, called the *realized covariation* between X^ℓ and X^r. As $h \to 0$, the RC limiting value is $[X^\ell, X^r]_T \doteq \mathrm{IC} + \sum_{s\in[0,T]} \Delta X_s^\ell \Delta X_s^r$, called the *quadratic covariation* (QC) of X^ℓ and X^r, where $\mathrm{IC} \doteq \sum_{k=1}^d \int_0^T \sigma_s^{\ell,k}\sigma_s^{r,k}\mathrm{d}s$. $[X^\ell, X^r]_T$ measures how the two components of X covariate, accounting for both the Brownian and the jump risks. For instance, if the Brownian parts of X^ℓ, X^r are, respectively, $\sigma_1 W^\ell$, $\sigma_2[\rho W^\ell + \sqrt{1-\rho^2}W^r]$ with càdlàg coefficients, then $\mathrm{IC} = \int_0^T \rho_s\sigma_{1s}\sigma_{2s}\,\mathrm{d}s$.

Each term $\Delta X_s^\ell \Delta X_s^r$ is called a *cojump*, because it is nonzero only if both assets ℓ and r jumped at time s. An important application of QC is determining the eventual *orthogonality* (QC $\equiv 0$) of two square integrable martingales, which is strictly tied with their stochastic independence. In particular, the presence of cojumps of (X^ℓ, X^r) indicates dependence between their jump components (Cont and Tankov (2004) in the case of Lévy processes). Thus, cojumping is for jump processes the analogous concept to the correlation coefficient for two correlated BMs, and models the financial effect of the contagion arising from sudden happenings (such as the propagation of a crash or the contagion of a default) or shocks of common fundamentals underlying the assets. See Lahaye et al. (2011) for an analysis of the determinants of cojumps of specific assets.

How the returns of the assets in a portfolio covariate influences the global return and thus portfolio risk management and selection (Das and Uppal, 2004). As mentioned in the univariate case, the risk premium of a derivative product written on jumping assets is shown to be composed of two parts (see Bjork et al. (1997), Equation 20, p. 222) accounting in different ways for the Brownian and for the jump risks, which has an impact in the pricing of the product.

This highlights the importance of separately estimating IC and the sum of the cojumps. Clearly, the estimation of the first allows estimating the second, for example, by subtracting $\hat{IC}$ from RC, and thus allows measuring the jump risk.

Multivariate extensions of the estimation of IV in nonparametric frameworks and in the presence of jumps in assets returns have only, as far as we know, been done using *bipower covariation* by Barndorff-Nielsen and Shephard (2004c), *threshold realized covariation* by Mancini and Gobbi (2012), or *outlyingness weighted QC* by Boudt et al. (2010). All three methods require having synchronous observations, while in practice, especially with HF or UHF data, this is not that realistic. If one needs the log-price X^ℓ at time t_i, one of the used approaches is to take the (log of the) last transaction price level that the asset reached before (or at) t_i. But, as is quite clear from Figure 1 in Park and Linton (2012), when h is very small, this implies that many returns will be 0 and RC will tend to 0 when $h \to 0$ (this is the Epps effect: see Barndorff-Nielsen and Shephard (2006a). Some devices have been adopted in the literature to synchronize bivariate data (Barndorff-Nielsen et al., 2008; Hayashi and Yoshidam, 2005) in order to recover consistent estimation of the IC of a BSM. In Mancini and Gobbi (2012), it is shown that a modified threshold RC, using the Hayashi and Yoshida selection criterion, consistently estimates IC in the presence of both asynchronous data and of FA jumps.

17.3 Testing for the Presence of Jumps

Within the same framework as in Equation 17.1, with X observed discretely, many different devices have been invented in the literature to test for the presence of jumps in asset prices. We remark that we can only analyze one path of X, the one of which we can observe the states X_{t_i} on the time horizon $[0, T]$. Thus, concluding that no jumps occurred does not mean that the DGP contains no jump parts at all, but simply that no jumps occurred for that ω and in that time horizon. Further, as argued in different ways by Lee and Hannig (2010) and Lee and Ploberger (Lee and Ploberger), if we try to identify the jump sizes through the increments $\Delta_i X$, then, because of the Lèvy law for BM paths, the eventual jumps in $]t_{i-1}, t_i]$ with sizes less than $\bar{H} \doteq \sup_{t\in]t_{i-1},t_i]} |\sigma_t|\sqrt{2h\ln(1/h)}$ will inevitably be confused with the variations of the BSM part of X.

We concentrate on the existing nonparametric tests. In most cases, the following assumptions are required, methodologies are adopted, and results are obtained: T is 1 day, and intraday evenly spaced (in time) returns are used; the theoretical framework only allows for FA jumps; microstructure noise is absent; the hypothesis H_0 of the absence of jumps within the interval $[0, T]$ is tested versus H_1 that some jumps occurred; the size of the test is established theoretically while the power is shown on simulated data; the speed of convergence of the test statistic under the null is $\sqrt{h}$ and the limit in distribution of its standardized version is a standard Gaussian r.v. We remark when one of these is not the case in the following list of methods. Note that, by the Itô formula, t is a jump time for an asset price S iff it is such for the log-price X.

Since Eraker et al. (2003), testing for jumps in volatility has become important. This problem is in principle more difficult than testing for the presence of jumps in X, as σ is not observable. As far as we know, no work in nonparametric frameworks has been done in this direction, while Jacod and Todorov (2010) test for cojumps in spot price and volatility. We only concentrate on testing for jumps in returns.

17.3.1 CONFIDENCE INTERVALS

The following tests are obtained by finding a statistic S_n, constructed with the observed returns, which behaves differently in the presence than in the absence of jumps. In most cases, S_n tends to 0 in probability in the absence of jumps while it tends to ∞ (or to a constant number $A > 0$) in their presence. Clearly, in order to accept or reject the hypothesis H_0 of no jumps, it is necessary to establish when S_n is significantly different from 0. So we need to find a confidence interval containing 0 and such that when S_n falls outside, we can "safely" reject H_0. Construction of confidence intervals is made possible using CLTs. If under H_0 our S_n converges in distribution to a centered r.v. Z with known law (usually Gaussian or mixed Gaussian), confidence intervals are obtained through the quantiles of such a law. Tabulation of all quantiles is easily retrieved only for standardized laws. If Z has constant variance V then the standardized $S_n/\sqrt{V}$ tends in distribution to $Z/\sqrt{V}$ with unit variance (Chung, 1974). However, if V is a r.v. then the convergence in distribution of $S_n/\sqrt{V}$ is not guaranteed anymore if we only have the convergence in distribution of S_n. If on the contrary the convergence of S_n is a little bit stronger, such as 'stable convergence in law' (see its definition and properties, e.g., in Jacod (2007)), then the convergence in law of the standardized statistic is ensured and rigorous construction of confidence intervals is permitted. We finally remark that a test is feasible when the asymptotic variance V is in turn estimable using the observations of X. If V_n converges in probability to V then stable convergence in law also implies that $S_n/\sqrt{V_n}$ stably tends to $Z/\sqrt{V}$.

17.3.2 TESTS BASED ON $\hat{\text{IV}}_n - \text{RV}_n$ OR ON $1 - \hat{\text{IV}}_n/\text{RV}_n$

Under the null of no jumps, $\hat{\text{IV}}_n - \text{RV}_n \xrightarrow{P} 0$, while in the presence of jumps $\hat{\text{IV}}_n - \text{RV}_n \xrightarrow{P} -\sum_{s\leq T}(\Delta X_s)^2 < 0$, so that, when standardizing by the proper convergence speed (typically $\sqrt{h}$), the last statistics explode to infinity. Tests based on $\hat{\text{IV}}_n - \text{RV}_n$ take the name of *linear tests*; however, in some cases simple transformations of a linear test have been shown to perform better in finite samples of simulated data. In particular, the *ratio tests* are based on $1 - \hat{\text{IV}}_n/\text{RV}_n$, which tends to 0 in probability under H_0 and tends to $1 - \text{IV}/(\text{IV} + [J, J]_T) > 0$ under H_1. Consequently also this quantity, once normalized by $\sqrt{h}$, explodes under H_1. The asymptotic theory for the ratio test is directly obtained from the one for the linear test by simply using the 'delta method.' We indicate the various tests with simply the initial letters of the their inventors names.

Barndorff-Nielsen and Shephard test (Barndorff-Nielsen and Shephard, 2006b). Under the same assumptions as for Equation 17.6, the following ratio test statistic is defined

$$\mathcal{S}_n^{\mathrm{BS}} \doteq \frac{1 - \mathrm{BPV}_n/\mathrm{RV}_n}{\sqrt{\dfrac{h \cdot \vartheta_{\mathrm{BPV}} \mathrm{MPV}_n^{1,1,1,1}}{\mathrm{BPV}_n^2}}}.$$

X jumps iff $\mathcal{S}_n^{\mathrm{BS}}$ is significantly different from 0. The authors analyze also adjusted ratio, linear, and log versions of this test. $\mathcal{S}_n^{\mathrm{BS}}$ is asymptotically standard Gaussian under the null H_0 of no jumps. The rejection region is thus given by $\{\mathcal{S}_n^{\mathrm{BS}} > 1.64\}$, which under H_0 has asymptotic probability equal to 5%.

Corsi, Pirino, and Renò test (Corsi et al., 2010). Under the assumptions mentioned after Equation 17.8, a statistic similar to $\mathcal{S}_n^{\mathrm{BS}}$ is proposed, but where the returns are replaced by thresholded returns in BPV_n and the needed MPVs. To improve the finite sample performance of the test, the authors use tripower variation in place of quadpower variation and make a correction to the threshold elimination criterion by substituting $E[|\sigma\Delta_i W|^r|(\sigma\Delta_i W)^2 > 9\sigma^2 h]$ for $|\Delta_i X|^r$ when the return is over the threshold function, rather than excluding it. This conditional expectation is explicitly given in the paper and is used with $\hat{\sigma}_{t_i}$ in place of σ, where $\hat{\sigma}_{t_i}^2$ is a threshold recursive estimator of spot volatility, constructed as explained in Section 17.2.3. The same asymptotic theory is obtained as for $\mathcal{S}_n^{\mathrm{BS}}$ and the same type of rejection region is considered but with varying levels. The authors find that, unlike for the pure estimation purpose, the correction is essential to improve the size of this test.

Christensen and Podolskij (Christensen and Podolskij, 2010) use the asymptotic results on the range-based estimator $\mathrm{RBV}_{n,m}$ to modify the ratio test $\mathcal{S}_n^{\mathrm{BS}}$ by replacing BPV_n with $\mathrm{RBV}_{n,m}$, $\mathrm{MPV}_n^{1,1,1,1}$ by the range-based analogous $RQQ_{n,m}$, where the absolute returns $|\Delta_{i-k}X|$ are replaced by $s_{X,i-k,h,m}$ and ϑ_{BPV} by a proper constant ν_m based on the moments $\lambda_{r,m}$ of the BM range. The test is still asymptotically Gaussian under the null, and, on simulated data, the authors show that there is no evidence of size distortion and that the test has higher power than the BS test. An observation step of $h = 20$ s is considered but microstructure noise is not accounted for, and the $n = mN = 1170$ considered intraday observations are divided into a varying number $N = 39, 78, 390$ of blocks of sizes $m = 30, 15, 3$.

Jiang and Oomen test (Jiang and Oomen, 2008). The drift coefficient of X is specified by $a_t = \alpha_t - \lambda_t \eta_t - V_t/2$, where λ_t is the instantaneous jump intensity and η_t is the mean of the jump size of $S = \exp(X)$. This specification and the Itô formula imply that $\int_0^T 2\mathrm{d}S_t/S_{t-} - \mathrm{d}X_t = \mathrm{IV}_T + 2\sum_{t\le T}(\mathrm{e}^{\Delta X_t} - 1 - \frac{1}{2}(\Delta X_t)^2 - \Delta X_t)$, thus, under H_0, the discretized version of the left-hand side gives an estimate of IV. For this reason, the authors define and study the test statistic

$$\mathcal{S}_n^{\text{JO}} = \left[2 \sum_{i=1}^{n} \frac{S_{t_i} - S_{t_{i-1}}}{S_{t_{i-1}}} - 2 \ln \frac{S_T}{S_0} \right] - \text{RV}_n,$$

which tends to 0 under H_0, and to a jumps driven term otherwise. Because a Taylor expansion of $\mathcal{S}_n^{\text{JO}}$ only involves third and higher powers of the returns, whose expectation has a magnitude order of h, the $\mathcal{S}_n^{\text{JO}}$ speed of convergence to 0 under H_0 is h rather than the usual $\sqrt{h}$. However, in finite samples, we cannot state that the JO test dominates the BS ones (Dumitru and Urga, 2011). Under general predictable α coefficient and strictly positive càdlàg σ, the standardized $\mathcal{S}_n^{\text{JO}}/h$ is asymptotically standard Gaussian under H_0. AVar$(\mathcal{S}_n^{\text{JO}}/h)$ is a constant multiple of the integrated *sexticity* $\int_0^T \sigma_t^6 dt$, which is consistently estimated using MPVs. The test rejection region is similar to that for the BS test.

17.3.3 TESTS BASED ON NORMALIZED RETURNS

When a (big) jump arrives within $]t_{i-1}, t_i]$, the realized return is expected to be much higher than that due only to Brownian innovations, if h is small. So in order to test for the presence of jumps, one could look at the magnitude of $|\Delta_i X|$. However, an increment $\Delta_i(\sigma \cdot W)$ could still realize high absolute values, if the volatility coefficient was high within $]t_{i-1}, t_i]$. So it is natural to standardize $\Delta_i X$ by a measure of the local volatility. This also makes comparable increments $\Delta_i(\sigma \cdot W)$ relative to different intervals $]t_{i-1}, t_i]$ among which the volatility could be highly different. The idea is in fact the same pursued to construct TBV (when comparing $(\Delta_i X)^2$ with $9\hat{\sigma}_{t_i}^2 h$ in order to establish whether $\Delta_i X$ has to be included within the estimator of IV) and ROWV. Thus, the statistics

$$\mathcal{T}_i^2 = \frac{(\Delta_i X)^2}{h \cdot \hat{\sigma}_{t_i}^2}, \quad i = 1, \ldots, n$$

are considered, (we indicate ...) $\mathcal{T}_i = \Delta_i X / (\sqrt{h}\hat{\sigma}_i)$, as under the null hypothesis of no jumps $\mathcal{T}_i^2 \sim \frac{(\Delta_i W)^2}{h}$, that is, $\mathcal{T}_i^2$ asymptotically have law $\chi^2(1)$. On the contrary, under H_1, if one jump occurs, we have $\mathcal{T}_i^2 >> \frac{(\Delta_i W)^2}{h}$ for sufficiently small h, as the jump size is nonzero while the denominator of $\mathcal{T}_i^2$ tends to 0. If more jumps with different signs occur within $]t_{i-1}, t_i]$, it is possible that the sum of their contributions remains small, thus making it difficult to recognize their presence. However, under FA jumps for sufficiently small h, each $]t_{i-1}, t_i]$ will contain at most one jump.

In order to construct $\mathcal{T}_i^2$, spot $\sigma_{t_i}^2$ needs to be estimated, and the four tests in this category differ in the choice of how to estimate it. Three of them use a *local window* of returns $\Delta_{i+j} X, j = -K, \ldots, -1$ with $K \to \infty$ in such a way that $hK \to 0$. For the sake of greater theoretical tractability, three of the four tests assume some degree of smoothness for the sample paths of a and σ, in particular, their continuity in time is required. This is somewhat restrictive, as for some assets, empirical evidence exists that σ does jump (Jacod and Todorov, 2010).

S. Lee and Mykland (Lee and Mykland, 2008) base $\hat{\sigma}^2_{ih}$ on BPV computed within a local window with $K \sim h^{\alpha}, \alpha \in]-1, -1/2[$:

$$\hat{\sigma}^2_{t_i} \doteq \frac{2}{\pi} \frac{\mathrm{BPV}_n(t_{i-1}) - \mathrm{BPV}_n(t_{i-K+1})}{h(K-2)}.$$

In fact, this behaves asymptotically like $c\int_{t_{i-K+1}}^{t_i} \sigma_s^2 ds/(h(K-2)) \sim c\sigma^2_{t_{i-K+1}}$ with some constants c. Because for the underlying process a and σ are assumed to be a.s. continuous in t, the fluctuations of their paths are not too wild, and we have $\sigma^2_{t_{i-K+1}} \sim \sigma^2_{t_{i-1}} \sim \sigma^2_{t_i}$. Under the null of no jumps, the T_is are shown to behave asymptotically as Gaussian independent r.v.s and the asymptotic Gumbel distribution of $\max_{i=1,\ldots,n} |T_i|$ is explicitly given. On the contrary, under the alternative hypothesis H_1 of FA jumps, for each $i = 1, \ldots, n$ if a jump occurs within $]t_{i-1}, t_i]$ the statistic $|T_i|$ explodes to infinity. Consequently, the following rejection region is established

$$\frac{\max_i |T_i| - C(n)}{S(n)} > \beta^{\star}$$

with constants $C(n), S(n)$ explicitly given in terms of n and proper critical level $\beta^{\star}$. The authors asses the optimal choice of the parameter K on simulated data and verify the performance of the test. Interestingly, the test is applied to study the dynamics of jump arrivals, and empirical evidence of jump clustering is found in foreign currency exchange markets.

Andersen, Bollerslev and Dobrev (Andersen et al., 2007) keep the BPV criterion to estimate the local squared volatility; however, their test differs from the LM one in three respects. First, $\sigma^2_{t_i}$ is estimated using all the data $\Delta_j X, j = 1, \ldots, n$ within the day ($T = 1$ day), rather than within a smaller local window. So the denominator is the same for all the statistics T_i^2. In particular, unlike the LM procedure, in order to detect whether a jump occurred within $]t_{i-1}, t_i]$, the single intraday return $\Delta_i X$ at the numerator of T_i^2 is not necessarily the last of the data set used to estimate $\sigma^2_{t_i}$. Secondly, the detection of jumps is conducted at two different levels. On the one hand, the authors analyze the occurrence of at least one jump within the day by rejecting this hypothesis if there exists an $i \in \{1, \ldots, n\}$ such that $|T_i| > C$, for some critical level $C > 0$. On the other hand, the occurrence of multiple intraday jumps is investigated by considering the jump-adjusted returns $\{\Delta_i X I_{\{|T_i| > C\}}\}_{i=1,\ldots,n}$ and by verifying, through a variety of specific tests, whether these behave like the tail of a vector of n i.i.d. Gaussian r.v.s Z_i, as asymptotically would have to be the case, by the property that $\int_0^t \sigma_s dW_s$ is a time changed Brownian motion B_{IV_t}. If the size of the first test is set to $\alpha = P\{\exists i \in \{1, \ldots, n\} : |Z_i| > C\} = 1 - P\{|Z_i| \leq C, i = 1, \ldots, n\} = 1 - P\{|Z_i| \leq C\}^n$ then C is the $1/2 + (1-\alpha)^h/2$ quantile of the standard Gaussian law, and the confidence interval $[-C, C]$ for the hypothesis of no jumps in $]t_{i-1}, t_i]$ has level $P\{|Z_i| \leq C\} = (1-\alpha)^h$. The size and power of the test are verified on simulated models with càdlàg σ, but without drift, and compared with the size and power of the BS test. Thirdly, the empirical application of the test is performed using 2-min returns, so adjustments for the presence of microstructure noise are made as detailed in the next section, with the aim of assessing the empirical validity of an SM model with FA jumps for a record of SPX prices.

Boudt et al. (2011) argue that when long local windows, such as one or more days, are needed in finite samples, a better performance is expected for the LM and ABD tests if the spot volatility daily periodicity is accounted for. They propose to correct the spot variance estimators by a factor f_i, which is a jump-robust estimator of the intraday periodicity in volatility.

S. Lee and Hannig (Lee and Hannig, 2010) extend the previous analysis in the presence of possibly IA jumps. The jump component of X is assumed to be in the Lévy class. The drift coefficient a is 0 and σ is assumed to have continuous paths. Spot σ^2 is estimated similarly as in Aït-Sahalia and Jacod (2009) by

$$\hat{\sigma}^2_{t_i} \doteq \frac{\text{TRV}_n(t_{i-1}) - \text{TRV}_n(t_{i-K-1})}{hK},$$

where TRV is used in place of BPV. For all i, this $\hat{\sigma}^2_{t_i}$ is a consistent estimator, for any $K \to \infty$, with $hK \to 0$. In order to identify presence and arrival times of the jumps of X, the authors apply the same methodology as in Lee and Mykland (2008); however, they remark that through it, for a given time step h, we can only unearth jumps bigger than the previously mentioned $\bar{H}$. Note that the smaller the considered h, the smaller $\overline{H}$. However, the authors interestingly propose a method to detect also the presence of jumps smaller than $\bar{H}$ with fixed h, consisting in making the QQ-plot of all the statistics $\mathcal{T}_{K+1}, \ldots, \mathcal{T}_n$, which under the null asymptotically behave like i.i.d. Gaussian r.v.s. Therefore, a significant deviation of the QQ-plot from the 45° line indicates deviation of the model from the null. In order to evaluate the impact of errors due to the finiteness of the available samples, a ***blue envelope*** of the admissible deviations of the QQ-plot under the null is formed using simulations. Further, when the data QQ-plot leads to reject the null of no jumps, the location of the small jumps is established through a devised 'belief measure' $b(t_i)$, which is close to 0 under the null of no jumps, and is close to 1 if a jump occurred in $]t_{i-1}, t_i]$. This investigation allows us to establish whether FA jumps are sufficient or not to describe a given data set. The authors show in their simulation study that UHF data is needed to obtain reliable performance of the tests; however, the effect of the microstructure noise in finite samples is not clear. A comparison is also conducted with the following $\mathcal{S}_n^{\text{AJ}}$ test, which shares the same problem of requiring UHF data to be reliable. To avoid having recourse to UHF data, Lee and Hannig apply their tests to 5-min empirical data but which span a very long-time horizon, and find that jump components with IA have to be incorporated in models for some US indices as well as for individual stocks included therein. Interestingly, they find that the two different classes of assets have different IA jump components.

T. Lee and Ploberger test (Lee and Ploberger, 2010) is similar in spirit to the LM one, as the presence of a jump is guessed if $\max_{i=K+1,\ldots,n} \mathcal{T}_i^2$ is too large. However, here $\hat{\sigma}_{t_i}^2$ is given by

$$\hat{\sigma}_{t_i}^2 = \frac{\sum_{j=i-K}^{i-1}(\Delta_j X)^2}{Kh},$$

a simple RV based on the local window of the K returns preceding t_i. In fact, for $K \to \infty$ such that $Kh \to 0$, we have $\hat{\sigma}_{t_i}^2 I_{\{t \in]t_{i-1},t_i]\}} \to \sigma_{t-}^2$ even if no bipower or threshold are applied (Ngo and Ogawa, 2009). Assuming that the coefficients a and σ of X are diffusions and $K \geq \ln n$, the size and power of the test are theoretically obtained. The rejection region is $\{\max_i \mathcal{T}_i^2 > C\}$, where the critical level C for obtaining an asymptotic size of α is shown to be the solution of some explicit moment condition for the r.v. $\frac{\sum_{j=i-K}^{i-1} Z_j^2}{K}$, where Z_j are i.i.d. standard normal. By manipulating the equation, C turns out to have a magnitude of the order of $\ln n$. The authors state that for any fixed $\varepsilon > 0$, the test is consistent against jumps with size greater than or equal to $(1+\varepsilon)\sigma_t\sqrt{2h\ln(1/h)}$, and this property is called *rate-optimality* of the test. LP study the finite sample performance of the test on simulated HF and UHF data and make comparisons with the AJ, BS, and LM tests. They also comparatively apply the test to empirical HF data and find evidence of jumps in many assets, and interestingly they verify the theoretical finding that, at a higher frequency, the number of detected jumps should be higher, as the "confusing" level $\sqrt{2h\ln(1/h)}$ decreases.

17.3.4 PV-BASED TESTS

Ait-Sahalia and Jacod in Aït-Sahalia and Jacod (2009) consider the test statistic

$$\mathcal{S}_n^{\mathrm{AJ}} = \frac{\mathrm{PV}_n(p, kh)}{\mathrm{PV}_n(p, h)},$$

with any power $p > 2$ and staggering fixed constant $k \geq 2$. If jumps are present, as $h \to 0$ both the involved power variations converge to the same limit $\sum_{s \leq T} |\Delta X_s|^p$. As a result, their ratio converges in probability to 1. On the other hand, if no jumps are present, the sum of the pth power of the jump sizes is 0 and then both power variations in $\mathcal{S}_n^{\mathrm{AJ}}$ tend to 0. However, the exact speed at which they converge depends on the sampling interval kh, and $\mathcal{S}_n^{\mathrm{AJ}}$ tends in probability to $k^{p/2-1}$, due to the difference between the two sampling frequencies. The considered X model is quite general, allowing for IA jumps. Two tests are constructed using $\mathcal{S}_n^{\mathrm{AJ}}$, one for the hypothesis H_0 of the absence of jumps in $[0, T]$, and the other one for the hypothesis H_0 that some jumps occurred. The asymptotic theory is developed for the two tests, both under H_0 as well as under H_1.

Podolskij and Ziggel (Podolskij and Ziggel, 2010) bootstrap power variations of X and construct a test using the statistic

$$\mathcal{S}_n^{\mathrm{PZ}} = n^{\frac{p-1}{2}} \sum_{i=1}^{n} |\Delta_i X|^p (1 - \eta_i I_{\{|\Delta_i X|^2 \le c h^{\alpha}\}}),$$

where η_i are i.i.d. r.v.s independent of X, with mean 1 and finite variance, $p \ge 2, c > 0, \alpha \in [0, 1]$. If no jumps occur, then asymptotically all the increments $\Delta_i X$ are below the threshold and $\mathcal{S}_n^{\mathrm{PZ}}$ behaves like $\tilde{\mathcal{S}}_n^{\mathrm{PZ}} = n^{\frac{p-1}{2}} \sum_{i=1}^{n} |\Delta_i X|^p (1 - \eta_i)$. Conditionally on X, $\tilde{\mathcal{S}}_n^{PZ}$ has expectation 0 and variance $n^{p-1} \sum_{i=1}^{n} |\Delta_i X|^{2p} \mathrm{Var}[\eta_i]$. The latter coincides with a constant factor times a scaled power variation of X, and converges in probability to a constant multiple of $\mu_{2p} \int_0^T |\sigma_s|^{2p} ds$. That implies, through a Berry–Esseen argument, the conditional stable convergence of $\mathcal{S}_n^{\mathrm{PZ}}$ to a mixed Gaussian r.v.. On the other hand, if $]t_{i-1}, t_i]$ contains a jump time, then asymptotically the η_i-term is not included within $\mathcal{S}_n^{\mathrm{PZ}}$, and $\Delta_i X$ contributes only by $|\Delta_i X|^p$. By Equation 17.5, $\mathcal{S}_n^{\mathrm{PZ}}/n^{(p-1)/2} \to \sum_{s \le T} |\Delta X_s|^p$, implying explosion of $\mathcal{S}_n^{\mathrm{PZ}}$. The rejection region is given by $\{\mathcal{S}_n^{\mathrm{PZ}}/\hat{V}_n > C\}$, where the normalizing factor $\hat{V}_n$ estimates the asymptotic variance of $\mathcal{S}_n^{\mathrm{PZ}}$ and makes $\mathcal{S}_n^{\mathrm{PZ}}/\hat{V}_n$ asymptotically Gaussian.

This test is applicable to the widest possible class of Itô SMs, also allowing for IA jumps. The asymptotic theory is developed both under H_0 of no jumps and under H_1. The test can asymptotically reach any desired level and is consistent. Proper choice of η_i distribution and threshold parameters is discussed in the paper. An extensive simulation study compares the performance of the test with the BS and AJ ones.

17.3.4.1 Remarks. 1. In Bajgrowicz and Scaillet (2010), a tool to assess the number of detected jumps is proposed when implementing for L days any daily test statistics $\mathcal{S}_n$ that, as the adjusted ratio test of BNS or the AJ test, satisfy given conditions. If for each day t, $\mathcal{S}_{n,t}, t = 1, \ldots, L$ is implemented based on n observations per day and (L, n) jointly tend to ∞ under a given constraint, then the authors suggest classifying as spurious all the jumps for which $\mathcal{S}_{n,t}$ is below the universal threshold $\sqrt{2 \log L}$. In fact this latter bound is asymptotically the expected maximum absolute value of a sequence of L independent standard normal r.v.s, and is a natural threshold for $\max_{t=1,\ldots,L} \mathcal{S}_{n,t}$ under the null of no jumps. Recall that the maximal intraday statistic $\max_{i=1,\ldots,n} |T_i|$ of LM is asymptotically Gumbel distributed. This implies that $P(\max_{i=1,\ldots,n} |T_i| \le \sqrt{2 \ln n}) \sim \mathrm{e}^{-1}$, and note that it is not a special case of the result $P(\max_{t=1,\ldots,L} |\mathcal{S}_{n,t}| \le \sqrt{2 \ln L}) \sim \mathrm{e}^{-1/(\sqrt{\pi \ln L})}$ in Bajgrowicz and Scaillet (2010), neither for $L = 1$ nor for $L = n$ and $n = 1$, due to the failure of the constraint for (L, n) when $n = 1$.

2. **Local power**. In some cases, the *local power* of the proposed test is studied. A sequence of alternative hypothesis H_1^n is considered such that, as $n \to \infty$, H_1^n gets closer and closer to H_0. For instance, in Lee and Ploberger (Lee and Ploberger, 2011), $H_0 : X_t \equiv W_t$ is tested versus $H_1^n : X_t = W_t + c_n I_{\{\tau \le t\}}$, where

$c_n = O(\sqrt{\frac{1}{n}\log n}) \to 0$ and τ is a finite positive r.v. We say that $H_1^n \to H_0$. This choice of moving alternative hypotheses stresses the capability of the test to correctly recognize a jump. If $\{S_n > C\}$ is the rejection region of the test of the hypothesis H_0, the local power is the limiting behavior of $P\{S_n > C|H_1^n\}$ as $n \to \infty$, and gives a measure of the test detection capability. Most importantly, it offers a criterion for comparing different tests through their capability measures. LP and PZ analyze the local power of their respective tests and both compare them with the local powers of the BS and AJ tests. Local power properties of many tests (e.g., LM) have not been studied.

17.3.5 TESTS BASED ON SIGNATURE PLOTS

In order to construct the two following tests, the whole plot of some transformations of $\mathrm{PV}_n(p, kh)$ as a function of p is considered. In both tests, we have that jumps in $X(\omega)$ occurred within $[0, T]$ iff such a curve displays a kink at some point p.

Woerner (Woerner, 2006a) defines the *log-power variation* function

$$b_n(p) \doteq \frac{\ln(h \cdot \mathrm{PV}_n(p, h))}{p \ln h},$$

and shows its different limiting behaviors for $h \to 0$ when X falls into different classes or when we choose different powers p. Even models beyond the SM framework are considered. In particular, $b_n(p)$ tends in probability to $1/2$ if X has continuous paths and possibly stochastic volatility while the limit is $1/2 \wedge 1/p$ if X is a model of the Ornstein–Uhlenbeck type with both Brownian term and Lévy jumps. Thus, Woerner proposes taking $p >> 2$ and concluding that X jumps iff $b_n(p)$ is close to $1/p$. If on the contrary $b_n(p)$ is close to $1/2$ then X is consistent with a continuous paths model. The assumptions on X are the ones under which the consistency of scaled power variations is guaranteed. CLTs for $b_n(p)$ are established under some further restrictions on the model (e.g., a BG index $<$ 1) or on the allowed range for p. These CLT results are, however, important, as they provide confidence intervals to support the decision based on $b_n(p)$.

With a similar logic, **Todorov and Tauchen** (Todorov and Tauchen, 2010a) define the following *activity signature* function

$$b_n(p) = \frac{p \log k}{\log k + \log[\mathrm{PV}_n(p, kh)] - \log[\mathrm{PV}_n(p, h)]}, p > 0.$$

As a consequence of Theorem 1 therein, when X is a pure jump process with constant BG index β then $b_n(p)$ consistently estimates β, as $h \to 0$. However, the behavior of $b_n(p)$ turns out to be a useful tool for any Itô SM with possibly IA jumps but constant BG index. In fact, $\forall p > 0$, $b_n(p)$ converges in probability to 2 if X contains a Brownian term and no jumps; to $p \vee 2, \forall p > 0$, if X contains $\sigma \cdot W$ plus jumps; and to $p \vee \beta$ if X is driven by a pure jump process. Thus, the test is performed by visually inspecting the graph of $b_n(p)$. No theoretical confidence intervals are given for this test, but a simulation study is performed. The authors remark that the presence of additive i.i.d. noise would destroy all information, because $b_n(p)$ would diverge for all $p > 0$. Fortunately, implementation of the test on simulated 5-min observations is already able to provide good information.

17.3.6 TESTS BASED ON OBSERVATION OF OPTION PRICES

Tests based on the behavior of the prices of options subscribed on X in fact investigate the presence of jumps in the "risk-neutral" model for X (see Cont and Tankov (2004) for option pricing principles). However, as a consequence of the Itô formula, indicating by Q the risk-neutral pricing probability, because P and Q are equivalent, the paths of X are continuous under Q iff they are such under the ***historical probability*** P.

Aït-Sahalia (Aït-Sahalia, 2002) establishes a positivity condition, which is necessarily satisfied by the ***transition density*** of a time-homogeneous Markov process X with continuous paths (which, in particular, has coefficients $\tilde{a}_t \equiv \tilde{a}(X_t), \tilde{\sigma}_t \equiv \tilde{\sigma}(X_t)$). The P-transition density $p(\tau, y, x)$ of X is the conditional probability density that $\forall t \; X_{t+\tau} = y$ given that $X_t = x$. This function is not directly observable, but the risk-neutral "transition density" q can be estimated starting from the cross-sectional prices at T $\{C(K), K \in \mathbb{R}\}$ of European call options on X with different strike prices K and fixed maturity $T + \tau$, knowing the log-price $X_T = x$. In fact, q turns out to coincide with the second derivative in K of C. Thus, if the estimated q does not verify the given positivity condition then options data is not compatible with a Q-Markov time-homogeneous DGP with continuous paths. Whether then X is also P-Markov and time-homogeneous depends on the form of the density $\mathrm{d}Q/\mathrm{d}P$.

Carr and Wu (Carr and Wu, 2003) consider a general Itô SM model as in Equation 17.1. Under some boundedness conditions on σ_t and on the jump sizes, CW find that option prices on X tend to 0, as the time to maturity (τ) tends to 0, at a rate which varies substantially if jumps are present or not. The authors concentrate in particular on at the money and out of the money (OTM) European call options. For instance, the price at T of an OTM option tends to 0 at the exponential rate $\mathrm{e}^{-c/\tau}$ in the absence of jumps, and at rate τ otherwise. This is explained as follows: the price in T of an option depends on the probability that the price of the underlying X stays close to or distant from the strike within the time period $[T, T + \tau]$, because the payoff is $(X_{T+\tau} - K)_+$. Such a distance is basically different in short periods of length τ if X can jump or not.

17.3.6.1 Remarks. 1. Aït-Sahalia (2002) and Carr and Wu (2003) do not derive confidence intervals for their jump statistics. However, a whole function (transition density as a function of the strikes in the first case and option prices as function of the time to maturity in the second case) is plotted and the global behavior can be visually inspected, similarly as for the test in Todorov and Tauchen (2010a).

2. An important difference between these last two tests and the previously mentioned ones, based on observations of X, is that the former ones rely on a model for the future $[T, T + \tau]$ of X, which is a model on which the market bets. On the contrary, time-series-based methods rely on a model for the realized past of the DGP on $[0, T]$. In this case, as the traders construct their strategies at present to hedge the future risks or to speculate on future states of the returns, they in fact bet on the "stationarity" of the behavior of X.

17.3.7 INDIRECT TEST FOR THE PRESENCE OF JUMPS

Testing for the presence of cojumps in the components of a bivariate asset is an indirect (but partial) way to test for jumps in each component. If one finds that the asset of interest X cojumps with some other assets then X necessarily jumps. However, if X did not cojump, it could still be the case that X has jumps.

Barndorff-Nielsen and Shephard (2004c) extend the concept of bipower variation to a bivariate framework to detect for simultaneous jumps in asset prices. Note that on the contrary the test for cojumps in asset prices in Jacod and Todorov (2009), the test for cojumps among X and σ in Jacod and Todorov (2010) and the tests for the existence of functional relations among the jump sizes of X and σ in Jacod et al. (2010) are not indirect tests for the presence of jumps in X, because all of them assume that one already found some jumps in X.

17.3.7.1 In the Presence of Noise. Some of the mentioned tests have good finite sample performance already with 5-min data, while other tests need UHF data and have been adjusted to be robust to the presence of microstructure noise. Clearly, the rate at which the adjusted test statistics converge turns out to be $n^{-1/4}$ rather than the typical rate $n^{-1/2}$ of the no noise case. In most cases, additive i.i.d. noise is considered, while in Aït-Sahalia and Jacod (2010b), Podolskij and Ziggel (2010), and Jacod et al. (2010), more realistic noise processes are allowed. The problem has been tackled in five ways: staggering (applied to the BS test, see Huang and Tauchen (2005)); properly plugging $\hat{\sigma}_\varepsilon^2$ into the test statistic in order to eliminate the bias induced by the noise (applied to the JO and ABD tests, see Jiang and Oomen (2008) and Andersen et al. (2007)); preaveraging the returns (applied to the PZ and AJ tests, see Podolskij and Ziggel (2010), Aït-Sahalia and Jacod (2010b)); preaveraging and then staggering (applied to the BS test, see Podolskij and Vetter (2009a)); and applying a generalized preaveraging and then using an AJ type test (Jacod et al., 2010).

17.3.8 COMPARISONS

Dumitru and Urga (2011) conduct a very accurate and interesting comparison of the AJ, BS, LM, ABD, JO, and PZ tests, both on simulated and on empirical data. The authors check on simulations the size and power of the tests using different sampling frequencies, levels of volatility, persistence in volatility, degree of contamination with microstructure noise (assumed to be additive i.i.d. Gaussian), and jump sizes and intensity, with jumps assumed of FA. The authors also propose a finite sample bias correction to improve the tests performance and conclude the overall superiority of the LM and ABD tests, but remark on the importance of using also the others in order to integrate information on the DGP. They also apply the tests to high frequency data on US Treasury bonds.

Theodosiou and Zikes (2011) compare, using Monte Carlo data, different versions of the BS, CPR, PZ, JO, and AJ tests, two versions of a MedRV-based test and the LM test. Scenarios are covered of both FA and IA fV jumps, stochastic volatility models with continuous and discontinuous volatility sample paths, microstructure noise allowed to be autocorrelated but assumed to be independent from X, infrequent trading, and deterministic diurnal volatility. The simulation results reveal important differences in terms of size and power among the different test procedures and the differences vary across the DGPs. There are jump detection disagreements among the tests and different sensitivities to both zero returns and noise effects. An empirical application to HF samples of exchange rates, individual stocks, and of the SPX index, confirms the disagreement of the various tests about jump occurrence

In Schwert (2009), the AJ, BS, LM, JO, and noise-adjusted JO tests are compared using empirical data of 10 stocks of the S&P100 index. Also, in this analysis the number and timing of the jumps are found to differ dramatically across the different tests when applied to the same data, and the author concludes that this can indicate that each test identifies different types of jumps in the data, so again to have a better picture on the DGP, no one of the tests should be ignored.

Comparisons are missing, as far as we know, with the following tests: range based (Christensen and Podolskij, 2010), LH (Lee and Hannig, 2010), LP (Lee and Ploberger), the noise-adjusted bipower-type test (Podolskij and Vetter, 2009a), and the two different noise robustifications of the AJ test (Aït-Sahalia and Jacod, 2010b; Jacod et al., 2010).

17.4 Conclusions

We reviewed all the methods in the literature we are aware of about nonparametric estimation of IV and testing for the presence of jumps in asset prices within the framework of general Itô SM models evolving in continuous time but which are observable only discretely. The inconsistencies arising in the application of the estimation and jump detection methods to simulated and empirical data show how difficult the asset prices modeling issue is, while trying to account for realistic features (e.g., microstructure noise) immediately gives rise to increasing technical difficulties in reaching the theoretical results needed for the practical application of the methods. We summarize here some open problems we became aware of while reviewing this literature. On the IV estimation side, an efficient rate nonparametric estimator is missing in the presence of iV jumps. On the detection of jumps side, the local power of the LM test has not been studied; nonparametric tests for jumps in the spot volatility, based on time series, are missing; deepening our comparative study of the different estimators' performances and completing the comparison picture of the existing tests in the literature would be interesting.

Acknowledgments

We thank Kris Boudt, Giampiero Maria Gallo, Jean Jacod, Roel Oomen, Mark Podolskij, and Viktor Todorov for important consultations. We are especially grateful to Roberto Renò for constant support, and to Dobrislav Dobrev who implemented his generalized range estimator on our simulated data, allowing us to check the Francesco algorithm and to complete our comparisons in Table 17.2.

CHAPTER EIGHTEEN

Nonparametric Tests for Intraday Jumps: Impact of Periodicity and Microstructure Noise

KRIS BOUDT, JONATHAN CORNELISSEN, CHRISTOPHE CROUX, and SÉBASTIEN LAURENT

18.1 Introduction

The occurrence of jumps is of particular interest in many practical financial applications. For example, jumps have distinctly different implications for the valuation of derivatives (Merton, 1976a,b), risk measurement and management (Duffie and Pan, 2001), as well as asset allocation (Jarrow and Rosenfeld, 1984).

To learn about the features of jump arrivals and their associated market information, a variety of formal tests have been developed to identify the presence of jumps, most of them being typically designed for the analysis of low frequency data (see e.g., Aït-Sahalia, 2002; Carr and Wu, 2003; Johannes 2004; Wang 1995, among others). However, the most natural and direct way to learn about jumps is by studying high frequency or intraday data.

Handbook of Volatility Models and Their Applications, First Edition.
Edited by Luc Bauwens, Christian Hafner, and Sebastien Laurent.

The earliest contributions in the identification of jumps using intraday data include those of Barndorff-Nielsen and Shephard (2004b) and (2006b), who developed a jump robust measure of the daily integrated variance called realized bipower variation. They provide a convenient nonparametric framework that uses the difference between the realized variance and the bipower variation to measure the contribution of jumps to total return variation and for classifying days on which jumps have or have not occurred.

However, for many financial applications, the presence of jumps needs to be detected over very short time intervals, such as 5 min. Over these intervals, there are often not enough observations to test for jumps using the difference between an estimator of the total return variance and a jump robust variance estimate. Recently, Andersen et al. (2007) and Lee and Mykland (2008) independently developed an alternative nonparametric test, which directly tests whether a given high frequency return has a jump component. The proposed jump test statistic in Andersen et al. (2007) and Lee and Mykland (2008) is the same and corresponds to the absolute high frequency return, standardized by a robust estimate of its volatility. As such, this test makes it possible to identify the exact timing of the jump and to characterize the jump size distribution and stochastic jump intensity.

The nonparametric jump test of Andersen et al. (2007) and Lee and Mykland (2008) (or extensions of it, such as in Lee and Hannig (2010)), has enabled researchers to study the relation between jumps and various financial and macroeconomic variables (see e.g., Bollerslev et al., 2008; Todorov, 2010 among others). For instance, Tauchen and Zhou (2011) investigate the market variance riskpremium and Lahaye et al. (2011) study the relation between macroeconomic announcements and jumps.

It is common to implement the jump test of Andersen et al. (2007) and Lee and Mykland (2008) using a rescaled version of a jump robust estimate of the daily integrated variance as an approximation for the variance of the high frequency return. The approximation error is small when the volatility is approximately constant over the day. As noted by Andersen et al. (2007) and Bollerslev et al. (2008), among others, this assumption is at odds with the overwhelming evidence of a strong periodic pattern in intraday volatility. Boudt et al. (2010) show that accounting for periodicity greatly improves the accuracy of intraday jump detection methods. It increases the power to detect the relatively small jumps occurring at times for which volatility is periodically low and reduces the number of spurious jump detections at times of periodically high volatility.

Andersen et al. (2007), Boudt et al. (2010), and Lee and Mykland (2008) assume that the log-prices are observed without measurement error. It is, however, more realistic to consider that the logarithm of the recorded asset price is actually the sum of the logarithm of the so-called efficient price and a noise component that is induced by microstructure frictions. Aït-Sahalia et al. (2011) divide the sources of microstructure noise into the following three groups: (i) frictions inherent in the trading process such as bid-ask bounces, discreteness of price changes, and rounding; (ii) informational effects such as the gradual response of prices to a block trade or inventory control effects; and (iii) measurement or data recording errors such as prices entered as zero or misplaced decimal points. In this chapter, we analyze the sensitivity of intraday jump tests to the presence of both intraday periodicity and microstructure noise in the data.

The effect of microstructure noise on estimators of the integrated variance and covariance has been widely studied (Bandi and Russell, 2008; Barndorff-Nielsen et al., 2008; Li and Mykland, 2007; Podolskij and Vetter, 2009b; Zhang, 2011). Accounting for microstructure noise in nonparametric jump detection has been recently studied by Bos et al. (2009) and Boudt and Zhang (2010).

The goal of this chapter is to illustrate the effect of periodicity and microstructure noise on the nonparametric detection of intraday jumps, emphasizing the interaction between both effects. We proceed as follows. Sections 18.2 and 18.3 state the model settings and describe the jump statistic. We then compare the different implementations of the test on simulated data and stock price data in Sections 18.4 and 18.5. Section 18.6 concludes the discussion.

18.2 Model

In essence, a price jump is a significant discontinuity in the price process. To define what is meant by "significant discontinuity," we need an underlying price model. We suppose that the log-price process $\{X_t\}$ is a combination of a latent log-price process $\{\tilde{X}_t\}$ and a noise process $\{\varepsilon_t^X\}$:

$$X_t = \tilde{X}_t + \varepsilon_t^X. \tag{18.1}$$

The latent process $\tilde{X}_t$ is supposed to be a Brownian semimartingale process with finite activity jumps. This means that it can be decomposed into a drift, a stochastic volatility diffusion, and a jump component

$$d\tilde{X}_t = \mu_t dt + \sigma_t dW_t + K_t dq_t, \tag{18.2}$$

where μ_t is the drift term with a continuous and locally finite variation sample path, σ_t is a strictly positive spot volatility process, and W_t is a standard Brownian motion. The component $K_t dq_t$ refers to the pure jump component, where $dq_t = 1$ if there is a jump at time t and is 0 otherwise, and K_t represents the jump size. The jump process is supposed to be independent of the diffusion process and to have finite activity, which means that the number of jumps over any interval of time is finite with probability 1.

For applications, one is often interested in price jump detection at a given frequency Δ, such as 2 min (Boudt et al. 2010) or 5 min (Lahaye et al., 2011; Lee and Mykland, 2008). This requires computation of returns on an equispaced calendar time grid, with last price interpolation. We normalize the length of 1 day to unity and focus on the day [0,1]. Let us denote $r_{i,\Delta} = X_{i\Delta} - X_{(i-1)\Delta}$, the corresponding returns being sampled at the frequency Δ, for $i = 1, \dots, \lfloor 1/\Delta \rfloor$.[1]

[1] The function $\lfloor \cdot \rfloor$ returns the largest integer less than or equal to its argument.

If there is no jump in the interval $[(i-1)\Delta, i\Delta]$, we have that

$$r_{i,\Delta} = \tilde{X}_{i\Delta} - \tilde{X}_{(i-1)\Delta} + \varepsilon^{X}_{i\Delta} - \varepsilon^{X}_{(i-1)\Delta}$$
$$= \int_{(i-1)\Delta}^{i\Delta} \mu_s ds + \int_{(i-1)\Delta}^{i\Delta} \sigma_s dW_s + \varepsilon^{X}_{i\Delta} - \varepsilon^{X}_{(i-1)\Delta}.$$

Throughout, we operate with sufficiently high frequency return series such that the mean process can be safely ignored.

We impose two high level assumptions on the microstructure noise: (i) ε^{X}_{t} is independent of the X process and (ii) $\varepsilon_X \overset{i.i.d.}{\sim} N(0, \sigma^2_{\varepsilon X})$. Under these assumptions, we have that for Δ sufficiently small, the high frequency return $r_{i,\Delta}$ is still normally distributed in the presence of noise (but absence of jumps), with variance equal to the sum of the integrated variance over $[(i-1)\Delta, i\Delta]$ and two times the noise variance

$$\frac{r_{i,\Delta}}{\left[\int_{(i-1)\Delta}^{i\Delta} \sigma_s^2 ds + 2\sigma^2_{\varepsilon X}\right]^{\frac{1}{2}}} \sim N(0,1). \tag{18.3}$$

The result in Equation 18.3 suggests to detect the presence of a jump in $r_{i,\Delta}$ whenever the standardized high frequency return exceeds an extreme quantile of the normal distribution. This requires an estimation of $\int_{(i-1)\Delta}^{i\Delta} \sigma_s^2 ds$. One possible avenue is to use local volatility estimates based on moving windows and kernel weights, as in Kristensen (2010), Mattiussi and Renò (2010), Renó (2006), and Lee and Mykland (2008).

An alternative is to impose more structure on the spot volatility process. Andersen and Bollerslev (1997b) and Taylor and Xu (1997) assume that the local volatility equals the daily volatility corrected for the intraday periodic pattern

$$\int_{(i-1)\Delta}^{i\Delta} \sigma_s^2 ds = f^2_{i,\Delta} \Delta \int_0^1 \sigma_s^2 ds. \tag{18.4}$$

The periodicity factor $f_{i,\Delta}$ is supposed to be a deterministic function of periodic variables such as the time of the day, the day of the week, and macroeconomic news announcements. The decomposition (Eq. 18.4) is unique under the standardization condition that the squared periodicity factor has a mean of one over the day.

18.3 Price Jump Detection Method

In this section, we first discuss the different building blocks for the construction of a jump detection method under the assumption that the high frequency returns $r_{i,\Delta}$ follow the model given by Equations 18.3 and 18.4. We need an estimator of the noise variance, the integrated variance, and the periodicity factor. Next, we present several jump test statistics based on these estimates. Finally, we discuss the choice of the critical value.

18.3.1 ESTIMATION OF THE NOISE VARIANCE

Estimators of the noise variance $\sigma^2_{\varepsilon X}$ are typically based on prices sampled in transaction time. Let us suppose that the log-price process is observed at time points $0 \leq t_1 < t_2 < \cdots < t_{n+1} \leq 1$, yielding the observations $X_{t_1}, X_{t_2}, \ldots, X_{t_{n+1}}$. Zhang et al. (2005) show that the noise variance is consistently estimated by $1/(2n)$ times the difference between the realized variance computed on the tick-by-tick log-price changes and the two-time-scale realized volatility (TSRV):

$$\hat{\sigma}^2_{\varepsilon X} = \frac{1}{2n}([X,X]^{(\text{all})} - \text{TSRV}) \xrightarrow{p} \sigma^2_{\varepsilon X}. \tag{18.5}$$

Let us briefly discuss the TSRV. It has two components, namely, the realized variance computed on the tick-by-tick returns and the averaged realized variance computed on returns sampled at a lower time scale. The realized variance calculated on the tick-by-tick returns is

$$[X,X]^{(\text{all})} = \sum_{i=1}^{n}(X_{t_{i+1}} - X_{t_i})^2.$$

The TSRV of Zhang et al. (2005) is based on partitioning the whole sample into K subsamples, with K being an integer. Let the average K subsampled realized variance be denoted as

$$[X,X]^{(\text{avg})} = \frac{1}{K}\sum_{i=1}^{n-K+1}\left(X_{t_{i+K}} - X_{t_i}\right)^2.$$

The TSRV is defined as the difference between the averaged realized variance computed over K step apart subsampled observations and the adjusted realized variance computed using all observations

$$\text{TSRV} = \left(1 - \frac{\overline{n}}{n}\right)^{-1}\left([X,X]^{(\text{avg})} - \frac{\overline{n}}{n}[X,X]^{(\text{all})}\right), \tag{18.6}$$

where $\overline{n} = (n - K + 1)/K$. Taking the difference between $[X,X]^{(avg)}$ and $\frac{\overline{n}}{n}[X,X]^{(\text{all})}$ cancels the effect of the microstructure noise. The factor $(1 - \overline{n}/n)^{-1}$ is a coefficient to adjust for finite sample bias.

18.3.2 ROBUST ESTIMATORS OF THE INTEGRATED VARIANCE

Several propositions have been made over the years to estimate the integrated variance (see Patton and Sheppard, 2009b for a general review). To guarantee a high power of the jump tests, we need to restrict ourselves to jump robust estimators, otherwise jumps will inflate the variance estimate and deflate the jump statistic based on Equation (18.3). Presence of multiple jumps within a day might lead to a failure of detecting the smaller jumps, a phenomenon called "outlier masking" in the robustness literature (Davies and Gather 1993). For simplicity, and like in Andersen et al. (2007), Lee and Mykland (2008), and Boudt et al. (2010), we estimate the integrated variance using returns sampled at the same frequency as the one at which jumps need to be detected, namely, Δ. In empirical work, the realized bipower variation (BPV) of Barndorff-Nielsen and Shephard (2004b) is especially popular

$$\text{BPV}_\Delta = \frac{\pi}{2}\frac{M_\Delta}{M_\Delta - 1}\sum_{i=2}^{M_\Delta} |r_{i,\Delta}||r_{i-1,\Delta}|, \tag{18.7}$$

with $M_\Delta = \lfloor 1/\Delta \rfloor$.

In the presence of microstructure noise, the BPV estimates the integrated variance plus the noise variation in the returns used to compute the integrated variance (i.e., $\int_0^1 \sigma_s^2 ds + 2M_\Delta \sigma_{\varepsilon X}^2$). This bias can be easily corrected for by using the following bias-adjusted version of the BPV

$$\text{BPV}^*_\Delta = \text{BPV}_\Delta - 2M_\Delta \hat{\sigma}^2_{\varepsilon X}. \tag{18.8}$$

This estimator is directly related to the class of two-time-scale realized variance estimators proposed by Zhang et al. (2005). Note that the lower the sampling frequency, the smaller is M_Δ and thus also the bias correction in Equation 18.8. Alternatively, one could use the modulated bipower variation described in Podolskij and Vetter (2009b), or the robust TSRV of Boudt and Zhang (2010).

18.3.3 PERIODICITY ESTIMATION

Under the model (Eqs. 18.3 and 18.4), but without microstructure noise, the periodicity factor corresponds to the standard deviation of the standardized returns $\bar{r}_{i,\Delta} = r_{i,\Delta}/(\widehat{IV}/M_\Delta)^{1/2}$, with $\widehat{IV}$ being an estimator of the integrated variance such as the bipower variation in Equation 18.7. Taylor and Xu (1997) propose the following estimation procedure for f_i. First, collect all the standardized returns having standard deviation f_i. Denote these $\bar{r}_{1,i}, \ldots, \bar{r}_{n_i,i}$, with n_i being the number of standardized returns having standard deviation f_i. Then, compute their standard deviations, that is, $\text{SD}_{i,\Delta} = \sqrt{\frac{1}{n_i}\sum_{j=1}^{n_i} \bar{r}_{j,i}^2}$. Finally, their estimator is a standardized version of these periodicity estimates

$$\hat{f}^{\text{SD}}_{i,\Delta} = \frac{\text{SD}_{i,\Delta}}{\sqrt{\frac{1}{M_\Delta}\sum_{j=1}^{M_\Delta} \text{SD}^2_{j,\Delta}}}. \tag{18.9}$$

Andersen and Bollerslev (1997b) show that more efficient estimates can be obtained if the whole time series dimension of the data is used for the estimation of the periodicity process. They consider the regression equation

$$\log|\bar{r}_{i,\Delta}| - c = \log f_{i,\Delta} + \varepsilon_{i,\Delta}, \tag{18.10}$$

where the error term $\varepsilon_{i,\Delta}$ is i.i.d. distributed with mean zero and having the density function of the centered absolute value of the log of a standard normal

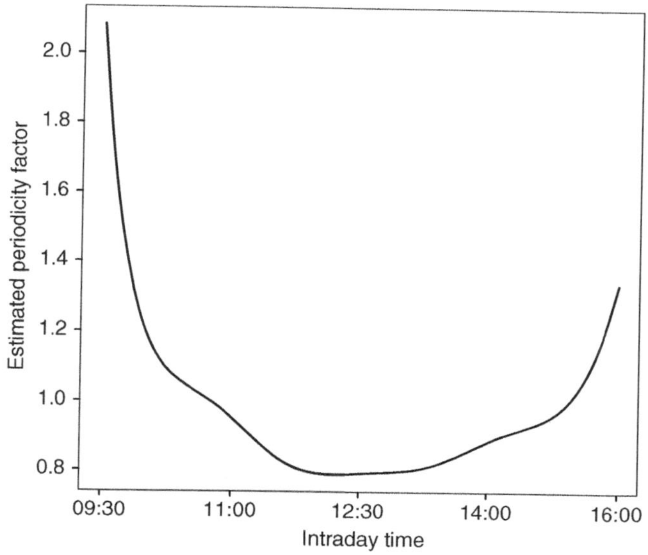

FIGURE 18.1 **Intraday plot of estimated 2-min intraday periodicity factors for General Electric.**

random variable, and $c = -0.63518$. Andersen and Bollerslev (1997b) then proposed to model $\log f_{i,\Delta}$ as a linear function of a vector of variables x_i (such as sinusoidal and polynomial transformations of the time of the day)

$$\log f_{i,\Delta} = x'_{i,\Delta}\theta_*, \tag{18.11}$$

with θ_* the true parameter value. Boudt et al. (2010) propose a jump robust regression estimator for this model called the "truncated maximum likelihood" periodicity estimate. Let us call the resulting periodicity estimates $\hat{f}_{i,\Delta}$. Figure 18.1 plots this estimate for the GE stock based on the 2-min return data in 2008, extracted from the NYSE trades and quotes database.[2] Note the clear U-shape induced by the opening, lunch, and closing of the stock market. This periodicity estimate is close to the pattern that one would obtain using 5-min returns and therefore seems to be robust to microstructure noise.[3]

[2]The periodicity factor is estimated using the default implementation in the R package RTAQ (Cornelissen and Boudt 2010).

[3]The periodicity estimates mentioned above assume that, in the absence of jumps, the standardized return $r_{i,\Delta}(IV/M_\Delta)^{-1/2}$ is normally distributed with variance f_i^2. In presence of microstructure noise, its variance is, however, $f_i^2 + 2M_\Delta\sigma_\varepsilon^2/IV$. Thus, it seems that the smaller the sampling frequency, the larger may be the bias introduced by the noise in the periodicity estimation. An analysis of this bias and the development of a periodicity estimate that is robust to microstructure noise and jumps is left for further research. Of course, given the smoothness of the periodicity pattern for equity and foreign exchange data, the parameter θ_* can always be estimated at a lower frequency than the one at which jumps need to be detected.

18.3.4 JUMP TEST STATISTICS

The model in Equations 18.3 and 18.4 suggests three statistics. The first one implicitly assumes the absence of an intraday volatility pattern and microstructure noise, namely:

$$I_{i,\Delta} = \frac{|r_{i,\Delta}|}{\sqrt{M_{\Delta}^{-1}\mathrm{BPV}_{\Delta}}}. \tag{18.12}$$

This test statistic is closely related to the original test proposed by Andersen et al. (2007) and Lee and Mykland (2008).[4] Note that the denominator in $I_{i,\Delta}$ estimates $\int_{(i-1)\Delta}^{i\Delta} \sigma_s^2 \mathrm{d}s + 2\sigma_{\varepsilon X}^2$, while the variance of $r_{i,\Delta}$ is $f_{i,\Delta}^2 \int_{(i-1)\Delta}^{i\Delta} \sigma_s^2 \mathrm{d}s + 2\sigma_{\varepsilon X}^2$ in the absence of jumps. It follows that jump detection based on the I-test in Equation 18.12s overdetects (underdetects) jumps when volatility is periodically high (low).

Boudt et al. (2010) propose the following adjustment:

$$J_{i,\Delta} = \frac{|r_{i,\Delta}|}{\hat{f}_{i,\Delta}\sqrt{M_{\Delta}^{-1}\mathrm{BPV}_{\Delta}}}. \tag{18.13}$$

This version of the test implicitly assumes that the microstructure noise follows the same periodic pattern as the spot volatility of the underlying efficient price process. This is inconsistent with the assumption that the variance of the microstructure noise is constant over the day. For this reason, we also consider a third statistic, which is consistent with the model in Equations 18.3 and 18.4

$$Z_{i,\Delta} = \frac{|r_{i,\Delta}|}{\sqrt{\hat{f}_{i,\Delta}^2 M_{\Delta}^{-1}\mathrm{BPV}_{\Delta}^* + 2\hat{\sigma}_{\varepsilon X}^2}}. \tag{18.14}$$

Note the use of BPV_{Δ}^* instead of BPV_{Δ}.

18.3.5 CRITICAL VALUE

The presence of a jump in $r_{i,\Delta}$ is detected when the jump test statistic exceeds a critical value. There are several possibilities of choosing this threshold. A straightforward jump detection rule is that return $r_{i,\Delta}$ is affected by a jump if the test statistic exceeds the $1 - \alpha/2$ quantile of the standard Gaussian distribution. This rule has a probability of type I error (detect that $r_{i,\Delta}$ is affected by jumps, if in reality $r_{i,\Delta}$ is not affected by jumps) equal to α. Its disadvantage

[4]Alternatively, sliding local windows centered around $r_{i,\Delta}$ could be used for the estimation of $\int_{(i-1)\Delta}^{i\Delta} \sigma_s^2 \mathrm{d}s$. If returns are sampled at frequencies of 1 h, 30 min, 15 min, or 5 min, Lee and Mykland (2008) recommend to use local windows containing 78, 110, 156, or 270 observations, respectively. These numbers correspond to the smallest number of observations for which jumps will have a negligible effect on the realized bipower variation. For simplicity, we always take local windows of 1 day.

is that the expected number of false positives becomes large. For example, with $M_\Delta = 195$ intraday returns per day and $\alpha = 0.01$, one expects to detect about $0.01 \cdot 195 \approx 2$ jumps per day, even if no single jump has occurred. Lee and Mykland (2008) call these false positives "spurious jump detections."

For this reason, Andersen et al. (2007) and Lee and Mykland (2008) propose to control the size of multiple jump detection tests. Andersen et al. (2007) use a Šidák correction to control for the number of spurious jumps detected per day. Under this approach, the rejection threshold is given by the $[1-(1-\alpha)^\Delta]/2$ quantile of the Gaussian distribution. Lee and Mykland (2008) use a different way to control for the size of multiple tests. They advocate to use the extreme value theory result that the maximum of L i.i.d. realizations of the absolute value of a standard normal random variable is asymptotically (for $L \to \infty$) Gumbel distributed. More specifically, in the absence of jumps, the probability that the maximum of any set of L test statistics exceeds

$$g_{L,\alpha} = -\log(-\log(1-\alpha))b_L + c_L, \tag{18.15}$$

with $b_L = 1/\sqrt{2}\log L$ and $c_L = (2\log L)^{1/2} - [\log\pi + \log(\log L)]/[2(2\log L)^{1/2}]$, is about α. All returns for which the test statistic exceeds this critical value $g_{L,\alpha}$ are then declared as being affected by jumps. In the sequel to the paper, we set $L = M_\Delta = 195$. This corresponds to testing for the joint null hypothesis of no jumps over one day, for a market that is open 6.5 hours a day with returns sampled every 2 min. We set $\alpha = 1\%$. For these values of L, Δ, and α, the rejection threshold used in Andersen et al. (2007) and Lee and Mykland (2008) equals approximately 4.049 and 4.232, respectively.

18.4 Simulation Study

This section consists of two parts. First, we illustrate the intraday differences in the values of the I, J, and Z statistics defined in Section 18.3 and discuss how these differences affect the size and power of the test. Second, we apply these three test statistics to a simulated price process and investigate their properties on daily and intraday levels.

18.4.1 INTRADAY DIFFERENCES IN THE VALUE OF THE TEST STATISTICS

Through stylized examples, we illustrate here the intraday differences between I, J, and Z. This graphical analysis will shed light on the differences in size and power of testing for jumps using these three statistics. We make abstraction of estimation error by assuming that $\int_0^1 \sigma^2(s)ds = \mathrm{BPV}^*_\Delta = 1, \sigma^2_{\varepsilon X} = \hat{\sigma}^2_{\varepsilon X} = 0.001$ and the periodicity factor $f_{i,\Delta} = \hat{f}_{i,\Delta}$ is as shown in Figure 18.1. Returns are sampled every 2 min.[5]

[5]We assume that the market is open 6.5 hours a day, resulting in 195 returns a day.

We first consider the case where the high frequency return $r_{i,\Delta}$ is generated by the model (Eqs. 18.3 and 18.4), but is relatively large, that is, we set $|r_{i,\Delta}|$ to 3.719 (the 99.99% quantile of the Gaussian distribution) times the volatility $\sqrt{f_{i,\Delta}^2 \Delta \int_0^1 \sigma^2(s)ds + 2\sigma_{\varepsilon X}^2}$. Because of the periodicity component, $|r_{i,\Delta}|$ fluctuates throughout the day, while the threshold remains constant. Figure 18.2 reports the values of $I_{i,\Delta}, J_{i,\Delta}$, and $Z_{i,\Delta}$ during 1 day. The value of $Z_{i,\Delta}$ obviously remains constant at 3.719 and serves as the benchmark. The value of $I_{i,\Delta}$ fluctuates substantially throughout the day, because the periodicity pattern is ignored. Note that if we use the threshold of 4.232, we detect all returns between 09:30 EST and 10:06 EST as spurious jumps based on $I_{i,\Delta}$. The value of $J_{i,\Delta}$ also fluctuates throughout the day. Instead of keeping the noise variance component constant at $2\sigma_{\varepsilon X}^2$, it implicitly sets it to $2f_{i,\Delta}^2\sigma_{\varepsilon X}^2$. It follows, as can be seen in Figure 18.2, that spurious jump detection will increase around noon.

A return takes extreme values when it is affected by a jump. These are the returns that we would like to detect. We consider a large return whose diffusion component is zero: $|r_{i,\Delta}| = 0.35$, for $i = 1, \ldots, M_\Delta$. Figure 18.3 plots the intraday evolution of the corresponding $I_{i,\Delta}$, $J_{i,\Delta}$, and $Z_{i,\Delta}$ test statistics. While $I_{i,\Delta} = 4.15$, for all $i = 1, \ldots, 195$, the value of $J_{i,\Delta}$ and $Z_{i,\Delta}$ fluctuates throughout the day because these test statistics take into account the periodicity pattern. Note that $J_{i,\Delta}$ detects more jumps than $Z_{i,\Delta}$ during the middle of a trading day and less during the opening and closing periods. In contrast to $Z_{i,\Delta}$, $J_{i,\Delta}$ does not take into account the noise variance separately, and hence

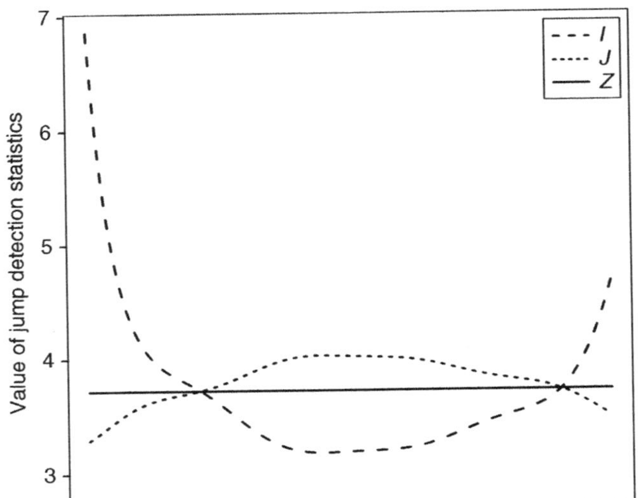

FIGURE 18.2 Effect of periodicity on the value of the I, J, and Z jump test statistics when $r_{i,\Delta} = 3.719\sqrt{f_{i,\Delta}^2 \Delta \int_0^1 \sigma^2(s)ds + 2\sigma_{\varepsilon X}^2}$. The critical value for jump detection is 4.232.

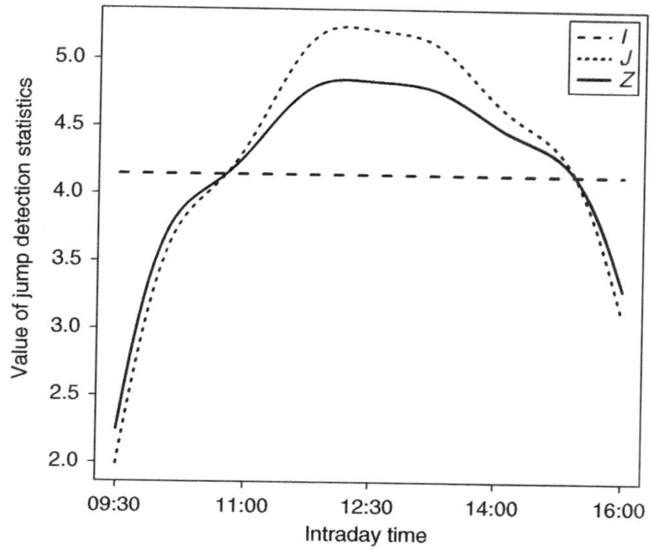

FIGURE 18.3 Effect of periodicity on the value of the I, J, and Z jump test statistics when $|r_{i,\Delta}| = 0.35$. The critical value for jump detection is 4.232.

overestimates (underestimates) the return volatility when $f_{i,\Delta} > 1$ ($f_{i,\Delta} < 1$), which explains this observation.

These stylized examples showed that the differences in the value of the I, J, and Z test statistics can thus be substantial at the intraday level. Under the model in Equations (18.3 and 18.4), we advise to use $Z_{i,\Delta}$ to detect jumps, as it correctly takes into account the noise variance and periodicity pattern.

18.4.2 COMPARISON OF SIZE AND POWER

The previous subsection indicated that the differences between the size and power of the I, J, and Z test statistics in 18.12–18.14 can be substantial on an intraday scale. This does not necessarily imply big differences on an aggregated basis, since the overdetection of jumps during a certain part of the day can be offset by the underdetection during another part of the day. In the next part, we evaluate the effective size and power of the three test statistics for a general log-price process with stochastic volatility, intraday periodicity, and finite activity jumps. We first describe the simulation setup and then discuss the results.

18.4.3 SIMULATION SETUP

We simulate a log-price process for 1000 days, with the time interval of 1 day standardized to $t \in [0, 1]$. The log-price series are simulated from the jump diffusion model in Huang and Tauchen (2005)

$$\begin{cases} X_t = \tilde{X}_t + \varepsilon_t^X \\ d\tilde{X}_t = \mu_X dt + f_t \exp(\beta_0 + \beta_1 v_t^X) dW_t^X + dJ_t^X \\ dv_t^X = \alpha_v v_t^X dt + dB_t^X \\ \text{Corr}(dW_X, dB_X) = \gamma, \end{cases}$$

where γ is the leverage correlation, v_t^X is a stochastic volatility process, f_t accounts for the intraday periodicity, and J_t^X is a compound Poisson process with jump intensity λ. For the diffusion, the parameters $(\mu_X, \beta_0, \beta_1, \gamma, \lambda)$ are set to $(0.03, -5/16, 1/8, -0.3, 2)$. The jump tests in Equations 18.12–18.14 implicitly proxy the stochastic volatility component by a constant (the daily integrated variance). To study the effect of this approximation on the size and power of the tests, we consider three types of spot volatility dynamics: a very persistent stochastic volatility ($\alpha_{v_1} = -0.00137$) with and without a periodic pattern and a less persistent stochastic volatility process ($\alpha_{v_2} = -1.386$) without periodicity. The absence of a periodic pattern means that $f_t = 1$. In the presence of periodicity, we implement the periodicity factor estimated for the GE stock during 2008, which is shown in Figure 18.1. The initial value of v_t^X for each day is drawn from a normal distribution $N(0, (-\alpha_{v_1} - \alpha_{v_2})^{-1})$. The size of the jumps is modeled as the product of the realization of a uniformly distributed random variable on $([-2, -1] \cup [1, 2])/\sqrt{2\lambda}$ and the mean value of the spot volatility process of that day. We assume the noise $\varepsilon_t^X \overset{i.i.d}{\sim} N(0, \sigma_{\varepsilon_X^2})$. We consider a low noise variance of $\sigma_{\varepsilon_X}^2 = 0.001$ and a high noise variance of $\sigma_{\varepsilon_X}^2 = 0.005$.

The diffusion part of the model is simulated with an increment of 1 s per tick using the Euler Scheme. We use independent Poisson sampling schemes such that the intertransaction times are exponentially distributed with on an average one transaction every 5 s. We align the price series to a regular 2-min grid, using the previous tick approach.

18.4.4 RESULTS

Table 18.1 reports the "effective size" and "effective power" of the I, J, and Z statistics. These effective size and power statistics correspond to the proportion of spuriously detected jumps and the proportion of actual jumps that have been detected with success.

A jump component is detected in a return when the test statistic exceeds 4.2322. Under the model (Eqs. 18.3 and 18.4), we therefore expect a size of $2(1 - \Phi(4.232)) \approx 2.32e - 5$. Because we estimate the volatility of the deseasonalized returns with the daily integrated variance, the actual effective size is slightly higher in the presence of time-varying stochastic volatility. To see the effect of periodicity on the size and power of the jump test statistics, we compute the size and power not only as an aggregate over the entire day but also for the intraday times when the periodicity factor is the highest (market opening

TABLE 18.1 Effective Size and Power of the I, J, and Z Jump Tests with Rejection Threshold Equal to 4.232.

Noise variance $\sigma^2_{\varepsilon X}$		Zero	Zero	Zero	Small	Small	Small	Large	Large	Large
Periodicity f_t		No	No	Yes	No	No	Yes	No	No	Yes
Persistence of v_t^X		High	Low	High	High	Low	High	High	Low	High
		Size $\times 10{,}000$								
I	9:30-16:00	2.80	3.52	5.70	2.80	3.32	3.47	3.16	3.68	2.28
	9:30-10:30, 15:00-16:00	2.69	3.20	9.93	2.86	2.19	4.71	3.37	3.53	3.03
	12:00-13:30	2.47	2.47	4.04	2.25	3.14	3.37	2.25	2.92	2.47
J	9:30-16:00	2.80	3.52	3.68	2.80	3.32	2.95	3.16	3.68	2.33
	9:30-10:30, 15:00-16:00	2.69	3.20	3.20	2.86	2.19	3.03	3.37	3.53	2.86
	12:00-13:30	2.47	2.47	4.27	2.25	3.14	3.37	2.25	2.92	2.70
Z	9:30-16:00	2.80	3.52	3.63	2.80	3.32	3.00	3.16	3.68	2.28
	9:30-10:30, 15:00-16:00	2.69	3.20	3.20	2.86	2.19	3.20	3.37	3.53	3.03
	12:00-13:30	2.47	2.47	4.04	2.25	3.14	3.37	2.25	2.92	2.47
		Power $\times 100$								
I	9:30-16:00	97.11	96.28	96.15	97.11	96.28	96.20	92.02	91.25	77.73
	9:30-10:30, 15:00-16:00	97.08	96.50	96.22	95.98	97.41	95.85	90.13	91.65	87.33
	12:00-13:30	97.07	97.30	95.90	97.12	96.53	95.19	91.90	90.87	64.47
J	9:30-16:00	97.11	96.28	96.15	97.11	96.28	96.67	91.97	91.15	79.24
	9:30-10:30, 15:00-16:00	97.08	96.50	96.22	95.98	97.41	95.66	90.03	91.32	86.45
	12:00-13:30	97.07	97.30	95.90	97.12	96.53	96.78	91.90	90.87	68.87
Z	9:30-16:00	97.11	96.28	96.15	97.11	96.28	96.62	92.02	91.15	78.10
	9:30-10:30, 15:00-16:00	97.08	96.50	96.22	95.98	97.41	95.66	90.13	91.32	86.77
	12:00-13:30	97.07	97.30	95.90	97.12	96.53	96.57	91.90	90.87	65.61

between 9:30 and 10:30 EST and market closing between 15:00 and 16:00 EST) and the lowest (lunch time between 12:00 and 13:00 EST).

Consider first the case of no microstructure noise in columns 1–3 of Table 18.1. Note that when the spot volatility is highly persistent and shows no periodicity, the size of the test (2.8e − 5) is the closest to the one expected under the model (Eqs. 18.3 and 18.4). In absence of periodicity in volatility, the size and the power of the I, J, and Z test statistics are very similar. In the third column, we allow for periodicity and see that the size of the I-statistic (5.70e − 5) is too high. Moreover, it detects many more spurious jumps at times of high periodicity (size of 9.93e − 5) than at times of low periodicity (size of 4.04e − 5). This is not the case for the J and Z statistics for which the size is similar for all intraday periods. Regarding the power of the tests, we see in columns 1–3 that the choice of test statistics has little influence. The power is the highest when the volatility process is persistent.

Consider now the case with microstructure noise. The numerator of the I, J, and Z statistic is then the square of the log-difference in the efficient price plus the noise terms. For the contamination with the small microstructure noise, there is little significant effect on the size and power of the jump test statistics. The presence of large noise, however, reduces significantly the power of the jump test statistics. From the last column, it seems that in the joint presence of a large noise variance and a strong periodic pattern in volatility, the I, J, and Z statistics all have a substantial higher power when the periodicity is high rather than when it is low.

18.5 Comparison on NYSE Stock Prices

The effect of accounting for periodicity in intraday jump detection of foreign exchange data was studied by Boudt et al. (2010). They find that it reduces the number of jumps detected at times of periodically high volatility, on the one hand, and leads to a significant increase in the number of jumps detected at times of periodically low volatility, on the other hand. Here, we extend this finding to jumps detected in stock prices.

Our data is from the New York Stock Exchange Trades and Quotes database. The sample contains 624 trading days ranging from July 2, 2007, to December 31, 2009.[6] We consider 27 Dow Jones Industrial Average constituents at the beginning of 2008.[7] The trading session runs from 9:30 EST until 16:00 EST (390 minutes). We force these price series to a regular 2-min grid by previous tick interpolation. We compare the average total number of 2-min jumps detected using the I, J, and Z statistics in Equations 18.12–18.14 for each 30-min interval of a trading day.

Figure 18.4 plots the average (over the 624 days and 27 stocks in the sample) number of detected jumps (in 2-min returns) per 30-min interval. The number of detected jumps can take values between 0 (no jumps detected in the 30-min interval) and 15 (every 2-min return in the 30-min interval has a jump). First note the U-shape in the intraday plot of number of jump detections using the I-statistic. This is in contrast with the rather uniform distribution of jump detections based on the J and Z statistics, which correct for the intraday periodicity. We clearly see that during opening hours, the I statistic detects more jumps than the J and Z statistics. The biggest difference is observed for the first 30-min interval, where the I statistic detects about 1 jump per stock every 2 days on average, while the J and Z statistics only detect on an average about 1 jump

[6]We removed half trading days from our sample, namely 2007-07-03, 2007-11-23, 2007-12-24, 2008-07-03, 2008-11-28, 2008-12-24, 2009-11-27, and 2009-12-24. Before the analysis, the data is cleaned using the step-by-step procedure proposed in Barndorff-Nielsen et al. (2009) and Brownlees and Gallo (2006), and implemented in the R package RTAQ (Cornelissen and Boudt 2010).

[7]Tickers of the stocks in the sample are: AA, AXP, BA, C, CAT, DD, DIS, GE, HD, HON, HPQ, IBM, INTC, JNJ, JPM, KO, MCD, MMM, MO, MRK, MSFT, PFE, PG, UTX, VZ, WMT, XOM. Because of too many missing observations, AIG, GM, and T were removed from our sample.

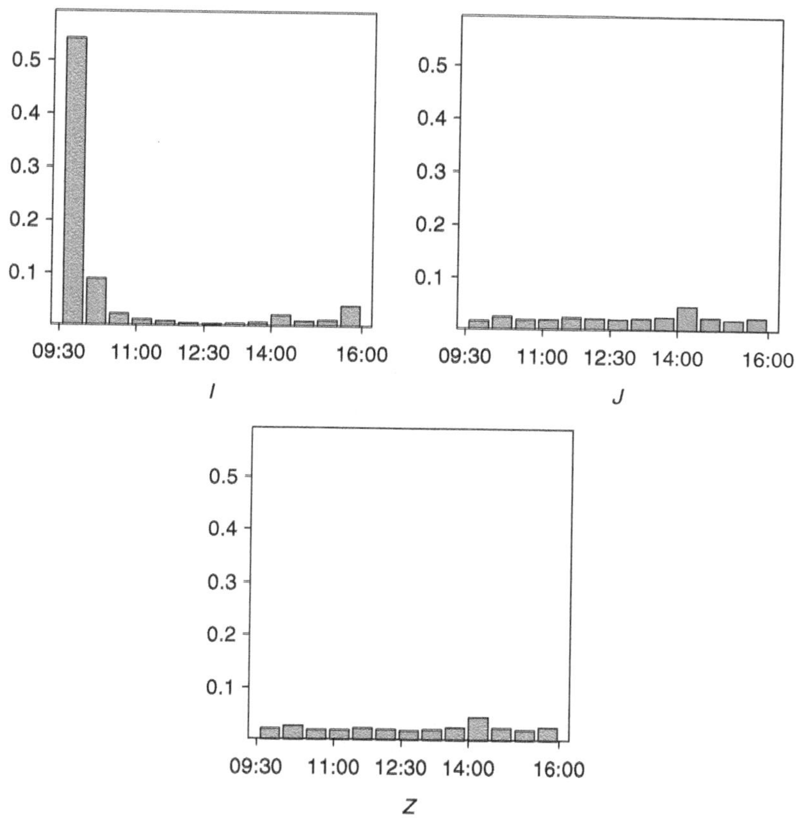

FIGURE 18.4 **Intraday plot of the number of 2-min intervals with jumps per 30 mins, averaged over 27 Dow Jones Industrial Average stocks and the 624 days in the sample.**

per stock every 66 and 50 days, respectively. When averaged over the entire day, we find that the I test statistic detects more than twice as many jumps than the J and Z statistics.

The pairwise percentage differences between the three tests are plotted in Figure 18.5. Panels (a), (b), and (c) compare the percentage difference of using I versus J, I versus Z, and Z versus J, respectively. In all cases, we observe a U-shaped pattern, similar to the periodicity pattern shown in Figure 18.1. Because of ignoring the intraday periodicity pattern, I detects up to 35 times more jumps during the opening period and up to 80% less jumps during noon, than the two other test statistics. Let us now focus on the comparison between Z and J. Since we find smaller differences here, it is reasonable to argue that the empirical impact of taking periodicity into account is larger than the impact of separating the continuous and noise variance in the denominator of the test statistic. The J statistic falsely imposes a periodic pattern on the noise variance, while the Z statistic keeps it constant over the day. As one can expect, shifting

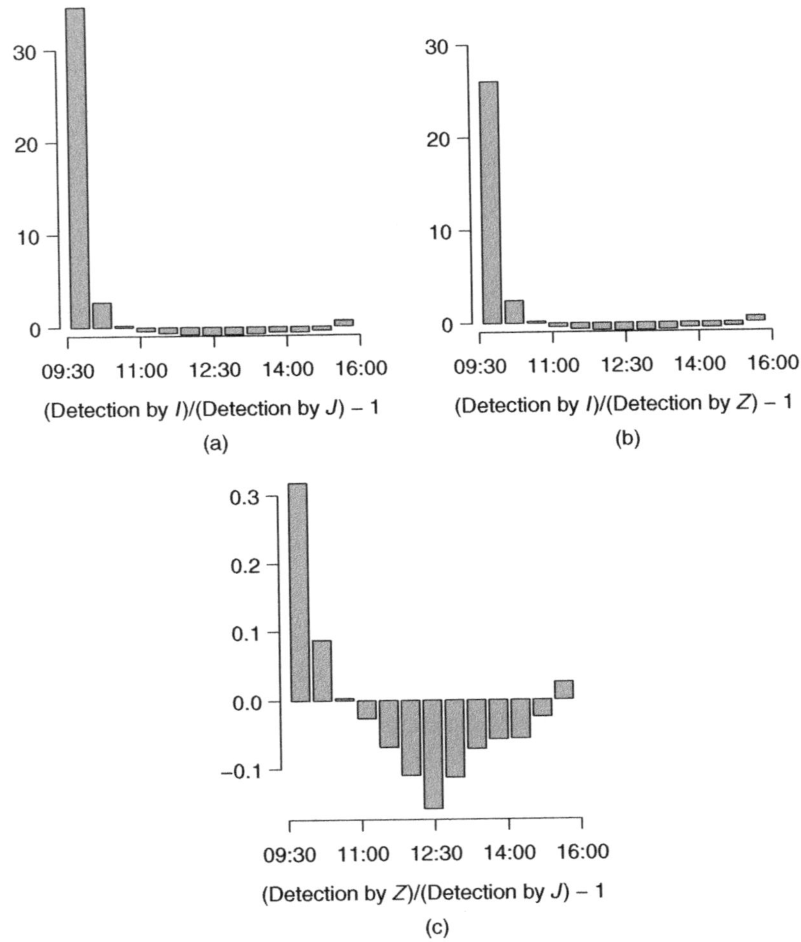

FIGURE 18.5 Pairwise differences of the number of jumps detected by two test statistics.

from J to Z, we detect more jumps during the opening period and less jumps during noon.

18.6 Conclusion

In this chapter, we review the literature on nonparametric tests for jumps in high frequency price series. High frequency financial returns are typically affected by (i) microstructure noise and (ii) a U-shaped periodic variation of intraday volatility. We discuss and illustrate the impact that these two features have on the jump detection statistic of Andersen et al. (2007) and Lee and Mykland (2008). Ignoring periodicity is shown to induce large size and power distortions of the jump detection statistic at the intraday level. Adjusted test statistics, taking into account the presence of noise in the data, are presented, which overcome this issue. Throughout the chapter, we made a strong parametric assumption on the noise process, namely, that it is i.i.d.-normal with constant variance and is independent of the process generating the efficient price. Relaxing this assumption is left for further research.

CHAPTER NINETEEN

Volatility Forecasts Evaluation and Comparison

FRANCESCO VIOLANTE and SÉBASTIEN LAURENT

19.1 Introduction

In this chapter, we review recent developments on volatility forecasts evaluation and comparison based on inference of moments of functions of predictions and prediction errors. We consider one-step-ahead forecasts of both univariate and multivariate volatility models, although the results can be easily extended to the multistep-ahead case. Depending on the purpose of the analysis, the forecaster may be interested in evaluating a single model, two models, or several models. When the object of the analysis is the forecasting accuracy of a single model, the quality of the model can be measured by the correlation between prediction and realizations. A common method that falls in this category is the Mincer-Zarnowitz (MZ) regression (Mincer and Zarnowitz, 1969), which involves regressing the realization of a variable on a constant and its forecast. Alternatively, the forecaster may aim to compare two or more models. Examples of tests for pairwise comparison have been proposed by Diebold and Mariano (1995) and West (1996) and were later generalized by Giacomini and White (2006). The multiple comparison problem can be tackled in different ways. We distinguish between two different approaches, namely, the multiple comparison

Handbook of Volatility Models and Their Applications, First Edition.
Edited by Luc Bauwens, Christian Hafner, and Sebastien Laurent.

with control (e.g., the reality check for data snooping of White (2000) and the superior predictive ability (SPA) test of Hansen and Lunde (2005a)), where a benchmark forecast is chosen ex-ante and compared to all the others to assess whether any of the competing forecasts outperforms the benchmark, and the multiple comparison without control (e.g., the model confidence set (MCS) test of Hansen et al. (2011)), where all the forecasts are compared against each other and poor performing models excluded.

A common problem in the evaluation of point forecasts is the comparison of nested models. In fact, depending on the forecasting scheme used to produce the sequence of out-of-sample observations, most of the tests for predictive ability discussed here may not apply, in the sense that the distribution under the null turns out to be degenerate in some cases and the test may suffer from serious size distortions. In this chapter, we consider the three most commonly used forecasting schemes (West, 2006). Let us denote by $\mathcal{T} + T$ the total sample size, where $\mathcal{T}$ is the estimation sample and T is the forecast evaluation sample. In the recursive scheme, the sample used to estimate the parameters of the model grows as the forecaster makes predictions for successive observations, that is, at each step $i = 1, \ldots, T - 1$ the forecast is based on all past information. In the rolling scheme, the sequence of T forecasts is based on parameters estimated using a rolling sample of fixed size $\mathcal{T}$. In the fixed scheme, the parameters of the model are estimated only once using data from 1 to $\mathcal{T}$. Then, the estimates are used to generate all forecasts, that is, at each step, $\mathcal{T} + 1, \mathcal{T} + 2, \ldots, \mathcal{T} + T - 1$, only the data are updated with the new information.

In this chapter, we essentially focus on the rolling and fixed forecasting schemes. In fact, as discussed in the following sections, the recursive scheme can be problematic when evaluating forecasts generated by nested models. Furthermore, the rolling and fixed schemes, other than allowing for the comparison of nested models, (Giacomini and White, 2006) also present other advantages. The rolling scheme is, in fact, rather appealing in case of heterogeneneity of the data or parameter drifts that cannot be easily modeled explicitly, whereas the fixed scheme can be useful when it is difficult to carry out parameter estimation. This is often the case, for instance, when comparing multivariate volatility models, where the large number of parameters makes the rolling scheme computationally challenging and time consuming, see Laurent et al. (2011) for an example where a combination of rolling and fixed schemes is used. A number of examples of applications using each of the three schemes can be found in West (2006).

Another problem, which characterizes the comparison of volatility forecasts, is the fact that the target variable is latent. Thus, the evaluation of forecasts or forecast errors has to be done with respect to some ex-post estimator. Typically, this problem is solved using a conditionally unbiased (and possibly consistent) estimator as, for example, the squared innovations, the realized volatility or kernels (see Andersen and Bollerslev, 1998 and the further developments by Barndorff-Nielsen and Shephard, 2002b; Zhang et al., 2005; Zhou, 1996; Barndorff-Nielsen et al., 2008 among the others) and their multivariate extension (Andersen et al., 2003; Barndorff-Nielsen et al., 2008; Hansen and Lunde, 2006b, or yet using range-based variance estimators (Parkinson, 1980; Garman and Klass, 1980; Brandt and Diebold, 2006). In the remainder of the chapter, we refer to the ex-post volatility estimator as the volatility proxy. However, it is not always true that using a conditionally unbiased proxy will lead, asymptotically, to the same outcome that would be obtained if the true volatility was observed. Hansen and Lunde (2006a) show that when the evaluation is based on a target observed with error, the choice of the evaluation criterion becomes critical in order to avoid a distorted outcome. The problem of consistency, sometimes referred to as *robustness*, of the ordering between two or more volatility forecasts has been further developed in Patton (2011), Patton and Sheppard (2009a) and Laurent et al. (2009).

Finally, since in most methods discussed here the evaluation of volatility forecasts relies, more or less explicitly, on the ranking implied by a statistical loss function and on the choice of a volatility proxy, we discuss the properties of a number of admissible loss functions and elaborate on the value of high precision proxies. In particular, if the ranking is nonrobust to the noise in the proxy (i.e., is subject to potential distortions), the inference on models' predictive accuracy will be incorrect even if the testing procedure is formally valid. If instead the ranking is robust, the presence of noise in the proxy is likely to affect the power of the test, but not its asymptotic size.

The rest of the chapter is organized as follows. In Section 19.2, we introduce the basic notation used throughout the chapter. In Section 19.3, we discuss the evaluation of the predictive accuracy of single forecasts. In Section 19.4, we introduce the problem of forecast evaluation under imperfect volatility proxies and provide a number of admissible loss functions. In Sections 19.5 and 19.6, we discuss methods for pairwise and multiple forecast comparison, respectively. In Section 19.7 we illustrate using artificial data the latent variable problem and its impact on the inference on forecast accuracy. In Sections 19.8, we conclude and discuss directions for further research.

19.2 Notation

We now introduce the basic notation and definitions used throughout the chapter. Let us define $t = 1, \ldots, T$, the time index of the forecast sample of size T. Let r_t be a scalar random variable whose conditional variance, $E[r_t^2|\Im_{t-1}] = E_{t-1}[r_t^2] = \sigma_t$, is of interest (to simplify the exposition, we assume that $E[r_t|\Im_{t-1}] = E_{t-1}[r_t] = 0$). The set $\Im_{t-1}$ denotes the information set at time $t-1$ and contains, for instance, past realizations of r_t. In financial applications, r_t typically represents a sequence of returns, that is, the first difference of logarithmic prices, of some financial asset. We also assume that $r_t|\Im_{t-1} \sim F(0, \sigma_t)$, where F is some distribution with zero-mean and finite variance. The (set of) variance forecast(s) (sometimes referred to as *models*) is denoted by h_t ($h_{k,t} \in \mathcal{H}$, $k = 1, \ldots, m$).

In the multivariate case, the variable of interest is the variance matrix, denoted $\Sigma_t = E_{t-1}[\mathbf{r}_t\mathbf{r}_t']$ where $\mathbf{r}_t$ is a $(N \times 1)$ random vector with $\mathbf{r}_t|\Im_{t-1} \sim F(\mathbf{0}, \Sigma_t)$ and Σ_t, whose typical element indexed by $i, j = 1, \ldots, N$ is denoted $\sigma_{ij,t}$ and is symmetric and positive-definite. The volatility forecasts are denoted

$H_{k,t} \in \mathcal{H}^{N\times N}$, with typical element $h_{ij,k,t}$, $i,j = 1,\ldots,N$, where $\mathcal{H}^{N\times N}$ is a compact subset of the space of symmetric and positive-definite matrices $R_{++}^{N\times N}$.

The forecast accuracy is usually evaluated by means of a loss function denoted as $L : R_{++} \times \mathcal{H} \to R_{+}$ where R_{+} and R_{++} correspond respectively to the nonnegative and positive portions of the real line and $\mathcal{H}$ is a compact subset of R_{++} identifying the set of volatility forecasts. In the multivariate case, the loss is defined as $L : R_{++}^{N\times N} \times \mathcal{H}^{N\times N} \to R^{+}$. Note that in both the univariate and multivariate cases, the first argument of the loss function is the true variance or some proxy of it, whereas the second is a volatility forecast.

As underlined in the previous section, owing to the latent nature of the variable of interest, the evaluation of the model forecasts has to rely on a volatility proxy, denoted $\hat{\sigma}_t$ and $\hat{\Sigma}_t$, respectively, in the univariate and multivariate cases. The only property that we require for the volatility proxy is conditional unbiasedness, that is, $E_{t-1}[\hat{\sigma}_t] = \sigma_t$ and $E_{t-1}[\hat{\Sigma}_t] = \Sigma_t \;\; \forall t$, respectively. Throughout the chapter, we consider the forecasts as observable. However, the forecasts may be biased or inaccurate in any way (because of parameter uncertainty, misspecification, etc.). About the volatility proxy, if not otherwise stated, we only assume that at least one conditionally unbiased proxy is available. In some specific cases, we also require the stronger assumption of consistency or the availability of a sequence of proxies that can be ordered in terms of their accuracy.

A simple variance proxy commonly used in the financial literature is the squared return, or the outer product of the return vector in the multivariate case. However, we discourage the use of such estimator for two reasons. First, although, under mild hypotheses, such proxy is conditionally unbiased for the latent variance, it is extremely noisy, which makes it unsuited in many situations. In fact, the scarce informative content of the volatility proxy could render difficult to assess the statistical relevance of the forecast performances and thus to discriminate between them. Second, even for the smallest multivariate dimension, $N = 2$, this proxy violates the positive-definiteness requirement of the volatility proxy. Other variance proxies based on realized moments are discussed in Andersen and Bollerslev (1998), Barndorff-Nielsen and Shephard (2002b), Zhang et al. (2005), Zhou (1996), Andersen et al. (2003), Hansen and Lunde (2006b), Barndorff-Nielsen et al. (2008), and Barndorff-Nielsen et al. (2008). Range-based variance estimators can be found in Parkinson (1980), Garman and Klass (1980), and Brandt and Diebold (2006).

19.3 Single Forecast Evaluation

A simple method for evaluating the accuracy of a volatility forecast is the well-known MZ regression (Mincer and Zarnowitz, 1969). This approach requires the estimation of the coefficients of regression of the target on a constant and a time series of forecasts, that is,

$$\sigma_t = \alpha + \beta h_t + \varepsilon_t \qquad \forall t = 1,\ldots,T. \tag{19.1}$$

The null hypothesis of optimality of the forecast can be written as $H^0 : \alpha = 0 \cup \beta = 1$. Given the latent nature of the target variable, the regression in Equation 19.1 is unfeasible. Substituting the true variance with some conditionally unbiased proxy, $\hat{\sigma}_t = \sigma_t + \eta_t$ with $E_{t-1}[\eta_t] = 0$, we can rewrite Equation 19.1 as

$$\hat{\sigma}_t = \alpha + \beta h_t + e_t, \tag{19.2}$$

where the innovations are $e_t = \eta_t + \varepsilon_t$. Since $\hat{\sigma}_t$ is a conditionally unbiased estimator of the true variance, Equation 19.2 yields unbiased estimates of α and β. The MZ regression allows to evaluate two different aspects of the volatility forecast. First, the MZ regression allows to test the presence of systematic over- or underpredictions, that is, whether the forecast is biased, by testing the joint hypothesis $H^0 : \alpha = 0 \cup \beta = 1$. Second, being the R^2 of Equation 19.2, an indicator of the correlation between the realization and the forecast, it can be used as an evaluation criterion of the accuracy of the forecast.

Since the variance of the innovation term e_t in Equation 19.2 depends on the accuracy of the volatility proxy, when a high quality proxy is available, the regression parameters are estimated more accurately. Also the R^2 of the regression in Equation 19.2, $-\text{Cov}(\hat{\sigma}_t, h_t)^2/(\text{Var}(\hat{\sigma}_t)\text{Var}(h_t))$, results penalized as the quality of the proxy deteriorates, see Andersen and Bollerslev (1998) for an analytical example.

The R^2 of the MZ regression has often been used as a criterion for ordering over a set of volatility forecasts (Andersen and Bollerslev, 1998; Andersen et al., 2003). Furthermore, to respond to the concern that few extreme observations can drive the forecast evaluation, many authors have argued in favor of MZ regressions on transformations of σ_t (and consequently $\hat{\sigma}_t$ and h_t), for instance, $\log(\hat{\sigma}_t)$ on $\log(h_t)$ or $|r_t|$ on $\sqrt{h_t}$ (see Pagan and Schwert (1990), Jorion (1995), Bollerslev and Wright (2001) among others for some examples).

Although appealing, this approach suffers from an important weakness. In fact, as pointed out by Andersen et al. (2005), transformed unbiased forecasts for the latent variance are not generally unbiased for the transformed proxy, $\hat{\sigma}_t$. However, allowing for $\alpha \neq 0$ and/or $\beta \neq 1$ in the MZ regression of the volatility proxy on the transformed forecasts explicitly corrects what would appear as signal of bias in the forecasts. Analytical examples under different distributional assumption for the volatility proxy can be found in Patton and Sheppard (2009a). It is important to point out that these drawbacks are only due to the substitution of the true volatility by the proxy. For the unfeasible transformed regression, that is, if the true volatility was observable, the null $H^0 : \alpha = 0 \cup \beta = 1$ would still apply for the transformed regression.

Also related to the use of transformations of the variables of interest, Hansen and Lunde (2006a) show that due to the latent variable problem, the R^2 of the MZ regression based on transformed variables is not always adequate and may lead to a perverse ordering. They established that the sufficient condition for the R^2 to be a valid criterion is $E_{t-1}[\sigma_t - \hat{\sigma}_t](\partial^i \phi(\sigma_t)/\partial \sigma_t^i) = c_i$ for some constant c_i, $\forall t = 1, 2, \ldots$ and $i \in N$ and where $\phi(\cdot)$ represents the transformation of the dependent variable and the regressor, for example, log, square, square root. This condition validates the use of the MZ regression in level and also, for example, of the quadratic transformation, that is, $\phi(x) = x^2$, although in the latter case, as pointed out by Andersen et al. (2005), the quadratic transformation of an unbiased forecast will not generally result to be unbiased for $\hat{\sigma}_t^2$, but rejects, for example, the log-regression.[1]

Another suitable property for a good forecast is that the forecasts or forecast errors are uncorrelated with other series or more generally with any other information available at the time the forecast is made. If this is not the case, then it would be possible to use such information to produce superior forecasts (Mincer and Zarnowitz, 1969; Figlewsky and Wachtel, 1981; Zarnowitz, 1985; and Keane and Runkle, 1990). Furthermore, including additional variables, such as lagged values of the volatility or of the standardized volatility, sign indicators or yet transformations and combinations of these variables allow to detect whether nonlinearities, asymmetries, and persistence have been neglected. This approach is called *augmented MZ regression*, where the augmentation consists, in addition to the right hand side of Equation 19.2, the term $\mathbf{z}_t\gamma$, where $\mathbf{z}_t$ represents the set of measurable additional regressors. The relevant null hypothesis becomes $H^0 : \alpha = 0 \cup \beta = 1 \cup \gamma = 0$.

Other than a test for unbiasedness and forecast accuracy, the MZ regression can also be viewed as a test of efficiency, that is, $E[h_t(\hat{\sigma}_t - h_t)] = 0$. In fact, if forecasts and forecast errors are correlated, then it would be possible to produce superior forecasts by exploiting this relationship. From Equation 19.2, we have

$$\hat{\sigma}_t - h_t = \alpha + (\beta - 1)h_t + e_t \tag{19.3}$$

and therefore,

$$E[h_t(\hat{\sigma}_t - h_t)] = \alpha E[h_t] + (\beta - 1)E[h_t^2] + E[h_t e_t] = 0, \tag{19.4}$$

when $\alpha = 0$ and $\beta = 1$.

The results outlined above can be directly extended, with few exceptions to the multivariate case. A simple approach is to consider the unique elements of the true variance matrix (proxy) and of the covariance forecast. The feasible MZ regression can be written as

$$\text{vech}(\hat{\Sigma}_t) = \boldsymbol{\alpha} + \text{diag}(\boldsymbol{\beta})\text{vech}(H_t) + \boldsymbol{e}_t, \tag{19.5}$$

[1]Note that although according to Hansen and Lunde (2006a) the R^2 of the quadratic MZ regression is a robust criterion, in the sense that it leaves the ranking between volatility forecasts unaffected when the latent variance is substituted by a proxy, the quadratic transformation of an unbiased forecast does not generally result to be unbiased for the quadratic transformation of the volatility proxy, $\hat{\sigma}_t$ Andersen et al., 2005. As an example let us assume $r_t|\Im_{t-1} \sim N(0, \sigma_t)$ and consider the volatility proxy $\hat{\sigma}_t = r_t^2$. The quadratic MZ regression ($\phi(x) = x^2$) can be written as $(\hat{\sigma}_t)^2 = \alpha + \beta h_t^2 + e_t$. Under the null $H^0 : h_t = \sigma_t \; a.s. \; \forall t$ the population values of the parameters are $\alpha = 0$ and $\beta = 3$. For the unfeasible transformed regression, that is, if the true volatility was observable, the null $H^0 : \alpha = 0 \cup \beta = 1$ would still apply for the transformed regression.

where $\boldsymbol{\alpha}$ and $\boldsymbol{\beta}$ are $(N(N+1)/2 \times 1)$ vectors of parameters, vech(·) is the half-vector operator, and diag(·) is the operator that transforms a vector into a square diagonal matrix with the vector along the diagonal. Equation 19.5 can be estimated by seemingly unrelated regression techniques. Then, a joint test that $\boldsymbol{\alpha} = \mathbf{0}$ and $\boldsymbol{\beta} = \mathbf{1}$ can be performed. As pointed out by Patton and Sheppard (2009a), the large dimension of the system may adversely affect the finite-sample properties of the joint test. The solution proposed to reduce the parameter space is to impose in Equation 19.5 the parameter constrains $\alpha_i = \alpha$ and $\beta_i = \beta \; \forall i = 1, \ldots, N(N+1)/2$.

19.4 Loss Functions and the Latent Variable Problem

An ideal approach to the evaluation of forecast performances is the comparison of expected losses evaluated with respect to the true variance. However, as noted in Section 19.3, the latent nature of the conditional variance makes it difficult to evaluate the performances of volatility forecasts. The latent variable problem can be solved, at least partly, by substituting the true conditional variance by some ex-post estimator based on observed quantities as they become available. Examples of volatility proxies have been provided in Section 19.1.

Obviously, a good volatility proxy must be conditionally unbiased. However, as first noted by Andersen and Bollerslev (1998) and Andersen et al. (2005), it is not always the case that the evaluation of forecast performances using a conditionally unbiased proxy will lead, asymptotically, to the same outcome that would be obtained if the true volatility was used. Hansen and Lunde (2006a), focusing on a qualitative assessment (ordering) of volatility forecasts, show that when the evaluation is based on a target observed with error, the choice of the evaluation criterion becomes critical in order to avoid a perverse outcome. They define the theoretical framework for the analysis of the ordering of stochastic sequences and provide conditions on the functional form of the loss function, which ensure consistency between the ordering based on a volatility proxy and the one based on the true, but latent, variance.

Let us define the precision, measured in terms of expected loss, of some generic volatility forecast, $h_{k,t}$, with respect to the true variance as $E[L(\sigma_t, h_{k,t})]$. The aim is to seek conditions that ensure consistency of the ranking (equivalence of the ordering) between any two forecasts k and j when a conditionally unbiased proxy is substituted to the true variance, that is,

$$E[L(\sigma_t, h_{k,t})] \leq E[L(\sigma_t, h_{j,t})] \Leftrightarrow E[L(\hat{\sigma}_t, h_{k,t})] \leq E[L(\hat{\sigma}_t, h_{j,t})], \qquad (19.6)$$

where k and j refer to two competing volatility forecasts. The violation of Equation 19.6 is defined as objective bias. A sufficient condition to ensure Equation 19.6 is the following

$$\frac{\partial^2 L(\sigma_t, h_t)}{(\partial \sigma_t)^2} \quad \text{exists and does not depend on } h_t. \qquad (19.7)$$

It follows immediately that Equation 19.7 rejects evaluation criteria commonly used in applied work such as absolute deviations, root of squared errors, or proportional error loss functions, whereas it validates the use of squared errors. Numerous examples of loss functions violating Equation 19.7 are discussed by Hansen and Lunde (2006a), Patton (2011), Patton and Sheppard (2009a), and Laurent et al. (2009). See also Section 19.7 for an analytical illustration.

Focusing on the univariate dimension, Patton (2011) provides analytical results for the undesirable outcome that arises when using a loss function that violates Equation 19.7, under different distributional assumptions for the returns and considering different volatility proxies and for a number of commonly used loss functions. Furthermore, building upon Hansen and Lunde (2006a), he provides necessary and sufficient conditions on the functional form for the loss function (defined within the class of homogeneous statistical loss functions that can be expressed as means of each period loss), ensuring consistency of the ordering when using a proxy. The following family of functions represents the entire subset of consistent homogeneous loss functions, with degree of homogeneity given by ξ[2]

$$L(\hat{\sigma}_t, h_t) = \begin{cases} \dfrac{1}{(\xi-1)\xi}\left(\hat{\sigma}_t^{\xi} - h_t^{\xi}\right) - \dfrac{1}{\xi-1} h_t^{\xi-1}(\hat{\sigma}_t - h_t) & \text{for } \xi \notin (0,1) \\ h_t - \hat{\sigma}_t + \hat{\sigma}_t \log \dfrac{\hat{\sigma}_t}{h_t} & \text{for } \xi = 1 \\ \dfrac{\hat{\sigma}_t}{h_t} - \log \dfrac{\hat{\sigma}_t}{h_t} - 1 & \text{for } \xi = 0 \end{cases}. \tag{19.8}$$

The loss function in Equation 19.8 can take a variety of shapes: symmetric ($\xi = 2$ corresponds to the mean squared prediction error loss function) and asymmetric with penalty on overpredictions ($\xi > 2$) or underpredictions ($\xi < 2$). The set of consistent loss functions in Equation 19.8 relates to the class of linear exponential densities of Gouriéroux et al. (1984) and, as noted by Laurent et al. (2009), it partially coincides with the subset of homogeneous loss functions associated with the most important linear exponential densities.[3] In fact, for $\xi = 0, 1, 2$, the function can be alternatively derived from the objective functions of the Gaussian, Poisson and Gamma densities, respectively (see Gouriéroux and Monfort (1995) for details).

The first of the generalizations to the multivariate case has been proposed by Patton and Sheppard (2009a). Laurent et al. (2009) completed this setting and provided a general framework for the evaluation of variance matrices. They identifies a number of robust vector and matrix loss functions and provide an insight into their properties, interpretation, and geometrical representation.

---

[2]Recall that a function is homogeneous if it has a multiplicative scaling behavior, that is, if $f : X \rightarrow Y$ and ξ integer, then f is homogeneous of degree ξ if $f(kx) = k^{\xi} f(x), \forall k > 0$.

[3]Recall that a function $f(x)$ is homogeneous of degree α if it satisfies $f(kx) = k^{\alpha} f(x)$ for all nonzero k.

In the multivariate case, the sufficient condition in Equation 19.6 becomes

$$\frac{\partial^2 L(\Sigma_t, H_t)}{\partial \sigma_{l,t} \partial \sigma_{m,t}} \quad \text{finite and independent of } H_t \ \forall l, m = 1, \ldots, N(N+1)/2, \tag{19.9}$$

where $\sigma_{l,t}$ is the lth element of the vector $\boldsymbol{\sigma}_t = \text{vech}(\Sigma_t)$. Given Equation 19.9, a generalized necessary and sufficient functional form for the loss functions is

$$L(\hat{\Sigma}_t, H_t) = \tilde{C}(H_t) - \tilde{C}(\hat{\Sigma}_t) + C(H_t)'\text{vech}(\hat{\Sigma}_t - H_t), \tag{19.10}$$

where $\tilde{C}(\cdot) : R_{++}^{N\times N} \to R_+$ with

$$C(H_t) = \begin{bmatrix} \frac{\partial \tilde{C}(H_t)}{\partial h_{1,t}} \\ \vdots \\ \frac{\partial \tilde{C}(H_t)}{\partial h_{K,t}} \end{bmatrix}, \quad C'(H_t) = \begin{bmatrix} \frac{\partial \tilde{C}(H_t)}{\partial h_{1,t}\partial h_{1,t}} & \cdots & \frac{\partial \tilde{C}(H_t)}{\partial h_{1,t}\partial h_{K,t}} \\ \vdots & \ddots & \\ \frac{\partial \tilde{C}(H_t)}{\partial h_{K,t}\partial h_{1,t}} & & \frac{\partial \tilde{C}(H_t)}{\partial h_{K,t}\partial h_{K,t}} \end{bmatrix}, \tag{19.11}$$

where $C(\cdot)$ and $C'(\cdot)$ are the gradient and the hessian of $\tilde{C}(\cdot)$ respectively, with respect to the $K = N(N+1)/2$ unique elements of H_t, denoted $\mathbf{h}_t = \text{vech}(H_t)$, and $C'(H_t)$ is negative-definite. The general form in Equation 19.10 is related to the linear exponential matrix densities and represents the family of the Bregman matrix divergences criteria. Well-known loss functions belonging to this family are the Frobenius distance, the von Neumann divergence, and the Stein loss function (also called *LogDet* or *Burg divergence*).

From Equation 19.10, Laurent et al. (2009) identified the entire subset of homogeneous ($\xi = 2$) loss functions based on forecast errors, that is, $(\Sigma_t - H_t)$, which can be expressed as

$$L(\hat{\Sigma}_t, H_t) = L(\hat{\Sigma}_t - H_t) = \text{vech}(\hat{\Sigma}_t - H_t)'\hat{\Lambda}\text{vech}(\hat{\Sigma}_t - H_t), \tag{19.12}$$

where $\hat{\Lambda}$ is a positive-definite matrix of constants that defines the weights assigned to the elements of the forecast error matrix. The loss function in Equation 19.12 nests a number of MSE (mean squared error)-type loss functions, defined on both vector and matrix spaces, for example, (weighted) Euclidean distance on the half-vectorization of the forecast error matrix or Frobenius distance on the difference of realized and predicted variance matrices, Σ_t and H_t.

Unlike the univariate case, where an analytical expression is available for the entire class of consistent loss functions, in the multivariate case, such generalization is unfeasible because there are infinite combinations of forecasts and forecast errors, hence of functions $\tilde{C}(\cdot)$, that satisfy Equation 19.10. However, given Equation 19.10, application-specific loss functions can be easily derived. Laurent et al. (2009) provide and discuss a number of examples.

Finally, Laurent et al. (2009) also show that, under the higher level assumption of consistency of the volatility proxy, the distortion introduced in the ordering when using an inconsistent loss function tends to disappear as the quality of the proxy improves. Since often nonrobust loss functions have other desirable properties that are useful in applications, for example, downweighting extreme forecast errors, they may still be used, provided the volatility proxy is sufficiently accurate.

In the following sections, we review a number of tests for forecast evaluation where performances are evaluated by means of a statistical loss function. Although most of the methodologies discussed are valid under a general loss function, we remind that in empirical applications, when the true variance is substituted by a proxy, the loss function should be chosen, depending on the setting, according to the Equations 19.8 and 19.10.

19.5 Pairwise Comparison

The first approach to pairwise comparison that we consider is the test of equal predictive ability proposed by Ashley et al. (1980) as a generalization of the approach introduced by Granger and Newbold (1977). The test is based on the comparison of the mean square errors (MSE) of a pair of forecasts with respect to the target. Let us define $e_{k,t} = \sigma_t - h_{k,t}$ the forecast error and $L_{k,t}^{\mathrm{MSE}} = T^{-1}\sum_t e_{k,t}^2$ the mean square forecast error of some model k with respect to σ_t. Then, when comparing the performance of model k to some other model j, simple algebra yields

$$L_{k,t}^{\mathrm{MSE}} - L_{j,t}^{\mathrm{MSE}} = (\mathrm{Var}(e_{k,t}) - \mathrm{Var}(e_{j,t})) + (\bar{e}_k^2 - \bar{e}_j^2), \tag{19.13}$$

where $\bar{e}_i = T^{-1}\sum_t e_{i,t}$. Let us now define $D_t = e_{k,t} - e_{j,t}$, $S_t = e_{k,t} + e_{j,t}$ and $\bar{D}$, $\bar{S}$ their empirical means. Then, (19.13) can be rewritten as

$$L_{k,t}^{\mathrm{MSE}} - L_{j,t}^{\mathrm{MSE}} = \mathrm{Cov}(D_t, S_t) + \bar{D}\bar{S}. \tag{19.14}$$

A test of equal predictive ability, or more precisely equal MSE, corresponds to testing the null hypothesis

$$H^0 : \mathrm{Cov}(D_t, S_t) = 0 \cup \bar{D} = 0. \tag{19.15}$$

Note that Equation 19.15 implies that the forecasts can be biased. In fact, $\bar{D}_t = 0$ does not require $e_{k,t} = e_{j,t} = 0$ but only that the biases are equal in size and sign. The null hypothesis in Equation 19.15 is equivalent to testing the null hypothesis $H^0 : \alpha = 0 \cup \beta = 0$ in the following regression

$$D_t = \alpha + \beta(S_t - \bar{S}) + \varepsilon_t. \tag{19.16}$$

If the forecast errors have zero-mean, that is, they are both unbiased, and under the additional assumption that they are normally distributed and uncorrelated, the test of equal MSE is equivalent to the test proposed by Granger and Newbold

(1977), henceforth GN, that is,

$$\text{GN} - T = \frac{\rho}{\sqrt{(T-1)^{-1}(1-\rho)^2}} \sim t_{T-1}, \tag{19.17}$$

where $\rho = \text{Cov}(D_t, S_t)/\sqrt{\text{Var}(D_t)\text{Var}(S_t)}$ and t_{T-1} is the Student t distribution with $T-1$ degrees of freedom.

The extension to the multivariate case is straightforward. In fact, the MSE can computed using the Euclidean distance, $L^E_{k,t} = T^{-1}\sum_t[\sum_{i\leq j} e^2_{ij,k,t}]$, $i,j = 1,\ldots,N$ or the Frobenius distance, $L^F_{k,t} = T^{-1}\sum_t[\sum_{i,j} e^2_{ij,k,t}]$, $i,j = 1,\ldots,N$, although it is worth noting that in the latter case the covariance forecast errors are double-weighted. Given that these loss functions can be expressed as a linear combination of MSEs on the unique element or on all elements of the forecast error matrix, a joint test on the coefficient of the pooled regression $D_{ij,t}$ on $(S_{ij,t} - \bar{S})$ can be performed using standard panel data techniques.

Another approach to pairwise comparison that we consider is the test of equal predictive ability proposed by Diebold and Mariano (1995), henceforth DM, and was further refined by West (1996), McCracken (2000, 2007) Clark and McCracken (2001, 2005) Corradi et al. (2001), Clark and West (2006, 2007), The DM test is a very general procedure[4] designed to compare two rival forecasts in terms of their forecasting accuracy using a general loss function. The measure of predictive accuracy, that is, the loss function, can be specified according to the definition of optimality adopted by the forecaster.

Consider a loss function as defined in Section 19.2 and define the loss differential between model k and j as

$$d_t = L(\sigma_t, h_{k,t}) - L(\sigma_t, h_{j,t}), \tag{19.18}$$

in the univariate case, and

$$d_t = L(\Sigma_t, H_{k,t}) - L(\Sigma_t, H_{j,t}), \tag{19.19}$$

in the multivariate case. Since in either case the loss function is scalar valued, we can more generally refer to the notation $d_t = L_{i,t} - L_{j,t}$. Under the assumption that d_t is stationary, $E[d_t]$ is well defined and allows for the formulation of the null hypothesis of equal predictive ability $H^0 : E[d_t] = 0$. The test takes the form of a t-statistic, that is,

$$\text{DM} - T = \frac{\sqrt{T}\bar{d}}{\sqrt{\omega}} \overset{a}{\sim} N(0,1), \tag{19.20}$$

where $\bar{d} = T^{-1}\sum_t d_t$ and $\omega = \lim_{t\to\infty} \text{Var}(\sqrt{T}\bar{d})$ is its asymptotic variance. A natural estimator of ω is the sample variance of d_t, though, this estimator is consistent only if the loss differentials are serially uncorrelated. Since this is

[4]It does not require zero-mean forecast errors (hence the forecasts can be biased), specific distributional assumptions, or zero-serial correlation for the forecast errors.

not generally the case, a suitable heteroskedasticity and autocorrelation consistent estimator, such as the Newey-West variance estimator, is preferable.

It is worth noting that the aim of the DM type tests is to infer about $E[d_t(\theta_0)]$ using $T^{-1}\sum_t d_t(\theta_0)$, where θ_0 represents the model parameter population values, and thus, these tests are based on asymptotics, requiring the size of the estimation sample $\mathcal{T}$ and the forecast evaluation sample T to grow to infinity at the same rate.[5] Since this type of asymptotics relies on parameter population values, the comparison of nested models is obviously not allowed, because the asymptotic distribution of the statistic under the null turns out to be degenerate (identically zero) when the restricted model is true. A solution to this problem has been provided by McCracken (2007) and Clark and McCracken (2005) (CM), who argue that although $T^{-1}\sum_t d_t(\hat{\theta}) - E[d_t(\theta_0)] \underset{p}{\rightarrow} 0$ when models are nested, $T^{-1}\sum_t d_t(\hat{\theta})$ is a nondegenerate random variable. On the basis of this argument, they suggest several statistics suited for testing equal predictive accuracy, whose distribution is nonstandard and depends on the parameter uncertainty. To obtain the distribution under the null hypothesis, Clark and McCracken (2009) propose an asymptotically valid procedure based on bootstrap sampling.

To allow for a unified treatment of nested and nonnested models, Giacomini and White (2006) (henceforth GW) suggest to approach the problem of the forecast evaluation as a problem of inference about conditional (rather than unconditional) expectations of forecast errors. The GW test is a test of finite-sample predictive ability. Giacomini and White (2006) construct a test for conditional equal predictive accuracy based on asymptotics in which the estimation error is a permanent component of the forecast error. Rather than focusing on unconditional expectations, their approach aims at inferring about conditional expectations of forecast errors, that is, inferring about $E[d_t(\hat{\theta})]$ using $T^{-1}\sum_t d_t(\hat{\theta})$. The GW approach tests the null hypothesis of equal predictive ability

$$E[L(\sigma_t, h_{k,t}^{\tau_k}(\hat{\theta}_{k,t}^{\tau_k})) - L(\sigma_t, h_{j,t}^{\tau_j}(\hat{\theta}_{j,t}^{\tau_k}))|\Im_{t-1}] \equiv E[d_{\mathcal{T},t}|\Im_{t-1}] = 0, \qquad (19.21)$$

where, for $i = k, j$, $h_{i,t}^{\tau_i}(\hat{\theta}_{i,t}^{\tau_i})$ are $\Im_{t-1}$-measurable forecasts, τ_i is size of the estimation window, possibly different for each model, and $\mathcal{T} = \max(\tau_k, \tau_j)$. Since under the null hypothesis, $\{d_{\mathcal{T},t}, \Im_t\}$ is a martingale difference sequence, Equation 19.21 is equivalent to $E[\delta_{t-1}d_{\mathcal{T},t}] = 0$, where δ_{t-1}, referred to as *the test function*, is a $\Im_{t-1}$-measurable vector of dimension q. By invoking standard asymptotic normality arguments, the GW test takes the form of a Wald-type statistic

$$\mathrm{GW} - T_{\mathcal{T}}^{\delta} = T\left(T^{-1}\sum_{t=1}^{T}\delta_{t-1}d_{\mathcal{T},t}\right)'\hat{\Omega}^{-1}\left(T^{-1}\sum_{t=1}^{T}\delta_{t-1}d_{\mathcal{T},t}\right), \qquad (19.22)$$

---

[5]Such asymptotics apply naturally under a recursive forecasts scheme, where the sample used to estimate the parameters of the model grows at the same rate as the forecast sample, that is, at each step t the forecast is based on all available information up to $t-1$. Additional assumptions for asymptotics based on rolling and fixed schemes, where the estimation sample increases with the overall sample size, are given in West (1996).

where $\hat{\Omega}$ is a consistent estimator of the variance of $\delta_{t-1}d_{T,t}$. The statistic is asymptotically χ^2_q under the null hypothesis.

An example of test function suggested by Giacomini and White (2006) is $\delta_t = (1, d_{T,t})'$, which allows to test jointly for equal predictive ability and lack of serial correlation in the loss differentials. Note that in the case where $\tau_k = \tau_j$ and $\delta_t = 1\ \forall t$, the GW test is equivalent to a "conditional" DM test with forecasts evaluated using the rolling window forecast scheme. Apart from this simple case, we are not aware of any other application of the GW approach (e.g., allowing for more sophisticated test functions, $\tau_k \neq \tau_j$, time-dependent estimation windows, different forecasting rules/methods, or yet different estimation procedures for each model).

Clearly, the GW asymptotics hold when the size of the estimation sample is fixed and the forecast sample grows, that is, $\mathcal{T}$ fixed, $T \rightarrow \infty$, as well as under a rolling scheme[6] and, in general, to any limited memory estimator.

19.6 Multiple Comparison

When multiple alternative forecasts are available, it is of interest to test whether a specific forecast (hereafter the benchmark), selected independently from the data, produces systematically superior (at least equivalent) performances with respect to the rival models. In this case, we aim to test the null hypothesis that the benchmark is not inferior to any other alternative. This approach, called *multiple comparison with control*, differs from the techniques discussed in Section 19.5 for two reasons. First, the multiple comparison allows to recognize the multiplicity effect, that is, statistical relevance of all comparisons between the benchmark and each of the alternative models, and calls for a test of multiple hypotheses to control for the size of the overall testing procedure. Second, while Section 19.5 involves tests of equal predictive ability, the choice of a control requires a test of SPA. The distinction is crucial because while the former leads to simple null hypotheses, that is, testing equalities, the latter leads to composite hypotheses, that is, testing (weak) inequalities. The main complication in composite hypotheses testing is that (asymptotic) distributions typically depend on nuisance parameters, hence the distribution under the null is not unique.

To simplify the exposition, the notation used in this section only refers the univariate dimension. Since all the techniques discussed hereafter are based on comparisons of forecast performances measured by some statistical loss function, the extension to the multivariate case, as noted in Section 19.5, is straightforward and only involves an appropriate redefinition of the loss function, namely, $L : R^{N\times N}_{++} \times \mathcal{H}^{N\times N} \rightarrow R_+$. Issues related to the choice of the loss function and to the latent variable problem have been discussed in Section 19.4.

The first approach that we consider is the reality check for data snooping of White (2000) (hereafter RC). Let us define the loss differential between the

[6]The sequence of $\mathcal{T}$ parameters is generated using the most recent information, for example, a rolling sample of fixed size $\mathcal{T}$.

benchmark, $h_{0,t}$, and some rival forecast, $h_{k,t}$ $k = 1, \ldots, m$ as

$$d_{k,t} = L(\sigma_t, h_{0,t}) - L(\sigma_t, h_{k,t}) \tag{19.23}$$

and $\mathbf{d}_t = (d_{1,t}, \ldots, d_{m,t})$. Provided that $\mathbf{d}_t$ is (strictly) stationary, $E[\mathbf{d}_t]$ is well defined, and the null hypothesis of interest takes the form

$$H^0 : E[\mathbf{d}_t] \leq \mathbf{0}, \quad \text{(or equivalently} \quad H^0 : \max_k E[d_{k,t}] \leq 0) \tag{19.24}$$

that is, the benchmark is superior to the best alternative. Clearly, the null hypothesis in Equation 19.24 is a multiple hypothesis, that is, the intersection of the one-sided individual hypotheses $E[d_{k,t}] \leq 0$. The RC statistic takes the form

$$\text{RC} - T = \max_k(\sqrt{T}\,\bar{d}_k), \tag{19.25}$$

where $\bar{d}_k = T^{-1} \sum_{t=1}^{T} d_{k,t}$. Note that as in Diebold and Mariano (1995), the RC test is based on asymptotics, which require the parameters of the model-based forecasts to converge to their population values, thus not allowing for the comparison of nested models. Using similar arguments of Giacomini and White (2006), Hansen (2005) extends the procedure to the comparison of nested models. The framework defined in Hansen (2005) is well suited when parameters are estimated once, that is, fixed scheme, or using a moving window (of fixed or time-dependent size or yet of different size for each model), that is, rolling schemes, whereas the comparison of models with parameters that are estimated recursively is not accommodated.

Given strict stationary of $\mathbf{d}_t$, White (2000) invokes conditions provided in West (1996) that lead to

$$\sqrt{T}(\bar{\mathbf{d}} - E[\mathbf{d}_t]) \xrightarrow{d} \text{N}(0, \Omega). \tag{19.26}$$

The challenge when implementing the RC test is that Equation 19.25 has an asymptotic distribution under the null hypothesis depending on the nuisance parameters $E[\mathbf{d}_t]$ and Ω. One way to proceed is to substitute a consistent estimator for Ω and employ the least favorable configuration (LFC) over the values of $E[\mathbf{d}_t]$ that satisfy the null hypothesis. From Equation 19.24, it is clear that the least favorable value to the alternative is $E[\mathbf{d}_t] = 0$, which presumes that all alternatives are as good as the benchmark. However, the distribution of Equation 19.25, that is, the extreme value of a vector of correlated normal variables, is unknown. White (2000) suggests two ways to obtain the distribution under the LFC for the alternative, namely, the Monte Carlo Reality Check (simulated inference) and the Bootstrap Reality Check (bootstrap inference). We refer the readers to White (2000) for further details on the two methods.

Using a similar approach, Hansen (2005) proposes a new test for SPA. His framework differs from White (2000) in two ways. First, he proposes a different statistic based on studentized quantities to alleviate the substantial loss of power that the RC can suffer because of the inclusion of poor and irrelevant forecasts.

Second, he employs a sample-dependent distribution under the null. The latter is based on a procedure that incorporates additional sample information in order to identify the relevant alternatives. In fact, while the procedure based on the LFC suggested in White (2000) implicitly relies on an asymptotic distribution under the null hypothesis that assumes $E[d_{k,t}] = 0$ for all k, Hansen (2005) points out that all negative values of $E[d_{k,t}]$ have also to be considered since they conform with the null hypothesis.

The new statistic takes the form

$$\mathrm{SPA} - T = \max\left[\max_k \frac{\sqrt{T}\bar{d}_k}{\sqrt{\hat{\omega}_k}}, 0\right], \tag{19.27}$$

where $\hat{\omega}_k$ is some consistent estimator of $\omega_k = \lim_{t\to\infty} \mathrm{Var}(\sqrt{T}\bar{d}_k)$, i.e. the kth diagonal element of Ω. The null distribution of the SPA statistic is based on $\sqrt{T}\bar{\mathbf{d}} \xrightarrow{d} \mathrm{N}(\hat{\boldsymbol{\mu}}^c, \hat{\Omega})$, where $\hat{\boldsymbol{\mu}}^c$ is a consistent estimator of $\boldsymbol{\mu} = E[\mathbf{d}_t]$ that conforms with the null hypothesis. The suggested estimator is

$$\hat{\mu}_k^c = \bar{d}_k 1_{\{\sqrt{T}\bar{d}_k/\hat{\omega}_k \le -(2\log\log T)^{1/2}\}}, \tag{19.28}$$

where $1_{\{.\}}$ denotes the indicator function. The threshold $(2 \log\log T)^{1/2}$ in Equation 19.28 represents the slowest rate that captures all alternatives with $\mu_k = 0$. More generally, any threshold in the interval $[(2\log\log T)^{1/2},\ T^{1/2-\varepsilon}]$, for any $\varepsilon > 0$ also produces a valid test and guarantees that all poor models are discarded asymptotically. For instance, Hansen (2005) proposes the value $0.25\,T^{0.25}$. Furthermore, since different threshold rates lead to different p-values in finite samples, Hansen (2005) also provides a lower and upper bound for the SPA p-values. These p-values can be obtained using $\hat{\mu}_k^l = \min(\bar{d}_k, 0)$ and $\hat{\mu}_k^u = 0$, where the latter yields a distribution under the null based on the LFC principle.[7] Hansen (2005) also provides a detailed description of the bootstrap scheme used to obtain the distribution under the null hypothesis.

Clearly, when comparing volatility models, the choice of a benchmark is not obvious. Furthermore, especially when the set of competing models is large, such applications may not yield a single model that is significantly superior to the alternatives because the data may not be sufficiently informative to give an univocal answer. In this case, the forecaster may aim to reduce the set of competing models to a smaller set that is guaranteed to contain the best forecasting model at a given confidence level. This approach, known as *multiple comparison without control*, suggests a comparison of all models with each other. It differs from the techniques discussed above for two reasons. First, the procedure does not require a benchmark to be specified. Second, the testing procedure generally relies on simple hypotheses, that is, equalities.

Hansen et al. (2011) construct a sequential test of equal predictive ability, dubbed MCS, which, given an initial set of forecasts M^0, allows to (i) test the

[7]In the latter case, the distribution under the null is obtained using the same arguments as in White (2000). The difference here stands in the fact that the variable of interest is the maximum of studentized quantities, whereas in White (2000), it is the maximum of nonstudentized quantities.

null that no forecast is distinguishable from any other; (ii) discard any inferior forecasts if they exist; and (iii) characterize the set of models that are (equivalent to each other and) superior to all the discarded models. The set of surviving model is called MCS and can be interpreted as a confidence interval for the forecasts in that it is the set containing the best forecast at some confidence level.

Designed around the testing principle of Pantula (1989) to ensure that sequential testing does not affect the overall size of the test, the MCS test involves a sequence of tests for equal predictive ability. Given M^0, the starting hypothesis is that all models in M^0 have equal forecasting performances. The relative performance of each pair of forecasts is measured by $d_{k,j,t} = L(\sigma_t, h_{k,t}) - L(\sigma_t, h_{j,t})$, for all $k, j \in M^0$ and $k \neq j$. Under the assumption that $d_{k,j,t}$ is stationary, the null hypothesis of equal predictive ability takes the form

$$H^0 : E[d_{k,j,t}] = 0 \qquad \forall k, j \in M^0. \tag{19.29}$$

If the null of equal predictive ability is rejected at a given confidence level α, then an elimination rule is called to remove the worst performing model. The equal predictive ability test is then repeated until the nonrejection of the null, while keeping the confidence level α fixed at each iteration, thus allowing to construct a $(1-\alpha)$-confidence set, $M^* \equiv \{k \in M_0 : E(d_{k,j,t}) \leq 0 \forall\, j \in M^0\}$, for the best model in M^0.

Let $\mathbf{L}_t$ be the $(m \times 1)$ vector of sample performances $L(\sigma_t, h_{k,t})$, $k \in M$ and $\iota_\perp$ the $(m \times (m-1))$ orthogonal complement of an m-dimensional vector of ones, where m is the dimension of M. Then, the vector $\iota'_\perp \mathbf{L}_t$ can be viewed as $m-1$ relevant contrasts, as each element can be obtained as a linear combination of $d_{k,j,t}$, $k, j \in M$, which has mean zero under the null (Eq. 19.29). Hence, Equation 19.29 is equivalent to $E[\iota'_\perp \mathbf{L}_t] = 0$, and under strict stationarity of $d_{k,j,t}$, it holds that $T^{-1/2}\sum_{t=1}^{T} \iota'_\perp \mathbf{L}_t$ is asymptotically normal with mean 0 and covariance matrix $\Omega = \lim_{t\to\infty} \mathrm{Var}(T^{-1/2}\sum_{t=1}^{T} \iota'_\perp \mathbf{L}_t)$. Thus, it seems natural to employ traditional quadratic-form-type tests as

$$\mathrm{MCS} - T_Q = T\left(T^{-1}\sum_{t=1}^{T} \iota'_\perp \mathbf{L}_t\right)' \hat{\Omega}^+ \left(T^{-1}\sum_{t=1}^{T} \iota'_\perp \mathbf{L}_t\right) \tag{19.30}$$

and

$$\mathrm{MCS} - T_F = \frac{T-q}{q(T-1)}\,\mathrm{MCS} - T_Q, \tag{19.31}$$

where $\hat{\Omega}$ is some consistent estimator of Ω, $q = \mathrm{rank}(\hat{\Omega})$ denotes the number of linearly independent contrasts, and $\hat{\Omega}^+$ denotes the More-Penrose pseudoinverse of $\hat{\Omega}$. The statistic in Equation 19.30 is asymptotically χ^2_q, whereas Equation 19.31 is asymptotically $F_{q,T-q}$ under the null hypothesis, as the subscripts Q (quadratic) and F (F-distributed) suggest.

However, when m is large, it might be difficult to obtain an accurate estimate of Ω. Alternatively, Hansen et al. (2011) also propose three simpler statistics that only require the estimation of the diagonal elements of Ω. The drawback is that their distribution under the null becomes nonstandard. To this respect, Hansen et al. (2011) provide a detailed description of the bootstrap scheme employed to solve the nuisance parameter problem and to obtain the distribution under the null hypothesis. Similarly to the SPA, the three statistics are expressed as functions of studentized quantities.

The first statistic is a sum of deviations (hence the subscript) from the common average. Under the null hypothesis $H^0 = E[\bar{d}_k] = 0,\ \forall k \in M$, the statistic takes the form[8]

$$\mathrm{MCS} - T_D = \frac{1}{m}\sum_{k\in M} t_k^2, \tag{19.32}$$

where $t_k = \sqrt{T}\bar{d}_k/\sqrt{\hat{\omega}_k^D}$, $k = 1, \ldots, m$, $\bar{d}_k = m^{-1}\Sigma_{j\in M}\bar{d}_{k,j}$ is the contrast of model i's sample loss with respect to the average across all models, and $\bar{d}_{k,j} = T^{-1}\Sigma_{t=1}^{T} d_{k,j,t}$ is the sample loss differential between models k and j. The variances $\hat{\omega}_k^D$ are consistent estimators of $\omega_k^D = \lim_{t\to\infty}\mathrm{Var}(\sqrt{T}\bar{d}_k)$. The remaining two statistics, dubbed range and semiquadratic, take the forms

$$\mathrm{MCS} - T_R = \max_{k,j\in M}|t_{k,j}| \quad \text{and} \quad \mathrm{MCS} - T_{SQ} = \frac{1}{m}\sum_{k,j\in M} t_{k,j}^2, \tag{19.33}$$

respectively, where $t_{k,j} = \sqrt{T}\bar{d}_{k,j}/\sqrt{\hat{\omega}_s^R}$, $k,j = 1, \ldots, m$, $k \neq j$ and $s = 1, \ldots, m(m-1)$ and the variances $\hat{\omega}_s^R$ are consistent estimators of $\omega_s^R = \mathrm{Avar}(\sqrt{T}\bar{d}_{k,j})$.

If the null hypothesis is rejected, then Hansen et al. (2011) suggest the use of the following elimination rule $\mathcal{E}_M = \arg\max_{k\in M} t_k$, which excludes the model with the largest standardized excess loss relative to the average across models. The iterative testing procedure ends as soon as there is the first nonrejection or obviously, if all forecasts but one have been recursively eliminated. Finally, the MCS p-value is equal to $p_i = \max(p_{i-1}, p(i))$, $i = 1, \ldots, m$, where p_i is the p-value of the test under the null hypothesis $H_{M^i}^0$, that is, at the ith step of the iteration process. By convention, when there is only one surviving model, the p-value is $p_m = 1$. The tests for multiple comparison mentioned in this section are implemented in Hansen and Lunde (2010).

19.7 Consistency of the Ordering and Inference on Forecast Performances

In this section, we illustrate, using a Monte Carlo simulation, to what extent the latent variable problem induces distortions in the ranking and affects the inference on forecast accuracy.

We focus on univariate volatility models, whereas a similar exercise based on the comparison of multivariate models is presented in Laurent et al. (2009) and Laurent et al. (2011).

[8]Note that this null hypothesis is equivalent to Equation 19.29.

The forecast performances are measured by the following two loss functions

1. L_{MSE}: $L(\hat{\sigma}_t, h_{k,t}) = (\hat{\sigma}_t - h_{k,t})^2$ (MSE)
2. L_{LMSE}: $L(\hat{\sigma}_t, h_{k,t}) = (log(\hat{\sigma}_t) - log(h_{k,t}))^2$ (MSE of the log transform).

Note that while L_{MSE} belongs to the family defined in Equation 19.8 with $\xi = 2$ (henceforth referred to as *robust*), it is straightforward to show that L_{LMSE} violates Equation 19.7 (henceforth "nonrobust"), that is,

$$L'_{\text{LMSE}} = \frac{\partial L(\sigma_t, h_t)}{\partial \sigma_t} = 2\frac{\log(\sigma_t / h_{k,t})}{\sigma_t}$$

$$L''_{\text{LMSE}} = \frac{\partial^2 L(\sigma_t, h_t)}{(\partial \sigma_t)^2} = 2\frac{1 - \log(\sigma_t / h_{k,t})}{\sigma_t^2},$$

with the second derivative depending on $h_{k,t}$. The choice of L_{LMSE} is not coincidental. Patton (2011) quantifies, under different assumption on the distribution of the returns, the bias with respect to the optimal forecast when using this loss function. To illustrate the centrality of the role of the quality of the volatility proxy when the evaluation of forecast performances is based on a loss function that violates (19.7) consider the conditional expectation of the second-order Taylor expansion of L_{LMSE} around the true value σ_t, that is,

$$E[L_{\text{LMSE}}(\hat{\sigma}_t, h_{k,t}) \mid \Im_{t-1}] \approx L_{\text{LMSE}}(\sigma_t, h_{k,t}) + L'_{\text{LMSE}} E[\eta_t \mid \Im_{t-1}] + 0.5 L''_{\text{LMSE}}(\sigma_t, h_t) E[\eta_t^2 \mid \Im_{t-1}],$$

where $\eta_t = (\hat{\sigma}_t - \sigma_t)$, σ_t and $h_{k,t}$ are $\Im_{t-1}$ measurable, and since the volatility proxy is required to be conditionally unbiased, $E[\eta_t \mid \Im_{t-1}] = 0$ and $E[\eta_t^2 \mid \Im_{t-1}] < \infty$ is the conditional variance of the proxy. Let us now define

$$\begin{aligned}
\Delta(h_{k,t}) &= E[L_{LMS}(\hat{\sigma}_t, h_{k,t}) \mid \Im_{t-1}] - L_{\text{LMSE}}(\sigma_t, h_{k,t}) \\
&= 0.5 L''_{\text{LMSE}}(\sigma_t, h_{k,t}) E[\eta_t^2 \mid \Im_{t-1}] \\
\Delta(h_{j,t}) &= E[L(\hat{\sigma}_t, h_{j,t}) \mid \Im_{t-1}] - L_{\text{LMSE}}(\sigma_t, h_{j,t})] \\
&= 0.5 L''_{\text{LMSE}}(\sigma_t, h_{j,t}) E[\eta_t^2 \mid \Im_{t-1}]
\end{aligned}$$

for a pair of forecast k and j. Then we have

$$\Delta(h_{k,t}) - \Delta(h_{j,t}) = 0.5 \left(L''_{\text{LMSE}}(\sigma_t, h_{k,t}) - L''_{\text{LMSE}}(\sigma_t, h_{j,t}) \right) E[\eta_t^2 \mid \Im_{t-1}] \neq 0.$$

Since, apart from coincidental cancelation, $L''_{\text{LMSE}}(\sigma_t, h_{k,t}) \neq L''_{\text{LMSE}}(\sigma_t, h_{j,t})$, the order implied by the proxy is likely to differ from the one implied by the true variance and the bias in the ranking is more likely to appear as the quality of the proxy deteriorates. On the other hand, the true ordering is likely to be preserved as the proxy becomes nearly perfect, that is, $E[\eta_t^2 \mid \Im_{t-1}] \rightarrow 0$.

We generate artificial data from an Exponential GARCH (0,1) (EGARCH) diffusion (see Nelson, 1991a for details), that is,

$$\begin{bmatrix} \mathrm{d}p(t) \\ \mathrm{d}\log(\sigma(t)) \end{bmatrix} = \begin{bmatrix} 0 \\ -0.1 - 0.05\log(\sigma(t)) \end{bmatrix} \mathrm{d}t + \begin{bmatrix} \sigma(t) & -0.1\sqrt{\sigma(t)} \\ -0.1\sqrt{\sigma(t)} & 0.01 + 0.04(1 - 2/\pi) \end{bmatrix}^{1/2} \begin{bmatrix} \mathrm{d}W_1(t) \\ \mathrm{d}W_2(t) \end{bmatrix}, \tag{19.34}$$

where $\mathrm{d}W_i(t)$, $i = 1, 2$ are two independent Brownian motions. The simulation is based on 500 replications. Using an Euler discretization scheme of Equation 19.34, we approximate the continuous time process by generating 7200 observations per day. All the competing models are estimated using the quasi-maximum likelihood estimator using data aggregated at daily frequency. The estimation is based on a fixed sample of size equal to 1500 days. The forecast evaluation sample amounts to 1000 days, which are used for the one-step-ahead forecast evaluation. All programs have been written using OxMetrics (Doornik, (2009a) by the authors. The estimation of the models and the MCS has been performed using G@RCH (Laurent, 2009) and MULCOM (Hansen and Lunde, 2010), respectively.

The set of competing models includes Exponential GARCH (EGARCH) (Nelson, 1991b), GARCH (Bollerslev, 1986), GJR-GARCH (Glosten et al., 1993), Integrated GARCH (IGARCH) (Engle and Bollerslev (1986)), RiskMetrics (Morgan 1996), and 2-Components Threshold Garch (2CThGarch) (Engle and Lee, 1999) models. The latent variance is computed as $\sigma_t = \int_{t-1}^{t} \sigma(u)\mathrm{d}u$, $t \in \mathbb{N}$. The proxy is the realized variance of Andersen and Bollerslev (1998), that is, the sum of intraday squared returns, and is computed using returns sampled at 14 different frequencies ranging from 1 min to 1 day. The proxy is denoted $\hat{\sigma}_{t,\delta}$, where $\delta = 1\mathrm{m}, 5\,\mathrm{m}, \ldots, 1\mathrm{h}, \ldots, 1\mathrm{d}$ represents the sampling frequency. In this setting, the realized variance estimator is conditionally unbiased, allows to control for the accuracy of the proxy (through the level of aggregation of the data δ), and is also consistent, that is, $\hat{\sigma}_{t,\delta} \underset{p}{\rightarrow} \sigma_t$ as $\delta \rightarrow 0$. The underlying ordering implied by a given loss function, whether it is robust or not, is identified by ranking forecasts with respect to the true variance, σ_t (denoted as $\delta = 0$ in Fig. 19.1).

Figure 19.1a represents the ranking based on the average sample performances (over the 500 replications) implied by the robust loss function, L_{MSE}, for the true variance ($\delta = 0$) and various levels of precision for the proxy ($\delta = 1$ m to $\delta = 1$ d). The ranking appears stable, and the loss differentials between models remain constant independent of the level of accuracy of the proxy. Thus, the ranking obtained under $\hat{\sigma}_{t,\delta}$ is consistent for the one under the true conditional variance σ_t, for all values of δ.

When looking at the nonrobust loss function, L_{LMSE}, the evidence of the objective bias is striking. In fact, although the consistency of the proxy ensures

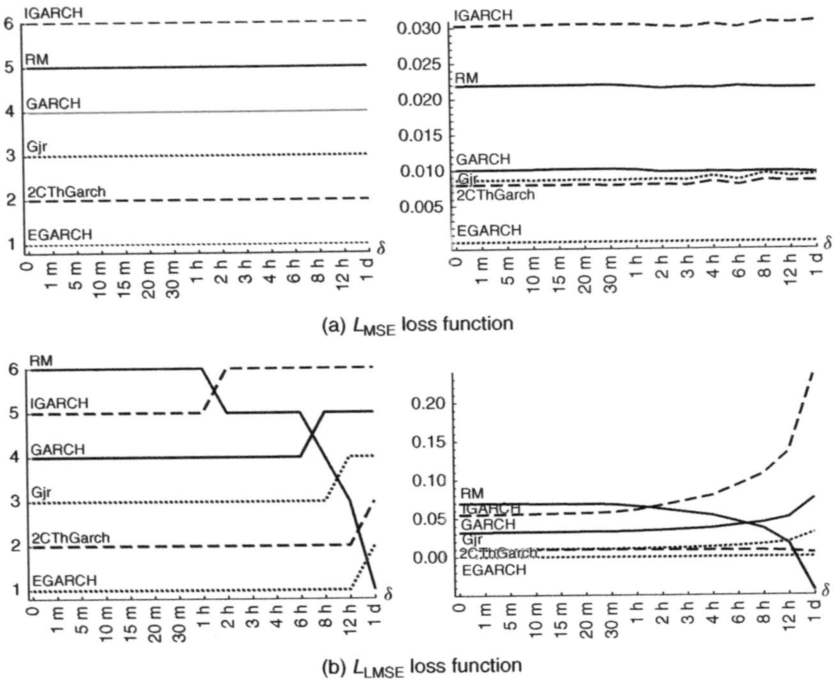

FIGURE 19.1 **Ranking implied by L_{MSE} and L_{LMSE}. Ranking based on average performances (left) and average loss differentials from EGARCH (right).**

convergence of the proxy-based ordering to the true one as $\delta \to 0$, which is the case when the ranking is based on $\hat{\sigma}_{t,\delta}$ computed using returns sampled at frequency higher than 1 h (Fig. 19.1b), as the quality of the proxy deteriorates, inferior models emerge. The relative performances of inferior models seem to improve rapidly and we observe major distortions at all levels of the ranking.

We now compare the forecast performances of our set of models using the MCS test. Ideally the MCS, that is, the set of superior models, should be a singleton containing the true process, that is, the EGARCH. However, as the quality of the proxy deteriorates, losses and thus loss differentials become less informative, which in turn makes more difficult to efficiently discriminate between models. Consequently, we expect the set of superior models to grow in size as δ increases. Figure 19.2 reports two statistics, the frequency at which the Egarch is in the MCS, which shows the size properties of the test (left), and the average number of models in the MCS, which is informative about the power properties of the test (right). As before, the results are reported as a function of the precision of the proxy, δ. The levels of confidence considered are $\alpha = [0.25, 0.1]$. The statistic considered is the MCS $- T_D$. The number of bootstrap samples used to obtain the distribution under the null is set to 1000.

When considering the robust L_{MSE}, and the evaluation is based on an accurate proxy, the MCS approach is able to correctly separate between superior

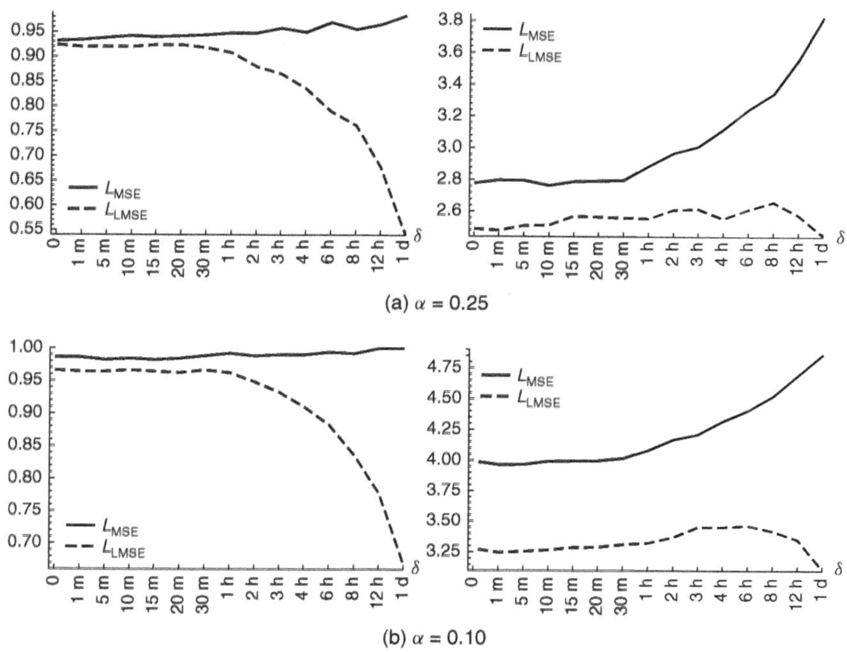

FIGURE 19.2 **Size (left) and power (right) indicators for the MCS test under L_{MSE} (solid) and L_{LMSE} (dashed).**

and poor performing models. The deterioration of the precision of the proxy only translates into a loss of power, that is, a larger MCS. In fact, the MCS includes the true model with probability that converges to one. These results clearly demonstrate the value of high precision proxies. Estimators based on relatively high frequency returns provide sensible gains in power. The inference based on the nonrobust L_{LMSE} is reliable only when a highly accurate proxy is available. In this case, as the quality of the proxy deteriorates, we identify on average a smaller MCS, but the probability that the set of superior models contains the true model reduces dramatically. As expected, the threshold, in terms of accuracy of the proxy, after which the MCS under L_{LMSE} breaks down coincides with $\delta = 1\text{h}$, that is, when the objective bias starts affecting the ranking (Fig. 19.1b).

Concluding, although the MCS testing procedure is formally valid, an unfortunate choice of the loss function can lead to undesired outcomes and results in an incorrect identification of the set of superior models.

19.8 Conclusion

In this chapter, we provide an overview of methods for volatility forecast evaluation and comparison. We consider both the univariate and multivariate settings. We discuss a large variety of methodologies that can be classified into three groups, namely, methods for the evaluation of the forecasting accuracy of single forecast, methods for pairwise comparison, and methods for multiple comparison.

We pay particular attention to the problems that arise because of the latent nature of the conditional variance. In fact, being the variance unobservable, the actual evaluation of the volatility forecasts, usually involving a loss function, requires the use of some proxy. Since this substitution may introduce dramatic distortions in the ordering between forecasts under evaluation, which can be avoided by an appropriate choice of the loss function, we elaborate on the admissible functional form of the loss function and discuss some examples.

We also emphasize the importance of high precision proxies. In fact, even if the forecast under evaluation is highly informative, the variable of interest is always some measure of forecast error. The informativeness of the latter, which allows to efficiently distinguish between superior and poor models, depends crucially on the quality of the proxy.

We show, using artificial data, how both size and power properties of some of the most well-known tests for predictive accuracy behave under both robust and nonrobust loss functions and different levels of accuracy of the volatility proxy.

In this chapter, we focused on methodologies for forecast evaluation and comparison where the forecast accuracy is measured by a statistical criterion, that is, means of functions of predictions and prediction errors. At some point, the forecaster might be interested in the economic evaluation of the forecasts, for instance, by means of an utility or a profit function or yet any other economically meaningful application-specific evaluation criterion. However, to date a comprehensive investigation of the properties of economic loss function has not been addressed yet. In particular, the robustness of the ordering when the evaluation is based on an imperfect volatility proxy remains an open issue and should be further investigated.

Bibliography

Aas, K. and D. Berg (2009). Models for construction of multivariate dependence-a comparison study. European Journal of Finance 15, 639–659.

Aas, K., C. Czado, A. Frigessi, and H. Bakken (2009). Pair-copula constructions of multiple dependence. Insurance: Mathematics and Economics 44, 182–198.

Abadir, K., W. Distaso, and F. Žikeš (2010). Model-Free Estimation of Large Variance Matrices. Technical report, Rimini Centre for Economic Analysis.

Abramowitz, M. and I. A. Stegun (1972). Handbook of Mathematical Functions. New York: Dover Publications.

Abramson, A. and I. Cohen (2007). On the stationarity of Markov–switching GARCH processes. Econometric Theory 23, 485–500.

Adanu, K. (2006). Optimizing the GARCH model—an application of two global and two local search methods. Computational Economics 28, 277–290.

Adrian, T. and J. Rosenberg (2008). Stock returns and volatility: Pricing the short-run and long-run components of market risk. Journal of Finance 63, 2997–3030.

Ahoniemi, K. and M. Lanne (2009). Joint modeling of call and put implied volatility. International Journal of Forecasting 25, 239–258.

Aielli, G. (2009). Dynamic conditional correlations: on properties and estimation. University of Florence Working Paper. Available at SSRN: http://ssrn.com/abstract=1507743.

Aït-Sahalia, Y. (2002). Telling from discrete data whether the underlying continuous-time model is a diffusion. Journal of Finance 57, 2075–2112.

Aït-Sahalia, Y., J. Fan, and D. Xiu (2010). High frequency covariance estimates with noisy and asynchronous financial data. Journal of the American Statistical Association 105, 1504–1517.

Aït-Sahalia, Y. and J. Jacod (2008). Fisher's information for discretely sampled Lévy processes. Econometrica 76, 727–761.

Aït-Sahalia, Y. and J. Jacod (2009). Testing for jumps in a discretely observed process. Annals of Statistics 37, 184–222.

Aït-Sahalia, Y. and J. Jacod (2010a). Analyzing the spectrum of asset returns: Jump and volatility components in high frequency data. Journal of Economic Literature (forthcoming).

Handbook of Volatility Models and Their Applications, First Edition.
Edited by Luc Bauwens, Christian Hafner, and Sebastien Laurent.

Aït-Sahalia, Y, J. Jacod, and J. Li (2010b). Testing for jumps in noisy high frequency data. Journal of Econometrics, working paper.

Aït-Sahalia, Y. and J. Jacod (2011). Testing whether jumps have finite or infinite activity. Annals of Statistics 39, 1689–1719.

Aït-Sahalia, Y. and A. Lo (1998). Nonparametric estimation of state-price-densities implicit in financial asset prices. The Journal of Finance 53, 499–547.

Aït-Sahalia, Y. and L. Mancini (2008). Out of sample forecasts of quadratic variation. Journal of Econometrics 147, 17–33.

Aït-Sahalia, Y. and P. A. Mykland (2003). The effects of random and discrete sampling when estimating continuous-time diffusions. Econometrica 71, 483–549.

Aït-Sahalia, Y., P. A. Mykland, and L. Zhang (2005). How often to sample a continuous-time process in the presence of market microstructure noise. Review of Financial Studies 18, 351–416.

Aït-Sahalia, Y., P. A. Mykland, and L. Zhang (2011). Ultra high frequency volatility estimation with dependent microstructure noise. Journal of Econometrics 160, 160–175.

Aït-Sahalia, Y. and D. Xiu (2012). Likelihood-based volatility estimators in the presence of market microstructure noise. In L. Bauwens, C. Hafner, and S. Laurent (Eds.), Handbook of Volatility Models and Their Applications. pp. 347–361. John Wiley & Sons.

Aït-Sahalia, Y. and J. Yu (2009). High frequency market microstructure noise estimates and liquidity measures. Annals of Applied Statistics 3, 422–457.

Alexander, C. (2001). Orthogonal GARCH. In C. Alexander (Ed.), Mastering Risk, Vol. 2. Prentice Hall.

Alexander, C. (2008). Practical Financial Econometrics. Chichester: John Wiley & Sons.

Alexander, C. and A. M. Chibumba (1997). Multivariate orthogonal factor GARCH. Mimeo, University of Sussex.

Alexander, C. and E. Lazar (2006). Normal mixture garch(1,1): Applications to exchange rate modelling. Journal of Applied Econometrics 21, 307–336.

Alexander, C. and E. Lazar (2009). Modelling regime–specific stock price volatility. Oxford Bulletin of Economics and Statistics 71, 761–797.

Alizadeh, S., M. W. Brandt, and F. X. Diebold (2002). Range-based estimation of stochastic volatility models. Journal of Finance 57, 1047–1091.

Almgren, R. and N. Chriss (2001). Optimal execution of portfolio transactions. Working Paper, University of Toronto.

Alper, C., S. Fendoglu, and B. Saltoglu (2008). Forecasting stock market volatilities using MIDAS regressions: An application to the emerging markets. Technical report, MPRA Paper No. 7460.

Amado, C. and T. Teräsvirta (2011). Modelling volatility by variance decomposition. CREATES Research Paper 2011–1, Aarhus University.

Amilon, H. (2003). GARCH estimation and discrete stock prices: An application to low-priced Australian stocks. Economics Letters 81, 215–222.

Amisano, G. and R. Giacomini (2007). Comparing density forecasts via weighted likelihood ratio tests. Journal of Business and Economic Statistics 25, 177–190.

Andersen, T. G. (1994). Stochastic autoregressive volatility: A framework for volatility modelling. Mathematical Finance 4, 75–102.

Andersen, T. G. (2009). Stochastic volatility. Encyclopedia of Complexity and System Science. Springer Verlag.

Andersen, T. G. and L. Benzoni (2009). Realized volatility. In T. Andersen, R. Davis, and J. Kreiß (Eds.), Handbook of Financial Time Series, pp. 365–400. Springer Verlag.

Andersen, T. G. and T. Bollerslev (1997a). Heterogeneous information arrivals and return volatility dynamics: uncovering the long-run in high frequency returns. Journal of Finance 52, 975–1005.

Andersen, T. G. and T. Bollerslev (1997b). Intraday periodicity and volatility persistence in financial markets. Journal of Empirical Finance 4, 115–158.

Andersen, T. G. and T. Bollerslev (1998). Answering the skeptics: Yes, standard volatility models do provide accurate forecasts. International Economic Review 39, 885–905.

Andersen, T. G., T. Bollerslev, P. F. Christoffersen, and F. X. Diebold (2006). Volatility and correlation forecasting. In G. Elliott, C. W. J. Granger, and A. Timmermann (Eds.), Handbook of Economic Forecasting. North Holland.

Andersen, T. G., T. Bollerslev, F. Diebold, and P. Labys (2000). Exchange rate returns standardized by realized volatility are (nearly) Gaussian. Multinational Finance Journal 4, 159–179.

Andersen, T. G., T. Bollerslev, F. Diebold, and P. Labys (2001a). The distribution of exchange rate volatility. Journal of the American Statistical Association 96, 42–55.

Andersen, T. G., T. Bollerslev, and F. X. Diebold (2007). Roughing it up: Including jump components in the measurement, modeling, and forecasting of return volatility. The Review of Economics and Statistics 89, 701–720.

Andersen, T. G., T. Bollerslev, and F. X. Diebold (2010). Parametric and nonparametric volatility measurement. In Y. Aït-Sahalia and L. P. Hansen (Eds.), Handbook of Financial Econometrics. Amsterdam: North-Holland.

Andersen, T. G., T. Bollerslev, F. X. Diebold, and H. Ebens (2001). The distribution of realized stock return volatility. Journal of Financial Economics 61, 43–76.

Andersen, T. G., T. Bollerslev, F. X. Diebold, and P. Labys (2001b). The distribution of realized exchange rate volatility. Journal of the American Statistical Association 96, 42–55.

Andersen, T. G., T. Bollerslev, F. X. Diebold, and P. Labys (2003). Modeling and forecasting realized volatility. Econometrica 71, 579–625.

Andersen, T. G., T. Bollerslev, and D. Dobrev (2007). No-arbitrage semi-martingale restrictions for continuous-time volatility models subject to leverage effects, jumps and i.i.d. noise: theory and testable distributional implications. Journal of Econometrics 138, 125–180.

Andersen, T. G., T. Bollerslev, and N. Meddahi (2005). Correcting the errors: Volatility forecast evaluation using high-frequency data and realized volatility. Econometrica 73, 279–296.

Andersen, T. G., T. Bollerslev, F. X. Dieboldc, and G. Wu (2005). A framework for exploring the macroeconomic determinants of systematic risk. American Economic Review 95, 398–404.

Andersen, T. G., H.-J. Chung, and B. E. Sorensen (1999). Efficient method of moments estimation of a stochastic volatility model: A Monte Carlo study. Journal of Econometrics 91, 61–87.

Andersen, T. G., R. A. Davis, J.-P. Kreiß, and T. Mikosch (2009). Handbook of Financial Time Series. Berlin: Springer.

Andersen, T. G., D. Dobrev, and E. Schaumburg (2009). Duration based volatility estimation. In Global COE Hi-Stat Discussion, paper series 034, Hitotsubashi University.

Andersen, T. G., D. Dobrev, and E. Schaumburg (2010). Jump-robust volatility estimation using nearest neighbor truncation. NBER Working Paper No. w15533, ssrn.com. (forthcoming 'Journal of Econometrics').

Andersen, T. G., D. Dobrev, and E. Schaumburg (2011). Integrated quarticity estimation: theory and practical implementation. Working Paper.

Andersen, T. G. and B. Sorensen (1996). GMM estimation of a stochastic volatility model: A Monte Carlo study. Journal of Business and Economic Statistics 14, 329–352.

Anderson, H. M., K. Nam, and F. Vahid (1999). Asymmetric Nonlinear Smooth Transition GARCH Models. In P. Rothman (Ed.), Nonlinear time series analysis of economic and financial data, pp. 191–207. Boston: Kluwer.

Andreou, E. and E. Ghysels (2002). Rolling-Sample Volatility Estimators. Journal of Business and Economic Statistics 20, 363–376.

Andreou, E. and E. Ghysels (2009). Structural breaks in financial time series. In T. G. Andersen, R. A. Davis, J.-P. Kreiss, and T. Mikosch (Eds.), Handbook of Financial Time Series, pp. 839–870. Berlin: Springer.

Andreou, E., E. Ghysels, and A. Kourtellos (2010a). Regression models with mixed sampling frequencies. Journal of Econometrics 158, 246–261.

Andreou, E., E. Ghysels, and A. Kourtellos (2010b). Should macroeconomic forecasters use daily financial data and how? Discussion Paper Universities of Cyprus and North Carolina.

Andrews, D. W. K. (1993). Tests for parameter instability and structural change with unknown change point. Econometrica 61, 821–856.

Ane, T. and L. Ureche-Rangau (2006). Stock market dynamics in a regime-switching asymmetric power GARCH model. International Review of Financial Analysis 15, 109–129.

Ang, A. and G. Bekaert (2002). International asset allocation with regime shifts. Review of Financial Studies 15, 1137–87.

Ang, A. and J. Chen (2002). Asymmetric correlations of equity portfolios. Journal of Financial Economics 63, 443–94.

Angelidis, T., A. Benos, and S. Degiannakis (2004). The use of GARCH models in VaR estimation. Statistical Methodology 1–2, 105–128.

Aragó, V. and E. Salvador (2010). Re-examining the risk-return relationship: The influence of financial crisis (2007–2009). Technical report, Discussion Paper, Universitat Jaume I, Spain.

Ardia, D. (2009). Bayesian estimation of a Markov–switching threshold asymmetric GARCH model with Student-t innovations. Econometrics Journal 12, 105–126.

Armesto, M., K. Engemann, and M. Owyang (2010). Forecasting with mixed frequencies. Federal Reserve Bank of St. Louis Review (forthcoming).

Arneodo, A., J. Muzy, and D. Sornette (1998). Casual cascade in stock market from the "infrared" to the "ultraviolet". European Physical Journal B 2, 277.

Asai, M. and M. McAleer (2005). Dynamic asymmetric leverage in stochastic volatility models. Econometric Reviews 24, 317–332.

Asai, M. and M. McAleer (2006). Asymmetric multivariate stochastic volatility. Econometric Reviews 25, 453–473.

Asai, M. and M. McAleer (2009). The structure of dynamic correlations in multivariate stochastic volatility models. Journal of Econometrics 150, 182–192.

Asai, M., M. McAleer, and J. Yu (2006). Multivariate stochastic volatility: A review. Econometric Reviews 25, 145–175.

Ashley, R., C. Granger, and R. Schmelensee (1980). Advertising and aggregate consumption: An analysis of causality. Econometrica 48, 1149–1168.

Audrino, F. and P. Bühlmann (2001). Tree-structured GARCH models. Journal of the Royal Statistical Society, Series B 63, 727–744.

Audrino, F. and P. Bühlmann (2003). Volatility estimation with functional gradient descent for very high-dimensional financial time series. Journal of Computational Finance 6, 1–26.

Audrino, F. and P. Bühlmann (2009). Splines for financial volatility. Journal of the Royal Statistical Society: Series B (Statistical Methodology) 71, 655–670.

Audrino, F. and F. Corsi (2010). Modelling tick-by-tick realized correlations. Computational Statistics and Data Analysis 54, 2372–2382.

Audrino, F. and F. Trojani (2006). Estimating and predicting multivariate volatility regimes in global stock markets. Journal of Applied Econometrics 21, 345–369.

Ausin, M. C. and P. Galeano (2007). Bayesian estimation of the Gaussian mixture GARCH models. Computational Statistics and Data Analysis 51, 2636–2652.

Azzalini, A. (1985). A class of distributions which includes the normal ones. Scandinavian Journal of Statistics 12, 171–178.

Back, K. (1991). Asset pricing for general processes. Journal of Mathematical Economics 20, 371–395.

Bacry, E., L. Duvernet, and J. Muzy (2010). Continuous-time skewed multifractal processes as a model for financial returns. Journal of Applied Probability (forthcoming).

Badescu, A., R. Kulperger, and E. Lazar (2008). Option Valuation with Normal Mixture GARCH Models. Studies in Nonlinear Dynamics & Econometrics 12, 5.

Baele, L., G. Bekaert, and K. Inghelbrecht (2010). The determinants of stock and bond return comovements. Review of Financial Studies 23, 2374–2428.

Bai, J., E. Ghysels, and J. Wright (2009). State space models and midas regressions. Working paper, NY Fed, UNC and Johns Hopkins.

Bai, J. and S. Ng (2002). Determining the number of factors in approximate factor models. Econometrica 70, 191–221.

Bai, X., J. R. Russell, and G. C. Tiao (2003). Kurtosis of GARCH and stochastic volatility models with non–normal innovations. Journal of Econometrics 114, 349–360.

Baillie, R., T. Bollerslev, and H. Mikkelsen (1996). Fractionally integrated generalized autoregressive conditional heteroskedasticity. Journal of Econometrics 74, 3–30.

Baillie, R. and C. Morana (2009). Modeling long memory and structural breaks in conditional variances: an adaptive FIGARCH approach. Journal of Economic Dynamics and Control 33, 1577–1592.

Baillie, R. T. and R. P. DeGennaro (1990). Stock returns and volatility. Journal of Financial and Quantitative Analysis 25, 203–214.

Bajgrowicz, P. and O. Scaillet (2011). Detecting spurious jumps in high frequency data. Working Paper.

Bali, T. G. and L. Peng (2006). Is there a risk-return tradeoff? Journal of Applied Econometrics 21, 1169–1198.

Bandi, F. M. and T. Nguyen (2003). On the functional estimation of jump-diffusion models. J. Econometrics 116, 293–328.

Bandi, F. M. and P. C. B. Phillips (2003). Fully nonparametric estimation of scalar diffusion models. Econometrica 71, 241–83.

Bandi, F. M. and R. Renó (2010). Non-parametric stochastic volatility. www.ssrn.com.

Bandi, F. M. and J. Russell (2011). Market microstructure noise, integrated variance estimators, and the accuracy of asymptotic approximations. Journal of Econometrics 160, 145–159.

Bandi, F. M. and J. R. Russell (2005). Realized covariation, realized beta and microstructure noise. Working Paper, Graduate School of Business, University of Chicago.

Bandi, F. M. and J. R. Russell (2006). Separating microstructure noise from volatility. Journal of Financial Economics 79, 655–692.

Bandi, F. M. and J. R. Russell (2008). Microstructure noise, realized volatility and optimal sampling. Review of Economic Studies 75, 339–369.

Bandi, F. M., J. R. Russell, and C. Yang (2008). Realized volatility forecasting and option pricing. Journal of Econometrics 147, 34–46.

Banerjee, A. and G. Urga (2005). Modelling structural breaks, long memory and stock market volatility: An overview. Journal of Econometrics 129, 1–34.

Bannouh, K., M. Martens, R. Oomen, and D. van Dijk (2009). Realized factor models for vast dimensional covariance estimation. Technical report, University of Amsterdam.

Barigozzi, M., C. T. Brownlees, G. M. Gallo, and D. Veredas (2010). Disentangling systemic and idiosyncratic volatility for large panels of assets. A seminonparametric vector multiplicative error model. Technical report, ECARES.

Barndorff-Nielsen, O. E., J. M. Corcuera, and M. Podolskij (2011). Multipower variation for brownian semi-stationary processes. Bernoulli 17, 1159–1194.

Barndorff-Nielsen, O. E., S. Gravensen, J. Jacod, M. Podolskij, and N. Shephard (2006). A central limit theorem for realised power and bipower variation of continuous semimartingales. From Stochastic Calculus to Mathematical Finance: The Shiryaev Festschrift, pp. 33–68. Germany: Springer.

Barndorff-Nielsen, O. E., S. Graversen, and N. Shephard (2004). Power variation and stochastic volatility: A review and some new results. Journal of Applied Probability 41A, 133–143.

Barndorff-Nielsen, O. E., P. Hansen, A. Lunde, and N. Shephard (2008). Designing realized kernels to measure the ex post variation of equity prices in the presence of noise. Econometrica 76, 1481–1536.

Barndorff-Nielsen, O. E., P. R. Hansen, A. Lunde, and N. Shephard (2011). Multivariate realised kernels: Consistent positive semi-definite estimators of the covariation of equity prices with noise and non-synchronous trading. Journal of Econometrics 162, 149–169.

Barndorff-Nielsen, O. E., P. R. Hansen, A. Lunde, and N. Shephard (2009). Realized kernels in practice: Trades and quotes. Econometrics Journal 12, C1–C32.

Barndorff-Nielsen, O. E. and N. Shephard (2001). Non-Gaussian Ornstein-Uhlenbeck-based models and some of their uses in financial economics. Journal of the Royal Statistical Society: Series B (Statistical Methodology) 63, 167–241.

Barndorff-Nielsen, O. E. and N. Shephard (2002a). Econometric analysis of realized volatility and its use in estimating stochastic volatility models. Journal of the Royal Statistical Society, Series B 64, 253–280.

Barndorff-Nielsen, O. E. and N. Shephard (2002b). Estimating quadratic variation using realised volatility. Journal of Applied Econometrics 17, 457–477.

Barndorff-Nielsen, O. E. and N. Shephard (2003). Power variation with stochastic volatility and jumps. Discussion paper, Nuffield College.

Barndorff-Nielsen, O. E. and N. Shephard (2004a). Econometric analysis of realised covariation: High frequency based covariance, regression and correlation in financial economics. Econometrica 72, 885–925.

Barndorff-Nielsen, O. E. and N. Shephard (2004b). Power and bipower variation with stochastic volatility and jumps (with discussion). Journal of Financial Econometrics 2, 1–37.

Barndorff-Nielsen, O. E. and N. Shephard (2004c). Measuring the impact of jumps in multivariate price processes using bipower covariation. Nuffield College, Oxford University.

Barndorff-Nielsen, O. E. and N. Shephard (2006a). Advanced in Economics and Econometrics. Theory and Applications. Ninth World Congress, Chapter Variation, jumps and high frequency data in financial econometrics. Cambridge University Press.

Barndorff-Nielsen, O. E. and N. Shephard (2006b). Econometrics of testing for jumps in financial economics using bipower variation. Journal of Financial Econometrics 4, 1–30.

Barndorff-Nielsen, O. E. and N. Shephard (2006c). Impact of jumps on returns and realised variances: econometric analysis of time-deformed lévy processes. Journal of Econometrics 131, 217–252.

Barndorff-Nielsen, O. E., N. Shephard, and M. Winkel (2006). Limit theorems for multipower variation in the presence of jumps. Stochastic Processes and Their Applications 116, 796–806.

Barndorff-Nielsen, O. E. and R. Stelzer (2009). The multivariate supOU stochastic volatility model. CREATES Research Paper 2009-42, School of Economics and Management Aarhus University.

Bartlett, M. S. (1946). On the theoretical specification of sampling properties of autocorrelated time series. Journal of the Royal Statistical Society, Supplement 8, 27–41.

Bates, D. (2000). Post-'87 crash fears in the S &P 500 futures option market. Journal of Econometrics 94, 181–238.

Bauer, G. H. and K. Vorkink (2011). Forecasting multivariate realized stock market volatility. Journal of Econometrics 160, 93–101.

Bauwens, L., W. Ben Omrane, and P. Giot (2005). News announcements, market activity and volatility in the euro/dollar foreign exchange market. Journal of International Money and Finance 24, 1108–1125.

Bauwens, L., A. Dufays, and J. V. Rombouts (2011). Marginal likelihood for Markov-switching and change-point GARCH models. CORE Discussion Paper 2011/13.

Bauwens, L. and P. Giot (2000). The logarithmic ACD model: An application to the bid-ask quote process of three NYSE stocks. Annalesd'Économie et de Statistique 60, 117–149.

Bauwens, L., C. Hafner, and S. Laurent (2012). Volatility models. In L. Bauwens, C. Hafner, and S. Laurent (Eds.), Handbook of Volatility Models and Their Applications, pp. 1–45. John Wiley & Sons.

Bauwens, L., C. M. Hafner, and J. V. K. Rombouts (2007). Multivariate mixed normal conditional heteroskedasticity. Computational Statistics & Data Analysis 51, 3551–3566.

Bauwens, L. and S. Laurent (2005). A new class of multivariate skew densities, with application to GARCH models. Journal of Business and Economic Statistics 23, 346–354.

Bauwens, L., S. Laurent, and J. Rombouts (2003). Multivariate GARCH models: A survey. CORE DP 2003/31.

Bauwens, L., S. Laurent, and J. V. K. Rombouts (2006). Multivariate GARCH models: A survey. Journal of Applied Econometrics 21, 79–109.

Bauwens, L. and M. Lubrano (2002). Bayesian option pricing using asymmetric GARCH models. Journal of Empirical Finance 9, 321–342.

Bauwens, L., A. Preminger, and J. V. K. Rombouts (2006). Regime-switching GARCH models. CORE Discussion Paper 2006/11, Center for Operations Research and Econometrics, Université Catholique de Louvain.

Bauwens, L., A. Preminger, and J. V. K. Rombouts (2010). Theory and inference for a Markov switching GARCH models. Econometrics Journal 13, 218–244.

Bauwens, L. and J. Rombouts (2004). Econometrics. In J. Gentle, W. Haerdle, and Y. Mori (Eds.), Handbook of Computational Statistics. Springer.

Bauwens, L. and J. V. K. Rombouts (2007a). Bayesian clustering of many GARCH models. Econometric Reviews 26, 365–386.

Bauwens, L. and J. V. K. Rombouts (2007b). Bayesian inference for the mixed conditional heteroskedasticity model. Econometrics Journal 10, 408–425.

Bauwens, L. and G. Storti (2009). A component GARCH model with time varying weights. Studies in Nonlinear Dynamics and Econometrics 13, 2, Article 1.

Bauwens, L., G. Storti, and F. Violante (2012). CAW-DCC: A dynamic model for vast realized covariance matrices. Forthcoming CORE Discussion Paper.

Bedford, T. and R. M. Cooke (2002). Vines-a new graphical model for dependent random variables. Annals of Statistics 30, 1031–1068.

Bekaert, G. and S. F. Gray (1998). Target zones and exchange rates: An empirical investigation. Journal of International Economics 45, 1–35.

Bekaert, G. and C. R. Harvey (1997). Emerging equity market volatility. Journal of Financial Economics 43, 29–77.

Bera, A. and M. Higgins (1993). ARCH models: Properties, estimation and testing. Journal of Economic Surveys 7, 305–362.

Bera, A. and S. Kim (2002). Testing constancy of correlation and other specifications of the BGARCH model with an application to international equity returns. Journal of Empirical Finance 9, 171–195.

Berg, A. (1999). The Asia Crisis: Causes, Policy Responses and Outcomes. IMF Working Paper No. WP/99/138.

Berkowitz, J. (2001a). The accuracy of density forecasts in risk management. Journal of Business and Economic Statistics 19, 465–474.

Berkowitz, J. (2001b). Testing density forecasts, with applications to risk management. Journal of Business and Economic Statistics 19, 465–474.

Bhanzali, R. (1999). Parameter estimation and model selection for multistep prediction of a time series: A review. In S. Ghosh (Ed.), Asymptotics, Nonparametrics, and Time Series. Marcel Dekker.

Bianco, S., F. Corsi, and R. Renó (2009). Intraday LeBaron effects. Proceedings of the National Academy of Sciences of the United States of America 106, 11439–11443.

Bickel, P. and E. Levina (2008). Regularized estimation of large covariance matrices. Annals of Statistics 36, 199–227.

Billio, M. and M. Caporin (2006). A generalized dynamic conditional correlation model for portfolio risk evaluation. Working Paper 2006–53, Department of Economics, University of Venice "Ca' Foscari".

Bjork, T., Y. Kabanov, and W. Runggaldier (1997). Bond market structure in the presence of marked point processes. Mathematical Finance 7, 211–223.

Black, F. (1976). Studies of stock market volatility changes. Proceedings of the American Statistical Assiciation, Business and Economic Statistics Section 1, 177–181.

Bollerslev, T. (1986). Generalized autoregressive conditional heteroskedasticity. Journal of Econometrics 31, 307–327.

Bollerslev, T. (1987). A conditional heteroskedastic model for speculative prices and rates of return. Review of Economics and Statistics 69, 542–547.

Bollerslev, T. (1990). Modelling the coherence in short-run nominal exchange rates: A multivariate generalized ARCH model. Review of Economics and Statistics 72, 498–505.

Bollerslev, T. (2008). Glossary to ARCH (GARCH). Research paper 2008–49, CREATES.

Bollerslev, T., R. Y. Chou, and K. F. Kroner (1992). ARCH modeling in finance. Journal of Econometrics 52, 5–59.

Bollerslev, T., R. Engle, and D. Nelson (1994). ARCH models. In R. Engle, and D. McFadden (Eds.), Handbook of Econometrics, Chapter 49, pp. 2959–3038. Amsterdam: North Holland.

Bollerslev, T., R. F. Engle, and J. M. Wooldridge (1988). A capital asset pricing model with time-varying covariances. Journal of Political Economy 96, 116–131.

Bollerslev, T., M. Gibson, and H. Zhou (2010). Dynamic estimation of volatility risk premia and investor risk aversion from option-implied and realized volatilities. Journal of Econometrics 160, 235–245.

Bollerslev, T., U. Kretschmer, C. Pigorsch, and G. Tauchen (2009). A discrete-time model for daily S&P500 returns and realized variations: jumps and leverage effects. Journal of Econometrics 150, 151–166.

Bollerslev, T., T. H. Law, and G. Tauchen (2008). Risk, jumps, and diversification. Journal of Econometrics 144, 234–256.

Bollerslev, T., J. Litvinova, and G. Tauchen (2006). Leverage and volatility feedback effects in high-frequency data. Journal of Financial Econometrics 4, 353.

Bollerslev, T., G. Tauchen, and H. Zhou (2008). Expected stock returns and variance risk premia. Review of Financial Studies 22, 4463–4492.

Bollerslev, T. and J. M. Wooldridge (1992). Quasi-maxmimum likelihood estimation and inference in dynamic models with time-varying covariances. Econometric Reviews 11, 143–172.

Bollerslev, T. and J. Wright (2001). High-frequency data, frequency domain inference and volatility forecasting. Review of Economics and Statistics 83, 596–602.

Bollerslev, T. and Y. B. Zhang (2003). Measuring and modeling systematic risk in factor pricing models using high-frequency data. Journal of Empirical Finance 10, 533–558.

Bollerslev, T. and H. Zhou (2002). Estimating stochastic volatility diffusion using conditional moments of integrated volatility. Journal of Econometrics 109, 33–65.

Bonato, M., M. Caporin, and A. Ranaldo (2009). Forecasting realized (co) variances with a block structure Wishart autoregressive model. Working Papers.

Bond, S. (2001). A review of asymmetric conditional density functions in autoregressive conditional heteroscedasticity models. In J. Knight, and S. Satchell (Eds.), Return Distributions in Finance, pp. 21–46. Portsmouth, NH: Butterworth-Heinemann.

Booth, G. G., T. Martikainen, and Y. Tse (1997). Price and Volatility Spillovers in Scandinavian Stock Markets. Journal of Banking and Finance 21, 811–823.

Bos, C. S (2012). Relating stochastic volatility estimation methods. In L. Bauwens, C. Hafner, and S. Laurent (Eds.), Handbook of Volatility Models and Their Applications, pp. 147–173. John Wiley & Sons.

Bos, C. S. and P. Gould (2007). Dynamic correlations and optimal hedge ratios. Discussion Paper TI 07–025/4, Tinbergen Institute.

Bos, C. S., P. Janus, and S. J. Koopman (2012). Spot variance path estimation and its application to high frequency jump testing. Journal of Financial Econometrics 10 (forthcoming).

Bos, C. S. and N. Shephard (2006). Inference for adaptive time series models: Stochastic volatility and conditionally Gaussian state space form. Econometric Reviews 25, 219–244.

Boudt, K., J. Cornelissen, C. Croux, and S. Laurent (2012). Nonparametric tests for intraday jumps: Impact of periodicity and microstructure noise. In L. Bauwens, C. Hafner, and S. Laurent (Eds.), Handbook of Volatility Models and Their Applications, pp. 447–462. John Wiley & Sons.

Boudt, K., C. Croux, and S. Laurent (2010). Outlyingness weighted quadratic covariation. Journal of Financial Econometrics, 9, 657–684.

Boudt, K., C. Croux, and S. Laurent (2011). Robust estimation of intraweek periodicity in volatility and jump detection. Journal of Empirical Finance 18, 353–367.

Boudt, K., H. Ghys, and M. Petitjean (2010). Intraday liquidity dynamics of the DJIA stocks around price jumps. Mimeo.

Boudt, K. and J. Zhang (2010). Jump robust two time scale covariance estimation and realized volatility budgets. Mimeo.

Bougerol, P. and N. Picard (1992). Stationarity of GARCH processes and of some nonnegative time series. Journal of Econometrics 52, 115–127.

Boussama, F. (2000). Asymptotic normality for the quasi-maximum likelihood estimator of a GARCH model. Comptes Rendus de l'Académie des Sciences de Paris, Série I 331, 81–84.

Brandt, M. W. and F. X. Diebold (2006). A no-arbitrage approach to range-based estimation of return covariances and correlations. Journal of Busines 79, 61–73.

Breiman, L., J. Friedman, C. J. Stone, and R. A. Olshen (1984). Classification and regression trees. Chapman & Hall/CRC.

Breiman, L. and J. H. Friedman (1985). Estimating optimal transformations for multiple regression and correlation (with discussion). Journal of the American Statistical Association 80, 580–619.

Briner, B. and G. Connor (2008). How much structure is best? a comparison of market model, factor model and unstructured equity covariance matrices. Journal of Risk 10, 3–30.

Britten-Jones, M. and A. Neuberger (2000). Option prices, implied price processes, and stochastic volatility. Journal of Finance 55, 839–866.

Broda, S. and M. S. Paolella (2009). CHICAGO: A Fast and Accurate Method for Portfolio Risk Calculation. Journal of Financial Econometrics 7, 412–436.

Broda, S. A., M. Haas, J. Krause, M. S. Paolella, and S. C. Steude (2012). Stable mixture GARCH models. To appear: Annals of Econometrics. (The Journal of Econometrics).

Brooks, C., S. P. Burke, and G. Persand (2001). Benchmarks and the accuracy of GARCH model estimation. International Journal of Forecasting 17, 45–56.

Brooks, R., R. W. Faff, M. D. McKenzie, and H. Mitchell (2000). A multi-country study of power ARCH models and national stock market returns. Journal of International Money and Finance 19, 377–397.

Broto, C. and E. Ruiz (2004). Estimation methods for stochastic volatility models: A survey. Journal of Economic Surveys 18, 613–649.

Brown, D. P. and M. A. Ferreira (2003). The information in the idiosyncratic volatility of small firms. Working paper, Univesrity of Wisconsin and ISCTE.

Brownlees (2010). On the relation between firm characteristics and volatility dynamics with an application to the 2007–2009 financial crisis. Technical report.

Brownlees, C. T., F. Cipollini, and G. M. Gallo (2011a). Intra-daily volume modeling and prediction for algorithmic trading. Journal of Financial Econometrics (forthcoming).

Brownlees, C. T., F. Cipollini, and G. M. Gallo (2012). Multiplicative error models. In L. Bauwens, C. Hafner, and S. Laurent (Eds.), Handbook of Volatility Models and Their Applications, pp. 225–247. John Wiley & Sons.

Brownlees, C. T., R. Engle, and B. T. Kelly (2010). A practical guide to volatility forecasting through calm and storm. Technical report, Department of Finance, NYU.

Brownlees, C. T. and G. M. Gallo (2006). Financial econometric analysis at ultra-high frequency: Data handling concerns. Computational Statistics & Data Analysis 51, 2232–2245.

Brownlees, C. T. and G. M. Gallo (2010). Comparison of volatility measures: A risk management perspective. Journal of Financial Econometrics 8, 29–56.

Buja, A., T. Hastie, and R. Tibshirani (1989). Linear smoothers and additive models (with discussion). The Annals of Statistics 17, 453–555.

Cai, J. (1994). A Markov model of switching-regime ARCH. Journal of Business and Economics Statistics 12, 309–316.

Cai, Z., J. Fan, and R. Li (2000). Efficient estimation and inference for varying-coefficient models. Journal of the American Statistical Association 95, 888–902.

Cai, Z., J. Fan, and Q. Yao (2000). Functional-coefficient regression models for nonlinear time series. Journal of the American Statistical Association 95, 941–956.

Calvet, L. and A. Fisher (2004). How to forecast long-run volatility: Regime switching and the estimation of multifractal processes. Journal of Financial Econometrics 2, 49–83.

Campbell, J. Y. (1987). Stock returns and the term structure. Journal of Financial Economics 18, 373–399.

Campbell, J. Y. and L. Hentschel (1992). No news is good news: An asymmetric model of changing volatility in stock returns. Journal of Financial Economics 31, 281–318.

Campbell, J. Y., A. W. Lo, and A. C. MacKinlay (1997). The Econometrics of Financial Markets. Princeton: Princeton Univeristy Press.

Caporin, M. (2008). Evaluating Value-at-Risk measures in presence of long memory conditional volatility. Journal of Risk 10, 79–110.

Caporin, M. and M. McAleer (2009). Do we really need both BEKK and DCC? A tale of two covariance models. Available at SSRN: http://ssrn.com/abstract=1338190.

Caporin, M. and M. McAleer (2010). Ranking multivariate GARCH models by problem dimension. Available at SSRN: http://ssrn.com/abstract = 1601236.

Caporin, M. and M. McAleer (2012). Model selection and testing of conditional and stochastic volatility models. In L. Bauwens, C. Hafner, and S. Laurent (Eds.), Handbook of Volatility Models and Their Applications, pp. 199–221. John Wiley & Sons.

Cappiello, L., R. Engle, and K. Sheppard (2006). Asymmetric dynamics in the correlations of global equity and bond returns. Journal of Financial Econometrics 4, 537–572.

Carnero, M., D. Pena, and E. Ruiz (2004). Persistence and kurtosis in GARCH and stochastic volatility models. Journal of Financial Econometrics 2, 319–342.

Carpantier, J.-F. (2010). Commodities inventory effect. CORE DP 2010/40.

Carr, P., H. Geman, D. Madan, and M. Yor (2002). The fine structure of asset returns: An empirical investigation. Journal of Business 75, 305–332.

Carr, P., H. Geman, D. B. Madan, and M. Yor (2005). Pricing options on realized variance. Finance and Stochastics 9, 453–475.

Carr, P. and L. Wu (2003). What type of process underlies options? A simple robust test. Journal of Finance 58, 2581–2610.

Carr, P. and L. Wu (2009). Variance risk premiums. Review of Financial Studies 22, 1311–1341.

Carroll, R. J., J. Fan, I. Gijbels, and M. P. Wand (1997). Generalized partially linear single-index models. Journal of the American Statistical Association 92, 477–489.

Carroll, R. J., W. Härdle, and E. Mammen (2002). Estimation in an additive model when the components are linked parametrically. Econometric Theory 18, 886–912.

Carroll, R. J. and D. Ruppert (1988). Transformation and Weighting in Regression. New York: Chapman and Hall.

Carter, C. K. and R. Kohn (1994). On Gibbs sampling for state space models. Biometrika 81, 541–553.

Carter, C. K. and R. Kohn (1997). Semiparametric Bayesian inference for time series with mixed spectra. Journal of the Royal Statistical Society, Series B 59, 255–268.

Caulet, R. and A. Péguin-Feissolle (2000). Un testd'hétéroscédasticité conditionnelle inspiré de la modélisation en termes de réseaux neuronaux artificiels. Annales déconomie et de Statistique 59, 178–197.

Cavaliere, G. (2004). Unit root tests under time-varying variances. Econometric Reviews 23, 259–292.

Chaboud, A., B. Chiquoine, E. Hjalmarsson, and C. Vega (2009). Rise of the machines: Algorithmic trading in the foreign exchange market. Board of Governors International Finance Discussion paper no 980.

Chan, D., R. Kohn, and C. Kirby (2006). Multivariate stochastic volatility models with correlated errors. Econometric Reviews 25, 245–274.

Chan, L. K., J. Karceski, and J. Lakonishok (1999). On portfolio optimization: Forecasting covariances and choosing the risk model. Review of Financial Studies 12, 937–974.

Chen, C.-C. and M.-Y. Hung (2010). Option pricing under Markov–switching GARCH processes. Journal of Futures Markets 30, 444–464.

Chen, G., Y. K. Choi, and Y. Zhou (2005). Nonparametric estimation of structural change points in volatility models for time series. Journal of Econometrics 126, 79–114.

Chen, J. and A. K. Gupta (1997). Testing and locating variance changepoints with application to stock prices. Journal of the American Statistical Association 92, 739–747.

Chen, J., H. Hong, and J. C. Stein (2001). Forecasting Crashes: Trading Volume, Past Returns and Conditional Skewness in Stock Prices. Journal of Financial Economics 61, 345–381.

Chen, X. and Y. Fan (2006). Estimation and model selection of semiparametric copula-based multivariate dynamic models under copula misspecification. Journal of Econometrics 135, 125–154.

Chen, X. and E. Ghysels (2011). News-good or bad-and its impact on volatility forecasts over multiple horizons. Review of Financial Studies 24, 46–81.

Chen, X., E. Ghysels, and F. Wang (2009a). On the role of intra-daily seasonality in HYBRID GARCH models. Technical report, Journal of Time Series Econometrics (forthcoming).

Chen, X., E. Ghysels, and F. Wang (2009b). The HYBRID GARCH class of models. Technical report, Working Paper, UNC.

Cheng, X., P. L. H. Yu, and W. K. Li (2009). On a dynamic mixture GARCH model. Journal of Forecasting 28, 247–265.

Chernov, M., A. Ronald Gallant, E. Ghysels, and G. Tauchen (2003). Alternative models for stock price dynamics. Journal of Econometrics 116, 225–257.

Cherubini, U., E. Luciano, and W. Vecchiato (2004). Copula Methods in Finance. West Sussex, England: John Wiley & Sons.

Chevillon, C. and D. Hendry (2005). Non-parametric direct multi-step estimation for forecasting economic processes. International Journal of Forecasting 21, 201–218.

Chib, S. (1998). Estimation and comparison of multiple change-point models. Journal of Econometrics 86, 221–241.

Chib, S., F. Nardari, and N. Shephard (2006). Analysis of high dimensional multivariate stochastic volatility models. Journal of Econometrics 134, 341–371.

Chib, S., Y. Omori, and M. Asai (2009). Multivariate stochastic volatility. In T. Andersen, R. Davis, J.-P. Kreiss, and T. Mikosch (Eds.), Handbook of Financial Time Series, pp. 365–400. New York: Springer-Verlag.

Chiriac, R. and V. Voev (2011). Modelling and forecasting multivariate realized volatility. Journal of Applied Econometrics 26, 922–947.

Chollete, L., A. Heinen, and A. Valdesogo (2009). Modeling international financial returns with a multivariate regime-switching copula. Journal of Financial Econometrics 7, 437–480.

Chou, R. (1992). Volatility persistence and stock valuations: some empirical evidence using GARCH. Journal of Applied Econometrics 3, 279–294.

Chou, R. Y. (2005). Forecasting financial volatilities with extreme values: The conditional autoregressive range (CARR) model. Journal of Money, Credit and Banking 37, 561–582.

Christensen, B. J., C. M. Dahl, and E. M. Iglesias (2008). Semiparametric inference in a GARCH-in-mean model. CREATES Research Paper 2008-46, School of Economics and Management, University of Aarhus.

Christensen, K., S. Kinnebrock, and M. Podolskij (2010). Pre-averaging estimators of the ex-post covariance matrix in noisy diffusion models with non-synchronous data. Journal of Econometrics 159, 116–133.

Christensen, K., S. Kinnebrock, and M. Podolskij (2010a). Pre-averaging estimators of the ex-post covariance matrix in noisy diffusion models with non-synchronous data. Journal of Econometrics, 159, 116–133.

Christensen, K., R. Oomen, and M. Podolskij (2010b). Realised quantile-based estimation of the integrated variance. Journal of Econometrics 159, 74–98.

Christensen, K. and M. Podolskij (2007). Realised range-based estimation of integrated variance. Journal of Econometrics 141, 323–349.

Christensen, K. and M. Podolskij (2010). Range-based estimation of quadratic variation. ssrn.com.

Christensen, K., M. Podolskij, and M. Vetter (2009). Bias-correcting the realised range-based variance in the presence of market microstructure noise. Finance and Stochastics 13, 239–268.

Christie, A. A. (1982). The stochastic behavior of common stock variances: Value, leverage and interest rate effects. Journal of Financial Economics 10, 407–432.

Christoffersen, P. (1998). Evaluating interval forecasts. International Economic Review 39, 841–862.

Christoffersen, P. and F. Diebold (2000). How relevant is volatility forecasting for financial risk management? Review of Economics and Statistics 82, 12–22.

Christoffersen, P., R. Elkamhi, B. Feunou, and K. Jacobs (2010). Option valuation with conditional heteroskedasticity and non-normality. Review Financial Studies 23, 2139–2183.

Chu, C.-S. (1995). Detecting parameter shift in GARCH models. Econometric Reviews 14, 241–266.

Chung, K. (1974). A course in probability theory. London: Academic Press Inc.

Cipollini, F., R. Engle, and G. Gallo (2006). Vector multiplicative error models: representation and inference.

Cipollini, F., R. F. Engle, and G. M. Gallo (2007). A model for multivariate non-negative valued processes in financial econometrics. Technical Report 2007/16.

Cipollini, F., R. F. Engle, and G. M. Gallo (2009). Semiparametric vector MEM. Econometrics Working Papers Archive wp200903, Universitá degli Studi di Firenze, Dipartimento di Statistica "G. Parenti".

Cipollini, F. and G. M. Gallo (2010). Automated variable selection in vector multiplicative error models. Computational Statistics & Data Analysis 54, 2470–2486.

Cížek, P., W. Härdle, and V. Spokoiny (2009). Adaptive pointwise estimation in time-inhomogeneous conditional heteroscedasticity models. Economic Journal 12, 248–271.

Cížek, P. and V. Spokoiny (2009). Varying coefficient GARCH-models. In T. G. Andersen, R. A. Davis, J.-P. Kreiss, and T. Mikosch (Eds.), Handbook of Financial Time Series, pp. 169–185. New York: Springer.

Clark, P. K. (1973). A subordinated stochastic process model with fixed variance for speculative prices. Econometrica 41, 135–156.

Clark, T. and M. McCracken (2005). Evaluating direct multistep forecasts. Econometric Reviews 24, 369–404.

Clark, T. and M. McCracken (2009). Nested forecast model comparisons: A new approach to testing equal accuracy. Federal Reserve of St. Louis Working Paper.

Clark, T. and K. West (2006). Using out-of-sample mean squared prediction errors to test the martingale difference hypothesis. Journal of Econometrics 135, 155–186.

Clark, T. and K. West (2007). Approximately normal tests for equal predictive accuracy in nested models. Journal of Econometrics 138, 291–311.

Clark, T. E. and M. McCracken (2001). Tests for equal forecast accuracy and encompassing for nested models. Journal of Econometrics 105, 85–110.

Clements, A., M. Doolan, S. Hurn, and M. Becker (2009a). On the efficacy of techniques for evaluating multivariate volatility forecasts. NCER Working Paper.

Clements, A., M. Doolan, S. Hurn, and R. Becker (2009b). Evaluating multivariate volatility forecasts. Technical report, NCER Working Paper Series.

Clements, M., A. Galvsimao, and J. Kim (2008). Quantile forecasts of daily exchange rate returns from forecasts of realized volatility. Journal of Empirical Finance 15, 729–750.

Clements, M. and D. Hendry (1996). Mutli-step estimation for forecasting. Oxford Bulletin of Economics and Statistics 58, 657–684.

Cohen, K., G. A. Hawawini, S. F. Maier, R. A. Schwartz, and D. K. Whitcomb (1983). Friction in the trading process and the estimation of systematic risk. Journal of Financial Economics 12, 263–278.

Colacito, R., R. F. Engle, and E. Ghysels (2011). A component model for dynamic correlations. Journal of Econometrics. doi: 10.1016/j.jeconom.2011.02.013.

Comte, F., J. Dedecker, and M. L. Taupin (2008). Adaptive density estimation for general ARCH models. Econometric Theory 24, 1628–1662.

Comte, F. and E. Renault (1998). Long memory in continuous-time stochastic volatility models. Mathematical Finance 8, 291–323.

Conrad, C. and E. Mammen (2008). Nonparametric regression on latent covariates with an application to semiparametric GARCH-in-mean models. Working paper 0473, Department of Economics, University of Heidelberg.

Cont, R. and C. Mancini (2011). Non-parametric tests for pathwise properties of semimartingales. Bernoulli 17, 781–813.

Cont, R. and P. Tankov (2004). Financial Modelling with Jump Processes. London: CRC Press.

Cornelissen, J. and K. Boudt (2010). RTAQ: Tools for the analysis of trades and quotes in R. package version 0.1.

Corradi, V. and W. Distaso (2006). Semi-parametric comparison of stochastic volatility models using realized measures. Review of Economic Studies 73, 635–667.

Corradi, V., N. Swanson, and C. Olivetti (2001). Predictive ability with cointegrated variables. Journal of Econometrics 104, 315–358.

Corsi, F. (2009). A simple approximate long-memory model of realized volatility. Journal of Financial Econometrics 7, 174–196.

Corsi, F. and F. Audrino (2008). Realized covariance tick-by-tick in presence of rounded time stamps and general microstructure effects. Unpublished manuscript, University of St. Gallen.

Corsi, F., F. Audrino, and R. Reno (2012). HAR modeling for realized volatility forecasting. In L. Bauwens, C. Hafner, and S. Laurent (Eds.), Handbook of Volatility Models and Their Applications, pp. 363–381. John Wiley & Sons.

Corsi, F., D. La Vecchia, and N. Fusari (2010). Realizing smiles: Pricing options with realized volatility. Journal of Financial Economics (forthcoming).

Corsi, F., S. Mittnik, C. Pigorsch, and U. Pigorsch (2008). The volatility of realized volatility. Econometric Reviews 27, 1–33.

Corsi, F., D. Pirino, and R. Renó (2010). Threshold bipower variation and the impact of jumps on volatility forecasting. Journal of Econometrics 159, 276–288.

Corsi, F. and R. Renó (2010). Discrete-time volatility forecasting with persistent leverage effect and the link with continuous-time volatility modeling. Journal of Business and Economic Statistics (forthcoming).

Cox, D. (1961). Tests of separate families of hypotheses. In Proceedings of the Fourth Berkeley Symposium on Mathematical Statistics and Probability, Vol. 1, pp. 105–123. Berkeley: University of California Press.

Cox, D. (1962). Further results on tests of separate families of hypotheses. Journal of the Royal Statistical Society-Series B 24, 406–424.

Cox, J. and S. Ross (1976). The valuation of options for alternative stochastic processes. Journal of Financial Economics 3, 145–166.

Creal, D., S. Koopman, and J. Lucas (2008). A general framework for observation driven time-varying parameter models. Technical report, Tinbergen Institute.

Curci, G. and F. Corsi (2010). Discrete sine transform for multi-scales realized volatility measures. Quantitative Finance (forthcoming). Available online: 24 Jun 2011, DOI:10.1080/14697688.2010.490561.

Dacorogna, M., U. Müller, R. Davé, R. Olsen, and O. Pictet (1998). Modelling short-term volatility with GARCH and HARCH models. In "Nonlinear Modelling of High Frequency Financial Time Series", C. Dunis, and B. Zhou (Eds.), pp. 161–76, Chichester: John Wiley & Sons, Ltd.

Dahlhaus, R. (1996). On the Kullback-Leibler information divergence of locally stationary processes. Stochastic Processes and their Applications 62, 139–168.

Dahlhaus, R. (1997). Fitting time series models to nonstationary processes. The Annals of Statistics 25, 1–37.

Dahlhaus, R. (2000). A likelihood approximation for locally stationary processes. The Annals of Statistics 28, 1762–1794.

Dahlhaus, R. and W. Polonik (2009). Empirical spectral processes for locally stationary time series. Bernoulli 15, 1–39.

Dahlhaus, R. and S. Subba Rao (2006). Statistical inference for time-varying ARCH processes. The Annals of Statistics 34, 1075–1114.

Dahlhaus, R. and S. Subba Rao (2007). A recursive online algorithm for the estimation of time-varying ARCH parameters. Bernoulli 13, 389–422.

Danielsson, J. (1994). Stochastic volatility in asset prices: Estimation by simulated maximum likelihood. Journal of Econometrics 64, 375–400.

Danielsson, J. (1998). Multivariate stochastic volatility models: Estimation and comparison with VGARCH models. Journal of Empirical Finance 5, 155–173.

Das, S. and R. Uppal (2004). Systemic risk and international portfolio choice. The Journal of Finance 59, 2809–2834.

Davidson, J. (2004). Forecasting Markov–switching dynamic, conditionally heteroskedastic processes. Statistics & Probability Letters 68, 137–147.

Davies, L. and U. Gather (1993). The identifcation of multiple outliers. Journal of the American Statistical Association 88, 782–792.

Davies, R. B. (1977). Hypothesis testing when a nuisance parameter is present only under the alternative. Biometrika 64, 247–254.

Day, N. E. (1969). Estimating the components of a mixture of normal distributions. Biometrika 56, 463–474.

De Jong, F. and T. Nijman (1997). High frequency analysis of lead-lag relationships between financial markets. Journal of Empirical Finance 4, 259–277.

De Jong, P. and N. Shephard (1995). The simulation smoother for time series models. Biometrika 82, 339–350.

De Luca, G. and G. M. Gallo (2010). A time-varying mixing multiplicative error model for realized volatility. Econometrics Working Papers Archive wp2010_03, Universitá degli Studi di Firenze: Dipartimento di Statistica "G. Parenti".

de Pooter, M., M. Martens, and D. van Dijk (2008). Predicting the daily covariance matrix of s &p100 stocks using intraday data-but which frequency to use? Econometric Reviews 27, 199–229.

de Vilder, R. and M. Visser (2008). Ranking and Combining Volatility Proxies for GARCH and Stochastic Volatility Models. MPRA paper 11001.

Dean, W. G. and R. W. Faff (2008). Evidence of feedback trading with Markov switching regimes. Review of Quantitative Finance and Accounting 30, 133–151.

de B. Harris, F. H., T. H. McInish, G. L. Shoesmith, and R. A. Wood (1995). Cointegration, error correction, and price discovery on informationally linked security markets. Journal of Financial and Quantitative Analysis 30, 563–581.

Degennaro, R. and R. Shrieves (1997). Public information releases, private information arrival and volatility in the foreign exchange market. Journal of Empirical Finance 4, 295–315.

Dehay, D. and J. Leškow (1996). Testing stationarity for stock market data. Economics Letter 50, 205–212.

Della Corte, P., L. Sarno, and I. Tsiakas (2009). An economic evaluation of empirical exchange rate models. Review of Financial Studies 22, 3491–3530.

Demeterfi, K., E. Derman, M. Kamal, and J. Zou (1999). More than you ever wanted to know about volatility swaps. Technical report. Research notes, Goldman Sachs.

DeMiguel, V., L. Garlappi, F. Nogales, and R. Uppal (2009). A generalized approach to portfolio optimization: Improving performance by constraining portfolio norms. Management Science 55, 798–812.

DeMiguel, V., L. Garlappi, and R. Uppal (2009). Optimal versus naive diversification: How inefficient is the 1/N portfolio strategy? Review of Financial Studies 22, 1915.

Dias, A. and P. Embrechts (2004). Dynamic copula models for multivariate high-frequency data in finance. Technical report.

Diebold, F. X. (1986). Modeling the persistence of conditional variances: A comment. Econometric Reviews 5, 51–56.

Diebold, F. X. (2004). The Nobel memorial price for R.F. Engle. Scandinavian Journal of Economics 106, 165–185.

Diebold, F. X., A. Hickman, A. Inoue, and T. Schuermann (1997). Converting 1-day volatility to h-day volatility: Scaling by $\sqrt{h}$ is worse than you think. mimeo, University of Pennsylvania.

Diebold, F. X. and J. A. Lopez (1995). Modeling volatility dynamics. In K. V. Hoover (Ed.), Macroeconometrics: Developments, Tensions and Prospects, pp. 427–472. Boston/Dordrecht/London: Kluwer Academic Press.

Diebold, F. X. and R. S. Mariano (1995). Comparing predictive accuracy. Journal of Business and Economic Statistics 13, 253–263.

Diebold, F. X. and K. Yilmaz (2009). Measuring financial asset return and volatility spillovers, with application to global equity markets. The Economic Journal 119, 158–171.

Ding, Z. and C. Granger (1996). Modeling volatility persistence of speculative returns: A new approach. Journal of Econometrics 73, 185–215.

Ding, Z., C. W. Granger, and R. F. Engle (1993). A long memory property of stock market returns and a new model. Journal of Empirical Finance 1, 83–106.

Disatnik, D. and S. Benninga (2007). Shrinking the covariance matrix. The Journal of Portfolio Management 33, 55–63.

Dobrev, D. (2007). Capturing volatility from large price moves: generalized range theory and applications. Working Paper, Kellogg School of Management, Northwestern University.

Domowitz, I. and H. White (1982). Misspecified models with dependent observations. Journal of Econometrics 20, 35–58.

Donaldson, R. G. and M. Kamstra (1997). An artificial neural network-GARCH model for international stock return volatility. Journal of Empirical Finance 4, 17–46.

Doornik, J. A. (2009b). Ox6: An Object-Oriented Matrix Programming Language. London: Timberlake Consultants Ltd.

Driessen, J., P. Maenhout, and G. Vilkov (2009). Option-implied correlations and the price of correlation risk. Journal of Finance 64, 1377–1406.

Drost, F. and T. Nijman (1993). Temporal aggregation of GARCH processes. Econometrica, 909–927.

Drost, F. and B. Werker (1996). Closing the GARCH gap: Continuous time GARCH modeling. Journal of Econometrics 74, 31–57.

Drost, F. C. and C. A. J. Klaassen (1997). Efficient estimation in semiparametric GARCH models. Journal of Econometrics 8, 193–221.

Drost, F. C., C. A. J. Klaassen, and B. J. M. Werker (1997). Adaptive estimation in time-series models. The Annals of Statistics 25, 786–817.

Duan, J. (1995). The GARCH option pricing model. Mathematical Finance 5, 13–32.

Duan, J.-C. (1997). Augmented GARCH(p,q) process and its diffusion limit. Journal of Econometrics 79, 97–127.

Dubins, L. and G. Schwartz (1965). On continuous martingale. Proceedings of the National Academy of Sciences of the United States of America 53, 913–916.

Dueker, M. J. (1997). Markov switching in GARCH processes and mean-reverting stock-market volatility. Journal of Business and Economic Statistics 15, 26–34.

Duffie, D. and J. Pan (1997). An overview of Value-at-Risk. Journal of Derivatives 4, 7–49.

Duffie, D. and J. Pan (2001). Analytical Value-at-Risk with jumps and credit risks. Finance and Stochastics 5, 155–180.

Dufour, J. and P. Valéry (2006). On a simple two-stage closed form estimator for a stochastic volatility in a general linear regression. Advances in Econometrics 20, 259–288.

Dumitru, A. and G. Urga (2011). Identifying jumps in financial assests: A comparison between nonparametric jump tests. Journal of business and Economic Statistics. Available on www.ssrn.com (forthcoming).

Durbin, J. and S. J. Koopman (1997). Monte Carlo maximum likelihood estimation for non-Gaussian state space models. Biometrika 84, 669–684.

Durbin, J. and S. J. Koopman (2002). A simple and efficient simulation smoother for state space time series analysis. Biometrika 89, 603–615.

Elie, L. and T. Jeantheau (1995). Consistance dans les modéles hétéroscédastiques. Comptes Rendus de l'Académie des Sciences, Série I 320, 1255–1258.

Embrechts, P., R. Frey, and A. McNeil (1999). Credit risk models: An overview. Journal of Banking and Finance 24, 59–117.

Embrechts, P., C. Klüppelberg, and T. Mikosch (1997). Modelling Extremal Events for Insurance and Finance. New York: Springer.

Embrechts, P., A. McNeil, and D. Straumann (2001). Correlation and dependence in risk management: Properties and pitfalls. Technical report, Departement Mathematik, ETHZ.

Engle, R. and R. Colacito (2006a). Testing and evaluating dynamic correlations for asset allocation. Journal of Business and Economic Statistics 22, 367–381.

Engle, R. F. (1982a). Autoregressive conditional heteroscedasticity with estimates of the variance of United Kingdom inflation. Econometrica 50, 987–1007.

Engle, R. F. (1982b). A general approach to Lagrange multiplier model diagnostics. Journal of Econometrics 20, 83–104.

Engle, R. F. (1990). Stock volatility and the crash of '87: Discussion. Review of Financial Studies 3, 103–106.

Engle, R. F. (2001). GARCH 101: The use of ARCH/GARCH models in applied econometrics. Journal of Economic Perspectives 15, 157–168.

Engle, R. F. (2002a). Dynamic conditional correlation: A simple class of multivariate generalized autoregressive conditional heteroskedasticity models. Journal of Business and Economic Statistics 20, 339–350.

Engle, R. F. (2002b). New frontiers for ARCH models. Journal of Applied Econometrics 17, 425–446.

Engle, R. F. (2004). Risk and volatility: Econometric models and financial practice. American Economic Review 94, 405–420.

Engle, R. F. (2009a). Anticipating Correlations: A New Paradigm for Risk Management. Princeton Univeristy Press.

Engle, R. F. (2009b). High dimenson dynamic correlation. The Methodology and Practice of Econometrics: A Festschrift in Honour of David F. Hendry. Oxford University Press.

Engle, R. F. (2011). Long term skewness and systemic risk. Journal of Financial Econometrics 9, 437–468.

Engle, R. F. and T. Bollerslev (1986). Modeling the persistence of conditional variances. Econometric Reviews 5, 1–50.

Engle, R. F. and R. Colacito (2006). Testing and valuing dynamic correlations for asset allocation. Journal of Business and Economic Statistics, 238–253.

Engle, R. F. and G. M. Gallo (2006). A multiple indicators model for volatility using intra-daily data. Journal of Econometrics 131, 3–27.

Engle, R. F., G. M. Gallo, and M. Velucchi (2011). Volatility spillovers in East Asian financial markets: A MEM based approach. Review of Economics and Statistics (forthcoming).

Engle, R. F., E. Ghysels, and B. Sohn (2008). On the economic sources of stock market volatility. Discussion Paper NYU and UNC.

Engle, R. F. and G. Gonzalez-Rivera (1991). Semiparametric ARCH models. Journal of Business and Economic Statistics 9, 345–359.

Engle, R. F., C. W. J. Granger, and D. Kraft (1984). Combining competing forecasts of inflation with a bivariate ARCH model. Journal of Economic Dynamics and Control 8, 151–165.

Engle, R. F. and B. Kelly (2008). Dynamic equicorrelation. Available at SSRN: http://ssrn.com/abstract = 1098969.

Engle, R. F. and F. Kroner (1995). Multivariate simultaneous generalized ARCH. Econometric Theory 11, 122–150.

Engle, R. F. and G. J. Lee (1999). A permanent and transitory component model of stock return volatility. In R. F. Engle, and H. White (Eds.), Cointegration, Causality, and Forecasting: A Festschrift in Honor of Clive W. J. Granger, pp. 475–497. Oxford: Oxford University Press.

Engle, R. F., D. M. Lilien, and R. P. Robins (1987). Estimating time varying risk premia in the term structure: the ARCH-M model. Econometrica 55, 391–407.

Engle, R. F. and S. Manganelli (2004). CAViaR: Conditional autoregressive Value-at-Risk by regression quantiles. Journal of Business & Economic Statistics, 22, 367–381.

Engle, R. F. and J. Mezrich (1996). GARCH for groups. Risk 9, 36–40.

Engle, R. F. and C. Mustafa (1992). Implied ARCH models from option prices. Journal of Econometrics 52, 289–311.

Engle, R. F. and V. K. Ng (1993). Measuring and testing the impact of news on volatility. Journal of Finance 48, 1749–1778.

Engle, R. F., V. K. Ng, and M. Rothschild (1990). Asset pricing with a factor-ARCH covariance structure: Empirical estimates for treasury bills. Journal of Econometrics 45, 213–238.

Engle, R. F. and A. Patton (2001). What good is a volatility model? Quantitative Finance 1, 237–245.

Engle, R. F. and J. Rangel (2008). The spline-GARCH model for low-frequency volatility and its global macroeconomic causes. Review of Financial Studies 21, 1187–1222.

Engle, R. F. and J. R. Russell (1998). Autoregressive conditional duration: A new model for irregularly spaced transaction data. Econometrica 66, 1127–62.

Engle, R. F., N. Shephard, and K. Sheppard (2008). Fitting vast dimensional time-varying covariance models. Economics Series Working Papers 403, Department of Economics, University of Oxford, Oxford.

Engle, R. F. and K. Sheppard (2001). Theorical and empirical properties of dynamic conditional correlation multivariate GARCH. Mimeo, UCSD.

Epps, T. W. (1979). Comovements in stock prices in the very short run. Journal of the American Statistical Association 74, 291–296.

Eraker, B., M. Johannes, and N. Polson (2003). The impact of jumps in equity index volatility and returns. Journal of Finance 58, 1269–1300.

Es, B. V., P. Spreij, and H. V. Zanten (2005). Nonparametric volatility density estimation for discrete time models. Journal of Nonparametric Statistics 17, 237–249.

Eun, C. S. and S. Shim (1989). International transmission of stock market movements. Journal of Financial and Quantitative Analysis 24, 241–256.

Fama, E. (1963). Mandelbrot and the stable Paretian distributions. Journal of Business 36, 420–429.

Fama, E. (1965). The behaviour of stock market prices. Journal of Business 38, 34–105.

Fama, E. F. and K. R. French (1992). The cross-section of expected stock returns. Journal of Finance 47, 427–465.

Fama, E. F. and K. R. French (1993). Common risk factors in the returns to stocks and bonds. Journal of financial economics 33, 3–56.

Fan, J., Y. Fan, and J. Lv (2008). High dimensional covariance matrix estimation using a factor model. Journal of Econometrics 147, 186–197.

Fan, J. and I. Gijbels (1996). Local Polynomial Modelling and its Applications. London: Chapman and Hall.

Fan, J., Y. Li, and K. Yu (2010). Vast volatility matrix estimation using high frequency data for portfolio selection. Technical report, Princeton University.

Fan, J. and Y. Wang (2007). Multi-scale jump and volatility analysis for high-frequency financial data. Journal of American Statistical Association 102, 1349–1362.

Fan, J. and Q. Yao (1998). Efficient estimation of conditional variance functions in stochastic regression. Biometrika 85, 645–660.

Fan, J., Q. Yao, and Z. Cai (2003). Adaptive varying-coefficient linear models. Journal of the Royal Statistical Society, Series B 65, 57–80.

Fan, J., J. Zhang, and K. Yu (2009). Asset allocation and risk assessment with gross exposure constraints for vast portfolios. Preprint, Princeton University.

Fang, K.-T. and B.-Q. Fang (1988). Some families of multivariate symmetric distributions related to exponential distribution. Journal of Multivariate Analysis 24, 109–122.

Feng, Y. (2004). Simultaneously modelling conditional heteroskedasticity and scale change. Econometric Theory 20, 563–596.

Fermanian, J.-D. and O. Scaillet (2005). Some statistical pitfalls in copula modeling for financial applications. In E. Klein (Ed.), Capital Formation, Governance and Banking, pp. 57–72. New York: Nova Science Publishers.

Fernandez, C., J. Osiewalski, and M. F. Steel (1995). Modelling and inference with v–spherical distributions. Journal of the American Statistical Association 90, 1331–1340.

Figlewsky, S. and P. Wachtel (1981). The formation of inflationary expectation. Review of Economics and Statistics 63, 1–10.

Findley, D. (1983). On the use of multiple models of multi-period forecasting. Proceedings of the Business and Statistics Section, Americal Statistical Association 37, 528–531.

Findley, D. (1985). Model selection for multi-step-ahead forecasting. In S. Ghosh, and P. Young (Eds.), Proceedings of the 7th Symposium on Identification and System Parameter Estimation, pp. 1039–1044. Oxford: Pergamon.

Fiorentini, G., G. Calzolari, and L. Panattoni (1996). Analytic derivatives and the computation of GARCH estimates. Journal of Applied Econometrics 11, 399–417.

Fleming, J., C. Kirby, and B. Ostdiek (2001). The economic value of volatility timing. Journal of Finance 56, 329–352.

Fleming, J., C. Kirby, and B. Ostdiek (2003). The economic value of volatility timing using realized volatility. Journal of Financial Economics 67, 473–509.

Fornari, F. and A. Mele (1997). Sign- and volatility-switching ARCH models: Theory and applications to international stock markets. Journal of Applied Econometrics 12, 49–65.

Forsberg, L. and E. Ghysels (2007). Why do absolute returns predict volatility so well? Journal of Financial Econometrics 5, 31–67.

Foster, D. P. and D. B. Nelson (1996, January). Continuous record asymptotics for rolling sample variance estimators. Econometrica 64, 139–74.

Francq, C., L. Horvath, and J.-M. Zakoïan (2009). Merits and drawbacks of variance targeting in GARCH models. Technical report.

Francq, C., M. Roussignol, and J.-M. Zakoïan (2001). Conditional heteroskedasticity driven by hidden markov chains. Journal of Time Series Analysis 22, 197–220.

Francq, C. and J. Zakoïan (2009). Bartlett's formula for a general class of nonlinear processes. Journal of Time Series Analysis 30, 449–465.

Francq, C. and J.-M. Zakoïan (2001). Stationarity of multivariate Markov–switching ARMA models. Journal of Econometrics 102, 339–364.

Francq, C. and J.-M. Zakoïan (2005). The L2–structures of standard and switching–regime GARCH models. Stochastic Processes and their Applications 115, 1557–1582.

Francq, C. and J.-M. Zakoïan (2008). Deriving the autocovariances of powers of Markov–switching GARCH models, with applications to statistical inference. Computational Statistics & Data Analysis 52, 3027–3046.

Francq, C. and J.-M. Zakoïan (2010). GARCH Models: Structure, Statistical Inference and Financial Applications. John Wiley & Sons.

Franses, P., M. van der Leij, and R. Paap (2008). A simple test for GARCH against a stochastic volatility model. Journal of Financial Econometrics 6, 291–306.

Franses, P. H., R. Paap, and M. van der Leij (2002). Modelling and forecasting level shifts in absolute returns. Journal of Applied Econometrics 17, 601–616.

French, K., G. Schwert, and R. Stambaugh (1987). Expected stock returns and volatility. Journal of Financial Economics 19, 3–29.

Fridmann, M. and L. Harris (1998). A maximum likelihood approach for non-Gaussian stochastic volatility models. Journal of Business and Economic Statistics 16, 284–291.

Frühwirth-Schnatter, S. (2006). Finite Mixture and Markov Switching Models. New York: Springer.

Fryźlewicz, P., T. Sapatinas, and S. Subba Rao (2008). Normalized least-squares estimation in time-varying ARCH models. The Annals of Statistics 36, 742–786.

Fryźlewicz, P., S. Van Bellegem, and R. von Sachs (2003). Forecasting non-stationary time series by wavelet process modelling. The Annals of the Institute of Statistical Mathematics 65, 737–764.

Fukasawa, M. (2010). Realized volatility with stochastic sampling. Stochastic Processes and Their Applications 120, 829–852.

Gallant, A. R., D. Hsieh, and G. Tauchen (1997). Estimation of stochastic volatility models with diagnostics. Journal of Econometrics 81, 159–192.

Gallant, A. R., C.-T. Hsu, and G. Tauchen (1999). Using daily range data to calibrate volatility diffusions and extract the forward integrated variance. restat 81, 617–631.

Gallant, A. R. and D. W. Nychka (1987). Seminonparametric maximum likelihood estimation. Econometrica 55, 363–390.

Gallant, A. R. and G. Tauchen (1996). Which moments to match? Econometric Theory 12, 657–681.

Garcia, R. and N. Meddahi (2006). Comment. Journal of Business and Economic Statistics 24, 184–192.

Garcia, R. and G. Tsafack (2007). Dependence structure and extreme comovements in international equity and bond markets with portfolio diversification effects. Technical report, CIRANO.

Garman, M. and M. Klass (1980). On the estimation of securities price volatilities. Journal of Business 53, 67–78.

Gatheral, J. and R. C. A. Oomen (2010). Zero-intelligence realized variance estimation. Finance and Stochastics 14, 249–283.

Gerety, M. S. and H. Mulherin (1994). Price formation on stock exchanges: The evolution of trading within the day. Review of Financial Studies 6, 23–56.

Geweke, J. (1986). Modelling the persistence of conditional variance: A comment. Econometric Reviews 5, 57–61.

Geweke, J. and G. Amisano (2011). Hierarchical Markov normal mixture models with applications to financial asset returns. Journal of Applied Econometrics 26, 1–29.

Geweke, J. and S. Porter-Hudak (1983). The estimation and application of long memory time series models. Journal of Time Series Analysis 4, 221–238.

Ghysels, E., A. Harvey, and E. Renault (1996). Stochastic volatility. In G. Maddala, and C. Rao (Eds.), Handbook of Statistics, pp. 119–191. Amsterdam: Elsevier Science.

Ghysels, E., A. Rubia, and R. Valkanov (2008). Multi-period forecasts of volatility: Direct, iterated, and mixed-data approaches. Working Paper, UCSD and UNC.

Ghysels, E., P. Santa-Clara, and R. Valkanov (2002). The MIDAS touch: Mixed data sampling regression models. Working paper, UNC and UCLA.

Ghysels, E., P. Santa-Clara, and R. Valkanov (2005). There is a risk-return tradeoff after all. Journal of Financial Economics 76, 509–548.

Ghysels, E., P. Santa-Clara, and R. Valkanov (2006a). Predicting volatility: getting the most out of return data sampled at different frequencies. Journal of Econometrics 131, 59–95.

Ghysels, E., P. Santa-Clara, and R. Valkanov (2006b). Predicting volatility: getting the most out of return data sampled at different frequencies. Journal of Econometrics 131, 59–95.

Ghysels, E., P. Santa-Clara, and R. Valkanov (2006c). Predicting volatility: how to get the most out of returns data sampled at different frequencies. Journal of Econometrics 131, 59–95.

Ghysels, E. and A. Sinko (2006). Comment on Realized variance and market microstructure noise by Peter Hansen and Asger Lunde. Journal of Business and Economic Statistics 24, 192–194.

Ghysels, E. and A. Sinko (2011). Volatility forecasting and microstructure noise. Journal of Econometrics 160, 257–271.

Ghysels, E., A. Sinko, and R. Valkanov (2006). Midas regressions: Further results and new directions. Econometric Reviews 26, 53–90.

Ghysels, E. and R. Valkanov (2012). Forecasting volatility with MIDAS. In L. Bauwens, C. Hafner, and S. Laurent (Eds.), Handbook of Volatility Models and Their Applications, pp. 383–401. John Wiley & Sons.

Giacomini, E., W. Härdle, and V. Spokoiny (2009). Inhomogeneous dependency modelling with time varying copulae. Journal of Business and Economic Statistics 27, 224–234.

Giacomini, R. and H. White (2006). Tests of conditional predictive ability. Econometrica 74, 1545–1578.

Giannikis, D., I. D. Vrontos, and P. Dellaportas (2008). Modelling nonlinearities and heavy tails via threshold normal mixture GARCH models. Computational Statistics and Data Analysis 52, 1549–1571.

Giot, P. and S. Laurent (2003). Value-at-risk for long and short positions. Journal of Applied Econometrics 18, 641–663.

Giot, P. and S. Laurent (2004). Modelling daily value–at–risk using realized volatility and ARCH type models. Journal of Empirical Finance 11, 379–398.

Giraitis, L., R. Leipus, and D. Surgailis (2006). Recent advances in ARCH modelling. In A. Kirman, and G. Teyssiére (Eds.), Long Memory in Economics, pp. 3–38. Springer.

Glad, I. K. (1998). Parametrically guided non-parametric regression. Scandinavian Journal of Statistics 25, 649–668.

Glosten, L., R. Jagannathan, and D. Runkle (1993). On the relation between expected value and the volatility of the nominal excess return on stocks. Journal of Finance 48, 1779–1801.

Gloter, A. and J. Jacod (2000). Diffusions with measurement errors: I-local asymptotic normality and II-optimal estimators. Technical report, Université de Paris-6.

Gloter, A. and J. Jacod (2001). Diffusions with measurement errors. part 1: Local asymptotic normality. ESAIM: Probability and Statistics 5, 225–242.

Goffe, W. L., G. D. Ferrier, and J. Rogers (1994). Global optimization of statistical functions with simulated annealing. Journal of Econometrics 60, 65–99.

Golosnoy, V., B. Gribisch, and R. Liesenfeld (2010). The conditional autoregressive Wishart model for multivariate stock market volatility. Economics Working paper 2010–07, Christian-Albrechts-University of Kiel, Department of Economics.

Gonćalves, S. and N. Meddahi (2011). Box-Cox transforms for realized volatility. Journal of Econometrics 160, 129–144.

Gonzalez-Rivera, G. (1998). Smooth transition GARCH models. Studies in Nonlinear Dynamics and Econometrics 3, 161–178.

Goodhart, C. and M. O'Hara (1997). High frequency data in financial markets: Issues and applications. Journal of Empirical Finance 4, 73–114.

Gosh, A. and O. Linton (2007). Consistent estimation of the risk-return trade off in the presence of measurement error. Working paper, London School of Economics.

Gouriéroux, C. (1997). ARCH Models and Financial Applications. Cambridge: Springer Verlag.

Gouriéroux, C. (2006). Continuous time Wishart process for stochastic risk. Econometric Reviews 25, 177–217.

Gouriéroux, C., J. Jasiak, and R. Sufana (2009). The Wishart autoregressive process of multivariate stochastic volatility. Journal of Econometrics 150, 167–181.

Gouriéroux, C. and A. Monfort (1995). Statistics and Econometric Models. Cambridge University Press.

Gouriéroux, C., A. Monfort, and A. Trognon (1984). Pseudo maximum likelihood methods theory. Econometrica 52, 681–700.

Granger, C. (1980). Long memory relationships and the aggregation of dynamic models. Journal of Econometrics 14, 227–238.

Granger, C. and P. Newbold (1977). Forecasting Economic Time Series. London: Academic Press.

Gray, S. F. (1996). Modeling the conditional distribution of interest rates as a regime-switching process. Journal of Financial Economics 42, 27–62.

Greene, W. H. (2011). Econometric Analysis (7th ed.). New Jersey: Prentice Hall.

Greenspan, A. (2009). We need a better cushion against risk. Financial Times, March 26.

Griffin, J. and R. Oomen (2008). Sampling returns for realized variance calculations: Tick time or transaction time? Econometric Reviews 27, 230–253.

Griffin, J. E. and R. C. A. Oomen (2011). Covariance measurement in the presence of non- synchronous trading and market microstructure noise. Journal of Econometrics 160, 58–68.

Guillaume, D. M., M. M. Dacorogna, R. R. Dave, U. A. Muller, R. B. Olsen, and O. V. Pictet (1997). From the bird's eye to the microscope: A survey of new stylized facts of the intra-daily foreign exchange markets. Finance Stochastics 1, 95–129.

Haas, M. (2008). The autocorrelation structure of the Markov-switching asymmetric power GARCH process. Statistics & Probability Letters 78, 1480–1489.

Haas, M. (2009). Value–at–Risk via mixture distributions reconsidered. Applied Mathematics and Computation 215, 2103–2119.

Haas, M. (2010a). Covariance forecasts and long-run correlations in a Markov-switching model for dynamic correlations. Finance Research Letters 7, 86–97.

Haas, M. (2010b). Skew–normal mixture and Markov–switching GARCH processes. Studies in Nonlinear Dynamics & Econometrics 14, Article 1.

Haas, M. and S. Mittnik (2009). Portfolio selection with common correlation mixture models. In G. Bol, S. T. Rachev, and R. Würth (Eds.), Risk Assessment: Decisions in Banking and Finance, pp. 47–76. Heidelberg: Springer.

Haas, M., S. Mittnik, and B. Mizrach (2006). Assessing central bank credibility during the EMS crises: Comparing option and spot market-based forecasts. Journal of Financial Stability 2, 28–54.

Haas, M., S. Mittnik, and M. Paolella (2004a). Mixed normal conditional heteroskedasticity. Journal of Financial Econometrics 2, 211–250.

Haas, M., S. Mittnik, and M. Paolella (2004b). A new approach to Markov-switching GARCH models. Journal of Financial Econometrics 2, 493–530.

Haas, M., S. Mittnik, and M. S. Paolella (2009). Asymmetric multivariate normal mixture GARCH. Computational Statistics & Data Analysis 53, 2129–2154.

Haas, M., S. Mittnik, M. S. Paolella, and S. C. Steude (2006). A nalyzing and Exploiting Asymmetries in the News Impact Curve. FINRISK Working Paper No. 256.

Haas, M. and M. Paolella (2012). Mixture and regime-switching GARCH models. In L. Bauwens, C. Hafner, and S. Laurent (Eds.), Handbook of Volatility Models and Their Applications, pp. 71–102. John Wiley & Sons.

Haerdle, W. and A. Tsybakov (1997). Local polynomial estimators of the volatility function in nonparametric autoregression. Journal of Econometrics 81, 223–242.

Hafner, C. M. (1998). Estimating high frequency foreign exchange rate volatility with nonparametric ARCH models. Journal of Statistical Planning and Inference 68, 247–269.

Hafner, C. M. (2008). GARCH modeling. In R. Meyers (Ed.), Encyclopedia of Complexity and Systems Science. Springer.

Hafner, C. M. and P. Franses (2009). A generalized dynamic conditional correlation model: Simulation and application to many assets. Econometric Reviews 28, 612–631.

Hafner, C. M. and H. Herwartz (2001). Option pricing under linear autoregressive dynamics, heteroskedasticity and conditional leptokurtosis. Journal of Empirical Finance 8, 1–34.

Hafner, C. M. and O. B. Linton (2010). Efficient estimation of a multivariate multiplicative volatility model. Journal of Econometrics 159, 55–73.

Hafner, C. M. and H. Manner (2010). Dynamic stochastic copula models: Estimation, inference and applications. Journal of Applied Econometrics (forthcoming). Article first published online: 30 Jun 2010 . DOI: 10.1002/jae.1197.

Hafner, C. M. and A. Preminger (2010). Deciding between GARCH and stochastic volatility using strong decision rules. Journal of Statistical Planning and Inference 140, 791–805.

Hafner, C. M. and O. Reznikova (2010a). Efficient estimation of a semiparametric dynamic copula model. Computational Statistics and Data Analysis 54, 2609–2627.

Hafner, C. M. and O. Reznikova (2010b). On the estimation of dynamic conditional correlation models. Computational Statistics & Data Analysis. doi: 10.1016/j.csda.2010.09.022.

Hafner, C. M. and J. V. K. Rombouts (2007). Semiparametric multivariate volatility models. Econometric Theory 23, 251–280.

Hafner, C. M., D. van Dijk, and P. H. Franses (2006). Semiparametric modelling of correlation dynamics. In D. Terrell, and T. B. Fomby (Eds.), Econometric Analysis of Financial and Economic Time Series, pp. 59–103. Amsterdam: Emerald Group Publishing Limited.

Hagerud, G. (1997). A New Non-Linear GARCH Model. Stockholm: EFI Economic Research Institute.

Hall, R. E. (1979). Stochastic implication of the life cycle-permanent income hypothesis: theory and evidence. Journal of Political Economy 86, 971–987.

Hamao, Y., R. W. Masulis, and V. Ng (1990). Correlations in Price Changes and Volatility Across International Stock Markets. Review of Financial Studies 3, 281–307.

Hamilton, J. D. (1989). A new approach to the economic analysis of nonstationary time series and the business cycle. Econometrica 57, 357–384.

Hamilton, J. D. (1991). A quasi-Bayesian approach to estimating parameters for mixtures of normal distributions. Journal of Business and Economic Statistics 9, 21–39.

Hamilton, J. D. (1994). Time Series Analysis. Princeton, New Jersey: Princeton University Press.

Hamilton, J. D. (2008). Regime switching models. In S. N. Durlauf, and L. E. Blume (Eds.), New Palgrave Dictionary of Economics (2nd ed.) Vol. 7, pp. 53–57. Houndmills: Palgrave Macmillan.

Hamilton, J. D. and R. Susmel (1994). Autoregressive conditional heteroskedasticity and changes in regime. Journal of Econometrics 64, 307–333.

Han, Y. (2006). The economic value of volatility modelling: Asset allocation with a high dimensional dynamic latent factor multivariate stochastic volatility model. Review of Financial Studies 19, 237–271.

Hansen, B. E. (1994). Autoregressive conditional density estimation. International Economic Review 35, 705–730.

Hansen, B. E. (1996). Inference when a nuisance parameter is not identified under the null hypothesis. Econometrica 64, 413–430.

Hansen, P. R. (2005). A test for superior predictive ability. Journal of Business and Economic Statistics 23, 365–380.

Hansen, P. R., Z. A. Huang, and H. H. Shek (2011). Realized GARCH: A complete model of returns and realized measures of volatility. Journal of Applied Econometrics (forthcoming). Article first published online : 17 Mar 2011, DOI: 10.1002/jae.1234.

Hansen, P. R., J. Large, and A. Lunde (2008). Moving average-based estimators of integrated variance. Econometric Reviews 27, 79–111.

Hansen, P. R. and A. Lunde (2005a). A forecast comparison of volatility models: Does anything beat A GARCH(1,1)? Journal of Applied Econometrics 20, 873–889.

Hansen, P. R. and A. Lunde (2005b). A realized variance for the whole day based on intermittent high-frequency data. Journal of Financial Econometrics 3, 525–554.

Hansen, P. R. and A. Lunde (2006a). Consistent ranking of volatility models. Journal of Econometrics 131, 97–121.

Hansen, P. R. and A. Lunde (2006b). Realized variance and market microstructure noise. Journal of Business & Economic Statistics 24, 127–161.

Hansen, P. R. and A. Lunde (2010). Mulcom 2.00, an ox*tm* software package for multiple comparisons, http://mit.econ.au.dk/vip_htm/alunde/mulcom/mulcom.htm.

Hansen, P. R., A. Lunde, and J. Nason (2003). Choosing the best volatility models: the model confidence set approach. Oxford Bulletin of Economics and Statistics 65, 839–861.

Hansen, P. R., A. Lunde, and J. M. Nason (2011). The model confidence set. Econometrica 79, 453–497.

Härdle, W. A. Okhrin, O. and Y. Okhrin (2010). Time varying hierarchical Archimedean copulae. Technical report, SFB 649 Discussion Paper 2010–018.

Härdle, W., H. Herwartz, and V. Spokoiny (2003). Time inhomogeneous multiple volatility modeling. Journal of Financial Econometrics 1, 55–99.

Harris, L. (1986). A transaction data study of weekly and intradaily patterns in stock returns. Journal of Financial Economics 16, 99–117.

Harvey, A., E. Ruiz, and N. Shephard (1994). Multivariate stochastic variance models. Review of Economic Studies 61, 247–264.

Harvey, A. and N. Shephard (1996). Estimation of an asymmetric stochastic volatility model for asset returns. Journal of Business and Economic Statistics 14, 429–434.

Harvey, A. C. (1989). Forecasting, Structural Time Series Models and the Kalman Filter. Cambridge: Cambridge University Press.

Harvey, C. R. (2001). The specification of conditional expectations. Journal of Empirical Finance 8, 573–638.

Harvey, C. R. and A. Siddique (1999). Autoregressive conditional skewness. Journal of Financial and Quantitative Analysis 34, 465–487.

Harvey, C. R. and A. Siddique (2000). Conditional skewness in asset pricing tests. Journal of Finance 55, 1263–1295.

Hashmi, A. R. and A. S. Tay (2007). Global and regional sources of risk in equity markets: evidence from factor models with time-varying conditional skewness. Journal of International Money and Finance 26, 430–453.

Hashmi, A. R. and A. S. Tay (2012). Mean, volatility and skewness spillovers in equity markets. In L. Bauwens, C. Hafner, and S. Laurent (Eds.), Handbook of Volatility Models and Their Applications, pp. 127–145. John Wiley & Sons.

Hastie, T. and R. Tibshirani (1987). Generalized additive models: Some applications. Journal of the American Statistical Association 82, 371–386.

Hastie, T. and R. Tibshirani (1990). Generalized Additive models. London: Chapman and Hall.

Hautsch, N. (2008). Capturing common components in high-frequency financial time series: A multivariate stochastic multiplicative error model. Journal of Economic Dynamics and Control 32, 3978–4015.

Hautsch, N., L. M. Kyj, and R. C. Oomen (2009). A Blocking and Regularization Approach to High Dimensional Realized Covariance Estimation. Working paper series, Humbolt-Universität zu Berlin.

Hautsch, N., P. Malec, and M. Schienle (2010). Capturing the zero: A new class of zero–augmented distributions and multiplicative error processes. Technical report, Humboldt Universität zu Berlin. SFB 649, DP 2010–055.

Hayashi, T., J. Jacod, and N. Yoshida (2011). Irregular sampling and central limit theorems for power variations: The continuous case. Working Paper. Annales de l'Institut Henri Poincaré, Probabilité et Statistique 47(4) 1197–1218.

Hayashi, T. and N. Yoshida (2005). On covariance estimation of non-synchronously observed diffusion processes. Bernoulli 11, 359–379.

He, C., H. Malmsten, and T. Teräsvirta (2008). Higher-order dependence in the general Power ARCH process and the role of power parameter. In Shalabh X. and

C. Heumann (Eds.), Recent Advances in Linear Models and Related Areas, pp. 231–251. Heidelberg: Physica-Verlag.

He, C., A. Silvennoinen, and T. Teräsvirta (2008). Parameterizing unconditional skewness in models for financial time series. Journal of Financial Econometrics 6, 208–230.

He, C. and T. Teräsvirta (1999a). Properties of moments of a family of GARCH processes. Journal of Econometrics 92, 173–192.

He, C. and T. Teräsvirta (1999b). Statistical properties of the asymmetric power ARCH process. In R. F. Engle, and H. White (Eds.), Cointegration, causality and forecasting. A Festschrift in Honour of Clive W.J. Granger, pp. 462–474. Oxford: Oxford University Press.

He, Z. and J. M. Maheu (2010). Real time detection of structural breaks in GARCH models. Computational Statistics & Data Analysis 54, 2628–2640.

Heinen, A. and A. Valdesogo (2009). Asymmetric CAPM dependence for large dimensions: The canonical vine autoregressive copula model. Technical report, available at SSRN.

Heinen, A. and A. Valdesogo (2012). Copula-based volatility models. In L. Bauwens, C. Hafner, and S. Laurent (Eds.), Handbook of Volatility Models and Their Applications, pp. 293–315. John Wiley & Sons.

Hendershott, T., C. Jones, and A. Menkveld (2010). Does algorithmic trading improve liquidity? Working Paper.

Hendershott, T. and R. Riordan (2009). Algorithmic trading and information. NET Institute, Working paper #09–08, Berkeley.

Henneke, J. S., S. T. Rachev, F. J. Fabozzi, and M. Nikolov (2011). MCMC-based estimation of Markov switching ARMA-GARCH models. Applied Economics 43, 259–271.

Hentschel, L. (1995). All in the family. Nesting symmetric and asymmetric GARCH models. Journal of Financial Economics 39, 71–104.

Higgins, M. L. and A. K. Bera (1992). A class of nonlinear ARCH models. International Economic Review 33, 137–158.

Hillebrand, E. (2005). Neglecting parameter changes in GARCH models. Journal of Econometrics 129, 121–138.

Hjort, N. and I. K. Glad (1995). Nonparametric density estimation with parametric start. The Annals of Statistics 23, 882–904.

Hoffman, D. and A. R. Pagan (1989). Post-sample prediction tests for generalized method of moment estimators. Oxford Bulletin of Economics & Statistics 51, 333–343.

Hong, H. and B. Preston (2005). Nonnested model selection criteria. Stanford University, Department of Economics, Working paper, Stanford.

Huang, X. and G. Tauchen (2005). The relative contribution of jumps to total price variance. Journal of Financial Econometrics 3, 456–499.

Ichimura, H. (1993). Semiparametric least squares (SLS) and weighted SLS estimation of single-index models. Journal of Econometrics 58, 71–120.

Ikeda, N. and S. Watanabe (1981). Stochastic differential equations and diffusion processes. North Holland: Kodansha.

Ishihara, T. and Y. Omori (2011). Efficient Bayesian estimation of a multivariate stochastic volatility model with cross leverage and heavy-tailed errors. Computational Statistics and Data Analysis (in press). Available online 27 July 2010.

Itkin, A. and P. Carr (2010). Pricing swaps and options on quadratic variation under stochastic time change models-discrete observations case. Review of Derivative Research 13, 141–176.

Jackwerth, J. and M. Rubinstein (1996). Recovering probability distributions from contemporaneous security prices. The Journal of Finance 51, 1611–1631.

Jacod, J. (2007). Statistics and high-frequency data. Lecture Notes, SEMSTAT in La Manga (Spain) Availability: ETH/Paris Summer School (in press).

Jacod, J. (2008). Asymptotic properties of realized power variations and associated functions of semimartingales. Stochastic Processes and Their Applications 118, 517–559.

Jacod, J., C. Kluppelberg, and G. Muller (2010). Testing for uncorrelation or for functional relationship between price and volatility jumps. working paper.

Jacod, J., Y. Li, P. A. Mykland, M. Podolskij, and M. Vetter (2009). Microstructure noise in the continuous case: The pre-averaging approach. Stochastic Processes and Their Applications 119, 2249–2276.

Jacod, J., M. Podolskij, and M. Vetter (2010). Limit theorems for moving averages of discretized processes plus noise. Annals of Statistics 38, 1478–1545.

Jacod, J. and P. Protter (1998). Asymptotic error distributions for the euler method for stochastic differential equations. The Annals of Probability 26, 267–307.

Jacod, J. and A. Shiryaev (2003). Limit Theorems for Stochastic Processes (2nd ed.) Berlin: Springer-Verlag.

Jacod, J. and V. Todorov (2009). Testing for common arrival of jumps for discretely observed multidimensional processes. Annals of Statistics 37, 1792–1838.

Jacod, J. and V. Todorov (2010). Do price and volatility jump together? Annals of Applied Probability 20, 1425–1469.

Jacquier, A. and S. Slaoui (2007). Variance dispersion and correlation swaps.

Jacquier, E., N. Polson, and P. Rossi (1994). Bayesian analysis of stochastic volatility models (with discussion). Journal of Business and Economic Statistics 12, 371–417.

Jacquier, E., N. Polson, and P. Rossi (2004). Bayseian analysis of stochastic volatility models with fat tails and correlated errors. Journal of Econometrics 122, 185–212.

Jagannathan, R. and T. Ma (2003). Risk reduction in large portfolios: Why imposing the wrong constraints helps. The Journal of Finance 58, 1651–1684.

James, W. and C. Stein (1956). Estimation with quadratic loss. In Proceedings of the Fourth Berkeley Symposium on Mathematical Statistics and Probability: held at the Statistical Laboratory, University of California, June 30-July 30, 1960, pp. 361. University of California Press, Berkeley.

Jarrow, R. A. and E. R. Rosenfeld (1984). Jump risks and the intertemporal capital asset pricing model. Journal of Business 57, 337–351.

Jiang, G. J. and R. C. Oomen (2008). Testing for jumps when asset prices are observed with noise-A "swap variance" approach. Journal of Econometrics 144, 352–370.

Jiang, G. J. and Y. S. Tian (2005). The model-free implied volatility and its information content. Review of Financial Studies 18, 1305–42.

Jin, X. and J. Maheu (2010). Modelling realized covariances and returns. Working Papers.

Joe, H. (1996). Families, of m-variate distributions with given margins and m(m-1)/2 bivariate dependence parameters. In L. Rüschendorf, B. Schweitzer, and

M. Taylor (Eds.), Distributions with Fixed Marginals and Related Topics. Lecture Notes–Monograph Series, Vol. 28. Hayward, CA: Institute of Mathematical Statistics.

Joe, H. (1997). Multivariate models and dependence concepts. London, New York: Chapman and Hall/CRC.

Joe, H. (2005). Asymptotic efficiency of the two-stage estimation method for copula-based models. Journal of Multivariate Analysis 94, 401–419.

Joe, H. and J. J. Xu (1996). The estimation method of inference functions for margins for multivariate models. Technical report, Technical Report no. 166, Department of Statistics, University of British Columbia.

Johannes, M. (2004). The statistical and economic role of jumps in continuous-time interest rate models. Journal of Finance 59, 227–260.

Jondeau, E. and M. Rockinger (2003). Conditional volatility, skewness and kurtosis: existence, persistence and comovements. Journal of Economic Dynamics and Control 27, 1699–1737.

Jondeau, E. and M. Rockinger (2006). The copula-GARCH model of conditional dependencies: An international stock market application. Journal of International Money and Finance 25, 827–853.

Jondeau, E. and M. Rockinger (2009). The impact of news on higher moments. Journal of Financial Econometrics 7, 77–105.

Jorion, P. (1995). Predicting volatility in the foreign exchange market. Journal of Finance 50, 507–528.

Jorion, P. (1996). Risk and turnover in the foreign exchange market. In J. Frankel, G. Galli, and A. Giovanni (Eds.), The Microstructure of Foreign Exchange Markets. The University of Chicago Press.

Jungbacker, B. and S. J. Koopman (2007). Monte Carlo estimation for nonlinear non-Gaussian state space models. Biometrika 94, 827–839.

Kallsen, J. and M. Taqqu (1998). Option pricing in ARCH-type models. Mathematical Finance 8, 13–26.

Kalnina, I. (2011). Subsampling high frequency data. Journal of Econometrics 161, 262–283.

Kalnina, I. and O. Linton (2008). Estimating quadratic variation consistently in the presence of endogenous and diurnal measurement error. Journal of Econometrics 147, 47–59.

Karatzas, I. and S. Shreve (2005). Brownian Motion and Stochastic Calculus. New York: Springer-Verlag.

Kasa, K. (1992). Common Stochastic Trends in International Stock Markets. Journal of Monetary Economics 29, 95–124.

Kaufmann, S. and S. Frühwirth-Schnatter (2002). Bayesian analysis of switching ARCH models. Journal of Time Series Analysis 23, 425–458.

Kaufmann, S. and M. Scheicher (2006). A switching ARCH model for the German DAX index. Studies in Nonlinear Dynamics & Econometrics 10, Article 3.

Keane, M. and D. Runkle (1990). Testing the rationality of price forecasts: New evidence from panel data. American Economic Review 80, 714–735.

Kim, C. (1994). Dynamic linear models with Markov switching. Journal of Econometrics 60, 1–22.

Kim, C.-J. and C. R. Nelson (1999). Has the U.S. economy become more stable? A Bayesian approach based on a Markov-switching model of the business cycle. The Review of Economics and Statistics 81, 608–616.

Kim, S., N. Shephard, and S. Chib (1998). Stochastic volatility: Likelihood inference and comparison with ARCH models. Review of Economic Studies 65, 361–393.

Kim, W. and O. Linton (2004). The LIVE method for generalized additive volatility models. Econometric Theory 20, 1094–1139.

Kinnebrock, S. and M. Podolskij (2008). Estimation of the quadratic covariation matrix in noisy diffusion models. Technical report, Oxford-Man Institute, University of Oxford.

Klaassen, F. (2002). Improving GARCH volatility forecasts with regime–switching GARCH. Empirical Economics 27, 363–394.

Kleidon, A. and I. Werner (1996). U.K. and U.S. trading of British cross-listed stocks: an intraday analysis of market integration. Review of Financial Studies 9, 619–684.

Kobayashi, M. and X. Shi (2005). Testing for EGARCH against stochastic volatility models. Journal of Time Series Analysis 26, 135–150.

Kock, A. B. and T. Teräsvirta (2011). Forecasting with nonlinear time series models. In M. P. Clements, and D. F. Hendry (Eds.), Oxford Handbook of Economic Forecasting, pp. 61–87. Oxford: Oxford University Press.

Koopman, S. J. (1993). Disturbance smoother for state space models. Biometrika 80, 117–126.

Koopman, S. J., B. Jungbacker, and E. Hol (2005). Forecasting daily variability of the S &P 100 stock index using historical, realised and implied volatility measurements. Journal of Applied Econometrics 20, 311–323.

Koopman, S. J., N. Shephard, and D. Creal (2009). Testing the assumptions behind importance sampling. Journal of Econometrics 149, 2–11.

Koopman, S. J., N. Shephard, and J. A. Doornik (2008). SsfPack 3.0: Statistical algorithms for models in state space form. London: Timberlake Consultants Ltd.

Koutmos, G. and G. G. Booth (1995). Asymmetric volatility transmission in international stock markets. Journal of International Money and Finance 14, 747–762.

Kraft, D. and R. Engle (1982). Autoregressive conditional heteroskedasticity in multiple time series. Unpublished manuscript, Department of Economics, UCSD.

Krämer, W. (2008). Long memory with Markov–switching GARCH. Economics Letters 99, 390–392.

Krämer, W. and B. Tameze-Azamo (2007). Structural change and estimated persistence in the GARCH(1,1)-model. Economics Letters 97, 17–23.

Krause, J. and M. S. Paolella (2011). Augmented likelihood estimation for mixture models. Working Paper, University of Zurich.

Kristensen, D. (2010). Nonparametric filtering of the realized spot volatility: A kernel-based approach. Econometric Theory 26, 60–93.

Kristensen, D. and O. Linton (2004). Consistent standard errors for target variance approach to GARCH estimation. Econometric Theory 20, 990–993.

Kroner, K. F. and V. K. Ng (1998). Modelling asymmetric comovements of asset returns. The Review of Financial Studies 11, 817–844.

Kuester, K., S. Mittnik, and M. S. Paolella (2006). Value-at-Risk prediction: A comparison of alternative strategies. Journal of Financial Econometrics 4, 53–89.

Kupiec, P. H. (1995). Techniques for verifying the accuracy of risk management models. Journal of Derivatives 3, 73–84.

Kyj, L. M., B. Ostdiek, and K. Ensor (2009). Covariance Estimation in Dynamic Portfolio Optimization: A Realized Single Factor Model. Working paper series, Humbolt-Universität zu Berlin.

Lahaye, B. E. (1992). The likelihood ratio test under nonstandard conditions: Testing the Markov switching model of GNP. Journal of Applied Econometrics 7, S61–S82.

Lahaye, J., S. Laurent, and C. Neely (2011). Jumps, cojumps and macro announcements. Journal of Applied Econometrics 26, 893–921.

Lamoureux, C. G. and W. D. Lastrapes (1990). Persistence in variance, structural change, and the garch model. Journal of Business and Economic Statistics 8, 225–234.

Lange, T. and A. Rahbek (2009). An introduction to regime switching time series models. In T. G. Andersen, R. A. Davis, J.-P. Kreiß, and T. Mikosch (Eds.), Handbook of Financial Time Series, pp. 871–887. Berlin: Springer.

Lanne, M. (2006). A mixture multiplicative error model for realized volatility. Journal of Financial Econometrics 4, 594–616.

Lanne, M. and P. Saikkonen (2005). Nonlinear GARCH models for highly persistent volatility. Econometrics Journal 8, 251–276.

Lanne, M. and P. Saikkonen (2007). A multivariate generalized orthogonal factor GARCH model. Journal of Business and Economic Statistics 25, 61–75.

Laurent, S. (2009). G@RCH 6, Estimating and Forecasting ARCH Models. Timberlake Consultants.

Laurent, S., J. Rombouts, and F. Violante (2011). On the forecasting accuracy of multivariate GARCH models. Journal of Applied Econometrics. 26, n/a. doi: 10.1002/jae.1248.

Laurent, S., J. V. K. Rombouts, and F. Violante (2009). On loss functions and ranking forecasting performances of multivariate volatility models. Working paper 2009s-45, Cirano.

LeBaron, B. (2001). Stochastic volatility as a simple generator of financial power-laws and long memory. Quantitative Finance 1, 621–31.

Ledford, A. W. and J. A. Tawn (1997). Statistics for near independence in multivariate extreme values. Biometrika 55, 169–187.

Ledoit, O., P. Santa-Clara, and M. Wolf (2003). Flexible multivariate GARCH modeling with an application to international stock markets. Review of Economics and Statistics 85, 735–747.

Ledoit, O. and M. Wolf (2003). Improved estimation of the covariance matrix of stock returns with an application to portfolio selection. Journal of Empirical Finance 10, 603–621.

Ledoit, O. and M. Wolf (2004a). A well-conditioned estimator for large-dimensional covariance matrices. Journal of Multivariate Analysis 88, 365–411.

Ledoit, O. and M. Wolf (2004b). Honey, i shrunk the sample covariance matrix. The Journal of Portfolio Management 30, 110–119.

Lee, H.-T. (2009). A copula–based regime–switching GARCH model for optimal futures hedging. Journal of Futures Markets 29, 946–972.

Lee, J. and B. Brorsen (1997). A non-nested test of GARCH vs. EGARCH models. Applied Economics Letters 4, 765–768.

Lee, S. S. and J. Hannig (2010). Detecting jumps from Lévy jump diffusion processes. Journal of Financial Economics 96, 271–290.

Lee, S. S. and P. A. Mykland (2008). Jumps in financial markets: A new nonparametric test and jump dynamics. Review of Financial Studies 21, 2535–2563.

Lee, T. and W. Ploberger (2011). Rate optimal tests for jumps in diffusion processes. Working paper.

Lee, T.-H., H. White, and C. W. J. Granger (1993). Testing for neglected nonlinearity in time series models: A comparison of neural network methods and alternative tests. Journal of Econometrics 56, 269–290.

León, Á., J. Nave, and G. Rubio (2007). The relationship between risk and expected return in europe. Journal of Banking and Finance 31, 495–512.

Lepingle, D. (1976). La variation d'ordre p des semimartingales. Zeitshrift fur Wahrscheinlichkeitstheorie und Verwandte Gebiete 36, 295–316.

Lepski, O. (1990). On a problem of adaptive estimation in Gaussian white noise. Theory of Probability and Applications 35, 454–470.

Levine, M. and J. Li (2007). Local instrumental variable (LIVE) method for the generalized additive-interactive nonlinear volatility model. Working paper, Department of Statistics, Purdue University.

Li, C. W. and W. K. Li (1996). On a double threshold autoregressive heteroskedasticity time series model. Journal of Applied Econometrics 11, 253–274.

Li, D. X. and H. J. Turtle (2000). Semiparametric ARCH models: an estimating function approach. Journal of Business and Economic Statistics 18, 174–186.

Li, Q. and J. S. Racine (2007). Nonparametric Econometrics: Theory and Practice. New Jersey: Princeton University Press.

Li, W., S. Ling, and M. McAleer (2002). Recent theoretical results for time series models with GARCH errors. Journal of Economic Surveys 16, 245–269.

Li, Y. and P. A. Mykland (2007). Are volatility estimators robust to modeling assumptions? Bernouilli 13, 601–622.

Liesenfeld, R. and J.-F. Richard (2003). Univariate and multivariate stochastic volatility models: Estimation and diagnostics. Journal of Empirical Finance 10, 505–531.

Liesenfeld, R. and J.-F. Richard (2006). Classical and Bayesian analysis of univariate and multivariate stochastic volatility models. Econometric Reviews 25, 335–360.

Liesenfeld, R. and J.-F. Richard (2008). Improving MCMC, using efficient importance sampling. Computational Statistics and Data Analysis 53, 272–288.

Lin, J. and C. Granger (1994). Model selection for multiperiod forecasts. Journal of Forecasting 13, 1–9.

Lin, W. L., R. F. Engle, and T. Ito (1994). Do bulls and bears move across the borders? International transmission of stock returns and volatility. Review of Financial Studies 7, 507–538.

Ling, S. and W. K. Li (1997). Diagnostic checking of nonlinear multivariate time series with multivariate ARCH errors. Journal of Time Series Analysis 18, 447–464.

Ling, S. and M. McAleer (2000). Statistics and Finance: An Interface, Chapter Testing GARCH versus E-GARCH, pp. 226–242. London: Imperial College Press.

Ling, S. and M. McAleer (2002). Stationarity and the existence of moments of a family of GARCH processes. Journal of Econometrics 106, 109–117.

Ling, S. and M. McAleer (2003). On adaptive estimating nonstationary ARMA models with GARCH errors. The Annals of Statistics 31, 642–674.

Ling, S. and H. Tong (2005). Testing for a linear MA model against threshold MA models. Annals of Statistics 33, 2529–2552.

Ling, S., H. Tong, and D. Li (2007). Ergodicity and invertibility of threshold moving average models. Bernoulli 13, 161–168.

Lintner, J. (1965). The valuation of risk assets and the selection of risky investments in stock portfolios and capital budgets. The Review of Economics and Statistics 47, 13–37.

Linton, O. B. (1993). Adaptive estimation in ARCH models. Econometric Theory 9, 539–569.

Linton, O. B. (1997). Efficient estimation of additive nonparametric regression models. Biometrika 84, 469–473.

Linton, O. B. (2009). Semiparametric and nonparametric ARCH modeling. In T. G. Andersen, R. A. Davis, J.-P. Kreiß, and T. Mikosch (Eds.), Handbook of Financial Time Series, pp. 157–167. Berlin, Germany: Springer.

Linton, O. B. and E. Mammen (2005). Estimating semiparametric ARCH(∞) models by kernel smoothing methods. Econometrica 73, 771–836.

Linton, O. B. and J. P. Nielsen (1995). A kernel method of estimating structured nonparametric regression based on marginal integration. Biometrika 82, 93–100.

Linton, O. B. and B. Perron (2003). The shape of the risk premium: evidence from a semiparametric generalized autoregressive conditional heteroscedasticity model. Journal of Business and Economic Statistics 21, 354–367.

Linton, O. B. and Y. Yan (2011). Semi- and nonparametric ARCH processes. Journal of Probability and Statistics, 1–17.

Liu, C. and J. M. Maheu (2009). Forecasting realized volatility: A Bayesian model-averaging approach. Journal of Applied Econometrics 24, 709–733.

Liu, J.-C. (2006). Stationarity of a Markov–switching GARCH model. Journal of Financial Econometrics 4, 573–593.

Liu, J.-C. (2007). Stationarity for a Markov–switching Box–Cox transformed threshold GARCH process. Statistics and Probability Letters 77, 1428–1438.

Liu, J.-C. (2009a). Integrated Markov–switching GARCH processes. Econometric Theory 25, 1277–1288.

Liu, Q. (2009b). On portfolio optimization: How and when do we benefit from high-frequency data? Journal of Applied Econometrics 24, 560–582.

Lo, A. A. MacKinlay (1990). An econometric analysis of nonsynchronous trading. Journal of Econometrics 45, 181–211.

Lo, A. W. (1991). Long-term memory in stock market prices. Econometrica 59, 1279–1313.

Lockwood, L. J. and S. C. Linn (1990). An examination of stock market return volatility during overnight and intraday periods 1964–1989. Journal of Finance 45, 591–601.

Long, X., L. Su, and A. Ullah (2011). Estimation and forecasting of dynamic conditional covariance: A semiparametric multivariate model. Journal of Business and Economic Statistics 29, 109–125.

Longin, F. and B. Solnik (1995). Is the correlation in international equity returns constant: 1960–1990? Journal of International Money and Finance 14, 3–26.

Longin, F. and B. Solnik (2001). Extreme correlation of international equity markets. Journal of Finance 56, 649–76.

Lopez, J. (1999). Regulatory evaluation of value-at-risk models. Journal of Risk 1, 37–64.

Lopez, J. (2001). Evaluating the predictive accuracy of volatility models. Journal of Forecasting 20, 87–109.

Loretan, M. and P. C. B. Phillips (1994). Testing the covariance stationarity of heavy-tailed time series: An overview of the theory with applications to several financial datasets. Journal of Empirical Finance 1, 211–248.

Loynes, R. M. (1968). On the concept of the spectrum for nonstationary processes. Journal of the Royal Statistical Society: Series B (Statistical Methodology) 30, 1–30.

Lubrano, M. (2001). Smooth transition GARCH models: A Bayesian perspective. Recherches Economiques de Louvain 67, 257–287.

Lundbergh, S. and T. Teräsvirta (2002). Evaluating GARCH models. Journal of Econometrics 110, 417–435.

Lütkepohl, H. (2005). New Introduction to Multiple Time Series Analysis. Berlin Heidelberg: Springer.

Luukkonen, R., P. Saikkonen, and T. Teräsvirta (1988). Testing linearity against smooth transition autoregressive models. Biometrika 75, 491–499.

Lynch, P. and G. Zumbach (2003). Market heterogeneities and the causal structure of volatility. Quantitative Finance 3, 320–331.

Madan, D. (2001). Handbook of Mathematical Finance: Option Pricing, Interest Rates and Risk Management, pp. 105–153. Cambridge, UK: Cambridge University Press.

Malliavin, P. and M. E. Mancino (2009). Fourier series method for nonparametric estimation of multivariate volatility. The Annals of Statistics 37, 1983–2010.

Mammen, E., O. B. Linton, and J. Nielson (1999). The existence and asymptotic properties of a backfitting projection algorithm under weak conditions. The Annals of Statistics 27, 1443–1490.

Mancini, C. (2001). Disentangling the jumps of the diffusion in a geometric jumping brownian motion. Giornale dell'Istituto Italiano degli Attuari LXIV, 19–47.

Mancini, C. (2004). Estimation of the parameters of jump of a general poisson-diffusion model. Scandinavian Actuarial Journal 1, 42–52.

Mancini, C. (2008). Optimal threshold for the estimator of integrated variance. Working paper.

Mancini, C. (2009). Non-parametric threshold estimation for models with stochastic diffusion coefficient and jumps. Scandinavian Journal of Statistics 36, 270–296.

Mancini, C. (2011a). Speed of convergence of the threshold estimator of integrated variance. Stochastic Processes and Their Applications 121, 845–855.

Mancini, C. (2011b, working paper). Test for the relevance of noise in observed data. Technical report. Available on www.ssrn.com.

Mancini, C. and F. Calvori (2012). Jumps. In L. Bauwens, C. Hafner, and S. Laurent (Eds.), Handbook of Volatility Models and Their Applications, pp. 403–445. John Wiley & Sons.

Mancini, C. and F. Gobbi (2012). Identifying the brownian covariation from the co-jumps given discrete observations. Econometric Theory. http://ideas.repec.org/.

Mancini, C., V. Mattiussi, and R. Renò (2011). Spot volatility estimation using delta sequences. Mimeo. Working paper.

Mancino, M. and S. Sanfelici (2011). Estimating covariance via Fourier method in the presence of asynchronous trading and microstructure noise. Journal of Financial Econometrics 9, 367–408.

Mandelbrot, B. (1963). The variation of certain speculative prices. Journal of Business 36, 394–419.

Mandelbrot, B. and H. Taylor (1967). On the distribution of stock price differences. Operations Research 15, 1057–1062.

Manganelli, S. (2005). Duration, volume and volatility impact of trades. Journal of Financial Markets 8, 377–399.

Manner, H. and O. Reznikonva. Time-varying copulas: A survey. Econometrics Reviews (forthcoming). DOI:10.1080/07474938.2011.608042. Available online 31 Oct 2011.

Marcellino, M., J. Stock, and M. Watson (2006). A comparison of direct and iterated multistep ar methods for forecasting macroeconomic time series. Journal of Econometrics 135, 499–526.

Marcucci, J. (2005). Forecasting stock market volatility with regime–switching GARCH models. Studies in Nonlinear Dynamics & Econometrics 9, Article 6.

Markowitz, H. (1952). Portfolio selection. Journal of Finance 7, 77–91.

Markowitz, H. (1959). Portfolio Selection: Efficient Diversification of Investments. John Wiley.

Markwat, T., E. Kole, and D. van Dijk (2009). Time variation in asset return dependence: Strength or structure? Technical report, ERIM Report Series 2009–052.

Martins-Filho, C., S. Mishra, and A. Ullah (2008). A class of improved parametrically guided nonparametric regression estimators. Econometrics Reviews 27, 542–573.

McAleer, M. (2005). Automated inference and learning in modeling financial volatility. Econometric Theory 21, 232–261.

McAleer, M., F. Chan, and D. Marinova (2007). An econometric analysis of asymmetric volatility: theory and applications to patents. Journal of Econometrics 139, 259–284.

McAleer, A. and M. Medeiros (2008a). A multiple regime smooth transition heterogeneous autoregressive model for long memory and asymmetries. Journal of Econometrics 147, 104–119.

McAleer, M. and M. C. Medeiros (2008b). Realized volatility. A Review Econometric Reviews 27, 10–45.

McConnell, M. M. and G. P. Quiros (2000). Output fluctuations in the United States: What had changed since the early 1980s? American Economic Review 90, 1464–1476.

McCracken, M. (2000). Robust out-of-sample inference. Journal of Econometrics 99, 195–223.

McCracken, M. (2007). Asymptotics for out-of-sample tests of granger causality. Journal of Econometrics 140, 719–752.

McInish, T. H. and R. A. Wood (1992). An analysis of intraday patterns in bid/ask spreads for nyse stocks. Journal of Finance 47, 753–764.

McLachlan, G. J. and D. Peel (2000). Finite Mixture Models. New York: John Wiley & Sons.

McNeil, A. J., R. Frey, and P. Embrechts (2006). Quantitative Risk Management: Concepts, Techniques and Tools. Princeton: Princeton University Press.

McNeil, A. J. and J. Nešlehová (2009). Multivariate Archimedean copulas, d-monotone functions and L1-norm symmetric distributions. Annals of Statistics 37, 3059–3097.

Meddahi, N. (2002). A theoretical comparison between integrated and realized volatility. Journal of Applied Econometrics 17, 479–508.

Medeiros, M. C. and A. Veiga (2009). Modeling multiple regimes in financial volatility with a flexible coefficient GARCH(1,1) models. Econometric Theory 25, 117–161.

Meitz, M. and P. Saikkonen (2008). Ergodicity, mixing, and existence of moments of a class of Markov models with applications to GARCH and ACD models. Econometric Theory 24, 1291–1320.

Meitz, M. and P. Saikkonen (2011). Parameter estimation in nonlinear AR-GARCH models. Econometric Theory 27, 1236–1278.

Melino, A. and S. Turnbull (1990). Pricing foreign currency options with stochastic volatility. Journal of Econometrics 45, 239–265.

Melvin, M. and X. Yin (2000). Public information arrival, exchange rate volatility and quote frequency. The Economic Journal 110, 644–661.

Mercurio, D. and V. Spokoiny (2004). Statistical inference for time-inhomogenous volatility models. Annals of Statistics 32, 577–602.

Merton, R. (1980). On estimating the expected return on the market: An exploratory investigation. Journal of Financial Economics 8, 323–361.

Merton, R. C. (1973). An intertemporal capital asset pricing model. Econometrica 41, 867–887.

Merton, R. C. (1976a). The impact on option pricing of specification error in the underlying stock price returns. Journal of Finance 31, 333–350.

Merton, R. C. (1976b). Option pricing when underlying stock returns are discontinuous. Journal of Financial Economics 3, 125–144.

Mikosch, T. and C. St ăric ă (2004). Nonstationarities in financial time series, the long-range dependence, and the IGARCH effects. The Review of Economics and Statistics 86, 378–390.

Mincer, J. and V. Zarnowitz (1969). The evaluation of economic forecasts. In J. Mincer (Ed.), Economic Forecasts and Expectations. New York: Columbia University Press.

Mishra, S., L. Su, and A. Ullah (2010). Semiparametric estimator of time series conditional variance. Journal of Business and Economic Statistics 28, 256–274.

Mittnik, S. and M. S. Paolella (2000). Conditional density and Value-at-Risk prediction of Asian currency exchange rates. Journal of Forecasting 19, 313–333.

Morgan J.P. (1996). Riskmetrics Technical Document (4th ed.) New York: J.P.Morgan.

Morillas, P. M. (2005). A method to obtain new copulas from a given one. Metrika 61, 169–184.

Muller, U., M. Dacorogna, R. Davé, R. Olsen, O. Pictet, and J. von Weizsacker (1997). Volatilities of different time resolutions-analyzing the dynamics of market components. Journal of Empirical Finance 4, 213–239.

Murata, Y. (1977). Mathematics for Stability and Optimization of Economic Systems. New York: Academic Press.

Mykland, A. and N. Shephard (2010). Econometric analysis of financial jumps using efficient bipower variation.

Mykland, P. and L. Zhang (2006). Anova for diffusions and ito processes. The Annals of Statistics 34, 1931–1963.

Neely, C. J. (1999). Target zones and conditional volatility: The role of realignments. Journal of Empirical Finance 6, 177–192.

Nelsen, R. (1999). An Introduction to Copulas, Lecture Notes in Statistics. New York: Springer-Verlag New York, Inc.

Nelson, C. R. and C. I. Plosser (1982). Trends and random walks in macroeconomic time series: Some evidence and implications. Journal of Monetary Economics 10, 139–162.

Nelson, D. B. (1990). Stationarity and persistence in the GARCH (1,1) model. Econometric Theory 6, 318–334.

Nelson, D. B. (1991a). ARCH models as diffusion approximations. Journal of Econometrics 45, 7–38.

Nelson, D. B. (1991b). Conditional heteroskedasticity in asset returns: A new approach. Econometrica 59, 347–370.

Nelson, D. B. and C. Q. Cao (1992). Inequality constraints in the univariate GARCH model. Journal of Business and Economic Statistics 10, 229–235.

Neumann, M. and R. von Sachs (1997). Wavelet thresholding in anisotropic function classes and application to adaptive estimation of evolutionary spectra. The Annals of Statistics 25, 38–76.

Newey, W. K. (1994). Kernel estimation of partial means and a general variance estimator. Econometric Theory 10, 233–253.

Newey, W. K. and D. McFadden (1994). Large sample estimation and hypothesis testing. In R. F. Engle, and D. McFadden (Eds.), Handbook of Econometrics, Vol. 4, Chapter 36, pp. 2111–2245. North–Holland.

Newey, W. K. and D. G. Steigerwald (1997). Asymptotic bias for quasi-maximum-likelihood estimators in conditional heteroskedasticity models. Econometrica 65, 587–599.

Newey, W. K. and K. D. West (1987). A simple, positive semi-definite, heterosketasticity and autocorrelation consistent covariance matrix. Econometrica 55, 703–708.

Ng, A. (2000). Volatility Spillover Effects from Japan and the US to the Pacific-Basin. Journal of International Money and Finance 19, 207–233.

Ngo, H. L. and S. Ogawa (2009). A central limit theorem for the functional estimation of the spot volatility. Monte Carlo Methods and Applications 15, 353–380.

Nguyen, T. M. (2007). A new efficient algorithm for the analysis with non-linear and non-Gaussian state space models. Master's thesis, Department of Econometrics & O.R., FEWEB, VU University Amsterdam.

Noh, J., R. Engle, and A. Kane (1994). Forecasting volatility and option prices of the S&P500 index. Journal of Derivatives 2, 17–30.

Noss, J. (2007). The econometrics of optimal execution in an order-driven market. Technical report, Nuffield College, Oxford University, Master's Thesis.

Okimoto, T. (2008). New evidence of asymmetric dependence structures in international equity markets. Journal of Financial and Quantitative Analysis 43, 787–815.

Omori, Y., S. Chib, N. Shephard, and J. Nakajima (2007). Stochastic volatility with leverage: Fast and efficient likelihood inference. Journal of Econometrics 140, 425–449.

Omori, Y. and T. Ishihara (2012). Multivariate stochastic volatility models. In L. Bauwens, C. Hafner, and S. Laurent (Eds.), Handbook of Volatility Models and Their Applications, pp. 175–197. John Wiley & Sons.

Omori, Y. and T. Watanabe (2008). Block sampler and posterior mode estimation for asymmetric stochastic volatility models. Computational Statistics & Data Analysis 52, 2892–2910.

Oomen, R. (2010). High-dimensional covariance forecasting for short intra-day horizons. Quantitative Finance 10, 1–13.

Opsomer, J. D. and D. Ruppert (1997). Fitting a bivariate additive model by local polynomial regression. The Annals of Statistics 25, 186–211.

Osiewalski, J. (2009). New hybrid models of multivariate volatility (a Bayesian perspective). Przeglad Statystycny 56, 15–22.

Osiewalski, J. and A. Pajor (2009). Bayesian analysis for hybrid MSF-SBEKK models of multivariate volatility. Central European Journal of Economic Modelling and Econometrics 1, 179–202.

Pagan, A. (1996). The econometrics of financial markets. Journal of Empirical Finance 3, 15–102.

Pagan, A. and Y. S. Hong (1991). Nonparametric estimation and the risk premium. In W. A. Barnett, J. Powell, and G. E. Tauchen (Eds.), Nonparametric and Semiparametric Methods in Econometrics and Statistics, pp. 51–75. Cambridge: Cambridge University Press.

Pagan, A. and G. Schwert (1990). Alternative models for conditional stock volatility. Journal of Econometrics 45, 267–290.

Pagan, A. and A. Ullah (1988). The econometric analysis of models with risk premium. Journal of Applied Econometrics 3, 87–105.

Pagan, A. and A. Ullah (1999). Nonparametric Econometrics. Cambridge: Cambridge University Press.

Page, C. H. (1952). Instantaneous power spectrum. Journal of Applied Physics 23, 103–106.

Pakel, C., N. Shephard, and K. Sheppard (2010). Nuisance parameters, composite likelihoods and a panel of GARCH models. Statistica Sinica. forthcoming.

Palandri, A. (2006). Consistent realized covariance for asynchronous observations contaminated by market microstructure noise. Unpublished Manuscript.

Palm, F. (1996). GARCH models of volatility. In G. Maddala, and C. Rao (Eds.), Handbook of Statistics, pp. 209–240. Amsterdam: Elsevier Science.

Pantula, S. (1986). Modelling the persistence of conditional variance: A comment. Econometric Reviews 5, 71–73.

Pantula, S. (1989). Testing for unit roots in time series data. Econometric Theory 5, 256–271.

Paolella, M. S. (2010). ALRIGHT: Asymmetric large-scale (I)GARCH with hetero-tails. Working Paper, University of Zurich.

Paolella, M. S. (2011). Multivariate asset return prediction with mixture models. University of Zurich.

Paolella, M. S. and S. C. Steude (2008). Risk Prediction: A DWARF-like Approach. Journal of Risk Model Validation 2, 25–43.

Paolella, M. S. and L. Taschini (2008). An Econometric Analysis of Emission Trading Allowances. Journal of Banking and Finance 32, 2022–2032.

Park, S. and O. Linton (2011a). Frequency domain estimator of quadratic covariation matrix for noisy and asynchronous high frequency data. Working Paper, London School of Economics.

Park, S. and O. Linton (2012). Realized volatility: Theory and application. In L. Bauwens, C. Hafner, and S. Laurent (Eds.), Handbook of Volatility Models and Their Applications, pp. 319–345. John Wiley & Sons.

Parke, W. R. and G. A. Waters (2007). An evolutionary game theory explanation of ARCH effects. Journal of Economic Dynamics and Control 31, 2234–2262.

Parkinson, M. (1980). The extreme value method for estimating the variance of the rate of returns. Journal of Business 53, 61–68.

Patton, A. J. (2004). On the out-of-sample importance of skewness and asymmetric dependence for asset allocation. Journal of Financial Econometrics 2, 130–168.

Patton, A. J. (2006a). Estimation of multivariate models for time series of possibly different lengths. Journal of Applied Econometrics 21, 147–173.

Patton, A. J. (2006b). Modelling asymmetric exchange rate dependence. International Economic Review 47, 527–556.

Patton, A. J. (2009). Copula-based models for financial time series. In T. G. Andersen, R. A. Davis, J.-P. Kreiß, and T. Mikosch (Eds.), Handbook of Financial Time Series, pp. 767–785. Berlin: Springer.

Patton, A. J. (2011). Volatility forecast comparison using imperfect volatility proxies. Journal of Econometrics 160, 246–256.

Patton, A. J. and K. Sheppard (2009a). Evaluating volatility and correlation forecasts. In T. Andersen, R. Davis, J.-P. Kreiss, and T. Mikosch (Eds.), Handbook of Financial Time Series. Springer Verlag.

Patton, A. J. and K. Sheppard (2009b). Optimal combinations of realised volatility estimators. International Journal of Forecasting 25, 218–238.

Péguin-Feissolle, A. (1999). A comparison of the power of some tests for conditional heteroscedasticity. Economics Letters 63, 5–17.

Pelletier, D. (2006). Regime switching for dynamic correlations. Journal of Econometrics 131, 445–473.

Perez-Quiros, G. and A. Timmermann (2001). Business Cycle Asymmetries in Stock Returns: Evidence from Higher Order Moments and Conditional Densities. Journal of Econometrics 103, 259–306.

Perron, P. (1989). The great crash, the oil price shock and the unit root hypothesis. Econometrica 57, 1361–1401.

Peters, R. T. and R. G. de Vilder (2006). Testing the continuous semimartingale hypothesis for the s &p 500. Journal of Business & Economic Statistics 24, 444–454.

Philipov, A. and M. E. Glickman (2006a). Factor multivariate stochastic volatility via Wishart processes. Econometric Reviews 25, 311–334.

Philipov, A. and M. E. Glickman (2006b). Multivariate stochastic volatility via Wishart processes. Journal of Business and Economic Statistics 24, 313–328.

Phillips, P. C. B. (1987). Time series regression with a unit root. Econometrica 55, 277–301.

Phillips, P. C. B. and J. Yu (2009a). A two-stage realized volatility approach to estimation of diffusion processes with discrete data. Journal of Econometrics 150, 139–150.

Phillips, P. C. B. and J. Yu (2009b). ML estimation of continuous time models. In T. G. Andersen, R. A. Davis, J. P. Kreiss, and T. Mikosch (Eds.), Handbook of Financial Time Series, pp. 497–527. Springer.

Pigorsch, C. and R. Stelzer (2009). A multivariate Ornstein-Uhlenbeck type stochastic volatility model. unpubliched manuscript.

Podolskij, M. and M. Vetter (2009a). Bipower-type estimation in a noisy diffusion setting. Stochastic Processes and Their Applications 119, 2803–2831.

Podolskij, M. and M. Vetter (2009b). Estimation of volatility functionals in the simultaneous presence of microstructure noise and jumps. Bernoulli 15, 634–658.

Podolskij, M. and D. Ziggel (2010). New tests for jumps in semimartingale models. Statistical Inference for Stochastic Processes 13, 15–41.

Polzehl, J. and V. Spokoiny (2006). Varying coefficient GARCH versus local constant volatility modelling: Comparison of the predictive power. SFB 649 Discussion Papers SFB649DP2006–033, Humboldt University.

Poskitt, D. S. and S.-H. Chung (1996). Markov chain models, time series analysis and extreme value theory. Advances in Applied Probability 28, 405–425.

Priestley, M. B. (1965). Evolutionary spectra and nonstationary processes. Journal of the Royal Statistical Society: Series B (Statistical Methodology) 27, 204–237.

Protter, P. (1990). Stochastic Integration and Differential Equations. A New Approach. Berlin Heidelberg, Germany: Springer-Verlag.

Protter, P. (2005). Stochastic integration and differential equations. Springer.

Rabemananjara, R. and J. M. Zakoïan (1993). Threshold ARCH models and asymmetries in volatility. Journal of Applied Econometrics 8, 31–49.

Ramchand, L. and R. Susmel (1998). Volatility and cross correlation across major stock markets. Journal of Empirical Finance 17, 581–610.

Rangel, J. G. and R. F. Engle (2009). The factor-spline-GARCH model for high and low frequency correlations. Banco de Mexico Working Papers 2009–03.

Rappoport, P. and L. Reichlin (1989). Segmented trends and nonstationary time series. The Economic Journal 99, 168–177.

Renó, R. (2003). A closer look at the Epps effect. International Journal of Theoretical and Applied Finance 6, 87–102.

Renó, R. (2006). Nonparametric estimation of stochastic volatility models. Economics Letters 90, 390–395.

Revuz, D. and M. Yor (2001). Continuous martingales and Brownian motion. Germany: Springer.

Richard, J.-F. and W. Zhang (2007). Efficient high-dimensional importance sampling. Journal of Econometrics 141, 1385–1411.

Rissanen, J. (1978). Modeling by shortest data description. Automatica 14, 465–471.

Rockinger, M. and E. Jondeau (2001). Conditional Dependency of Financial Series: An Application of Copulas. HEC Department of Finance Working Paper No. 723.

Rockinger, M. and E. Jondeau (2002). Entropy densities with an application to autoregressive conditional skewness and kurtosis. Journal of Econometrics 106, 119–142.

Rodriguez, J. (2007). Measuring financial contagion: A copula approach. Journal of Empirical Finance 14, 401–423.

Roll, R. (1984). A simple model of the implicit bid-ask spread in an efficient market. The Journal of Finance 39, 1127–1139.

Rombouts, J. and L. Stentoft (2011). Multivariate option pricing with time varying volatility and correlations. Journal of Banking and Finance 35, 2267–2281.

Rombouts, J. V. and L. Stentoft (2010). Option pricing with asymmetric heteroskedastic normal mixture models. CREATES Research Papers 2010–44, School of Economics and Management, University of Aarhus.

Rombouts, J. V. K. and M. Bouaddi (2009). Mixed exponential power asymmetric conditional heteroskedasticity. Studies in Nonlinear Dynamics & Econometrics 13, Article 3.

Rombouts, J. V. K. and L. Stentoft (2009, February). Bayesian Option Pricing Using Mixed Normal Heteroskedasticity Models. CREATES Research Papers 2009–07, School of Economics and Management, University of Aarhus.

Rosenblatt, M. (1952). Remarks on a multivariate transformation. Annals of Mathematical Statistics 23, 470–472.

Ross, S. A. (1976). The arbitrage theory of capital asset pricing. Journal of Economic Theory 13, 341–360.

Rydén, T., T. Teräsvirta, and S. Åsbrink (1998). Stylized facts of daily return series and the hidden Markov model. Journal of Applied Econometrics 13, 217–244.

Sajjad, R., J. Coakley, and J. C. Nankervis (2008). Markov–switching GARCH modelling of Value–at–Risk. Studies in Nonlinear Dynamics & Econometrics 12, Article 7.

Sandmann, G. and S. J. Koopman (1998). Estimation of stochastic volatility models via Monte Carlo maximum likelihood. Journal of Econometrics 87, 271–301.

Savu, C. and M. Trede (2006). Hierearchical Archimedean copulas. Technical report, International Conference on High Frequency, Konstanz.

Scharth, M. and M. Medeiros (2009). Asymmetric effects and long memory in the volatility of dow jones stocks. International Journal of Forecasting 25, 304–327.

Scholes, M. and J. Williams (1977). Estimating betas from nonsynchronous data. Journal of Financial Economics 5, 181–212.

Schwarz, G. (1978). Estimating the dimension of a model. Annals of Statistics 6, 461–464.

Schwert, G. (1989a). Business cycles, financial crises, and stock volatility. Carnegie-Rochester Conference on Public Policy 39, 83–126.

Schwert, G. W. (1989b). Why does stock market volatility change over time. The Journal of Finance 44, 1115–1153.

Schwert, M. (2009). Hop, skip and jump-what are modern "jump" tests finding in stock returns? Available on www.ssrn.com.

Schwert, W. (1990). Stock volatility and the crash of '87. Review of Financial Studies 3, 77–102.

Sensier, M. and D. van Dijk (2004). Testing for volatility changes in the U.S. macroeconomic time series. The Review of Economics and Statistics 86, 833–839.

Sentana, E. (1995). Quadratic ARCH models. Review of Economic Studies 62, 639–661.

Severini, T. A. and J. G. Staniswalis (1994). Quasi-likelihood estimation in semiparametric models. Journal of the American Statistical Association 89, 501–511.

Sharapov, I. (1997). Advances in multigrid optimization methods with applications. PhD thesis, Univeristy of California, Los Angeles.

Sharpe, W. (1964). Capital asset prices: A theory of market equilibrium under conditions of risk. Journal of Finance 19, 425–442.

Shephard, N. (1996). Statistical Aspects of ARCH and Stochastic Volatility,. In D. R. Cox, D. V. Hinkley, and O. E. Barndorff-Nielsen (Eds.). Econometrics, Finance and Other Fields, Time Series Models, Chapter 1, pp. 1–67. London: Chapman & Hall.

Shephard, N. (2005). Stochastic volatility: Selected readings. Oxford, UK: Oxford University Press.

Shephard, N. and M. K. Pitt (1997). Likelihood analysis of non-Gaussian measurement time series. Biometrika 84, 653–667.

Shephard, N. and K. Sheppard (2010). Realising the future: Forecasting with high frequency based volatility (HEAVY) models. Journal of Applied Econometrics 25, 197–231.

Shephard, N. G. and T. G. Andersen (2009). Stochastic volatility: Origins and overview. In T. G. Andersen, R. A. Davis, J.-P. Kreiss, and T. Mikosch (Eds.), Handbook of Financial Time Series, pp. 233–254. New York: Springer.

Sheppard, K. (2006). Realized covariance and scrambling. Unpublished Manuscript.

Sheppard, K. (2012). Forecasting high dimensional covariance matrices. In L. Bauwens, C. Hafner, and S. Laurent (Eds.), Handbook of Volatility Models and Their Applications, pp. 103–125. John Wiley & Sons.

Shiryaev, A. N. (1999). Essentials of Stochastic Finance: Facts, Models and Theory. Singapore: World Scientific.

Silvennoinen, A. and T. Teräsvirta (2009). Multivariate GARCH models. In T. G. Andersen, R. A. Davis, J.-P. Kreiss, and T. Mikosch (Eds.), Handbook of Financial Time Series, pp. 201–228. New York: Springer.

Silvennoinen, A. and T. Teräsvirta (2005). Multivariate autoregressive conditional heteroskedasticity with smooth transitions in conditional correlations. SSE/EFI Working Paper Series in Economics and Finance 577.

Silvennoinen, A. and T. Teräsvirta (2007). Multivariate autoregressive conditional heteroskedasticity with the double smooth transition in conditional correlation GARCH model. SSE/EFI Working Paper Series in Economics and Finance 625.

Silverman, R. A. (1957). Locally stationary random processes. IRE Transactions on Information Theory 3, 182–187.

Sinko, A., M. Sockin, and E. Ghysels (2010). Matlab toolbox for midas regressions. Available at www.unc.edu/eghysels/Software_datasets.html.

Siu, D. T. L. and J. Okunev (2009). Forecasting exchange rate volatility: A multiple horizon comparison using historical, realized and implied volatility measures. Journal of Forecasting 28, 165–486.

Sklar, A. (1959). Fonctions de répartitionán dimensions et leurs marges. Pub. Inst. Statist. Univ. Paris 8, 229–231.

Smith, A. F. M. and A. E. Gelfand (1992). Bayesian statistics without tears: A sampling-resampling perspective. The American Statistician 46, 84–88.

Smith, M. and A. Pitts (2006). Foreign exchange intervention by the Bank of Japan: Bayesian analysis using a bivariate stochastic volatility model. Econometric Reviews 25, 425–451.

So, M. K. P. and C. Y. Choi (2009). A threshold factor multivariate stochastic volatility model. Journal of Forecasting 28–8, 712–735.

So, M. K. P., W. K. Li, and K. Lam (1997). Multivariate modelling of the autoregressive random variance process. Journal of Time Series Analysis 18, 429–446.

So, M. K. P., W. K. Li, and K. Lam (2002). A threshold stochastic volatility model. Journal of Forecasting 21, 473–500.

Song, P. X.-K., Y. Fan, and J. D. Kalbfleisch (2005). Maximization by parts in likelihood inference. Journal of the American Statistical Association 100, 1145–1157.

Spokoiny, V. (2009). Multiscale local change point detection with applications to Value-at-Risk. The Annals of Statistics 37, 1405–1436.

Stentoft, L. (2008). Option pricing using realized volatility. CREATES Research Papers with number 2008–13.

Stock, J. H. and M. W. Watson (2007). Introduction to Econometrics (2nd ed.). New Jersey: Prentice Hall.

Su, L., A. Ullah, S. Mishra, and Y. Wang (2012). Nonparametric and semiparametric volatility models: Specification, estimation, and testing. In L. Bauwens, C. Hafner, and S. Laurent (Eds.), Handbook of Volatility Models and Their Applications, pp. 269–291. John Wiley & Sons.

Sun, Y. and T. Stengos (2006). Semiparametric efficient adaptive estimation of asymmetric GARCH models. Journal of Econometrics 133, 373–386.

Takahashi, M., Y. Omori, and T. Watanabe (2009). Estimating stochastic volatility models using daily returns and realized volatility simultaneously. Computational Statistics and Data Analysis 53–6, 2404–2426.

Tang, K. and W. Xiong (2010). Index investment and financialization of commodities. Technical report, Princeton University.

Tashman, A. (2010). A regime–switching approach to model–based stress testing. Journal of Risk Model Validation 3, 89–101.

Tashman, A. and R. J. Frey (2009). Modeling risk in arbitrage strategies using finite mixtures. Quantitative Finance 9, 495–503.

Tauchen, G. and M. Pitts (1983). The price variability-volume relationship on speculative markets. Econometrica 51, 485–505.

Tauchen, G. and H. Zhou (2011). Realized jumps on financial markets and predicting credit spreads. Journal of Econometrics 160, 102–118.

Tay, A. S. and K. F. Wallis (2000). Density forecasting: A survey. Journal of Forecasting 19, 124–143.

Taylor, S. J. (1982). Financial returns modelled by the product of two stochastic processes, A study of daily sugar prices 1961–79. In O. D. Anderson (Ed.), Time Series Analysis: Theory and Practice 1, pp. 203–226. Amsterdam: North-Holland.

Taylor, S. J. (1986). Modelling Financial Time Series. New York: John Wiley & Sons.

Taylor, S. J. and X. Xu (1997). The incremental volatility information in one million foreign exchange quotations. Journal of Empirical Finance 4, 317–340.

Teräsvirta, T. (1994). Specification, estimation, and evaluation of smooth transition autoregressive models. Journal of the American Statistical Association 89, 208–218.

Teräsvirta, T. (2006). Forecasting economic variables with nonlinear models. In G. Elliott, C. W. J. Granger, and A. Timmermann (Eds.), Handbook of Economic Forecasting, Vol. 1, pp. 413–457. Amsterdam: Elsevier.

Teräsvirta, T. (2009). An introduction to univariate GARCH models. In T. G. Andersen, R. A. Davis, J.-P. Kreiß, and T. Mikosch (Eds.), Handbook of Financial Time Series, pp. 17–42. Berlin: Springer.

Teräsvirta, T., C.-F. Lin, and C. W. J. Granger (1993). Power of the neural network linearity test. Journal of Time Series Analysis 14, 309–323.

Teräsvirta, T., D. Tjøstheim, and C. W. J. Granger (2010). Modelling Nonlinear Economic Time Series. Oxford: Oxford University Press.

Teräsvirta, T. (2012). Nonlinear models for autoregressive conditional heteroskedasticity. In L. Bauwens, C. Hafner, and S. Laurent (Eds.), Handbook of Volatility Models and Their Applications, pp. 49–69. John Wiley & Sons.

Theodosiou, M. and F. Zikes (2011). A comprehensive comparison of alternative tests for jumps in asset prices. www.ssrn.com.

Thomakos, D. D. and T. Wang (2003). Realized volatility in the futures markets. Journal of Empirical Finance 10, 321–353.

Timmermann, A. (2000). Density forecasting in economics and finance. Journal of Forecasting 19, 231–234.

Timmermann, A. (2000). Moments of Markov switching models. Journal of Econometrics 96, 75–11.

Tjøstheim, D. and B. H. Auestad (1994). Nonparametric identification of nonlinear time series: projections. Journal of the American Statistical Association 89, 1398–1409.

Todorov, V. (2009). Estimation of continuous-time stochastic volatility models with jumps using high-frequency data. Journal of Econometrics 148, 131–148.

Todorov, V. (2010). Variance risk-premium dynamics: The role of jumps. Review of financial studies 23, 345–383.

Todorov, V. and G. Tauchen (2010a). Activity signature functions for high-frequency data analysis. Journal of Econometrics 154, 125–138.

Todorov, V. and G. Tauchen (2010b). The realized Laplace transform of volatility. Working Paper, KGSM.

Todorov, V., G. Tauchen, and I. Grynkiv (2010). Realized Laplace transforms for estimation of jump diffusive volatility models. Working Paper, KGSM.

Triantafyllopoulos, K. (2008). Multivariate stochastic volatility with Bayesian dynamic linear models. Journal of Statistical Planning and Inference 138, 1031–1037.

Tsay, R. (2002). Analysis of Financial Time Series. New York: John Wiley & Sons.

Tsay, R. S. (2005). Analysis of Financial Time Series: Financial Econometrics (2 ed.). New York: John Wiley & Sons.

Tse, Y. K. (2000). A test for constant correlations in a multivariate GARCH models. Journal of Econometrics 98, 107–127.

Tse, Y. K. and A. K. C. Tsui (2002). A multivariate GARCH model with time-varying correlations. Journal of Business and Economic Statistics 20, 351–362.

Tse, Y. K. and P. S. L. Yip (2003). The Impacts of Hong Kong's Currency Board Reforms on the Interbank Market. Journal of Banking and Finance 27, 2273–2296.

Turner, C. M., R. Startz, and C. R. Nelson (1989). A Markov model of heteroskedasticity, risk, and learning in the stock market. Journal of Financial Economics 25, 3–22.

Van Bellegem, S. (2012). Locally stationary volatility modelling. In L. Bauwens, C. Hafner, and S. Laurent (Eds.), Handbook of Volatility Models and Their Applications, pp. 249–268. John Wiley & Sons.

Van Bellegem, S. and R. Dahlhaus (2006). Semiparametric estimation by model selection for locally stationary processes. Journal of the Royal Statistical Society: Series B (Statistical Methodology) 68, 721–764.

Van Bellegem, S. and R. von Sachs (2004). Forecasting economic time series with unconditional time-varying variance. International Journal of Forecasting 20, 611–627.

Van Bellegem, S. and R. von Sachs (2006). Locally adaptive estimation of evolutionary wavelet spectra. The Annals of Statistics 36, 1879–1924.

van der Weide, R. (2002). GO-GARCH: A multivariate generalized orthogonal GARCH models. Journal of Applied Econometrics 17, 549–564.

Verbeek, M. (2008). A Guide to Modern Econometrics (3rd ed.). John Wiley & Sons.

Vetter, M. (2010). Limit theorems for bipower variation of semimartingales. Stochastic Processes and Their Applications 120, 22–38.

Violante, F. and S. Laurent (2012). Volatility forecasts evaluation and comparison; A survey. In L. Bauwens, C. Hafner, and S. Laurent (Eds.), Handbook of Volatility Models and Their Applications, pp. 465–485. John Wiley & Sons.

Visser, M. (2008). GARCH parameter estimation using high-frequency data. MPRA paper 9076.

Vlaar, P. J. G. and F. C. Palm (1993). The message in weekly exchange rates in the european monetary system: Mean reversion, conditional heteroscedasticity, and jumps. Journal of Business and Economic Statistics 11, 351–360.

Voev, V. (2007). Dynamic modeling of large-dimensional covariance matrices. In L. Bauwens, W. Pohlmeier, and D. Veredas (Eds.), In High Frequency Financial Econometrics: Recent Developments (1st edn), pp. 293–312. Heidelberg: Physica–Verlag.

Voev, V. (2009). On the economic evaluation of volatility forecasts. CREATES Research Papers 2009–56, School of Economics and Management, University of Aarhus.

Voev, V. and A. Lunde (2007). Integrated covariance estimation using high-frequency data in the presence of noise. Journal of Financial Econometrics 5, 68–104.

Vrontos, I., P. Dellaportas, and D. Politis (2003). A full-factor multivariate GARCH model. Econometrics Journal 6, 311–333.

Vuong, Q. (1989). Likelihood-ratio tests for model selection and non-nested hypotheses. Econometrica 57, 307–333.

Wago, H. (2004). Bayesian estimation of smooth transition GARCH model using Gibbs sampling. Mathematics and Computers in Simulation 64, 63–78.

Wang, Y. (1995). Jump and sharp cusp detection by wavelets. Biometrika 82, 385–397.

Wang, Y. and J. Zou (2009). Vast volatility matrix estimation for high-frequency financial data. Annals of Statistics 38, 943–978.

Watanabe, T. and Y. Omori (2004). A multi-move sampler for estimating non-Gaussian times series models: Comments on Shephard and Pitt (1997). Biometrika 91, 246–248.

West, K. (1996). Asymptotic inference about predictive ability. Econometrica 64, 1067–1084.

West, K. (2006). Forecasts evaluation. In G. Elliot, C. Granger, and A. Timmermann (Eds.), Handbook of Economic Forecasting. Amsterdam: North-Holland.

West, K. and D. Cho (1995). The predictive ability of several models of exchange rate volatility. Journal of Econometrics 69, 367–391.

Whelan, N. (2004). Sampling from Archimedean copulas. Quantitative Finance 4, 339–352.

White, H. (1982). Maximum likelihood estimation of misspecified models. Econometrica 50, 1–25.

White, H. (2000). A reality check for data snooping. Econometrica 68, 1097–1126.

White, H. L. and I. Domowitz (1984). Nonlinear regression with dependent observations. Econometrica 52, 143–161.

Woerner, J. (2006a). Analyzing the fine structure of continuous time stochastic processes. working paper University of Gottingen.

Woerner, J. (2006b). Power and Multipower variation: inference for high-frequency data. Stochastic Finance, pp. 343–364. USA: Springer.

Wong, C. S. and W. K. Li (2001a). On a logistic mixture autoregressive model. Biometrika 88, 833–846.

Wong, C. S. and W. K. Li (2001b). On a mixture autoregressive conditional heteroscedastic model. Journal of the American Statistical Association 96, 982–985.

Wood, R., T. Mcinish, and K. Ord (1985). An investigation of transactions data for NYSE stocks. Journal of Finance 3, 723–739.

Wooldridge, J. M. (1994). Estimation and inference for dependent processes. In R. F. Engle, and D. McFadden (Eds.), Handbook of Econometrics, Vol. 4, Chapter 45, pp. 2639–2738. Elsevier.

Wooldridge, J. M. (2009). Introductory Econometrics: A Modern Approach (4th ed.). Mason, OH: South-Western Cengage Learning.

Wright, J. and H. Zhou (2009). Bond risk premia and realized jump risk. Journal of Banking & Finance 33, 2333–2345.

Wu, C. and J. C. Lee (2007). Estimation of a utility-based asset pricing model using normal mixture GARCH(1,1). Economic Modelling 24, 329–349.

Wu, L. (2010). Variance dynamics: Joint evidence from options and high-frequency returns. Journal of Econometrics, 160, 280–287.

Xekalaki, E. and S. Degiannakis (2010). ARCH Models for Financial Applications. John Wiley & Sons.

Xia, Y., H. Tong, and W. K. Li (2002). Single-index volatility models and estimation. Statistica Sinica 12, 785–799.

Xiao, Z. and L. R. Lima (2007). Testing covariance stationarity. Econometric Reviews 26, 643–667.

Xiu, D. (2010). Quasi-maximum likelihood estimation of volatility with high frequency data. Journal of Econometrics 159, 235–250.

Yang, L. (2006). A semiparametric GARCH model for foreign exchange volatility. Journal of Econometrics 130, 365–384.

Yang, L., W. Härdle, and J. Nielsen (1999). Nonparametric autoregression with multiplicative volatility and additive mean. Journal of Time Series Analysis 20, 579–604.

Yang, M. (2000). Some properties of vector autoregressive processes with Markov–switching coefficients. Econometric Theory 16, 23–43.

Yao, J.-F. and J.-G. Attali (2000). On stability of nonlinear ar processes with Markov switching. Advances in Applied Probability 32, 394–407.

Yu, J. (2005). On leverage in a stochastic volatility model. Journal of Econometrics 127, 165–178.

Yu, J. and R. Meyer (2006). Multivariate stochastic volatility models: Bayesian estimation and model comparison. Econometric Reviews 25, 361–384.

Yu, J. and P. C. B. Phillips (2001). A Gaussian approach for estimating continuous time models of short term interest rates. The Econometrics Journal 4, 211–225.

Zakoian, J.-M. (1994). Threshold heteroskedastic models. Journal of Economic Dynamics and Control 18, 931–955.

Zarnowitz, V. (1985). Rational expectations and macroeconomic forecasts. Journal of The American Statistical Association 100, 1394–1411.

Zhang, L. (2006). Efficient estimation of stochastic volatility using noisy observations: A multi-scale approach. Bernoulli 12, 1019–1043.

Zhang, L. (2006a). Stochastic volatility using noisy observations: A multi-scale approach. Bernoulli 12, 1019–1043.

Zhang, L. (2011). Estimating covariation: Epps effect and microstructure noise. Journal of Econometrics 160, 33–47.

Zhang, L., P. A. Mykland, and Y. Aït-Sahalia (2005). A tale of two time scales: Determining integrated volatility with noisy high-frequency data. Journal of the American Statistical Association 100, 1394–1411.

Zhang, L., P. A. Mykland, and Y. Aït-Sahalia (2011). Edgeworth expansions for realized rolatility and related estimators. Journal of Econometrics 160, 160–175.

Zhang, Z., W. K. Li, and K. C. Yuen (2006). On a mixture GARCH time-series models. Journal of Time Series Analysis 27, 577–597.

Zhou, B. (1996). High-frequency data and volatility in foreign exchange rates. Journal of Business and Economic Statistics 14, 45–52.

Ziegelmann, F. A. (2002). Nonparametric estimation of volatility functions: the local exponential estimator. Econometric Theory 18, 985–991.

Zivot, E. (2009). Practical issues in the analysis of univariate GARCH models. In T. G. Andersen, R. A. Davis, J.-P. Kreiss, and T. Mikosch (Eds.), Handbook of Financial Time Series, pp. 113–155. New York: Springer.

Zumbach, G. (2007). The RiskMetrics 2006 methodology. Technical report, RiskMetrics Group.

Index

Handbook of Volatility Models and Their Applications, First Edition.
Edited by Luc Bauwens, Christian Hafner, and Sebastien Laurent.

Printed and bound by CPI Group (UK) Ltd, Croydon, CR0 4YY

16/09/2026

14963413-0008